CALL OF EMPIRE

Call of Empire

From the Highlands to Hindostan

ALEXANDER CHARLES BAILLIE

McGill-Queen's University Press
Montreal & Kingston · London · Chicago

ISBN 978-0-7735-5124-4 (cloth)
ISBN 978-0-7735-5206-7 (ePDF)
ISBN 978-0-7735-5207-4 (ePUB)

Legal deposit fourth quarter 2017
Bibliothèque nationale du Québec

Printed in Canada on acid-free paper that is 100% ancient forest free
(100% post-consumer recycled), processed chlorine free

McGill-Queen's University Press acknowledges the support of the Canada
Council for the Arts for our publishing program. We also acknowledge the
financial support of the Government of Canada through the Canada Book
Fund for our publishing activities.

Library and Archives Canada Cataloguing in Publication

Baillie, Alexander Charles, 1939–, author
Call of empire: from the Highlands to Hindostan/Alexander Charles Baillie.

Includes bibliographical references and index.
Issued in print and electronic formats.
ISBN 978-0-7735-5124-4 (cloth). – ISBN 978-0-7735-5206-7 (ePDF). –
ISBN 978-0-7735-5207-4 (ePUB)

1. East India Company. 2. Baillie family. 3. British – India – History –
18th century. 4. British – India – History – 19th century. 5. Great Britain –
Colonies – India – History – 19th century. 6. Great Britain – Colonies –
India – History – 18th century. 7. India – Economic conditions – 18th century.
8. India – Economic conditions – 19th century. 9. India – Ethnic relations –
History – 18th century. 10. India – Ethnic relations – History – 19th century.
11. India – History, Military – 18th century. 12. India – History, Military –
19th century. I. Title.

DS463.B35 2017   954.02'9   C2017-904054-5
                                          C2017-904055-3

This book was typeset by Marquis Interscript in 10.5/13 Sabon.

For my grandchildren

Contents

Preface

By some act of serendipity, a chest that had lain in oblivion for almost a century and a half in the Inverness Library appeared at the Highland Archive Centre in 2002. The staff of the centre had yet to examine, in any detail, the contents of the chest when my son Jonathan, who was completing his doctorate at Imperial College, London, wandered onto the premises to enquire as to the existence of any materials on the Baillies of Leys or Dunain. Fiona MacLeod, the senior archivist, recalled that a recently received chest contained Baillie correspondence and directed Jonathan to it. Since we were reasonably familiar with our family history as a result of my uncle Donald Baillie's extensive genealogical research, Jonathan approached the ancient chest with keen anticipation. Nor was he disappointed. The letters were indeed those of five generations of our Dunain and Leys ancestors. Moreover, the chest contained in excess of two thousand letters and a good many of them were written to or from various family members in India.

Excited by the promise of this treasure trove, Jonathan and I lost no time in engaging a local researcher, Sandra Bardwell, to summarize and classify the correspondence. The sheer number of letters meant that her task would be long and laborious. Upon completion of the project in 2003, Sandra stoked our mounting enthusiasm by reporting that, in her opinion, the contents of the chest dating from 1720 to 1869 constituted the most comprehensive collection of Highland correspondence from that era.

This discovery, together with a considerable collection of family letters and other material in the National Archives of Scotland, the University of Cambridge, and the Oriental and India Office Collection of the British Library, was the genesis of my determination to document the lives of my forebears, who, with more or less success over a span of four generations, had sought their fortunes in India. I had been aware of an Indian connection but not the rationale for it, the details thereof, nor the sheer number of Baillies engaged in the service of the East India Company. This epistolary cornucopia promised to cast an abundance of light on my ancestors' activities in India. Admittedly, they were minor cogs in the wheels of empire, but, at the least, their letters would provide considerable insight into their personalities and lives while also offering a contemporary view of social, political, and military events.

Thus began a quest that took me around the globe, to Scotland, India, and Ireland. This book is the product of all my research and travel. A large portion of it consists of lengthy quotations from Baillie correspondence; for this I offer no apology, because, in my view, these quotations offer a fascinating window into a long-lost world. All the quotations are reproduced verbatim, with the occasional editorial insertion (punctuation, editorial explanations in square brackets, and the like) as an aid to the reader. To assist the reader further, I include a glossary of Anglo-Indian and Scottish terms; a "Cast of Supporting Characters," which provides short profiles of some of the individuals mentioned in passing in the book; and a list giving the modern equivalents of place names used in British India (I decided to use the latter rather than the modern versions in the interests of narrative clarity).

I faced two challenges in telling this story. First, I struggled with some of the language and attitudes expressed in the letters. To readers today, the European sense of entitlement and racial superiority that we encounter in these letters is unacceptable, to put it mildly. Yet I hesitated to act as censor, since to do so would undercut my objective of providing as complete and accurate a picture of an era of British and imperial history as possible. In the end, I left the offensive statements intact, trusting that readers would be able to place them in their proper context.

The other problem was just as difficult. The correspondence refers to countless Baillies and Baillie relatives, and the sheer number of characters with the same names – William, John, Alexander – recurring frequently is confusing even to family members. How could this story be made comprehensible? Ultimately, I determined to focus on the lives of the two Baillies who accomplished the most and who are still commemorated in a modest fashion in India today. They are Colonel William Baillie, the 12th Laird of Dunain, who, after a distinguished military career, died in an Indian prison in Seringapatam; and his nephew, Colonel John Baillie of Leys, who, in large part, secured the province of Bundelcund for the

East India Company and later served as the British resident at Lucknow, in the Indian state of Oude. Two more individuals are featured in supporting roles: William's brother and heir, Colonel John Baillie, the 13th Laird of Dunain, who died in Ireland attempting to thwart a threatened Napoleonic invasion; and their nephew and my great-great-great-grandfather, Colonel Alexander Baillie, who, of all four generations of our family, spent the most years in India.

I recognize that these four Baillies, fascinating though they are to me, may have little interest to those outside my family. For that reason, I have attempted to relate their lives to the world in which they lived. In this regard, I have naturally emphasized Scotland and India, but, because the letters demonstrate a detailed knowledge of events beyond those two countries, my story also touches upon the European continent, the West Indies, and the American colonies.

The book begins by placing my family in the context of eighteenth-century Scotland. I offer here a brief snapshot of Scotland at that time, tracing its historical evolution and describing the prevailing socio-economic conditions, particularly in Inverness. Then, in the remainder of the book, I follow the lives of the four Baillies previously mentioned, attempting throughout to relate their stories to the larger Scottish and Indian context. India, in particular, receives much attention, as is only fitting. Along the way, I examine the fabric of Indian society when Europeans first arrived, the expanding British presence in the country, and the relationship both between the natives of India and the East India Company and between the Company and the government of Great Britain and its colonial representatives. It is a tangled, complicated story, but one cannot understand the Baillies without coming to terms with it. The two were inseparable.

CRZ

I have incurred a number of debts in writing this book. During my time in Inverness, Fiona McLeod of the Highland Archive Centre thoughtfully arranged to introduce me to Keeta Campbell, who had earlier become intrigued with Colonel William Baillie. Keeta had spent a good deal of time researching his life in Edinburgh's National Archives and had written an unpublished manuscript of the subject. Needless to say, I was delighted when Keeta graciously presented me with a copy. For this, I thank her deeply. Fiona McLeod herself was unstinting in her assistance while Sandra Bardwell succinctly and accurately summarized the letters in the chest and Allison Mowat, through her diligent research, uncovered a good deal of additional information on our Scottish ancestors. My fifth cousin, John Baillie, and my ninth cousin once removed, the Honourable Alexander Baillie, provided otherwise unavailable paintings, cameos, and insights into the lives of my ancestors, and my ever-patient editor, Curtis Fahey, brought an objectivity to what should and should not be included and was instrumental in shaping the story. I particularly want to thank my son Jonathan, without whose continuing research this work would not have been possible, and Anna Porter, without whose advice and encouragement the manuscript would not have been published.

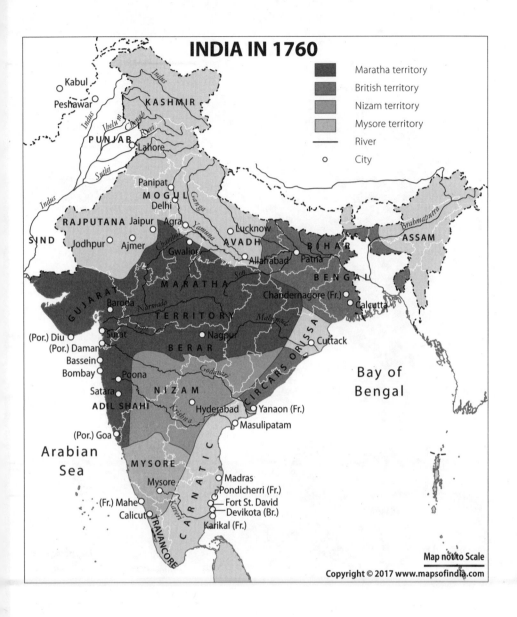

INDIA IN 1760

Legend:
- Maratha territory
- British territory
- Nizam territory
- Mysore territory
- River
- City

Kabul
Peshawar
KASHMIR
Indus
Jhelum
Chenab
Ravi
PUNJAB
Lahore
Sutlej
Indus
Panipat
MOGUL
Delhi
Ganga
RAJPUTANA Jaipur Agra
SIND
Jodhpur Ajmer
Gwalior
Chambal
Yamuna
AVADH
Lucknow
BIHAR
ASSAM
Brahmaputra
Allahabad Patna
Son
BENGAL
MARATHA
Chandernagore (Fr.)
Calcutta
GUJARAT
Baroda
Narmada
TERRITORY
Mahanadi
ORISSA
CIRCARS
(Por.) Diu
Surat
Nagpur
Cuttack
(Por.) Daman
BERAR
Bassein
Bombay
Godavari
Poona
Satara
NIZAM
ADIL SHAHI
Krishna
Hyderabad
Yanaon (Fr.)
(Por.) Goa
Masulipatam
Arabian
Sea
MYSORE
CARNATIC
Mysore
Madras
Pondicherri (Fr.)
(Fr.) Mahe
Fort St. David
Devikota (Br.)
Calicut
Kaveri
Karikal (Fr.)
TRAVANCORE

Bay of
Bengal

Map not to Scale
Copyright © 2017 www.mapsofindia.com

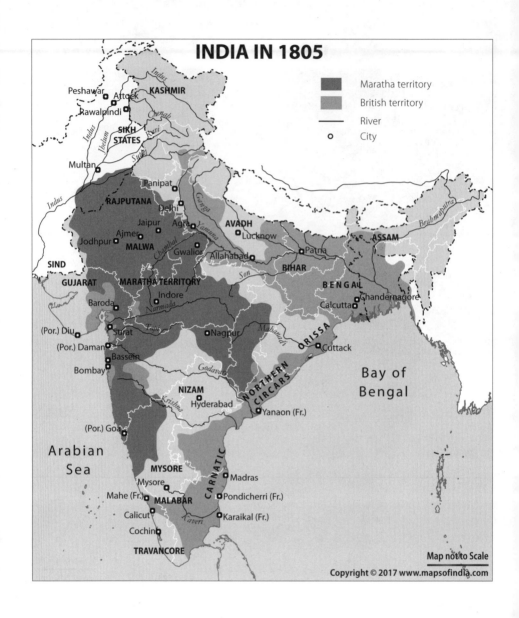

INDIA IN 1805

Legend:
- ■ Maratha territory
- ▨ British territory
- — River
- ○ City

Peshawar
Attock
Rawalpindi
KASHMIR
Indus
Chenab
Ravi
SIKH STATES
Jhelum
Sutlej
Indus
Multan
Panipat
RAJPUTANA
Delhi
Jaipur
Agra
AVADH
Lucknow
Ganga
Yamuna
ASSAM
Brahmaputra
Ajmer
Jodhpur
MALWA
Gwalior
Allahabad
Chambal
SIND
GUJARAT
MARATHA TERRITORY
Indore
Son
BIHAR
Patna
BENGAL
Chandernagore
Baroda
Narmada
Calcutta
(Por.) Diu
Surat
Tapi
Nagpur
Mahanadi
ORISSA
Cuttack
(Por.) Daman
Bassein
Bombay
Godavari
NORTHERN CIRCARS
NIZAM
Krishna
Hyderabad
Yanaon (Fr.)

Bay of Bengal

(Por.) Goa

Arabian Sea

MYSORE
Mysore
Madras
Mahe (Fr.)
MALABAR
Pondicherri (Fr.)
Calicut
Kaveri
Karaikal (Fr.)
Cochin
TRAVANCORE

CARNATIC

Map not to Scale

Copyright © 2017 www.mapsofindia.com

Cawdor Castle. The home of Colonel William Baillie's great-grandfather, Sir Hugh Campbell. It is a popular tourist destination as the supposed setting for William Shakespeare's thane of Cawdor. Photographed by the author.

Ann Baillie of Leys (1738–1776). The daughter of
Alexander Baillie XI of Dunain and his wife, Anne
Campbell. Ann was the wife of George Baillie of Leys
and the mother of Colonels Alexander and John.
Courtesy of the Honourable Alexander Baillie.

Cameo of Colonel William Baillie XII of Dunain
(1739–1782). Son of Alexander Baillie XI of Dunain
and his wife, Anne Campbell. He was an officer of
the East India Company. Courtesy of the Honourable
Alexander Baillie.

Mohammed Ali Khan, Nawab of Arcot. The East India Company placed Mohammed Ali on the throne of Arcot and he remained a constant, if undependable, ally throughout the Anglo-Mysore wars. Courtesy of the Scottish National Portrait Gallery, Edinburgh.

Tipu Sultan, the son of Hyder Ali. He continued his father's wars with the East India Company until his defeat and death in 1799. Courtesy of the Victoria and Albert Museum.

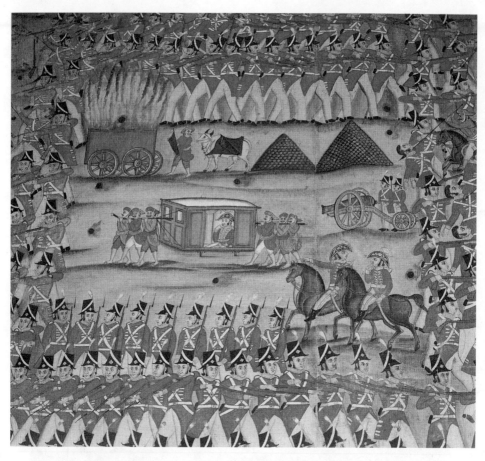

The Battle of Pollilur, 1780. Detail of a mural at Tipu Sultan's Summer Palace depicting the defeat of William Baillie owing to the destruction of his ammunition tumbrils. Courtesy of the Mary Evans Picture Library.

Cenotaph at Seringapatam. Erected in memory of Colonel William Baillie XII of Dunain, who died in Hyder Ali's prison, by his nephew, Colonel John Baillie of Leys. Photographed by the author.

Baillie of Dunain

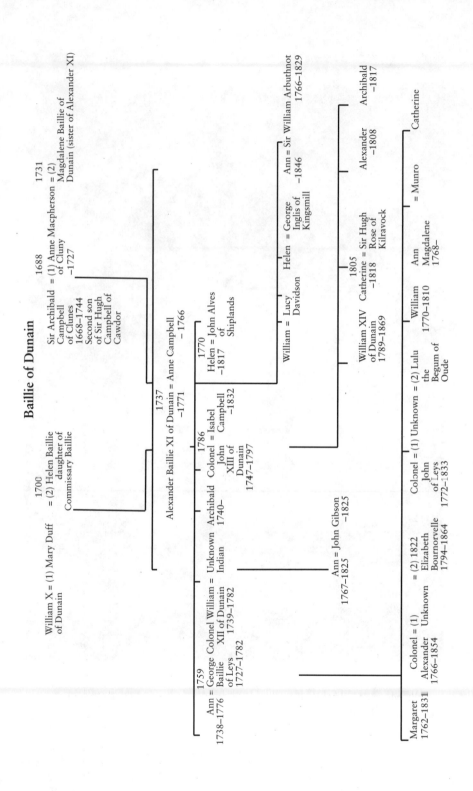

Baillie of Leys

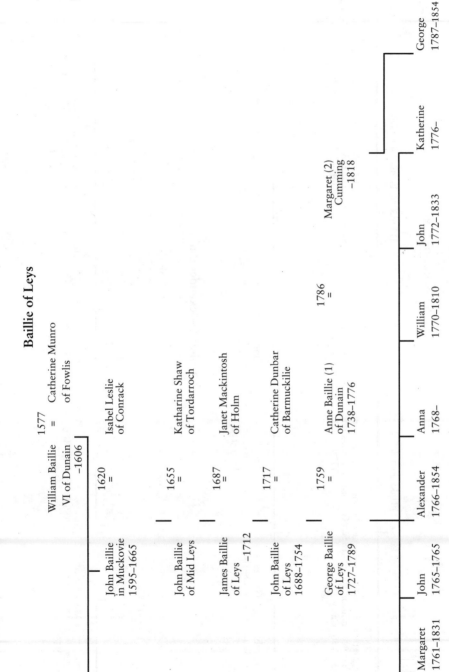

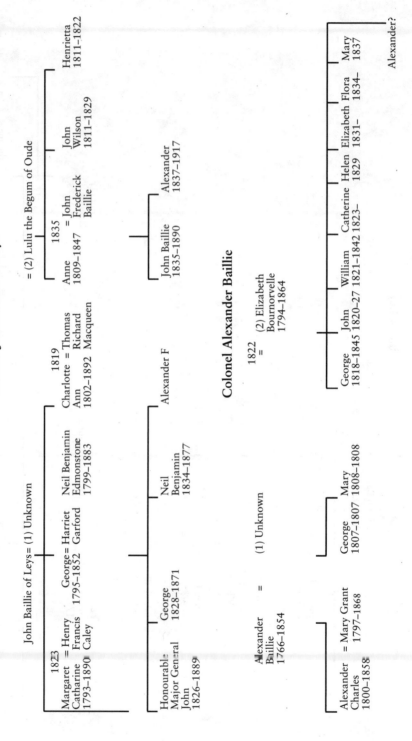

Colonel John Baillie of Leys

John Baillie of Leys = (1) Unknown

= (2) Lulu the Begum of Oude

Margaret Catharine 1793–1890 = Henry Francis Caley | George 1795–1852 = Harriet Garford | Neil Benjamin Edmonstone 1799–1883 | Charlotte Ann 1802–1892 = Thomas Richard Macqueen (1819) | Anne 1809–1847 = John Frederick Baillie (1835) | John Wilson 1811–1829 | Henrietta 1811–1822

1823

Honourable Major General John 1826–1889 | George 1828–1871 | Neil Benjamin 1834–1877 | Alexander F

John Baillie 1835–1890 | Alexander 1837–1917

Colonel Alexander Baillie

Alexander Baillie 1766–1854 = (1) Unknown

= (2) Elizabeth Bournorvelle 1794–1864 (1822)

Alexander Charles 1800–1858 = Mary Grant 1797–1868

George 1807–1807 | Mary 1808–1808

George 1818–1845 | John 1820–27 | William 1821–1842 | Catherine 1823– | Helen 1829 | Elizabeth 1831– | Flora 1834– | Mary 1837

Alexander?

CALL OF EMPIRE

Culloden's Children

It is never difficult to distinguish between a Scotsman with a grievance and a ray of sunshine.

P.G. Wodehouse

As King George II's third son, Prince William Augustus, reviled by Scots to this day as Cumberland the Butcher, broke the rebel clans on the bloody field of Culloden, William Baillie was a robust and precocious six-year-old living in Inverness. As the heir of Alexander, the 11th Laird of Dunain, he bore his paternal grandfather's name, in accordance with tradition. William would have been largely oblivious to the devastation wrought only a short distance from his home and similarly oblivious to the opportunities the Hanoverian integration of Scotland into the British Empire would provide to enterprising and adventurous young Scots. Clearly, he was even more unaware of the fate that awaited him on a subcontinent thousands of miles from Inverness.

As his Clan Chattan kinsmen and neighbours marched unwaveringly across Culloden Moor to a slaughter that time and nostalgia would enshrine in myth, the young boy could barely appreciate the concept of warfare let alone the profound impact of the Rising of 1745, popularly known as "the Forty-Five," and its aftermath. His family, however, awaited the outcome with trepidation. For the gentry of Inverness, whether Hanoverian or Jacobite in their sympathies, had been compromised by the presence in their midst of the son of the Stuart Pretender. The charismatic but ultimately callow Charles Edward Stuart had marched his army into the Highland capital and been greeted ecstatically by a goodly portion of the populace. The inveterate and unrepentant Jacobite Francis Oliphant of Gask was, in retrospect, given to hyperbole and undue optimism when he informed his sister: "His entry into Inverness ressembled in some respects that of our Saviour into Jerusalem, the day being Palm Sunday, and the crowds of people who followed crying 'Great Prince, deliver us.' Our Highlanders have returned in greater numbers, and more zealous than ever, so that far from our dear Prince's affairs being worse, they were never in a better condition. We are in a country which is inaccessible to the enemy, unless they wish to expose themselves to perish in detail as they approved each time they tried to penetrate."[1]

Understandably, the pressure to declare for the Stuarts was unrelenting. Yet countering the Jacobite momentum was the reality that the leading families, having prospered, at least relatively, under the Hanoverians and being heavily Protestant in their faith, had the most to lose from a Stuart restoration. These families were torn in their allegiance as siblings, let alone neighbours, opted for one or the other faction. Undoubtedly, many would have preferred to remain neutral but that choice grew ever more elusive as the Stuart adherents became more and more insistent.

William's father, the ranking Baillie in the Highlands, was reasonably successful in treading that fine line. Alexander was a delightful ditherer who could write an entire letter with no apparent substance but those attributes may have served him well in this particular situation. He "took no part in the Rising of 1745 further than doing what he could to succour distressed Jacobites, and the shelter and nourishment afforded by the 'Soul Mor' [Great Soul] of Dunain were consistently spoken of."[2] Those actions clearly evidenced his empathy for his Clan Chattan kinsmen. However, when in March General Sir John O'Sullivan, the prince's quartermaster and adjutant-general, ordered Alexander "upon pain of fire and sword to send to the castle of Inverness the number of 8 horses with as many carts before 8 o'clock tomorrow morning and signify their arrival to Capt. McLoghlan store keeper in the castle,"[3] the laird would have done so begrudgingly inasmuch as he was an intimate and, through his grandmother Isobel Forbes, the second cousin of Lord President Duncan Forbes, George II's man in the north.

As a Protestant and extensive landowner, Dunain's sympathies would naturally incline toward the House of Hanover. On the other hand, his kinsman, Hugh Baillie, the 3rd Laird of Dochfour, was in a more delicate position. Hugh's grandfather had been a younger son of Alexander, the 7th Laird of Dunain, but the Dochfour family had become closely intertwined with the notoriously Catholic and Jacobite Fraser clan. Indeed, Hugh had married a Fraser, as had his father and grandfather. In the laird's absence, the wily Simon Fraser, chief of Clan Fraser, visited the estate to beseech Dochfour's wife, Emilia, to convince her husband to declare for the Bonnie Prince. The charm of Simon Fraser was difficult to resist. In his youth he had kidnapped and forcibly married the widow of the 9th Lord Lovat, a woman who subsequently doted upon her abductor. However, the audacity of the act obliged him to flee the country for some time. While Simon "the Fox" had a history of playing both sides in the struggles between the Hanoverians and the Jacobites, he strongly supported Charles Edward Stuart in the Forty-Five. Nevertheless, Dochfour resisted his kinsman's impassioned blandishments.[4] He sought to remain outside the fray and, from the vantage of a low hill, hand in hand with his six-year-old son Evan, watched the cannon of the Duke of Cumberland wreak carnage on Drunmossie Moor. And, undoubtedly, father and young son also watched helplessly as the Hanoverian troops torched their estate. Tainted by his proximity to his Fraser in-laws, and denounced as a papist and traitor, Dochfour suffered disaster: his lands were declared forfeit, and they were regained only a decade later, in good part, through the dogged persistence of Duncan Forbes.

Had he not providentially been practising law in Edinburgh as a writer to the Signet, John Baillie of Leys would have been in the most invidious position. Leys was another cadet branch of the Baillies of Dunain through a younger son of William, the 6th Laird of Dunain, and their estate was nestled in the midst of Clan Chattan lands. The various septs of Clan Chattan, among whom were the Mackintoshes, MacGillivrays, MacPhersons, Shaws, Farquharsons, MacBains, and Davidsons, were the most avid and determined proponents of a Stuart restoration. They had been in the forefront of "the Fifteen," an earlier Jacobite insurrection in 1715. In order to atone for their role in that rebellion and to earn a living, many Clan Chattan men joined the 43rd Royal Highland Regiment, more commonly known as the Black Watch. The regiment had been formed to enforce Hanoverian control and to check depredations in the north. At the time the recruits had been assured that their service would be limited to Scotland but subsequently the Black Watch was directed to London. Through a tragic misunderstanding, many of the men deserted under the erroneous assumption that they were to be shipped to America. The British authorities, insensitive to, or unaware of, the circumstances, felt compelled to enforce discipline and executed three of the deserters. All three, Malcolm and Samuel MacPherson and Farquhar Shaw, belonged to Clan Chattan. The government's decision to assign one hundred of the deserters to foreign garrison duty only reinforced the Highlanders' impressions that the government had from the outset intended to deceive them. The seething resentment of the clan over these executions and colonial postings was a cardinal contributor to the Rising of 1745. The chief of Clan Chattan at the time was Angus Mackintosh, who served as a captain in the Black Watch. Angus remained loyal to George II but his wife, "Colonel" Anne of Farquharson, in a startling display of feminine independence, rallied Clan Chattan to the Jacobite cause. That the only standard the victors failed to capture at Culloden was that of Clan Chattan underlined the clan's resolve. The successful Inverness merchant and four-time provost John Hossack observed that "the brunt of the battle fell on Clan Chattan."[5]

John of Leys's mother was Janet Mackintosh of Holme, his grand-mother Katharine Shaw of Tordarroch, and he was related by marriage and tied as godparent to the MacGillivrays and MacBains, all of whom belonged to Clan Chattan. Moreover, John had amicable relations and a dependency on the Catholic Frasers in his capacity as factor to Simon Fraser, Lord Lovat. Yet Leys was a Protestant and inclined, like Dunain, toward the stability provided by the Hanoverians. The experience of John's neighbours, the Robertsons of Inshes, underscored how fortunate John was in his Edinburgh residence. On her return from Inverness the afternoon of 16 April, Robertson's wife was confronted by the horrific sight of sixteen men, a number of whom were her brothers, lying dead before her door,[6] an experience that was particularly appalling since her son served in Cumberland's army.

Obviously, the Baillies were not alone in balancing opposing forces. For example, a kinsman, Hugh Rose, the 16th Baron of Kilravock, after entertaining the Young Pretender to dinner, encountered the triumphant Duke of Cumberland. The duke reputedly observed, "You have had my cousin here."[7] With great trepidation Rose limply explained that such was the custom in Scotland. To his immense relief, Cumberland agreed that Rose could hardly refuse to acknowledge Charles as a prince.

Culloden, the last full-scale battle on British soil, was over in an hour and when the extent of the victory became evident, the Baillies under-stood that life in the Highlands had been irreparably altered. Yet they could scarcely conceive how significantly the Hanoverian victory would shape their future. Culloden and its aftermath gave rise to a chain of events which would provide all three branches of the family – Dunain, Dochfour, and Leys – with substantial wealth and prestige but it would also result in the demise, at least in the Highlands, of two of the three.

CR

The Scottish Wars of Independence in the thirteenth and fourteenth centuries had wrought havoc in the land in which William Baillie would later be born. Through it all, Scottish resilience and martial ardour were reinforced by a clan system that was well established by the eleventh century. The clans were evident in both the Lowlands and Highlands but were much more deeply embedded in the latter. Clanship was a peculiarly Scottish institution, one that developed as a means of providing protection and security to groups of people living in a specific place. Clan members were often, but not necessarily, related; however, over time, they tended to adopt the surname of the chief. The chief furnished protection and, in return, required military service, collected rents, and arbitrated disputes. At the outset, the chief held the lands in trust for the members of the clan. In that sense, clanship, in which the lowest man on the social strata shared a common bond with his chief, differed radically from the more hierarchical feudal model. The two concepts became intertwined, however, as Robert Bruce, during the Wars of Independence, sought to strengthen his position by awarding grants of land to the clans, thereby buttressing the position of clan chiefs and the elites around them.

By the dawn of the eighteenth century, the clans had outlived their purpose. While the Lowlands were experiencing change, the Highlands seemed permanently mired in the pastoral stage. "In his natural habitat, surrounded by his henchmen, his bard, his piper and his servants or gillies, the Highland chieftain could be an awe-inspiring figure. What generally struck most outsiders, however, was the shabbiness and poverty of the chief's existence. Like his followers, he was a product of a fundamental and intractable poverty."[8] Rents rose as the economies of large-scale cattle ranching squeezed out small tenants and sheep began to play a greater role. The financial return from sheep was markedly higher than that from cattle and the economies of scale were at least as significant. Moreover, the major graziers were able to furnish the landlord a secure and stable income, whereas the small tenants not infrequently required forbearance. While on most of the estates "gradual and relentless displacement rather than mass eviction was the norm ... taken together, the numbers involved were very great and suggest a systematic process of enforced movement."[9] The most notorious of what became known as the Highland Clearances were carried out by the Duke of Sutherland. Between 1807 and 1821, Sutherland's agents relocated six to ten thousand people to subsistence crofting settlements on the coast. It is difficult to envisage evictions akin to the clearances taking place in England or Europe, where small landowners with legal rights and privileges accumulated over centuries presented almost insurmountable obstacles to land clearance on a major scale.

Religion was another distinguishing characteristic of Scotland. During the Reformation of the sixteenth century, John Knox introduced Presbyterianism, a form of Calvinism, to Scotland. The new religion was austere, but offsetting its structures against most forms of enjoyment – music, dancing, gambling – was the direct access to God promised through the written word of the Bible. In the event, while Presbyterianism experienced broad popular support in the Lowlands, it proved less appealing beyond the urban enclaves of the Highlands where the people tended to remain loyal to the Catholic faith or follow their chiefs into the Episcopal fold. The Kirk, as the Presbyterian Church was called, eventually triumphed but at the cost of a country torn apart by violence and anarchy.[10]

Presbyterianism had a profoundly egalitarian impact on Scottish education and society. The country already prided itself on a distinguished tradition of higher education. The University of St Andrews was founded in 1413, Glasgow in 1451, Aberdeen in 1495, and Edinburgh in 1583. However, with the advent of Presbyterianism, literacy acquired a greater significance in that it enabled direct communication with God. In 1616 the Kirk persuaded the Scottish Parliament to enact a law requiring every parish to establish a school.[11] Parliament later rendered the creation of such schools more feasible by levying a tax on local landowners to finance them and reaffirmed that initiative through additional legislation in 1696. Accordingly, although basic education was not as advanced in the Highlands, by the end of the seventeenth century there existed a school in virtually every Lowland parish. And by the later eighteenth century almost 84 per cent of the Highland parishes had schools.[12]

While the scholar who pegged Scotland's literacy rate at an incredulous 65 per cent[13] may have been given to hyperbole, the state of literacy was unquestionably significant enough that Scots were better prepared than many of their contemporaries to make their mark in the world. In particular, the parish schools equipped students with a proficiency in Latin which qualified them for admission to college. Higher education proved relatively affordable, the annual tuition fee of £5 per annum being one-tenth of their English equivalents, Cambridge and Oxford. As a result, the students were more representative of society than in other European countries and the number attending colleges trebled in the years between 1720 and 1840. By 1750, the quality of education provided by Scottish universities compared favourably with anything offered in Europe. As religious censorship waned and education flourished, Scotland, and especially Edinburgh, became a vibrant intellectual centre. Adam Smith and David Hume wrote not just for the cognoscenti but for the general public. "Even a person of relatively modest means has his own collection of books, and what he couldn't afford, he could get at the local lending library, which by 1750 virtually every town of any size enjoyed."[14] This egalitarian spirit pervades Scottish society to this day and is poignantly given voice by the poet Robbie Burns's "a man's a man for a' that."

The Scots had hoped that the assumption of the English crown as James I by their king, James VI, in 1603 would give rise to trade and other opportunities. Yet the two countries, each with its own Parliament, remained sharply divided. Toward the end of the seventeenth century, resentment of the English surfaced in a rebellion led by John Graham of Claverhouse, "Bonnie Dundee," privy councillor of Scotland, who inflicted a severe defeat on William III's much larger force at Killiecrankie in 1689. However, fortuitously for the new monarch, Claverhouse lost his life and the rebellion its momentum. Following William's victory over James II in 1690 at the Battle of the Boyne in Ireland, the Highland chiefs yielded to the inevitable. They dutifully began swearing oaths of allegiance to William in return for a pardon. The notorious Massacre of Glencoe on 13 February 1692, in which thirty-eight unsuspecting members of Clan MacDonald were murdered by their Campbell guests in retaliation for their tardiness in pledging allegiance to William and Mary, underlined William's determination to enforce loyalty to him and sped up the oath-swearing process.

Gradually, as Scotland became more and more a Protestant nation, the abiding friction between it and England shifted from religion and politics to economics. English merchants had prospered by making the transition from the traditional wool and cloth trade to an economy based on the re-export of sugar, tobacco, pepper, molasses, and cotton from America and Asia to the rest of Europe. Meanwhile, Scotland remained immured in its subsistence-level agricultural economy. In the late seventeenth century, England and other European nations sensed an opportunity to undercut their trading rivals by the aggressive use of prohibitive tariffs. Scotland found itself at a severe disadvantage as its major trading goods – skins, grains, wool, and coal – were neither scarce in, nor vital to, foreign markets. England then sought to solidify its advantage by passing the Navigation Acts, the object of which was to secure its merchants' control over the Atlantic and Asian markets. In an effort to sustain that mastery, England built and resolutely maintained the paramount navy on the planet. The Navigation Acts exacerbated the

Scottish plight since, despite a shared monarch, the lowly Scots were excluded from trade with England's empire.

The Scots had made various attempts to create their own empire but were blocked, for example, when Nova Scotia was returned to France by Charles I in the 1632 Treaty of Saint-Germain-en-Laye. When a series of poor harvests struck in 1695, Scotland suffered disproportionately. The English and Dutch were able to import food in return for manufactured goods but agricultural Scotland had little to offer. Its situation was further aggravated by England's participation in the Anglo-Dutch Wars (1652–54, 1665–67, and 1672–74), the Nine Years' War (1688–97), and the War of the Spanish Succession (1701–14). These wars, primarily directed at two of Scotland's principal trading partners, Holland and France, had a devastating effect on the country's commerce. Foiled by the English in their attempts to create an effective trading company through the Company of Scotland Trading to Africa and the Indies, the Scots, in 1696, authorized that company to found a colony in Darien, a malaria-infested swamp claimed by the Spanish. The Darien adventure was the brainchild of William Paterson, a visionary Scot who, with markedly more success, founded the Bank of England. In the end, Darien failed miserably, thwarted both by English merchants and by the English Parliament, which prized the alliance with Spain.[15]

With many of Scotland's leading families mortgaging their estates to raise the entire £400,000 required for the venture (a sum that constituted roughly 50 per cent of the country's available capital), five ships, "amidst ... tears and prayers and praises,"[16] sailed from Leith with twelve hundred settlers on 17 July 1698. From the moment they landed on 30 October, everything went awry. The colonists were short of provisions. Nor were they likely to obtain additional supplies. William, their indifferent sovereign, in deference to the Spaniards, instructed the English settlements in the Caribbean to refrain from supplying Darien. At the same time, Spain reasserted its right to territory it regarded as part of Panama. Malaria and starvation decimated the colony. Four hundred settlers died within seven months. The colony was abandoned in July 1699, but in a comedy of errors six more ships had already sailed from Leith with thirteen hundred additional settlers and a third fleet of five ships departed for the colony shortly thereafter. The aroused Spanish blockaded Darien until the beleaguered Scots surrendered. The hapless colonists fled Darien for the last time, ending a fiasco that doomed any further Scottish aspirations to empire.

The ill-starred Darien enterprise, combined with a spate of poor harvests, caused great distress in Scotland. Darien cost the country more than two thousand lives and in excess of £200,000. In addition, Darien broke the Bank of Scotland, which suspended payments in 1704. Arthur Herman effectively captured the prevailing sentiment: "With the Kingdom's finances in tatters, and its agriculture in the grip of famine and starvation, Scotland's ruin was complete."[17] In their reduced circumstances, the Scots were vulnerable to English overtures. Many Scots concluded that they could not succeed in foreign trade without the assistance of their southern neighbour. They had absorbed the painful lesson that, if their common sovereign had to choose between the two countries, he would inevitably rule in favour of the richer and more populous. On the other side, union appealed to the English as a means of retaining Scotland in the English, rather than the French, orbit and of ensuring that Scotland did not provide a staging ground for an attempted Stuart restoration. The enduring fear of the English in the event of a conflict with France was a Scottish stab in the back.[18]

The southerners employed both the carrot and the stick. The Scottish Parliament endeavoured to gain access to trade with the empire by passing the Act of Security in 1703. The act stipulated that Scotland would not, in future, be bound to accept the same monarch as the English unless Scotland was accorded free trade with England and its colonies. When royal assent of the act was refused, the Scottish Parliament declined to raise taxes and threatened to withdraw troops from the Duke of Marlborough's army in France. The English Parliament responded in 1704 with the Alien Act, which provided for the seizure of Scottish assets in England and banned all imports from Scotland unless the Scots agreed to full union. On the other hand, as an incentive, the English, who would contribute thirty-five times the Scottish amount to the public purse, offered £398,085 to reimburse the Darien investors and to support Scottish industry.

In its effort to merge the two countries, the crown blatantly selected both negotiating teams based on their willingness to endorse "an incorporating Union." Not unexpectedly, the appropriately bribed Scots, by a vote of 110 to 69 on 16 January 1707, grudgingly acceded to the Treaty of Union. And grudgingly is the operative word, since the Scots deeply resented relinquishing their Parliament in Edinburgh for what they perceived as a paltry 45 of the 558 seats in the British House of Commons and 16 in the House of Lords. Westminster further humiliated the Scots by two gratuitous measures: it abolished the Scottish Privy Council and undermined the Kirk's claim to a Presbyterian religious monopoly in Scotland by passing the Act of Toleration. In fact, it is arguable that the first stirrings of Jacobitism were inspired less by loyalty to the hapless Stuarts than by resistance to the transfer of power from Edinburgh to London.

In any event, while Andrew Fletcher may have been extreme in portraying Scotland as "only fit for the slaves who sold it,"[19] enthusiasm for the union was wanting among the Scots. Resentment once more threatened to erupt into full-scale hostilities with the outbreak of the War of the Spanish Succession. In 1708 the French sent a fleet and ten thousand troops to accompany James Stuart, the Old Pretender, to the Scottish coast. A larger English fleet under Admiral George Byng intercepted the French force. Much to James's chagrin, the French retreated across the channel. Then, shortly after acceding to the throne, the Hanoverian George I in 1715 not only sacked his Scottish secretary of state, John Erskine, Earl of Mar, but also publicly snubbed that influential public servant. Mar proved a weighty adversary. Almost immediately, he declared for the Stuarts and raised a substantial army. However, fortuitously for the House of Hanover, Mar, as a military commander, proved indecisive and ultimately wanting. After a series of fiascoes and defeats, the Fifteen collapsed, with Mar retreating to Perth and the Old Pretender boarding a ship for France.

Recognizing that renewed war with France or Spain could prove a catalyst for a further rising on behalf of the Stuarts, the lord president of Scotland, Duncan Forbes, advocated appointing the chiefs of the disaffected clans as senior officers of regiments serving in foreign lands. "If the government preengages the Highlanders in the manner I propose, they will not only serve well against the enemy abroad, but will be hostages for the good behaviour of their relations at home, and I am persuaded it will be almost impossible to raise a rebellion in the Highlands."[20] But London ignored Forbes's prescient advice. At the same time, the British government fomented Scottish disaffection by imposing a heavy excise duty and raising taxes to finance its European wars. To add insult to injury, some of these taxes were in direct violation of the Act of Union.

The government proceeded to alienate the Scottish elite even further by restricting patronage to a favoured few of its most ardent supporters. Accordingly, when the Young Pretender, Charles Edward Stuart, landed in Scotland with visions of French and English reinforcements, he found a receptive audience. His father, the Old Pretender, had issued proclamations designed to arouse Scottish anti-union sentiment while guaranteeing the free practice of the Presbyterian religion. Charles took a similar approach. He exploited particular Scottish grievances – the increased taxes since the union, the construction of forts to control the country, and the disarming of the Highlanders following the Fifteen – and appealed to Scottish pride. "We see a nation always famous for valour reduced to the condition of a province, under the specious presence of an Union with a more powerful neighbor."[21] Thus, the Hanoverians had unwittingly enabled the Stuarts to "pose as champions of Scottish nationalism and defenders of Scottish liberty."[22]

Many fawned over Charles Edward, comparing him to that quintessential Scottish hero, Robert Bruce. Forbes lamented: "All Jacobites, how prudent so ever, became mad; all doubtful people became Jacobites; and all Bankrupts became heroes, and talk'd nothing but hereditary rights and victory; and what was more grievous to men of gallantry, and if you will believe me, much more mischievous to the publick, all the fine Ladys if you will except one or two became passionately fond of the young Adventurer, and used all their Arts, and industry for him, in the most intemperate manner."[23] Nevertheless, despite the ecstatic welcome, the number of his adherents did not meet the Bonnie Prince's expectations. Forbes had performed laudably in calming the clans, the majority of whom had gradually converted to Presbyterianism. Lord Elcho observed in a reflective moment: "He [Charles Edward] was joind upon his Entring the Abby by the Earl of Kelly, Lord Balmerino, Mr. Hepburn of Keith, Mr. Lockart, younger of Carnwarth and several other Gentlemen of distinction, but not one of the Mob who were so fond of seeing him Ever ask'd to Enlist in his Service, and when he marched to fight Cope he had not one of them in his army."[24] While the members of the "Mob" may not have been in evidence around Charles Stuart, the gentlemen cited by Elcho were committed rebels if also pragmatic ones; with the exception of Balmerino, they escaped with their lives and even their estates. George Lockart, who as an attainted rebel stood to forfeit his estates on his father's death, even staged his own death and funeral in Paris so that his untainted younger brother could inherit the family lands.

Charles Edward bested the British commander-in-chief in Scotland, Sir John Cope, at Prestonpans. He then set out from Dalkeith with five hundred cavalry and six thousand foot soldiers, half of whom were Highlanders. Failing to rally the numbers anticipated on his progress south, Charles's force gradually diminished, though he did penetrate to within 127 miles of London before his commanders lost confidence and retreated north. The rest of the sorry episode is well known. Charles Edward took Inverness, which Forbes had held for George II, and on 17 April 1746, disdaining the advice of Lord George Murray, the victor of Prestonpans and his most able commander, lined up his malnourished and exhausted army to face the enemy. The ground chosen for the confrontation, Culloden Moor, was singularly ill-suited to a Highland charge but ideal for the Duke of Cumberland's artillery. The debacle was over in an hour. One thousand of the Jacobite Highlanders lay dead and the rest attempted to take refuge where they could.

Cumberland earned his sobriquet "the Butcher" in the wake of the victory. The duke ordered that the wounded rebels be slain. "All the wounded on the field of battle were killed on the Thursday; and the wounded in houses were carried to the field on Friday, where they were killed."[25] Cumberland reputedly instructed a young James Wolfe, the future conqueror of Quebec, to shoot a wounded Highlander lying on the field, a command to which Wolfe responded that Cumberland could have his commission but not his honour. The victors pursued the rebels, or anyone resembling a rebel, relentlessly, torching whole communities and indiscriminately imprisoning both the guilty and guiltless in inhumane conditions. They were led in this savage retribution by the brutish Henry "Hangman" Hawley, rumoured to be a natural son of George II. Cumberland was a hero in England, where his countrymen granted him a £25,000 annual stipend and Handel composed "All Hail the Conquering Hero," but was celebrated less expansively in Scotland. Whereas the English styled a flower "Sweet William," the Scots designated a weed "Stinking Willy."

In the wake of the Forty-Five, the British built a series of military roads to control the Highlands, confiscated rebel estates, and, through the Act of Proscription in 1747, outlawed Highland dress. They also banned the possession of arms and undermined the authority of the clan chieftains by abolishing their traditional rights. These measures applied indiscriminately to all Scots despite the fact that only a minority of Highlanders had fought on behalf of the Young Pretender and despite the active presence in Cumberland's army at the Battle of Culloden of four Scottish regiments. Twenty-two clans had rallied for the Bonnie Prince while only ten supported George II, but, reinforcing the contention that the Forty-Five was, in good part, a reaction to economic conditions, those ten were by far the more prosperous. In fact, the combined annual income of the clans championing the Stuarts totalled a miserable £1,500.

Reflecting the general sentiment, John Hossack wrote to Duncan Forbes in the south: "We are all accounted Rebells, we have no persons to complain to, nor do we expect redress."[26] The Scots were devastated and in disarray following the Forty-Five but time and integration with England would in a relatively few years burnish Scottish prospects. "The aftermath of Culloden, in effect a military occupation by a suspicious regime, was traumatic in the short term and the harbinger of deeper, long-term changes, as the Hanoverian government embarked on a strategy to draw the Highlands as fully as possible into the mainstream of British life."[27]

☙

After Culloden, the opportunities of empire became more apparent to the Scots. Fifty years after the union, Edinburgh was thriving. The Scotophobe Samuel Johnson claimed that "the best prospect a Scotsman ever sees is the high road to London,"[28] and indeed a good many Scots were drawn there. Like their counterparts in America, they seemed to appreciate the commercial opportunities afforded by a laissez-faire private sector more readily than did English or European merchants. Increasingly, they grasped that "if hunting and gathering and pastoral-nomadic Scotland chained people to a life of destitution and ignorance, commercial Scotland opened them up to the rest of the world, and the rest of Britain."[29] The union not only created the largest free-trade zone in Europe but also gave Scotland access to the extensive English colonies. Sir Gilbert Elliot, Lord Minto, concluded: "Since the year 1746 ... a most surprising revolution has happened in the affairs of the country. The whole system of our trade, husbandry and manufactures ... began to advance with such rapid and general progression, as almost exceeds the bounds of probability."[30] By 1755, the Glasgow merchants had gained control of the tobacco trade and Scottish trade overall had more than doubled. Edinburgh prided itself as the centre of the much vaunted Scottish Enlightenment. There was a general recognition that "in place of empty titles and an insignificant pomp, they [the Scots] have acquired the more solid blessings of security, liberty and riches."[31] Scottish self-confidence had risen to the point that the distinguished author Robert Louis Stevenson mused, "It [Edinburgh] is what Paris ought to be,"[32] and the esteemed philosopher David Hume posed the question: "Is it not strange that at a time when we have lost our Princes, our Parliament, our independent Government ... are unhappy in our accent and ... speak a very corrupt Dialect of the

Tongue which we make use of, is it not strange I say, that in these Circumstances, we shou'd really be the People most distinguished for Literature in Europe."[33] Reassuringly, it was a sentiment shared not only by the Scots. Voltaire asserted that "it is to Scotland that we look for our idea of civilization,"[34] and the normally acerbic Horace Walpole opined: "Scotland is the most accomplished country in Europe."[35]

The union, in time, gave rise to a new world of expansive opportunity. "Instead of becoming a trap, the Act of Union launched an economic boom. In the span of a single generation it would transform Scotland from a Third World country into a modern society, and open up a cultural and social revolution. Far from finding themselves slaves to the English, as opponents had prophesied, Scots experienced an unprecedented freedom and mobility. For the first time, the term growth began to apply to Scottish society, in every sense of the word."[36] At the most basic level, the union presented lucrative career prospects to aspiring Scots. In the aftermath of the Forty-Five young Scots readily adapted to the broad array of opportunities offered throughout the empire and took full advantage. The East India Company (EIC) became an effective Scottish fiefdom; Scots established Jardine Matheson and many of the other great trading companies; and Scots built the Canadian railways, established its banks, and dominated the fur trade.

None of this was preordained. A relatively barren, sparsely populated, and impoverished society entering into a union with the world's most advanced economy, and a union in which political power lay in the partner's capital city, risked becoming a dependent satellite. Why is it, then, that Scotland, unlike Ireland, thrived in the aftermath of union? There are many reasons. First, the Scottish educational system prepared young Scots to compete effectively with their English counterparts. Secondly, England had sought union to attain political and military security and entertained little in the way of economic ambitions north of the border. Thirdly, Scotland had built diverse trading relationships and was not overly dependent on the English market; for example, in 1700 less than 50 per cent of Scottish trade was with England whereas Ireland was dependent on England for 75 to 80 per cent of its trade. That commercial experience meant that the Scots were well positioned to take full advantage of access to England's empire. Finally, members of the Scottish elite, to a much greater extent than their Irish counterparts, were committed to economic growth. They provided the impetus for agrarian reform and industrial and financial innovation, and they readily adapted the more advanced technology available in England to their needs and were soon improving on it.

As the country thrived, the Scots appeared to have fully integrated politically and economically with their powerful southern neighbour. A Scot, James Thomson, wrote "Rule Britannia" and other Scottish literati extolled Britain's virtues. Street names such as Hanover, George, Queen, and Frederick in Scotland's cities proclaimed the loyalty of the governing classes. Yet the Scots did retain a distinct identity rooted in their religion, their reliance on civil law, and their system of education. All classes from the lowest to the highest conversed in the Scottish dialect and revelled in John Barbour's and Blind Harry's poems praising Bruce and Wallace. Gradually, as any thought of a Jacobite menace receded and as the Highland warriors were increasingly seen in England as a staunch bulwark against the French and their republican values, "the Jacobite myth, with its potent mixture of themes of love, loyalty, exile and loss,"[37] came to represent a heroic Scottish past that was not only politically acceptable but also a rallying point for the entire British nation.

No Scottish family better illustrated Scotland's transformation after 1745 than the Baillies. In their eagerness to take advantage of all that the empire offered, in their complete absorption of English values yet, at the same time, their continuing Scottishness, the Baillies were the embodiment of the new Scotland, as the story that follows will demonstrate.

2

No Great Mischief

They change their skies but not their souls who run across
the sea.

Horace

Scotland was restless and very much a subordinate partner in Great
Britain when William Baillie, the first son of Alexander, 11th Laird, and
his wife, Anne Campbell, was born on 18 October 1739 in Inverness-
shire on the family estate of Dunain, a Gaelic name meaning Hill of the
Bird. William was the scion of a long-established Highland family. The
Baillies had run "an honoured course in the neighbourhood of the burgh
of Inverness"[1] since 1452 when Alexander, the 1st Laird, was granted
the baronies of Dunain, Dochfour, Leys, and Torbreck, part of the castle
lands of Inverness, by his maternal cousin, Alexander Gordon, the 1st Earl
of Huntly. This grant was in recognition of Alexander's assistance at the
Battle of Brechin against the Earl of Crawford, Alexander Lindsay, who
had rebelled against King James II. Alexander, 1st Laird of Dunain, married Catherine, the daughter of Duncan Grant of Freuchy, chief of the
Grants, and their descendants married into many of the prominent local
families in the area, including the Forbes of Culloden, the Roses of
Kilravock, the Munros of Fowlis, the Dunbars of Moray, the Frasers
of Phopachy, the Mackintoshes of Holm, and the Shaws of Tordarroch.
William's mother, Anne, was the third daughter of Sir Archibald Campbell
of Clunes, the second son of Sir Hugh Campbell of Calder, Shakespeare's
Thane of Cawdor.

The original Dunain line gave rise to the cadet Baillie families of
Dochfour, Leys, and Torbreck, and one observer could report in the late
nineteenth century that "Baillie of Dunain, the parent stock of all the
Baillies, is the oldest heritor by a considerable way in the parish of
Inverness."[2] At their zenith, the Baillies were large landowners, owning

the estates of Dunain, Dochfour, Leys, Torbreck, Balrobert, Garvamore, and Dochnacraig, while also holding a number of important local posts, including that of constable, sheriff and deputy sheriff, provost, and commissioner. Their story was not without sensational elements. According to family lore, the oldest son of Sir William Baillie of Lamington fled to Inverness as a result of an incident which is depicted in graphic detail in an aged holograph found in the papers of Baillie of Olivebank in 1792.

Baillie of Hoprig, Lamington and Penston was a branch of the Baliols Lords of Galloway. Hoprig[,] by marrying the daughter of the famous Sir William Wallace regent of Scotland, got the estate of Lamington. Their second son was the first of the house of Carphin of whom Jerviston or Jerviswood – Baillie of Hoprig in earlier days about 600 or 700 years ago – had two sons and one daughter and as was the custom in those days families of rank had a chaplain or priest in their families and this gentleman had the assurance to use too much freedom with the young lady for which reason the two young gentlemen, being exasperated for his so doing[,] deprived him of the opportunity of being guilty of the trespass in future by depriving him of his manhood[,] for which cause the church of the gentrie of that cast in those days having so much power[,] they, these two brothers of the said lady[,] were obliged to fly. The one went to the north toward Inverness the other to the west country toward Lamington and to this day it is a doubt which of the two was the oldest or chief of the family, Baillie of Dunain at Inverness or Baillie of Lamington in Lanarkshire, but the south Baillie having the best estate pretends to the chiefship though it is disputed and suspected much that the north brother was the eldest and this with many other mysteries of the present world must remain doubtful or secret till doomsday.[3]

Though Alexander, the 11th laird, was overtly conscious of his illustrious heritage,[4] time and Culloden had exacted a toll on the family. They retained some of their social prominence but their land had been subdivided among cadet branches and, despite the £250 dowry Anne Campbell had brought to the marriage, debts weighed heavily upon the remaining property. In all likelihood, the debt was the result of several factors, notably the general economic malaise in Scotland, the acquisition of property forfeited by Jacobite families after Culloden, Torbreck's debts (for which Alexander, as the heir of his father, was a guarantor), and Alexander's complacency. In his correspondence, Alexander dwelt on his debts but gave little evidence of any activity to alleviate them. One of his many creditors was his future son-in-law, George Baillie of Leys, whose frustration is evident:

> That I am a little displeased, at your returning no answer to a letter I wrote you ... & which I know you received, is certainly true – but it is likewise true, that I have at present, not in my power to lend money or have it lying out, in any bodies hands at interest; because dr. sir you know I have no less than £2,000 ster'g of patrimony to pay younger children; and it will take all my bonds in, to pay off that ... will any friend stand in the way of my doing so – tis really what I would not expect, at least of Dunain; more especially as you told me last time we were together; that at, or about this time, you were to get some money; and if I wanted ye payd of my debt to acquaint you ... at present I'm under an absolute necessity to raise money and therefore hope & depend upon you at farthest ag't the payment next month tho if sooner so much the better. Miss Anne your daughter or no young lass will have me till I get my affairs settled & put in order wh makes me in a hurry as I want much to be married.[5]

Much of how the family incurred its debts is speculation but there is no uncertainty as to one part of the story. John, the son-in-law of William, 8th Laird of Dunain, acquired Torbreck and Balrobert from his father-in-law. Though he held the lucrative positions of deputy sheriff of Inverness and factor for the Gordons and for lands administered by the commissioners for forfeited estates, he left his affairs in such an embarrassed state that his son, Captain William, was forced to sell Torbreck and Balrobert to the Frasers in 1758. Whatever the exact amount of the contingent debt, it was sufficient to cause Alexander a good deal of anxiety. Alexander's distant kinsman, Cosmo, 3rd Duke of Gordon, was the primary creditor of Torbreck and his actions prompted the following plea from Dunain in 1750:

> I beg leave to trouble your Grace to acquaint you with my situation with my regard to my engagement with your Grace as cautioner for Mr. Baillie of Torbreck your late Factor.
>   I am informed your Grace has sent positive orders to your doers to put a caution in execution against us and imprison us till your Grace

is pay'd of the debt due by us. I must own this is but just and I wish it was in my power to do it imedeatly but the situation of this country is such that men of much better funds than I can not raise the fifth part of your debt on any security but the sale of lands. I am at present leading an adjudication against Torbreck for my relief which is the most effectual and only method I can see for your Grace's payment and which I hope your Grace will approve of and order your doer to concur with me. For though your Grace shou'd throw me in prison I wou'd certainly rott there before I cou'd raise your money without selling the little thing I have to support myself and small family which I hope your Grace will not think just till first all methods are taken to make Torbreck[,] who is the principal debtor and who alone squandered your rents[,] sell his lands for your payment and whatever his funds come short of your debt I will cheerfully make up tho' I reduce myself to my shirt. I know your Grace's predecessors wou'd not see me unjustly oppress'd nor I hope will you but order your doer to stop any further personal diligence against me and goe on in any other method against him or both of us that will soonest make your payment effectual.[6]

The following letter from his cousin John would have assuaged any fear of imprisonment but Dunain's contingent obligation remained a pressing worry: "I have the favour of your post with relation to the Duke of Gordon's debt agst Torbreck in which you are engaged and am sorry for it. When the notice was sent north I am sure I was informed by some of the Duke's doers that they did not intend to stress you, which may have been the reason why I did not write on that subject ... No doubt you have a relief from Torbreck and I hope he is not yet so far in debt that he or his estate can repay you and if diligence can operate your relief I do not see you can be blamed."[7]

William was baptized in Inverness, the de facto capital of the Highlands and the winter residence for many of the local gentry. Daniel Defoe, the author of *Robinson Crusoe*, thought Inverness in the 1690s "a pleasant, clean, and well-built Town: there are some merchants in it, and a good Share of Trade. It consists of two Parishes, and two large handsome Streets; but it has no public buildings of any Note."[8] He also observed that the inhabitants spoke a pure form of English. They may have felt a notch above the Gaelic-speaking Highlanders, since, although they themselves were proficient in Gaelic, another visitor noted: "The natives do not call themselves Highlanders ... because they speak English."[9] The city exported salmon from the Ness, herring "of an inferior kind" from the Firth, cordage, sacking, and linen but had experienced a gradual decline since 1700. That decline was exacerbated by dismal harvests in 1739 and 1740 and shortly thereafter the devastation wrought by the Forty-Five. Nevertheless, in William's youth, Inverness experienced a marked economic recovery, stimulated by money the victorious army circulated after Culloden, the influx of wealth from the East and West Indies, the establishment of manufacturers, and the improvements in agriculture. By 1791, Inverness and its surrounding parish boasted a population of 7,930, three banks, a printer, a covered market, two tanneries, a tawning works, two tallow chandleries, a soap-boiling works, a brickworks, a hemp factory, a thread works, four stills, twelve brewers, and a thriving salmon fishery.[10]

Identifying, in its pretensions, more with Edinburgh than the surrounding Highlands, the town fathers of Inverness placed an emphasis on education. In 1664 they established a new grammar school which drew from the better-off elements of society. Then in 1727, under the auspices of the Society for the Propagation of Christian Knowledge, Inverness launched Raining's School, which catered to a broader spectrum of the population and offered classes in reading, writing, English, Latin, arithmetic, and church music. In addition, as the gentry increasingly recognized the value of education in preparing young men for careers in the rapidly expanding British Empire, they determined, in 1787, to create a "seminary of learning" and raised £6,277 in local subscriptions to found the Inverness Academy. By that time the town also had ten "more humble schools," which by law the local landowners were required to finance, to provide a basic education to youngsters who could not afford the fees levied at the academy. Reinforcing literacy, Scotland's General Assembly in 1704 provided for libraries throughout the Highlands. In short, while he predated the academy, William had local access to a quality of education that had been unavailable to his father and that difference is abundantly evident in the correspondence of those two generations. Some of William's own nephews were young enough to attend the Inverness Academy and many of his grand-nephews took advantage of that opportunity.

Over time William acquired two sisters, Anne and Helen (Nelly), and two brothers, John and Archibald, the latter of whom died in infancy. Irrespective of the additional siblings, William remained the favoured son, as evidenced by his father's lament to Fraser of Balnain that his wife "has the thing verie much at heart for carring on the education of her favourite son who is now at colege and in a more expensive way than we can easily bear."[11] William was an intelligent, conscientious, and handsome young man. He entered King's College, Aberdeen, in 1754, won the prize in mathematics, and graduated in 1758. Subsequently he attended the University of Edinburgh with a view to practising law. However, other opportunities beckoned brightly.

As the English continually expanded their empire, they experienced a heightened need for armed forces but begrudged the cost of mercenaries. As late as 1757, the ministry in London was content to send gangs throughout Scotland to impress sailors and to dispatch Scottish regiments to North America but remained reluctant to trust Scotland with its own defence against invasion or insurrection. This apprehension palpably manifested itself when, at the outset of war with France, Parliament passed a militia act providing for conscription by ballot but specifically excluding the inconstant Scots. Yet, while many English thought it folly to arm Highland Jacobites, economic necessity gradually eroded their resistance, as did Sir Edward Hawke's destruction of the French fleet at Quiberon Bay on 20 November 1759. That battle quashed any prospect of effective French support for a Jacobite rising and, incidentally, also prevented the French fleet from reinforcing Quebec against Wolfe's onslaught on the Plains of Abraham.

Wolfe, who, as we have seen, served in the Forty-Five under Cumberland, presumably reflected the English perception of the "weasel" Scot when, five years after Culloden, he cynically wrote Captain William Rickson. "I should imagine that two or three independent Highland companies might be of use; they are hardy, intrepid, accustomed to a rough country, and no great mischief if they fall. How can you better employ a secret enemy than by making his end conducive to the common good? If this sentiment should take wind, what an execrable and bloody being should I be considered here in the midst of Popery and Jacobitism!"[12] By then, the Highlanders had developed a reputation as formidable warriors, a reputation that extends to the present day.[13]

Besides military service, there was another route to advancement for ambitious Scots. That route was commerce, the horizons of which expanded considerably with the growth of the British Empire. As a result of the opportunities offered by the empire, prodigious wealth was no longer the exclusive purview of the landed gentry. Sir Robert Clive decisively defeated a massive Indian army at Plassey in 1757 and returned to Britain in 1760 with a fortune of £300,000 and a quit-rent on lands near Calcutta of £27,000 per annum for life. Paul Benfield, Sir Robert Fletcher, and Sir Francis Sykes were other men who returned from India with astounding fortunes which they employed to secure seats at Westminster. They were quickly dubbed nabobs, a mangling of the name for the Muslim princes who ruled several Indian states. These parvenus congregated in "Nabobery," located on Harley and Wimpole streets south of Regent's Park, and were known initially as the "Bengal Club" and later as the "Bengal Squad." The nabobs had a pronounced impact on society, constituting as they did, together with the West Indian planters, the first example of wealth independent of both the state and the urban merchant class. Furthermore, they had become acclimatized to command in India and presumed to continue in that vein in Britain. Accordingly, the nabobs aroused considerable envy, particularly when they utilized their fortunes to acquire magnificent estates; Old Masters paintings and classical antiquities, the escalating demand for which gave rise to great auction houses still in operation today, Christie's and Sotheby's; and positions in Parliament.

By 1779, the nabobs controlled twenty-six seats in the House of Commons. That number had almost doubled to forty-five seats in another five years, and by the time of the 1812–18 ministry of Robert Jenkinson, Lord Liverpool, who was himself of Anglo-Indian extraction, sixty-three members had served in India.[14] Their increasing prominence provoked resentment, as Wyatt Tilby points out:

> The nabobs, as the latter were commonly called in England, were for many reasons a most unpopular class of men. They did not generally come of high family, yet their wealth enabled them to outshine the heads of old country houses. That wealth could buy them everything save breeding and respect; and they attempted to cover the deficiency, after the manner of the upstart all the world over, by insolence. Accustomed to command in India, they assumed an overbearing tone at home. Their demeanour naturally aroused the furious resentment of all those particles of society which they had displaced; the aspiring snob and the lofty patrician were for once allied in detesting a common foe.[15]

Even Prime Minister William Pitt, whose family's prominence was based on an Indian fortune, seconded that sentiment and evinced the sense of entitlement of the landed classes. "The riches of Asia have been poured in upon us, and have brought with them not only Asiatic luxury, but Asiatic principles of Government. Without connections, without any natural interest in the soil, the importers of foreign gold have forced their way into Parliament, by such a torrent of private corruption, as no hereditary fortune could resist."[16]

The hostility endured. Half a century later, the ardent reformer William Cobbett vented: "It is a duty to God and Man to put the nabobs on the coal without delay. They have long been cooking and devouring the wretched people of both England and India."[17] Clive waved a red flag at the parliamentary bull investigating his revenue grant from the nawab of Bengal, the hapless Mir Jafar. "By God, Mr. Chairman at this moment I stand astonished by my own moderation."[18] By 1772, the scathing satirist Samuel Foote's play *The Nabob* had become a popular hit. The central character, Sir Matthew Mite, who sought to buy respectability by entering the House of Commons, was a blatant parody of Clive. Nor were the riches limited to Britain. When Elihu Yale was dismissed as governor of Madras in 1692 for corruption and trading for his own account, he donated part of his considerable fortune to the Collegiate School of Connecticut, which, in appreciation of the gift, adopted the name Yale College.

While, as Macaulay observed, the nabobs may have inflated the price of everything from fresh eggs to rotten boroughs, the resulting envy did not detract William's generation from its eagerness to emulate the nabobs and join the East India Company. "In Bengal and to a lesser extent, the Carnatic, the Company was seen to have in its gift a dazzling new array of appointments by means of which aspirants whether civilian or military and regardless of age, experience or ability could expect to acquire such wealth as would sustain the comforts of opulence and the fruits of influence for several generations to come. Calcutta had become a veritable Klondike."[19] The lure of empire was potent, particularly to striving and often impoverished Scots. John Maynard Keynes later marvelled at the phenomenon: "Escape was possible for any man of capacity or character at all exceeding the average, into the middle and upper classes."[20] Or as Kevin Phillips more colourfully observes: "Braw lads raised on cold oatmeal were now spooning sturgeon eggs."[21]

Yet it was not only the East Indies that attracted young Scots bound on improving their lot. As early as 1733, Kenneth, the brother of William, 10th Laird of Dunain, had planted a family offshoot in America, sailing to Georgia with its founder, James Edward Oglethorpe. Alexander Baillie, the eldest son and heir of Hugh Baillie of Dochfour, and the cousin of William, son of the 11th laird, sailed to Nevis in 1751 to work for James Smith's merchant company, Smith and Lambert. He was, naturally, intent on reaping some of the riches of the West Indies. To put those riches in perspective, Dochfour's island of Nevis accounted for three times more British imports than did New York in the years 1714–73 while imports from Jamaica in 1773 were five times greater than those of all the American colonies.[22] A few months after his arrival, Dochfour suggested to Dunain that success would elude the vast majority of his countrymen seeking their fortune in this tropical climate.

> An epidemick fever … raged round the Islands about Christmas and snatched off numbers of the natives, as well as Europeans; this came to compleat their distress after a violent hurricane they had in September. That rooted up almost all their sugarcane beatt still there … and drove ashore in Antigua, Montserrat, St. Christopher and this island above seventy sail of merchantmen and a great many more in Jamaica besides several small craft that were sunk in the different roads before they could unmoor and make out to see, but these evils are common once a year, for which reasons no ships stay or come here in September or October, but last year the hurricane came sooner than usual and the ships were long a loading by reason of a very indifferent sugar crop.
>
> The heat of the climate was on my first arrival very uneasy and disagreeable, but custom and a loss of some Scotch beef makes it now more tolerable. Besides when I see so many of my poor country-men who come abroad with very laudable intentions and may be truly said to earn their bread with the sweat of their brows, toiling and fatiguing in the field, exposed to the excessive heatt of the sun from morning to evening after a parcel of Negroes and find it a very difficult matter to make both ends of the year meet, it gives me com-fort to think that my lott is at least as good as thousands of theirs and that by arms and industry something may in time be made of it. Though I really believe several make it now as easily and with less anxiety and disappointments in more northern climates, and that entirely owing to the great numbers that from all nations would resort hither, from a very mistaken notion indeed that gold may be got for the gathering of it. There is no people more deceived in this respect than the Scots, who flock to the foreign settlements in num-bers every year, and I am sorry to say that I have hitherto seen few of them in a capacity to return, nor really do such as are seem to incline it much, for they as commonly come abroad young and before they are well able to judge for themselves, these countries grow naturally dear to them with their age for they are remarkable for their spirit

and resolution in all vicissitudes of fortune, an instance of this I had occasion to see last week, being at St. Christopher's. And in company with a young man from Dumfries, who after complaining bitterly of his ill luck since he came here told me he designed immediately for Jamaica, what, says I, for that cursed place that has been the grave of so many of our countrymen. He answered that he knew very well it was the grave of nineteen in twenty of such of them as went there, but as there was no encouragement for young people here and that he had done his best to no purpose for some time already, he would cheerfully run the risk of twenty to one for a fortune rather than go home a beggar ...

You'll expect before I finish my letter, I shall say something of the ladies, being full of making my fortune that way before I left Scotland, well, you must know that I have not yet had the pleasure of seeing many whose charms made any incurable impressions on my heart; I don't know whether it is owing to the disagreeableness of being restricted to one continual bedfellow in these hotter climates and almost suffocated with the effluvia of tobacco, or to their fortunes not answering expectations, but I protest the Negro wenches are much handsomer and friendlier in my eyes in all respects and for all the purposes you please, and I am sorry to observe that in all appearance the married men think so too for their honour be it spoken there is not one in forty of them but keeps one or more of them in chints and calicoes out of the field and for what purpose I leave you to judge.[23]

But success did not elude Alexander for long. He proved highly entrepreneurial in a broad array of undertakings. While still working for James Smith in 1753, Alexander described to Dunain his intention to utilize the first money he saved to purchase a small vessel to trade rum from St Kitts to Inverness. "In short, I see so many chances in a man's making money in that way to one against him, and such a benefit arising to the country by having their superfluities taken away, and their foreign goods bought cheap, which they now pay freight from, and extravagant prices at Glasgow for, that I'm resolved, whenever God puts it in my power, to have a small vessel, and try that trade in person."[24] That initiative did not materialize but others did. Alexander married Smith's daughter and in 1755 brought a younger brother, James, to St Kitt's. Shortly thereafter, they formed a new trading company, Smith and Baillies. The brothers bought the plantation Hermitage in Granada, which James managed while Alexander continued to operate from St Kitts. By 1770, a third brother had joined them and they began operating as the trading house Alexander, James and Evan Baillie. The firm and the brothers prospered to the extent that, when Britain legislated an end to slavery in 1834, the Dochfour family received £110,000 from the government as compensation for the slaves they had "lost." James later acquired Northbrook Plantation in Demerara. In 1775 he moved to London and in 1792 entered Westminster as the MP for Horsham.

Even by 1758 Alexander's prosperity was sufficiently evident that Dunain was despondently petitioning his kinsman to hire his son, William. At the same time, Dunain was clearly having difficulty reconciling himself to William's possible departure. William, on the other hand, had recognized that he was much more likely to restore Dunain's fortunes by venturing abroad than by wrestling with the estate itself. Alexander wrote, with a "verie heavie heart":

> My son Willie on whom I placed too much of my affection thinks my situation too contracted for both of us ... his plan is to go to St. Kitt's with a dependence on you. But what success you have had or how far you might be useful to him I know not. But one thing I am sure of that he and I would be greatly disappointed if you faild in that friendship we would expect. Upon the whole pray let me have your advice with regard to my son and when you intend being in this country, as I truly long to see you. I am now greatly distressed with the thoughts of parting with the person my hopes was mostly fix'd upon and if you do not give me some consolation either by your advice, or comeing soon home I am the next thing to certain as I am now on the decline of life it will hurry me to that state from which there is no looking back.[25]

The empire's bounty was brought home even more tangibly in 1758 when a son of Fraser of Phopachy, James Fraser, who had amassed a large fortune in the West Indies, purchased the ancient Baillie lands of Torbreck and Balrobert at the judicial sale instigated by the creditors of John Baillie of Torbreck. Meanwhile, nothing came of William's plans for a new start in St Kitts, and while I would like to think that moral revulsion at slavery in the West Indies may have prompted a change of heart, that may be asking too much of a young aspiring Scot in the mid-eighteenth century. In any event, as tension with France intensified, other opportunities seemed possible.

In 1757 Alexander Montgomerie, Earl of Eglinton, obtained a commission to raise the 77th Highland Regiment and Simon Fraser of Lovat, the nineteenth chief of Clan Fraser, surmounting his role at Culloden and his father's execution on Tower Hill, was given a commission for the 78th Regiment. As it turned out, Simon Fraser more than redeemed his family's Jacobite past. His regiment, together with the Louisbourg Grenadiers, formed the spine of Wolfe's attack against Quebec, and subsequently Fraser raised his eponymous 71st Highlanders to fight in the American Revolutionary War. Eventually, Fraser petitioned Parliament for the return of his estates, a petition that was granted in recognition of his service to the crown. In addition, Fraser represented Inverness-shire in Parliament from 1761 to 1782.

Highlanders, including William Baillie's family, were actively engaged in the Seven Years' War. Captain Charles Baillie, a cousin of William, fell on 8 June 1758 while leading one hundred Highland grenadiers in the capture of Louisburg, and another cousin of William, Lieutenant William Baillie of Torbreck of the 42nd Highlanders, was one of 551 redcoats and provincials who perished in General James Abercromby's ill-judged frontal assault at Ticonderoga on 8 July of the same year.

In view of the global nature of the conflict, and in an action that would shape William's career, the directors of the venerable East India Company responded to the French threat by petitioning for more European soldiers in India. Whatever the cause, by December 1758, William was residing with a Mr Grant in Edinburgh in an attempt to obtain a commission in the army. He wrote that month to his penurious father pleading for funds for food and rent and seeking introductions to great men. "I wrote you two or three past ago to which I have yet got no return which makes me suspect you either have not been well or have been waiting for some money to send … when you are at leisure just write me two or three lines to let me know how you do. If you happen to have a note or two why send it without waiting for sums."[26] A few days later, William reported: "I would fain hope our scheme may take place but there is no doing things in too great a hurry for such ado commonly come worst speed."[27] This was also the year in which William of Torbreck's death at Ticonderoga brought that family's financial difficulties to a head, prompting William's observation in the same letter: "But if Torbreck should go to the Devil … I hope we may live to overtake him and all who just now keep high heads." Like all sons of Scottish fathers, however, he added: "If you can send a little money without distressing yourself it will not be unacceptable as I would not chuse to trouble Mr. Grant but as little as possible."[28]

William's efforts were rewarded when Catherine, the Dowager Duchess of Gordon and widow of Dunain's primary creditor, sought to affirm her loyalty to the Hanoverians despite, or rather because of, her Culloden-tainted relatives. (Her father, William Gordon, had died in Edinburgh in 1746, having travelled there to declare for Bonnie Prince Charlie.) She raised the 89th Regiment under her second husband, Staats Morris, an American who would faithfully serve the British as a major-general in the American Revolution even though his brother Lewis and half-brother Gouverneur were distinguished Patriots. William wrote his father from Edinburgh that the wealthy West Indian merchant and British parlia-mentarian Sir Alexander Grant of Dalvey had sent details of his com-mission in the 89th Regiment, which "cannot happen for a month or two & therefore he thinks it would be as well for me to be in the north for these two months as spending my money here to no purpose."[29] Again, the subject of finances arose: "I believe it will take 8 or 9 pound to clear me of this town which I acknowledge is double the sum I ought to have occation to ask just now considering your yearly income but I hope some day I may be able to compensate your goodness to me which was always more than any son could in reason expect from a parent."[30] Owing to the Duchess of Gordon's sponsorship, Inverness-shire was well represented in the 89th. Hector Munro, whose life, for better or worse, would be intertwined with William's, was appointed a major in the regiment, William's bosom friend William McGillivray of Dunmaglass gained a captaincy, and eventually, on 18 October 1759, William acquired a 2nd lieutenantship.

Though he did not realize it at the time, William Baillie was on the verge of a life-determining journey.

3

Eastward Ho!

I don't like abroad. I've been there.

George V

In January 1760 William, accompanied partway by his father, set out to join the 89th Regiment in Elgin. Shortly thereafter, Dunain prophetically wrote: "As Mr. Pope says[,] though the curtain is drawn for a little twixt you and me I would fain hope it is possible we may meet once more. But if it should happen that you do not overtake your old father or mother our blessings is conveyed to you in the strongest terms in these few lines and to them you have a good title as you never disobliged us and may He who is blessed and rules the world take care of you. I will not now as you are going to the care of providence give any fatherly advices but your mother and I are of belief you will think of us with that friendship we naturally ought to expect."[1] William responded on 6 February from Aberdeen, outlining the route marched and adding: "I yesterday arrived here together wt the rest of the gentlemen in very good health after a march of four day ... The Colonel and the Duchess are just arrived. The Duchess goes directly for London and the Colonel remains here for some days in order to march wt us to Kingshorn where we are to ship for the Thames."[2]

Rumours ran rampant as to the ultimate destination of the 89th. At first, they expected to replace a regiment bound for Germany. Then William reported home that they had anticipated travelling to Portsmouth and thence to the East Indies but had received a counter-order to proceed to Hastings. In the interim, the East India ships had departed and that destination was seemingly rendered moot. Speculation then refocused on Germany and the defence of George II's cherished Hanover. William, who had never before ventured beyond the borders of Scotland, ended his letter: "And be assured that now I am at some distance, I think more of the banks of the Ness than ever I did in my life."[3]

Ultimately, as the French threat escalated, the entreaties of the East India Company prevailed and on 23 April William embarked from Spithead on the *Admiral Watson* for what, he believed, was Bombay. In an age when there was a high probability that those at home would never again see relatives or friends bound for Asia or America, there was an understandable hunger for news coupled with the nagging thought that the other party in any epistolary exchange wrote too infrequently. William wrote his parents shortly after setting sail for India:

By a letter Dunmaglass had yesterday from his sister I understand you have been uneasie at not hearing from me. But I think the uneas- iness ought to be rather of my side for this now is the fourth letter I have wrote since I came to England without receiving one. Upon Monday last we march'd from Chissister and embark'd immediately, and tho I was very happy in Capt. [George] Morrison's company being only Second Lieut: desired that according to Major Scot's promise I might be made first so he immediately put me into Dunmaglass on that account. He and I are the only officers on board this ship and tho it be the smallest I believe it is the newest and best of the four.

I hope by this time Mr. Baillie [Evan] has receiv'd my letter and is satisfied of the necessity I was under of drawing ... There has been only about two or three and twenty deserted from the five companies one of which number little Baillie the shoemaker. Make so if he ever makes his appearance in the north I beg you to remember him. You can have an opportunity of writing me by another fleet that sails from here about a month hence wt. the rest of the regiment for Bombay. So I beg you not lose the opportunity.[4]

After a voyage of five months, the *Admiral Watson* arrived not at Bombay but at Madras on 1 September 1760. William wrote his father describing the long trip and, revealingly, conveying his compliments to Dunmaglass's sister, Annie McGillivray:

Upon the first of September our ship arriv'd at Madrass on this coast after a four month's voyage ... On the 23rd of April we set sail from Spithead with a fine gale ... without anything extraordinary except the heat which indeed troubled us much as we were here for a few days becalmed ... But on the 22d of June we had a very hard gale with rain, thunder and lightning which made a division of our Fleet

for next morning we cou'd see only the Leatham. However, we did
not mind that much as we suppos'd we shou'd meet soon and that
our separation was only going to their steering a point or two different from us and to our great joy so it happened for just 30 days
after ... we met our old consorts ... a good deal to the eastward of
the Cape of Good Hope ... On twenty ninth we made the land of
Mohilla ... an island on the east coast of Africa for we kept between
Madagascar and the main land. Here it was designed we should
water. But either through a mistake or design, I am apt to believe the
latter (as the sooner we get India the better our captain's market)[,]
we steered a different course all night and in the morning there was
no land to be seen, about twelve o'clock we saw land again but it
prov'd to be the island of Comoro where no ships ever land, so we
bore away for India ... The Prince Edward and Sandwich sheered off
too[,] I suppose to get before and make the better market. So that
now there remained only the Leatham and us. On the second of
August in the evening I saw 4 sail of large ships making towards us
and gaining upon us fast. In the night we sailing better than the
Leatham got off leaving her in the very heart of them and as we supposed taken, we continuing our voyage on the 23d of August made
the island of Ceylon and so coasted it allong till the 1st of Sept'r.
when ... we arriv'd. The other ships in company with those four sail
of men of war which we left the Leatham with and look'd to be enemies arriv'd at Cudalore the 4 of September ...

   Now if I could give you any account of what sort of country and
climate this I would willingly. The shortest I think is this. That when
a man comes first into this country his chance for living the first
month is 3 to 1 against him but afterward if he has anything of a
tolerable constitution his chance is very good. This is reckoned the
healthiest part of the whole country. Our pay here is very good, to
a Lieut. it will be about 200 a year and to others in proportion to
their rank.

   Our Gentlemen are some of them well and some ill, however there
is none in a bad way. Give my complts. to Miss Annie McGillivray
and tell her that my good friend her brother is very well ... I thank
God since I have come here I have been extremely healthy ... As now
I think I have nothing else to say I wou'd beg it of you as my greatest
request to take good care of yourself, and to Mama the rest that they
wou'd do the same, for I can tell you I expect to be yet as happy
on the banks of the Ness as ever. But then I assure you my greatest

happiness will be seeing you and all well, and to see that is my great
and only desire. When you write me which I beg will be as soon as
you have an opportunity you'l be so good as acquaint of every thing
that has happened in the country since I left it and upon what footing things are.[5]

Nothing in his sparsely populated and impoverished homeland would
have prepared William Baillie for what greeted him on his arrival in
Madras. India in 1760 was a vast subcontinent encompassing what today
are the nations of India, Pakistan, and Bangladesh. It was a fertile and
resource-rich country with a population approximating 200 million at a
time when the entirety of Europe did not exceed 180 million. With its
abundance of precious stones, spices, cotton yarns and cloth, sugar,
indigo dye, silks, and saltpetre, India accounted for 24.4 per cent of
world gross domestic product.[6] The subcontinent was protected by the
Himalayan mountain range to the northeast and the waters of the Bay of
Bengal, the Indian Ocean, and the Arabian Sea to the east, south, and
west. However, India's wealth attracted invaders intent on conquest or
merely plunder and they all penetrated the country through its vulnerable
northwest passages.

For most of its later medieval and modern history, it was India's fate to
be on the receiving end of foreign influences. Following the establishment
of a series of Turkish-ruled Islamic sultanates throughout India in the
thirteenth and fourteenth centuries, Persian became the language of government across much of the region, and Persian cultural standards, in art,
dress, and etiquette, were adopted even in Hindu courts. But, for at least
seven hundred years before then, from about 400 AD to 1200 AD, India
was a large-scale and confident exporter of its own diverse civilization in
all its forms, and the rest of Asia was the eager and willing recipient of a
startlingly comprehensive mass transfer of Indian culture, religion, art,
music, technology, astronomy, mythology, language, and literature.[7] In
fact, during those centuries, India's influence in southeast and central
Asia and, to some extent, China was comparable to that of Greece on
Aegean Turkey and Rome and later in the remainder of Europe. Moreover,
that dispersion of its philosophies, political ideas, and architectural forms
was implemented not by conquest but by cultural sophistication, one of
the earliest examples of "soft" power in action.

At the time the British were first drawn to India, it was ruled by the
Mughals. Their first emperor, Babur, was a Muslim of mixed Turkic-
Mongolian heritage who claimed descent from both Tamerlaine the

Great and Genghiz Khan. Babur had subjugated much of the country following his victory at the Battle of Panipat in 1526. The early Mughal emperors, particularly Akbar, had provided capable government and enlightened leadership. Akbar accommodated his predominantly Hindu subjects by refraining from forced conversion to Islam, by including practitioners of all religions in high government positions, by permitting the Hindu states to conduct their own internal affairs, and by marrying a Hindu princess from Jaipur. This approach gave rise to almost two centuries of relative peace in which the economy flourished. However, the sixth emperor, Aurangzeb, alienated many of his Hindu subjects by discarding the pluralist policies of his predecessors. Aurangzeb was able to crush dissent and annex further territories but upon his death in 1707 the empire began its long decline. His heirs and their heirs fought among themselves, Mughal governors and the Hindu Marathas gradually asserted and achieved independence, assorted Indian states attacked each other in an attempt to expand their territories, and the world's two leading military powers, Britain and France, inexorably expanded their presence. The Mughal emperor in Delhi retained a nominal but symbolic power until the last emperor, Bahadur Shah, was bundled off to Burma in 1857 following the suppression of the Great Mutiny.

India at this time consisted of a profusion of semi-independent kingdoms. There were various levels of independence; for example, the rajah of Tanjore owed allegiance to the nawab of Arcot, who, in turn, acknowledged the nizam of Hyderabad as his overlord, with the nizam deputizing for the Mughal emperor. For foreigners, the proliferation of these states with their curious titles and pomp and ceremony added immensely to the country's exoticism. In addition to the nizams of Hyderabad, the country's indigenous rulers included the nawabs of Oude, the chhatrapatis of Bhonsla, the peshwas of the Marathas, the ranas of Jhansi, the wālis of Swat, the maharajahs of Baroda, the rajahs of Jath, the maharanas of Mewar, the maharaos of Cutch, the maharawals of Banswara, and the thakoor sahibs of Palitana. Over time the British appealed to the Indian obsession with hierarchy by developing a complex set of fine distinctions, with the princes eligible for appointment to British orders of chivalry and those of the higher-ranking states entitled to military salutes of between three and twenty-one guns.

The number of princely states was fluid as the more powerful sought to extend their territories in ongoing internecine conflicts, aspiring warriors declared independence from their particular overlord, and the British increasingly imposed direct rule on conquered lands. At the time

of William's arrival, the British had not yet amassed extensive landholdings but in 1765 the Mughal emperor granted them the diwani of Bengal,
Bihar, and Orissa. With that award, the British became the de facto rulers
of much of the lower Gangetic plain. Over the years, the British either
dispensed with an intermediary and annexed territory directly, as in
Oude, Delhi, the Sindh, Punjab, and Kashmir, or negotiated subsidiary
alliances with the local princes whereby the prince acknowledged the
hegemony of the British in return for military protection. These alliances,
for example, Hyderabad, Mysore, Jaipur, and, until 1856, Oude, appealed
to the British, who saw them as a way of avoiding the economic costs of
direct rule while also obliging native rulers to gain the political support
of the populace. Despite continuing annexation of Indian territory by
the British, there remained 565 princely states at the time of partition
in 1947.

But that was all in the future. In the 1760s, as the Mughal empire continued its steady decline, a few native princes consolidated adjoining
territories and became the primary powers on the subcontinent. An
accomplished warrior and administrator, Mahadeo Rao, assumed the
mantle of the peshwa of the Hindu Marathas in 1761; Hyder Ali, the bane
of the British and William in particular, usurped the throne of the Wodeyar
kings of Mysore in the same year; Nizam Ali ousted his brother in 1762 to
reign as nizam of Hyderabad and soubah of the Deccan; Mohammed Ali
succeeded as nawab of Arcot in 1749 and prevailed in the southeast; and
Shuja-ood-Dowla had reigned as nawab of Oude since 1732.

As if all this were not alien enough to William, he also encountered
other unusual customs. First there was the country's religion. Although
the emperor and the preponderance of his senior officers were Muslim,
the dominant religion was Hinduism, practised by roughly 80 per cent of
the population. Unlike Christianity, Judaism, and Islam, Hinduism has
no single founder, no single scripture, no consensus as to doctrine, and a
multitude of deities which emanate from a supreme being, Bhagavan or
Ishvara, who takes three forms: Shiva, the destroyer; Brahma, the cre-
ator; and Vishnu, the preserver. Hindus believe that existence is a cycle of
birth, death, and rebirth governed by karma (action). In that cycle the
nature of a person's next incarnation is heavily dependent on his or her
conduct in the previous life.

To Europeans, one of the most repugnant aspects of Hinduism was the
caste system, which appears to date from the Aryan invasions of circa
2000 BC. This caste system rigidly stratifies society into four main
classifications, with a fifth, the *dalits* or untouchables, outside it. The

brahmins are the spiritual and intellectual leaders, the kshatriyas are the warriors and administrators, the vaisyas are the craftsmen, artisans, and farmers, and the shudras are the unskilled labourers. There are innumerable subcastes within the four classifications. Caste, which is determined by birth, defines one's choice of occupation, one's rank within society, one's dietary and social interactions, one's choice of marriage partner, and one's access to religious, educational, and basic facilities.

The lot of the untouchables was much worse than that of any other group. They were condemned to work in occupations perceived as ritually impure, such as leatherwork, butchering, and removal of rubbish, animal carcasses, and human waste. Other castes believed that the pollution resulting from such activity was contagious. As a result, the other castes ostracized the dalits and subjected them to severe discrimination. They were segregated from others in seating at village functions, in schools, and in burial grounds, and they were prohibited from eating with other castes, from entering temples and the homes of other castes, and from using common village paths and properties. Given that opportunities were naturally greater for Muslims in a predominantly Muslim-ruled country, and given the severe disadvantages experienced by the lower castes and untouchables, it is surprising that more Indians did not convert to Islam.

In the eyes of Europeans, an even worse aspect of Hindu culture was the custom of suttee whereby the wife was burnt on the funeral pyre of her deceased husband. Theoretically, the practice was voluntary, but if the widow refused to participate in the ritual, she was ostracized by her family and community. Suttee was outlawed by the British in their territories in 1829 and in the princely states over the next few decades until Queen Victoria banned it throughout India in 1861.

By the time William stepped ashore, the Anglo-French conflict was in full swing. Since May, Sir Eyre Coote had been besieging Pondicherry, the centre of French power in India. Coote was an Irish veteran who was beloved and respected by his men. He had supported the Hanoverians in the Forty-Five, had distinguished himself at Plassey under Clive, would inflict a severe defeat on the French at Pondicherry and Wandiwash, and would, against overwhelming odds, defeat Hyder Ali at Porto Novo and at the Second Battle of Pollilur. He was to die at Madras while carrying on the Second Anglo-Mysore War.

For years, the cities of Madras and Pondicherry had borne the brunt of the hostilities on the subcontinent. A blockade by the Count de la Bourdonnais had enabled the capture of Madras in 1746. The city had

been restored to the British in the ensuing peace treaty but only after a
ransom payment of £440,000. With the resumption of war, the British
grasped the opportunity to revenge themselves on their erstwhile rivals.
William, with a wing of Colonel Staats Morris's 89th Regiment, disem-
barked at Cuddalore on 2 September to reinforce Coote.[8]

Britain's primary ally in the south of India was the nawab of Arcot,
Mohammed Ali, a tall and imposing man of great charm. British assistance had placed him on the throne of Arcot at the expense of his French-
backed adversary. Later, when the Mughal emperor released Mohammed
Ali from the suzerainty of the soubah of the Deccan, that same British
assistance enabled him to assume the most prestigious title in the south
of India, that of nawab of the Carnatic. As a result, Mohammed Ali
remained loyal, in his way, to Britain and the EIC, but he was notorious
for neglecting his commitments. In the present conflict, however, he
proved of inestimable value. Indeed, the nawab deprived the French of
their last hope by neutralizing the Marathas through a payment of twenty
lakhs of rupees. After that, the conquest of Pondicherry was merely a
matter of time, and William, with the 89th, continued to lay siege to the
city until starvation drove the governor general, the former Jacobite
Comte de Lally, to surrender in early 1761, an act that led to the ill-fated
Lally's trial and execution for treason by his superiors in France.

Following this success, the Company demolished the fortifications of
Pondicherry and proceeded to strip the French of their remaining possessions in India. Tayaga-Durgam fell on 4 February, Mahé on 9 February,
and Gingee on 5 April. From Fort St George, William provided a colour-
ful account of the fall of Pondicherry, remarked on the prospect of prize
money from the "Black King or Nabob" – Mohammed Ali – and once
more relayed his "compliments to Nannie McGillivray."

> I now write you from Fort St. George where we arriv'd a day
> or two ago all in good health and spirits from the taking of
> Pondicherry the chief settlement of the French on this coast.
> We ... began our approaches and batteries agst. it on the tenth of
> September 1760 and from there we continued coming nearer and
> nearer till the fifteenth of January 1761 when it surrendered. It is
> a place by nature very strong by reason of a great deal of water
> which surrounds it and well fortified by art. And it would not only
> cost us a great number of men but the company a vast expense had
> not their provisions run short for they were resolv'd to defend to
> the last, and when we took possession of it there was but one day's

provision in it. The loss of our whole army during the siege was only one officer and two artilery men ...

It is said we are to have some prize money and presents from the Black King or Nabob for taking it, and indeed it is [not] improbable for when we took it, there was in it godowns of great value and vast quantities of stores and ammunition, and for the guns that were mounted on the walls they were innumerable. However I'll believe it when I receive the money and not till then.

There is nothing else extraordinary to acquaint you with, for whether we stay and garison this place or go else where, we know nothing about only this, that there is only one triffeling place more to be taken belonging to the French on this coast, called Gingee which I suppose the Companies' Troops can take without the assistance of the King's Forces[;] we are in hopes that by this time there is a peace and that we shall be call'd home soon.

About two months ago we had the certain news of the second division commanded by Major [Hector] Munro were at Anjango and we are in daily expectations of them here. Pray give my compliments to Nannie McGillivray and tell her her Brother is very well, and I beg you may use her as civily as possible, for I assure you her Brother has been my particular friend ever since we have been together and has endeavour'd to show it on all occasions ... I beg when you write you will let me know every little thing that has happened since I left the country either wt. respect to your own affairs or any thing else that may occur ... I add no more but that where ever I am if at any time I am serious my thoughts are mostly about Inverness.[9]

Following the victory at Pondicherry, William settled at Fort St George, the headquarters for the army in the Madras Presidency, which encompassed a good part of southeastern India. The EIC's interest in Madras dated to 1639 when Francis Day, the Company's factor at Masulipatnam, purchased a square-mile building plot at the village of Madraspatnam from a local naik. The Hindu lord of the Carnatic, the rajah of Chandragiri, then confirmed the acquisition and the Company commenced construction of Fort St George. When the rajah was overthrown by Abdullah Qutb Shah, the Muslim sultan of Golconda in 1646, the Company secured a fresh title from the new overlord. Then, when the Mughal Emperor Aurangzeb in turn dethroned the sultan in 1687, the emperor renewed the EIC's title. By the time of William's arrival, Madras was the primary British city in southern India and the second largest city in Britain's empire.

In roughly the same era, William Hodges, the British landscape painter who visited India at the bequest of Warren Hastings, depicted Madras in glowing terms:

> The English town, rising from within Fort St. George[,] has from the sea a rich and beautiful appearance; the houses being covered with a stucco called chunam, which in itself is nearly as compact as the finest marble, and, as it bears as fine a polish, is equally splendid with that elegant material. The stile of the buildings is in general handsome. They consist of long colonnades, with open porticoes, and flat roofs, and offer to the eye an appearance similar to what we may conceive of a Grecian city in the age of Alexander. The clear, blue, cloudless sky, the polished white buildings, the bright sandy beach and the dark green sea, present a combination totally new to the eye of an Englishman, just arrived from London, who, accustomed to the site of rolling masses of clouds floating in a damp atmosphere … cannot … but contemplate the difference with delight: and the eye thus gratified, the mind soon assumes a gay and tranquil habit, an allegorist to the pleasing objects with which it is surrounded.[10]

But appearances were deceiving. Of the thirty ensigns commissioned in India in 1775, only sixteen survived to become lieutenants in 1780 although the only campaign was that against Pondicherry, which fell without assault. Of every one hundred arriving in Madras, fifty would die within five years.[11] In the words of one writer, "Calcutta, particularly in the damp, hot season, was as mortal a place as a man could choose to live in. Compared to these, Madras possessed a healthy climate. But it was only by comparison. Middle-aged arrivals were almost certain to die within the year. Experience teaches us to verify this general observation that men's lives advanced to or nigh the age of 40 are very precarious in such a climate."[12] Nor was the climate the sole provocation. Innes Munro noted: "Those who are new to this climate are cruelly harassed in the night-time by mosquito flies. No precaution whatever can prevent them from preying upon the ruddy cheeks of a flesh-coloured European, as they have such a particular relish for foreign blood that they will never desist from their pursuit until all the rouge is completely extracted, leaving their victim a miserable object, with his face swelled over, his eyes in bumps like the small-pox and ulcers in the legs, that with some do not close up for several months. The sting is fully as poisonous as that of a bee."[13] Munro clearly was not seduced by the romance of India for he went on to observe: "Providence surely never intended that Europeans should carry their conquests thus far from their native shores; for their immigration hither is certainly meant as a punishment and scourge. No one, in my opinion, that could exist in his native country, would ever wish to spend the best, or indeed, any, part of his life in this, were he once sensible of the difference. Even the allurements of wealth can be no compensation for the risks and hardships incident in a climate so foreign to his constitution, if life and happiness be his principal desire."[14]

A fellow officer arriving in Bengal agreed. "It is a common observation that the English Gentlemen ... are too apt to indulge their appetites so that it has become a saying they live like Englishmen, and die like rotten sheep. Of 84 rank and file which our company consisted off, on our arrival we had but thirty four remaining in three months, a convincing proof how fatal this climate is to Europeans. The most adult and robust, are most particularly unhealthy."[15] At the other end of the spectrum, James Baillie, Dochfour's second son, observed: "I am astonished that any person can think of injuring there children so much who are not born to independent fortunes, as to keep them after their Education in so compleat and in such a miserable country when they have such a country as Grenada, St. Vincent or the other West India islands to send them to, or what do you think of the East Indies for a change."[16]

We do not have much in the way of William's initial impressions of the native Indians, but, in an attempt to convey a sense of the country and its indigenous people, he sent home the following account written by the same anonymous officer in Bengal quoted above:

The inhabitants of Bengal wear turbans on their heads, and a piece of cotton cloth rolled round their loins, all the rest of the body is naked, the better sort wear a habit like a night gown. They are divided into a great number of tribes or casts, I mean the Gentoos, who are the original possessors of the country, the Moors (whose religion is Mahomedan) are intruders only. The Gentoos, tho pagans[,] yet have a confused idea of one supreme being and a future state; many of them adopt the opinions of Pythagoras. They are a gentle, harmless & inoffensive people, adhering strictly to their own antient customs & manners, notwithstanding the Moors, who conquered them, are almost as numerous as themselves. Simple indeed in their diet, but not so in their tempers, being greatly addicted to overreaching, & they think it meritorious to impose on a white man. They are slender in their persons, & very agreeably featured. A very barbarous custom prevails among them, quite inconsistent with their character, & that is, they burn the living wives, with their deceased husbands.

When the husband is laid upon the pile, his wife must stretch herself on his body, & her eldest son, or nearest male relation sets the first torch to it. Several instances of this happened while I was at Calcutta. If the woman declines, or absolutely refuses to comply with this custom; they won't compel but excommunicate her [from] her Tribe or Cast after which life becomes indeed a burthen so that the poor unhappy woman is forced to chuse either to be burnt or starve ...

Should any European enter their houses, they imagine them to be polluted, neither will they eat or drink any thing that has been touched by Europeans or even Moors whom they hate, & not without reason, for they are a lazy, haughty people, oppressing without mercy where they have any power.[17]

Munro's view of Indians was as follows: "It seems to be an invariable maxim with all of them to prey as much as possible upon Europeans, being contented with that mode of retaliation for the conquest of their country."[18] Likewise, the historical writer Robert Orme, reflecting the prevailing prejudices of the day, described Indians as "a most enervated inhabitant of the globe. He shudders at the sight of blood, and is of pusillanimity only to be excused and accounted for by the great delicacy of his configuration. He is so slight as to give him no chance of opposing with success the onset of an inhabitant of more northern regions."[19] Ironically, that same year, 1761, the most able challenger the British would confront in India, Hyder Ali, de facto usurped the throne of Mysore and proved eminently capable of resisting the British.

As for the Europeans living in Madras, the anonymous officer quoted by William Baillie found them singularly lacking in civility and generosity of spirit. Whether or not this assessment was warranted, his concluding sentence rings true. "The people of these settlements live in astonishing luxury, but notwithstanding have very little politeness among them[;] one seldom meets with a father & son two brothers, uncle or nephew or even cousins in one settlement, and as they have no ties of blood to cement their friendships; tis no wonder we find them so selfish. Every man's fortune seems to depend on the death, ruin, or removal of another."[20] The Company sought to control the deportment of its employees but that proved an increasingly uphill battle. "In 1754 the Company could still order the Governor and Council and all their servants, civil and military, to attend church every Sunday, unless they were sick; and enjoin the governor and Council to attend the morals and way of life of all under them; but it was no longer possible to enforce these provisions."[21]

By year's end, William was aboard the *Seaford* with his boon companion, Alexander Godsman, and 250 soldiers.[22] The EIC was intent on seizing the island of Mauritius which the French had renamed Île de France at the time they captured it from the Dutch. The seizure of Mauritius would eliminate all French influence in the east but the invasion was apparently aborted and the island did not become a British colony until 1810. In a letter to his father, William described this latest episode of his life in India:

The Seaford a 20 gun ship arriv'd at Madras in July, with an express from the Admiralty that Commodore Kepple with a fleet and troops were to be sent with all expedition to attack the Mauritius (an island about two hundred miles to the westward of where we are now and a very rich French settlement)[,] desiring as many of the ships that were in India as cou'd be spared to sail directly to meet them at St. Augustine's Bay, on the island of Madagascar. But by an after express by ye Alderney sloop of war ... the island of Diego Rays [Rodrigues, an outer island of the present day Republic of Mauritius] was fixed on for the rendezvous. When the first express arriv'd at Madras there was Commodore Tiddeman wt. four sail of the line there, he being scarse of marines petitioned the Governor for some land forces to supply this deficiency: so we to the number of two hundred and fifty, besides officers[,] were immediately embark'd. We sailed the fifth of August and without meeting any thing extraordinary arriv'd at Diego Rays the 16th of September. Soon after our arrival we were joined by Admiral Cornish wt. the rest of the India fleet. This island is a place where shipping generally (who are bound for the Indies) put in for water & turtles. It produces nothing else worth mentioning ... We cruised of[f] it till the 1st inst when giving over all hopes of Mr. Kepple we again set sail but where next God knows; only we hope for Madagascar in order to get some fresh stock, for this month past we have lived entirely on salt water provisions.

All your acquaintances in the regiment are very well. There is only Mr. Godsman and I in this ship and we are quite happy together. I beg you'l acquaint his sister that my good friend Cap't. McGillivray is very well. The prize money I mentioned to you in my last we had

reason to expect is quite out of hand & I am afraid it will turn to
nothing. Pray give my compliments to all who will be so good as to
ask for me, and to every body at home in particular and let me beg
that you will all think of me as seldome as possible, for I thank God
I have health, and money enough to serve me, which last I hope I will
always have without troubling you, so that taking care of yourselves
ought to be your chief care, for I assure you if ever I return to the
banks of the Ness which I don't at all despare of; seeing you all alive
will be greater happiness to me than any thing else whatsoever, and
wtout that I shall care very little for it. I beg you'l write me as often
as you can get an opportunity and let me know not only how all my
friends are but likewise how your own affairs go on. For I assure you
the most triffiling thing you can think of will be very agreeable and
acceptable. I hope to hear of Nelly's being well married, and Jock a
good scollar, remember me particularly to Nance of the Leys.[23]

This letter was the last to mention Annie McGillivray. It may well have
been that William's attentions were diverted elsewhere by that time. For
her part, Annie may have determined to await William's return, for she
never married and spent her days managing her brother's household.

Meanwhile, at home, Dunain's debts and financial anxieties continued
to accumulate. On what proved to be an unduly optimistic assessment,
John Fraser wrote to Dunain in December 1760 that the Torbreck affair
had turned out as well as they could have wished.[24] However, a year later
a harsh reality struck home when Dunain received a demand as guarantor for the late Torbreck.[25] The Dunain estate would be challenged to
generate sufficient funds to honour the claims against Alexander as guarantor, let alone retire or even reduce his debts, since its rentals that year
exceeded its expenses by the slimmest of margins.[26]

Back in India, as British arms prevailed on the subcontinent, the EIC,
despite the claim of its erstwhile ally, Mohammed Ali of Arcot, restored
Tanjore to its hereditary ruler. Mohammed Ali was dependent on the
British for his succession to the throne of his late father, Anwaradean
Khan, a succession that had been hotly contested by the French nominee,
Chanda Sahib. Nevertheless, the nawab was often slow to act in the
Company's interest. Accordingly, the EIC decided that it, in turn, should
not become overly dependent on the nawab. The Company rationalized
that Mohammed Ali would be placated by his recognition in the Treaty
of Paris, which concluded the Seven Years' War, as nawab of the Carnatic,
the paramount title in the south of India. This designation naturally

antagonized the nizam of Hyderabad, who asserted suzerainty over the nawab's territory, and, with greater long-term repercussions, Hyder Ali of Mysore. In any case, to compensate Mohammed Ali for the loss of Tanjore, the local rajah paid him twenty-six lakhs of rupees.[27] This payment was immediately applied to reduce the nawab's debts to the Company, but it had little impact in that regard as the Company proved exceedingly adept at creating new obligations. In all, Mohammed Ali paid the Company £1,425,000 in the space of three years and a reasonable valuation of the ceded territory would augment the effective payment by £4,440,000. That is an astonishing sum when we consider that the EIC army never surpassed three thousand Europeans and eight thousand sepoys, of which two thousand were the nawab's troops. Even more reprehensible was the Company's failure to attribute any value to the ceded territory in determining the nawab's outstanding debts.

The Treaty of Paris in February 1763 stripped France of all claims on the Coromandel coast, restored Pondicherry and Chandernagore to France, and triggered the recall of all His Majesty's regiments. Afterwards, no British army troops graced Indian soil until Lord Macleod's Highlanders (1st Battalion of the 73rd Foot) landed in the fateful year of 1780.[28] The same treaty also returned the lucrative trading centre of Manila to Spain. William wrote his father in June evidencing a tinge of envy for the "pretty little fortunes" earned by the troops who had conquered Manila in 1762 and bemoaning the likelihood of his being called home with little to show for his sojourn in the east.

I now write I believe for the last time from India in answer to your letter dated in October 1761, the only I have receiv'd since I left Scotland, and indeed before it arriv'd I was afraid I shou'd never have one for which reason I did not write you by the ships that went from here last year. All us soldiers (I mean of our regiment) have been much disappointed in this country, for instead of making rich as we expected and as I believe I let you understand by some of my letters, we had reason to expect. If we are brought upon ye peace, most of us will I believe return just as poor as when we came out, excepting our half pay, a very fine bargain for scorching in this country three or four years.

I fancy I need not tell you how successful our arms have been at Manilla, there indeed even subalterns have made pretty little fortunes. Our regiment I believe exceeds all the regiments that ever

came to India in bad luck. As to our great expectations from
Pondicherry I believe they will turn to nothing.

According to your desire I send inclosed a list of my recruits that
are alive. The effects of those who died, as they left no wills[,] fell to
the Captains of the different companies they belonged to. So in case
any of their friends should enquire about what they might have left[,]
this must sattisfie them as it was impossible for me to help it, it being
an established rule in the Army. Coll: Morris and all our regiment to
about 100 men are at Bombay ... We shall all if we are not called
home go to Bombay in Septr. next. We have had no deaths or prefer-
ments since my last, all our people are so strong that for my own
part I almost give up any hopes of a step [up], which if I do not
get before I go home, I shall curse the army while I live. Poor
Dunmaglass has lately been very ill but is now a little better ...
I wish all the poor people (I mean the tenants) well. I long vastly to
be among them but there is a thing or two that must happen first
wtout which it wou'd not tho' agreeable, make me at all so happy.[29]

4

Baillie-ki-Paltan

More than any other time in our history, we face a crossroads.
One path leads to despair and total hopelessness, the other
to total extinction. Let us pray we have the wisdom to choose
correctly.

Woody Allen

As it happened, William did not leave India. He may have experienced a change of heart relative to his expectations or he may merely have been reluctant to return home empty-handed after "scorching in this country three or four years." When the 89th regiment embarked for Britain on 21 December 1763, the disenchanted lieutenant resigned his commission and joined the military arm of the East India Company.

Generally, those who sought their fortunes in the outer reaches of the British Empire were the younger sons of the landed gentry. Sir Walter Scott described the EIC as "the Corn Chest for Scotland where we poor gentry must send our youngest sons as we send our black cattle to the South."[1] On the other hand, the eldest generally stayed home to understudy or manage the estate. William, as Alexander's eldest son, proved an exception. He may have enlisted with the EIC in order to earn enough money to discharge his father's debts, but regardless, as with so many other men of his age, William's decision to enlist in the EIC changed the course of his life.

The East India Company was a leviathan with extensive commercial and political tentacles. An enterprise focused initially on the spice trade, it had been chartered by Queen Elizabeth I on 31 December 1600 as the Governor and Company of Merchants of London Trading to the East Indies. The spice trade had long been dominated by the Spanish and Portuguese, but the defeat of the Spanish Armada in 1588 gave the English an opportunity to gain a foothold. The crown granted the new company a trading monopoly over an astounding expanse of territory, all lands to the east of the Cape of Good Hope and to the west of the Straits of Magellan.

The first EIC mission to India landed in Surat, the principal Mughal port, in 1608. William Hawkins, who led the expedition, failed to wrest trading concessions from Jahangir, the emperor at the time. However, various demonstrations of English sea power, particularly the defeat of the Portuguese at the Battle of Swally, convinced the emperor to grant the EIC the right to establish a trading post at Surat in 1612. The Company purchased a small plot of land at Madras from the naik of Wandiwash in 1639, acquired Bombay as part of the dowry of the Portuguese Catherine of Braganza upon her marriage to Charles II in 1665, and established a permanent settlement on the Hooghly River near the village of Kalikata in 1690. The English were irritants but the Mughals tolerated their presence as a quid pro quo for protecting their shipping on the adjacent seas. Eventually, in 1716, the EIC, by threatening to close the Surat factory upon which the Mughals depended for bullion shipments, obtained a firman giving it trading privileges in the Mughal Empire. This firman granted lasting title to the most extensive commercial and territorial concessions ever accorded a foreign power.

In view of the sizable capital requirements and risks involved, the original charter awarded the Company a monopoly for fifteen years but the hefty profits realized by the EIC in the India trade prompted James I to grant subsidiary licences to potential English competitors. At the same time, however, James renewed the Company's charter in 1609, as did Oliver Cromwell in 1657 and Charles II in 1670. In a foretaste of the future, Charles II further empowered the Company to acquire territory, mint money, command troops, form alliances, conduct war and peace, and exercise civil and criminal jurisdiction in its lands.

Monopoly was acceptable to the crown because the Company's imports yielded customs duties of £20,000 in a good year, and, over time, Charles II and his brother James were able to borrow from the Company £150,000, much of which remains unpaid to this day. Yet the EIC's monopoly status was in jeopardy since both the public and Parliament were convinced that the Company was impoverishing the country by exporting silver bullion and importing only luxury goods while manufacturers believed that increased competition would improve the prospects for their products. Under pressure to relinquish their monopoly and having suffered severely from Cromwell's Dutch wars, the EIC directors in 1657 voted to liquidate. The government, dreading the consequences of the

Company's failure, backed down and renewed the E I C's charter with its monopoly intact. Nevertheless, demands for open trade in India continued unabated, with the result that in 1694 Parliament passed a deregulating act permitting any English entities to engage in the India trade. Four years later, Parliament authorized a competing company with a state-backed indemnity of £2,000,000. However, the principals of the E I C subscribed for £315,000 of the issue and dominated the new firm. In practice, it soon became evident that there was little effective competition and by 1708 the E I C had folded the upstart into the renamed but undeterred United Company of Merchants Trading to the East Indies. The Company gradually edged out other European rivals to dominate trade in the two principal countries of interest, India and China. Through a combination of substantive representation in Parliament, a liberal sprinkling of Company shares to M P s, and continual loans to the government, the E I C was able to retain its monopoly of trade with India to 1813 and China to 1833.

By the end of the seventeenth century, the E I C had divided India into three presidencies, Madras, Bengal, and Bombay. Each president, or governor, was assisted by a council of ten senior merchants domiciled in the relevant city. In Britain the Court of Directors, on behalf of the Court of Proprietors, administered the operations of the "Grandest Society of Merchants of the Universe" from East India House, an unimposing building on the south side of Leadenhall Street in the city of London. The twenty-four-person Court of Directors managed the venerable Company through ten committees. Each proprietor with a holding of £500 was entitled to one vote and those with £2,000 in shareholdings were eligible to stand for the directorate. The E I C was the largest private employer in Britain's empire and one of the few offering the prospect of a sizable fortune. Accordingly, aspirants competed avidly for the Company's "writerships" and military appointments. Every year the directors were entitled to nominate a certain number of applicants as writers, cadets, surgeons, chaplains, home officers, and warehouse labourers. The clannish Scottish directors were notorious for reserving those appointments for the exclusive benefit of their fellow countrymen.

For years the Company considered itself solely a commercial enterprise, primarily dealing in cotton, silk, indigo, pepper and other spices, sugar, salt, saltpetre, tea, and opium. Following the E I C's expulsion from Bantam in present day Indonesia, however, the Court of Directors concluded that trading exclusively as merchants carried undue risk. "Prosperity and permanence depended on the Company operating in the east as a sovereign power with secure bases, adequate firepower and efficient government."[2] Nevertheless, the Company would have been content merely to fortify its primary posts and other modest landholdings had it not been for three factors. First, the disintegration of Mughal power following the death of Aurangzeb in 1707 ended a period of relative peace and meant that the EIC was compelled to deal, not with one recognized central power, but with numerous demanding and often contending local princes. Secondly, by 1719, France had established itself in India through the Compagnie des Indes, and, with the onset of the War of the Austrian Succession in 1744, the English and French found themselves on opposing sides. When the nawab of Hyderabad awarded the French the northern Circars in return for military assistance, France held the largest European-owned territory in India. The most objectionable provocation, however, was the nawab of Bengal's award of trading concessions to the French equal to those accorded the British after countless years of patient lobbying.

Finally, the superiority of European arms radically altered the balance of power on the subcontinent. While Indian military training had scarcely advanced during almost two centuries of relative tranquility under Mughal rule, European arms had been finely honed by incessant conflict. "Warfare in India was still a sport; in Europe it had become a science."[3] Indian recognition of this reality, together with rivalry among the native rulers themselves, enabled both the English and French to exercise much more authority than their numbers would warrant. By supporting one prince or another, the Europeans were able to maintain a balance of power and determine particular outcomes.

Gradually, the Company accepted that it had to intervene militarily to secure its trade. In 1756 Siraj-ood-Dowla, the nawab of Bengal, seized the EIC factories at Kasimbazar and Calcutta in response to what he regarded as flagrant violations of the emperor's firman. That seizure cost the EIC an estimated £2,000,000 and the death of 123 Company officials and dependants in the notorious Black Hole of Calcutta. At the same time, Siraj extended assistance to the Company's French enemies. Robert Clive reacted by taking the French factory at Chandernagore and by then defeating Siraj-ood-Dowla at the decisive and celebrated Battle of Plassey in 1757. When Hector Munro, although vastly outnumbered, routed the combined forces of the nawabs of Bengal and Oude and of the Mughal emperor in 1764, the emperor, Shah Alam II, signed the Treaty of Allahabad awarding to the EIC the revenue-collection rights in Bengal, Bihar, and Orissa. By a single treaty the Company acquired financial authority and political and military control over one-eighth of India. Moreover, the Company was also fortunate to be on the winning side in the first global conflict, the Seven Years' War. The Treaty of Paris in 1763 restricted the French to the enclaves of Pondicherry, Mahé, Yanam, and Chandernagore in India and effectively muted any Gallic threat by precluding a military presence in those outposts.

The EIC was a behemoth that pervaded all walks of life. It established the still thriving entrepôts of Hong Kong and Singapore and, at its apex, governed more subjects than any country with the exception of China, boasted the globe's largest merchant navy, and, almost inconceivably, controlled 50 per cent of world trade. Just as it intervened militarily in India to secure its commerce, the Company interceded in politics to safeguard its interests at home. Not only were there no fewer than sixty-three EIC servants or alumni holding seats at Westminster by the 1810s, but Horace Walpole had claimed as early as 1767 that at least one-third of the sitting MPs owned Company shares or, more flamboyantly, were "dipped in this traffic."[4] In an attempt to illustrate the Company's economic significance to Britain, Clive, in 1769, informed the House of Commons that the Company in this first phase had taken possession of a "rich, populous, fruitful country in extent beyond France and Spain united."[5] By 1833, the EIC controlled over 500,000 square miles in India, with ninety-three million British subjects paying over £22 million in annual taxation. To place the magnitude of the Indian accomplishment in context, Richard Wellesley, during his tenure as governor general from 1798 to 1805, conquered more territory than Napoleon did in Europe.

Besides exerting considerable influence in Parliament and effecting a shift in socio-economic power throughout the country, the Company, via its imports, altered habits of dress and diet. While silk and opium were utilized by a rarefied socio-economic class, muslins, tea, and spices were worn or consumed by people of all walks of life. The tea involved in that most iconic event of the American Revolution, the Boston Tea Party, belonged to the EIC; in fact, the Tea Act, awarding a monopoly of tea sales in the colonies, was an effort by Lord North's ministry to restore the Company's finances, which had been devastated by a famine in Bengal and the Seven Years' War. Moreover, the London money market arose from the EIC's requirement for Spanish rials. "It is no exaggeration to say that East India business generated the London money market just as it did the London docks."[6] Had it not been for the development of the money market, London would not have become the world's pre-eminent financial centre in the nineteenth century, a status it shares today with

New York. Finally, the Company provided a major new source of funding to sustain British initiatives. Indeed, Chatham grandiloquently viewed the riches of the Indies as "a gift from heaven" sent to offset the debts incurred in the Seven Years' War and thus secure "the redemption of a nation."[7]

There are many aspects of the British role in India that are difficult to comprehend, not least of which is the extent of the humiliation – and at times outright cruelty – inflicted on a subject people by an imperial power. The most astonishing feature of this story, however, is the fact that territorial acquisitions and the extension of British rule throughout the subcontinent was a process driven not by the state but by a private corporation. For many years, that process occasioned virtually no debate. But, gradually, a new view took hold. The Carnatic Wars of the 1740s through the 1760s and Wellesley's campaigns at the turn of the century, by transforming European trading companies into political powers through the outright acquisition of territory and the imposition of subsidiary alliances on several of the princely states, underlined the full scope of the Company's influence in India. Politicians at Westminster slowly came to conclude that Parliament should be involved in issues pertaining to subject peoples. "Playing on that old resentment against the Company's monopoly, on the growing unease about its management of its Indian territories, and on the jealousies being roused by the nouveau riche 'Nawabs' of the Bengal Squad, the Ministry sensed a popular cause. But how to wrest this providential windfall from the Company posed serious problems."[8]

In 1783 William Pitt was inclined to challenge the Company's right to hold territory but he failed to win support from his divided ministry. Such an assault on the Company faced numerous practical obstacles. For example, if the Company's chartered rights were violated, other chartered bodies would rally to the defence of the EIC. Moreover, if the offices or income of the diwani accrued to the state, George III would stoop to the role of a feudatory of the Mughal emperor. The secretary of the treasury and Britain's leading authority on Indian affairs in the later eighteenth century, John Robinson, objected strenuously to the British government's assumption of responsibility for India. He was convinced that there were bound to be "errors" in the administration of such a distant territory and that it was preferable to blame the Company's directors rather than the king's ministers for those "errors." Finally, there was concern that "a state takeover would confer such a reservoir of desirable patronage on the King and his ministers as to enable them to buy off all opposition and thus subvert the constitution and possibly subordinate domestic priorities to the exigencies of Indian policy."[9]

Preceding ministries had understandably preferred a negotiated settlement with the EIC. These negotiations gave rise in 1767 to an extension of the Company's charter in return for a £400,000 annual payment to the treasury and some constraints on splitting shares and raising the dividend. These measures had little impact on the Company but did establish a precedent for parliamentary interference in its internal affairs. That interference became more pronounced as rumours of Company abuses and reports of a devastating famine in Bengal – in which an estimated ten million people starved to death – reached Britain. The EIC was clearly not culpable for the natural disaster but Company officials did little to alleviate the impact and aggravated the crisis by raising land taxes 10 per cent to compensate for lost revenues.

The famine severely depleted the Company's revenues at a time when military and administrative costs were soaring. Its finances were under further pressure from the £400,000 subsidy to Parliament and the ever-mounting demand for dividend increases. In dire straits, the Company suspended its dividend and applied to the government for a £1,000,000 loan. It received its loan but at the cost of the 1773 Regulating Act, which appropriated more powers to the government. The act established a governing council in Calcutta with a majority nominated by Parliament, set up a supreme court whose judges were appointed by the crown, provided the government with access to all India correspondence related to revenue, political, and military issues, and gave the governor general authority over the subsidiary presidencies. At the suggestion of the first governor general, Warren Hastings, the act also sought to limit the egregious profiteering practised by the Company's servants. Despite the EIC's unenviable bargaining position, the act's provisions were vaguely phrased and subject to interpretation. At the time, John Robinson, was concerned that the Regulating Act had "neither given the state a definite control over the Company, nor the Directors a direct control over their servants, nor the Governor-General a definite control over his Council, nor the Calcutta Presidency a definite control over Madras and Bombay."[10]

There followed a number of attempts to rein in the Company but all were for naught until Pitt's India Bill of 1784 enshrined the ascendancy of Parliament. The governor general became a royal appointment, his authority over his Council and the subsidiary presidencies was confirmed, and a Board of Control appointed by Parliament was created to "superintend, direct and controul" the Company's possessions. This board, comprised of a secretary of state, the chancellor of the exchequer, and four privy councillors nominated by the king, reduced the hitherto proudly independent Company to a mere branch of the civil service. The Company then entered a long period of decline during which it surrendered its monopoly of the India trade, recognized the suzerainty of the crown in its territories (1813), relinquished its remaining mon-opolies, and yielded full power and authority over its possessions to the Board of Control (1833). Then, in the wake of the Indian Mutiny of 1857, Parliament assumed the Company's possessions and armed forces. This relic of another age lingered on until its dissolution in 1874 but its legacy permeates British and Indian life to this day. In an ironic twist of fate, the moribund company was acquired in 2005 by a Jain from Palanpur, Sanjiv Mehta, who now operates the East India Company as an upscale retail outlet in London's West End.

℈

William was one of five lieutenants to receive a captain's commission in return for inducing fifty soldiers from the royal regiments to enlist in the EIC's military arm.[11] On 2 April 1764 he was gazetted captain of the 5th Battalion of Coast Sepoys, which was "called for many years by his men who admired and loved him the Baillie-Ki-Paltan."[12] The 5th Battalion, which William would command until 1771, had been formed in September 1759 and was largely comprised of Muslims since, with the exception of the Marathas, the Hindus were not, generally speaking, attuned to military life. These sepoys were a splendid sight. A lieutenant in William's regiment allegedly observed that "the uniforms had a very military appearance. They consisted of a light red infantry jacket, a white waistcoat and a blue turban placed in a soldier like man-ner upon the head, edged around with tape of the same colour as the facings and having a tassel at the lower corner. He has a long blue sash, lightly girded around his loins with the edge passing between his legs and fastened behind. He wears a pair of white drawers, tightly fitted, coming half way down his thigh and being coloured at the lower end with a blue dye. It appears to be scalloped all round. A pair of sandals on his feet, white crossbelts, a firelock and a bayonet completes his uniform."[13]

The newly minted captain's financial circumstances improved mark-edly, commanding as he did an income of £300 per annum. William's first military assignment as an officer of the EIC was the siege of Madura. Like any other campaign, the siege would have begun on almost a festive note as the British officers embarked with their extensive entourages. William would have been accompanied by a cook, a stableboy, a barber, a man to wash and another to iron his clothes, a grasscutter, and, in the absence of bullocks, a number of coolies to transport his considerable baggage.

This particular encounter took place because Muhammad Yusuf, a subject of Mohammed Ali and hitherto an able and loyal ally of the EIC, had rebelled against the nawab and proclaimed himself ruler of Madura. In all likelihood, Yusuf would have remained faithful to the Company and a partial check on the nawab's growing power had not the Madras Council chosen to back Mohammed Ali, who, not coincidentally, was also the source of many of their private fortunes. As it turned out, the siege was not a prolonged affair as, recognizing the inevitable, Yusuf's officers delivered him to the Company. Madura surrendered on 14 October 1764 and the nawab lost no time in executing Yusuf.

There is little Baillie correspondence in the archival records for 1764 and 1765 save notification that Dunain had obtained a modest sinecure as collector of supply for Inverness and protracted exchanges with the 89th's agent, Henry Drummond, seeking to recover arrears and half-pay claimed by William. Major Hector Munro had deducted twelve months' subsistence for William and another party commencing 26 October although William's resignation from the regiment was effective 21 December. Drummond was unable to provide an abstract of Lieutenant Baillie's accounts,[14] further frustrating any reckoning. William's colleague Alexander Godsman, who had been handling the matter on William's behalf, replied, in thinly veiled exasperation, to an enquiry from an overzealous agent of Dunain.

I am very sorry to learn that Mr. Baillie of Dunain shou'd be so extremely uneasy about his son's arrears, which in your let. you say "I must 'ere now have recover'd, and whereof £40 falls to Dunain's share." To be sure it all falls very justly to Dunain's share if the sum was ten thousand pounds, for I have not the smallest title or pretence to half a farthing of it. Whatever strain his son wrote in to me, he was long 'ere now well convinced, that I never would make a handle of what he said in his letter, to curtail any part of whatever arrears might be due to him: which I hope you'l be kind enough to signify to Dunain at your convenience. If you or Dunain are of opinion that you can recover the arrears sooner than I, I shall inclose the power of attorney to you and send it in course of post and to make you or him certain that I have receiv'd no part of it already nor any thing in lieu thereof, you may please direct a letter to Henry Drummond Esq. (Great George's Street, Westminster Lond.) who is agent to the 89th Regiment and who will satisfy you on that point. I do assure you had I receiv'd any part of it, it shou'd not have rested a day in my custody, however it will only cost the trouble of a letter to be sure.[15]

Munro, understandably, had more on his mind than junior officers' arrears. The nawab of Bengal, Mir Qasim, had rebelled against the British – to whom he was indebted for the throne – and sought refuge with Shuja-ood-Dowla, the nawab of Oude. We have no evidence that William participated in the events that ensued, but it is highly probable that he did – or at least followed them with interest.

The allure of Mir Qasim's treasure and his own natural aversion to the EIC, which he perceived as his main rival for control over the Mughal throne in Delhi, proved irresistible to Shuja-ood-Dowla. The forces of the two nawabs and the emperor greatly outnumbered those of the Company. Nevertheless, Major John Carnac routed Shuja-ood-Dowla's army. Despite his impressive victory, Carnac, slow to move and preoccupied with his dignity, was censured by his masters for not pursuing the enemy and was superseded by Hector Munro. Malleson is devastating in his assessment of the unfortunate Carnac:

Major Carnac was not one of the glorious illustrations of the old Indian army. He possessed few of the qualities which are required in a general. Careful of his own comfort, absorbed by a love of the acquisition of money ... he displayed neither energy nor enterprise. With far greater means at his disposal than Major Adams (his predecessor), he accomplished much less. He paid but little attention to the comfort of his troops, who, however, disliked him less on that account than for the distrust he evinced on many occasions of their capacity to beat the enemy. The intense dislike felt towards him by his officers and men, and which can be traced in all the correspondence of the time, was increased by the semi-regal state with which, whilst careless for others, he shrouded himself.[16]

Carnac did prove victorious on a number of occasions but, as we will see later, would be dismissed by the EIC for his role in the ignominious Treaty of Wadgaon in 1779.

Upon assuming command, Munro quickly asserted control. Faced with a second sepoy mutiny, he summarily blasted twenty-five of the offenders from cannon, a salutary display that effectively discouraged future challenges to his authority. Then, Munro, with a force of six hundred Europeans, fifty-one hundred sepoys, and twenty pieces of artillery, pursued the enemy across the Tone River. Shuja-ood-Dowla's much larger forces, approximately ten thousand infantry and twenty thousand cavalry, held back, thereby providing the British time to form their lines. Despite effective Indian artillery, Munro's troops stormed the trenches and decisively vanquished the enemy at Buxar. Even though British losses of five hundred sepoys and one hundred Europeans were higher than the number of casualties previously sustained "against black troops,"[17] and Shuja-ood-Dowla himself escaped to Allahabad, Munro became the hero of Buxar.

A rehabilitated Carnac then succeeded the bound-for-Britain Munro and secured Shuja's surrender on 11 June 1765. Shuja-ood-Dowla signed a treaty with the Company, paid fifty lakhs for the cost of the war (although the Company's expenses were less than a fifth of that amount), and regained his lands. But the governor of Bengal, Robert Clive, obliged Shuja-ood-Dowla to relinquish the province of Allahabad to provide for the subsistence of the EIC troops stationed in Oude, ostensibly to protect the nawab.

Subsequently, the British gradually but inexorably circumscribed the nawab's powers, and by 1774 the EIC had imposed a British resident on Oude.[18] Despite British encouragement to shed the last vestiges of Mughal rule by proclaiming himself king of Oude in 1819, the nawab, in reality, reigned over a British puppet state. Finally, in 1856, the British ended the charade by ejecting the last nawab, Wajid Ali Shah, from the throne and annexing Oude. Conventional wisdom attributes the outbreak of the Indian Mutiny of 1857 to the natives' fear of pork and beef contaminating newly issued ammunition, but it is much more likely that the real catalyst was the annexation of Oude in conjunction with the shabby treatment of the popular Wajid Ali, who was also a poet, a playwright, a dancer, and a patron of the arts. That would explain why Oude supplied a disproportionately large number of the mutineers, why the rebellion was centred there, and why, following their victory, the British wreaked such devastation in Lucknow, the principal city in that state.

On 12 August 1765, shortly after Buxar, Alam II, the Mughal shah and king of Delhi, granted to the Company the northern Circars, although these lands were occupied by the nizam of Hyderabad, Nizam Ali, one of

India's most powerful princes.[19] The nizam subsequently agreed to cede the disputed territory with the exception of Guntur in return for the annual sum of nine lakhs of rupees and the Company's military assistance in attacking Hyder Ali of Mysore. The Circars would become a major bone of contention, with the Company on one side and the nizam and Hyder Ali on the other, but at the time the Circars were bestowed with much flourish and showmanship.

> Whereas Salabat Jung Bahadur, Soubah of the Decan, conferred the Circar of Siccacole, etc. on the French Company; and that, in consequence of its not being confirmed by us, either by Firmaum or otherwise, the high, mighty, glorious Chiefs of the Khans, chosen by the Omrahs, Sepoys, Surdars truly faithful, worthy of receiving favours and of obligations, are invariable and never-failing friends and well-wishers, the English Company (having sent a large force for that purpose) did expel the French there from; we, therefore, in consideration of the fidelity and good wishes of the above high, mighty, etc., etc. English Company have, from our throne, the basis of the world, given them the aforementioned Circars by way of Iniam or free gift ... It is incumbent, therefore, on your Sons, Omrahs, Viziers, Governors, Muttasseddees ... both now and hereafter, forever and ever; to use your endeavours in the strengthening and carrying into an execution this our most high command, and to cede and give up to the above-mentioned English Company, their heirs and descendants, forever and ever, the aforesaid Circars.[20]

In the midst of these grand events, William had more mundane matters on his mind. Initially, at least, far from helping alleviate his father's debts, he had financial concerns of his own. In an undated letter, Evan Baillie, Dochfour's third son, gently admonished Dunain to put his finances in better order. Evan had returned from his successful venture with his brothers in the West Indies and continued his trade from Bristol, where he served as sheriff, alderman, and MP. He wrote Dunain: "Duncan Grant has acquainted you of the demands from your Son. He goes a far voyage wherein I heartily wish him success. It is to Bengal in India ... & this it seems made his demands necessary and I have honor'd them directly in cash. There is nothing less to my liking than to see your debt encreased either to myself or another. Great pleasure it would give me to see them diminish'd and discharg'd, which I wish may soon happen."[21]

Lacking any mail from home, William felt abandoned by his family. We have very little record of him until 1766, when Godsman, having returned to Britain with the 89th, informed Dunain that William's Pondicherry prize money (just over £20) had finally materialized.[22] That may or may not have been the first of William's remittances to trim Dunain's debts but thereafter the payments flowed freely. On 12 June of that same year, William's first nephew, Alexander, was born to George and Anne Baillie of Leys. Anne was the elder of William's sisters and had married her fourth cousin once removed, George, the scion of a cadet branch of Dunain. George was a tight-fisted and stubborn individual who spent a good deal of his time in Edinburgh practising law as a writer to the Signet. Their son, Alexander, would prove to be the first of the next generation to follow in William's footsteps by pursuing a career in the EIC.

CR

Meanwhile, in southern India, the man who was to prove William's nemesis (as William was, in good part, to prove his), Hyder Ali, was emerging as a formidable adversary. Hyder Ali, who would become the most able indigenous military strategist and the most serious challenge to British rule in India, was reputedly born in 1722 at Boodicotta. His father, Fateh Mohammed, fell in battle supporting the nawab of Arcot shortly after Hyder's birth and he and his brother were raised by his uncle, the keladar of Bangalore. Hyder's daring and resolution, combined with the tactical and strategic vision displayed at the victory over the French and Chanda Sahib at Deonhalli, brought him to the attention of Krishnaraja II, the Hindu ruler of Mysore. Hyder became a protégé of Krishnaraja, who granted him ever greater responsibility, and his military skills and cunning enabled him to supplant the hereditary Wodeyar monarchs as the de facto ruler of Mysore in 1761. Krishnaraja II's son, Nanjaraj, inherited the de jure throne in 1766; however, Hyder Ali substituted the more pliant brother Chamaraja Wodeyar VIII as the professed sovereign after Nanjaraj was poisoned, purportedly by Hyder Ali himself. Chamaraja, in turn, was strangled in his bath in 1776 and replaced on the throne by a mere infant, Khasa Chamaraja Wodeyar IX, who succumbed to smallpox or, in turn, was murdered by Hyder Ali.

Hyder was tall and robust and, for a native of India, of a fair and florid complexion. "With a prominent and rather aquiline nose, and small eyes, there was in his countenance a mixture of stern[n]ess and gentleness; but the leading impression on the minds of those who described it, was that of terror; an inference resulting, perhaps, as much from experience as from physiognomy. His voice was mellow and musical, and on ordinary occasions, he spoke in a subdued tone. In dress, he exhibited rather an extravagant mixture of the soldier and the fop."[23] Although illiterate and cruel, Hyder was a skilled strategist and lacked any sentiment whatsoever, weighing everything in the balance of utility. He possessed great vigour of mind and body and burst through the prejudices of education and restraints of habit to adopt whatever improvements or ideas would advance Mysorean interests. While Hyder quickly recognized the superiority of European military training and enlisted French officers to instruct his forces, he also took advantage of Indian talents both traditional and original. The native cavalry's ability to engage and disengage with great speed is an example of the former while Hyder's innovations in rocketry illustrate the latter. Indeed, Hyder's development of rocketry techniques would prove decisive in his fateful encounter with William at Pollilur in 1780. Hyder Ali well merited the following assessment: "The career of Hyder Ali was eventful and adventurous. His success was equal to the highest ambition, as a usurper and a trader in war. The British encountered no such antagonist to their conquest or supremacy in their Indian enterprises."[24]

Had Hyder Ali been in a position to do so, he would undoubtedly have aided the French at Pondicherry in 1760, but he read the tea leaves and took no part in the conflict. Later, the recognition of Mohammed Ali as nawab of the Carnatic by the Treaty of Paris in 1763 angered Hyder Ali, who had never forgiven the nawab for reneging on his promise to cede Trichinopoly to Mysore in return for the assistance provided by Mysorean troops. The First Anglo-Mysore War of 1767–69 ensued and was concluded by the Treaty of Madras, which established a mutual defence pact between Hyder Ali and the EIC. When Hyder Ali was attacked by the Marathas in 1769, he berated the Company's equivocation when he called for assistance under the terms of the treaty: "That in case any enemy raises disturbances either in your country or mine, both are to join in the expulsion of such an enemy; for where friendship exists in perfection, the countries of each are one. I hope, therefore, from this time you will begin to reflect on all this and acquaint me with the result, as, after the enemy's penetrating either into yours or my country, you are then pleading an excuse that you must consult with the Governors of Bengal and Bombay, and be of no benefits; the saying, you know, expresses, that 'the remedy should precede the disease.'"[25]

Hyder pursued his demand that Madras honour its obligations on 7 March 1770: "In consideration of the union between us, the Army and Artillery which are with me are your own; notwithstanding, out of regard to the firm agreement mentioned in the Treaty between us, if the Company be but pleased it is then a small force to join and act in concert with me to save the good appearance, and to be talked of by the people, it will be very proper. It is a thing very apparent, that the good harmony and the sincere friendship between the Company and myself, will be beneficial to many affairs, and be a means to strike a terror into the Enemy, and to increase the friendship and regulate the affairs of both parties."[26]

Hyder Ali's specific request was for 300 Europeans, 3,000 sepoys, and the usual train of artillery.[27] The Madras Council debated the issue. A supremely self-assured Sir John Lindsay, recently arrived with plenipotentiary powers from London to investigate the dealings between the EIC and the native princes, argued consistently, albeit with little knowledge of conditions in India, that the Company should support Hyder's antagonists, the Marathas. In the end, the Council dithered and deferred. That betrayal, more than any other action, antagonized Hyder Ali and transformed him into a permanent enemy of the British. The final straw, which led to his invasion of the Carnatic, was the Company's attack in 1778 on the French trading post of Mahé, an enclave Hyder considered under his protection. Thus, by reneging on this relatively minor commitment, the discharge of which would almost assuredly have bound Hyder to the British, the Madras Council brought upon itself years of strife during which Hyder and his son, Tipu Sultan, posed a severe threat to British hegemony in India.

At the outset, William was very much a junior cog in the contest against Hyder Ali. That contest began in 1767 when, as a condition of their acquisition of the northern Circars, the government at Madras entered into a treaty with two of the subcontinent's most powerful princes, the soubah of the Deccan, Nizam Ali, and Mahadeo Rao's Marathas, to deal with that constant thorn in their side, Hyder Ali.

Nizam Ali was the fourth son of Nizam Asaf Jah I. He gained fame as a Mughal commander by routing and forcing a peace upon the Marathas at the Third Battle of Panipat in 1761. The following year he overthrew his brother to become soubah of the Deccan and nizam of Hyderabad. When the Treaty of Paris reinstated Salabat Jung on the throne of Hyderabad in 1763, Nizam Ali responded by executing the unfortunate Salabat. Over time, the once formidable Nizam Ali became more cautious, and, owing to his unsuccessful intrigues with the French, defeat at the hands of the Marathas, and fear of Hyder Ali, entered into an alliance with the British that essentially made him their creature. He remained on the throne of Hyderabad until his death by natural causes in 1803.

Mahadeo Rao's Marathas were a Hindu warrior confederacy from the western Deccan which, at its zenith in the eighteenth century, controlled much of the Indian subcontinent. They rose to prominence in the seventeenth century under the leadership of Shivaji, who challenged, with a good deal of success, the Mughal Empire. In order to administer the Maratha regime effectively, Shivaji's grandson appointed a peshwa or prime minister whose descendants henceforth ruled the Marathas. They remained the pre-eminent native power in India until defeated by the British in the Anglo-Maratha Wars which ended in 1818.

Mahadeo Rao had ascended to the musnud as fourth peshwa of the Marathas following his father's death at the Third Battle of Panipat. The defeat left the Maratha Empire in chaos, during which Mahadeo was ousted by his uncle, Ragonaut Rao. However, Ragonaut's ostensible ally, Nizam Ali, kept encroaching on Maratha territory. Mahadeo defeated the nizam and subsequently negotiated an accord with his former enemy. His goal was to recover Maratha lands from Hyder Ali but in this he was continually undermined by Ragonaut Rao. Finally, Mahadeo Rao captured his uncle in 1768 and was able to consolidate and enlarge the Maratha Empire. In an effort to manage an expanding empire, he granted semi-autonomy to his most stalwart allies, the Gaekwads of Baroda, the Holkars of Indore and Malwa, the Scindias of Gwalior, and the Bhonslas of Nagpur. These groups became the basis of the Maratha Confederacy. Mahadeo was one of the most able and respected Indian rulers and it was a tragedy for his people that he succumbed to tuberculosis at the tender age of twenty-seven in 1772.

In the action against Hyder Ali, the British contingent of 500 European infantry, 5 battalions of sepoys, including William's Baillie-Ki-Paltan, 30 European dragoons, and 16 pieces of artillery was led by the new commander-in-chief, Brigadier-General Joseph Smith. Smith, an avowed mentor to William, was well versed in the culture of the East India Company. He was the son of Joseph Smith, a former gunner of Fort St George, and had been commissioned as an ensign in the EIC in 1749, rising to major by 1760. Smith joined Nizam Ali's forces entering Mysore on 29 April. The soubah marched at a leisurely pace and Smith sought, with limited success, to goad him to greater exertion by emphasizing that the Marathas, having taken the field first, might conquer Seringapatam and seize the greater part of the spoils. But the Marathas were inconstant allies whose behaviour was denounced in scathing terms by one, admittedly biased, European: "A Mahratta is utterly destitute of the generosity and point of honour which belongs to a bold robber; equally destitute of mercy and of shame, he will haggle in selling the rags of a beggar he has plundered or overreached; and is versatile as the occasion offers, to swagger as a bully or to cringe as a merchant when he dares not rob."[28]

In fact, unbeknownst to Smith, the Marathas were sufficiently sated in their quest for plunder that Hyder was able to negotiate a separate truce. He paid six lakhs of rupees immediately with an equal amount due in six months and ceded to the Marathas the country he had entrusted to his brother-in-law. Hyder further intimidated the soubah by displaying his troops and bringing his cannon and firepower to bear. Nizam Ali's dewan, or prime minister, convinced him to treat with Hyder. To remove Smith and the bulk of the Company's troops, the dewan suggested to General Smith that he protect his supply routes from Arcot by securing the places which ensured free passage. Smith, increasingly suspicious of what was transpiring, grasped the opportunity to extract his troops from an untenable position. He immediately secured the mud forts of Vaniambaddy, Kaveripatnam, and Tiruppattur but was repulsed at the Fort of Krishnagiri. However, as Nizam Ali was still officially the Company's ally and the Council in Madras persisted in regarding him as such, Smith was forced, as a token of good faith, to leave William with three battalions of sepoys and six cannon in the Nizam's camp near Seringapatam.[29] Apprehension grew as the pay of William's troops fell into arrears. The officers entertained visions of the sepoys mutinying and defecting to either Hyder or Nizam Ali's army.

Smith, to no avail, pleaded with the Madras Council to seek peace with Hyder Ali, but at the same time dispatched William's fellow captain, Henry Cosby, with five hundred soldiers and twelve dragoons to deliver the arrears to William's men. Cosby rose to the challenge, as he would do on many occasions in the future. He marched three hundred and fifty miles in thirteen days and was able to deliver the money owing to the stranded troops. Still, although Cosby's funds had paid the arrearages, William and his men remained in a precarious position. They were subject to attack by both his antagonist and his purported ally with virtually no prospect of reinforcement.

William's jemindar, Ibrahim Beg, ingratiated himself with the soubah's forces and was able to confirm Smith's suspicions. The soubah and Hyder Ali had indeed come to terms and were planning to invade the Carnatic

with the intent of deposing Mohammed Ali and installing Hyder Ali's
son, Tipu Sultan, as the nabob of Arcot by virtue of his status as the prospective son-in-law of the pretender Mahfouz Khan. Mahfouz Khan was
Mohammed Ali's older brother and therefore the lawful heir of their
father, Anwaradean Khan. Tipu would continue his father's vendetta
against the EIC, and while he proved an even more implacable enemy of
the British, he was never the threat his father proved to be. Malleson was
puzzled that

> the memory of the cruel, narrow-minded, and bigoted Tipu Sultan is
> revered much more than the memory of his able and liberal-minded
> father ... Bigotry rules the Muhammadan world. And although the
> bigots lost the empires which their far-sighted and liberal ancestors
> had won, the Muhammadan world has pardoned the temporal loss,
> and, whilst it pays no heed to the qualities of the founders, still
> venerates the piety of those who undid the founders' work! Tipu,
> cruel and vulgarly ambitious, possessed none of the great qualities
> of his father. He was a poor soldier; never, as had been the wont of
> Hyder, inspiring his soldiers by personal leading. He did not lead, he
> sent his soldiers to the attack.[30]

Notwithstanding Malleson's puzzlement, Tipu Sultan would remain a
threat to the British until his death in the Fourth Anglo-Mysore War
in 1799.

Since their dispute was with Mohammed Ali and not his ally, the
Company, Hyder Ali and the nizam sought to neutralize the British in the
forthcoming conflict. It was perhaps for that reason that the nizam permitted William to withdraw with his men, on the rationale that, having
resolved his differences with Hyder Ali, he had no further occasion for
their services. Smith's army had pulled back to Vaniambaddy, where Smith
lamented to Lord Clive that Madras was not only ignoring his pleas for
reinforcements and provisions to defend the territory from the imminent
threat but, influenced by Mohammed Ali's undue assurances that the
nizam would continue the war, had blithely ordered him to share his scarce
provisions with his supposed allies. The dilatory Council delivered those
instructions only three days before Hyder and the nizam launched their
attack on the Carnatic. Hyder's brother-in-law, Makhdum Ali, slipped
through a pass, the existence of which was unknown to the British. He
managed to drive off the bulk of Smith's cattle and destroy a considerable
amount of his cavalry. The loss of the cattle delayed Smith's march and

enabled Hyder and the nizam to recapture Kaveripatnam. With their massive numerical advantage, sixty-five thousand troops against Smith's six hundred Europeans and five battalions of sepoys, the enemy threatened to overwhelm the Carnatic. Hyder sought to prevent the British from marching through Changana Pass but Cosby again came to the rescue, taking the key village and occupying the main hill while the advance guard cleared the pass. Smith rushed his troops to the hill to reinforce Cosby and repulsed several of Hyder's determined attacks. With the arrival of the last two guns, the Grenadier Battalion commanded by Captain William Baillie led a decisive rout of Hyder's army.[31] In the Battle of Changana Pass, Hyder and his allies suffered two thousand killed while Smith's casualties were limited to one hundred and seventy killed and wounded. Then, at the Battle of Rajahcoopun, although Hyder Ali's cavalry captured some of Smith's provisions, it was an unqualified victory for the British, whose twenty casualties contrasted markedly with Hyder's fifteen hundred.

On 8 September, Smith was reinforced by Colonel John Wood's troops from Trichinopoly. Owing to lack of provisions, Joseph Smith had fallen back to Trinomallee, which Mohammed Ali had undertaken to supply. Though this capricious ally again neglected his commitments, fortune favoured Smith, whose troops fortuitously discovered an ample supply of underground provisions. Hyder and the nizam, under the delusion the British were reduced to the last extremity for want of food, concluded that Smith's outflanking movement was a retreat toward Arcot and, throwing caution to the winds, fell upon the British wing and rear. However, the British were prepared and inflicted another severe defeat on the native princes.

Regardless of the setback, Hyder remained in a favourable position to surround an inferior force. Yet he was so disconcerted by the failure of his original plan that he failed to move the bulk of his artillery into firing range. With Hyder's cannon effectively out of action, the immense disparity in numbers did not faze the sepoys and "did not prevent our men from marching on with a firmness that will forever do them honour, for, notwithstanding all the efforts from cannon, musketry, rockets, and horse, they could not discompose our lines."[32] Smith singled out for praise the 8th Regiment under William Cooke, the 5th under William Baillie, and the 6th under Cosby, who "advanced with such rapidity, and gave so brisk a fire that the enemy's Sepoys could not stand it, but were obliged to quit their position and run."[33]

The British victory was sufficiently decisive that Hyder, having lost the greater part of his baggage and cannon, was forced to withdraw from the

Carnatic. William played a critical role defending high ground and leading his 5th Battalion.[34] The contest persisted, although an uprising in Malabar and offensive action by the Company's army in Bengal forced Hyder and the nizam to attend to their separate interests. Hyder Ali struck again in November when he took Tripatore and Vaniambaddy, but Smith expeditiously recaptured both. On Christmas Day, with Hyder incessantly harassing the EIC troops, William, under Major Thomas Fitzgerald's command, was sent to accompany supplies coming from Trinomallee. Hyder foresaw an opportunity to intercept the supplies and, under the illusion he was attacking a single battalion, led the charge himself with four thousand cavalry, two thousand infantry, and five guns. William's 5th was subjected to the first onslaught and stood firm in the face of overwhelming odds.[35] Hyder's horse was shot from under him and he was struck by a bullet through his turban. He retreated hastily into the Singarpettah Pass with the loss of over four thousand men and sixty-four guns. Fitzgerald reported: "Hyder Ali[,] judging that disappointing the army of this supply would benefit him in proportion to the distress it would be attended to with us, moved in person with the power of his troops to intercept it. About 5 yesterday evening he attacked us with more resolution than I ever saw his men show on any occasion … his horse made a most resolute charge on the 5th Battalion which stood firm on its ground."[36]

Around this time, the nizam acquired intelligence that Colonel Joseph Peach was travelling by sea from Bombay to attack the northern Circars. This threat further unsettled him and on 23 February 1768 he signed a separate peace. Under its terms, the EIC agreed to provide him with military assistance if he was attacked. The Company also achieved a reduction in the tribute it paid for the northern Circars, from nine lakhs in perpetuity to seven lakhs for six years.[37] In return, the nizam agreed that Mohammed Ali, the nabob of Arcot, was no longer subordinate to him and was entitled to the diwani of Mysore should he be able to wrest it from Hyder Ali.

The separate treaty with the nizam undermined Hyder Ali's position, enabling the Company's forces, including the 5th Battalion, to subdue the Fort of Krishnagiri on 2 May 1768. After Hyder narrowly escaped defeat, through Wood's ineptitude, at the hands of the combined forces of Smith and Wood, he sought peace with an offer to pay ten lakhs of rupees and to cede the Baramahal. However, the Madras Council, seldom missing the opportunity to miss an opportunity, rejected his overtures and the First Anglo-Mysore War dragged on indecisively. Then, in October, Hyder recaptured Mulbagal. Wood hastened to the rescue but was repulsed. Smith came to Wood's support on 7 October, forcing Hyder to withdraw. The wrong-footed Madras councillors ordered Smith to Kolar, ostensibly to consult with them but in reality to grant Colonel Wood an opportunity to shine in the field. In that respect, after a series of mishaps and missteps, Wood's light was wretchedly extinguished. Displaying "an incompetence worthy of his patrons,"[38] he was tried for misappropriation and misconduct in the field and cashiered.

In December 1768, encouraged by Wood's blunders, Hyder descended into the Baramahal and captured several poorly garrisoned forts. Smith resumed command the following February while Madras opened negotiations. Hyder spurned the terms offered and appeared with six thousand horse and two hundred foot within five miles of the city, having traversed one hundred and thirty miles in three and a half days. Smith was in rapid pursuit and came within twelve miles of St Thomas Mount. However, bowing to Hyder's demands, the craven Council forbade Smith to approach any farther. It then concluded what Smith, who had earlier encouraged the Council to pursue Hyder's peace overtures, thought a prejudicial treaty. Hostilities ended on 3 April 1769. Under the terms of the treaty, the EIC and Hyder Ali agreed to the restoration of all territories and a mutual-defence pact that subsequently gave rise to much animosity.

The Company ought to have learned a clear lesson from this experience. "The interests of the three Indian powers were mutually destructive. The one certain thing about the situation was that an alliance between any two of them against the third would be only temporary, and would be dissolved by its own success. In these circumstances the obvious course for the English was to avoid entanglements with any of the parties. What they did was to ally themselves first with the Nizam, then with Hyder, and then with a party of the Mahrattas, without any clear ideas of the responsibilities to which they were pledging themselves, and without the vigour to carry out the responsibilities which they had undertaken."[39]

It had been an eventful year for William Baillie, giving him an opportunity to display his military abilities while also introducing him, in a particularly brutal way, to the machinations of Anglo-Indian politics.

5

Brothers in Arms

I have been through some terrible things in my life, some of
which actually happened.

Mark Twain

Despite a recession caused by the First Anglo-Mysore War, William was
evidently growing more enamoured of India and its prospects for he sent
word home requesting that his brother, John, join him. Robert Munro,
a friend of William's and a cousin of Hector Munro, informed Dunain in
a letter dated 19 December 1767:

> Your son, Captain Baillie[,] came down from the armie to Ft
> St George purposely to see me September last was a twelvemonth.
> I have the pleasure to acquint you that he is in perfect good health
> and in as good a way as any younge man in India. He commands a
> battalion of seapoys or countrie troops which is verie lucrative and
> I do assure you he is in the greatest esteem with all the people on
> that side of India. I mean the Governor and Councell, both sivel and
> militarye. In short I do not know any of my acquaintance in that part
> of the world that promises or deserves prosperity so much as he
> does. I have a particular charge from him by all means to carie out
> his brother to him where he has it in his power to be of much greater
> service to him than anything that can happen to him at home, which
> with your and Mrs. Baillie's concert I am to have him out with me
> about this time twelvemonths.[1]

This was not the first mention of John's move to India. A month earlier,
William Fraser, who, despite his atrocious spelling and contorted grammar, served as Dunain's adviser on educational matters, had suggested
that John should undertake a demanding course of study on his voyage
to India. John "should be directly yoak'd to French, as the most generall

language[,] and to bookkeeping and numbers, and when he takes his passage, he may by himself in the course of his voyage make some progress in
both" and "he should otherwise amuse himself with reading when he is
not otherwise employed."[2] Even earlier, Fraser had written Dunain from
Edinburgh, "this place of smoak and business," remarking: "The best service you can do your boy is, that … you see to get him to acquire a fine fair
hand of write & figure well. It will do him more service in the world than
all the scholastick learning you can give him, unless he discover an uncommon genius for being a scholar & making his bread in that way: there is
nothing gets a young man an outlet for bread so soon as to write & figure
well, all kinds of businesses run on young people with these accomplishments and I have seen severall young people from Inverness have fine
hands tho' more of them a good time ago than of late."[3]

   John, as a younger brother, had grown up somewhat in William's
shadow. Like William, he attended King's College in Aberdeen, but,
unlike him, John did not garner academic prizes. At the same time, while
he was a reliable and devoted companion, John does not appear to have
possessed his elder brother's consummate interpersonal skills. In any
event, the two were close, and John's excitement grew at the prospect
of joining William. The family brought to bear whatever influence it
could exert, with the result that John obtained an appointment to the
EIC through the assistance of Sir Alexander Grant of Dalvey.[4] Colonel
Archibald Campbell, the EIC's chief engineer in Bengal, suggested that
"Jock" should not sail until the end of 1768 owing to the abundance of
candidates for posts,[5] and, in any case, it appeared that John could not be
sent to India before December.[6] Nevertheless, in November 1768, John
wrote from onboard ship that Sir Alexander Grant had again come to his
aid by arranging to place him on the first vessel bound for India.[7]

   John's departure meant another, albeit temporary, financial setback for
Dunain, since John had to resort to a further draw on his father in order to
pay for his passage to India. After his arrival in Madras in late December,
he wrote home: "I have been this two or three days abroad, we have 10 or
12 dish of meat every day to dinner and everything else in proportion. I
wrote Nelly from Gravesend what money I have drawn on you for I assure
you it vexes me to the heart the distress it must be to you to pay it. But I
trust in God once arrived in India my brother will remit home as much
money as will make the latter part of your days pretty easy and I give you
my word and my honour that whatever comes of me I will do all in my
power to make you all happy by having the happiness of seeing himself."[8]

CR

Dunain's grief at parting with his second son would have been assuaged by the prospect of further reductions of his debts. Robert Munro, in the same letter as quoted above, reported that although Captain Baillie "is struck from the half pay list, as he remain'd behind the Regiment in India without the King's livery," Godsman was in receipt of £50 from William and Munro already held a balance of £4.8, the total of which would shortly be forwarded to Dunain. William's father would also have taken consolation from the words of one of his creditors, Robert Sandilands, who wrote that the captain "may bring the sheaves, as well as the laurels with him"[9] when he returned to Inverness and that Dunain will "in few years have the comfort to see both your sons return in health and affluence and your family restored to as flourishing a post as ever it held at the greatest height of its former glory."[10] As a creditor of Dunain's, it was not unnatural that the "sheaves" and the "affluence" would be foremost in Sandilands's thoughts. Alexander's pride in his elder son shone through in a letter to James Grant. "I thank you heartily for your enquiry about my son. I heard from him a fortnight ago when he acquainted me he had more health and money than I can assure you his father has."[11] Moreover, Dunain would have revelled in the praise that General Joseph Smith lavished on William in his report to the Court of Directors in April 1768. Robert Munro wrote Dunain: "I have pleasure to acquaint you that I heard a letter read to the proprietors of India stocks, by the Secretary to the Companies, a letter written from Coll'n. Smith who commands the armie giving an acco't of his marches and counter marches, and his engagement wt. Hederanage, in which letter he gives your son great honnour on his galant behaviour. He commanded eight companies of the grenadiers of Sepoys."[12]

It was also in 1768 that the saga of the execrable Airds began. On 4 January, Donald Campbell of Airds, a Highland officer who had fought on the winning side at Culloden, wrote to Dunain requesting that William assist Airds's son Donald, then embarking for India. "I am happy to understand ... that your son William is in so good a way in the East Indies, may he arrive at the highest rank of military grandeur in that part of the globe and return home a rich Nabob. My son Donald is now at London so far on his way to that country, and will I believe saile the end of this or beginning next month, and it will be a favour done me that you write your son by him, recommending Donald to his acquaintance and notice, and so I am told your youngest son also goes. I wish the youngsters meet at London and saile on the same bottom."[13] Such a request was not uncommon, particularly in Scotland, and the implicit understanding was that the petitioner would stand guarantor for any debts incurred. Dunain relayed the appeal to William, who readily complied. Unfortunately, young Campbell suffered an untimely death and left debts outstanding.

The amount must have been meaningful for in a letter home dated 8 October 1769 William commented that the enclosed bill together with the demand on Airds should ensure the Baillies' financial comfort until his return to Inverness. This letter also indicates that, by now, William was apparently becoming more beguiled by the riches of the Indies, since he suggested, for the first time, that his cousin Francis also join the brothers: "The inland I make no doubt will be payable agreeable to its tenor and will at least I hope with the demand upon Airds help to make you and my Mother cosy until we have ye happiness of once more meeting ... If Frank cou'd be sent out as a Volunteer I wou'd with pleasure take care of him until he was provided for, but there is no other sphere in which he cou'd come to this country with any tollerable prospects. I shou'd think it might be done. My Brother is well & I hope will soon be a Lieutenant." The letter ended with a postscript mentioning the planned celebration of William's thirtieth birthday: "As to John I give you my word without partiality I find in him every thing I cou'd desire either as a Brother or as a friend. We intend both being very merry the 17th of this month."[14]

Notwithstanding William's best intentions, his parents' financial security was less secure than he had envisaged. By 29 January 1770, Arthur Cuthbert, William's agent in Madras, had forwarded two bills owed by the deceased Donald Campbell, and by 20 August Airds had sent a whingeing letter reneging on his son's debts:

I had your favour of the 15th late last night and am very sensible
of your kind concern for the loss of my son which you may believe
could not but affect his mother and me however resigned. Yet we
must and ought to be submissive to the will of Providence. I am also
extremely sensible of your son Cap't Baily's civilitys to Donald and
I shall never forget the obligations he laid me under on that account.
Tho' at same time as things are circumstanced, I should from my
heart wish he had been more reserved as to the advance of money,
as I doubt not you will judge with me, that I sett out my son on
such footing that he needed make no money demand, without being
more expensive than my circumstances could afford or his necessity
require ... I hope from the above state, you will allow that I did for
Donald much above what I could afford to a younger son, consistent

with any justice to my other children. Though happy your son Cap't Baillie is in such point of view as to be in condition to serve his friends, yet sorry I am that he in particular, or indeed any other, should be put to any inconveniency or loss by my son. I wrote Col. Arch'd Campbell in Bengal to see any effects left by him put to the best avail, and how far that goes, without regard to what I advanced for him above his patrimony, I am heartily disposed should go to pay his debts. But my expense otherwise of late, and other advances, however willing, puts it out of my power to do more.[15]

A chastened Dunain wrote to William that Airds was no gentleman and that he would have welcomed the funds for they would "be immediately applied to the discharge of our debts for my debts are yours. Dear Willie trust me and believe that I am as much your affectionate father as when we parted at Gordon Castle. Your mother is greatly failed as well as I am but our affection for you is the last thing that will leave us."[16] The last we hear of Airds is in a letter of 23 July 1772 from Margaret Campbell to Anne Baillie, the widow of Dunain, in which the former relates that her husband had determined that young Campbell's assets exceeded his debts and that Airds would soon be in touch with Mrs Baillie.[17] Yet, to no one's surprise, Airds failed even to honour this undertaking. William was genuinely shaken by Aird's deplorable behaviour and expressed his indignation and dismay. "Nothing could surprise me more than the behaviour of Campbell of Airds. I think it villainy beyond comparison that he shou'd refuse to pay money advanced in reality on his account to his son, otherwise in the utmost distress, nay even in want of the common necessarys of life ... I can hardly think him so devoid of principle but yet he can be shamed out of it."[18]

Other than the Airds incident, India was proving agreeable to the Baillie siblings. William found John "everything I could desire either as a brother or as a friend"[19] and they both looked forward to the arrival of their cousin, Francis Baillie. Frank was the son of Dunain's close relation Francis Baillie, tacksman (rent collector or tenant-in-chief bearing the clan chieftain's name) of Ballagan and, presumably, a first or second cousin of William and John. His mother, Margaret, lived at Dunain.

In a letter dated 20 January 1770 William reflected on the less appealing aspects of his assignment: "There is one Hinnegan of Carlisle who I hear has made some aplication to you about the amount of his Brother's effects who died in this country. I was under the necessity of being his executor as he belonged to our Regiment and shall, if he will give you a security against my being troubled further about, not only remitt the triffle his Brother left but also send him all the papers of his I cou'd ever find. Indeed, if I had not been at great pains there wou'd not have been sufficient to bury him, far less any thing to be remitted, though from that I claim no merit as I looked upon it, my duty."[20] Another duty arose from the expectation of relatives or acquaintances, no matter how distant, that an officer in India would take an interest in their sons lately arrived in India. Marie Baillie was married to a second cousin of Dunain, William Baillie of Ardmore, a younger brother of Hugh Baillie of Dochfour. Although Marie had never met William, her deceased son David had apparently been friendly with him. In any event, Marie wrote to William in 1777 pressing her demands on behalf of her son, who had tastes well beyond his station.

Though I have not the honour of a personal acquaintance yet I am no stranger to your character in life – while as a man of worth and a soldier, affordes the highest satisfaction, to all you are connected w't and to those of your country who share in your good fortune. Mr. Baillie and myself, who are much interested in your felicity, were made Happie unexpressibly so, by a letter from Mr. Andrew Ross, giving us accounts, that our young man, Simon, was so luckie as fall under your protection, a favourable circumstance indeed, for him, and his fond parents; and that being the case, we both rest satisfied, if he proves deserving that you will protect and countenance him, as your relation and namesake. As Mr. Baillie has already writ you and recommended both our boies to your friendship, we assure ourselves that your goodness of heart will lead you to give them a helping hand when needs require. I do not mean money, but your advice and friendship. Simon I fear has an expensive turn which if indulged must prove very unfavourable as he has not a shilling to depend on from this or any other quarter, further to what his indulgent good father may of his free choice bestow on him[,] he already having laid out on him, all that he has a just title to claim. It will be kind and good in you Sir, to curb as much as possible his inclination or genius as to an imoderate expense or contracting debt[, which] of all other disposi-tions [is] the most ruinous to a young man particularly in the army. Mild means I know from experience agrees best w't Simon's temper who is a warm hearted affectionate lively boie and do not want for parts, if he takes a right turn[,] but he is keen and hot tempered to a fault. As I have used the freedom to tell you my mind, and sentiments of Simon, will you good Sir, indulge a fond mother by telling her honestly by letter under your own hand, how my poor boie behaves as I am in dread about his conduct ... His brother John I have less fears about, he being a very advisable, honest boie. I dare say both of them by this time, grown stout lads. The death of my dear and valuable Capt. David Baillie has affected us in this family severlie, Simon and John, all great sufferers by the loss of so generous and good hearted a brother.[21]

By the time William received Marie's letter, he had come to like and respect her son John while also sharing a "fond" mother's concerns about Simon. "Your son John is well and without flatery in my opinion a very promising youth. I have told him again and again and you may rest assured, any thing in my power to assist him I will do most readily and not only in justice to so good a recommendation but realy from a likeing to him. I am truly sorry for my friend Captain David were he alive he would stand surety for what I promise in regard to his Brothers. Simon disliked either the climate or the service or perhaps both and return'd home in October last."[22]

In 1770 William noted that one of his kinsmen, a son of Sir Alexander Mackenzie of Coul, was returning home with a fortune of between £8,000 and £10,000. Some fortunes, however, were suspect and William had reason to believe that this was true of Coul. In any case, for his part and that of his brother, the continuing recession in India, accompanied as it was by a famine in which one-third of the population of Bengal died, was not sufficient to deter them from dwelling on their prospects for advancement and, ultimately, financial gain.

> Now as to our situation. John has not yet got a commission though in daily expectations of it and Wm. is the old Cap't still endeavouring by every (I hope fair) means to get that which wou'd carry them back to their parents and native country. The bill has been very slow on this coast for years past, and the last war has not a bit mended the matters. Had this not been the case, I shou'd have been at home long ago. However we have now only to wish for better times.
> Sir Alex'r Mackenzie's son had great luck at Bengal & yet nevertheless I do not envy him for by all accounts he has left the service with a very bad grace.
>   We have at present here the near prospect of an other war being daily threatened by the Mahrattas. A detachment of which John and

I make part marches tomorrow for Trichinopolly a place about two hundred miles to the southward to prevent any incursions on that quarter.[23]

That same year, 1770, John Alves, a doctor and son of Thomas Alves of Shiplands, married William's younger sister, Nelly. Alves brought with him three sons, Thomas, Alexander, and Archibald, and a daughter, Mary, from his previous marriage. As another example of the interconnectedness of the Inverness gentry, that earlier marriage had been to William and Nelly's cousin Jean Campbell. At least one of Alves's children, Archibald, remained closely interwined in later life with his Baillie half-siblings and cousins. Despite the pious platitudes strewn throughout his correspondence, John Alves proved a conscientious and tenacious steward of William's interests in Scotland.

In the same letter in which he announced his marriage, Alves conveyed the unwelcome news that William was not on the half-pay list despite the assurances of General Stringer Lawrence that he would not forfeit his army rank and half-pay by remaining in India. George Ross, the London agent of the 89th Regiment, had undertaken to enquire further into the matter and Alves assured William that his friends were renewing their efforts on his behalf.

Few of your friends I assure you have been more anxious for your success and prosperity, or happier upon hearing of it than I have been. Our acquaintance and former connexions entitled you to this, but now a nearer tye interests me in your welfare and happiness. Your Father's letter which accompanies this will inform you that upon the 13th March your sister Nelly and I were married at Dunain. Did not your distance from here render it impracticable to have your advice in a matter of this kind, I'm sure, whatever her inclination might be, she would never take a step of so much importance without your entire approbation, as I know there is not a person upon earth she so much values as she does you, or upon whose friendship and affection she so much relys. The match indeed cannot be considered by any of her friends, as advantageous to her in point of fortune; but, thank God, happiness is not necessarily connected with wealth. It can subsist without it: a decent competency is indeed necessary, and Providence, I trust, as it has hitherto done, will still continue to supply me with that. Nothing but personal attachment could have induced either of us to think of the other as a partner for life, and when this is founded upon a long and thorough acquaintance with each other's tempers and dispositions[,] it promises a longer duration and to produce a happier union than is attainable without it let the parties have never so much riches to boast of. Neither of us I hope will have cause to repent our choice – nothing I'm sure would make her do so, so soon as your disapproving it.[24]

Later that year, on 20 October, Alves briefed William that all attempts to recover his half-pay had been thwarted, as had been all efforts to shame Airds into honouring his son's debts. On a happier note, Nelly was pregnant,[25] and Alves enclosed a note from Dunain commenting: "I am of belief that you will have as much satisfaction of him [Alves] as a Brother-in-law as I have of him now as a second son, poor Jock only excepted."[26] The doctor provided some salacious local gossip reflecting on the manhood and integrity of Major Alexander Mackenzie of Coul. Time would effectively rebut the former charge, as Mackenzie sired an heir with his wife, Katherine Ramsay of Camno. Alves's opinion that Britain was on "the eve of a Spanish war" anticipated the outbreak of hostilities by a good nine years since Spain, while embittered by its losses sustained against Britain in the Seven Years' War, did not intervene on behalf of the American rebels until 1779. Portentously, Alves refers to two people, Hyder Ali and Hector Munro, who will play critical roles in William's future and launches the campaign to persuade William to return to his native country.

It gave me great pleasure to hear by it and other accounts that your health continues good, and your constitution unimpaired by the fatigues you must have undergone in the late war with Hyder Ali and the great heat of the climate you live in. Tho' these have not yet produced any sensible effects, yet they surely operate in some degree and in time will bring on an early old age with the infirmities that usually attend it. But I hope you will think even a small competency with health, preferable to greater riches without the power of enjoying them, and that you will take your measures accordingly.

I wrote you a letter ... It inform'd you that a few weeks before, your Sister Nelly had become my wife, and I have now the pleasure to add that I hope in a few months she will become a mother. Her health is not very good at present, owing partly to her pregnancy, but I hope she will get free of her burden and her complaints in due time. As she writes you herself I need not add any more.

I inform'd you in my last what steps had been taken with respect to your half pay affair. I'm sorry to say that our efforts have hitherto proved ineffectual, nor do I believe that any thing can be done till you return to Britain yourself, when I hope you will find no great difficulty in getting yourself repaid. As your Father is to write you fully with respect to your claim upon Airds, I need not say any thing on that subject. Tho' your debt is not strictly a legal one, yet surely it is a debt of honour, which every disinterested person of good sentiments will say ought to be repaid; yet I'm sorry to say, I have no great expectations from it.

For the same reason that you do not write of Indian politicks, I believe I must be silent as to the political transactions in this country. What is generally known here such as that we seem to be on the eve of a Spanish war ... Tho' Major Mackenzie came to Britain, he has not come north. But his Father and Mother have gone to Edin'gh to see him. There is talk of his returning to India again in the spring. As the family is so weak, he being the only son, most people seem surpris'd that he does not rather marry & settle in the country; but he may have reasons they don't know. By hints I have had from one that was very intimate with him, I suspect that tho' he did marry, he could not beget an heir to the estate. It is said here, that he has not yet got any thing considerable to be called a fortune.

Your acquaintance Bob Munro has been disappointed of a ship which he expected lately to get the command of. He is now here & goes up soon wt. his cousin, Col. Hector Munro[,] to Lond'n in order to push this affair further so that perhaps when you see him next, he will be a Cap't.[27]

The half-pay affair continued to weigh on William's mind and he let his father know that "I have by this ship sent a power of attorney, certificates etc. to one Mr. David Mitchell at Messrs. Annan & Calhoun's merchants of London who has been recommended to me as a diligent good lad if possible to recover my half pay. I beg if there has already any steps been taken towards the recovery he may be made acquainted with them." Mitchell was able to isolate the particular obstacle to William's receiving his half-pay claim but was no more successful than his predecessors in actually securing payment. Colonel Morris had left William's name off the regimental list when the 89th disbanded. William could qualify for payment only if Morris provided a certificate that William belonged to the regiment at the time it "broke."

Meanwhile, John had been forming his impressions of India, impressions that did not depict the natives of the country in an advantageous light. In a letter written in early 1771 in which he related his sense of the place to his father, John, then in Vellore, described India, if not its inhabitants, as a glass half full rather than half empty.

I'm sorry I'm now not well able to keep my promise in regard to giving a description to you of this country and its inhabitants. The reason is this[,] that without a knowledge of the country languages a man gets but a little account of them and what he does get is so very uncertain that it is hardly worth sending his friend or relation. And another thing is that they are in themselves such a poor miserable race there wou'd not be any thing very entertaining or that wou'd compensate his trouble in making such an enquiry. I do not make their opinion of (or behaviour to) us any rule for forming this idea of them because I do not altogether blame them for looking upon us as a set of people who have nothing to depend upon at home and therefore come here to destroy and pillage their country and consequently do not think themselves oblig'd to keep any faith with us. But as far as I can learn[,] they have very little principle among themselves and I have heard it frequently observ'd that they have not a word in their language to carry the idea of gratitude. They have some notion of a return for a benefit receiv'd but I do not believe they have that generous sensation which every man ought to have when he shows his benefactor his remembrance of the good office. They do not seem to have half the degree of passions we have the want of which prevents their exerting those parts which God Almighty has bestow'd upon them and makes them appear in a despicable light to us and I wou'd also infer from it that they cannot enjoy pleasure nor feel pain to half the degree we do. Indeed, for those eighteen months I have been in the country I never have seen one of them in a passion or rather in those momentary fits of madness which we are liable too. Upon the whole they are a poor sett not worth the saying any thing more of. As to the country it is a very fine one healthy and pleasant producing all the necessarys of life. I mean as pleasant as a country so hot as this can be to Europeans. For the mercury rises to between 95 and 100 degrees at twelve o'clock for three or four months in the year. The hottest time is about from the 15th of March till the later end of June. These are the months the land winds blow. In July we have frequently showers of rain which cools the weather a good deal. In

the later end of Septem'r or beginning of October the monsoons ...
and then we have fine cool clear weather for about three months.
They commonly sow the land in November and gather in the harvest
in Jan'y. The principal grain is rice of which they have great quantities. There are several other grains peculiar to the country. There's
but little wheat here. However, European gentlemen have plenty of it
and as to the country people they prefer rice. We have plenty of the
tropical fruits (which luckily for me I care little for). There's good
cattle both large and small. The horses are very fine but scarce and
consequently very dear ... I must observe one thing more of this
country. That it is the best in the world for a young man who has
nothing to depend upon as he is sure if he behaves himself properly
to get what he comes for. That is baring the great accident that every
man is liable too. And I assure you the risk of that is quite trifling.[28]

In 1771 William informed his father that he was in Madras with his
unit, by now renamed the 5th Carnatic Battalion, to prepare for a likely
campaign. If there were no immediate war with Spain or France, he
would, in all likelihood, be employed against the rajah of Tanjore, who
had not paid his yearly tribute to "our Nabob, Mohammed Ali." General
Smith had asked William to act as his brigade major but that was inferior
to his present position and William was balking. He added in a postscript: "I beg in future by the ships that sail in January some of the latest
Scotch magazines and newspapers be always sent me. John is well at
Vellore and shortly to be a Lieutenant."[29] The invasion of Tanjore commenced in September but was called off by Mohammed Ali once the
rajah agreed to pay the nawab fifty lakhs of rupees. To blunt the troops'
disappointment at a lost opportunity for prize money, Mohammed Ali,
oblivious as to the source of such funding, promised seven lakhs of rupees
to be shared by the EIC forces.

With the Tanjore expedition aborted and the Carnatic tranquil, William
once again lamented his want of political connections and mused about
returning to Scotland, albeit without a considerable fortune.

The Carnatick is at present in peace, promotion hardly to be expected,
and the few places of profit filled up by those who chance to have
interest with the Governor and Council of Madras. The little I have
had has always been through the military men, and from them at
present nothing is to be looked for. Letters to Mr. Hastings, second
in Council, and soon to be Governor, would help me much, but the

method by which these could be obtained, I can neither devise myself
nor direct my friends. At any rate, be assured I will not long be
absent, for I am entirely of opinion that a man had better return in
the flower of life with a small fortune wherewithal to make himself
and his friends happy, than with millions when, perhaps, he has not
the good luck to overtake them, or constitution to enjoy it himself.[30]

In fact, however, William and his finances were flourishing and the remittances from India began to flow in earnest. In February 1771 Arthur
Cuthbert, whom William had appointed as his agent in Madres, sent a
£400 bill of exchange to Dunain and said of William and John that they
were "perfectly well at Vellore[,] one of the inland garrisons."[31] Then, on
29 June, William's mother acknowledged, in a letter written by the soon-
to-be India-bound Francis Baillie, the receipt of another £853, with which
she intended to discharge some of her husband's creditors "in the manner
I think will be most agreeable to and for the interest of my said son
Captain Wm. Baillie."[32] For Dunain had succumbed to his ailments and
departed this world on 30 June 1771. William was now the 12th Laird of
Dunain and directly responsible for the estate and its debts. John Alves
informed William in November: "Your bill for £850.11sh which I then
told you your Father endorsed two days before his death has been duly
honoured and you will see by the enclosed state of debts how that money,
and a little more has been employed. Your last bill for £400 has been sent
to London and I have reason to believe has been accepted; but as it will
not be payable for near a twelve month to come I expect to receive your
answer to my last letters before that time with particular directions how
you would have this money laid out."[33]

The following month, George Baillie of Leys elaborated further on
Dunain's failing health over the course of the year and detailed a litany of
William's relatives' medical ailments. George wrote:

I certainly would have wrote to you on your Father's death had
I been there at home. That event happened most unexpectedly to us
all for undoubtedly this time two years as I think I wrote to your
Brother he was in remarkable good health & spirits but last winter
he failed much and in spring particularly all the month of March we
were much afraid of him tho' my wife's extraordinary bad share of
health rendered it impossible for us to attend him. However as soon
as she could come this length we were here and he seemed much
better. So that it being judged necessary for her to go to Peterhead he

urged our going directly which accordingly we did but were not long there when he dyed as I'm persuaded of a polypus for I can not conceive another cause for the so sudden change. You may believe this calamity greatly affected your Sister who continued all summer very ill so that I brought her to Ed'gh to have the best advice for her ...

Thank God she has mended ever since and is now pretty advanced with child. We have been here these two weeks with your Mama who is just scrambling only yet out of a fever in which I assure you we were all most dismally afraid of her. Nor do I think her out of danger yet tho' it's our most earnest desire she may live to welcome you home here. To say the truth if she does not, it must make some confusion which I most heartily wish may be prevented by your speedy arrival here where your personal presence I'm persuaded will give the greatest pleasure, and satisfaction to all the real well wishers of yourself and family ...

I should not omit to acquaint you that your Mother has managed hitherto most properly, altogether for the good of thye family making no separate interest but extinguishing the debts as fast as possible nor do I believe more can be done than she does ...

P.S. your name son is a very pretty child and walks stoutly.[34]

Another letter, written by Alves in January 1772, makes the standard plea for William to return home but adds that if "you find it necessary (and you must surely know your own affairs best) to remain a little longer where you are, it will be necessary that you send a factory or power of attorney. Your Mother and I do the best for you that we can, but we want a legal authority."[35]

In light of William's accession to the lairdship of Dunain, Alexander Baillie of Dochfour raised an issue which had been troubling Dunain before his death. Dochfour noted that the Dunain estate was limited to male heirs and that, given the risks inherent in both brothers serving in India, William should consider altering the provision to enable their sisters' children to inherit the estate. Otherwise, it would accrue to their Dochfour cousins. Such an alteration was well within William's power. Indeed, his father had expressed his desire to effect the change but the old procrastinator had not acted.

Our friend Alves has undoubtedly given you an account of your Father's decease & of the concerns of your family in a fuller manner than I could pretend to do, what therefore remains for me is only to console with you on the occasion which I sincerely do; the character of uprightness and goodness of heart which the honest man has left I am persuaded be of more joy to you than if he had bequeathed you a greater estate. That also may by the help of money be considerably improved & I pray God it may be handed down to his own Posterity, which he was very naturally anxious about.

I dare say it is known to you that the Estate of Dunain is limited to heirs male, not by entail but by a restriction any successor can alter; your Father in his lifetime & indeed within these twelve months past communicated to me his intention of altering the succession, so as in the case of yours & your Brother's demise the Estate shou'd fall to his own Grandchildren, & not to Mr. Alex'r Baillie writer in this place, who (in that event) wou'd be the heir male. Now my Dear Sir, I hope you will pardon my officiousness in medling unasked with these matters but it proceeds from a real love & affection which I bear to all your Father's children, & his own memory, & a pride & pleasure it wou'd afford to see a certainty that the family being always represented by his descendants. If I might therefore presume to recommend any thing to you, it wou'd be that (considering we are all mortal) you wou'd as soon as convenient execute a deed, making over the property of the Estate (in case of your own & Brother's & heirs of either of your body's failure) to such of your Sister's children as is most agreeable to yourself, it being entirely in your own power to dispose of it to any child or children of either of your Sisters. A settlement of this kind can be attended with no inconveniency in the event which all your friends ardently wish of y'r settling among them, and it will prevent a world of litigation & expense shou'd it please God that you or your Brother do not return to this country. I thought it my duty from our early acquaintance to mention this matter & particularly as from my knowledge, your Father had it so very much at heart.[36]

6

Affairs of the Heart

Never open a can of worms unless you plan to go fishing.

Proverb

It is difficult to gauge exactly when William took an Indian wife or bibi; nor do we know the woman's name. In any case, taking an Indian mistress was long an established practice and, at that time, carried very little social stigma in India. Indeed, the East India Company, in its early days, when its foothold in India was fragile, encouraged the growth of a Eurasian community as a bulwark of English influence. In 1687 the Court of Directors informed the head of the Madras Presidency: "The marriage of our soldiers to the Native women [is] a matter of such consequence to posterity that we shall be content to encourage it with some expense and have been thinking for the future to appoint a Pagoda to be paid to the Mother of any child that shall hereafter be born of any such future marriage, upon the day the child be christened if you think this small encouragement will increase the number of such marriages."[1] On the other hand, there remained sufficient residual racial prejudice that it was understood, if only implicitly, that an Indian liaison was not something about which one wrote home. Similarly, servants of the Company returning home would seldom mention their Anglo-Indian families.

Such relationships were inevitable given the influx of young single European males and the virtual absence of unmarried European women in that country. Many of these relationships were not formalized by marriage, discouraged as they were by the requirement since 1719 that the governor consent to the marriage of any Christian inhabitant of Madras. By that time, the rule was introduced to discourage marriage with poor girls of mixed and especially Portuguese blood on the rationale that "many of the young gentlemen in the Company's service [were] ... of good families in England, who would be very much scandalized by such marriages as were likely to be contracted here without the consent of the President."[2] Furthermore, a chaplain who consecrated unauthorized marriages courted dismissal. Such strictures appear not to have been routinely observed, however, and in fact the Company offered five rupees as a christening present for every child born to a soldier "and his invariably Indian wife."[3] The economics of keeping a mistress were so advantageous compared to Britain that one author has estimated that 75 per cent of single EIC employees in the eighteenth century had Indian mistresses and that there were fewer than three hundred European women in Bengal, for example, in the 1780s.[4] Moreover, many questioned whether those single European women who did reach India were what they claimed to be. "A great many young women, generally, Mantua makers, milliners, etc. come annually to this country in quest of husbands and are amazingly successful ... What these ladies have formerly been is very conspicuous in their behaviour, which is an awkward attempt, to appear what they never were. This & the distant voyage these bold adventuresses make, who seldom have any relations or friends or even acquaintances in the country & who came upon the strength of recommendation only, naturally creates suspicions, which break out into scandal."[5]

On the subcontinent there was no social cost to Anglo-Indian liaisons; on the contrary, there were advantages, since those with Indian connections were better equipped to interact with the native Mughal-dominated society. Furthermore, EIC employees were able to provide their progeny with ample opportunities in the Company. Reflecting on Madras circa 1760, Henry Dodwell observed: "Not half these men will be married; and of those married less than half would have European wives."[6] A letter, assuredly never intended for perusal in Britain, from William's younger brother, John, to the governor, Sir Thomas Rumbold, in late 1779 was indicative of how widespread mixed-race liaisons had become. However, it is unlikely that many were as fraught with personal peril and humiliation as John's encounter with a Mr Bedford. Which embarrassment was greater, his cuckolding or being thrice disarmed by Bedford, it is difficult to determine. In any event, John would presumably have been loath to disclose either.

> However unjustifiable my conduct may appear to you Hon'ble Sir
> as Governor and Chief Magistrate of Fort St. George, yet I hope
> these feelings as a man of honour which distinguish you so eminently
> in private life will upon this occasion induce you to listen to an

impartial and exact account of the unfortunate business I was
engaged in with Mr. Bedford.

A train of little circumstances made me suspect that Mr. Bedford
either had or wanted to have connections with a Portuguese girl I
keep. His servants I observed frequently lurking about my quarters
and their manner of coming and going was so particular that I
repeatedly signified to Mr. Frank Baillie and Lieut: [Nathaniel]
Daw[e]s my suspicion of their intentions. The girl and her servant
declared one day … upon my returning from the Granary Guard[,]
that two officers called at the window in my absence wishing to con-
verse with them and one of them appear'd in artillery uniforms.

Upon the 11th instant[,] having the Halaja gate Guard and
apprehending some advantage might be taken of my absence, I
lock'd the door of my quarters and put the key in my pocket. Near
one o'clock in the morning having the occasion to go home, to my
surprise I found the door open and on going into the room where
the girl was, I discover'd by her that she had just left the embrace
of some other man.

I said nothing to her that night. However in the morning on
questioning her, she bursting out in tears confessed the fact and
said it was Mr. Bedford who had been with her last night and she
at the same time acknowledged that he had connections with her
before when in the other quarters. Those confessions she afterwards repeated in his presence and that of Lieut: Mitchell and
Ensign Baillie. The seduction of a gentleman's girl is consider'd by
officers in general as so despicable and mean an act that a confession of the same subjects the offender either to be brought to a general court-martial for ungentlemanlike behaviour or at least to be
forever held in so contemptible a light as to be avoided by his
brother officers.

Knowing the above, I cou'd not suppose Mr. Bedford wou'd make
a confession the consequences of which wou'd prove so fatal to him.
I therefore plainly told him that he had committed an act so low
and unbecoming, that a denial was what wou'd naturally ensue. But
that to a man of honour there were such glaring and selfconvicing
proofs that denial served only to add presumption to meanness, the
reward of which among gentlemen is always a slap in the face which
I accordingly gave him. Mr. Bedford demanded of me satisfaction
which I agreed to give him.[7]

John then described what was a parody of a traditional duel. It began with each of them discharging three pistols followed by an unorthodox display of swordsmanship in which Bedford ran, from a considerable distance, full speed at John, causing the latter to drop his sword. This sequence took place not once but three times before some passersby halted the proceedings.

Such awkward moments notwithstanding, it was not until Charles, 1st Marquess Cornwallis, fresh from the loss of the American colonies at Yorktown, arrived as governor general in 1786 that an Indian liaison became a liability. Cornwallis served as governor general of India until 1793 and in 1805 he began a second term which was cut short by his death. As we shall see, he enacted significant reforms in India and defeated Tipu Sultan in the Third Anglo-Mysore War. But he was a man of his time. "The Governor-General was blinkered, unimaginative, racist and dull ... he was also honest, brave, humane and just. He embodied the Roman ideal of fair dealing and the British faith that character counted for more than intellect. He established the principle, which would be held sacred by Victorians, that imperial power involved moral responsibility."[8]

Smarting from his humiliation in America, Cornwallis was determined that the pattern should not be replicated in India. In his view, the root cause of the American Revolution was the development of a settled colonial class whose interests gradually diverged from those of the mother country. By precluding the emergence of such a class in India, Cornwallis felt he could ensure that Britain would retain its colonies in the East Indies. Accordingly, Cornwallis sought to discourage servants of the Company remaining in the country once they had completed their EIC assignment. That meant minimizing any ties to India. Accordingly, Cornwallis required that British-born subjects not in the employ of the Company or the crown post good behaviour bonds and stipulated that such persons could only lease, not purchase, land outside Calcutta. As always, family was the most powerful potential tie. In order to reduce the appeal of marriage, or indeed even a serious relationship, with a native woman, Cornwallis introduced a raft of legislation specifying that Indian women, whether wives or not, were excluded from Company social events and that the mixed-race progeny of these liaisons could not earn a position above clerk in the Company's civil department or above lieutenant in its military arm. In 1790 Cornwallis barred natives from holding Company offices worth more than £500 per annum and sepoys from obtaining commissions. On 19 April 1791 the Court of Directors decreed that "no person the son of a Native Indian shall henceforward be appointed by this Court to employment in the civil, military or marine service of the Company."[9] Latterly, the Company even required a certificate that applicants for commissions were not the sons of native Indians. In 1795 it explicitly stipulated that employees have two European parents except for "pipers, drummers, bandsmen and farriers."[10] Anglo-Indians suffered further economic disadvantage since they were not permitted to own land. Ironically, what began as a pragmatic policy by Cornwallis accentuated the differences between the races and led to increasingly rigid discrimination.

Cornwallis's initiatives were inevitably reinforced by a combination of socio-economic and political factors. Conversion to and assimilation into the local culture became less of an enticement for preferment in India as British power waxed while that of the Mughals waned. At the same time, as the allure of employment with the Company grew, the directors sought to reserve commissions and writerships for their friends and relatives. As a result, there were fewer positions available to Anglo-Indians. The belief of senior EIC officers that the appointment of Eurasians would dilute native respect for Company officials further undermined the prospects for Anglo-Indians. Finally, an influx of European women and missionaries discouraged Indian liaisons. Indeed, William Dalrymple has observed that biographies of eighteenth-century worthies were revised in the following century to excise any reference to Indian wives.[11] The growing rigidity of the racial divide and the limited prospects for mixed-race children in India led more and more well-to-do fathers to send their natural children to be raised and educated in Britain.

However, those developments lay in the future and the birth of William's Anglo-Indian daughter, Ann, on 20 August 1767 was a cause of celebration. Ann was a winning child whom William sent to London for her education. Shipping young sons to Britain was a common practice among officers and senior civil servants but it was unusual to provide for a daughter in this manner. Such provision was particularly challenging at this time because the East India Company was coping with a severe recession caused by the credit crisis of 1772. The panic, which began in London, resulted in substantial losses for the Company and a severe drop in its share price.

On 29 May 1775 William remitted £500 through his London agent, David Mitchell, and noted: "The cause of my writing at present is a little daughter of mine whom you'll find consigned to your care in the Nottingham or the Colebrooke to sail this month from Madras[,] her name is Ann fair haired about 8 years old. Mr. Arthur Cuthbert, my new

Madras attorney & friend[,] will transmitt you letters to the Lady
Mistress of the seminary she is to be placed at and a bill at the same time
for money enough to support her untill an opportunity offers of remit-
ting more. Your particular care of what may relate to her will confer a
lasting obligation on me."[12] Then in December, an associate of William's,
H. Woodhouse, reported that Ann, or Nancy to her intimates, had left
Cuddalore for Madras to embark on her European adventure.

> Your dear little girl is set out on her tour to Europe ... so I hope the
> dear child has got safe to Madras w'ch I have wrote to know, as I
> must own I am greatly interested in her welfare & love her as much
> as possibly I could a child of my own for it's a most amiable baby &
> you lose a great pleasure in not seeing her before she embarqued.
> Mrs. Woodhouse made her a cake, & supply'd her with every thing
> she could possibly want on the road, & sent her under the care of
> one of my orderley's, a very careful good fellow. I was sorry I had no
> female I could trust her to the care of, but I have none, but her old
> slow girl Catharina who has not turn'd out quite right, & indeed
> lay in at the time Nancy went. However the person Mrs. Cuthbert
> sent, will I dare say take great care of her. Mrs. Woodhouse sent in
> Nancy's trunk, a list of all her things, a copy of w'ch she desires me
> to enclose you, which was it for a child of her own she thinks more
> than sufficient for the voyage ... as to what care & attention I may
> have paid to that sweet child, it has been one of my chiefest amuse-
> ments & greatest pleasures, as well as Mrs. Woodhouse's, you are
> then very little oblig'd to us, & if we can ever in any shape add to
> the dear thing[']s future happyness it will add to ours ...
>   After hav'g paid little Nancy's dancing master, & provided her
> necessarys for the voyage, & Mrs. Woodhouse still has some pagodas
> remaining, w'ch she will acc't to you for.[13]

Nancy set sail for London on 1 January 1776 with a £100 bill and an
introduction to David Mitchell. On her arrival in London, she began
boarding at Mrs Curtis's school.[14] William's correspondence with Mitchell
is sprinkled with tender references to Nancy. In September 1777 he wrote:
"I cannot sufficiently express my obligations for your kind attentions in
general to my wishes but most particularly so in your care of my little girl.
I beg no expense be spared in making her accomplished and any present
as occasionally thought proper, an amount to the governess or govern-
esses I shall pay with the greatest satisfaction."[15] Mitchell apparently

took William's expressed desires literally since Ann's expenses for board and education rose markedly from the £11 for the half-year ending 16 March 1777 to £18.6 for the half-year ending the next March.[16] Then in October 1778 William explained to Mitchell that he did not, at present, have any mode of making remittances and entreated him: "If the money in your hands shou'd be out before any more of mine reaches England I trust you will advance for my little girl ... Mr. Cuthbert sent you for her by care of the China ships this last season two pairs carded muslins, 2 ditto flower'd & 4 pieces white handkerchiefs ... take care of my dear Nancy." "I shall never disapprove any cash expended on my Nancy – the pearls as they are low valued, I would not have sold – let them be made up in a necklace or bracelets or earrings or any way they may answer for her."[17]

When Ann wrote to her father in January 1779, she brought to light the existence of a larger family by ending her letter with "duty to mama and love to brother."[18] In the same letter she wrote that she had spent Christmas with a Mr Speediman and his sister-in-law, Miss Webster. She also recommended the bearer of the letter, James, Speediman's youngest son, who was bound for Madras as a cadet. William had earlier asked Mitchell to assure Speediman that he would do everything in his power to assist his son in recognition of the kindness they had shown Ann.[19] William did arrange an appointment for James, but unfortunately, it was to the young man's detriment for he was captured and died of his wounds in Hyder Ali's prisons following the Battle of Pollilur.

In October 1779 William conveyed to Mitchell a bill for £150 for Nancy and £50 for Frank's mother,[20] and he also wrote a most affecting letter to his daughter. It contains his first reference, albeit a melancholy one, to the existence of Ann's siblings. His manner of conveying the news of her mother and siblings' death seems cold-hearted but death was a constant companion in those days and particularly on the Indian sub-continent. The letter read:

I have been happy in the receipt of many of your letters and return my thanks for the handsome purse and waistcoat you sent me. Continue to be a good girl paying attention to Mrs. Curtis's advice and your education & you shall have everything from me you can wish for. Mr. Mitchell has my instructions for this purpose as proof you may ask a receipt if he has not given them to you already, for pearls in his possession sufficient to make you a necklace or a pair of bracelets. Your little brother and sister died ... about eighteen

months ago and your mother soon after of a putrid liver. Nevertheless[,] while your uncle or father is alive you have nothing to fear
either of them will be sufficient to afford you protection & supply
your wants. This from my dear Nancy your affectionate father.[21]

Meanwhile, William received a succession of pleas to return home. One
came from his cousin, Archibald Campbell, who appears to have been his
closest boyhood friend, in early 1772.[22]

It is now so long since I have had the pleasure to hear from you that
I begin to fear, length of time and distance of place may wear us
quite out of acquaintance ... The melancholy account of your
Father's death you have had from Dr. Alves together with a state of
your family affairs in this part of the world, which makes it needless
for me to say any thing on the subject, further than to inform you,
that the draughts you sent were duely honoured (that on Airds only
excepted) and the proceeds of them immediately apply'd towards
payment of debts, agreeable to your instructions; and I verily believe,
that (next to seeing you and Jock safely returned) there is nothing
earthly my Aunt has so much at heart, as clearing off all incumbrances, and in so far as she can contribute to it making your situation comfortable & agreeable, when you arrive; I'm sorry to inform
you, that she is in a very weak way at present, having but lately
recovered of a rheumatick fever, which brought her to the gates of
death; and though she is now free of fever, or any acute complaint,
yet her advanced time of life, joined to this unfavourable season of
the year, must not only retard her recovery, but make it the more precarious. I really wish that you cou'd now think of coming home, for
though I would fain hope, my Aunt may get the better of this, yet
you are to consider, that to one at her period of life, every winter
must be a kind of climaterick; & shou'd you be so unlucky as to lose
her, while matters are on their present footing, it might create great
confusion, no other person here, being either so well vers'd in your
affairs, or equally safe to take a hearty concern in them ... I dare
say you'll allow, that it is better to sit down contentedly with a
moderate living, while you can have a prospect of health and years
to enjoy it, than to return with a great one, in the decline of life,
deprived of those friends who wou'd have participated of your happiness and deprived of your relish for those very aims, for which
you amassed it: This you know is no uncommon case, but I hope it

will not be yours ... Death has already deprived us of so many relations & friends, that unless you hasten home, you may be a stranger
in your own country, when you return ... As for myself, I am (thank
God) much as you left me, excepting that change, which is the natu-
ral effect of so many additional years: I lodge however more comfortably, having lately built a new house, which you'll allow I needed,
and in the heart of which, I long to see you.[23]

Dr Alves wrote in a similar vein. While devoting the bulk of his missive
to his mother-in-law's health, he could not resist a jab at the much
maligned Mackenzie of Coul:

I do all I can to assist your Mother, who is extremely zealous and
careful of your interests, and I hope you will not have any reason to
disapprove of our conduct. In my last I told you she was just beginning to recover of a severe fever. She is still weak, but I think mending slowly and now able to sit in her chair for two hours. The season
of the year indeed is against her, but you may be sure nothing in our
power will be omitted that can in the least contribute to her health.
Had it pleas'd God to deprive us of her at this time we must have
been at a loss for want of a paper authority to act for you. She
indeed has not a legal authority, but then it will pass unquestioned
sooner than any body's else. Should you, contrary to our earnest
wishes and expectations, resolve to remain some time longer in India,
you must certainly send a power of attorney or factory, as I mentioned in my last, and particular directions how you would have
matters conducted in your absence ... Your Sister & George are well
at the Leyes. Nelly says she is to give me a few lines to inclose for
you, so let her speak for herself, she will surely say some thing of her
son. She raves about him from morning to night, and dreams of him
from night to morning. Jock won't believe it but it is very certain
that she would prefer passing an evening in play with William than
to the most brilliant assembly or card party she could go to. At this
moment I hear her singing to him when she ought to be writing her
letter to you ... I heard this day that Col. Mackenzie Coul is just
going back again to India, and to be station'd at Madras, so that
you will have an opportunity of renewing your acquaintance with
him. I did not see him when he was in this country, but I hear he
is very plausible. Speaking however and acting with propriety are
two very different things.[24]

While William's kinsmen were bombarding him with pleas to return to Inverness, John wrote to his mother on 18 February 1772 describing the siege of Tanjore – an episode to be discussed later – and setting out his ever-optimistic expectation of an impending promotion. The most welcome aspect of John's letter was his confirmation that William had sent Dr Alves and Archibald Campbell the long-sought power of attorney.

> Although I have not heard from you since my arrival in this country yet I do not suppose you have in the least forgot me. At the same time I own your writing wou'd be a particular satisfaction. My Brother has wrote several letters by this ship and sent a power of attorney to Dr. Alves and Mr. Campbell to act for him. I dare say they are the persons you wou'd choose were you to appoint them yourself. He has notwithstanding desir'd them always to act with your approbation.
>
> As to his own going home it is at present impossible except he was to throw away that opportunity he has been labouring for these thirteen years past. He has lived with General Smith those four or five months and had double pay as Brigade Major. Besides he is now close upon a Majority. That being the case I'm sure you'll not be surpris'd at his staying a little longer in this country.
>
> As for me I am still the Ensign but expect a step in a few weeks, I believe I might say days. During the expedition against Tanjore I had double pay and if the army was to take the field I think I'd be pretty sure of the same again, perhaps better.[25]

While not mentioned in John's letter, Hector Munro, whose financial setbacks had induced him to accept a commission from the EIC, as opposed to his preferred royal regiment, had been working to advance John's rank. Munro undertook such activity to bolster his influence in the Inverness Burghs, which, despite his active service in India, he continued to represent in Parliament until 1801.[26]

In November 1772 Nelly provided William more news and gossip. William obviously had encouraged his mother to move to town or a less burdensome residence, but Nelly emphasized their mother's determination to stay at Dunain and manage it on William's behalf. In addition, she mentioned the political aspirations of Cosmo Gordon's third son, Lord George. He was eventually successful, entering Westminster in 1774 as MP for Ludgershall. Yet he proved to be less than the ideal parliamentarian, gaining a reputation for criticizing all and sundry and eventually being imprisoned for fomenting the "Gordon Riots" against Catholic emancipation. Finally, she apprised William of his friend Dunmaglass's good fortune in that his cousin Lachlan MacGillivray had gifted him his Hutchinson Island plantation.

As several ships arrived this season without bringing any letter from you and I know you was on the expedition to Tanjore you cannot imagine how miserable I was with apprehension about Jock and you. At length however I was relieved by your letter of Feb'y last which tho' they give me no near prospect of seeing you soon, have made me quite easy and happy. I hope some lucky stroke will soon enable you to make us all more so by coming home ... I daresay your plan with regard to our Mother would be the best, but she has all allong shown such a desire for living at Dunain, that it would be no purpose to endeavour to separate her from it: I think in that case it would be worth your while to give directions about enclosing the hill and planting it, or any of the other moors about, as even a year or two in advance will be something gained, and make the place sooner what you would wish it to be. I own it would give one great pleasure to see some improvements going on at Dunain, especially with the prospect of seeing you soon there.

As you directed I will endeavour to recollect all the little anecdotes which has happened in this neighbourhood since I wrote last. I used to be more particular in writing Jock as he was later from this country and would know the people better. I will begin with the marriages: your cousin Lachlan McIntosh Balnespick to Miss Anny McIntosh, the Laird's niece ... I let you to wit that the young Laird of Kilravock is for certain to marry Anny Fraser the shoemaker's daughter; it has made a great noise in the country for some time past, but it is very near a conclusion now. She is really very pretty and I daresay will make a better wife than the present lady who has I believe contributed a great deal to the destruction of the family: they have sold within these ten years thirty thousand pounds worth of land and their debt is not yet payed.

The great Sir Alexander Grant of Dalvey died last summer and was carried by sea to Finchorn and burried with great pomp at Dilne: our town has declared itself in favour of his late antagonist Colonel Munro who is our present member for the burroughs. It is thought the Duke of Gordon will make this country for his Brother, Lord George ... I wrote Jock last April that James Baillie Dochfour was come home and married to Miss Campbell Glenure; he has since taken a lease of the place Muniach where he is to live in the summer, and in town for the winter. The Baillies now muster so strong here that I wish you would come home to be provost amongst them. Mr. Baillie Dochfour is really a Magistrate. Your old Cap't. Dunmaglass has gone to America to take possession of a small estate given him by a cousin of his in that country, he is to be back next year.

As I have come almost to my last page it is now time I should say something of your little nameson; he was lately inoculated for the small pox and had the disease very favourably. He begins to run about and speak little words; he's a perfect master of signs and is much admired by every body, indeed it is no wonder for he is really a pretty little creature. I could say a great deal more on this subject but having I am afraid exhausted your patience all ready.[27]

In January of the following year, 1773, Archibald Campbell again asked for a power of attorney to manage William's affairs, not realizing that William had already acceded to this request. He also conceded that William's mother would be hurt by such a move. "I do not believe you could mortify her [more] than by putting the management of your affairs in any other channel."[28] When he did provide such a power of attorney, William wrote to reassure his mother. "My Brother and I thank God enjoy most excellent constitutions & being inured to the climate run no risk I hope of leaving this world untill we have accomplished our now only wish of seeing you & our Sisters once more in an independent way. I have appointed during my absence which I hope will not be long Dr. Alves & Mr. Campbell Managers with strict injunctions which by & by I think to them almost unnecessary to comply with your desire in every thing that may be agreeable to you."[29] At some point, William added Alexander Godsman as a third party.

Later in 1773, Archibald intensified the pressure on William to return home. He enumerated all the drawbacks and risks of remaining in India and, as an incentive, even suggested a particular heiress to whom William should "hasten home and lay siege." The object of the proposed siege was Anne Brodie of Lethen. Anne had inherited the family estates when her fifteen-year-old brother John died in Nice in 1773. She became the 8th Laird of Lethen and died unmarried in 1805, never having succumbed to anyone's siege.

Last week Dr. Alves deliver'd me your obliging letter of the 10th March ult'e, and an other to my Wife of said date, acquainting her of some presents you had been so kind as to send her, for which we return you our hearty thanks. My Wife wou'd have writ you herself, but thought it needless to put you to the expense of postage, for what cou'd amount to no more than assurances of her regard and friendship. I can hardly venture to affirm with truth, that I am pleased at your present prospect of preferment, because so far as it may retard your coming to the country I certainly regret it. I can now from experience inform you, that after forty, 'tis but a gradual decay ... if you mean therefore to marry with propriety, and wish to see your succession grown up, you have little time my friend to lose; add to this, that if you remain in these hot climates till the decline of life, you will be less able to bear a cold one when you return. Let me seriously ask you if you wou'd not rather have £5,000 & a son to inherit it, than double that sum to leave to some distant collateral heir ... let this then rouse you from your golden dream, if nothing else can ... Doctor Alves ... might justly take exception to your writing me any thing which I cou'd not shew him, and indeed I cou'd wish, that in all your letters to him and me, you wou'd mention him as the person on whose diligence and activity you chiefly confide, for though I hope I need not assure you of my sincere friendship, and inclination to serve you, yet I am too conscious of my own indolence to desire you depend so much on my activity, as you might naturally expect, or as I wou'd incline ... Frank Baillie, I understand, goes over to you by this fleet, which is entirely a deed of his own, having conceived so strong a desire to go to you, that it wou'd have made him unhappy to baulk him: if I thought there was any occasion to recommend him to you, I freely cou'd as one of whom I have a good opinion, and I believe will be deserving of any encouragement you are pleased to shew him ... Lethen's only Son died lately at Nice, where he had been sent for the recovery of his health, and by Lethen's settlement, the eldest daughter (aged seventeen) now succeeds to the estate. Why won't you hasten home and lay siege to her?[30]

Shortly thereafter, John Alves briefed William on the latter's affairs in Inverness, observing that your "settlement on your old Mamie has made the old woman happier than any Nabobess in India."[31] Alves, in addition, informed William that Frank Baillie's mother had waived her life interest in the income that Dunain had willed to her, thereby providing Frank with the means to travel to join his cousins in India. Frank had, indeed, resigned his apprenticeship with Alexander Murray and was preparing to leave for Madras. In February 1774 Frank wrote his Aunt Anne from London that he was likely to board ship by the end of the week. He briefed his aunt frequently on the progress of his voyage and finally, in September, notified her that he had arrived and had been treated handsomely by her sons.

> I arrived here on the nineteenth Aug't and on the morning of the twentieth came ashore. The first house I went to was Mr. Anderson's who receiv'd me very kindly and though I was not quite so lucky as to meet with either of your sons here, yet they took care that I should not be destitute upon my arrival, for I received a letter from each of them and I do assure you Dear Madam that were both of them my Brothers twenty times they could not write me more affectionately than they have done. Major Baillie ordered me money & every necessary I could want. He also ordered me new clothes and desired Doctor Anderson how soon I got ready to introduce me to General Smith, as he has solicited him for a commission for me. I was last night at the General's but did not find him at home. Therefore I go there this night again, and I expect in fortnight to be appointed to Major Baillie's Regiment. He is now at Ellore which is four or five hundred miles from here ... He & his Brother are in perfect health ... This climate is very hot but it has agreed with me very well as yet for I have not been an hour sick since I left England except for one little cold I brought from the Cape which I cured with a drink of water gruel made of your meal some of which I have yet.[32]

The year 1773 had begun with much debate in Parliament as to the fate of the East India Company. The EIC's independence was then very much in jeopardy. Its finances had been strained by military activity in Bengal and the financial panic of 1772 in London. In addition, or perhaps because of those events, various abuses were coming to light. In the following letter, written in January 1773, John Alves outlined the substance of the EIC debate and, in his sound analysis of the plight of France, foreshadowed the French Revolution. In passing, Alves mentioned the Russo-Turkish War of 1768–74, which brought the southern Ukraine, northern Caucasus, and Crimea within Russia's orbit; the first partition of Poland among Russia, Prussia, and Austria; and the coup d'état by Gustav III in

Sweden. For someone living in the far north, he demonstrated a firm grasp and broad knowledge of the relevant issues of the day and an eye for the foibles of politicians.

Your India affairs have engaged the attention of our Ministry and Parliament very much of late. A committee of Parliament has, for some time, been examining into the state of the Company and the conduct of its servants for several years back, and tho' they have not yet made their report, a great many abuses are said to have subsisted in India, and still to subsist, so as to render the interposition of our legislative authority necessary, and indeed it is the opinion of many, that Government means to take the territory & revenues belonging to the Company in India into their own hands leaving only the commercial part to them, as being most properly their province; should this be the case you would all become King's troops. What makes it the more probable is, that the Ministry has got a stop put to the Company's sending out any supervisors this year, tho' they had come to a resolution to do it, and had even chosen six persons (from among the directors chiefly) who were to go out in that character. A bill however was brought in to Parliament & made to pass as soon as the forms would admit, restraining them for a limited time from sending out any supervisors to India. How things may turn out it is hard to say; but one thing is certain that the Company is at present very much straiten'd for cash and put to their shifts to answer the demands upon them, and that their affairs seem to be near a crisis. One of the causes assigned for their want of cash is the immense sums that have been laid out upon fortifications in India, particularly in Bengal. You seem to have been in great apprehensions from the French in India, but I hope without sufficient grounds, at least if I may judge from the present situation of that people at home. Their treasury was quite exhausted and their navy ruined at the end of last war, and they have not been able to repair them till this day. Their finances are in great disorder; their publick credit not good; the people groaning under a heavy load of taxes; the greatest number of the Provincial Parliaments, with the Princes of the Blood at their head in a professed & open opposition to the measures of the Court, the King endeavouring to make the Parliaments mere courts of justice, and to render his own dominion absolute, and the Parliament struggling for some share in legislation, and a little remains of that authority which they enjoyed formerly when the Government was feudal. In short they are so poor at present and have so much to do at home that I scarce think they will attempt any great matters abroad.

I had some thoughts of giving you a short sketch of the present state of the other European powers, but I find I won't have time and indeed it little concerns you just now to know that the Turks & Russians have been carrying on a bloody war for three years past, and are now holding a congress to bring about a peace. That the king of Prussia, the Austrians & Russians have taken possession of Poland & are going to divide it among them. That Sweden from being a limited has this year become an absolute monarchy etc. etc.

Probably you will like better to hear something of the political state of this country. I mean of our own country. You know our present representative is Gen'l [Simon] Fraser who having resided for several years in Portugal and never attended Parliament, has neglected the interests of his constituents, and cool'd their attachment to him very much. The Duke of Gordon willing to make his advantage of this negligence of Gen'l Fraser's has set up his Brother L'd George as candidate for the country against the next general election and besides endeavouring to make friends of as many of the present freeholders as he can, he has split his own valuation (which is very considerable) as far as it would go and will have above 24 new barons of his own upon the roll before the election. On the other hand, Gen'l Fraser, sensible, tho' perhaps, too late of his misconduct, has within these few weeks come over from Portugal, with an intention not to return again, is now attending Parliament, and gives out that he is resolved to stand for the country. If he really will stand it must be because he has some assurance that the Ministry will favour him, for otherwise he would have no chance; and if so, it is hard to say how far that influence may go: the Gordons will not however readily give up the point now that they have laid out so much money upon it. The Grants have in appearance join'd the Duke upon this occasion, but it is an unnatural alliance, their political interests are opposite in other places and if the Ministry interfere, I dare say they will change sides. I shall let you know from time to time any thing material that is done in this contest. It is said the Duke of Argyle who has a good deal of valued rent in this country is to support Gen'l Fraser.[33]

Parliament did pass the Regulating Act, which circumscribed the Company's powers. The act provided that the crown could appoint the

Company's senior servants, designated Bengal as supreme over the other presidencies, required that India House forward any information for the attention of the government within fourteen days, and extended the term of directors from one to four years. Candidates who had served in India must reside in Britain for two years before seeking a directorship, and directors were required to step aside for a year before seeking re-election. The revisions to the charter restricted the scope of the EIC but did not constrain it commercially. Indeed, the act, in an attempt to restore the Company's finances, portentously granted the EIC an exclusive right to export tea to the American colonies.

It was also in 1773 that William and John took part in the siege of Tanjore. After abandoning his planned attack on Tanjore two years earlier, the nawab of the Carnatic, Mohammed Ali, soon began to refocus on that prize. Seeking to take advantage of the dissension following the death on 18 November 1772 of the Maratha chief Mahadeo Rao, Mohammed Ali decided to attack Tanjore, an ally of the Marathas. His pretext was that Thuljaji, the rajah of Tanjore, was selling and mortgaging properties belonging to him, had refused to pay the tribute owing to his overlord, and was forming connections with the French, Dutch, Danes, Hyder Ali, and the Marathas. Madras agreed and assembled a force at Trichinopoly under General Smith. Although about to depart for England, Smith had agreed to replace the twice-cashiered and again in disfavour Sir Robert Fletcher, who, as commander-in-chief, had proved a disappointment to all. After negotiating the payment of prize money by the nawab, Smith's troops set out for Tanjore on 31 July 1773. Fortuitously, the army was almost immediately available since the men were returning from a punitive expedition against the Marawar and Nalcooty Poligars who had been wreaking havoc in the Carnatic. By now, William Baillie had agreed to serve as Smith's brigade major, and on 17 September 1773 the army, with William in the forefront, took Tanjore with very few casualties. John was one of those casualties but soon fully recovered.

The Dutch now denied that they had been aiding the rajah, but their defence was weakened by the fact that they were then in possession of Nagore, which they claimed to have purchased from Thuljaji. The rajah had no right to dispose of Mohammed Ali's territory but the Dutch did not withdraw from Nagore until confronted by troops led by the combined forces of the nawab's son and General Smith. In this particular instance, the Company's interests coincided with those of Mohammed Ali since the British sought to eject any foreign rivals from the Coromandel Coast. Following the campaign, in February 1774, William wrote a letter home in which he dwelt on the potential prize money, speculating that it might be as much as 4,000 pagodas for majors, though it might not be fully discharged until the end of the year. The letter also touched on other matters, including the sad news of his nephew Billy's death and his mother's injured feelings over his granting of power of attorney to Alves and Cousin Archibald. On the latter point, the purpose had obviously not been communicated well, and as a result, William displayed unaccustomed exasperation with his brother-in-law. At the same time, although he was hopeful about further promotion, William's concern that superior connections would favour other aspiring officers remained in the forefront. In this case, he feared an officer named Fletcher would be promoted over him. It almost certainly was the same Fletcher who sparred with William for command of the Grenadiers in 1780 and shared William's fate at Pollilur that same year.

My Mother certainly was mistaken in the idea formed of the power of attorney and I have reason to think that mistake not lessen'd by some of my friends. This I have told her in a letter pretty plainly which no doubt you will have the perusal of. On reflection I think with you [that] even did she not chuse a country life it wou'd be better [to] carry on the farm for my account ... My Sister must call the next by a luckier name and I will consider him equally in my care w't the former ... During the course of last year our military on the coast have been in greater luck than usual. We again in the beginning of September attacked Tanjore and within six weeks made ourselves (by breach & storm) master of it with little more loss than at the former siege and much more advantage to every body. I led the storm with 200 grenadiers, supported by Col: Vaughan with about as many men and closed the scene with the loss of very few men in about 10 minutes. The Nabob got immense income and extensive possessions and we handsome prize money. A Subaltern's share 1,000 pag's, a Cap'tn's 2,000, a Major's 4,000 and so on in proportion to all ranks except the General who receives one lakh that is 100,000 pag's, a sum equal to ¼ of the whole. There was no body killed or wounded we are connected with except John. He had[,] by a horseman in a brush with their cavalry the 8th Sept'r. just before the commencement of the siege[,] the great tendon leading to the thumb of his right hand cut[;] however to the surprise of every body has recovered entirely the use of it again. The money is payable in March next though through the villainy of the Nabob it may probably be the end

of the year before it's all cleared off. He has grown to such a height
of riches and powers that finding Europeans I'm sorry to say rather
venal he does just what he pleases and in a few more years unless
curb'd likely to prove as dangerous to the Company as any other
black power in Hindostan. At present every thing promises peace
and tranquility in the Carnatick yet you find this dated from camp
of at least 7,000 men ...

I wrote you in May last of my promotion and have now the
pleasure to add that the prospect is fair for another step. A
Brother of Sir Robert Fletcher junior to me in the service goes
home in this ship with views I imagine of getting over many. Pray
shou'd you be able to learn how he plays his cards do not fail to
advertise me.

Peace reigns in Bengal and by the little war of last year the
Company have increased their revenues prodigiously.[34]

That prodigious enhancement of the EIC's revenues was a result of the
First Rohilla War, in which the nawab of Oude paid the Company forty
lakhs of rupees to assist in the subjugation of the Rohillas and in which
William, as we shall see later, fully participated. In the meantime, William
and his fellow officers could contemplate the prospect of prize money for
the fall of Tanjore. And contemplate it they did. General Smith's share of
the Tanjore ransom money would permit him to retire in England in relative comfort while the promised allocations to each officer were considerable. On the other hand, Mohammed Ali was notorious for committing
in the heat of a crisis and neglecting that commitment once the crisis had
passed. As events would prove, William had every reason to be sceptical
that the nawab would discharge his obligation within the contracted
time. In a letter to General Smith dated 4 December 1773, Mohammed
Ali referred to two earlier letters

wherein I expressed my resolution to pay this money to the army in
six months from the fall of the place – and that I had determined in
my own mind to set apart the first of the revenues of the conquered
countries for that purpose.

I have a most sacred regard to my word and I am fully resolved to
give every possible satisfaction to the army – but the great expense
which I have incurred on account of the opposition of the Dutch –
and also the immense demands made upon me for debts claimed
both by the Dutch and the Danes and others as contracted by

Thuljaji the late Rajah have involved me in difficulties which I could neither foresee nor prevent.

By such means I have been prevented from fulfilling my inclinations to the army ... However it is my full resolution that the ransom money shall become due to the army exactly six months from the fall of the place according to my promise ... I have now made assignments on certain countries to Mr. [Paul] Benfield for the full discharge of that money. He has my commands therefore to wait upon you ...

What can I say more?[35]

The nawab's undertaking was reassuring but few took his promises at face value. On behalf of Mohammed Ali, Benfield offered to pay the European enlisted men, the sepoys, and the lascars in full by 30 September 1774 and the officers by 31 March 1775. The prize-money negotiations then began in earnest. General Smith, recognizing the inability of the nawab to discharge his debt expeditiously, wrote to Major Humphrey Harper in January 1774 stating that, since the troops were assembled at Vellore, Harper should call together a captain and a subaltern from each corps in order to consider the nawab's offer and advise Smith of their reaction. Smith emphasized the urgency in view of the threatened incursion by the Marathas.

Of this you may assure the officers from me, that His Highness has not the power to fulfill his promise to the army by the 17th March; nay it's totally impossible for him to collect such an immense sum of ready money as wou'd be required to pay off our demands (not less than 7 lakhs of pag's) and since that is the case our business should be to obtain substantial and undeniable security for the money which he truly offers to give ... The unsettled state of this country, the great probability of its being increased & that soon – are circumstances that should prevail over every other to hasten our making an agreement that will secure our money ...

On our part no time is to be lost – remember that Mahrattas expected.[36]

Following that meeting, William and John were among the twelve officers who responded to Major Harper and who clearly bristled when the nawab referred to the payment as a "reward": "We readily acquiesce with the General that it is better to get ours properly secured provided

His Highness gives substantial and undeniable securities for the money, the time he requires will be granted, but it's expected he'll be fixed to that period of payment ... It's also expected that it will be totally put out of his power to swerve from or use any second plea of this nature ... We must also observe that in the Nabob's letter he makes use of the word reward which we think on this occasion is improperly apply'd & rather ungrateful to our feelings, as it's a fairly contracted bargain, and we presume much to His Highness's advantage."[37]

Upon receipt of the officers' letter, a meeting took place at Colonel Edward James's house. The officers were less than satisfied that the non-commissioned officers and soldiers should be paid before them. For that and other reasons, they formed a committee which included Major Baillie to confer with Paul Benfield to assess the nawab's proposals and determine the undeniable security. The officers camped at Chillaberry Plain endorsed this recommended approach with the observation, perhaps tongue in cheek, that "we should rely on His Highness, the Nabob's honour and well known integrity for the performance of the proposals which may hereafter be agreed upon between His Highness & the army, for the mode and time of payment of the said ransom money."[38]

On 14 February, Smith reported to majors Harper and Baillie that "Mr. Benfield waited upon me this morning, and gave such satisfactory answers respecting the deposit of jewels & valuables for the ransom money with an interest at BH Co. to commence from June, that I desire you will once more assemble the officers from different corps & know from them whether a deposit of jewels & valuables, properly valued, & placed in such hands as they will approve of, will be acceptable to them or not. As a very large part of my fortune is depending on the payment of this money – and as it's my determined resolution to leave India so soon as I can (wt. propriety) I wish to be informed with their final resolves."[39]

The officers, in a letter dated 24 February, expressed their appreciation for General Smith's efforts and encouraged him to persist in seeking payment of the Tanjore prize money. While the Maratha threat had receded, the officers wished to settle the business expeditiously. "We are fully impressed with your zeal in wishing to secure their just rights to an army that has been happy & successful under your command. And we are the more sensibly affected with these sentiments, at the apprehension of your departure from this country. The Nabob did us but justice in appearing pleased with our last letter. It was respectful to him as a Prince & favourable as a debtor. As the enemy that threatens distress to His Highness's government has now retreated, we hope, & expect that His Highness will

consider our former address, & adhere fully & faithfully to his engagements to the army."[40] On 8 March, Benfield wrote Smith undertaking to
resolve the Tanjore ransom money to the army's satisfaction and enclosing the following translation of a letter from His Highness explaining the
great equivocator's rationale for his actions:

When first I entered into an agreement with the army to pay the ran-
some money for Tanjore in the space of six months after it should be
taken by storm, I had not the least doubts of being able to discharge
the whole in the time specified which would have given me the greatest satisfaction. In this, however, I have been disappointed as the
disputes with the Dutch ... led me into such inconveniences that
to procure tranquility in these countries and to free myself of the
expense of keeping an army in the disputed territories, the extraordinary charges of which amounted to a lakh of pagodas a month
I found myself under the necessity of ... paying them in ready money
five lakhs and a half/5/2 of pagodas. These sums with the money
due to the Danes amounted to not less than eight lakhs of pagodas
which would have been more than sufficient to have answered every
demand of the army: but which I was prevented from applying to
that purpose by unavoidable necessity. I need not mention to you the
sufferings of a country in the time of war and what must be the consequences to the revenues by the presence of hostile armies. Such
have prevented me as yet from reaping the fruits of the advantages
gained to me by the army. And to add to the present inconveniences
heaven has denied us rain in its due season. I do not complain of
these: the one is the unavoidable consequences of war, and the other
is at the disposal of the Almighty: but I have stated every thing to
you plainly, to convince you that necessity, and neither intention nor
inclination[,] has been the cause of delaying payments of the ran-
some money ... But as it would have been derogatory to my honour
as Prince of the country to be oblidged to give security, and as I
wished to satisfy the army in every particular as far as it was in my
power; to reconcile both ... I have appointed Mr. Benfield to stand
between us: whom I am fully resolved to enable to give every satisfaction to the army that circumstances will allow.[41]

This time the officers were less sympathetic to the nawab's straitened
circumstances. They were frustrated by his effusive but ineffective
assurances and insulted that other creditors had been paid despite an

understanding that the army would rank first in line for payment. It particularly rankled that the Danes and Dutch, whom they had evicted from his territory, had taken precedence over them. They became more intransigent in their demands and responded to General Smith thusly:

> Your declared intention of never separating your interest from ours adds, if possible, to those ties of respect and gratitude, which bind us to our General & our friend. With General Smith at our head, if we have but a part of that success in transacting with, that we had in transacting for the Nabob, neither the commander nor the army can be disappointed. From the respect we owe the Nabob's connections with our country, we are sorry to observe that the perusal of His Highness's letter has afforded us very little satisfaction. We hope it has suffered in the translation in every respect ... we are compelled to observe that His Highness's arguments are no less deficient in consolation than they are ill chosen. His Highness has been pleased to observe in vindication of his inability to perform his promise to us that to purchase tranquility from the Dutch and satisfy the Danes he has expended a sum more than sufficient to have discharged our debt. His original engagement was to have paid us out of the first revenues of the conquest ... It is evident that money due to us has been expended by His Highness whether in the purchase of peace, of territory, or claims, it matters but little to our interest ...
>
> We beg of you Sir again to represent to His Highness in the strongest manner that without entertaining a very unfavourable idea of his Government from its extent, especially its late acquisitions[,] we must suppose it too full of resources not to enable him to render us soon that justice which is our right and which thro' the friendly interposition of our General & Commander we respect.[42]

With that, the file goes cold and we are left to speculate whether William ever received his 4,000 pagodas. The payment may well have been jeopardized, as recounted in the next chapter, by the Court of Directors' vehement disapproval of the delivery of Tanjore to Mohammed Ali and its insistence that Madras restore Thuljaji, the former rajah, to his throne. Despite Mohammed Ali's repeated claims to have paid "prize-money to the army on both expeditions," the nawab was exceedingly gifted in gilding the lily and equally skilled in deferring his debts – as the Baillie brothers would have cause to learn again in the future.

7

A Council of Incompetents

Half the lies our opponents tell about us are not true.

Sir Boyle Roche, MP

While General Smith's fear of a Maratha onslaught proved unwarranted, William did find himself dealing with the remnants of Maratha incursions. Although the Company had offered to assist the nawab, Shuja-ood-Dowla, under certain conditions, to drive the Marathas from Oude and its environs, the nawab had settled for the loan of a few pieces of cannon and, on his own, dispatched the Maratha hordes from his territories. He then turned his attention to another vexation. For the preceding three years, Shuja-ood-Dowla had protected the neighbouring Afghan Rohillas from the Maratha menace and expended significant sums in doing so. At the time they sought his assistance, the Rohillas had pledged to repay him. Yet, reminiscent of Mohammed Ali, the Rohillas evinced no inclination to honour that pledge once the Maratha threat had receded. As a result, Shuja-ood-Dowla decided to move against them, though not before gaining the approbation of the Mughal emperor. Under the terms of a secret agreement, Shuja-ood-Dowla would give to the emperor half of "such new territories as he might wrest from the possession of usurpers."[1] In turn, the emperor undertook to bestow the other half on the nawab. Without disclosing this agreement to the British, Shuja-ood-Dowla notified Governor General Hastings of his intention to evict the Rohillas from Rohilkand and, agreeing to the conditions under which the cooperation of a British force had previously been offered, requested that a brigade join him in the proposed expedition. In February 1774 the provisional commander-in-chief, Colonel Alexander Champion, received instructions to join the nawab at Shahabad. Champion marched with a disparate detachment that included William Baillie's Company of Artillery. In early April, Shuja-ood-Dowla arrived with an enormous army said to have numbered one hundred thousand men. He demanded of Hafiz Rahmat, the chief of the Rohillas, the monies due him for rescuing them. Hafiz recognized the justice of the nawab's claim and the fragility of his people's position. He implored his fractious countrymen to make an earnest effort to repay their obligation. "Hafiz attempted to inspire into the several leaders a resolution to act with unanimity and firmness in support of the common cause; but all his efforts were rendered void by the spirit of jealousy and faction already mentioned, which contributed to destroy them much more effectually than the sword of the enemy."[2] The Rohilla chieftains were unmoved by Hafiz's entreaties and refused to entertain any payment to the nawab. Further financial demands brought little response and on St George's Day, 23 April, Colonel Champion and the nawab routed the Rohillas near Miranpur Katra. Champion reported that the Rohilla army was forty thousand strong and that their losses, after a stout resistance, approximated two thousand. William was in the forefront of the battle and was singled out in Champion's report to the Court of Directors: "Captain Baillie and the Gentlemen of his Corps, in the service of the artillery, gave great satisfaction."[3] The Rohillas fled in disarray and took refuge in a mountainous region. They were a spent force which never again posed a meaningful threat to Oude.

By May 1774, Colonel Champion reported that Shuja-ood-Dowla controlled the whole of the Rohilla country. The resident, Nathaniel Middleton, accordingly sought the forty lakhs that Shuja-ood-Dowla had promised the Company. The nawab correctly countered that Faizullah Khan's army still remained on his borders and that, under his engagement with the Company, the forty lakhs were not due until he no longer required British military assistance. Providentially, Faizullah Khan soon made application to remain in Rohilkand as a tributary of the nawab. Hastings resisted such a settlement. His primary objective in supporting the nawab's expedition against the Rohillas had not been the forty lakhs of rupees but the securing of a buffer zone against future Maratha incursions. He believed that, in assuring the borders of an ally, the Company was safeguarding its own position. Hastings felt the delivery of the Rohilla country to Faizullah Khan subverted the overall rationale for the recent campaign. Nevertheless, the nawab concluded a treaty with Faizullah Khan wherein the latter would be recognized as the first nawab of Rampur and retain possession of that city and district, which had been bequeathed to him by his father, Ali Mohammad, the founder of Rohilkand. Faizullah was permitted a force of no more than five thousand men and undertook to render military service to the nawab whenever called upon. He also paid fifteen lakhs to Shuja-ood-Dowla, dispatched his excess troops from Rohilkand, and remained an obedient subject of the nawab for the remainder of his life.

Champion and the British soldiers relentlessly clamoured for prize money. Their relations, never close, with the nawab deteriorated. Eventually, to appease the troops and ensure that the British did not turn upon him, Shuja-ood-Dowla offered a gratuity of seven lakhs of rupees. Shortly thereafter, he further proposed a present of three lakhs to Colonel Champion and 50,000 rupees to the officers. Champion sought clearance for the troops to accept the gift but Hastings responded that the recent Regulating Act of 1773 precluded the acceptance of any presents by Company servants under any pretense whatsoever. Understandably, the officers and men reacted with a great deal of bitterness to the abolition of a long and cherished tradition. Once again William's visions of meaningful prize money proved illusory.

CR

We next encounter William in Ellore where shortages of supply frustrated him. In a letter dated 14 August 1774 to Governor Alexander Wynch in Madras, he pleaded: "Without what I have applied for and on the present footing I am afraid though always ready to do my utmost, the Battalion I command cannot be keep'd in that in India for constant necessary order and readiness for the field."[4] He was still in Ellore when he received another letter, dated 17 October, from his brother-in-law, John Alves, that touched upon several issues. Alves sought guidance as to what should be done with Dunain in the event his mother's death preceded William's return. By this time, William's advances had rendered the estate debt-free and Alves was lending the excess funds on his brother-in-law's behalf. The doctor also reported that Nelly was flouting convention and superstition by persisting in again naming a child after her elder brother. William, for his part, had enquired about the availability of the estate of Castlehill. However, Alves's uncle, the Abbé Seignelay Colbert, had been purchasing Castlehill's debts and had effectively eliminated any competitors in his quest to acquire that property. Colbert was in a position to do so since he had prospered as vicar-general of Toulouse and bishop of Rodez. He would later serve as secretary to King Louis XVIII. Accordingly, Alves encouraged William to consider purchasing the estate of Kynmylies, which George Ross of Pitkerrie and Cromarty, lacking heirs, had placed

on the market. Finally, General Fraser's lands forfeited in the Forty-Five
had been restored and the expected parliamentary contest between Fraser
and Lord George Gordon had been resolved to each other's satisfaction.
The resolution involved the creation of several baronetcies, one of which
apparently would have accrued to William had he been resident in
Inverness-shire.

I have the pleasure to inform you that Nelly has once more made
you an uncle. June 29 she became the Mother of another fine boy,
shorter in appearance than the former child, and hitherto he has
thriven extremely well ... All her friends were for giving the child
(as you too suggest) a different name from the former, but Nelly who
pays little regard to superstitious notions, was determin'd, should it
be in her power, while she had a Son to have a William and accordingly, you are again a namefather ...

The subject upon which I wanted your directions on a separate
paper in case it should please God to deprive us of your Mother
before you return home was, the house and farm of Dunain – what
should be done with them? Whether they should be sold or the farm
carried on for your own account and what should be done with the
furniture & papers? You may easily figure to yourself what situation
matters would be in at such a time & I wish'd for your directions
how to act but as the honest old lady has enjoy'd pretty good health
for some time past, I hope she will live to welcome you home. She is
just now here with us. She came in to drink your health with us on
your birthday. Tomorrow my good friend you will enter upon your
36th year – make haste home.

The estate of Castlehill about which you enquired has been long
under sequestration and ... it is hard to say when the sale might
come on. But my Uncle the Abbe Colbert (or Cuthbert) who has
lived in France for many years & who has considerable claims upon
the estate is now at Edin'g buying up the debts with a view to be the
purchaser at a sale which he intends to bring on directly ... There is
another estate however in the neighbourhood on the market which
would do ... I mean the estate of Kynmylies. The present rent is
£250. There is a good deal of young fir planting in a thriving condition which will be of value some years hence. The mains are all
enclos'd & planted, and the farm is in good order. Mr. Ross has
offer'd it for sale, but asks a high price nine or ten thousand pounds
but probably he would take less. I'm told he means to entail his

whole land estate, so that unless Kynmmylies should be sold in his lifetime, it will not be contestable afterwards.

I wrote to you last year of the political contest in this country between the Duke of Gordon & Gen'l. Fraser. A very happy change in the General's circumstances has taken place this year. He has had influence & address enough to obtain from Government a gift of his estate with consent of Parliament. His friends & the Duke have made a number of Barons & there was an appearance of a hard struggle but the sudden dissolution of Parliament which happen'd about a fortnight ago has brought matters to a crisis sooner than expected & the Duke has at present one or two of a majority upon the roll but the General's good genius has prevail'd again. He has got the Ministry to provide Lord Geo: Gordon with a seat for an English borough, and he himself will be return'd for this country without opposition. The Duke has split his whole valuation in this shire and made about 26 Barons upon this occasion.[5]

Dr Alves wrote again in April 1775 informing his brother-in-law that Kynmylies was no longer available. It had been purchased by William's third cousin Evan Baillie of Dochfour. In addition, for the first of many times, Alves described the state of rebellion in America. That conflict, resulting as it did in French intervention in support of the Americans, would have profound consequences for William in India. However, Alves wrote primarily to express concern that they had not heard from William for well over a year. The concern was understandable not only for familial reasons but also because John Alves and William's mother were attempting to anticipate the absent proprietor's wishes.

I ... now begin to long much for a letter from you having received none since that dated in Feb. 1774 which makes your Sister very unhappy, as two ships of war have arrived from Madras this spring. All your friends are well; your Mother, who is at present with us in very good health; Mrs. Baillie better than she has been for some time; Nelly without any complaints, & your little nameson a fine thriving boy; Mrs. Grant your Aunt at Stonyfield says he is the likest to your Father of any ever descended from him, and indeed the likeness is very striking.

In one of my former letters I told you that the estate of Kynmylies was in the market. I did not know then that it was so near being sold. Within these few weeks Evan Baillie, third son to Dochfour, who has been for 16 years in the West Indies & married a Creole lady there[,] has bought it for £10,000 ster'l. He is come over & settles at Bristol as a merch't ...

The spirit of emigration to America still continues in the Highlands & is said spreading & gaining strength. Many hundreds are going over this year from the Aird, Urquhart, Glenmoriston, Glengary Kintail & other parts besides many in the southwest parts of Scotland which is very strange considering the present confusion in America. The provinces of New England & Virginia are actually in rebellion & have an army in the field, and the whole continent seems to have united in an attempt to throw off their dependence on Great Britain. Government is sending over 8 regiments to reinforce the army there and a large fleet to block up their harbours and bring them in to order. What the events will bring I know not but fear a good deal of blood will be spilt before matters are settled.[6]

Nelly, in her continuing campaign, appended a fervent entreaty: "I thought to have written you a letter this night but am prevented by your Mother's coming in to us. I can however comprise all I have to say in two words which the old lady most heartily joins in to with Come Home. When we do not hear from you regularly my anxiety is very distressing; in a word my patience is quite worn out."[7]

In July 1775 William wrote to Alexander Godsman that he was very much relieved to hear from him that family and friends were well since he had received no other mail that season. The presents to which he refers in this letter had been seven years in transit, having first been lost and then shipped on a circuitous route via Jamaica before being "smuggled" into Britain. At the same time, William seemed optimistic that he would benefit from the military opportunities presenting themselves. The action he cited was the Battle of Adas, the initial engagement of the First Anglo-Maratha War. As William intimated, the result was such that both factions could claim victory. The First Anglo-Maratha War arose from the Bombay Council's ill-judged support of the usurper Ragonaut Rao. Ragonaut was a younger brother of the peshwa, Balaji Baji Rao. On the latter's death, he had his nephew, Narayan Rao, the reigning incumbent, assassinated. However, Narayan's widow gave birth to a posthumous son who became the de jure heir to the Maratha throne. Grasping the prospect of ruling as regents, twelve Maratha chiefs designated the child as peshwa. Ragonaut, in an effort to retain the throne, purchased British assistance by ceding Salsette and Bassein in the Treaty of Surat on 6 March 1775. These territorial cessions so alienated his fellow Marathas that Ragonaut became persona non grata and found himself almost entirely dependent on the Company's forces.

> The presents Mitchell tells me he has recover'd or at least some-
> thing in their likeness. All I shall say is I never sent any thing in my
> life from India that was not the very best of its kind. I write only at
> length once a year in January. This is just to inform you that the
> humans are well & that Frank got a commission about a week ago,
> and is now with my Brother at Ellore 300 miles to the north and
> actually an Ensign in the battl'n I command. I return to that place
> in a few days. India now promises better for the military than it has
> for some time past. At Bengal they have acquired the Corah prov-
> ince from the heir of Shuja-ood-Dowla, lately dead, amounting to
> 20 odd lakhs of rupees yearly for the Company and at Bombay
> they are engaged in a war in support of Ragonaut Rao against his
> nephew and the greater body of the Mahrattas. Hitherto they have
> been rather unsuccessful, but the more mischief the better for us red
> coat men. In an engagement the 15th May last they[,] though with
> victory so far as to make the enemy leave the field of battle[,] had
> two captains & 3 lieuts. killed, 4 subalterns wounded and seventy
> four noncommissioned & privates killed and wounded besides 3 or
> 400 Sepoys.[8]

Newly minted as an acting colonel, William, at the outset of 1776, finally provided his unqualified approval of Alves's management of his interests in Scotland. He encouraged his brother-in-law to proceed with any other improvements that he, Campbell, and Godsman agreed upon. Given Alves and Godsman's visceral dislike of each other, William must have concluded that any project upon which the three could agree would be in the estate's interests. At the same time, his irritation with Alves's London correspondent is palpable. However, on a lighter note, upon learning of William Chisholm's marriage to his Dochfour cousin, Catherine, William marvelled that a man nineteen years his senior could "be still adequate to the task." Finally, while William noted that the military actions of the First Anglo-Maratha War had subsided, the arrival of Lord Pigot as governor of Madras presaged the internecine struggles that would beset the Madras Council in the years ahead.

Your letters ... gave great joy to both my Brother and me but by
what mismanagement I cannot say the news papers and almanacks
never came to hand. I suspect your London correspondent is not so
careful as I could wish, a great loss for you can hardly conceive with
what pleasure and entertainment when they do come we often over-
haul them for months after the receipt. I am entirely satisfied with
the management of my many concerns. Planting the craig I likewise
approve & as I shall, I'm confident, any other improvements you w't
Mr. Campbell & Godsman think necessary & prudent. My neighbour of Kynmylies will no doubt be an agreeable one and it gives us
no small degree of comfort to learn of the good fortune of all the
Brothers – Chisholm's marriage with the Sister seems rather extraordinary at his time of life, truly he cannot ... be still adequate to such
a task, if he is, I being so long in a sultry debilitating clime must have
forgot the vigour & strength of sweat & brow ...

As my Mother now must require (what in reality she ought to have
had before) something to carry her about in a decent manner, I beg,
without mentioning it until the time of delivery, you purchase a han-
som new cart chair and pair and present to her as a small token of
the gratitude and affection of her son.

India is at peace without a near prospect of any disturbance. Lord
Pigot about three weeks ago arrived ... [as] president and governor
of Madras. The old actors being turned out without the least compliment from the Company. From his Lordship we expect (though yet
nothing certain happened) much good to the service being not only
able in himself but here universally from his former conduct much
loved and esteemed. Gen'l. Smith left us in October and Sir Robert
Fletcher as Commander-in-Chief succeeded him ...

My Brother and Frank are well ...

P.S. While writing this letter I have been appointed to act as Lt.-Col.
And hope soon to have a commission for that rank.[9]

Further, to John Alves's immense relief, William clarified matters by providing instructions to Alves and Godsman regarding the management of
the estate in the event of the death of his mother: "In case of my Mother's
death which God forbid at least untill I once more return. Without
Dr. Alves and Mr. Godsman choose it, the farm of Dunain to be let to
the highest bidder but with a particular clause relating to the care of the
stand, garden & planting. My Father's papers to be sealed up and every

other little matter my Mother may leave to me, untill you have all the particular leads from myself, the pictures to be preserved and taken care of. The household furniture and utensils to be sold ...This is all that occurs to me at present."[10]

Shortly thereafter, William wrote directly to his mother beseeching her to preserve her health pending his and John's return. For the first time since joining the EIC, he held out the prospect of his return in the not too distant future.

Nothing could please me more than the good accounts I had last year of your health. It was a cordial both to my Brother and me beyond any thing else we could possibly have had from my accounts. However, I think you seem too sparing of the necessary to the comforts of life, let it not, I pray, be so in future if you deny yourself the least that may be conducive to render it pleasing or agreeable assuredly you will give me the greatest anxiousness. My most genuine hope is finding you at Dunain to receive me on my return. I'm yet thank God as stout and hearty as when I left it and though I cannot ascertain exactly the time of my departure from India, in the nature of things and course of the service it cannot now be at any great distance. John is well and joins me in sincerest and best wishes to our Sisters and their husbands.[11]

The thought of quitting India may have been induced by his lack of advancement, which he must have found particularly galling given the experience of the officers superseding him. With the departure of General Smith for England, William felt he had lost his patron. Preoccupied with his circumscribed prospects of promotion, he expressed his concerns to the new commander-in-chief, Sir Robert Fletcher. He complained that two junior colonels had taken precedence over him and concluded with a request that Fletcher plead his situation with the "Hon'ble Board."[12] The preference given to well-connected newcomers, particularly in the matter of temporary brevets, continued to stick not only in William's craw but also that of his colleagues. His resentment again came to the fore in his lament to Arthur Cuthbert in January 1777 that Mathew Horne had been unfairly promoted over him.

I am in the old style but rather going down than up, still no command and of late the Gov't, though acting for a year past as Lieut. Col., put Matthew Horne, I suppose for his great case of Lord Pigot, over my

head. I take the liberty my friend to send you copy of my remonstrances given in not firm hopes of redress but merely to shew the
world my consciousness of the injury. [James] Stuart's answer you also
have ... but notwithstanding the cunning and civil answer, he avoids
carefully touching on the points which make in my favour ... My
friend I mention all this matter to you in case an opportunity should
offer, either through Gen'l Smith or other leading military men at the
India House, of helping me. I'm unfortunate by coming out so young
and living so long in the country. I cannot with propriety address a
single man in the directorate myself and in a body I fear notwithstanding the professions of almost all my military friends, I am little
known to them.[13]

William's objections, while seemingly valid, were complex. In any event,
the promotion of others clearly rankled. He felt that an artillery officer
lacked the experience to command infantry and groused that Colonel
James Stuart, who was slated to succeed Sir Robert Fletcher as commander-in-chief of the Madras establishment, had not really addressed
his objections. As it happened, Stuart's stint as the senior military officer
at Madras was short-lived as he quickly became embroiled in a bitter
controversy wherein he arrested Governor Pigot at the behest of the
Madras Council (the Mathew Horne whose promotion had upset William
was one of the officers charged with making this arrest). As soon as they
were apprised of this action, the Court of Directors suspended Stuart.
Accordingly, Stuart had more pressing matters on his mind than William's
petition. He did, however, in January 1777, undertake to place William's
complaint regarding Horne before the Board of Directors as soon as possible. At the same time, while he sympathized with William's aversion to
temporary brevets and had expressed his opinion that "the President &
Council here have no power or right to grant brevets of field officers
under any description,"[14] Stuart equivocated in particular cases.

William reported to Godsman that same month: "I'm still struggling
on as usual but ... the promotion very little more advanced than when I
wrote you last."[15] His frustration erupted again in September when
Henry Cosby was placed in command of two to three thousand infantry.
William sought redress from Governor John Whitehill and the Council.

A reflection, and I may venture to say unmerited, lately thrown not
only on myself but on the whole body of field officers on this establishment, Col: Braithwaite alone excepted, leads me at this time

much contrary to inclination, & reflecting on the multiplicity of business you are engaged in, to make application for redress. A grievance
of such nature, as must ever be corroding to the feelings of a man, no
less than the taking from me my character as a soldier which I have
been most tenacious of and hitherto have maintained for many years
in this service I hope with honour.

To be short and take up as little of your time as possible, I mean
the nomination of Captain Cosby (for I can hold him in no other
light when detached from his employ of Adjutant General) to command a detachment which from numbers the eldest officer in the
service might be proud of.

Some surely of your field officers are men of ability and have given
proof, the records of the Board will testify it. What then can have
given cause to launch an attack upon every right that to an officer
ought to be dear. If an accusation be laid in I am ready for myself
and request a publick trial ...

What I know and complain of is that between two & three thousand infantry with a proportionable train of artillery of the Hon'ble
Company's troops have taken the field, and under the command of a
captain who by the Court of Directors is appointed adjutant general,
and to hold the nominal rank of Lieut; Colonel only while he does
that particular duty.[16]

Meanwhile, William's comfort level could not have been enhanced by
the political turmoil in Madras. The dysfunction of the Madras Council,
touched upon in William's letters, was first evident in the Court of Directors' vehement disapproval of Governor Wynch's assault on Tanjore. The
directors were shocked the troops had been employed on such reprehensible services: "We do declare the last expedition unjustifiable, and your
conduct therein wholly inexcusable."[17] The Court concluded by disput-
ing Madras's claim that its actions had secured the EIC's position and
suggested that the possessions of the Company had been endangered by
its success in reducing Tanjore. The directors' rancour was sufficient that
they dismissed Wynch and appointed, in his place, Lord George Pigot,
with specific instructions to restore the rajah to power.

Having served an earlier term as governor, from 1755 to 1763, Pigot
ought to have been attuned to the political nuances of Madras but he was
blessed with the proverbial tin ear and remained oblivious to local sensibilities. Pigot doggedly strove to execute his instructions from the Court
of Directors but was continually thwarted by those who stood to benefit

from the nawab's retention of Tanjore. William, as a beneficiary of the presumably unpaid Tanjore prize money, could well have placed himself in that camp, but in fact he thought Pigot "our greatest hope," and aligned himself with the governor. Desperate not to relinquish Tanjore, Mohammed Ali appropriately bribed a number of the Madras councillors. They, in turn, dutifully produced fraudulent claims against Tanjore. The nawab's primary actor in the campaign was Paul Benfield, who had acted as his go-between in the prize-money negotiations. Benfield asserted large financial claims against Tanjore and Mohammed Ali, claims that could be jeopardized by the rajah's recovery of the state. Pigot gave scant credence to the purported claims, as he was well aware that Benfield had arrived in India with modest means and could not have amassed such a significant fortune with any semblance of virtue.

On 13 February 1776 the governor placed the rajah once again on the throne of his forebears. Nevertheless, the dissension on the Council became increasingly vehement and Pigot increasingly peremptory in his dealings. Finally, George Stratton, on behalf of the strong-willed if weak-witted Council, in an unprecedented flouting of established authority, ordered Colonel Stuart, the second in command of the military, to arrest Pigot and incarcerate him. Inevitably, such an act was bound to become a hotly debated topic in India and at India House. With a view to ensuring that the troops stationed at Fort St George did not intervene, the Council promised them a "donation" which, to no one's surprise, remained unpaid at year end. In September 1776 William wrote an eyewitness account of Pigot's arrest and imprisonment: "Since January we have had nothing of moment happen on this coast until the 24th of last month when Lord Pigot was made prisoner and Mr. Stratton, governor in his place. The combustion it caused is hardly yet over. I therefore cannot venture to write you primary causes or effects. Indeed, I presume you'll find enough from the published papers, it being one of the first instances of this happening either at home or abroad. His Lordship was seized by a party of arm'd men about a mile from his garrison between eight and nine at night and carry'd to St. Thomas Mount where he has remained prisoner ever since."[18]

Speculation ran rampant and William may or may not have been representative when he informed Mitchell: "Col. Stuart was a severe blow to me and many others as you will know by the published papers. Lord Pigot I imagine feels most[,] though it's said he bears his misfortune w't great fortitude."[19] In the same vein, William reported to Godsman the following January that the government was in a state of chaos:

India, at least, the Coast of Coromandel, is at present quite a house
of confusion from the late confinement of Lord Pigot and likely to
continue so some months longer. Great luck to our Honourable
Master there is no appearance of war from any quarter. Was there,
I know not what might happen.

The civil servants with whom by constitution the government
lies are all at loggerheads, the majority I think in favour of his
Lordship; however the present governor and council have the red
coats on their side and therefore must have the reins till we hear
from Leadenhall St.[20]

Pigot's arrest inevitably dominated public discussion in Madras, and, in
virtually every letter home, William mentioned the affair. In a letter to
Alves, he noted:

I have been moved to Vellore but whether for the better or worse is
hard to say. Changes of government especially when brought about
in the manner our late one has, blow prudence and good either to
the publick or the individual. The civil arm still as much if not
more divided about Lord Pigot and his confinement than ever.
Remonstrances and protests given in daily to the present President
& Council. Sending his Lordship home in the Lyoness now under
dispatch is in agitation. However, I am at a distance unconcerned.[21]

Yet again, in his January 1777 letter to Cuthbert already quoted, William
outlined the Pigot controversy.

Our great change of government no doubt by the ships of Sept'r and
October you had from my Brother … Since, it has been the strangest
scene of tangle and confusion at Madras you ever saw. Although Lord
Pigot has behaved himself with the greatest degree of propriety since
his confinement yet it has not prevented his well wishers and others
disaffected to the present Board making remonstrances & protests and
on every opportunity shewing their disapprobation at the manner at
the time of his being seized & made prisoner, now they talk of forcing
him home by the Lyoness and in consequence have received a fresh
address from about two & forty of the inhabitants of Madras shewing
the illegality of such an act. How it will end I cannot at this distance
say for few are fond of writing their sentiments since you know private matters at this season of the year engross much of business.[22]

Later, on 14 September, William elaborated in another letter to Alves:

> Mr. Whitehill, an old Councillor of Madras who went home about
> 18 months ago[,] return'd on the 31st Aug't with a new commission
> of government from our honourable masters which has effectively put
> an end to all our disputes. Col. Stuart is suspended for six months and
> all the Councillors, Lord Pigot's party as well as the others, order'd
> home[,] I suppose to answer for their conduct before the House of
> Commons. When [Thomas] Rumbold [the new governor] & Munro
> [the new commander-in-chief] comes they say the red coats will be
> hauled over the coals – God grant some of them I believe as well as
> the others. I mean the civilians play's a black game. By the by my
> friends need have no anxiety about me for I fortunately was not
> on Madras duty when the revolution happened, consequently not
> concerned therein.[23]

Upon learning of these developments, the Court of Directors ordered
Pigot reinstated as governor and then recalled the various instigators
to London for examination. However, by this time, Pigot had died in
prison and James Stuart had assumed the role of commander-in-chief
following Sir Robert Fletcher's death in December 1776. Of the new
governor, John Whitehill, William commented: "Mr. Whitehill arrived
the 31st August ... to the great astonishment of both partys (Lord Pigot's
friends as well as those who hold the government) and is now in as
peaceable possession of every power & authority appertaining to this
station as if no disputes had ever happen'd. The others are preparing for
a voyage home agreeable to the Company's orders."[24]

For an ambitious officer, like William, the rotation of governors and
military commanders in revolving-door fashion created uncertainty and
concern. Nevertheless, there were grounds for optimism since, upon his
recall, Stuart was replaced as commander-in-chief by Sir Hector Munro,
the hero of Buxar and William's "countryman and old major"[25] in the
89th Regiment. A further connection was Munro's representation since
1768 of the Inverness Burghs in Parliament, a position he retained while
in India. Alves, on 8 June 1777, conveyed the news that upon visiting his
friend Captain Ross, he ascertained that General Munro had just received
an order by express from the Court of Directors to set out for London the
next morning to enable him to embark immediately for India and that
"the lady of this house is so kind as to recommend you & your Brother
to the General's good offices, & Kilravock (with whom the General is

very much connected in the political way) was to do the same. I hope you will find the Gen'l your friend. As to his character in the military line I am no judge but I believe it is very well establish'd. As a private gentleman however, I know it is unexceptionable and I'm persuaded you will find him a very worthy honest man."[26] William sanguinely suggested to his London agent, David Mitchell, the following January that he was in hearty expectation of Munro and Rumbold's arrival.[27] However, as financial necessity rather than the prospect of glory drove Munro's decision to return to India, skepticism arose as to his energy and steadfastness under fire. One writer, A.P. Newton, remarks: "Munro was a man whose best days were long past; personally honest, he was also slow minded, irresolute in an emergency, unable to profit by the ideas of other people."[28] It was Munro's irresolution that would prove disastrous for William.

Q3

A couple of years earlier, in July 1775, William informed Alexander Godsman, who had become factor for the Duke of Gordon after the 1765 reduction of their former regiment, the 89th, that John had been commissioned an ensign in William's regiment and that "India now promises better for the military than it had done some time past ... the more mischief the better for us to have the enemy take the field of battle."[29] Godsman responded with news of Inverness and the resilience of the American rebels, with whom, like many Britons, he appeared to sympathize. He demonstrated shrewd analytical ability in recognizing that divisions of opinion in Britain encouraged the American rebels and rendered Britain's pursuit of the war less effective. The battle that Godsman mentioned as taking place on 17 June was that of Bunker Hill. While technically a British victory, General William Howe's forces suffered extensive casualties before dislodging the rebels on their third charge. Even then, the Americans retreated only for want of ammunition and the "victory" did not realize its objective of relieving the siege of Boston. In fact, this moral victory over British troops cemented the rebels' opposition to Great Britain and reassured them that their militia could capably acquit themselves in combat. The requirement for troops for the war in America built momentum for the rehabilitation of proscribed Scots and those tainted by the Forty-Five. General Fraser had already recovered much of his clan's land but furthered his family's claim by raising two battalions for service in America, while the MacGregors, whose name had been proscribed since 1603, recovered their right to its use by an act of Parliament and likewise offered to raise a regiment for the American war. As an aside, a cursory perusal of the letter suggests that Alves and Godsman were less than kindred spirits.

If it please God you come home well to this country, Mr. [Alexander of Dochfour] Baillie's being so close in your neighbourhood will be a very great acquirement to your happiness, for he is a most desirable man, both for a friend and a neighbour. His brother James is very lately gone from here to London, where his lady is, and, I hear he intends on soon going out to the West Indies on business. The third brother, Evan, is settled at Bristol in a company trade, and Duncan, the youngest, is in the West Indies.

Colonel Hugh Grant who came home very lately from Bengal, has brought home an immense fortune, and is just now going through the neighbourhood pricing estates, for he is resolved to be a purchase near this place ...

The present contest 'twixt Britain and her North America Colonies engages the attention of all ranks and degrees; whether Britain shall have the power to tax them or not, or whether the most valuable blessing of a free people shall only belong to themselves.

The only rencontre they have had with the King's troops worth pains of notice was on the 17th of June last; and, although they were defeat[ed], they discovered a far greater degree of courage and bravery than Britons believed them to be possessed of. There is a talk that some new regiments will be raised to send to New England, to assist the rest of the King's troops there to enforce obedience to the laws of the British Senate; should this take place I believe General Fraser will be pretty certain of getting the command of one of them, and will have the nomination of his own officers – he made an application to this purpose already, but matters had not come to that pitch to make reinforcements of that kind necessary, and hitherto have only augmented the companies at the rate of only twenty rank and file.

The Americans think themselves capable to repel any force Britain can send against them, and this notion may inspire them to hold out much longer than people imagine, and oblige Britain to raise several new regiments before they can be brought to order. The British Senate have been all along a good deal divided about the measures they ought to pursue, which has brought a stimulus to the courage of the Americans, and may serve to spin out the contest

longer than otherwise there was any reason to expect. The Clan of
Macgrigor have got their name restored by an act of the last Session,
and they have likewise offered to raise a regiment to go against the
Americans. Mr. Willox now takes the name of Macgrigor, and in case
raising of regiment takes place, he has great reason to expect a company in the Macgrigor Regiment ...

Mrs. Margt Baillie, upon receiving yr draft on London[,] was so
struck with a sense of gratitude towards you that all power of expression seemed to be lost for a time. In your last to the Doctor, you mentioned giving your nurse a year's rent; he observed that probably you
did not advert that they at present rented the Mills, beside the possession of land, and that both put together would be a very considerable
sum – that it is probable you did not advert to their having got something already, and that, therefore, it would be imprudent to make
them any advance at present. I agreed with him in this, but observed
that such a sum as they got formerly would do them a great service,
nor did I think you would grudge it in the least. He said, that when
it appeared their necessity was very pressing, something might be
bestowed, so in this position that matter stands ...

P.S ... [Your mother] is at present as well as can be expected; but
one at her time of life cannot be expected to have great strength.
She is, perhaps, one of the fondest parents in the universe, and all
her wishes are to live to see you. I don't recollect if I wrote you since
we took infestment and sasine for you on the lands of Dunain ...
I daresay the Doctor writes you punctually about your money
matters, and will send you exact from time to time how matters
stand. I mentioned twice to the Dr. that I could get the Duke's bond
for any money you might have to spare in this country, but, as he
did not seem to take any notice of my proposal, I did not speak of
it afterwards ... [30]

During that year Sir Alexander Grant of Dalvey, the heir of the long-time
M P for the Inverness Burghs intervened on William's behalf, and whether
or not his influence was the deciding factor, William received his long-
sought promotion to lieutenant-colonel on 29 December 1775. Shortly
thereafter, William informed Godsman of his appointment and his expectation of receiving the commission soon. Concerned that his tenants were
embarking for America, he entreated Godsman to encourage them to
remain at Dunain. When William's mentor, General Smith, had left India,

he had been replaced by Sir Robert Fletcher. Fletcher had been twice dismissed from the Company's service, the first time for insolence and the second for mutinying against Robert Clive. The Court of Directors, failing to learn from experience, reinstated Fletcher and sent him to India as commander-in-chief. William expressed his skepticism of Fletcher's talents and placed his hopes in Lord Pigot. In his assessment of Fletcher, he proved prescient as the new commander's arrogance exceeded any military skills, but his expectations of Pigot failed to materialize. In bemoaning the number of young men who had declined the Company's commissions and accepted employment with Mohammed Ali, William reflected the growing tendency of native rulers to enhance their military prowess by employing European officers. Indeed, William believed that the nawab's growing power and influence might well prove the greatest future threat to the Company.

Many many thanks to you for your letter of March last. Your management of my little farm is both clear and effective and I'm convinced made out with the greatest justice to my interest. Take care and encourage the poor people and do not let them be running to America. I would rather remitt half the rent. Puff them up and say I'll soon be amongst them when every indulgence imaginable will be shown them. Indeed, to tell you the truth[,] nothing cou'd give me more real pleasure and of course I am trying for it with all my might. The devil is there is no commanding what we wish. Patience and perseverance is the only mode and although I have been too long on the hunt, I cannot ultimately yet determine when my flitting will take place. My health and constitution are by no means impaired which ought at a great manner to set my friends at ease. Sooner or later they must see me[,] it being undoubtedly the main point at which all my thoughts are aim'd. The Coast of Coromandel at present affords little for expectation ... in any way. All is peace and no part at war. The Company and Nawab together are in possession of as much upon the present establishment as they can well manage and our governor general and Council seem little inclined to increase it. My friend, General Smith[,] left us in October and is succeeded by our countryman Sir Robert Fletcher who hitherto has had no opportunity to exhibit what talents he may have. Lord Pigot is our greatest hope ... They say he has powers to reduce the Nawab's service (a terrible irritant to the senior officers in the Company's troops for two or three years back) to its proper standard. You can hardly conceive to what a state of consequence Mohammed Ali has grown from the abject situation you remember him in at the siege of Pondicherry. His revenues so great & his forces so numerous what with the additional pay and batta he gives, many young men have declined commissions in the Company's to accept in his. Far from also being the humble servant of every English gentleman he met, there is not three on the Court besides Council he wou'd rise from his bed to receive. Nay his troops are so many in number and well disciplined, he is, in my opinion, rather of more terror to the Company than any thing else.[31]

In January 1776 Nelly resumed her pleas for William to return home; indeed, if anything, she became more strident on the subject.

Since I wrote you last spring I have not had the pleasure of a letter from you. I must confess to begin to be very uneasy at being so long unheard of John or you. But my great distress is that you do not seem to think seriously of coming home. One year after another comes to an end, but no prospect of your return: your stay in India seems to be endless. You are wasting your constitution by a bad climate and the fatigues of a military life, even should you escape the immediate danger attending it, and all for what you can very well do without. For God sake be satisfied and come home with health to enjoy what you have. Don't be angry with me for this great scold, I cannot help telling you my mind. I am now grown so very impatient to see you once settled at Dunain with a good wife.

I wrote you formerly that the chintz and muslin you was so good as [to] send us had been seized. They were afterwards bought for our account at the India house, and the muslins and shawl came here about a twelve month ago and were given to the persons they were directed to. It was necessary the chintz should be exported and, they were accordingly sent to Jamaica and lately smuggled back again and sent home where they arrived safe some weeks ago; they are indeed remarkably pretty.

The Doctor writes you all the publick news but leaves all the little country occurrences for me. Your cousin Sandy Duff is gone in to the army again a cap't in the 46 regiment and I daresay will go soon to America. Cap't. Duncan McPherson formerly of your regiment is gone in a cap't to the 42 who also go to America ... There is little new in the matrimonial way since I wrote last. The widow Culloden is married to an Aberdeenshire Laird and the

Laird of McLeod is soon to be married to Sir Idy's eldest daughter, a love match, but not a prudent one, his estate quite out at elbows and a part of it in the market.[32]

At the same time, John Alves wrote to update William on the plantings at Dunain and to ascertain William's intentions before any more such activity was undertaken. For the first time, Alves mentions, albeit indirectly, the impact of the plantings on the tenants' sheep and thus their livelihood. He thereby foreshadows the Highland Clearances, which accounted in good part for the continual emigration from Scotland to America despite the latter's unsettled conditions. While Nelly asserted that her husband left it to her to acquaint William with the news of the neighbourhood, the doctor indulged in a goodly portion of the local gossip, while also gently encouraging William to purchase Balnain's property since it was "pretty contiguous" to Dunain. Finally, Alves's observation that "the Gen'l will command most of the northern chieftains" is fascinating in that it affirms the cogency of Lord President Forbes's advice to the Hanoverians to diffuse potential support for the Stuarts by coopting the clans through enlisting their chiefs to fight in foreign wars. Whereas Forbes's advice would have reflected a deliberate policy on the government's part, this time it was a natural evolution of the integration of Scotland into Britain. Ironically, the sons and heirs of the very men who fought and fell at Culloden attempting to overthrow the Hanoverian monarchs were now at the forefront in championing the cause of George III.

Since your letter of Feb'y last we have not heard any thing from or of you, and begin to be anxious for the arrival of the next ships from India. In my last I told you that we propos'd inclosing the Craig of Dunain & planting it with firs. This work is now finish'd & it has taken 600,000 fir plants. Come home when you will, I presume you will be glad to have this done to your hand, and as plantations of this kind do not make a great show for some years, it is good to be in advance with them; however we will proceed no further without your own special orders and direction. Mr. Baillie Dochfour having lately purchas'd the feu of Dochfour from the Duke of Gordon this season has inclos'd the hill belonging to it & Dochcairn & planted a part of it also with firs, so that Ness-side will make a better appearance some years hence than it has hitherto done, especially as Mr. Baillie is to build a house there next season. Last summer

when I understood his intention of inclosing the hill, I went with
Mr. Godsman and some of your old people to view the Marches
there and Mr. Godsman was to be on his guard that no encroachments should be made upon your property. It would be a great saving to you in your future improvements that a part of the garden of
Dunain were appropriated to raising young nurseries of firs & forest
trees of different kinds ...

The Caledonian Mercury (the best Scots news paper) for the year
1775 accompany this to London in order to be forwarded to you,
together with a Scots Almanack to you & another to John & one
to Frank. By the papers you will see that our dispute with America
is now become a very serious matter indeed. The whole North
American continent is in open rebellion & in arms. An army of
30,000 men is to be sent out in the spring to subdue them. There is
nothing but recruiting going on here. The old Highland Regiment is
augmented to 1,200 men & Gen'l Fraser has got a regiment of
Highlanders to consist of two battalions of 1,000 each ... McLeod,
McIntosh, the young Chisholm Culcairn, Lochiel, and a Brother of
the Duchess of Gordon's are captains in this corps & Cluny one
of the majors, so that the Gen'l will command most of the northern
chieftains. The regiment must be compleat by the 25th of March
next, and to be sent directly to America.

Belnain died a few weeks ago and left a considerable fortune (near
£20,000) to three Daughters, the land estate about £300 a year to
the eldest who I hear is to be married to one Tytler a writer in Edin'g
who is to take the name of Fraser, but it is generally thought the
estate will be sold. I have no doubt but Mr. Baillie Dochfour will
have a view to it, or perhaps Colonel Grant Sheuglie who is lately
come home, but I wish rather you were master of it, as it is pretty
contiguous to your other property ...

I understand Godsman is to leave Dochfour next term and to have
a farm of the Duke's at Allnaskiach. He says the Duke would build
him a snug house there, but as his time in this country is uncertain, he
is not sure if he will enter upon building. He thinks rather of taking
George Baillie's house at Leyes which has been vacant for two years
with the farm which he would turn in to a graziery, but I believe if he
could get a company, he would gird on his sword once more.

As Nelly writes at this time and mentions deaths, marriages &
other country occurrences, I need say nothing of them. The year
1775 proved fatal to several old people in this neighbourhood, and

among the rest be my Father who died last March. Your Mother was in a very declining way about a month ago, but is now quite well again, & things at Dunain still in the old way.

Little Billy who has grown a stout lad sends you a kiss, and another to Uncle John.

P.S. As the new park & planting at Dunain makes it necessary for the bodies thereabout to part with their sheep[,] & Wm. Ross among the rest, we make it up to him by allowing him yearly (including his farm) the £5 you at first ordered for him, & for this he has the sole charge of the young planting, that no caller may hurt them. We shall take care that your nurse & old J. Gow, who is in a very declining way, shall not suffer for want.[33]

In June 1776 Archibald Campbell notified William of the distressing but not unexpected news of his mother's illness and death. A cold she had contracted in February developed into a tenacious cough and "feverish fits" to which she succumbed on 15 March. Her will left everything to William, with Godsman and Campbell as trustees. William was aware of the contents of the will, since Frank had taken a copy with him to India. Godsman would be renting the farm and Campbell advised that William confirm the bequests to his sisters. William's mother had verbally bequeathed her clothes to his sisters, her watch to Nelly, and her diamond ring and a lock of his father's hair to Anne. As the bequests had been verbal, William was entitled to object to them, "but I own I wish you to confirm them, not only in compliance to your Mother's intentions, but the value of the whole thing so inconsiderable, that it is not worthwhile to dispute them. Pray therefore (if you are of the same opinion) write your Sisters a few lines, giving up your right to these particulars as if you are to bestow them, 'tis best to do it with a good grace." His cousin closed by again imploring William to return. "Let me now repeat my earnest request, that you leave that rascally climate, and return to your native country, while you have yet a few friends remaining to participate your happiness, for without such what is life? You say that you expect to find these stout and healthy, if you come over by forty, but let me inform you for one, that I feel the approaches of old age so sensibly that every day is a memento mori; add to this, my sight so decay'd that without a pair of spectacles mounted on my nose, I am (as Milton says) ... presented with an universal blank. If you don't think of settling till it comes to this the whole riches of the Indies will afford you small comfort."[34] Alves followed a week later with the same news, adding that Frank's mother was staying with her sister and sister's daughter.[35] Then, their ten-year-old nephew, Alexander, wrote his uncles with news that was even more devastating for being unexpected. His mother, Anne, William's elder sister, had died on 14 September. If the deaths of 1776 did not spur the brothers to return to their native country soon, it was unlikely that anything else would.

> Will be kind enough to excuse this, being my first [letter,] as Papa is unable to write them himself, the dismal melancholy news, I with unspeakable grief acquaint them of my dearest Mama's death in a fever and angina the 14th of September. We had been for a year past happy in her being quite recovered of the lingering illness she was for a long time troubled with, but cut off I may say in a few hours, altogether unexpectedly. Papa joins all of us in kindest good wishes for your healths and safe homecoming, which must be the greatest comfort to us under our most heavy affliction. Comp'ts also to poor Cousin Franky. We feel much for you, was not all drowned in our own distress. Frank's Mother is kind enough to stay with us yet which makes both Papa and us as happy as we can be in our case.[36]

In September 1776, still unaware of the demise of his mother and sister, William wrote John Alves, congratulating him on the low cost of planting the Craig. He agreed with Alves's recommendation that the park to the south and west of the house be enclosed and planted, and instructed him to proceed. William also, as Alves had suggested, sought to ensure that his marches adjoining Dochfour's land be defended.[37] For his part, Alves reported that they had disposed of the household furniture at Dunain in an auction that, owing to the great variety of small articles, took two full days to complete. The sale of the household furniture after expenses brought in roughly £105.

That December, Alves conveyed the news that he and Archibald Campbell had leased the farm of Dunain to Alexander Godsman, although the doctor's distaste for the arrangement is evident in his reference to the rent from Godsman being less than that from an "indifferent tenant." Alves concluded his letter with reflections on the war in America and underlined the colonies' declaration of independence. He reported the British victories on Long Island and in New York City and described with remarkable accuracy the strategy for dividing the northern and southern colonies and stifling trade in an attempt to undermine the Americans' ability to sustain the rebellion. What he failed to foresee, and understandably so, was John Burgoyne's defeat at Saratoga. Alves felt that the French would be constrained by their considerable debt from openly assisting the American rebels. However, Saratoga instilled sufficient confidence in American prospects for the French to declare war on Britain.

The only unwelcome part of your letters was that wherein you desire in the event of your Mother's death, that Dunain be let, and the things there dispos'd of. This, as it seems to show that you have no immediate prospect of returning home we would have dispens'd with.

As Mr. Godsman is to send you particular accounts of the stocking, corn & cattle at Dunain by which you'll see how every thing was dispos'd of, I need say nothing on that subject; nor yet of the terms of Mr. Godsman's entry to Dunain, since he is also to send you a copy of the articles of agreement relative to that betwixt himself upon the one part, & Mr. Campbell & me as acting for you upon the other, in which every thing is particularly specified. Upon Mr. G's proposal these articles vary a little from our first plan; and no doubt the conditions are more favourable to Mr. G. than they would have been to any body else. The rent too is less than would have been got from an indifferent tenant, but we suppos'd these indulgences were agreeable to your intention. The household furniture at Dunain except the things already seal'd up, and perhaps a few of such as you might be desirous to keep, will be dispos'd of as you direct ...

When I wrote you last, I little thought I should have any further occasion this year to send you disagreeable acc'ts from this country. I'm heartily sorry however to have now to inform you of your Sister Mrs. Baillie's death. It was occasion'd by a fever & sore throat which carried her off in less than three days, last Sept'r. Her complaints were considered so little dangerous in the beginning, that we were not inform'd of her illness till about 20 hours before she expired: you may judge how much shock'd & surpris'd we were upon finding her condition so different from what we expected. Every thing you may believe was attempted that could be thought of in so short a time, but alas! It was too late. Nelly was so affected by this melancholy & unlook'd for event that her health suffered not a little. She is now better, however, and I hope a short time will restore her to her former state of health.

I shall write this season a letter to your Brother which will be deliver'd by a young man of the name of Fraser who has a sort of

connection with you. He was out last year as surgeon's mate to an
Indiaman and is to return this year in the same character, intending,
I believe, to remain in India, if he can. Any civilities you may show
him, will, I daresay[,] be well taken by his friends in this country &
I shall be very well pleas'd that you find him deserving your notice.
But I cannot, after saying even this much, omit putting you a little on
your guard, and telling you that some years ago, his character was
not quite unexceptionable; but he was then very young & thought-
less, and probably his poverty was an enemy to his virtue. I hope he
is since reform'd, but I do not by any means intend that this recommendation[,] such as it is, should lead you to any risk or expense
on his account: your advice & countenance may be of use to him,
and this is all the length I wish you to go, and even this only if you
find him deserving it.

I have little to acquaint you with at this time in the way of country
news ... Cap't Evan Baillie [William of Ardmore's son] is lately
appointed by the India Directors (your hon'ble masters) to return to
Bengal & resume the command of the Mughal cavalry.

In regard to publick affairs, the disputes in America still continue
and at length the Americans have thrown off their connection with
Britain & formally declar'd themselves independent. Lord Howe,
however & his Brother the General have been successful against
them of late, and have driven them from Long Island, New York etc.
The Generals [Guy] Carleton & Burgoyne too have driven them out
of Canada & are coming down upon the back settlements of New
England & New York, & when they join the Howes will effectively
prevent all intercourse between the New England & the Southern
Provinces, which with the total stoppage of their trade by our ships
of war will I hope soon bring them back to reason & their duty.
Meantime preparations are making for another campaign in
America. God grant a speedy issue to the dispute, for while it continues all parties must suffer. There was lately some appearance
of a French & Spanish war. These powers are suspected of secretly
assisting the Americans & some of their late operations seem'd
to indicate a design of taking advantage of our present distress'd
circumstances, & falling upon us while our whole army almost is
abroad. A strong fleet of observation however of 16 ships of the
line, is getting ready with all expedition & I hope the cloud is blown
over for the present; at least the French & Spanish Ministry are now
giving strong assurances of a pacifick disposition. Indeed, France is

so much loaded with debt that I believe she hardly has credit to raise a fund for carrying on a war ...

Your little namesake is well & is become a very entertaining companion since he began to prattle.[38]

The following year, in October 1777, Godsman described the war in America in a somewhat more pessimistic vein, but, like Alves, he did not anticipate French intervention. Indeed, Louis XVI would likely have fared much better had he thought more like these Highland Scots, given that the war in America left French finances in a shambles and thereby, it could be argued, prepared the ground for the revolution of 1789.

We continue to carry on the war with keenness against America, and their will seems to be equally good; what their abilities may be, time only can determine, for they have already done so much beyond what we expected they could do, that the wisest of our Ministry is not able to say what they cannot do – every skirmish which is generally in our favour, gives us hopes that they are soon to be brought to order, and the war finished; but by the underhand assistance of the French & Spaniards, they find resources, which in all probability will enable them to spin out the contest for another year or perhaps longer, and the event is hid in impenetrable darkness. We have a formidable fleet ready for action, which together with the poor state of the French finances obliges them to be cautious, and for ought I can see we have no chance of being engaged in a war soon.[39]

Francis now reappears, having been assigned to a battalion of sepoys in Tanjore country, "much as to try how he cou'd act on his own station as any thing else, by the by it is as good a station as he cou'd be on and you know he had me always within call."[40] At that time, William was presiding as president of a General Court Martial in Madras,[41] which, among other matters, sentenced John Forrester, a private of the 2nd Battalion, 2nd Regiment, "to receive 1,000 lashes of a cat o'nine tails in the usual manner" for desertion; and Edward Walker, a sergeant, to 1,200 lashes and degradation to the rank of private, coupled with the declaration that he would be "forever incapable of promotion in the Honourable Company's service."[42]

In September 1777 William told Godsman that he had obtained his first fixed command at the Fort of Poonamallee. "No report of war in India or the least publick disturbances. I was about two months ago for the first time appointed to fixed command, that of the small fort of Poonamallee consisting of about five hundred Europeans and 300 Sepoys and where I hope, no better offering, to keep my post some time more especially if our country man Munro & my old major shou'd prove my friend."[43]

The following March, William noted Hector Munro's appearance on the scene as well as that of the new governor. Sir Thomas Rumbold had served previously in India both in the military and as a councillor in Bengal where he amassed a sizable fortune. During his second posting, Rumbold seemed intent on multiplying that fortune.

> Mr. Rumbold & General Munro with all their train of followers arrived here the eighth of last month & thank God intestine brawls seem once more at an end on this establishment. There has been no particular act of government yet taken place to mark the line they mean to follow. However, as far as we can guess[,] unanimity in Council that great point seems determined as General Stuart will not be try'd here but order'd home or further suspended till the pleasure of the Directors be known.
>
> At Bengal is nothing extraordinary. At Bombay government intends a rupture soon with the Mahrattas & by way of dividing that great power making a broad diversion in favour of Ragonaut Rao who you know we deserted so shamefully lately [by the Treaty of Poorunder on 1 March 1776]. I am in hope of commanding a force from this Presidency shou'd I not succeed in getting some very lucrative garrison. I intend making a trip home by way of firming up my constitution & settling some little matters in the North.[44]

That was the first indication of a possible visit to Scotland but mentioning it to Mitchell in London clearly did not incur the same level of obligation as if William had conveyed that intention to his friends and family in Inverness. He relayed much the same information about his life in India to John Alves but, significantly, omitted any reference to a trip home.

> Peace is once more perfectly restored to the settlement of Fort St. George and from the mild steady demeanour of Mr. Rumbold are the people looking with pleasure forward ... The King of Tanjore & the Nawab's affairs engross much of their time. The former likely they will support in his just rights and the latter I hope bring to that proper sense of his obligations to the English Nation in general & to

the Company in particular which in his late attempts towards desperate & total independence, he seems to have forgot ... I am in good hope of commanding a force from this coast to assist [against the Marathas]. Shou'd Munro prove my friend I must succeed & assuredly in that case push hard for the long or short honour. John & Francis are well but poor – what's worse God only knows when they will be rich. My love to Nelly & her Billy & kind compliments to the rest of my friends.

P.S. The French too draw our attention towards the Malabar Coast. They have made lately a settlement at Charol a place near Bombay & granted them by the Mahrattas.[45]

The granting of Charol to the French by Peshwa Mahadeo Rao II's deputy, Nana Furnese, violated the treaty the Marathas had negotiated with the EIC. The incensed Bombay Council, still anxious to establish Ragonaut on the throne, prevailed over Calcutta's objections by highlighting the seriousness of the French threat. Bombay then sent an inadequate army to impose the hapless Ragonaut on the Marathas. The combined Maratha forces surrounded the British troops and compelled Colonel John Carnac to sign the ignominious Treaty of Wadgaon. By this treaty, the British renounced their support of Ragonaut, relinquished all the territorial acquisitions since 1773, and undertook to pay Mahadji Scindia 41,000 rupees. Governor General Hastings repudiated the convention on the grounds that Bombay was not legally empowered to sign such a treaty and sent the resolute and capable Thomas Goddard to harass the Marathas. Eventually, the Company inflicted such pain on Scindia that the latter sued for peace. The First Anglo-Maratha War then terminated with Hastings and Nana Furnese signing the Treaty of Salbai on 17 May 1782. William's sympathy lay with Bombay's ally Ragonaut Rao but history has proven far less kind to the ruthless usurper.

In October 1777 Godsman sent a chatty note updating William and acknowledging that his earlier letters may well have gone astray. He had entrusted them to "the care of my agent at London who was then become a very old man, and very inattentive to any little business for which charges were not commonly stated." He outlined the valuation of the utensils, crops, and materials turned over to him, reported on the plantings, and, in a reference that underlined the extent of the Highland Clearances then under way, suggested that William should enclose the pasture grounds in the Mouth of Caiplich since it would make a fine sheep walk and provide

good grazing for cattle; "in many parts of the Highlands, sheep have
become the cattle in vogue for stocking a farm; they think the profits arising from them are far greater than black cattle, and many Highland farms
on this account have risen to a monstrous rent." William's cousin
Alexander Baillie of Dochfour was "doing great things on that and his
other piece of Dochcairn. He has built a very neat house with wings, put
up a fine set of office houses, made out a fine garden of large extent, with
walls seventeen or eighteen feet high, and has peaches & apricots of many
various kinds of fruit growing there, and a thousand things that his Father
or Grandfather would not know the names of[;] he is himself a worthy
good man & I'm convinced you'll be happy in his acquaintance."
Conscious of William's concern for his tenants, Godsman concluded: "All
the poor men around here are well. Poor Anderson Elder still does any
little thing in the garden, and I keep a cow for him and show him such
kindness as I believe you wou'd wish me to do; but as he is now upon a
different footing from what he was formerly, we are to allow him so
many bolls of meal as may be necessary for his maintenance & charge the
same to your acc't for which he takes care of the little nursery that is
going on. The poor man cannot last it out long."[46]

Once more, the following February, Nelly pleaded with her brother to
return home for a wife although she made a point of excluding the
McKenzie ladies, leaving us to question the nature of their offence. In what
seemed to be the common assessment of George Baillie of Leys, Nelly had
little expectation their brother-in-law would do much for his children. She
conveyed news of their nephews and relayed a good deal of neighbourhood scuttlebutt, including some involving Simon Baillie, who had earlier
been the subject of his "concerned" mother's entreaties to William.

We have not had any letter from you or John for many months past
which considering the situation Madras is in at present, makes us not
a little uneasy about you. But I hope God will preserve you both and
send you home to the few that remains of your friends here. I would
forgive your long stay in India did you only do as your namesake
Simon Baillie has done, that is, to come home for a wife (I will say
I don't wish her to be a McKenzie lady) tho' I must own there is nothing in this world I so much wish for as to see or hear that you are
married and had a family. You should consider that twenty years in
India will soon make you an old man. Tho' I am happy to learn from
Simon that you look as young as ever and, thank God, keep good
health: long last. He does not say so much of poor John whose

constitution I am afraid is broken. I wish he could think of coming home even with a small fortune rather than lose his life in pursute of a large one. Simon Baillie has been very lucky for the short time he has been in India; he gives himself out for being worth five thousand pounds. The Doctor has wrote to you by him a few days ago. His wife and he can tell you what a stout little fellow your nameson is grown. We have been very lucky this year in having got the Doctor's two eldest sons taken off our hands at a less expense[,] poor fellows[,] than we could look for, tho' to be sure their education for some time past has been very heavy on our small funds. The eldest lad who is past seventeen, and has been at college for two years past, goes out to Jameca to the Doctor's cousin's, the Castlehill lad who makes very kind offers for him; the second boy is gone to London some weeks ago to his Uncle Thomas who has sent for him and is to bring him up to the English law entirely at his own expense. There is only Archie who remains who is a very promising boy about 14 years old. If you could do any thing for him in the East Indies (that is without putting yourself to much expense) I am sure his Father would be happy to have him under your protection. I would have mentioned them to you sooner but for fear of leading you into any inconvenience on there [sic] account, which is the last thing on earth I would wish to do.

Your Sister's children are all well. The eldest girl lives at Edinbrough with Mrs. Whittny. George lives at the Leyes with the rest and has a boy to teach them. They are all fine children. The second girl who is about 9 years old the Doctor wants me to take for some time for her education in town which I intend to do if I live till next winter. There is not much to be expected from there [sic] Father tho' he seems desirous to give the boys an education. Alick [or Aleck] is a very good scholar and I hope will turn out very well. The other two boys are beginning to read and promise to be good scholars likeways.[47]

Meanwhile, the war in America was having a profound impact throughout the British Empire and may have played a role in formalizing William's promotion to lieutenant-colonel, as suggested by the following note in the Court of Directors records for April 1778:

The board taking into consideration the case of field officers now doing the duty of those absent in England, it appears by the consultations of December 17, 1775 that Major Baillie, Major Fitzgerald and Major Nixon were appointed to do the duty of Lieutenant Colonel

Bonjour, Braithwaite and Bellingham then absent with no other advantage whatever other than the nominal rank of Lieutenant Colonel. Colonel Braithwaite arrived from England last year, but there was no account of Lieutenant Colonel Bonjour, or Lieutenant Colonel Bellingham and it is very doubtful whether they may return at all – as they have now been absent near three years. In these circumstances, the Board are of opinion and accordingly resolve that Major Baillie and Major Fitzgerald who are now doing their duty be appointed full Lieutenant Colonels to rank from the time they were given it in order to act as such – that their pay and gratuity as Lieutenant Colonels commence from the 25th of last month and that it be recommended to the Board of Directors.[48]

By then, William had let Alves know that he was unable to gauge when he would settle in Scotland. However, he did confirm his mother's verbal bequests to his sisters and, in a gesture certain to arouse Alves's and our curiosity, requested, without even hinting at the reason, that he turn whatever assets he could into cash.

My return is so very uncertain that I think every thing that can with propriety be turned into ready cash shou'd. If Mr. Godsman does not chuse the cattle & stacks of the farm, let them be sold with household furniture, plates etc. etc. to the highest bidder. The papers to remain as they are for the present in his care, also the pictures and any little family pieces there may be & ought not to be sold. You will easily understand what I mean by this though my memory is not sufficient for particulars. What has been given my Sisters I entirely approve and shou'd Nelly wish for much more she is as welcome as it's possible for a brother to make a favourite Sister & give her a hug for me.

I cou'd wish also, indeed, request not to speak in stronger terms that the money lent to Torbreck and James Francis Gortuley be called in and lodged in the bank or some place where it can be drawn from at a moment's warning. As I have the best reasons for this I beg it may be attended to. I will say explanatory that it's from no change in my circumstances either at home or abroad. Further wou'd answer no purpose in itself.[49]

The same month, William wrote Godsman outlining the particularly generous terms on which the latter would rent the Dunain farm and enquiring after his older sister's family:

You are becoming a perfect old Whig. Your long preachings & accounts of fodder, cattle etc., etc. are as unintelligible to me as the deepest problems of Euclid. I have observed in a letter to Dr. Alves that you have the house and farm of Dunain at the old rent with the care of the papers, pictures and what else may not be thought proper for sale on my account. The repairs will be charged to me and you may take my word ... I will not turn you out in a hurry. If you chuse the cattle or any thing else to be sold by auction take them and be accountable to myself only for the money. I have also to beg that, if possible, you send me yearly an acc't current of all my business and I'm sure in this both Mr. Campbell & the Doctor will willingly be most aiding and assisting ... May you long enjoy the beggar's pension is the sincere wish of your affect'e friend ...

I beg you'll let me know in your next how Mr. George Baillie & his family are. I feel much for the loss of my Sister and more so if possible for the children now she is gone.[50]

8

Command at Pondicherry

I concluded from the beginning that this would be the end and I
am right, for it's not half over.

Sir Boyle Roche, MP

The crisis in America had emboldened the Marathas, Hyder Ali Khan,
Nizam Ali Khan, Moodaji Bhonsla I, and many of the lesser princes.
With the clandestine support of the French, they sought to present a
united front against the British, who seemed at their most vulnerable. The
French provided supplies from Mauritius and Bourbon while an adventurer, the Chevalier St Lubin, undertook as early as May 1777 to bring
two regiments and one hundred French officers to the Maratha coast to
support Nana Furnese against Britain's ally Ragonaut Rao. Fortunately
for the Company, the united front proved anything but. Indeed, at this
precise moment, two of the confederates, Hyder Ali and the Marathas,
were at each other's throats.

But internal divisions were not restricted to the Indians. Each of the
three British presidencies seemed to negotiate transactions in its own nar-
row interests, often at the expense of the greater good. Nawab Mohammed
Ali of Arcot, together with his creditor-allies in Madras, envisioned an
alliance with the Marathas against Nizam Ali of Hyderabad and Hyder
Ali of Mysore, while Bombay sought an alliance with Hyder and Nizam
Ali against the Marathas. Furthermore, even had the Company proven
more adept in diplomacy, it inevitably was affected by the fortunes of
Great Britain itself.

The state of the national interests at home had at all times a material
influence on those of the Company; who derived pecuniary aid at
particular junctures by advances under votes of Parliament, which
advances were invariably repaid to the country. It was not, however,

so much from the want of money, as in the supply of physical force that they experienced the greatest difficulty. Their commerce suffered from the inadequacy of naval protection, and their European arm was essentially crippled in India, from the impossibility of procuring a sufficient number of recruits. Never were these effects more seriously felt than in the year 1778–9. Great Britain had to contend with her revolted colonies; the attempt to detach France from America failed, and British ships were seized in French ports without the country possessing the means of retaliation.[1]

Despite the success of British arms against the French in India, elsewhere Britain seemed more and more on the defensive. In this context, the native rulers in India became increasingly ready to bait the British lion, particularly when the lion's actions – whether those of the civil authorities or of the East India Company – seemed designed to alienate them.

ভ

The surrender of General John Burgoyne at Saratoga on October 1777 was a signal setback for the British in America, a setback that provided France with the confidence to declare war in support of the rebels. The native princes of India also sensed a decline in British power as the latter's losses mounted both in America and in Europe. In May 1780 one of William's fellow officers in India articulated Britain's sense of vulnerability and isolation:

The fleet in the West Indies disabled and the French fleet superior in ships in that quarter while England has to coup [sic] at home with the united Fleets of France and Spain far superior in number of ships and weight of mettle to any the British Nation can oppose to them[,] and I am afraid our admirals & captains poisoned with the seed of party sowen amongst them. In short the prospect of the West Indies Islands falling into the hands of France & Spain[,] the certainty of America's being lost and England threat[e]ned with an invasion at home is bringing that once great & warlike nation to a deplorable situation. And I think that were men at the helm of affairs in this country to conduct matters with prudence self disinterestedness and spirit the Company's territorial acquisitions in the East may at this juncture be considered as the most secure of any belonging to the Crown of Britain.[2]

As soon as the Company learned in June 1778 that war with France was imminent, Governor General Hastings took the offensive in an initiative calculated to eliminate the French presence on the subcontinent. He immediately ordered an attack on Pondicherry and occupied Chandernagore. By 8 August, Munro, with William at his side, was encamped on the Red Hills within four miles of Pondicherry. Munro gradually tightened the siege and was on the verge of a decisive assault on 17 October when a tsunami intervened. While Munro was resuming preparations to effect a breach, the French commander, General Guillaume Léonard de Bellecombe, indicated his intention to surrender. Bellecombe signed the articles of capitulation on 17 October. The Company's casualties, 260 Europeans and 646 sepoys, exceeded those of the defenders (322 Europeans and 146 sepoys killed and wounded). Nevertheless, it was a significant victory for the Company. "After a ten weeks' siege Pondicherry fell the 14th instant which I think secures honour to General Munro & tranquility to the Company on this coast."[3] The British captured "265 serviceable pieces of ordnance and 6,000 muskets."[4] William notified David Mitchell that same month that Munro had given him the command, "which if I can keep will I think turn out in some degree profitable as well as honourable."[5]

William's accident-prone brother, John, had acted as deputy quartermaster, 2nd Regiment, and experienced a head wound from a musket ball in the siege. He was succeeded as deputy quartermaster by Francis Baillie.[6] William went into further detail with Godsman. He had been slated to command an expedition to Bombay just as the French appearance in Charol had revived the conflict with the Marathas. Governor Rumbold had ordered fifty European infantry, fifty artillerymen, and the 2nd Battalion of sepoys to hold themselves in readiness to march under William's command with John as deputy quartermaster. However, the outbreak of hostilities in Europe altered the military's plans and William and John were diverted to Pondicherry. Losing no time, William led fifteen hundred Europeans and twelve thousand sepoys in an assault which captured the Bound Ridge. On 5 September, they seized Crakor Ground, then overran the towns to the north and south of Pondicherry. William had commanded the "whole grenadiers of the army for this siege."[7]

Aide-de-Camp James Campbell sent a notice requiring the French to deliver all arms and ammunition within twenty-four hours and promising freedom of religion and peaceful residence in Pondicherry to those who were willing "preter serment et fidelité a sa Majesté Brittanique."[8] The British took possession of the city on 25 October, allowing the defeated officers to retain their arms and the regiments their flags. The European officers and soldiers were sent to Madras where, according to the articles of capitulation, they were to be "properly accommodated; till such time as ships can be provided by the Government of Madras, to transport them to France; which shall be done as expeditiously as possible. The Caffres, Seapoys and Mallays shall deliver up their arms and be allowed to go where they please." General Bellecombe and Étienne-Claude Chevreau, the intendant and commissioner of the Marine at Pondicherry, were permitted to remain there until their departure for France, with Bellecombe entitled to take his effects comprised of papers, equipage, plate, and luggage including "a large picture of the King that was given to the said General."9 The British undertook not to force, or even solicit, the French troops to enter Britain's service and not to destroy the fortifications until in receipt of instructions from home.

William basked in the command of Pondicherry. In a letter to John Alves, he referred to Sir Edward Hughes, who had returned for a second tour of duty as commander-in-chief, East Indies station:

How shall I recount the changes of late in this part of the world. In consequence of a directive from the Lords of the Admiralty to Sir Edward Hughes & words to the same purpose from ye Company to their servants here we have at once seized every bit of French property in India. At Bengal it was an easy mark because the poor people had no fortifications. Here, though reduced, Pondicherry made a gallant defence, such as will ever do honour to Bellecombe, its commander. He was in some degree my friend for these months at least we lived though in different houses, in as much amity as possible for military men ... He wrote me a letter which I hand you a translation of for the perusal of my friends and I with pleasure add that since my commanding the place, I have given universal satisfaction to both sides. I have done justice to the French and never had the British interest out of mind.10

As the commanding officer, William was entitled to purchase certain goods at Government House in Pondicherry at a stipulated price and others at auction. Enterprising officers, in most cases, subsequently resold the items and William followed that practice, though there is no record of his profit in these transactions.11

While William savoured his good fortune, he also had to contend with petty squabbles. One French resident wrote to him as follows:

Mr. Comper, inhabitant of Pondicherry, this afternoon having a party at billiards with one of my friends was in the hight of the game when a Mr. Cair & another officer came in to the house where we were at our diversion, & took up one of the quies & was going to carry it away when the gentleman of the house begg'd he wou'd not take it away, he immediately quitted the quie & took up one of the balls with which we was at play, my friend & I begg'd he wou'd not disturb our game that he shou'd have the table immediately when the game was out, but he gave us the greatest abuse as possibly can be imagined & very much below the character of a gentleman & an officer; we likewise returned the same abuse & in the same language; both of the gentlemen set upon my friend & beat him in a cruel manner; it is very natural to suppose that I fled to the assistance of my friend & when I wanted to part them received a violent blow with a stick between the fore finger & thumb which caused the blood to flow; & I am sorry to say that I am affraid I shall lose the use of it for some time – the gentlemen immediately went home to their house ... & sent over a guard of Sepoys on purpose to conduct me to the guard – the Sepoys (by the officer's order) used us in the cruelest manner by striking us with the butt end of their musquets on our temples & head – after which they all dispersed. You Sir I now apply to for justice. True you are our conquerors, but we ought not to be treated like slaves as we are Christians & men – I humbly beg you will take this affair unto your consideration.[12]

In the meantime, despite the laurels he was gathering in India, William was thinking of home and wrote Nelly an apologetic letter in an attempt to placate her.

What shall I say my dear Sister to give you comfort or pleasure. What you look for every year is a letter from your Brother, acquainting you with his speedy intentions of returning to his Native Country. Without this every thing he writes seems dreary & unpleasant but to be writing you untruths or feeding you with false hopes constantly is almost equally bad. It is absolutely impossible for a military man in this country to say positively when or at what period he may be able to leave it. I was fully determined on paying you at least a visit in the course of this year, but the war broke out, and my Brother can affirm as well as myself that were I to ask leave now the Government so far from granting it would in all probability use me very ill for making the proposition. I have in my letter of this date to your husband said what you may depend upon to be true that you are never out of my mind and that I am always thinking how I may see you and the Banks of the Ness once more. John and Francis are both at Madras & well and no doubt will write you by this opportunity.[13]

For an officer concerned that his light shone only under a barrel, William must have been delighted to receive a letter from India's foremost soldier, Sir Eyre Coote, assuring him of his support. "I am thoroughly acquainted with your worth & military abilities; but were that not the case, the friendship & esteem which our worthy friend General Jos. Smith had for you, would be of sufficient inducement for me to assure you that I shall ever be most ready to do you every service in my power. You may expect soon to see the Governor & your humble servant with our families, as we mean to make a little excursion about the country."[14] At the same time, William unequivocally earned the respect of the French he had vanquished at Pondicherry. The commanding officer, General Bellecombe, wrote:

I cannot quit Pondicherry, Sir, without testifying, to you, the liveliest acknowledgement, & the greatest sensibility, of your proceedings towards this unfortunate colony & towards me – the yoke of arms could never be more perfectly softened than by the manner in which you govern this conquest – your actions since in it – the virtues that characterize the English nation – so fine a conduct, & so supported cannot hereafter contradict itself. I am so convinced of it, that I think I have no other wish to make, than that Pondicherry may remain under your command until this possession is returned to France – For my own part, Sir, I will never forget the marks of attention, & of personal distinctions which you have heaped upon Mad. Bellecombe & me – be persuaded that we will always retain the most precious remembrance of them – & that we will be immensely flattered by seeing Col. Baillie always amongst the number of our friends.[15]

In a postscript penned a few days later in Madras, Bellecombe added: "I wish you, Sir, good health, & I request you to believe that I will always with pleasure seize any opportunity that may offer to be of assistance to you."[16]

William was in good spirits, though he worried that the Company's position in India was threatened by the avarice of its officials. On 10 October 1779 he informed Alves of the utter destruction of the French power in India and went so far as to find even a Frenchman "a fine fellow":

You wou'd learn by my letters to Godsman of October last, that our arms had been successful against Pondicherry and your friends escaped without injury. John had a slight scratch but of it he soon recovered perfectly. The French nation have not now an inch of land in India and I'm sure it wou'd require a force they are not adequate to (without England be very unsuccessful indeed at home) reestablish themselves again in any part of it.

The country powers if not kept in proper order, it must be owing entirely to defects of our governments, and the incapacity and rapacious dispositions of the members which compose them. In my opinion the Company never were in as flourishing a state before.

Two of Sir Edward Hughes' squadrons are arriv'd at Madras, the Admiral Barker and Ganges but I believe we have no certain accounts of the rest further than that they were safe at the time they parted with them ...

Godsman wou'd also tell you I got the command of this conquest. I retain it still & of course you may suppose I have given satisfaction to the English government. The enclosed will give you an idea of the other side of the question. It is from a fine fellow, though a French man, and one who defended the place as long as possible in a most gallant manner. The plan, the works being destroy'd, is at present an open town.

I can say nothing certain of my Brother, Francis or myself. They are at present in Madras. Tell Nelly I am just as fond of her as when we parted & that I'm constantly consulting with myself how and when I may leave this country.[17]

On the same date, he wrote Mitchell that Pondicherry was no longer a fortification, that nine officers and fifty Highlanders were aboard Sir Edward Hughes's squadrons when they reached Madras on 14 September, and that Sir Eyre Coote was proceeding from Bengal to deal with the Marathas. Indeed, those troops on board Hughes's ships were the first royal troops to land in India since William's regiment had debarked in 1764. Unaware that he was shortly destined for the Guntoor Circar,

William mentioned that a body of English troops marching to reinforce the brother of Nizam Ali of Hyderabad, Bazalet Jung, had encountered William's perennial adversary, Hyder Ali, in Guntoor.[18]

CR

The capture of Pondicherry was a meaningful contribution to the war effort but beyond that the East India Company took exceptional steps to further the British interest. For one thing, it resolved to give three guineas to each of the first 2,000 able-bodied seamen, two guineas to each of the first 2,000 ordinary seamen, and 1 $^1/_2$ guineas to every able-bodied landsman who volunteered to serve in the fleet. These inducements were over and above all normal bounties. In addition, the Company undertook to build three seventy-four-gun ships of war.

On the other hand, the Company proved far from adept in its dealings with the native princes. Robert Clive had astutely cautioned: "The chief strength of the Mahrattas is horse, the chief strength of Hyder Ali is infantry, cannon and small arms; from the one you have nothing to apprehend, but ravages, and plundering, and loss of revenue; from the other extirpation."[19] However, Madras, oblivious to that warning, continued to treat Hyder Ali as a minor irritant rather than a formidable opponent to be placated. Hyder, still smarting from the Company's failure on two occasions to honour its mutual-defence obligations under the 1769 treaty, placed little value on its assurances. A significant victory at Adoni on 1 May 1779 strengthened his hand vis-à-vis the Marathas. Then, as soon as Hyder Ali became aware that the English and French had commenced hostilities, he moved quickly to secure a six-year peace with the Marathas. Nevertheless, despite his strong inclination to assist the French, the time required to conclude the Maratha treaty and the great distance to be traversed precluded Hyder Ali from aiding in the defence of Pondicherry.

In a provocation that outraged Hyder, Madras's Governor Rumbold imperiously informed him that the Company intended to evict the French from Mahé. Hyder, regarding that enclave as under his protection, responded bluntly: "I see you write concerning the French factory of Mahé: in my country there are factories belonging to the English, Dutch, Portuguese, Danes, and French, and besides, there are many merchants there who are considered as my subjects. If anyone entertains designs against those factories, I will, without doubt, take the best and most considerable methods to give them assistance."[20] Despite the candour of his response, the authorities at Madras complacently convinced themselves that Hyder had been intimidated by the rapidity and scale of the British victory at Pondicherry and that he would, accordingly, not intervene on Mahé's behalf. However, the Marathas' defeat of Company forces at Wadgaon, on 11 January 1779, with the loss of five hundred Europeans and three thousand sepoys, undercut any military cachet earned by the British at Pondicherry. The result was that Hyder Ali, "perceiving so glaring an instance of weakness and disgrace," was likely "encouraged openly to resist our proposed attempt on Mahé."[21] As for the Company's ally Mohammed Ali of Arcot, he feared that if the English attacked Mahé, Hyder Ali would overwhelm his and the Company's territory with the support of troops from French Mauritius.

Colonel John Braithwaite informed Bombay that Hyder Ali had engaged to send 34,000 troops, of whom 8,000 were cavalry, to the defence of the French outpost. Yet the British persisted in their strategy and in the short run proved successful. Hyder was distracted by the manoeuvrings of his supposed Maratha allies, and on 19 March 1779 Mahé fell to Braithwaite's troops, with Francis Baillie participating in the attack as a pioneer officer.[22] Braithwaite demolished the fortifications and abandoned Mahé in November.

The bumbling Bombay Presidency, in direct violation of the Treaty of Wadgaon, continued to alienate the Marathas by persevering in its support of Ragonaut Rao. For his part, Governor General Hastings's disavowal of what he believed was a humiliating treaty naturally rekindled hostilities. Indeed, the strong-willed if weak-witted Madras Council condemned Bombay's folly and lectured Hastings: "Thus, by ill-timed and unfortunate enterprise, the reputation of our arms is soiled and the friendship of the principal Indian States hazarded or lost forever, and that too at a period when we are engaged in a war that calls for the exertion of all our force, and the goodwill of every state in alliance with us."[23] Madras, then, in a fine example of the pot calling the kettle black, wrote the Court of Directors:

Before we were engaged in disputes with the Mahrattas, that nation turned all its views to the reduction of Hyder's power, and waged incessant war for that purpose; during many years, Hyder, by his superior and active genius was able to withstand their attacks, which, while very powerful, were of no long continuance; and whenever the Mahrattas quitted his country, he always found means to recover himself so far as to be prepared for the next invasion. In this perpetual

scene of warfare between the two first powers of India, your affairs
were everywhere carried on in perfect peace and security. Your force
was extremely respected and your friendship courted by the parties at
war, and by every other state in India. This was so precisely the situation in which we think you should and might easily have continued
that nothing could possibly have altered it, but the engagements
entered into by the Presidency of Bombay with Ragonaut Rao, and
the different attempts formed in consequence to overturn the reigning
Government at Poonah: the views of the Mahratta state became by
those means instantly turned from Hyder to the Company: they withdrew all their forces from his country to defend themselves against the
attacks of Ragonaut Rao and his allies. Hyder availed himself of this
opportunity to recover the conquests that had been made from him
by the Mahrattas, and to recompense himself by conquests upon him;
and the Mahrattas at length seeing no prospect of relief from their
wars with the English, were forced to conclude a treaty with Hyder,
which they made offensive, that they might have the benefits of his
assistance against us.[24]

While denouncing its fellow Presidency of Bombay, Madras continually confirmed its own dire reputation. "In the uncertain state of India in
the 18th Century, a crisis was certain sooner or later to confront every
European settlement; but whenever one confronted Madras, the English
Council there invariably proved themselves incompetent to deal with
it."[25] In a resounding affirmation of this proclivity, the Council at
Madras then provoked Nizam Ali into an otherwise unlikely alliance
with Hyder Ali.

Bazalet Jung held the territory of Guntoor Circar for life from his
brother, Nizam Ali, with an undertaking not to dispose of it without the
latter's consent. When the French sought to acquire Guntoor from
Bazalet Jung, he transferred the territory to Madras, a transfer of which
neither Bazalet Jung nor Madras informed the nizam. Simultaneously,
with astounding chutzpah, Governor Rumbold determined that by
employing a Savoyard mercenary, Henri de la Sale, who had styled himself Monsieur Lally after the former governor general of French India,
the Comte de Lally, Bazalet Jung had breached the treaty of 1769. This,
in turn, meant that Madras need not pay the tribute due Nizam Ali.
Oblivious to the danger he was courting, Rumbold stoked the fire by
agreeing to rent the Guntoor Circar to Mohammed Ali for ten years in
return for 270,500 Madras pagodas. Hastings naturally was scathingly

critical of Rumbold's Council for negotiating a treaty which was bound
to alienate a key British ally, Nizam Ali. He therefore overruled Rumbold,
insisting on the reinstatement of the tribute to Bazalet Jung, but the
nizam was so incensed at Madras's duplicity that he united with Hyder
Ali to oppose his erstwhile British allies. Hyder, with the nizam's blessing, sought to goad the British by leasing Guntoor from Bazalet Jung.

It is not in my power to consent to His Excellency's [the nizam's] giving up the Guntoor Circar to my old and bitter enemies, for it joins
to my country. If the English are put in possession, His Excellency
and I cannot agree ...
    What are the English whose names give so much alarm to the
people of this country? How did I encounter them when I was at
war with them? How often were they not defeated by my victorious troops? This is well known to everybody. Why should we be
so much afraid that their protection should be solicited? If His
Excellency and I are joined, we shall stand in fear of no one.[26]

Terrified of Hyder Ali, Bazalet Jung turned to his British allies for
assistance. Madras dispatched a detachment under the command of
Lieutenant-Colonel Humphrey Harper. However, as was its wont, the
Council neglected to obtain Hyder's permission to march troops through
his country to Bazalet Jung at Adoni, and when it did belatedly apply for
that permission, Hyder responded tongue in cheek in July 1779:

As a sincere friendship subsists between the Nabob Hyder Ali Khan
and the Company, you propose marching the troops under your
command to Adoni, through Duranall and Actour, which I understand. It gives as manifest as the sun, that a sincere friendship subsists between His Excellency and the Company, and that they have
no separate interest; it is, therefore, my duty to pay a regard to the
friendship they have for him; yet you will march your troops by
another road that this friendship may be preserved for there are
Sepoys stationed in that country, and some disputes and quarrels
may take place between your men and the Sepoys, who are of a very
quarrelsome disposition. I have so much regard for our friendship,
that I would not wish this to happen.[27]

Colonel Harper experienced repeated delays, which he attributed to a
lack of funds. Nevertheless, an impatient Madras Council, despite its

failure to provide for the army, questioned his rationale for withdrawing from the passes to Guntoor and showered him with niggling criticisms.[28] Brooking no excuses, Madras appointed Colonel William Baillie in Harper's stead. Before William's arrival, Bazalet Jung sent Harper instructions not to proceed farther. The nizam had threatened to destroy Bazalet Jung if he did not speedily discontinue all intercourse with the English and enforce their withdrawal from the country. Indeed, when Bazalet Jung attempted to join the British, his own troops insisted that he instead join his brother, the nizam.[29]

William assumed command on 21 November 1779 and found himself in a precarious position. He reported to Governor Rumbold that Bazalet's dewan, Fatulla Khan, had intimated "Bazalet Jung's wish that we should proceed notwithstanding the former [orders] which he had been under the necessity of writing and as appears to result from fear of his Brother & the delays of the Company's troops more than inclination or because he supposes it his interest."[30] Under that conviction, William planned to march to Adoni by the Cullachurroo Pass, which Nawab Mohammed Ali and Fatulla Khan considered the most feasible. Lally and his French troops were at Adoni and William undertook to tread cautiously until either hearing further from Rumbold or learning that Bazalet Jung had dismissed Lally and sent him "to a proper distance." William then wrote to Bazalet Jung to determine his intentions as to whether the Company's troops should enter his country. However, Bazalet Jung and Fatulla Khan replied firmly that they did not wish to entertain the Company's forces in their territory although Fatulla Khan "avers (if we can trust his information) that Bazalet Jung has been of dire necessity led to the step he has taken."[31] Subsequently, William related that the nizam had posted guards from the Ghat of Elysanum to Chintopilly on the north bank of the Kistna River "as if afraid of the detachment's passing that way into his country – At Commom, Hyder Ali between four & five thousand horse with one thousand Carnatic Peons seemingly watching our motions on that side – No intelligence from Adoni or Hyderabad of late date."[32] On 30 December, the Council at Madras instructed William that "it would be necessary for him to be upon his guard, in case of any attempts being made against the Guntoor Circar – that he should only protect their present possessions, and not act offensively against any power without positive orders; but that he was empowered, in case of any movement towards the Guntoor Circar, either from the Nizam or Hyder Ali, to call for the Sepoys, under Lieutenant Douglas, and for as many Sepoys as could be spared from the Masulipatam District."[33] Earlier that same month, William, with feigned conviction, had assured Mohammed Ali: "I trust at them to do their utmost – I mean Hyder Ali and the Soubah. The Company with the assistance of the Nabob of the Carnatic (Arcot), will always be overmatch for them. We have great resources, and must be strong indeed when the fleet arrives. This detachment is encamped at Macunda, waiting for further orders."[34]

Cognizant at last of the danger of a war on two or three fronts, Madras supported the Bengal Council's instructions to General Thomas Goddard to negotiate a peace with the Marathas.

A war with Hyder, let the event be ever so successful on our part, would distress the Carnatic beyond measure and prove a most expensive burthen on the Company; we sincerely, hope, therefore, that General Goddard may conclude a treaty with the Mahrattas, and thereby free the Company from the necessity of engaging the two most powerful estates of India at the same time; which will probably be the case if he fails in his negotiation: should we be at peace with the Mahrattas, Hyder will be afraid to disturb us, for, exclusive of our strength, which he could then have no hope of resisting, the determined enmity which the Mahrattas bear him, would induce him rather to court our friendship than to provoke us into hostilities; and this is precisely the state where we can only expect to preserve that tranquility in the Carnatic, which is so necessary to the affairs of the Company at all times, but especially at this juncture.[35]

Likewise, Governor General Hastings foresaw the risks of the three native powers uniting to oust the British interloper and instructed General Goddard to attempt to effect an arrangement with the Marathas along the lines of the 1776 Treaty of Poorunder. The Marathas had then refused any negotiations until Tanjore was restored to their kinsman, but by the time the rajah had been reinstated, they were even less conciliatory since they had humiliated the British at Wadgaon and were increasingly aware of the British setbacks in America and Europe. Accordingly, they would consent to conclude a peace only on the basis that "the English should deliver the person of Ragonaut Rao into the hands of their vakeel, and make immediate restitution of the Island of Salsette."[36]

Rumbold, still unable to grasp the extent of Hyder Ali's disdain for the Company, speculated that Mohammed Ali, through enmity to Hyder, might well be fabricating the latter's hostile intent and sent emissaries to Hyder to determine his plans. Hyder made clear that, while he had believed that the alliance with the Company would flourish, the Company itself – by, on more than one occasion, disowning its treaty obligations for mutual assistance, by attacking Mahé, and by sending troops to Bazalet Jung – seemed set on breaking with him. He concluded with the observation: "Formerly I was of opinion that the English excelled all other nations in sincerity and good faith; but, from late experience, I am convinced that they have no longer any pretensions to those virtues."[37]

In November 1779 Nawab Mohammed Ali of Arcot informed Madras of a treaty between Hyder Ali and the Marathas and acceded to by the nizam of Hyderabad. The intent was to attack the East India Company's possessions: "The measure lately pursued at Bengal and Bombay, in support of Ragonaut Rao, having drawn on the Company the resentment of the Mahratta state, given offence to Nizam Ali Khan, who is in friendship with that state, and a declared enemy to Ragonaut Rao, and opened a way to rupture with Hyder Ali, by promoting peace between him and the Mahrattas, and leaving him at liberty to execute the threats which he has denounced against the Carnatic, it has become a matter of serious importance with the Company to consider how they may best avert the evils that surround them, and what line of conduct it may be proper to adopt, for establishing their affairs in future upon a solid and permanent footing."[38] In short order, the nawab clarified the specifics of the treaty. Hyder Ali had agreed to pay twenty-five lakhs and give up particular territories to the Marathas; both Hyder Ali and the Marathas had undertaken not to negotiate a separate peace.

Goddard resigned himself to war with the Marathas. In preparation he negotiated a treaty with Futty Sing (Shrimant Rajashri Fatehsinrao Gaekwad), the maharajah of Baroda and ruler of Gujarat. Shortly thereafter, he cemented the alliance with Futty Sing by driving the Marathas from Ahmedabad and transferring the city to the maharajah. Goddard then proceeded to win significant victories against the Marathas. With only 700 or 800 troops he routed a 40,000-strong Maratha force on 2 April 1780 and then captured Bassein, Tarrapore, and Danow. Yet, despite Goddard's successes, a peace treaty with the Marathas remained elusive.

ॐ

While William remained perilously stranded in the Guntoor Circar, Baillie relatives were actively fighting or trading throughout the globe. In March 1779 his brother John, ever conscious of his honour, complained

to General Munro of the promotion of another officer and sought the
general's opinion of his services and character. Munro's reply would have
been great comfort to John. He said that he had no occasion to have
recourse to the opinion of others but it was enough for him to have witnessed John's actions "at the siege of Pondicherry where your services
were very conspicuous and where you received a wound when acting as
an Assistant Engineer. I was at that time so sensible of your merit as well
as that of other gentlemen during that long siege that I represented it to
the Government at Madras in the strongest terms. And I will now add
that if at any time I have it in my power to testify my regard for you, as
well as an opinion of you as a brave and gallant officer it will afford me
real satisfaction to do it."[39] The following year, on 25 March 1780, John
obtained the long-sought lieutenantcy for which William had paid £50.[40]

William's cousin James, a Dochfour Baillie, wrote for the purpose of
recommending a young relative, Peter Fraser, who may or may not have
been the same Fraser whose youthful poverty John Alves feared had been
an enemy to his virtue. The letter also conveyed news of the Dochfour
family and encouraged William to return to his native country where he
could place Dunain on a footing comparable to that of Dochfour, which
had been greatly improved by James's brother Alexander. James's comment about retaining the "Sugar Colonies" underlined how dependent
British economic well-being was on the fortunes of war.

> After the absence of so many years has, in a manner, made us strang-
> ers to each other, yet, I assure you, I have often, with pleasure look'd
> back to the days of our juvenile intimacy, & it has, from time to
> time, given me and all the well wishers of your family, very great
> satisfaction, to have such favourable accounts of your situation in
> India; your character is such, as will always command many friends,
> and I am happy to understand, that your present rank in the Service
> bids fair to insure you such a fortune, as will enable you soon to
> return to your native country in affluent circumstances, which you
> may believe, I wish very much to see. From the time we parted, in the
> 1755 to the year 1771, I was employed in the line of planting and
> commerce, in the Islands of St. Christopher & Grenada, and if this
> unfortunate war, in which we are engag'd, does not strip us of our
> Sugar Colonies, I may venture to say, that I have acquired a compe-
> tency, & what will enable me to live, with ease, in any part of the
> world[;] however from being long accustomed to a busy scene, I
> found an idle life irksome, &, therefore, in the beginning of seventy

five, I entered into business here, where you may depend, my best services will always be at your command. My Brother Alexander has resided chiefly, in the North, since his return from the West Indies, and has lately laid out a considerable amount of money, in buildings & improvements at Dochfour, where, I am sure, he would be very happy to take you by the hand; it is the first expensive establishment, on the Banks of the Ness, but, I hope, you will soon keep him in countenance, by turning your thoughts seriously towards the Rock of Dunain, where you have a very sufficient seat for amusements of this kind ...

Now I must beg leave to request your countenance & protection, to the bearer Peter Fraser a young relation of mine, who has very imprudently gone over as a common soldier in the Companies Service: he has some abilities, and having no manner of vice, that I know of, I have recommended him to General Munro, and will esteem it very kind in you to render him any services in your power.[41]

Another William Baillie, a less than erudite son of William's deceased sister Anne, wrote from Spanishtown, Jamaica, where he was working for their Inverness neighbour George Cuthbert of Castlehill, a successful merchant and the colony's provost marshall in 1785–88. "I hear my stepmother has got a young son. I can say no thing about it but it is for me not to depend upon nobody but do as well for my selfe as possible."[42] Finally, Torbreck's son, Lieutenant Robert Carnibe Baillie of the 3rd South Carolina Regiment, was killed at the siege of Savannah on 9 October 1779.[43]

9

Disaster

The cup of our trouble is running over, but, alas, it is not yet full.
Sir Boyle Roch, MP

In February 1780 William's detachment marched from the Guntoor Circar to Ellore, a small mud fort in Masulipatam. Meanwhile, at Madras, the government, though now aware of the dangers of war on a number of fronts at once, remained curiously blind to the full extent of Hyder's ambitions – to say nothing of his military preparations. It continued to dither, insensible to the imminent peril. In this respect, Innes Munro, newly arrived with Macleod's Highlanders, proved much better informed than the Madras Council. "These ideas of war originate from a report at present circulating through the country, and seriously alarming the inhabitants, that Hyder Ali, Nabob and General of the Mysore army, who is reputed to be an able officer, but a turbulent neighbour to the Carnatic, is intent upon breaking with us, that he may have some pretext to join in the general conflagration which now threatens the East India Company's affairs. It would appear, however, from the unsuspicious tranquility of the Madras Council, that the report is without foundation, though it seems to have raised among the natives in general an uncommon share of terror and dismay."[1] Moreover, an officer in William's detachment wrote to his brother: "The Nabob [Mohammed Ali of Arcot] was alarmed, but the Governor and Council secure in their own wisdom, were deaf to his repeated applications, and neglected assembling the army."[2]

For his part, Hyder Ali had gathered 100,000 troops as well as Monsieur Lally's Europeans, and encouraged by the reputed success of the French in Europe and the prospect of French reinforcements, determined "to ruin the Carnatic and to chastise the English. He had tried them already, and knew them well; they had no conduct; and even now, although he had assembled so great a force to enter into their country, they had not manifested the least glimmering of ability, and therefore now was the time to go against them."[3]

With detachment and little sympathy, Munro also analyzed just how it was that the British found themselves alone and without friends. Many today would take issue with his description of Muslims and others would contend that the British had been compelled to resort to territorial acquisition in order to protect their commercial interests as the order imposed by the Mughals waned. Nevertheless, the natives of India undoubtedly agreed with his description of British behaviour.

It appears by the first charter which those [EIC] merchants obtained from the Government, that the chief object in contemplation from voyaging hither was simply a commercial intercourse with the Indians, which then seemed to be the summit of their ambition. After obtaining, however, a thorough knowledge of the meek and pusillanimous disposition of these unfortunate natives, the inexhaustible wealth of their country, the vast superiority of European tactics to those of Asia; and having also compared, with an Indian's eye, their own slow progress in the accumulation of riches by fair and honest traffic, with the opulent and easy acquisitions that a less scrupulous conscience yielded to the Mahomedan conquerors; they were soon induced, by such rapacious considerations, to blend war with commerce, so naturally adopting the policy and deceitful manner of the Moors, that I believe nothing, but the act of circumcision was wanting to render them complete Mahomedans. This change first began by augmenting their forces, and afterwards lending them out as mercenaries to either Mahomedan or Gentoo [Hindu], as opportunity offered, eagerly[,] however, preferring the prince that would cede to them the most jaghirs and money as a recompense for their services. By this means they soon became so formidable and renowned in arms as to take responsibility of invasion, conquest, and innocent bloodshed, upon themselves, attacking the powers of India upon selfish speculation as their avarice and ambition dictated, and continuing wantonly to sport away the lives of their countrymen, until they had, by the most dishonourable acts of injustice and oppression, rendered the British name odious in all Indian courts, and usurped the immense territories now in their possession, which at present take no less than a standing army of one hundred thousand fighting men to defend them.[4]

By now, Governor Rumbold, having tested the Company's patience to the limit, was dismissed from the service for disposing of the Guntoor Circar to Mohammed Ali, an act certain to provoke both Hyder Ali and Nizam Ali. Hyder Ali held back from attacking the Carnatic until he had solidified his alliances; he planned his invasion of the Carnatic to take place in conjunction with the nizam's attack on the Northern Circars, with an assault on Bengal by Moodaji Bhonsla, the rajah of Berar (Nagpur), and with a resumption of the Marathas' conflict with the British, via the warriors Mahadaji Scindia and Tukojirao Holkar. However, the Marathas were fully occupied with Goddard's troops, the nizam, through timidity, refrained from molesting the Northern Circars, and Bhonsla failed to attack Bengal. Accordingly, while Bombay and Bengal were preoccupied with the Marathas, Hyder Ali was left to his own, albeit formidable, devices in the Carnatic.

The renowned parliamentarian Edmund Burke, who evidently had a great deal more regard for Hyder's abilities than did the Madras Council, aptly described the Mysorean ruler as the "black cloud that hung for a while on the declivities of the mountains, the menacing meteor which blackened all the horizon until it suddenly burst, and poured down the whole of its contents upon the plains of the Karnatic."[5] The black cloud burst with a vengeance upon those plains. "The hostile sword was drawn upon the 20th of July 1780; and these barbarians rushed like an impetuous torrent through the ghauts, dispersing themselves all over the Carnatic, like herds of furious animals in quest of their prey, and committing every act of cruelty and devastation that it was possible for savage minds to suggest."[6] Hyder Ali's vast army entered the Carnatic through the Shangamath Pass, laid waste to the countryside, plundered Conjeveram and Porto Novo, and laid siege to Mohammed Ali's capital, Arcot. Not until Conjeveram fell did the Madras Council give any credence to the possibility of an invasion; yet in eight days the country was overrun. Even the appearance on 24 July of Hyder Ali's cavalry at St Thomas Mount, three miles from Fort St George, did little to raise the government from its torpor. "Around that centre of British power, he certainly drew a line of merciless desolation, marked by the continuous blaze of flaming towns and villages."[7]

Instead of recognizing the severity of the threat and moving energetically to consolidate the Company's forces in a position of strength, Madras continued to think in terms of dispersing its troops. On 25 and 29 July 1780 it instructed Colonel Baillie to direct an attack on Cuddapah or some other of Hyder's possessions in those parts. Baillie, it stated, should seek to distress the enemy as much as possible and should contemplate reducing the Fort of Sedbout. His instructions also suggested that he should dispatch troops to Lieutenant James Douglas for the defence of Guntoor if expedient and send Captain George Smith's battalion to Madras if he could spare it. At that point, two Council members, Charles Smith and Samuel Johnson, vociferously dissented on the basis that Cuddapah was on the other side of the passes and it would be difficult to recall Colonel Baillie's forces should they be required for the defence of the Carnatic. They believed Baillie should be directed to join the rest of the army with all haste so as to thwart Hyder's ambitions in the Carnatic. John Whitehill, as acting governor, and General Munro disagreed on the basis that "Colonel Baillie might not only distress the enemy in that quarter, but oblige Hyder to withdraw part of his force from the Carnatic, and because it was doubtful if provisions could be immediately procured for a greater number than were now under marching orders."[8] The debate was pre-empted by William's correspondence outlining the difficulty of provisioning his troops owing to Hyder's cavalry to the south and the high level of the Kistna River to the north. He was also concerned that he could not much longer detain the bullocks required to march. Accordingly, Madras altered its instructions, ordering him to march toward the Mount "if he should be unable to subsist his detachment in the enemy's country, or from any other quarter."[9] Then, on 6 August, as William's troops were marching to attack Commom, a fort belonging to and bordering Hyder's territory, he received orders to set out immediately for Madras.

Munro, pleading poor health, thought that he could render more effective service by remaining in Madras and devolved his command to John Mackenzie, Lord Macleod, an able and experienced officer. The Council ordered Macleod to assemble the troops from Madras and Vellore at Eyecollam, near Conjeveram. He, in turn, took immediate exception to the proposed routes on 1 August, observing with uncanny foresight that

the rendezvous now intended might have been a properest before the invasion, but the march of those detachments by the routes proposed, would, at this critical juncture, render them liable to be attacked separately, and either the object of their junction rendered abortive, or some part of the army receive such a check, as, in his opinion, it would be imprudent to risk in the first outset of the war. And deeming the core assembled at Poonamallee to be the basis of the strength of the Carnatic, he thinks it ought not to move from the neighbourhood of the magazines and stores till joined by all the troops which could be drawn together, and enabled to march in sufficient force to act effectively in the field against the numerous cavalry of the enemy.[10]

Macleod recommended that Baillie march to the Carnatic without delay upon the prudential principle that, in a crisis, all the Company's strength should be concentrated at the centre.

Munro, stubbornly continuing to underrate his enemy, did not envisage the defence of Madras as his principal objective. Rather, seeking to prevent Hyder from gaining possession of the principal forts, he thought that the troops should be assembled near the scene of action. Munro anticipated little difficulty in gathering the troops together and noted that, if the Council should do him the honour of asking him to effect a junction, he would promise to perform. He was particularly confident because he believed that Hyder, with his cavalry, was still at Califpauk and therefore in no position to interfere with the assembling of the Company's troops. Although Smith and Johnson sided with Macleod, the majority opted to place the ageing hero of Buxar back in command.

◌঵

William arrived near Gomeraponda on 24 August, within twenty-five miles of Munro at St Thomas Mount, his original destination. The junction of the two forces could easily have been achieved the next day but Munro, succumbing to Mohammed Ali's repeated entreaties to protect his capital of Arcot, altered William's instructions to have him march fifty miles to Conjeveram. Had this "ill-advised order"[11] not seen the light of day, William and his troops would not have been vulnerable to Hyder's depredations. Further, absent Munro's order, the two armies could have joined forces on 25 August. "These obvious means of placing beyond the reach of accident the immediate formation of a respectable army," in the words of a nineteenth-century military historian, "were wantonly abandoned, by directing that officer [William] to pursue an independent route of upwards of fifty miles to Conjeveram, a measure not recommended by any speculative advantage that has ever been stated, and inexplicable by any conjecture, excepting that of attempting practically to justify an erroneous opinion."[12] The repeated reversal of marching orders was particularly frustrating given the challenges of transporting even a small army in India.[13]

William had with him 2,813 men, comprised of two companies of European infantry, three battalions, including the 1st and 11th Carnatic Native Infantry, and six sepoy companies of the 7th Carnatic and 2nd Circar with ten field-pieces. But the force was less impressive than it looked, since many of the sepoys were raw recruits hastily raised in the Circars. Even worse, countless numbers had deserted on the march south. William informed Governor Whitehill that he was marching the next day for Conjeveram. However, two days later, he reported that he had encountered unseasonably heavy rains and was stranded on the north banks of the Cortelcar. Two thousand of Hyder's troops had kept the detachment under constant observation but had not attempted any action. William did propose that, since the waters were not subsiding, he descend to the mouth of the river and be ferried by boat to Ennore, only thirteen miles from Madras, but received no reply. Finally, he crossed the river on the afternoon of 3 September. Munro's observation that William had been delayed seven days from crossing "a little dirty mullah or small rivulet" by "the greatest fall of rain ever known in this season of the year"[14] suggests that the flooding could not have been foreseen. Following the crossing, Mohammed Ali's secretary, relieved that forces were advancing to sustain Arcot, wrote to William: "The great attention which you have on all occasions shown to his Highness the Nawab, together with the regard which I have at all times expressed towards you, now induce me to write you a letter of congratulation on your having passed the River which impeded your progress, and on your being on the road to join General Sir Hector Munro, whose virtuous arm will, with the blessing of God, chastise the unprovoked insolence of Hyder Ali. The sense which both the Nawab and I have of your services are not unknown to Governor Whitehill and General Munro. It is a pleasure to call one's self the friend of a gallant officer."[15]

In the interim, by 17 August, Macleod had trekked from Poonamallee to the Mount where he was joined on the twenty-fourth by Colonel Braithwaite's contingent from Pondicherry. Munro appeared on 25 August. Ominously, as the troops set out for Conjeveram, Mohammed Ali's 1st Cavalry Regiment, whose wages were fourteen months in arrears, declined to march without some payment. The nawab's ameer refused to furnish any funds, whereupon the troops were dismounted and sent as prisoners to Madras. Shortly thereafter, four well-disciplined regiments of the nawab's cavalry, provoked by arrearages of pay, transferred to Hyder Ali's service. Then, upon their arrival at Conjeveram, the Company's forces learned that their

capricious ally, Mohammed Ali, had failed them once more: the promised provisions were nowhere to be found.

Munro noted that Hyder Ali had raised the siege of Arcot and was
encamped within two miles of him. The wily warrior tested Munro by a
feint to the right, and when no challenge arose, interposed his troops
between Munro and Baillie without a shot being fired. While Munro may
not have recognized the risk of allowing Hyder to position his troops
between the British forces, Hyder certainly appreciated the opportunity
Munro had granted him. Attacking the combined British forces was a
hazardous undertaking at best but if he could trap and demolish William's
small army before Munro could reinforce it, Hyder might well dominate
the Carnatic. In any event, he would have disposed of his long-time
adversary, Colonel Baillie.

Munro prepared to attack Hyder as soon as Baillie joined him but, by
allowing Hyder to position himself between the two British commanders,
rendered that juncture doubly difficult. As William marched toward
Munro, he encamped on 5 September at the village of Perambaucum,
which, flanked by trees and water, provided a strong defensive position.
Since crossing the Cortelcar, William had been continually harassed
by cavalry under the command of Hyder Ali's son, Tipu Sultan, cavalry
which was also laying waste to the surrounding countryside. Those inci-
dents had been manageable irritants. But the stakes rose as Hyder
instructed Tipu to launch a frontal assault on William with "the flower of
his army." And that is what he did at roughly 9:30 the next morning, leading a force that, according to one estimate, numbered ten thousand horse,
five thousand foot, and eight field guns.[16] William had only sixteen
hundred men and ten field guns at his disposal but acquitted himself
with aplomb. Tipu's troops formed into three columns and advanced in
orderly fashion until they came within five hundred yards, at which time
the Company's troops fired in unison, wreaking carnage among the
Mysoreans and causing them to flee in the utmost confusion. In the aftermath, Tipu continued to employ his field pieces but was unable to close
sufficiently to bring his musketry to bear. The battle continued until four
in the afternoon when Tipu ceded the field. It was a signal victory for
William. Tipu's losses approximated fourteen hundred,[17] and he reported
to his father that he had no hope of making any impression on Colonel
Baillie without further reinforcements.

Tipu then enraged European sensibilities by indiscriminately throwing
his own dead and wounded into a nearby house that he then set afire.[18]
Father and son would evidence similar compassion a year later when

Sir Eyre Coote offered to exchange the Mysorean prisoners captured at Tripasore for an equal number of Britons in Hyder's custody, only to have Hyder respond: "The men taken at Tripasore are faithless and unworthy, they know they dare not approach me; they are your prisoners and I advise you to put every one of them to death speedily."[19]

Despite routing Tipu's troops, William's position remained perilous. He had suffered the loss of 126 killed, wounded, or missing and lacked the conveyances to transport the wounded, and Hyder's entire army blocked any junction with Munro. On the morning of 7 September, William sent a note to General Munro that he had beaten off Tipu but had only the shirt on his back and a like deficiency in ammunition and provision. "I must plainly tell you, Sir, that you must come to me for I see it is impossible for my party to get to Conjeveram."[20] Interestingly, for want of a cipher, Munro and Baillie carried on much of this correspondence in Gaelic.

Despite the protestations of Lord Macleod and several of his brother officers that the entire army should remain intact and march to Baillie's relief, Munro concluded that proceeding with the entire army would jeopardize the transport that contained the bulk of his provisions, heavy guns, and baggage. Accordingly, he further divided his forces, dispatching Lieutenant-Colonel Fletcher with 1,007 men and a supply of ammunition to assist William's forces in reaching Munro's camp. Munro had included field guns in the order but Fletcher felt they would delay his journey. As Munro did not expect Fletcher to make Perambaucum until the evening of 9 September, he instructed William not to move until the night of the ninth, when he was to march with the entire army from Conjeveram. However, Fletcher made excellent progress, evading a trap set by his hircarrah, who had been suborned by Hyder. Indeed, Hyder's intelligence was flawless, for he was aware not only of the hour of Fletcher's march but also of the strength of his force and his lack of any cannon. Suspecting treachery, Fletcher astutely changed route and arrived, drums beating, at William's camp at daybreak of the ninth.

In retrospect, Fletcher may not have been the ideal officer to send to William's aid. The two of them had entered the Company's service at roughly the same time. William ranked in the army next above Fletcher, and while both were esteemed as officers of the first merit, "the patronage of the Commander in Chief was particularly engaged to Baillie."[21] William had requested that, as at Pondicherry, he command the Grenadiers. Munro had readily agreed. Fletcher sought, and was given, command of the Grenadiers until William joined the army at Conjeveram. "Their minds tho' they were always upon a footing of intimate friendship, were evidently tinged with no small degree of jealousy of each other." Thus, a just consideration of the above should have suggested the sending of the Grenadiers under an officer other than Fletcher. Worse, though "Lieutenant-Colonel Fletcher's party, natives as well as Europeans, were resolute, well-disciplined veterans – extremely well officered," he "and his senior officers had the greatest opinion of what they could achieve as well as too mean an opinion of the enemy."[22] Fletcher felt that his force could cut their way through Hyder Ali's army and frequently expressed his wish to encounter the enemy in broad daylight as if marching under cover of night was a disgrace. "Nor was Fletcher's bravery and ambition tempered by much experience or any reverse of fortune – Baillie was not less brave or ambitious of military glory – but he had much more experience – and he knew the strengths and weaknesses of the enemy's troops as well as his own, thoroughly."[23] As another assessment puts it: "Baillie was one of the Company's officers who had served for many years in India. A fine, upstanding, handsome man, he was keen on his profession and personally brave, but was very badly supported by the Council at Fort St. George; and to their parsimony and shifting policy were probably due his fatal indecision and his defeat at the Battle of Pollilur."[24]

At 7:00 on the evening of 9 September, Baillie's detachment set out for Conjeveram with drums silent so as not to alert Tipu, who had firmly inserted his forces between Baillie and Munro. Fletcher's party led. The following account of the Battle of Pollilur is attributed to General Macleod.

> The detachment had not proceeded above two miles, when the enemy began to annoy it with rockets and musketry. A mile further the enemy were discovered in force in the rear, and opened some guns there, which raked our line. Upon this Colonel Baillie made some change in his disposition, and discovering the situation of the enemy in the rear, fired a few rounds among them from two field-pieces, which dispersing them, he resumed his march. Soon after they again opened their guns upon his left at no great distance, and he ordered a corps of Grenadier Sepoys to move out to take them. But they were interrupted by a deep watercourse. Their guns were, however, soon silenced by the fire of ours. At the same time the fire of small arms and rockets on all sides was incessant, and the baggage people and followers became very troublesome, many of them being wounded. Some of the Sepoy corps became uneasy, many deserted,

and it was found difficult to maintain strict order and regularity on the march. 'Tis said that Colonel Fletcher and some of his gentlemen now again spoke to Baillie to halt until daylight, to which he agreed. It was about 11 at night when he halted at a top about 4 $^1/_2$ miles from Perambaucum, and 3 from Pollilur.

There are causes to believe that Baillie here, and General Munro at Conjeveram, were both deceived and betrayed, much about the same time by their hircarrahs. A Sepoy of the guides and a Brahmin hircarrah, that were with Colonel Baillie upon this occasion, attended me on the 28th August 1781 over the melancholy field of slaughter, [and] the Sepoy, giving an account of the fatal affair, told me, immediately as the detachment halted, Colonel Baillie dispatched his head hircarrah, with the strongest injunctions, and promises of great reward, for bringing certain intelligence to him, with all possible expedition, whether or not Hyder's army was near him, or moving towards him; and that the hircarrah returned between two and three in the morning, and most confidently assured the Colonel that Hyder with his army still lay near Conjeveram to oppose the General's army, that he had sent more horse to assist Tipu Sultan, but that no considerable force or artillery was arrived or expected. The Brahmin hircarrah checked the Sepoy while he was informing me of this circumstance, but the latter firmly insisted that it was true, adding, that if Colonel Baillie had not been betrayed by his hircarrah, he would have gone to the little fort of Tuckollim, then possessed by our people, and not above a mile from his right; and most evident it is, that Baillie would have done this in the night without any loss.[25]

Ensign Hodges and Innes Munro, among others, subsequently criticized William for halting.[26] Those two claimed that Fletcher urged William to continue the march during the night. Indeed, Captain Richard Chase "perfectly well remembered" that, when William halted, "Fletcher remarked that for his own part he was no advocate for halting but as Baillie was a good officer, he believed that he must have received some fresh intelligence which occasioned him to form this resolution."[27] Francis Gowdie, an officer who was captured at Pollilur but survived to command the 3rd Brigade in the final defeat of Tipu Sultan, was of the opinion that the "unsteady behaviour of the troops"[28] induced William to halt. However, the accounts conflict markedly, and, unfortunately, we shall never know what, if any, fresh intelligence William acquired that fateful night. In any event, while Hodges "points out the halts made by the detachment in the most particular manner ... it does not appear that these halts were unnecessary – several black officers that were in the action declared to me they frequently heard Colonel Fletcher and some of his officers urge Baillie to halt during the 9th – Fletcher imagined that they would in the face of day gain a glorious victory over a great part of Hyder's army – Baillie was not quite so sanguine, but had no doubt of our army being near him early in the morning."[29] Certainly, the delay did enable Tipu to seek further reinforcements from Hyder, but, even so, he had already concentrated his forces the previous day and placed them with three batteries directly in William's path.[30]

It is doubtful, therefore, that a night march would have saved the detachment. An objective observer presumably would have some sympathy for the decision to rest the troops during the night in view of Baillie's earlier message to Munro that the former was in no position to march and that Munro must come to him. That Fletcher's reinforcements did not bring sufficient litters to transport the wounded adds weight to that sentiment. Innes Munro, while critical of the halt, had earlier suggested that General Munro could not practically march at night in India and that was in a situation where no enemy troops were harassing him.

But to return to Macleod's account:

Between four and five in the morning [10 September] Colonel Baillie put the detachment again in motion ...

At daylight being in the avenue running west on the great road to Arcot ... the head of the detachment turned to the left into the plain between it and the small village of Pollilur. This was the field on which the enemy had planned their inevitable destruction, and as soon as the front appeared turning out of the avenue, the enemy began to play most furiously upon it, from the tops on the left, and divers stations all along in front, from so many guns that our people say, they could not guess at their number. Many fell before they had proceeded 300 yards over the plain. The ground was somewhat hollow here. Baillie halted and immediately sent out Captain Rumley with six companies of Sepoy Grenadiers to take five guns stationed behind a water-course. About 400 yards on the left of the detachment, he likewise sent the company of Marksmen as a reinforcement after the Grenadiers. Rumley took these guns, but by some fatality, they were neither used against the enemy nor spiked. The enemy immediately turned several pieces of cannon upon this party, and large bodies of horse advanced furiously. The Colonel made the

First Battalion move out a little, but the Grenadiers flew back
broken and confused. About the time that Baillie had arranged the
Grenadiers, a cannon ball grazed one of his legs, and not long thereafter two of his tumbrils were blown up by the enemy's shot, the
detachment, notwithstanding, maintained its steadiness, and repeatedly beat back the horse that attempted to cut in among them. The
enemy's cannon were so heavy and numerous that even had we
ammunition our small field-pieces could do very little against them.
Some people think it unaccountable that the detachment stood the
unremitting destruction by the enemy's artillery, for at least an hour
and a half, without making any attempt to extricate themselves. But
what could be done? All ranks of the shattered party were now most
sensible of their very critical situation. The commanding officer saw
that the black troops particularly were quite disheartened. The enemy's guns were judiciously placed in divers stations, behind trenches,
and great bodies of their best horse drawn up on both flanks in readiness to charge. Hyder overlooked the whole scene; this was his first
essay in the war. From what had already happened, as well as what
finally, in a moment decided the affair, it is evident, that any movement they could possibly attempt, would but accelerate their ruin. In
short, it appears plain that no measure could be devised or attempted
to overcome such superior force. The least disorder when on the
move, would probably determine the affair in a moment; besides,
they were fixed by the assured arrival – by the certain assistance –
of their friends. Had not they every reason to hope that their
General, with the army was by this time at hand, to relieve them?
What would be said of Colonel Baillie had he, in a desperate
attempt, lost his detachment at 7 or 8 o'clock, – in case General
Munro with the army had arrived at Pollilur at 10 o'clock. But to
return to these brave men, Colonel Fletcher near the rear of the
detachment, having something in view which is not known, called
aloud, "Come this way, Grenadiers."

Instantly the Sepoys, and, in short order, the whole detachment
broke and flew back in the utmost disorder and confusion. The horse
cut in among them as quick as thought, but Colonel Baillie rallied
a body of the intrepid Europeans upon a small spot of ground that
rose a little above the plain, at the distance of 300 yards from the
ground on which they broke. This handful faced every way and
drove off the horse. Colonel Fletcher and many others were cut
down on this occasion, and but a few of even the European officers

now appeared. There was not one black man to face the enemy. Such as fled beyond the spot on which the Europeans rallied were all put to the sword, as appeared by their bones, which covered the plain for about three quarters of a mile, when we went over it in August last.

All hopes of succour and relief now being exhausted, Colonel Baillie made a signal for surrendering, and a party of horse advanced, upon whom some of the Europeans fired, having no other idea than to sell their lives as dear as possible.

As the men's ammunition was now mostly expended, the horse rushed frequently on their bayonets. In one of these attempts, two horsemen seized upon Colonel Baillie, but his life was saved by his Brigade Major, Mr. Fraser, declaring to them who he was, and beseeching them not to kill him. This was instantly reported to Hyder, and he immediately ordered the slaughter to cease.

By all accounts, it was half-an-hour past 9 o'clock before this melancholy and most unfortunate affair was finally concluded, before the slaughter ceased and the few remaining brave men threw away their useless arms. Much about the same time the advanced guard of our army was within three miles of Pollilur – that is, about four miles from their distressed friends; but alas! Here they turned their backs upon this most hardy and resolute band, who, to the last moment, looked for their assistance.[31]

The end came as Hyder surrounded the British with forty thousand horse and French troops, while William had less than four hundred men and no prospect of being relieved. In an attempt to preserve what lives remained, William attached a white flag to his bayonet. Then, upon intimation that quarter would be given, he ordered his troops to lay down their guns. However, a few of his troops continued a desultory fire and "the enemy rushed upon them in the most savage and brutal manner, sparing neither age nor infancy, nor any condition of life; and, but for the humane interposition of the French commanders, Lally and Pimoran were employed and insisted with the conqueror to show mercy, the gallant remains of our little army must have fallen as sacrifice to that savage burst of blood with which the tyrant disgraced his victory."[32]

According to one historian: "Hyder's officers refused to attend to Colonel Baillie's signal, pointing to the Sepoys who in their confusion were still continuing to fire; this, however, being explained, they agreed to give quarter, and Colonel Baillie directed Captain Baird to order his men to ground their arms. The order was of course obeyed, and the instant it was so, the enemy's cavalry, commanded by Tipu Sultan in person, rushed upon the unarmed troops before they could recover themselves, chopping down every man within their reach. The greater part of Captain Baird's company were literally cut to pieces by these wretches."[33]

જી

Such was the catastrophe, for British arms, of the Battle of Pollilur on 10 September 1780. There are differing accounts of certain aspects of the battle. One contends that the French officers in Hyder Ali's service, Lally (who commanded the European infantry) and Pimoran (who led the artillery), thought Fletcher's march was a skilful manoeuvre to attack Hyder on both flanks and advised the Mysorean to retreat. Apparently, Hyder was inclined to approve the measure until two hircarrahs arrived from Conjeveram reporting that Munro's army was still encamped and making no preparations to move. Lally thought Munro's behaviour so extraordinary that he suspected they had been betrayed. However, Hyder "had exact and constant intelligence of everything that was done in the English camp"[34] and relied on that intelligence to order the bulk of his army to reinforce Tipu Sultan. Then, at four o'clock on the morning of 10 September, observing the inertia in the British camp, Hyder, leaving only irregular cavalry to "amuse" the army at Conjeveram, slipped away to join the attack on William.

Macleod ascribed little import to the destruction of the tumbrils and was reinforced in that view by a comment in a letter by John Baillie (no apparent relation), written, admittedly, four years after the battle: "Two of our tumbrils were quickly blown up, without however doing us any kind of mischief as was erroneously imagined. There was nothing in them but a few blunt cartridges."[35] On the other hand, Colonel Assur, a French officer who served under Hyder Ali, remarked that although Hyder's seventy-five cannon created great havoc in the square, the Mysorean, with "numbers of his best troops killed, & many more wounded; his infantry obliged to give way," began to contemplate retreat.

A movement which Baillie made to the right evidently shewing that he meant to attack the enemy's artillery & centre made Hyder still more apprehensive of the battle. He consulted Lally who told him a retreat was then too late; that the army from Conjeveram was probably advancing in the rear; & that they had no choice but to endeavour by their artillery & cavalry to break the detachment. At this

instant two tumbrils, one in front, the other on the right, blew up, &
made large openings in both lines, on which Hyder's brother-in-law
Meer Sahib with the Mughal cavalry made the first impression; they
were followed by the elephants & Mysore horse which completed
the overthrow. The Sepoys, amounting to better than 4 battalions,
were mostly cut to pieces. Col. Baillie, although much wounded,
rallied the Europeans, & once more formed them in square; with
this handful of men he gained an eminence (a small rising mound
on the plain) where, without ammunition, and most of his people
wounded, he resisted & repulsed thirteen separate attacks; but fresh
bodies of cavalry pouring in; they were broken without giving way.
And this officer says he saw many of our Europeans desperately
wounded, raising themselves from the ground to receive the enemy
on their bayonets.[36]

Other accounts second the significance of the tumbrils' loss. A biog-
rapher of Hyder Ali concludes: "The victory cost the Mysore army very
dear, as the slaughter of their best troops was immense; and nothing, but
the accident of the tumbrils could have saved Hyder from a total defeat.
Had the good genius of the English brought up their troops from
Conjeveram, during the battle, the Mysore army must have been inevitably ruined – not one battalion of foot or a single gun, would have probably escaped."[37] Hector Munro, in a report to the secretary of war,
related: "A wounded Sepoy came in who told me that Colonel Baillie was
defeated owing to three tumbrils having blown up. He is a gallant officer
and nothing but an accident which human invention or foresight could
not have guarded against occasioned the unfortunate disaster."[38] Another
commentator states that the tumbrils "blew up and the bonds of union of
the Colonel's force were broken up. The explosion was tremendous. It
shattered one side of the square, and stunned all the men comprising
it."[39] Following the destruction of the tumbrils, the sepoys were no longer
a disciplined fighting force, and so it may well be that the incident was
critical not because of the loss of the remaining ammunition but because
of the panic to which the explosion gave rise. The prominence of the
burning tumbrils in the murals at Tipu's summer palace suggests that the
victors, for their part, attributed great import to this incident. At the same
time, the immensity of the explosion implies that the tumbrils did indeed
contain a material amount of ammunition and all accounts appear to
agree on the severity of the explosion. In any event, whether or not there
was ample ammunition in the tumbrils, all parties agreed with the

unidentified officer who reported to his brother that, following the explosion, "our Guns became useless for want of ammunition."[40]

In the midst of the Battle of Pollilur, the essential question in the mind
of every British soldier was the whereabouts of General Munro. Given
that Munro's and Hyder Ali's armies were encamped within sight of each
other on the evening of the eighth, it was reasonable to suppose that
Munro would not allow Hyder to move without following closely at his
heels. On the sixth, when Tipu first attacked Baillie, Munro was "advan-
tageously encamped" to bring the enemy to action. Colonels Fletcher and
John Elphinstone exhorted Munro to do so and Macleod approved a
plan to attack Hyder. But Munro countermanded the order. On the seventh, Macleod, on his knees, urged Munro "in the strongest manner to
move to the relief of Colonel Baillie with the whole army,"[41] or at least
to allow him to march the remainder of his own troops to relieve his regiment, the 73rd. Anthony Sadleir, a member of the Madras Council but
also one of its most outspoken critics, believed that if Munro had joined
William, they would have prevailed handily. He could not understand
why Munro did not march to William's relief on the seventh regardless of
whether or not he had dispatched Colonel Fletcher.[42] Yet Munro dallied
for three days, fearing he lacked provisions to march. Hearing a "smart
cannonade" on the ninth, Munro prepared the troops to march but, as
the firing ceased about midnight, he, for some inexplicable reason which
baffled Lord Macleod, again instructed the men to rest on their arms until
further orders. As Macleod later said: "The reason or intelligence which
afterwards induced the General to alter his resolution were I make no
doubt very solid but are unknown to me."[43] Finally, Munro arose from
his lethargy and set the troops in motion on the tenth. They marched
within two miles of William. One writer concludes that, had Munro
advanced more promptly, Baillie's defeat would have, in all probability,
been converted into a victory.[44]

At noon on the tenth, Munro learned of William's destruction at
Pollilur. His confidence gave way to panic and he withdrew precipitately
to Conjeveram, where he destroyed four of his cannon and retreated to
Chingleput at the cost of much of the army's baggage. Concerns for the
safety of his baggage and provisions, which had prevented his marching
in force to William's rescue, no longer bore such importance. From
Chingleput, he fled to Fort St George. "So great was the panic that had
struck all orders of men in the Presidency of Madras, on this mournful
occasion, that if Hyder had immediately pursued and improvised his victory, the 10th of September might have proved the most unfortunate in

the annals of Britain."[45] While Munro proved unable to march the few miles to relieve William from the sixth to the tenth, he proved much more adept in retreat, traversing eighteen miles in a single day.

One of the survivors of the carnage reflected plaintively, in verse, on the failure to support the detachment:

On the 10th September
This is the day by fate decreed,
Britania's sons thereon shou'd bleed,
'twas on Ticcolam's fatal plain,
where many Britain there was slain,
Oh! Dire mishap alas Munro,
Some sad neglect caused all our woe,
there for thy aid long did we stay,
If thou hadst come, we'd won the day,
but now alas it is too late,
forc'd we are to submit to fate,
hark! what a dreadful shock; alas we're crost,
our last resource and all is lost,
ten thousand dangers now is near,
confusions voice aloud we hear,
our haughty foe applauds the sound,
and hurls distraction all around,
a doleful din of clashing arms,
and all the rage of wars alarms,
frail nature shrunk beneath the stroke,
to view such havock on her work.
This woeful day let fame record,
and join with us in one accord,
ye gods behold our deep distress,
and speedily our wrongs redress,
send ye some hero brave to swing the sword
and loyal hearts the Council Board.[46]

Francis Baillie, who was with Munro at Conjeveram, provided his account of the disaster to his relatives in Inverness. Albeit family, he furnished a personal but objective perspective on Munro's deficiencies and the atmosphere in Madras where every inhabitant of the city put on mourning and "extolled the characters of Colonel Fletcher and the brave officers and men who perished with him, and did justice to the valour of

Baillie,"[47] in contrast to the negligence and indolence of their general and the Council. However, as time would prove, Francis was dreadfully misled as to William's condition and treatment.

It's a long time since you have heard from me, and now I am afraid the following sheets will tire your patience; you have no doubt 'ere now heard of our misfortunes on this Coast yet give me leave to give you, what I think a just acc't of them. On the tenth of Sept'r about ten in the morning, Col. Baillie with about three thousand six hundred men were either killed, wounded or taken prisoners by Hyder Ali. His army consisted of fifty thousand men & by all accounts he had two & forty guns, whereas our troops had only ten; & even with this small number Hyder's army were repulsed two or three times before they got the better. A cannonade began about twelve o'clock the preceding night which continued some time & was very plainly heard in General Munro's camp. Had he marched at that time, as was expected, the troops being all lying on their arms, we would have come time enough to have obtained a most complete victory, instead of which he delayed marching untill the next morning half an hour after sun rise, so that by the time we got within five miles of the place of action the G'l. was informed that very superior numbers had got the better of the small force commanded by Col. B. after fighting most gallantly from day break till about ten o'clock; when the accounts of the defeat arrived, we retreated to Conjeveram, where we remained on our arms that night. About two in the morning of the eleventh we set out for Chingleput, a fort belonging to the Company and on our road to this place. That day we retreated or rather fled with the remains of our army & thirty two guns, the distance of twenty five miles. During this flight we lost the whole baggage of the army. We halted one day at Chingleput where we received a small reinforcement, after which the little army we had, quite disheartened[,] made a march of twenty seven miles which brought us to Saint Thomas's Mount, within nine miles of Fort St. George. The Battle of Buxar and the taking of Pondicherry, by which Sir Hector has acquired such laurels, will not now save his credit, for he has given very clear proofs at this time, that he has no idea of the profession of a soldier. You will think this extraordinary of a man who has come to such high rank, but it is the truth. The small army we have got is now in cantonments within a mile of Madras, in the garden houses belonging to the gentlemen of the place. We have now got

General Coote to command us; he came purposely from Bengal on account of the mismanagement here, and brought with him six hundred Europeans; we expected ten battalions of Sepoys to march over land, but it is feared that they cannot now be spared, as the Mahrattas give them enough to do there. Since we came here, Hyder has taken Arcot, the capital of our Nabob; it held out six weeks against his whole army, which now does not consist of less than one hundred thousand men. The number of troops in this place were one hundred & fifty Europeans belonging to us and about fifteen hundred fighting men belonging to the Nawab. Arcot is a large place & formerly the Nawabs used to reside in it, but since they found that money gave them great sway in our councils, they have taken up residence at Madras. There's a wall round the town of Arcot seven miles in circumference, with small bastions at different places, in the inside is a small fort or citadel, but not capable of any great resistance, after the town is taken.

By retiring to this fort our people got terms, which was, that they marched out with the honours of war, & were sent to this place on their parole not to serve against the enemy during the war. You now see that the loss of a few hours in not marching to the assistance of Col. B. when the cannonade was first heard, has cost us the most of the Carnatic; which General Coote with our small army, will find no easy matter to regain. I imagine in a month or two hence, we shall be able to take the field with about eight thousand men, black & white, of the latter near two thousand, and I make no doubt but we shall give a very good account of this tyrant. General Goddard who has been in the field against the Mahrattas on the Malabar Coast, is now ordered to enter Hyder's country on that side, his army consists of about ten thousand, so that in a little time, Hyder shall find enough to do; then as soon as Goddard enters his country, he must draw off the greatest part of his army out of the Carnatic. Since writing the above, there are accounts arrived here of eight battalions of Sepoys having marched from Bengal for this place; so that if they come safe, I think this same invader will get a good drubbing.

Col. Baillie is kept in his camp with two or three more officers; he is perfectly recovered of his wounds; is very much respected by Hyder as a brave & good officer, & at the same time well treated. His Brother & myself are with the army, here in cantonm'ts. He is now made a Capt. ... [and] I was six weeks ago promoted to the rank of Lieut. & we both are in good health.

The enclosed letter has been wrote some time ago, but no opportunity of forwarding it has offered untill now; the list of the killed & wounded is not very exact it being made out by report of some black men. But enclosed I send you one which was received a few days ago, from one of the officers prisoner with Hyder, you may depend upon the justness of it as I copied it from the original.[48]

While history is written by the victors, or at least the survivors, and William was criticized in various circles for halting at night, the brunt of the blame was borne by Munro, around whose neck the charges hung like a millstone. Fraser-Mackintosh notes Munro's "great imprudence" in sending Fletcher to reinforce William and then observes: "This was the Commander-in-chief's first error, which, like all his errors, arose from an indistinctness of judgment, and a facility to be led by designing men. Of that mischievous class, too many edged themselves into his councils, and the rest of his advisers, weak men, were total novices in Indian intrigue and warfare."[49] Nor did the government of Madras escape derisive criticism. Colonel Henry Cosby may have been representative. His forces having arrived from Tanjore and Trichinopoly too late to take part in the battle at Pollilur, Cosby believed that Munro's army would have fled to Madras itself had Cosby not joined the general at St Thomas Mount and strengthened his resolve. He wrote: "Our respectable Governor[']s chief time seems to be taken up with playing with Boys and making their Fortunes, in short his conduct is the most shameful you can conceive[;] he is now sending home his chief favorite Mr. Lewen to gloss over his wretched administration. He has contrived to keep the General on his side which of course gives him a dead Majority, Mr. [Anthony] Sadleir has been suspended for speaking the truth, and [Charles] Smith and [Samuel] Johnson are made mere Cyphers of by two men who have not the twentieth part of their abilities or zeal."[50]

For William's part, whether or not he should have halted, none criticized the bravery, competence, or determination with which the doomed detachment fought. The tributes were numerous:

History cannot reproduce an instance, for fortitude, cool intrepidity, and desperate resolution, to equal the exploits of this heroic band. In numbers now reduced to 500, they were opposed by no less than 100,000 enraged barbarians, who seldom ever grant quarter. The mind, in the contemplation of such a scene, and such a situation as theirs then was, is filled at once with admiration, with astonishment,

with horror, and with awe. To behold formidable and impenetrable
bodies of horse, of infantry, and of artillery, advancing from all
quarters, flaming savage fury, wielding the numerous instances of
slaughter, and darting destruction around, was a scene to appal even
something more than the strongest human resolution; but it was
beheld by this little band with the most undaunted and immovable
firmness. Distinct bodies of horse came on successively to the charge,
with strong parties and infantry placed in the intervals. Whole fire
was discharged in showers; but the deliberate and well-levelled pla-
toons of the British musketry had such a powerful effect as to repulse
several different attacks. Like the fueling waves of the ocean, however, when agitated by a storm, fresh columns incessantly poured in
upon them with redoubled fury, which at length brought so many to
the ground, and weakened their fire so considerably, that they were
unable longer to withstand the dreadful and tremendous mob; and
the field soon presented a picture of the most inhuman cruelties and
unexampled carnage.[51]

The gallantry of Colonel Baillie was undoubted; his virtues were
acknowledged by all; and his calamitous end must excite the sigh
of pity in every bosom not wholly unassailable, by the accumulated
misfortunes of another.[52]

A feat of arms perhaps unrivalled in the world's history.[53]

Coll. Assur in the presence of the Governor of Goa bestowed the
highest encomia upon Coll. Baillie & repeatedly said that every
manoeuvre which he made, shewed him to be an officer of great
experience, conduct & knowledge in his profession, and that he did
not think that any troops in the world could have displayed more
intrepidity & determined resolution than the troops under his command, both Europeans & Sepoys.[54]

The victors rode their horse and elephants over the scene of the slaughter. Those wounded British soldiers who were not trampled to death by
the animals suffered horribly, exposed during the day to an unforgiving
sun and, at night, to the ravages of fox, jackals, and tigers drawn to the
scene by the scent of human blood. Those who could walk were taken
prisoner and brought to Hyder Ali, who, still expecting that Munro
would attack, had retired six miles away from the battlefield to savour

his victory. William, stripped and wounded, was borne to Hyder's presence on a cannon. There, he and the other prisoners – along with the severed heads of some of their unfortunate friends – were presented to the victor of Pollilur, who gave rewards of ten rupees per live captive and five rupees per head. The Mysoreans even required that some prisoners carry the heads of their compatriots. Hyder taunted William, who retorted that he owed his victory to an accident of the tumbrils and that, otherwise, the British would have prevailed. "Your son will inform you that you owe the victory to our disaster rather than to our defeat."[55] Indeed, William answered with such spirit and contempt that Colonel Assur was "apprehensive that the insolent conqueror would have been provoked to an act of fatal barbarity."[56]

William was unfortunate in both his commanding officer and his adversary. Other British commanders had overcome vastly superior numbers. For example, Robert Clive at Plassey defeated a much larger army under Siraj-ood-Dowlah, the nawab of Bengal, and a younger and more vigorous Hector Munro had been victorious over the combined armies of the nawab of Bengal, the nawab of Oude, and the Mughal Emperor Shah Alam II. However, they and other British commanding officers had not encountered, as William did, the combination of overwhelming numbers, European-trained and equipped forces, and the most capable, shrewd, strategic, disciplined, innovative, and dispassionate warrior that India had produced, at least since the major Mughal emperors. With the exception of Hyder Ali, the native princes, at one time or another, had been compelled to submit to terms dictated by the East India Company. Besides the nawabs of Bengal and Oude and the Mughal emperor, Nizam Ali of Hyderabad had sued for peace in the First Anglo-Mysore War and had been easily intimidated by the Company's military power. The great Maratha chiefs, including Scindia, Bhonsla, and Holkar, all had accepted British terms. Even Hyder's son Tipu Sultan, as we shall see, would accede to Cornwallis's demands and deliver his sons as hostages to the British in the Third Anglo-Mysore War before he lost his life and kingdom in 1799. Only Hyder Ali was never decisively defeated or subjugated by the East India Company and only he consistently negotiated with the British as an equal.

10

Imprisonment and Death
at Seringapatam

If there's another world he lives in bliss. If not, he made the best
of this.

Robbie Burns

"The sequel was worthy of a commencement; every indignity that malice
could devise, every perversion that cruelty could inflict, awaited the
unhappy Europeans, who were destined for years to remain the prisoners
of Hyder Ali."[1] Of the 86 officers in William's detachment, 70 were killed
or wounded, and another 150 non-commissioned officers and privates
died in the battle. Colonel Assur further related that Hyder denied the
officers and men the common necessaries of life and subjected them "to
every species of bad usage."[2]

The conquerors provided a shell of a tent for Colonel Baillie and his
fifty-eight officers but not a scrap of straw or anything on which they
might lie. The tent accommodated only ten people with the result that the
vast majority suffered in the open. Hyder offered a paltry 500 rupees
(£50) to be divided among roughly that number of prisoners. William
refused that offer and eventually Hyder's dewan, Kistna-row, delivered a
still modest 1,000 rupees (as well as some cloth) which William divided
among his fellow captives: to each captain, 13 rupees; to the lieutenants,
9 rupees; to the ensigns, 7 rupees; and to each of the non-commissioned
officers and privates, 1 rupee. William was also able to prevail upon
Captain Pimoran, a sympathetic Frenchman in Hyder's service, to
advance 400 pagodas (£140) against William's draft drawn on Madras,
which proceeds William again distributed among his co-prisoners.

One prisoner, Lieutenant John Lindsay, noted that "some infamous
provisions were flung upon a large cloth upon the ground and we were

desired to eat that or want."[3] Although William and others were severely wounded, Hyder, after permitting one visit from two French surgeons with good intentions but rusted instruments, forbade further medical assistance or, for that matter, any civilities to the captives. Indeed, one Elliot, another European employed by Hyder, was beaten publicly for carrying necessaries to Colonel Baillie. Their prospects seemed abysmal and proved no less. For many Britons, the treatment meted to the unfortunate prisoners confirmed their stereotype of their ruthless Asiatic foe.

At a time when prisoners of war in other countries considered their misfortunes at an end by falling into the power of a generous foe, in whose camp, the unfortunate never failed to meet with sympathy and respect, the miseries of our unhappy countrymen were yet but in their rise. In the merciless hands of barbarous Mahomedans, persecutors of their religion and their colour, inured to cruelties and utter strangers to humanity, how dreary was the prospect which opened to their view! Their conquerors, swayed only by the blackest passions of the human heart, exhausted every art that might tend to humiliate and oppress the agonized feelings of their British prisoners. Smarting with the excruciating pain of undressed wounds, their spirits sinking under the repeated indignities and abuse which they hourly experienced; and not only denied the common necessaries of life, but stripped of every covering to shield them from the vicissitudes of the climate; their gloomy minds could suggest ideas only of perpetual slavery, of eternal separation from each other, their country, and their friends. And the misery, I believe, has seldom attained so afflicting a crisis. Wounded alike in body and mind, the termination of existence seemed the only good that was left them and the fate of those who had perished upon the bloody field appeared to them to be equally happy and enviable.[4]

On the morning of the twelfth, the British discovered that three of their officers had died of their wounds during the night and more had become delirious. William desperately pleaded for surgeons and provisions but was informed that they would be marching twelve miles closer to Arcot where necessities would be readily available. The conquerors provided conveyances for twenty of the severest cases and forced the others, regardless of the severity of their wounds, to walk. "Those that were not wounded in the limbs had no conveyances allowed them, but were beat along by the Sepoys and when no longer able to walk were dragged along with ropes."[5] Four more officers died during the ordeal. At one point in the march, Tipu Sultan approached William, complimenting him on his gallantry and counselling him to keep up his spirits since his defeat was attributable only to the uncertain fortunes of war. He assured William that his father, Hyder Ali, intended to provide handsomely for the captives and that they should lack nothing. He went so far as to suggest that, should William have any cause for complaint, he submit it directly to him. Yet his sincerity was suspect, for Tipu knew full well that William would never have any means of addressing him. At a resting place, Hyder did relent somewhat in response to entreaties from his French allies. However, the prisoners' position was becoming less and less tenable. Their wounds were full of dirt and sand and they had nothing but the bare ground to rest upon.

On 12 September the prisoners learned they were to be separated. Colonel Baillie, Captains Baird, Rumley, Lucas, Menteith, and Wragg, and Lieutenants Fraser and Lindsay were to remain in camp while the rest would undertake the 240-mile journey to Seringapatam by various routes. Twenty-three officers and the privates who could march were sent via Bangalore, while twenty-seven officers and all the privates who were badly wounded were transported to the fort of Arnee where they would recuperate until physically able to attempt the long trek. Approximately 393 men departed for prison, with the first contingent reaching Hyder's capital, Seringapatam, on 7 October.

Then, on 16 September, the guards informed William that all the remaining prisoners, with the exception of the three ranking officers, were to join their fellow prisoners on the march to Seringapatam. William chose Captain David Baird and Lieutenant John Lindsay to stay with him, but these three were also shortly dispatched to Seringapatam. Lindsay had not been attended by the surgeons and plunged into a violent fever. In the midst of the fever, he encountered one of his old servants, who had not eaten for two days and who undertook to care for Lindsay. Lindsay gave him "all my treasure amounting to 15 rupees to take care of for me, and desired him to go to the bazaar, and buy something for himself and me. He promised to return immediately, but the treacherous villain as soon as he had got my all, left me, and I never saw him afterwards. Baird, likewise, had been plundered of his wealth in much the same manner, but Baillie was so generous as to give us, out of what little he had remaining, a pagoda each."[6]

Lacking clothing and soap and plagued with vermin, the prisoners plodded on to Arcot. On the twenty-eighth, their spirits rose temporarily when, to their great joy and astonishment, there appeared in the prisoners' tent eight baskets of liquor. They were a present from a French gentleman William had befriended during his command at Pondicherry. The Frenchman had required William's signature acknowledging receipt of the gift, but shortly after William affixed his signature, Kistna-row removed the baskets which were never to be seen again. A few days later, Lindsay, still extremely ill, asked the commandant if they could rest for a couple of days to refresh themselves or else he would die before reaching Seringapatam. The commandant responded in a rage: "I might die and be damned – that he had received the Nawab's orders to send me to his capital, and that if I died on the road, he would tie a rope round my neck and drag me there."[7]

By 8 March 1781, William, Captain Rumley, and Lieutenant Fraser, the first two in irons, as they had been the entirety of their 240-mile journey from Arcot, arrived at what the prisoners dubbed "headquarters" and today bears the name Colonel Bailey's [sic] Dungeon, in Seringapatam. By 8 May, the myar placed all the officers, with the exception of Captain Baird, in irons, each pair weighing between eight and nine pounds. When the myar approached Baird, from whose right leg a bullet had just been extracted and whose open wound would not have withstood the irons, Captain Lucas sprang forward and remonstrated in no uncertain terms that death would be the result of barbarously fettering Baird in chains. The myar retorted that he had been given as many sets of irons as there were prisoners and that he was obliged to enchain everyone. Lucas then offered to wear two sets of chains to preserve his friend's life. That act of generosity moved the myar, drawing on the ancient Hindu occult principles of palmistry and astrology, to send the keladar to look into the "book of fate." The keladar returned to report that Captain Baird's fate was good and the myar, in consequence, left Baird without irons.

All of this suffering was bad enough, but what was even more terrifying to British sensitivities than the persistent torture, neglect, and chains was the prospect of forced conversion to the Muslim religion – along with the necessary corollary, circumcision. Hyder began to offer inducements to the British captives to convert, but, experiencing little success by that route, he undertook to achieve his objective by force. Of the prisoners held after Pollilur, 300 converted.[8] They were labelled "Children of the Nawab," had their right ears bored to wear the Muslim badge of slavery, a silver pearl, and, by royal decree, forfeited any right of release in the event of peace. Indeed, when peace came in 1784, Tipu Sultan retained "to the disgrace and scandal of the British name about

150 circumcised Europeans and 60 European artificers in open and direct violation of the treaty."⁹ Several British drummer boys were required to wear women's dress and entertain the court as dancing girls but the vast bulk of the converts was utilized to train Hyder's troops.

The reluctant converts were forcibly constrained, shaven, washed all over to purify them from the Christian faith, and forced to drink madjum, a potion of bang and opium. They were then subjected to "the detestable operation." The next day, one of the victims conveyed the following note to "headquarters": "All Mussulman, all lost, all undone forever. Adieu."¹⁰

The prisoners were distraught at the treatment of their fellow captives but even more shocked to learn that the victims – no doubt under pressure – had asked to have two of their old companions subjected to the same treatment, which was carried out on 31 October much against the inclinations of the two young men. The new Muslims were placed in a battalion with orders to observe the same discipline and subordination as those in the Company's service. The keladar determined that more Europeans would be of infinite service to his master and shortly thereafter, on 15 January, Hyder ordered thirteen more prisoners to undergo forced conversion. The following account by Sergeant John Maxwell Dempster, formerly of the Bengal artillery and who, exceptionally, volunteered to enter Hyder's service, describes in intimate detail the conversion ordeal.

On Wednesday the 19th of September the Bra[h]min and Myar came to our prison, and after falling in the men, he selected sixteen from the rest, smiths being prepared to knock off their irons, without giving us the smallest idea of what was to ensue, and conducted us to the kutcheree, where they informed us upon what account we were released, and in a very flattering manner requested us to take service. All their promises and tenders were rejected with disdain. They then changed their accent and threatened us in the severest manner. We were then conducted to a large square, the repository or seminary of those Carnatic boys that had been brought into slavery, whom you see every night at exercise. Upon our arrival there, how great was our surprise to find two English lads among the boys, who had been circumcised three months before our arrival, one of whom is a Mr. [Henry] Clarke, who had been an Ensign in the 2nd battalion, 2nd regiment; the other a private in the same regiment; they informed us immediately that we should be circumcised. They had scarce finished telling us this when the guard came in, accompanied by a barber. You, sir, who have delicate feelings, will conceive what our situation was, dragged to what every Christian in the universe utterly abhors, and surrounded by enemies whose very souls are many thousand times blacker than their visage. After some resistance on the part of every one of us, we were obliged at last to sit down and be shaved, after which we remained in the most cruel uncertainty for three or four hours, when our ill-favoured guard brought us a doze of majum each, and obliged us to take it. It wrought differently. Some were insensible: others were not. A little after sunset, a black surgeon, with thirty or forty caffres, seized and held us while the operation was performed. We remained under cure for a month, upon six cash per day, with mutton, rice, etc. The 30th October we were conducted to the kutcheree, and there examined if we would take those Carnatic slave boys and learn them their discipline, for which we should each of us receive one gold sanam per day, with provisions and cloaths.[11]

While Baillie's men were experiencing untold deprivation in Hyder's prisons, an intermediary told Tipu that his master was "much concerned to hear that Colonel Baillie and the rest of the officers whom you have taken prisoners, several of whom are the sons of people of distinction, suffer very great hardships, and have not even the common necessaries of life, such as clothes and food allowed them. He says that it is not the custom of Europeans, nor is it ever usual with great princes, to treat their prisoners in that manner, and wonders that Your Highness should adopt so unworthy a conduct." Tipu disingenuously responded: "They are in no want of food and raiment, let someone be sent on your part to see them, and Braithwaite who was taken in the Tanjore country is here in the camp, you may see him yourself. A sheep for ten men is their daily allowance, and upon this some that were lean when they were with you, are grown very fat since I have had them. They that have told you all this therefore have told you lies. And as to the other article, they have not to be sure fine clothes, but they are sufficiently supplied with white linen. You may tell your master to be perfectly easy upon this head, and when matters are made up between us I shall release them altogether."[12]

છ૨

Although William had languished in captivity for five months, John Alves in Inverness was unaware of his brother-in-law's plight when he wrote

him in February 1781 of local and family affairs. In this letter he reported
on the election to Parliament of Hector Munro and Lord Macleod, the
two officers who had argued so heatedly over William's fate at Pollilur.
Curiously, the Dochfour family tree does not record any heirs of the
Alexander mentioned in the letter, or, indeed, even a marriage. In fact, his
youngest brother, Evan, succeeded to the lairdship of Dochfour. Yet Alves
reported that Alexander had travelled to the West Indies to check on the
estates left to their son by Mrs Baillie's father and Alexander's first
employer, James Smith of Smith and Lambert. Indeed, Alexander's son,
Lieutenant-Colonel William Baillie, died on his passage to the West Indies
to join his regiment during his father's lifetime. Alves himself appeared to
be disposing of his own progeny admirably and at little cost. Beyond the
immediate neighbourhood, the "Dutch war" to which Alves refers was
the Fourth Anglo-Dutch War of 1780–84 and stemmed from the Dutch
support of the rebels in America. That assistance to the Americans
undoubtedly arose from Dutch resentment of the shift of commerce to
London and the resulting superior economic growth of Britain, whose
gross national product by 1780 surpassed that of the Dutch Republic.
The letter does illustrate the haphazard nature of mail delivery and the
challenges of conducting business at a distance.

Tho' I write two or three times every year, you have certainly not
received some of my letters, because you say you have not yet got
any general statement of your affairs in this country tho' I have twice
sent you a general acc't of your money matters. By Mr. Godsman's
acc'ts you see I receive annually the balance of your rents which is
put into the bank till I can settle it to advantage ... I will not however miss the occasion of letting you know that Nelly, her boy and
girl are well, as also George Baillie's family. We have lost all hope
now of seeing you till in peace as the Dutch war will no doubt give
employment to our forces in India ... And in the first place with
respect to politicks we have had a contest wherein General Fraser for
this country, Sir Hector Munro for the Borrows and Lord McLeod
for Ross Shire have come into Parliament without the least opposition owing partly I fancy to the disorder of his affairs for Sheriff
Campbell. Our friend has been disordered in his mind for more than
a twelve month past, nor is there any prospect of his amendment ...
Mr. Baillie Dochfour is at present in the West Indies whither he went
to look after his affairs, and the estates left to his son by Mr. Smith,
his wife's father who died last year. Mrs. Baillie and son spent the

winter at Edin'r, but I suppose the whole family will be at Dochfour
next summer. My eldest daughter, Mary[,] was lately married to Mr.
McIntosh of Holm who besides his small land property has a sinecure place in the Excise worth £140 per annum. Tom my oldest boy
is in Jamaica and I hope doing well. Alick and Archie are in London
with my brother who has put the former into business and is preparing the other for it.

My best comp'ts to them[,] however, in which Nelly also joins
as well as in the most fervent wishes for your welfare and speedy
return home.[13]

By May 1781, the Scottish relatives were well aware of William's dire
situation. "I hope long before this time your Brother's captivity is at an
end," John Alves wrote to John Baillie. "All the accounts in this country
both publick and private do justice to his merit and I flatter myself he will
soon reap the reward of it ... Your Sister and the children are well, but she
is most unhappy till she hears of your Brother's being releas'd and well."[14]
The following year, William's English agent, David Mitchell, wrote a letter expressing his anxiety for William's fate and proffering advice as to
his daughter Ann's future. The new ministry that Mitchell hoped would
effect an honourable peace with the American colonies was that of
William Petty, 2nd Earl of Shelburne and later Marquess of Lansdowne,
who became prime minister on 4 July 1782.

Both your Daughter and myself are very much concerned at not
receiving any letters from you ... however, our anxiety has been somewhat alleviated by the captain of that vessel informing me that, just
before he left Madras, he had heard you was in good health, and that
you and your fellow prisoners were much better treated of late, than at
first, which I, immediately, communicated to Doctor Alves, in answer
to his enquiries about you ... he says your Sister and all friends were
well, but very uneasy about your health & situation, your Brother not
having wrote them since January 1781. I most earnestly wish that
either he, or your attorney would write us by every conveyance untill
you are at liberty to do it yourself, which I pray God may be soon.
The Admiral Hughes Packet, dispatched from Madras the 2nd of
November last, was taken off the western islands, after sinking her
dispatches, by which we were deprived of all our letters by her.

Your Daughter is in very good health, and is now in town for the
holidays: as her education will be pretty near completed in a year, or

two more[,] and she will, then, be quite womanish[.] I think if you
continue in India, the best thing that can be done for her would be,
to have her out, and see her settled in life before you quit the country; I am sure her sensibility, and good nature will make her an excellent wife to a discreet man ...

   Enclosed is your acc't curr't, balance in your favour £78..8..8,
which cannot last long, as Miss Baillie's expenses in dress etc. will
increase as she grows older.

   We are in some expectations that our new ministry will soon be
able to bring about a peace, which I hope will be both honourable &
lasting; and flatter ourselves that the disputes in India are in a fair
train of being accommodated.[15]

In January 1783 Nelly wrote John imploring him to send any news
of William and alerting him of his nephew Alick's impending arrival
in Madras.

I cannot express the unhappy state of mind I have lived in these
two years past on account of my dear Brother's misfortunes as well
as the constant danger you are exposed to. I thought to have written
a long letter, but I find it is impossible, I have not the spirits for it.
I intended saying a great deal of my poor little ones, how promising
they are and particularly to introduce to your acquaintance the
youngest little girl Helen of whom probably you have never heard.
But I cannot proceed, the subject overpowers me, I must wait for
happier days. But why have you been so long silent, for God's sake
my d'r John write often and send me what comfort you can respecting poor William whose unhappy fate I lament every hour I live and
will never cease lamenting till I am assured that he is well and his
own master again ... I need say nothing of George's children as Aleck
is the bearer of this.[16]

A letter from Alves to John that same month further emphasized the
family's apprehension.

Since the date of your last letter [February 1781] it is now almost
two years ... That we have been inquisitive every time a dispatch
arrived from India you may easily believe, but the accounts we got
and the reports which have prevail'd upon such occasions by no
means served to relieve our anxiety. We have been told that your

Brother was treated with severity, & kept by the black savage whose prisoner he is, in very close confinement, and even in irons. This cursed report had well nigh cost poor Nelly her life, and tho' we collected several circumstances afterwards that rendered the account improbable, yet the idea frequently comes across her, and throws a damp on her spirits that nothing can get the better of, which too is much heightened by reflecting on the possibility of your falling into the same hands, as well as the constant danger you must be in and the fatigues you must suffer in the hazardous & distressing service you are upon. It was a relief to us lately to receive a letter from John McKay ... dated in June last, and from the mention he makes of your Brother, I can collect that at Madras nothing is known with certainty of him and his fellow prisoners ...

We think ourselves here on the eve of a peace, God grant it may be so, that you may have some respite from your fatigues, but particularly that your Brother's confinement may come to an end.[17]

While William was in prison, much was happening in India, little of which boded well for the British. In the Madras Presidency, Hyder had subdued Arcot, proclaimed himself nawab of the Carnatic, and overrun Kavalur, Tanjore, Trichinopoly, and Madura. There were prayers in mosques throughout India excoriating the British or what Nizam Ali of Hyderabad, in an intercepted letter, described as "a people worse than women ... a set of merchants without a name ... a handful of tradesmen who in their nature are like foxes."[18] However, Governor General Hastings, believing that a good offence is the best defence, determined to attack on all fronts and sent Sir Eyre Coote with 640 Europeans, fifteen lakhs of rupees, and a large supply of provisions to Madras. Coote also carried an order suspending Whitehill as acting governor of Madras. That suspension paved the way for Coote to direct the hostilities unobstructed by the Madras Council. In explaining Whitehill's removal to the Court of Directors in late 1780, Hastings let his frustration over Madras's treatment of an ally, the nizam of Hyderabad, come to the fore:

Whereas the belief of the Nizam Ali, that we were actually vested with the controul, which we declared ourselves to possess, but he distrusted the effect of that controul, since the orders which we had repeatedly given, and declared to him for the resolution of the Circar of Guntoor, had not only been disregarded, but Mr. Holland, who had been the instrument in the negotiation, had been punished by

them for the part which he had taken in it; the controlling power
which are vested in it by an act of the British legislature, had been,
in repeated instances, treated by the gentlemen at Fort St.
George with slight and disrespect, but in the present instance, they thought
proper to take more upon them; they defeated our acts by their
refusal to conform to them, and comply with our orders, where we
had a special right to them. The faith of this Government had been
pledged to the Nawab Nizam Ali Khan for the restoration of the
Guntoor Circar to Bazalet Jung; they were so informed, and
required to restore it. They did not restore it ... upon these grounds
we resolved on the tenth ultimo, to give effect to our commands and
to determine to exert the authority with which we were vested in
suspending Mr. Whitehill, the President of Fort St. George from the
Company's service.[19]

The alarm in Britain was considerable. The news of the catastrophe at
Pollilur in September 1780 had been followed by Cornwallis's surrender
at Yorktown on 19 October 1781, an event that extinguished any hope
that Britain could retain America. Horace Walpole bewailed: "India and
America are alike escaping."[20] The prime minister, Lord North, acknowledged that Pollilur "had engaged the attention of the world ... and had
given rise to so much public clamour and uneasiness."[21] Minorca and
Tobago had been lost. It seemed as if the empire was disintegrating on all
fronts. Britons began to question whether it had ever been realistic to
expect that a handful of British troops could command the subcontinent
of India and the other colonies Britain had accumulated. Gibbon's quip
that the empire was "an oak planted in a flower-pot"[22] aptly exposed its
fragility. That vulnerability loomed larger as the native armies became
trained in European warfare.

In the end, of course, Britain lost America but not India, at least for
another century and a half. The reasons why it failed in one country and
succeeded in the other are beyond the scope of this book; suffice to say
that, in the case of India, a history of submission to foreign conquerors,
the inability of Indian princes to unite against a common British foe, the
weak position of other European powers on the subcontinent (the French
had been expelled from Pondicherry, Mahé, and Chandigarh at the outset
of hostilities), widespread revulsion in Britain at perceived Indian atrocities, and the high quality of British military officers serving both the
crown and the East India Company were all factors working in favour of
the status quo.

In any event, what is clear is that the resolution of the situation in America enabled Britain to focus and bring its resources to bear on India. Indeed, far from signalling the collapse of Britain's empire, the revolution in America set in place a series of events that led to a vastly more powerful Britain and an aggrandized empire. Whereas the empire consisted of twenty-three colonies in 1792, the number had escalated to forty-three by the time of Napoleon's defeat at Waterloo in 1815.

Nebertheless, in late-eighteenth-century India, the hostilities dragged on. By 1781, the British were in dire straits and at one point, with the French fleet anchored off Pondicherry and English provisions exhausted, Hyder Ali was positioned to inflict a devastating defeat on the EIC's army. Fortunately, French Admiral Comte d'Orves departed for Mauritius upon learning of Sir Edward Hughes's approach with the British fleet. "Had the French Admiral left only two frigates to block up the road to Cuddalore, consequences might have happened as fatal to the interests of Great Britain in the East Indies as flowed in North America, from the convention of Saratoga."[23] Soon afterwards, Coote was repulsed with heavy casualties by Hyder at the Pagoda of Chillumbrum in June 1781. That success, despite the remonstrances of Tipu Sultan, convinced Hyder to offer battle to Coote at Porto Novo. On 1 July 1781 Coote deployed 8,000 rank and file and 60 cannon against Hyder's 60,000 to 100,000 troops and 47 field pieces. In short order, Coote managed to evade Hyder's redoubts and completely routed the latter's army. Hyder's losses were astonishing, both in quantity and in quality, ranging somewhere between 3,000 and 10,000 and including his favourite general and brother-in-law, Meer Sahib, who had been the first to break William's lines at Pollilur. In contrast, British losses were fewer than 400, with only one officer killed. Grievously for the beleaguered family, that officer was Lieutenant and Quartermaster Francis Baillie, the first of the family to die in India. Alves wrote to John Baillie:

> The accounts we have had of poor Frank's death have come to us
> through a channel that leaves no room to doubt of its truth. Indeed
> I have seen two men of the 73[d] Reg't that were in the same action
> in which he fell. This unlucky event gave Nelly & me much concern,
> and you may believe it was a heavy stroke indeed to his poor
> Mother. The loss of a promising and an only son could not miss to
> be affecting and the loss at the same time of her only means of sub-
> sistence was a sad aggravation! Before we had the acc't of his death,
> the last remittance he sent was exhausted. I had written to him that

I would not see her want, and I gave her a supply accordingly. Till
I hear from India, I shall continue to supply her wants out of your
Brother's funds which I hope he will approve. They are not many, as
she is a very moderate person, and she is so broken that I suppose
she will not continue long. If Frank left any thing, I dare say you will
take care of it for her.[24]

The unfortunate Frank left very little, the entire cash in his estate amounting to only 42 pagodas and 142 rupees, the equivalent of £15.[25]

Porto Novo not only marked a significant victory, it also served to
undermine the myth of Hyder's invincibility and to rejuvenate British
morale. "Although no trophies were gained, or prisoners made, the 1st of
July 1781, will ever be accounted an important day to the eastern branch
of the British empire. It broke the spell which was formed by the defeat
of Colonel Baillie, and destroyed that respect which the name of Hyder
Ali had obtained from the disastrous to this prosperous event, amongst
superstitious observers, whose opinions are formed by the impression of
striking events, more than by the deductions of reason."[26]

Nevertheless, the victory was not a turning point in the war as each
side jostled for supremacy. Coote followed up his victory with another
defeat of Hyder Ali at the Second Battle of Pollilur in August 1781.
Hyder's forces, for their part, captured Colonel Braithwaite and his
troops in the Tanjore country on 18 February 1782 and sent them to join
the other prisoners at Seringapatam. Then Hastings achieved a general
truce with the Marathas on 17 May 1782. By that point, the Company
had bought the neutrality of Moodaji Bhonsla, the rajah of Nagpur, while
Nizam Ali of Hyderabad preserved the peace. Only Hyder and the French
remained hostile. Tipu checked the EIC by capturing General Richard
Mathews and his troops at Bednore on 28 April 1783. Then a naval battle between the British fleet, under Admiral Edward Hughes, and the
French fleet, under Admiral Bailli de Suffren, occurred at Sadras in
February 1782. The results were indecisive, but the French fared better
than the British, landed troops at Porto Novo, and in league with Hyder
Ali, captured Cuddalore in April.

With neither side gaining advantage and his health deteriorating,
Hyder questioned his continual conflict with the British. "I shall pay
dearly for my arrogance; between me and the English there were perhaps
mutual grounds of dissatisfaction, but no cause for war, and I might have
made them my friends in spite of Mahommed Ali the most treacherous of
men. The defeat of many Baillies and Braithwaites will not destroy them.

I can ruin their resources by land but I cannot dry up the sea; and I must first be weary of a war in which I can gain nothing by fighting."[27] Indeed, the campaigns of 1782 took a toll on the health of two of the principal protagonists; Hyder Ali died of natural causes in December 1782, and Eyre Coote followed in April 1783. In his last message to his son, Hyder admonished him to negotiate peace: "I have gained nothing by the war with the English … if you, through fear of disturbances in your own kingdom, repair thither without having previously concluded peace with the English, they will certainly follow you and carry the war into your own country. On this account, therefore, it is better to make peace on whatever terms you can procure, and then go to your own country."[28] In the short term Hyder's advice fell on deaf ears, but even Tipu came to recognize the inevitable when news of the Treaty of Paris ending the American Revolutionary War reached India. Colonel William Fullarton's impending threat to Seringapatam persuaded Tipu to negotiate the Treaty of Mangalore in 1784, bringing to an end the Second Anglo-Mysore War and restoring the status quo ante bellum.

Meanwhile, in September 1783, upon learning that peace had been concluded and believing the reports of the captives' reasonably comfortable imprisonment in Mysore, David Mitchell wrote to William.

Since writing you the 16th Jan'y last, your Daughter and I have been made very happy to find by your Brother's letter to me, dated in camp the 29th August last, that you was in good health; and not doubting on your being released upon the news of the peace arriving in India, we most sincerely congratulate you upon the happy event, and flatter ourselves with the hope of seeing you soon in Old England, as being some little time in this climate would certainly prove very salutary to you after so long a confinement, and so many years hard service in India.

Mr. Brodie, in his letter of the 1st of September last, remitted me a bill for eighty pounds, which is paid, and shall be applied for the use of your Daughter, whom you will perceive by the inclosed is in good health, and spending her midsummer holidays in town with my friends: to have it from under your own hand that you have regained your freedom, and enjoy a good state of health would afford infinite pleasure and satisfaction to her.

P.S. The definitive treaties between England, France, Spain and America were signed by the plenipotentiaries at Paris on the 3rd instant, and

received here on the 6th to be ratified, and that with Holland is hourly
expected; when all are completed peace will be proclaimed in due
form, which I hope will be the means of restoring the same blessing all
over India.[29]

Peace treaty or not, both sides saw the cessation of hostilities as little more than a pause, with war to break out again at the first propitious moment. John reflected the prevailing attitude upon his arrival in
London in 1785: "The last Europe news through foreign gazettes is
that two grand allyances are form'd, one consisting of the English, the
Emperor of Russia, the Danes and some German princes; the other
France, Spain, Portugal, the Dutch, the Swedes and Prussia. Sir Hugh
Palliser said to come to India with five sail of the line ... Peace is finally
concluded at home and commissions coming out on the part of the different nations to settle matters in India. But war again soon expected.
Pitt has carried the bill respecting India affairs and has a small majority
in the House of Commons."[30] The bill to which John alluded was
the East India Company Act of 1784, commonly known as Pitt's India
Act, which, as recounted earlier, strengthened civilian control over
the Company.

With the conclusion of the war, the surviving prisoners in Mysorean
jails, roughly thirteen hundred British and two thousand sepoys, gained
their freedom. As noted earlier, the four hundred Europeans who, forcibly or otherwise, had become Muslims were not among those freed, for
Tipu Sultan, in blatant violation of the treaty, refused to release them.
Neither was William Baillie, who had succumbed to his wounds and neglect on 13 November 1782. His aide-de-camp, Captain Alexander Fraser,
wrote to John from prison that William had been ill for some months and
would, in all probability, have recovered if he had been given any medical
assistance. His burial was attended by a sole European.

You will probably have heard before you receive this of your
Brother's death, he died the 13th Nov. last after an illness of three
months & a half. His will and papers are in the possession of Doctor
Sinclair. Exclusive of his will, he has left legacies to the amount of
about three hundred & fifty pound sterling, three hundred of which
is to your Sister, Mrs. Alves. His last words to me concerning you
were, "I hope in God my Brother will live & get home. Tell him to go
home immediately and not be looking too high as I have been. He
can live like a prince in his own country." Brigade Major's pay while

in prison is an object to me as even in case of my death it will be great service to my brothers & sisters who you know stand in great need of it, perhaps your mentioning me to General [James] Stuart will be the means of securing it for me. I can say with great truth that had your Brother lived, obtained pay for me as his staff was little but very little of what he intended to do for me as you will know if ever I am released. I have a great deal to communicate to you relative to your Brother's demands on the Company but my present horrid situation will admit of my saying only I am my dear Baillie, most affectionately yours.

Capt. Rumley who is my prison companion desires his compliments to you.[31]

Unfortunately, neither Fraser nor Rumley lived to corroborate the Company's debts to William. They were poisoned by their captors in October 1783.

David Baird's cousin and a fellow prisoner, James Dalrymple, wrote that William Baillie was much worse treated than any of them. Hyder clearly was taking no chances with his long-time rival.

Colonel Baillie possessed great vigour of body and mind, being of a middling stature, well and firmly made, and animated on all occasions with calm and steady resolution. Before the unfortunate day that consigned him to a confinement, from which he was destined never to escape, he uniformly bore a character of an officer enterprising, brave, and judicious. As his merit and rank had rendered him an object of terror to the conqueror before he fell into his hands, so he became an object of barbarous resentment afterwards, and was treated, accordingly, with unusual marked severity. In the enemy's camp he was separated from his fellow prisoners, the Captains Rumley and Fraser[,] and thrown into irons even on his journey to Seringapatam from Arcot. On his arrival on his way to the capital [of] Hyder, at Bangalore[,] five guns were fired in order to assemble the people to insult his misfortunes. And during the whole course of his illness, he received not the least comfort or assistance from the advice of any physician.[32]

Upon learning of his brother's death, John wrote John Alves with the devastating news and dropped the bombshell that William had a daughter in England.

Necessity now obliges me to inform you of a melancholy truth. God knows it is so to me as well as you and my other relations. For altho' not rich, I had enough of my own and I flatter myself a mind above coveting or wishing for the property of any human being, far less that of an only Brother, who I will dare say was a credit to his country. Were he alive I would not speak in these terms but we may surely be permitted to say favourable truths of the dead tho' near relations. I will say no more on this melancholy subject but request that you will endeavour to keep poor Nelly alive (excuse my calling her so) until my return.

Having often in consequence of my Brother's desire a promise that in case any accident should befall him I would quit this country and having been informed by a letter from Seringapatam that the putting me in mind of that was his dying words. I am therefore determined to be amongst you as soon as possibly I can. I think in six months I shall be able to get away. I am to remain at Madras during that time doing my own private business, and therefore do not consider myself a military man. My Brother has made a will the contents of which I know not but believe he has left much in my power. His affection for Nelly was well known to me and you know she is my only Sister alive. More would be improper on this subject.

I have a Niece in or near London, a Daughter of my Brother's. She is under the care of Mr. David Mitchell, No. 13 Paper Buildings. I now in the most particular manner request that she may be brought carefully down there and be treated as far as 'tis in your power and my Sister's with every attention that would be shown were he married to her mother.

As in the course of a passage from hence to Europe many accidents may happen, I shall certainly make a will here before sailing and shall leave it in such hands that a copy will be transmitted to you and others in case of my death ... Once more take care of Nelly.[33]

The conclusion of the Second Anglo-Mysore War that cost William Baillie his life did nothing to dampen the internecine squabbling in Madras. In a letter written in February 1784 to one Brodie, John Baillie provided a first-hand account of just how dysfunctional the Madras government actually was – with Governor George Macartney on one side and General James Stuart on another – and how close the bickering had come to undoing the British cause in the recent conflict. John casts both parties in a poor light but his sympathy lies with Stuart. Macartney, he explains, jeopardized the EIC army's position at the second battle of Cuddalore, in June 1783, by withholding supplies and finally suspended Stuart, who, as we shall see later, nurtured his resentment and exacted revenge. As accomplished as he was, Macartney had a talent for alienating many with whom he came in contact. His sister-in-law cut to the quick: "There is but one thing he wants – feeling."[34] In his description of these events, John recognized that he may have crossed the line to indiscretion and requested that Brodie destroy the letter once he had digested it.

Immediately upon [Coote's] death the disputes between Lord MacCartney and General Stuart ran as high as they cou'd well do. On Sir Edward Hughes arrival from Bombay he immediately as soon as he cou'd take in water sail'd with 17 sail of the line and block'd up the harbour of Trincomally for two or three months. Suffren, during this time, having fortified the mouth of the harbour so as to make an attack on it impossible or at least improbable to succeed, remain'd quiet repairing his ships and refreshing his men[,] convinced that want of water and the sickness of his men would oblige Sir Edward Hughes to leave him. By the time both those events had nearly happen'd our army under General Stuart got to Cuddalore. Our fleet on intelligence thereof of our army being before Cuddalore came and anchor'd to windward of the port. You will here think it extraordinary how our army came to be so long in getting to Cuddalore as they march'd soon after our fleet sail'd for Trincomally. There is two causes – first mismanagement on General Stuart's end; 2ndly, private spite towards him in Lord MacCartney by not sending the ships and furnishing the other equipments. Suffren now finding the mouth of the harbour open, knowing the sickliness of our troops and perceiving the inevitable fall of Cuddalore[,] came out boldly with fourteen ships in high order. He, by manoeuvring, led Sir Edward from his station, made a half kind of fight with him and had such a superiority of fire owing to the state of his ships that it was necessary to say [that] want of water, perhaps that was really the case, obliged our fleet to come to Madras. Suffren then took up his station in Cuddalore Roads.

Our army on their arrival at Cuddalore having neglected taking the proper advantages of ground and by a lethargic disposition

unaccountably permitted the French to fortify themselves in lines
about a thousand yards outside of the fort. The attack on those
lines was a serious piece of service in which we had from a thousand to twelve hundred men killed and wounded. The French lost
considerably also but not nearly equal to us.

By the loss of twelve hundred effectives, sickness and a scarcity of
rice, a measure selling for one rupee, our army became so much
reduced that after the garrison of Cuddalore was reinforced by the
marines and seamen from Suffrein's fleet, I considered our army as
in a very dangerous situation. The least misfortune that cou'd have
befallen us was the loss of our battering train; the greatest losing part
of our baggage and leaving our sick and wounded to the mercy of
the enemy.

Worse than the above might have happen'd but I don't think they
cou'd have beat our army. At this unfortunate and critical moment in
our affairs what shou'd fortunately arrive but the preliminary articles
of peace which saved us from a disgrace which I'll venture to say
that had old Sir Eyre lived (with all his faults) never would have
happen'd. General Stuart was immediately order'd himself by sea to
Madras and the disputes between Lord MacCartney and him became
more and more violent. Each of the three great men wish'd to throw
the balance of the miscarriage at Cuddalore off his own shoulders
and it seem'd to me as far as I could observe that on a comparison of
acc'ts Lord MacCartney and Sir Edward Hughes thought it prudent
to go hand in glove and so General Stuart was ship'd off for
England. I must here observe that had not this happen'd I believe
Lord MacCartney wou'd have soon shared that fate by means of
General Stuart ... Tipu has been tampering and putting of time without doing any thing decisive respecting peace and our army marches
in a few days ... Ever since Stuart's departure Gov't here has had
constant disputes with the King's officer, sometimes right in my opinion and sometimes wrong. But taking it all and all if there is any
merit, I think the Company's servants here will be thought to carry
things with too high a hand and that Legislature at home will disapprove of their conduct. I know nothing further to inform you of
respecting publick affairs and have only to add respecting them
that I never laid myself so open before on paper. You had better
take notes from this letter, if worth your while, and destroy it
on receipt ...

Nothing can be more anxious than I am to get out of this unhappy country. I hope to leave in a month or two at most. How happy shall I be to have the pleasure of shaking hands with you in any part of Great Britain.[35]

Following Stuart's dismissal, Macartney wanted to appoint Sir John Burgoyne, the cousin of General John Burgoyne of Saratoga infamy, as the succeeding commander-in-chief, but Burgoyne refused on the basis that Stuart could be deprived of his command only by the king's order. Macartney then appointed Colonel Ross Lang, a long-serving officer with the Company, as commander-in-chief. In response, Burgoyne asserted his command of the king's troops and was supported in that regard by all the officers. Macartney then had Burgoyne arrested for "disobedience of orders and inciting to mutiny and sedition." Burgoyne was fully and honourably acquitted at a court-martial but died shortly thereafter. His contempt for Macartney was presumably shared by many: "For there is hardly one person whose misfortune it has been to have any transactions with you since the Right Honble the President's arrival, who has not had reason to curse the hour his ill stars doomed him to have any connections with his Lordship. His Highness the Nawab, the Supreme Board, the late gallant and much revered Commander-in-Chief Sir Eyre Coote, Sir Edward Hughes, General Stuart, myself, many others, both in public and private situations, are proofs undeniable that your consistency is one uniform and general plan of tyranny and oppression."[36] Burgoyne signalled his intent to call Macartney to account. "The time must come, and you know it, when ample justice must be done me, and when, divested of the plumes of government, you must answer for your conduct."[37] Upon Macartney's return to England in 1785, General Stuart challenged him to a duel. One-legged Stuart, propped against a tree, was only successful in wounding Macartney in the shoulder. Disgusted with himself, he sought to continue the duel but the seconds would not countenance it.

A few years of quiet after Macartney's departure proved to be the lull before the storm. Tipu Sultan revived the conflict in 1789 by invading the state of Travancore, a British ally. His adversary was happy to respond. Again, Innes Munro reflected the prevailing sentiment:

It is to be hoped that the treaty of peace, which the Company have lately completed with Tipu Sultan is only meant to be temporary.

Such I am certain, must be the wish of every Briton actuated by sentiments of patriotism, and capable of feeling the indignities, which have been uniformly heaped upon the British name. Can any Englishman read of the sufferings of his unfortunate countrymen in the different prisons of Mysore without dropping a tear of sympathy? Or, can he peruse the account of the repeated indignity and contempt with which his nation has been treated by the present usurper of Mysore, without being filled with indignation, and burning with sentiments of retaliation and revenge?[38]

With that, the Third Anglo-Mysore War commenced. In a letter to an unnamed correspondent in India, written when he himself was back in Scotland, John made his detestation of Tipu Sultan clear amidst references to the Russian empress, her lover, and Pitt's domination of Parliament. "I am not likely ever to see the Plains of Hindostan but I read with much anxiety the acc'ts now received from that quarter and if I can trust my own resolution, I think I cou'd serve as a volunteer for one day against that tyrant Tipu with much pleasure to myself. But I hope and pray he has enough against him and that you'll have it in your power to hang him on one of the gates of Madras by way of finishing the war ... Our late differences with the Court of Spain are patch'd up for the present but I think it highly likely that the ambition of the Empress Catharine and her stallion Potemkin will soon involve Europe in a war. Nothing but an impotent state of France can prevent it. Mr. Pitt all powerful in administration."[39]

Bolstered by the successful negotiation of the Tripartite Treaty with Nizam Ali and the Marathas, Cornwallis confronted and defeated Tipu Sultan on 15 May 1791 but then, short of provisions, withdrew toward Bangalore. There he was joined by Hurry Punt and Purseram Bhow's Marathas bearing ample supplies and roughly sixty thousand troops. The supplies may have proven more valuable to Cornwallis than the warriors. Despite their bellicose and imposing appearance, the Marathas were renowned for carefully husbanding their resources. A contemporary wrote: "Warfare, he [a Maratha] regarded as a legitimate means of plundering, but as his steed and spear represented his entire capital, and constituted his sole claim to employment, he sedulously avoided all conflict (which somewhat detracted from his merits as a combatant), and preferred flight to fight on every occasion of danger."[40] Or as a British army officer serving in India put it: "The guns are of all sorts and dimensions having names of their gods given to them, are painted in the most fantastic manner, and many of them held in esteem, and for the services they are said to have already performed for the state, cannot now be dispensed with although in every respect unfit for use. Were the guns even serviceable, the small supply of ammunition with which they are provided has always effectually prevented the Maratha artillery from being formidable to their enemies."[41]

The combined forces advanced, taking Nundydroog on 19 October and the hitherto impregnable fortress of Savendroog two months later. In February 1792 they arrived at Tipu's magnificent capital, Seringapatam. "It will readily be allowed that this insulated metropolis must have been the richest, most convenient and beautiful spot possessed in the present age by any native Prince in India."[42] At Seringapatam, Tipu deployed five thousand cavalry, forty to fifty thousand infantry, and four hundred cannon but proved unable to withstand Cornwallis and his allies, who overran Tipu's fortified camp and part of the island of Seringapatam. The British and allied losses were relatively modest while Tipu suffered twenty thousand killed, wounded, or missing, the latter mostly through desertions. Tipu sued for peace and by the Treaty of Madras on 26 February 1792 ceded half his territories to the Company and its allies, paid them 3 crores and 30 lakhs of rupees, and delivered two of his three oldest sons as hostages to Cornwallis.

But again the peace was short-lived. By 1798, Napoleon had formulated designs, albeit fanciful, on India and Tipu entered into furtive negotiations encouraging the French to attack the British in the subcontinent. François Ripaud, an adventurer, sought reinforcements for Tipu from the Comte de Malartic, the governor of Île de France (Mauritius). In an ironic turn of events, Ripaud formed a sixty-member Jacobin Club of Seringapatam and planted a tree of liberty in the despot's capital. Malartic disowned Ribaud but did agree to publish a proclamation allowing French volunteers to serve under Tipu. Although only 109 volunteered, the British obtained a copy of the proclamation and, at Jedda, intercepted a letter from Napoleon professing that he was "full of the desire to free you [Tipu] from the iron yoke of England."[43] Governor General Richard Wellesley, who was eager both to eradicate any French influence in India and to expand British possessions, concluded: "The evidence of meditated hostility was complete."[44] He utilized this provocation to eliminate Tipu once and for all and with that launched the Fourth Anglo-Mysore War.

The moment was propitious since Nelson's destruction of Napoleon's fleet at Aboukir on 1 August 1798 rendered any French attempts to reinforce Tipu moot. Furthermore, Wellesley had neutralized Nizam Ali through a subsidiary alliance with Hyderabad. The treaty, in addition, evicted the French from the nizam's territories and provided for a British military force in that state. Wellesley dispatched George Harris, an experienced and intrepid officer and veteran of the American Revolutionary War, to encamp in front of Seringapatam with General John Floyd and Nizam Ali.

Harris offered to suspend further hostilities but on terms that Tipu found unacceptable: that Tipu surrender half his territory, pay twenty million rupees, and deliver as hostages his four sons and four senior officers of Harris's choosing. However, when troops under the command of General James Stuart – not the James Stuart who had earlier arrested Governor Pigot but a Perthshire Scot who was a distant relative of William Baillie – arrived from the Bombay Presidency to reinforce Harris, Tipu offered to negotiate. Harris refused unless Tipu first conveyed the hostages and treasure to him. Since Tipu gave no indication of complying with Harris's conditions, the British and their allies resumed the attack and forced the "Tiger of Mysore" back to the fort of Seringapatam itself. Harris, with a fine sense of poetic justice, chose David Baird to launch the final onslaught. "The distinguished officer appointed to lead the assault beheld those walls, within which he had himself been immured in irons, during a tedious imprisonment of nearly four years; the faithless captivity and secret massacre of his countrymen were unhappily known to him from no borrowed sources, and the prospect of avenging the wrongs which he had witnessed and partaken, and of terminating, in one short hour, the future possibility of every similar outrage, formed a mass of reflections and of motives capable of rousing to the highest pitch of animation, a less ardent spirit than that of Major-General Baird."[45]

The Fourth Anglo-Mysore War culminated in the death of Tipu Sultan and the dismemberment of his kingdom. Baird discovered Tipu's body "under a vast heap of the slain,"[46] and David Wilkie's monumental painting of the scene depicts the grate of Colonel Baillie's Dungeon in which William had died and Baird had languished for four years. William's eldest nephew, Lieutenant Alexander Baillie, served under General Harris in the Battle of Seringapatam and would also have derived untold pleasure from avenging his uncle.

There were grand celebrations in British India. The prize money was extraordinary, over £1 million, and, for the first time, the EIC awarded commemorative medals to all ranks. Seringapatam and Tipu became part of British folklore. The East India Company directors presented Tipu's mechanical man-eating tiger, together with a French tricolour found in the fort, with due pomp and ceremony to King George III. That mechanical tiger remains a popular display item today in the Victoria and Albert Museum. Keats cited Tipu's tiger in *The Cap and Bells* and Wilkie Collins, in 1868, based the first detective novel in English literature, *The Moonstone*, on a cursed diamond looted at Seringapatam.

While Harris was presumably delighted with his barony of Seringapatam and Mysore and Belmont in the County of Kent, Wellesley was dismissive of his "Irish and pinchpeck" title of marquess and £5,000 per annum for twenty years. No shrinking violet, he made clear to the foreign secretary and future prime minister, Lord Grenville, that he expected and felt entitled to much more. "The manner in which I have conducted this war has been received with exultation, and even the most unqualified admiration in India; and ... you will gain much credit by conferring some high and brilliant honour upon me immediately. The Garter would be much more acceptable to me than any additional title, nor would any title be an object which should not raise me to the same rank which was given to Lord Cornwallis."[47]

The British were reluctant to divide Mysore between Nizam Ali and the East India Company. They believed that the nizam was barely capable of managing his existing lands and any increase in territory would provoke the Marathas. Accordingly, by the Treaty of Seringapatam, the British claimed the coast of Mysore and the Fort of Seringapatam while providing Nizam Ali a modest territory which he forfeited to the Company a few years later. It restored the rest of Tipu's empire to the Hindu Wodeyars, who had ruled prior to Hyder's usurpation in 1761. The Wodeyars provided enlightened leadership to Mysore and remained allied to the British until independence in 1947.

Hyder and Tipu were exceptionally able warriors and experienced considerable success against the British. Indeed, Hyder was arguably India's most capable military leader. It is, then, somewhat surprising that he and his son were not adopted by later Indian nationalists as exemplary icons in the Indian quest for independence. However, they were never popular, perhaps because of their ruthlessness or perhaps owing to their Muslim faith in a predominantly Hindu south. It may also be that Tipu overreached in proclaiming himself padshah (king) in 1786. He became the first to throw off the increasingly threadbare cloak of Mughal rule but alienated many by his attempt to establish his own caliphate. Today,

his legacy and that of his father is limited to the Gumtaz (their mausoleum), Tipu's Summer Palace in Seringapatam, and the ruins of Tipu's
palace in Bangalore. For one reason or another, Tipu Sultan has earned
the condescension of posterity and folklore, possibly apocryphal, has
it that his and Hyder Ali's descendants have been relegated to pulling
rickshaws in Calcutta.

The Seringapatam dungeon where Colonel Baillie and the other captured officers from the Battle of Pollilur were imprisoned. The cannon collapsed into the dungeon during the 1799 siege in which Tipu Sultan was killed. Photographed by the author.

General Sir David Baird Discovering the Body of Sultan Tippoo Sahib after Having Captured Seringapatam on the 4th May 1799 by David Wilkie. Baird stands above Colonel Bailey's (*sic*) Dungeon in which Baird was imprisoned for four years. Courtesy of the National Gallery of Scotland.

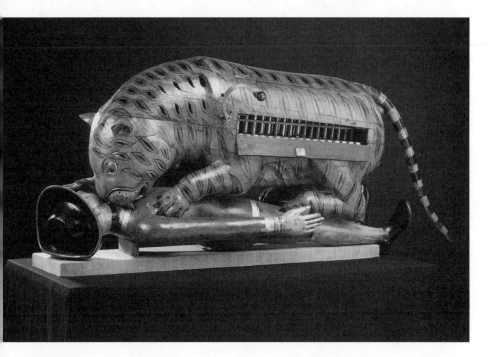

Tipu's mechanical man-eating tiger captured at Seringapatam in 1799 and now on display at the Victoria and Albert Museum. Courtesy of the Victoria and Albert Museum.

Sacred to the Memory of
IOHN BAILLIE Esq' of Dunean,
Colonel of the Regiment of Loyal Invernefs Fencibles.
He Died in this City on his march to Oppose
the Invading Enemy.
On the 31' of January 1797.
Aged 49'

Memorial to Colonel John Baillie XIII of Dunain. Plaque in St Canice's Cathedral in Kilkenny, Ireland, memorializing Colonel John's death as he led the Loyal Inverness Fencibles to repulse a Napoleonic invasion at Bantry Bay. Photographed by the author.

Colonel John Baillie of Leys (1772–1833). The fourth son of George and
Ann Baillie of Leys. He became a professor of Persian and Arabic languages
at the College of Fort William, agent for Bundelcund, resident at Lucknow,
a member of Parliament, and a director of the East India Company.
Photograph courtesy of John Baillie.

Margaret Baillie (1761–1831). The feisty eldest child of George
and Ann Baillie of Leys. She raised some of the Anglo-Indian sons of
her brother John and of his close friend Neil Benjamin Edmonstone
and later managed Colonel John's household. Courtesy of John Baillie.

Lulu, the Begum of Oude. A princess of the Court of Oude and believed to be the wife of the British resident, Colonel John Baillie of Leys. She was the mother of Anne, John Wilson, and Henrietta. It appears the Begum remained in Lucknow when Colonel John returned to Great Britain. Courtesy of John Baillie.

Anne, Henrietta, and John Wilson Baillie. The three children of Colonel John Baillie of Leys and his wife, the Begum of Oude. Courtesy of the Honourable Alexander Baillie.

The Baillie Guard Gate, Lucknow. Constructed by Saadat Ali Khan, nawab of Oude, in honour of the British resident, Colonel John Baillie of Leys. It constituted the entrance to the residency and became the iconic symbol of British resistance during the Indian Mutiny of 1857–59. Photographed by the author.

Leys Castle, Inverness. Designed by Samuel Beazley for Colonel John Baillie of Leys and completed after his death in 1833. Photographed by the author.

Homeward Bound

Where there's a will, there's a relative.
Anonymous

Upon receiving the news of his brother's death, John, who was serving as Sir Eyre Coote's aide-de-camp, sought leave to put William's affairs in order. The will to which Alexander Fraser alluded proved to be an eighteen-year-old document disposing of William's effects in India to one Dr Sinclair, a surgeon with the Company, should he die at the siege of Madura. At that time, William was imminently expecting to storm the city and hurriedly penned a note to Sinclair making him the "sole heir and executor to my little effects in India."[1] In the intervening years William's financial position had improved significantly but in lieu of any other will, Sinclair, when confronted by John, indicated his intention to claim William's entire property in India. John soon discovered that a subsequent will existed but he remained intensely disillusioned by Sinclair's ethics. He underscored his disdain for his former comrade to Alexander Godsman: "You will not only be surprised but astonished when I tell you your friend and mine not long ago, Mr. Sinclair[,] is not worthy the attention you pay him in your letter. The story is too long for me to relate now but I will tell it you when we meet. He is I think the most dangerous man I have met within life & I have seen a great many rogues since leaving Dunain."[2] That contempt for Sinclair was also reflected in John's correspondence putting his niece and David Mitchell on guard against any attempts by Sinclair to insinuate himself with them and to let them know that the only effect of the doctor's faithlessness was to hurt his own character. John elaborated:

You no doubt think I have neglected that attention which you had a right to expect as a friend. I acknowledge it but there has been more

cause than perhaps you imagine. Of all men I suppose Sinclair is
the last you would suppose capable of endeavouring to deprive me
of my just right. However, he has attempted it by endeavouring to
constitute the following letter wrote by my Brother during the siege
of Madura, into a will.

"My friend I have received your letter and have just time to tell you
that we expect every hour to be ordered to storm. Therefore in case
I shou'd be kill'd, I by this make you sole heir and executor to
my little effects in India. I wish you all health and happiness. I am
Dear Sinclair
Y'rs Will'm Baillie

                                        Camp 21st June 1764"

Less for me to make any comments; rather your own principles and
understanding will point out all I can say. When I first began to
suspect something I cou'd hardly believe it possible he was in earnest.
I therefore put the question pointedly and received a positive answer
that he intended to dispute with me the whole of my Brother's property in India. This I tell you on honour. On a subsequent will's being
found leaving me sole heir and executor, he told his friends ... that
he never intended prosecuting[,] being ashamed of his former avowal
& finding it wou'd not succeed. The above affair has given me much
vexation and prevented my paying attention to you and others which
I ought.
    My Brother's affairs are so confused that I fear I shall not get out
of India before Oct'b'r comes twelve months but I am still bent on
going as soon as possible.[3]

In any event, John Ferguson and William Pope, attorneys in Calcutta,
had opened a box of William's private papers and three small trunks that
had been in the care of a Mr Cumming. In them they found a short will
naming John sole executor and inheritor of William's estate. The will was
dated 28 July 1779 and contained a codicil dated 23 July 1780 raising
Ann's lump-sum inheritance.

                              Pondicherry the 28th July, 1779

I William Baillie eldest son and heir of Alex'r Baillie Esquire of
Dunain in the County of Inverness North Britain in case of my death

do hereby leave my dear Brother John Baillie my sole heir, executor ·
administrator and assign as to the Estate of Dunain and whatever
lands or monies etc. etc. at home or abroad I may die possessed of
or may be due to me[,] with this only proviso that he pay Miss Ann
Baillie, now in England and who I believe to be a natural Daughter
of mine[,] thirty pounds sterling a year untill she attains the age of
twenty (she was born the twentieth August 1767) and then finally
the sum of five hundred pounds sterling. This I declare to be my last
will and testament as witness by my hand & seal.

W'm Baillie

Signed & sealed in presence
of us
E W White
Richard Chase

 I hereby finding my fortunes rather increased since making the
above will given the said Miss Ann Baillie my natural Daughter
terms therein mentioned the sum of one thousand instead of
five hundred pounds sterling.

W'm Baillie

This addition wrote at Inneconda
On the 23rd day of July, 1780[4]

John's grief in the aftermath of his brother's death was compounded by
the demise of his mentor, Sir Eyre Coote. John expressed his inertia to a
soldier who had served in William's regiment. "Ever since my arrival
here[,] owing to the death of Sir Eyre & my brother, I have been in a total
state of indifference. However I now begin to awaken from that lethargy
and find it necessary to be busy preparing matters for my departure from
this country."[5] He was as good as his word. First he instructed Ferguson
and Pope to take good care of the small articles in the box regardless of
their limited material value since the keepsakes were worth a great deal
to him. Then he confirmed the verbal legacies left to Nelly and Margaret
Baillie, writing home: "I desired Mrs. Baillie, Frank's Mother, might
receive the same allowance as given by her Son. I think it was fifteen
pounds a year but am not sure as to the sum. I therefore think it necessary
to observe that my intention is she shall receive what you and Dr. Alves
judge sufficient to afford her the comforts of life with an assurance the
sum shall be continued." He also instructed that the small allowances to
different people at Dunain should remain in place and concluded: "You
mention a very severe season. Be assured that any indulgence you shew

the poor people on that acc't shall be approved by me."[6] He then set himself to the challenge of reconstructing William's financial position, writing to Mitchell in June 1783: "I know not what my Brother may prove
worth, in short all I can at present depend on, is the money in your hands
and what is due him by the Company; and the Company's debt I fear
I shall not soon recover."[7]

William's worth proved reassuring but John was, indeed, prescient in
his low expectations of the Company. The statement of known assets and
liabilities related to India totalled 36,000 pagodas exclusive of the prize
money owing a lieutenant-colonel from the conquest of Pondicherry.
That prize money was still owing in 1788, nine years after the fall of the
city. At the existing conversion rate, William's known Indian assets would
approximate £14,511. However, William had disbursed substantial
personal funds during the campaign and afterwards in prison. Those
amounts proved painstakingly difficult to determine since the individuals
in the best position to provide the information had died or were still prisoners in Mysore. John was able to ascertain the amounts held and administered by agents in Madras, and the balance with David Mitchell in
London. Laboriously, he put together a record of William's disbursements on behalf of the Company. He ascertained from captains Cornelius
Grant and David Baird that William had advanced 2,000 pagodas to pay
the troops and 1,000 for intelligence from the time he left Vellore in
September.[8] In time, performing a necessary but gruelling task, John was
able to obtain a record of disbursements totalling 11,260 pagodas, made
to William's detachment in July and August 1780.

There remained the question of William's daughter, Ann. John wrote
Mitchell in September 1783: "Be so good as assure my Niece that whatever provision is made for her, it shall not only be fulfilled but exceeded
by me and I shall be happy to do every thing in my power to make up as
far as I can her great loss."[9] He also implored Mitchell to send Ann north.
"I recommend to you in the strongest terms the carrying my Brother's
Daughter from London for fear of accidents and delivering her to my
Sister Mrs. Alves at Inverness with particular injunctions that she shall be
kept on a footing in point of dress and every other attention."[10] He then
sought to ensure that his sister Nelly was not taken by complete surprise
and at least provided some comfort with the news that her nephew,
Alexander (commonly known as Alick or Aleck), the first of the second
generation to seek his fortune in India, had arrived safely in Madras. He
wrote Nelly:

Having wrote fully to Dr. Alves and Mr. Godsman ... I have nothing
particular to mention now except that the finding you alive and well
will be a principal inducement for me to remain in that country if
I am fortunate enough to get there. I am doing my utmost to get
out of this country and have still some hopes of leaving it about
Christmas but cannot say with any certainty. This will be deliver'd
you by Lieut: Colonel Mckenzie with whom I have been on a
friendly footing for years. In case he has not already got there, he
carries down with him a niece of yours. It is unnecessary for me to
recommend her. Your fondness for her Father will surely induce you
to take much care of her. Alick Baillie is with me and well.[11]

John's promise to his brother to quit India should anything befall the latter weighed upon him and he was also "conscious myself that the very
existence of the little family I am connected with depends thereon."[12]
India had exacted a serious toll on John's health without bestowing the
fortune he sought. Indeed, even though he had saved £1,000 by living at
Sir Eyre Coote's house, he was compelled to borrow an additional £500
for his passage home on a Danish ship. John paid £710 for his passage
and that of a slave boy and two Europeans. For that, he had the use of
half the "great room" and every civility he could wish.

In the summer of 1785, John, at long last, landed in England. Three
years later, he notified the East India Company's Court of Directors of his
desire "to remain here until his health is re-established."[13] The Court, in
turn, directed Baillie and others to return to Madras by "early ships of
next season and ... informed [them that] should they fail to do so ... they
will be struck off the list of the army."[14] John was inclined against undertaking another tour of duty in India but hedged his bets by securing an
extension of his leave to the season of 1790.

Yet, as it happened, the hedge proved unnecessary since John adapted
easily to life in the Highlands and enthusiastically embraced his role as
the 13th Laird of Dunain. He married his cousin, Isabella, daughter and
only child of Archibald Campbell of Budgate, on 5 June 1786. Isabella
was no shrinking violet. As will become evident, she was "a lady of great
tenacity in her views, the only child of a simple couple, and during the
whole of her life dominating her parents, husband, and children."[15] There
must have been some ill will between John's niece, Margaret, the daughter of George and Anne Baillie, who was herself not without strong opinions, and his intended. Certainly, something prompted Margaret to write

Isabella: "When I say I wish you as happy as a state of mortality will submit off in the connexion you are about to form I hope my sincerity will not be doubted. Interested as I am in the welfare of an Uncle so decidedly high in my esteem and to whom I feel so grateful for his many favours, what pleasure I must experience at the prospect of his union with a woman whom I believe so calculated to promote his happiness." Margaret, however, seems to have declined the wedding invitation, for she sought to justify her refusal. "I imagined that[,] though you was kind enough to ask me[,] my accepting the invitation would not be entirely agreeable."[16]

In short order, John and Isabella produced three sons, Alexander, Archibald, and William, and two daughters, Katharine and Anne. The new laird of Dunain lived "on a small paternal property on which I have laid out a good [deal] of money."[17] He moved from the family home, the castle of Spioradail, to a thatched house high above Loch Ness. Then in 1790 John built Dunain House, which still stands today. He also moved quickly to recover the feu duty of Dunain which the Duke of Gordon had pledged to Baillie of Dochfour, a situation that irritated John since he could not comprehend why an estate should be wadsett, or leased, to anyone other than the proprietor, particularly when there was "no want of money."[18] In due course he was successful in purchasing the superiorities of Dunain, Dochgarroch, and Dochnacraig from the Duke of Gordon in 1794.[19]

John took an active role in the community. In 1792 he participated as a founder of and donor to the Inverness Academy, an institution that sought to provide a better and broader education than that offered by the existing grammar schools and to serve as a training ground for India-bound young men. The Baillie family benefited to some extent, since at least three of Dunain's great-nephews graduated from that academy. Among other endeavours, John established a bleaching mill at Dunaincroy. At the same time the contentious bent evidenced in India resurfaced in Inverness. Dunain became engaged in a complex legal dispute with his third cousin, Alexander Baillie of Dochfour, over the ownership of the lands of Easter and Wester Dochcairns, ostensibly acquired by the latter from Dunain's father. Another Dochfour cousin, Evan Baillie, claimed one-half of the march to the burn "with nothing to support but acts of occasional possession." That dispute was not settled until after the death of John's son, William, in 1869. On another occasion the burgh of Inverness sought to extend its right to cut peat at the Mount of Caiplich. Dunain, as the closest neighbour, would suffer most by this encroachment and sought to prevent it. In another confrontation, which occurred in 1790, Dunain appeared to provoke his neighbour Mrs Rose, who may well have been the future mother-in-law of Dunain's daughter, Katharine, in an arcane dispute about a church pew. In the words of William Todd:

The Duke [of Gordon] has of late had two letters from Mrs. Rose, since she went to Edinburgh, complaining of her having met with great incivility from Dunain or Mrs. Alves or some body or other about her seat in the church. You probably know the particulars better than I can tell you. She wishes the Duke to give her this seat – and she undertakes to free him of the whole rent; and at the same time to accommodate you and Miss Godsman with room in it for nothing. His Grace you may well suppose, is vexed to hear of Mrs. Rose's having met with any disturbances, more especially as it happened about the time he was her lodger – and he wishes, if possible, to get her provided with another seat – but at the same time, he is very unwilling to give offence to Dunain, who I told him, had been in possession of this seat for several years, in consequence of some compromise with you. He hopes that Mrs. Rose would be pleased if she got liberty from them to sit in his seat along with Dunain – and he bid me write to you, to wait upon Dunain, and let him know how much he is embarrassed by Mrs. Rose's application; and, that he will take it very kind if Dunain will give him liberty to write to Mrs. Rose that upon his return to Inverness she will have a right to a seat along with Dunain's family … and I beg you will write me such a letter, as his Grace can send to Mrs. Rose, in order to make her easy, if possible, or at any rate, to shew her that he wished to get her accommodated if it could be done without inconvenience to Dunain, with whom he wishes to live in the habits of friendship, and whom he would not wish to disoblige upon any acc't.[20]

Nevertheless, John's labours, which included the purchase of Shiplands as an accommodation to the Alves and extensive plantings, to restore the estate of Dunain were bearing fruit. A listing of the rentals and tenants of the properties for 1793 indicated that sixty-one tenants were contracted to provide an annual income of £423 to John. Although the notations in the margin suggest that not all the tenants were able to meet their obligations in full, the estate revenues and the inheritance from William would have allowed John and his family to live comfortably.

While John was too entrenched in Scotland to consider returning to India, his "military ardour ... did not suffer him long to remain inactive."[21] In 1793, as the conflict with France escalated, Dunain received a commission as a major in the Duke of Gordon's North Fencibles. As a result, he bore responsibility for recruiting a company of men, a not inconsiderable task as evidenced by correspondence from the duke's secretary. "As if we had not enough to do already with the Marquis's Regiment, you see we have now got an order to add one Major, one Cap't., a dozen of Lieutenants and two Ensigns, and four hundred men to your Corps of Fencibles. How we are to find these men altogether, the Lord knows. In the meantime, however, the Duke has to recommend the officers and as he is busy today, he bids me write to you to enquire if you have any of your able friends about Inverness, that you would wish to serve along with you, and under your own eye as Subalterns."[22] The Duke of Gordon's description of ten of his new men – hailing from London – as "terrible creatures as ever were"[23] bears witness to the difficulty of attracting recruits of any worth.

Recruiting also involved competitive intrigue, as outlined in a short note from John's cousin, Archibald Campbell, in 1793. "The bearer Will Mcintosh, my plough driver and a fine boy, goes to enlist with you as a soldier, but you must get him attested immediately, to prevent Holm who has accepted a commission in the Grant Fencibles from getting the start of you, for he has been tampering with him already. I have a prospect of starting some more game for you under my roof, but as a great deal must depend on expedition and secrecy, the sooner you appear in person the better, a man being always the best hero in his own cause. I heard nothing of your having accepted a commission till yesterday."[24]

Major Baillie extended his recruiting activities to Skye. There his efforts were assisted by an old friend from his days in India, Keith Macalister, who, from Inverness, encouraged his brother to lend Dunain a hand.

> This will be delivered to you by a recruiting party belonging to my friend Major John Baillie, Esq'e of Dunain[,] who wishes to raise men for the Duke of Gordon's Regiment in Sky. I have therefore to request that whenever this party make themselves known, you will render them every service in your power upon your estate and when they have occasion to go to a different part of the Island, that you also recommend them to the countenance & protection of your friends.
>
> Major Baillie was considered by us all, during his stay in India, one of our most particular friends and intimately acquainted with all

– and was of essential service to your own concerns in India since your Brother's death, altho' you don't know the circumstances.

When you have occasion to visit the town of Inverness, I wish exceedingly you would wait upon Major Baillie, who lives about a gun shot from the bridge at Dunain, is a considerable proprietor in the country, and would give you more real information regarding your county business in an hour than all your writers would in a year, besides the pleasure of getting acquainted with a most amiable & respectable family.[25]

Dunain was successful in raising a company of fencibles to the extent that John Woodford, colonel of the Gordon Highlanders, notified him that "the regiment was compleat, as we have at the least seventy men above our establishment"[26] and accordingly had ordered an end to recruiting efforts. The North Fencibles were soon dispatched to England to await further orders: "All the lads belonging to your company are in perfect good health, and well-behaved boys ... encamped ... in a remote part of this country where there is nothing to be got but at double price which you may be sure our lads do not like."[27] There were the inevitable squabbles as to precedence in rank between the English militia and the North Fencibles, who believed themselves entitled to precedence on the grounds that they, as opposed to the militia, were part of the standing army. Nor did the men "look so well as they did in Scotland as they are all burnt with the heat, and has not got their new clothes as yet."[28]

As evidence mounted that Napoleon was fomenting rebellion in an Ireland that was becoming increasingly unruly, the administration in London determined to strengthen British forces there. The Duke of Gordon recommended to Henry Dundas, the dispenser of patronage in north Britain and popularly known as the uncrowned king of Scotland, that Dunain raise a new regiment of fencibles to serve in Ireland. As a result, Dunain in 1794 was appointed colonel of the Loyal Inverness Regiment of Fencible Infantry, comprised of six hundred men. In the interests of speed, the duke begrudgingly permitted Dunain to take any of the men he had previously enlisted for the North Fencibles, provided the same number was returned in six months.

I took the liberty of recommending at the same time you and Major Gordon to his attention as good officers. I congratulate you on your promotion and with all my heart wish you both much success in your undertaking ...

As you say your promotion now rests with me I shall certainly not object to your taking with you such of the men as you originally brought to the Regiment, as voluntarily wish to go, you becoming bound to return me an equal number in the course of six months. But I expect that neither you nor Major Gordon will propose any thing further, either with regard to men or officers. And I wish to have it understood by all concerned that I shall positively withhold my consent from every future attempt that may be made to reduce the strength of my Regiment, and should any officer be inclined to leave it I shall not allow him to take a single man along with him upon any account.[29]

John was fortunate to have the patronage of the Duke of Gordon but it was not without its costs. The Loyal Inverness Regiment of Fencible Infantry may theoretically have been John's to command but the duke took a proprietorial interest in its composition, repeatedly peppering John with gratuitous advice and making the same rash offers against which he often warned.

I wrote you yesterday of Cap't Irvine having closed with me for the Majority for 40 men I hope you have wrote to him by return of post confirming it as I have the greatest certainty of your future approbation of such an acquisition & connection in the Reg't. If I had not closed with him yesterday I had an other very advanta- geous one from Cap't. Ayton[,] a very good fellow with a good Fifeshire estate of 7 or 800 per an. who would have accepted & been a very good Major also ... To have been better appointed than with Cap't. Irvine I do not think could scarcely have happened but failing him I would have strongly recommended the other & as we are very old & intimate acquaintance he says if he does not agree with some others about a Majority or L't. Colonelcy, I might let him know of our augmentation (if we ever come to so happy a pass) & that he might in that case raise you men to come in Second Major, rather than not be doing some thing in these times & as you have made no promises of the 2nd Majority to any of the Capt's. whose regimental rank you have not even fixed yet & as the gentle- man is an old officer & army rank, I w'd think it a good plan to bring him in 2nd Major in that event taking place & thereby get the addition of 30 or 40 men he would bring in with him, which you would not get by the promotion of any of the Capt's., none of whom have reason to expect it either. I just mention this to prevent rash promises.[30]

The corps, comprised of 34 officers, 62 non-commissioned officers, 22 drummers, and 570 privates, was established on 19 September 1795 and embarked for Ireland on 1 November to fend off a much anticipated Napoleonic invasion at Bantry Bay. The regiment settled in at Laughliston Camp near Dublin and then left for Kilkenny. Dunain never returned; the "advanced season in the middle of winter could not fail to prove fatal to a constitution so shattered by hard services and wounds as Coll: Baillie's. It accordingly, brought on a violent return of the liver complaint of which he died."[31] Dunain died on 1 February 1797 and was buried in St Canice's Cathedral at Kilkenny, where a plaque commemorates him to this day, albeit with an incorrect date of death:

Sacred to the Memory of
John Baillie Esqr of Dunean
Colonel of the Regiment of Loyal Inverness Fencibles.
He Died in this City on his march to Oppose
The Invading Enemy.
On the 31 of January 1797
Aged 49

The vaunted French fleet of thirty-six ships did manage to elude the British navy and appeared off Bantry Bay carrying General Hoche's 15,000 troops and the Irish rebel leader Wolff Tone. But by the time Hoche's ship belatedly joined the fleet, the weather had turned and a fierce "Protestant wind" scattered the French force on 27 December 1796.

Ostensibly, Dunain left the family in comfortable circumstances. The annual rents of heritable subjects were £481 while the estate inventory, drawn up by John Alves, was valued at £4,199. Although the foregoing did not include the value of the properties, the trustees determined to sell Shiplands and Dochnacraig, which were not adjacent to the main estate, in order to liquidate all or part of Dunain's debts. Dunain had paid substantial bounties to entice his recruits and had incurred significant expenses in outfitting and maintaining his regiment, expenses that remained outstanding at the time of his death. Resolution of those obligations dragged on and indeed the estate was not settled until 1809, a delay that caused considerable loss to his heirs. Isabella was still seeking assistance twelve years after John's death. She petitioned Charles Grant, the MP for Inverness and chairman of the EIC, for financial support through the freeholders of Inverness but to little avail.[32] The Company response was simply: "As the services of Coll: John Baillie were from his low rank in the army of a much less conspicuous nature than those of his Brother, a very few words will suffice on this subject. On the arrival of Sir E. Coote from Bengal Mr. Baillie was a Cap't. on the Madras Establishment."[33] John's expenses relative to the Fencibles must have been enormous since, despite £5,000 proceeds from the sale of Shiplands, £4,000 from land expropriated for the Caledonian Canal, and William's fortune, the estate of Dunain found itself in straitened circumstances.

Of the three sons and two daughters of John and Isabella, only Katharine married. On 3 October 1805 she became the bride of Sir Hugh Rose of Kilravock, the MP for Nairnshire. They had nine children.

Ҩ

A postscript is now in order concerning William's daughter and John's niece, Ann. We have little record of Ann's years in Inverness until she married John Gibson, whom she may have met when he served as surgeon to her uncle's Loyal Inverness Fencibles. Following John of Dunain's death, his widow, Isabella, obviously retained an ongoing interest in her niece's welfare and, in that regard, conducted extensive correspondence aimed at preventing Ann's inheritance falling into the hands of John Gibson and his family. She asked her confidant, Colonel Donald McLeod of Achagoyle, to convince Ann that the £1,000 bequest of her father should remain in her name and be administered for her benefit rather than by the Gibsons. In April 1806 Isabella's son William, who had attended the universities of Aberdeen and Edinburgh before apprenticing to Kenneth Mackenzie, writer to the Signet in Edinburgh, reported to his mother on the outcome of the colonel's visit.

> Coll. McLeod is now left town. Two days before he left I called upon him, when he informed me that he had just received a letter regarding payment of Mrs. Gibson's £1000, which he gave me to peruse. In consequence of this letter he paid the Gibsons a visit & had a private conversation with Mrs. G. on the subject, but before he could get her to open her mind upon the subject he was interrupted by the Dr.'s entrance. In the course of this conversation he made no mention of your letter, but sported his sentiments on the subject entirely as flowing from himself & not as suggested by any other person. The Coll. seems to think that the Dr. sh'd not have the management of the

money. That if put into the stocks which they seem to wish it should, it ought to be done in Mrs. Gibson's name alone. If these conditions are not agreed to, the Coll. thinks the principal should still be retained and the yearly interest alone paid to the Gibsons as it fell due.[34]

The next day, McLeod elaborated on his conversation with the Gibsons. His views had been largely summarized by William but he did emphasize his impression that Gibson was "quite bent on getting possession of the money – and that he is somewhat suspicious that I would be averse to that design on account of my regard to the true interest of Mrs. G. – yet it struck me that he was unable completely to disguise such feelings." McLeod then suggested that the £1,000 could not be placed at the disposal of either husband or wife, since Isabella had written that the marriage settlement provided a life rent only, with any residual to accrue to their children or, failing heirs, to Mrs Gibson alone. McLeod tactfully closed with a compliment to William: "When I tell you that these are William's sentiments and mine on the subject, I allow a just weight to his opinion, young lawyer as he is – for I am happy to assure you that he thinks soundly and solidly."[35]

It is not clear what transpired but Gibson continued for some time to draw interest on Ann's bond from Provost Thomas Gilzean, who managed the Dunain family's affairs. In a letter to Isabella in May 1806, Gibson alerted her of his intention to draw on the funds. He also offered a few comments on political affairs of the day. The "Doctor" to whom he refers was not a medical practitioner but Henry Addington, the son of a prominent society doctor. In 1801 George III, exercised by Pitt's espousal of Catholic emancipation, had prevailed upon Addington to replace Pitt as prime minister. However, several ministers, sympathetic to Pitt's Catholic policy, refused to serve under Addington. By 1804, Charles Montagu-Scott, Lord Dalkeith, and other members of Addington's party had turned against the unpopular prime minister and driven him from office. Gibson was prescient in his supposition that William Pitt would recover the prime ministership.

Lord Dalkeith & a number of other Scots members set off for London some time ago, with a wish I believe to turn out the Doctor, in which they have succeeded, of course I suppose Mr. Pitt will resume his former situation as Premier. He is certainly a very able man. I trust he will be directed to pursue such measures as will be most conducive to the interest of the Nation. It is well known that he and Buonaparte are sworn enemies ... Whereas you mention you

wish I had inform'd you sooner about matters, lest Whitsunday
should inconvenience the family, a month or two thereafter will
make no difference to me, so that any time between then, if possible
I shall forbear drawing on Mr. Gulzean for the interest of Mrs. G's.
bond, the amount of the bill which had so nearly caused a schism
between Mr. Gulzean and me.[36]

The following month, after examining the trust in some detail,
William reported to his mother. "As to the Gibson's money I suspect
that from the terms in which the deed is executed that it must be paid if
they wish it, this is likewise Mr. Mackenzie's opinion on the subject.
Indeed, upon reading the deed I think there would be no good reason
for this want of trust as it is the Dr's Father not himself who is trustee
for the fund in which case the old man could not without the most flagrant breach of trust appropriate it to his own or his family's use. And
altho' we know him to be a poor man we have every reason to suppose
him an honest man."[37]

Whatever happened to Ann's funds, Gibson did not leave her destitute.
In 1807 they immigrated to India, where, despite the dismal prospects for
assistant surgeons, John Gibson secured an appointment at Rungpore.
He let Isabella know that he had applied to join the Bengal Military Fund
for Widows, which, in the event of his death, would provide Ann with
£250 per annum in Britain or 300 rupees per month in India.

The Gibsons seemed to cope well in India and to have been accepted in
elite social circles. In a letter of 1808, Ann wrote:

Altho' we are going to Rungpore at present; Lord Minto has
promis'd the Doctor the first vacant situation in Calcutta that he
can, with any propriety, give him if he shou'd prefer it to Rungpore
... We have every prospect of being comfortable at Rungpore.
Dr. Todd who has just left that situation says it is by far the best climate in India and a very pleasant society during the cold weather.
They constantly find the winter here is from October to March,
during which time you see all the ladies dressed in fur ... and muffs.
We have met with great attention from several families here – but
there is no friendship in society in their style of visiting here. You
are oblig'd to make all your calls before 12 o'clock in this country
for after that hour it is not thought genteel. You are always ask'd to
commence parties to dinner which very seldom is got before eight
o'clock at the earliest and you generally separate before eleven.

You have very little of each other's company ... They give immense
dinners here. The tables absolutely groan under their load; the
fruits and vegetables are just coming in season, but they are nothing
equal to our European ones, in short I think there is nothing so
good here as at home.[38]

Gibson foresaw a meaningful commercial opportunity in indigo owing
to the increasing demand for blue dye in Europe. In 1809 he invested
10,000 rupees for a 50 per cent interest in a plantation four hundred
miles from Lucknow. By 1811, he could report: "I am at present very
busy dispatching to Calcutta my indigo & making up acc'ts. This year
has turned out as bad as last & according to custom, I must look forward
to another one next. We have now had three bad years."[39] After those
disappointing indigo crops, their spirits rose as Gibson began to prosper,
earning £900 per annum by 1812. However, as economical as the Gibsons
claimed to be, they could save virtually nothing. As Ann wrote in February
1812, mentioning in passing John Baillie, a nephew of William and John
who was then serving as the British resident at Lucknow:

The Resident wishes us very much to go to Lucknow in the cold
weather, but it is not easy to get leave of absence for 4 months, from
the distance being so great. It will take us a month going & an other
returning; Gibson was oblig'd to send his indigo home last year,
which is a very great draw back to his making a fortune quickly.
What he sent home in 1809 is not yet all sold. The crops this year
promise at present well, & if we cou'd only get it sold at Calcutta it
wou'd be a great ease & blessing to his mind. His present salary
from Government is 9 hundred pounds a year, & altho' it keeps us
very comfortably we cannot save any thing out of it, & yet we are
great economists. We do not have a single serv't that we can do without, & yet our servants' wages are £200 a year. John is at present at
one of his factories, this is his busy season of the year.[40]

In 1816 they moved to Lucknow so that Gibson could take up an
appointment as surgeon to the nawab of Oude, Ghazi-ood-din-Haider, at
an exceptionally attractive salary of 2,500 rupees per month. Their idyll
ended a decade later when, immediately following a breakfast at the residency, John contracted cholera. He died almost immediately and Ann
succumbed to the same disease the next day, on 8 August 1826. Ann died
intestate. The first inkling the relatives in Britain had of the Gibsons'

demise was a letter from the former resident's son, Ben, who had been in India since 1823. Margaret Baillie wrote:

We have this morning received a confirmation of the Gibson's melancholy fate. The much lamented news was communicated to us in a letter from Benjamin dated the 20th of Sept'r. He does not mention the day of their death but says Dr. Gibson was seized immediately after a public breakfast given by the Resident at Lucknow with violent pains in the bowels which speedily terminated in his disposition. Mrs. Gibson only survived him one day ... that fatal complaint cholera. Will you have the goodness to mention this sad termination & our uncertainty respecting these valuable friends to our cousin Lady Arbuthnot ... There are some particulars respecting the settlement of Gibson's funds which John will at more leisure communicate to you.[41]

John shed further, if far from complete, light on the Gibsons' fate. "We are all in this house destroyed beyond measure by the mournful intelligence of the death of both the Gibson's at Lucknow in August last of cholera. The melancholy event has been announced by private letter from Calcutta dated in September but I have no direct account of their illness and as my brother & son were both in Calcutta in September their total silence on the subject excites surprise tho' it does not encourage the hope that our worthy relations survive."[42]

Margaret reported in February 1825 that "Ben announced his receipt of the papers regarding Mrs. Gibson's estate but I suspect the other party will give all possible trouble."[43] We are left to speculate whether Margaret's troublesome "other party" is Gibson's family or the state, since, owing to Ann's illegitimacy, the government automatically fell heir to her assets. Her relatives, in turn, felt entitled to them. Accordingly, in late 1825 or early 1826, Ann's cousins posed the following questions to the eminent barrister Sir Samuel Sheperd ("cousin german" is another term for "first cousin"):

A was born in India an illegitimate child and sent to this Country to be educated where she married B and returned with him to Bengal where they resided for upwards of twenty years the last ten of which at Lucknow the court of a native Prince where B died leaving his wife A two thirds of his property soon after which A herself died at Lucknow without making any settlement. Query? Does A fortune fall to the Crown or does it go amongst her nearest relations.

Query 2. If A fortune should go to her nearest relations who are ten cousin germans would the children of another cousin german who has been sometime dead be entitled to their mother's share.

Query 3. Should A fortune fall to the Crown does it become the perquisite of persons in the public offices or does it go direct to the Crown and what share is generally allowed to the Relations or to whom should a petition be addressed.

Sheperd concluded that, since she was an Englishwoman, Ann's property would be distributed according to English law; and that, since she was illegitimate and childless, her property would revert to the crown. The crown, after taking the usual deductions, would distribute the remainder to those who would have been the deceased's next of kin except for the illegitimacy. The surviving cousins would share it equally among them, with no provision for the progeny of deceased cousins.[44]

One of the beneficiaries, Anne, the youngest daughter of John and Isabella, recorded the outcome of the attempts to secure Ann Gibson's fortune. Her sister Katharine Baillie Rose of Kilravock had predeceased Ann Gibson and, accordingly, her heirs were not eligible for any share of the estate. At the same time, Anne included a muddled account of her uncle's death given that the "Black Hole at Calcutta" was a notorious incident which took place twenty-four years before William's imprisonment in a city far removed from Calcutta.

Miss B has likewise been told that the money succeeded to us by the death of Mrs. Ann Gibson, a Cousin & D of her uncle Colonel W'm Baillie, an older Brother of her Father's who was taken prisoner when head of a division of the army at the time of the uprising and imprisoned in the Black Hole at Calcutta. A high ransom was offered by the British government but was not accepted of and then it was supposed he was poisoned. Mrs. Gibson his Daughter was illegitimate, and the Crown being heir to all she possessed I think 20,000. This the Crown retained and then the rest was divided amongst the ten cousins german, as next of kin, 5 of the Baillies, 3 of the Alves, my Brother and I, my Nieces and Nephews, their Mother being dead, they did not come in.[45]

Anne's cousin John provided a more coherent account. "I have altogether the pleasure of informing you that I have obtained the King's Warrant for distributing poor Mrs. Gibson's property and that your share of it in my hands at your command is the sum of £1,149-9 & somewhat less than a penny which latter I mean to keep to myself as my pay for my trouble ... My sister wrote to your mother some time ago regarding William's share of the money & I wait for her answer with impatience, as I fear the state of her health may have prevented her considering the subject."[46]

After considerable effort and time, and once the Exchequer had siphoned off its share, Ann Gibson's ten Scottish cousins prevailed and shared equally the remaining proceeds of her estate. The beneficiaries were the five offspring of Ann and George Baillie – Colonel Alexander, Colonel John, Margaret, Catharine, and Ann Munro; the three progeny of Helen and John Alves – William, Helen Inglis, and Ann Arbuthnot; and the two surviving children of John of Dunain – William and Anne.

Brain Fever in Baghdad

If we could see ourselves as others see us, we would never speak
to them again.

Anonymous

Of John and Isabella's three sons, Alexander died in childhood. The other
two boys, Archibald and William, had lives that were short, in the case of
Archibald, and tragic, in the case of William.

Following John's death, Isabella campaigned for an appointment in
India – preferably an EIC writership – for her second son, Archy. A close
friend of her late husband, Donald Macleod of Achagoyle, advised her
to approach Charles Grant, the local member of Parliament and chairman of the East India Company. Grant had influence and was adept at
exercising it on behalf of untold numbers of young men in the county.
Macleod wrote:

I presume indeed that it most naturally becomes you to apply personally to Coll: Grant, and to every individual within your reach
who has interest with Mr. Charles Grant. The appointment of a
writer in the East I'a Company's service is considered a very weighty
favour and for which underhand 4 & sometimes £5000 are paid. I
think you ought to address Mr. Charles Grant yourself and consider
whether it would not be proper that you enclosed your letter to
Mr. Ar'd Alves, who, as one of the guardians could wait on
Mr. Grant with it, and represent to him the state of the family and
its claims to the favourable attention of the Hon'ble Company.
The sooner all applications on the subject are made the better and
I hope you will get the gentlemen who promise their aid, to write to
Mr. Grant by a certain time. No more occurs to me on the subject at

present. My application will be among the first which Mr. Grant
will receive on Archy's account.[1]

Grant responded to Isabella's solicitations. "I have comparatively few
of those [civil] appointments to give & many applications – applications
too from persons I much respect & of great weight in the country. To
more than one of that description I have lately been oblig'd to send a
refusal. You will judge how much I must be embarrass'd when more are
to be serv'd than the means of service will allow ... The public merits of
your late husband & brother in law however known & acknowledg'd
will not produce the particular object you have in view, because the
patronage of appointments into the Company's service is the private
right of the Directors & they will of course prefer their own connections."[2] He did dangle the prospect of a military appointment for Archy,
but Isabella persisted in seeking a writership. She enlisted a number of
local dignitaries and secured a petition from the county on Archy's behalf.
Her opinionated niece, Margaret, expressed herself in no uncertain terms
as to Grant's shabby conduct despite her belief that Archy was a less than
diligent young man, particularly in comparison to Donald McLeod's son.
In all likelihood, she was accurate in her assessment of Archy, for, notwithstanding his education at King's College, Aberdeen, and Hertford
College, the preparatory school for the East India Company, Archy was
proving an irresponsible lad. On his academic pursuits, the report given
by his cousin Archibald Alves was lukewarm at best: "If I may judge from
the places he tells me he held at the examination, he is at least not below
par."[3] Margaret wrote:

As Colonel McLeod & William succeeded in procuring an application from the county, Mr. Grant can now surely have no further pretence for delaying Archie's appointment, indeed our worthy member
has in my opinion behaved extremely shabbily on this occasion ...
I trust poor Archie will yet do very well in Bengal, though not quite
so steady a young man as John McLeod. But I sometimes see those
wonderful boys turn out only neighbor like [mediocre] men, while
those who were not so promising at first astonish us a little in after
life. William is too fond of the society at Kilravock to give us much
of his company, however as he is getting a plan of Dunain made out,
business will sometimes force him to favour us with a visit, & a sight
of him always affords me pleasure, he surely is the most contented
mortal I ever saw for if we have only an egg for dinner, he seems

pleased & in good humour ... No news & indeed I am not in spirits
to narrate any if there were, being in dreadful anxiety about the merchant fleet, & the letter I received from Bengal was chiefly George's
not above half a page from John, to be sure there is the comfort of
knowing he was well in Sept'r, but I think he appears less anxious
about coming home than in former letters, which worries me not a
little, but in short I'm a discontented being & therefore justly punished in always having something to complain of.[4]

As Isabella pursued a writership for Archy, it became increasingly evident that he was deficient on a number of counts. William, very much the
elder brother, chided Archy to apply himself more diligently. His letter
reveals the stringency of the prevailing educational standards:

I am happy to hear that you are making some progress in your
classical pursuits. Of the difficulty of acquiring this species of learning you must be fully convinced; many years of the most ductile
period of our lives are employed in such attainments, surely then
the folly of suffering them to be so far forgotten as to render the
pitiful remains of no manner of use, and that too at the very period
of life when they are about to become of the most essential importance, is most unpardonable.
    In the profession which you have a prospect of entering upon, it is
as impossible to be in any manner successful without an acquaintance with the Oriental languages, as it would be to make a figure in
this country without speaking English, and to think of this without
first attaining a thorough mastery of Greek and Latin is quite absurd.
These are the roots of all foreign languages, and to attempt to proceed without a complete knowledge of them is a mere waste of time,
and must in the end prove abortive. In short to expect to make a
fortune without first qualifying yourself for your profession is vain.
Without application and exertion many years of your life may be
wasted without making a step towards independence, and with these
the way lies open to the rapid attainment of it. Surely with such an
alternative before you, you cannot hesitate![5]

Archy, apparently undismayed and unmoved by this reproach from his
brother, euphorically wrote his mother: "I am happy to inform you that
I have passed the examinations at the India House with flying colours[;]
it was very simple they examined my writing and asked me several

questions: 'where I had studied' and 'what proficiency I had made in my studies.' I was also asked to produce a certificate from the persons under whom I studied stating the nature of the education which I have received and the proficiency I have made and certifying as to my mental ability and my disposition and character."[6] Colonel Macleod appended a more jaundiced but realistic assessment of the "trifler's" prospects:

It is with great satisfaction I corroborate what Archy writes above respecting the examination before the Court of Directors. I did not however think it so simple a trial as he says. But we had real friends in Court. The worthy chairman has moreover, done every thing possible to have Archy appointed to Bengal, but he found it impracticable. I hope that by God's blessing we shall get through the more formidable examination by the professors on this day 8 days. I shall not conceal from you that I apprehend Archy has been strangely indulged in making light of every task proposed to him so that his mind is as yet incapable of serious application. If this unfortunate habit is not surmounted he will continue a trifler.[7]

The general view of Archy was anything but sanguine. Nevertheless, he passed muster in the examination by the professors but then jeopardized his writership by participating in a riot at Hertford College, following which all students were sent home. Archy assured his mother that none would lose his place but again his judgment was suspect. After examining Archy, Charles Grant informed him that he had acted poorly and that as a result his appointment could not be guaranteed. Yet Archy's optimism was proven well founded in the end, since he was allowed to return to Hertford and was assured that he would indeed receive a writership. William wrote expressing his satisfaction that Archy was enjoying Hertford, providing local gossip, and commenting on the novelty of the theatre in Inverness though he could not "say much in favour of the performers" and reported that "Mr. Rose's clarinet and mine have been dumb for several months now for want of a change of music and are likely to continue so."[8]

However, some event, presumably health-related, intervened to cause Archy to relinquish his appointment. Archy's cousin and one of his guardians, Archibald Alves, wrote:

In point of understanding and education I think him sufficiently calculated for the situation destined for him. He is more disqualified for it from bodily than mental causes, and I own to you in his present feeble state I think him unfit for any situation where the smallest exertion would be necessary. He is so weak that a walk of a mile tires him. From his appearance I thought it might have proceeded from some paralitic affliction, but from what I can gather from himself it is mere debility. It is to be hoped therefore, that when he has done growing his constitution may undergo a change and acquire strength to throw it off, which I heartily pray may be the case. Whether a warm climate is suited to him or not I cannot say, you no doubt have had medical opinions on the subject.[9]

William's observations to his mother seemed to corroborate Alves's explanation. "I think your plan of getting Mr. MacQueen to pass the summer with Archy is a very good one. I have not consulted Dr. Baillie but I think there may be some satisfaction in doing so, altho' I really believe little aid can be expected from medicine in Archy's complicated case."[10] Dr Matthew Baillie, although not a close relative, was a distinguished professor of anatomy, the author of the first systematic textbook of pathology, and physician to George III. By 1810, Archy appears to have joined a bank in or near London. He died six years later, in 1816.

❈

Archy's brother William had initially resolved on a legal career, but, to the consternation of his mother and Donald Macleod, he soon decided to abandon the law and enter the army. Macleod observed: "There is no prospect either at home or abroad of seeing to a reputable and advantageous rank – but by the special influence of great men – or by the advances of large sums of money."[11] Large sums of money were beyond consideration; an income statement for Dunain as of 3 September 1807 indicated that expenditures exceeded revenues by £10 per annum and debt obligations amounted to £4,300.[12] Indeed, the estate was obviously in jeopardy, for it had been scheduled for judicial sale at a recent Court of Session and only the sale of the Shiplands property and a windfall from the Caledonian Canal's appropriation of a portion of the Dunain estate, together with the exertions of Colonel Macleod and Archibald Alves, had held the creditors at bay.

There was, however, more than meets the eye to William's decision to renounce the law, for his mother and Macleod were soon engrossed in correspondence concerning the young man's "unfortunate attachment"

to an Inglis girl, an attachment that supposedly imperilled the estate. It is
not clear why marriage to the young Inglis woman would trigger the sale
of Dunain unless creditors had been patient in the hope that William's
future wife would bring a substantial dowry to settle the debts. In any
event, Donald Macleod did not portray the Inglis girl's mother in the
most attractive of lights:

> You seem to despair of William's being weaned from what I cannot
> help considering a most unfortunate attachment – never despair –
> who knows what change two years may bring about in his mind.
> I doubt if you have made a return to Mrs. Inglis' letter – but
> Mr. Arbuthnot as well as myself thinks you ought. You have the fair-
> est ground and the most urgent cause for declaring your feelings to
> that lady on the misfortune with which your son is threatened by
> the intimacy to which he was encouraged in her family. Mrs. Inglis'
> letter, I think, clearly betrays an artful and assuming address, and a
> shallow understanding destitute of the least tinge of good principles.
> A person of little experience in the world must be sensible how very
> readily a youth in W'm's situation may be led to indulge an attach-
> ment of this nature, however obvious it may be to an unbyassed
> observer, that in the event, it will deprive him of a landed property
> which rendered his forefathers respectable for centuries back.
> Probably Mrs. I. does not imagine that the state of the Dunain family
> affairs is such, that as soon as the young couple can accomplish their
> delusive projects, the estate must be sold. She writes you that "when
> your son avowed to her his partiality for her daughter," that she
> asked him "if his mother knew of the matter, he replied that she did,
> but that she strongly objected chiefly on account of his youth." She,
> however, "considers herself excused from every imputation of clan-
> destinely encouraging the connection" because "on her asking him if
> his mother knew of his continuing his visits, he said, she did nor did
> he mean to conceal them." Now, in my humble opinion, this, which
> Mrs. Inglis affects to consider a sufficient apology for the counte-
> nance which she clandestinely gave to the growing passions of the
> young people, should, if she were under the influence of just feelings,
> have determined her on an early communication with the other
> widowed mother on the subject most interesting to both. The youth
> told her that his mother strongly objected. Yet it is evident, nor does
> Mrs. I. attempt to gloss the affair[,] that her conduct continued to
> encourage the son to disregard his mother's strong objections and to

indulge his imprudent partiality for her daughter. It may be referred to Mrs. I.'s prudence and tender regard for her daughter whether or not the intended connection bears any rational prospect of permanent happiness.[13]

The reverberations of William's "imprudent partiality" extended to Bengal. Once Ann Gibson learned she had been implicated in the affair, she immediately wrote to Isabella seeking to absolve herself and her husband of any culpability:

Altho' I wrote to you only a few weeks ago I can not resist from writing again, from having heard that a report had been circulated (to our great surprise) that Gibson & I, were not only acquaint'd with William's attachment, but had been the chief promoters of it. Be assured my dear Mrs. B if I had had, the least suspicion or idea of it, I shou'd have immediately inform'd you for altho' I have a great regard for the Inglis family, & wou'd think any man lucky in getting ... Inglis, I never cou'd have approved of William's forming a connection at so early a period of life & with his estate in debt. Gibson & I feel very much hurt, at you & Margaret having given credit to it, as I was in hopes both of you were convinced of our sincere attachment to my ever dear Uncle's family to suspect us, of undermining any of your wishes, & I am sure my dear William & the Inglis's will have candour enough to clear us of such an infamous fabrication. No doubt William saw them first at our house, as they were my intimate friends long before he came to Edin, but it was not to follow, that he was to fall in love with them & I am sure that while we were in Edin no such attachment existed, or else W and she had more cunning than most young people at their age, for he never paid them the least attention before us, or did we ever hear he did at any other place. The girls & Mrs. Inglis have always correspond'd with Gibson & me since coming to this country & except in one letter, they never mention'd his name, & then Helen Inglis merely said, they had, had, a very pleasant walk a few days before she wrote me ... I cannot conceive what malicious person cou'd have told Miss Baillie (I wish you wou'd tell me who it was) as it cou'd have been done, with no other vein, but to separate families which they envied having been so long firmly attached in affection & friendship & particularly when we were at too great a distance to vindicate ourselves. However, I trust these malicious intentions will not succeed in

making any difference between us as I have always felt a special
affection for you & a sisterly one for all your family. Gibson means
to write you on the subject as he really feels very much hurt.[14]

Isabella succeeded in sundering the young people's nuptial plans, an
achievement she might later have had grounds to regret.

Following this mini-tempest, Isabella and William undertook an active
campaign to secure the writership that had been intended for Archy.
William expressed a sense of urgency when writing to Charles Grant in
1810: "I am within two months of the age after which young men are
excluded from the enjoyment of a civil appointment in the East India
Company service."[15] Shortly thereafter, he managed to secure an inter-
view with Grant and surmised from the conversation that the transfer
would be accomplished. Grant advised him to send a letter stating his
case and to attend India House for the Court of Directors meeting on
28 December, at which time he would receive a decision regarding his
petition. Grant had earlier suggested that William would be required to
sit for an examination by the Hertford professors, but since the school
had recessed until February, that obstacle had been eliminated – or so it
seemed. Word soon came down that William was required to take an
examination with Dr Henley, the only professor currently at Hertford. "I
have understood from Mr. Grant this morning," William wrote his
mother, "that the transfer of Archy's writership to me is at length procured tho' the strictness of their rules is such that an examination will still
be necessary. From some hints thrown out by Mr. Grant however I have
reason to think it may be got through. The examination is to take place
at the Hertford College. The professors there are all absent at present
except Dr. Henley who is therefore to be my sole examinator."[16] In due
course, Margaret confirmed to Isabella that William had, in fact, secured
the writership. "William wrote you on Thursday that he had got his
appointment & I have now the pleasure to say that his examination is
actually over. He read a chapter in the Greek Testament & several passages in Sallust to the entire satisfaction of Dr. Henley. There are still
some certificates required of William's attendance at the Colleges of
Edin'g & Aberdeen, which he has already written for."[17]

Macleod congratulated Isabella on William's success and pointed out
that since each director prized the ability to bestow a writership, the record of her late brother-in-law and husband, worthy though it may have
been, accounted for little and that in fact Charles Grant, although much
maligned by Margaret, had played a critical role. He also stressed that,

once in India, William should introduce himself to Sir James Mackintosh, who was then serving as chief judge in Bombay and would eventually be appointed commissioner of Indian affairs.

I suppose it is ten or 12 days since you heard of William's complete success ... In this business, from first to last, we are solely obliged to the exertions of Mr. Charles Grant[,] more so indeed than I imagined some time ago for I was led to adopt the idea that the Court of Directors, in consideration of the merits and misfortunes of Coll's W'm & J Baillie had given the writership to Archy but that could not be done without depriving an individual director of his right. Therefore that appointment was the gift of Mr. Grant solely and Wm's being preferred to Archd's appointment is also owing to his strenuous exertions. From this brief statement you will perceive how much your family owes to Mr. Grant.

Yesterday I had a second letter from W'm. He has determined by Mr. Grant's advice to proceed for Bombay about the end of next month. To be properly prepared for the voyage will require all his diligence. The passage money and fitting out will cost between £250 & £300 ...

He goes for Madras by one of the April fleet. I hope you'll be able to procure such a letter for Sir James Macintosh as will essentially engage his exertions in favour of W'm. Sir James has great influence and if W'm has but an opportunity, he will recommend himself.[18]

William began preparing for the passage. "There are ships to sail for Bombay about the end of February and as any further delay can answer no purpose, I should think it best to embrace that opportunity if possible ... In case I should sail so soon it will be necessary to lose no time in sending up cotton shirts or any thing else that may be useful. I shall also wish to have all my music sent to me of which I have endeavoured to give a list on the other side ... Indeed, altho' you have some reason to complain of me for carrying on my correspondence so much by proxy I was for a while in London that I was constantly writing letters or trotting to the India House."[19]

As his departure for India drew near, William reported that his writership would be in Bombay and that he should know shortly the details of his passage. "I cannot sail by the ships in which I originally thought of going as the luggage and passengers were ordered on board above ten days ago which is somewhat earlier than was expected. I am now therefore in the act of settling my passage on board the Scaleby Castle[,] a large ship recommended to me by Mr. C. Grant. It is to sail about the beginning of next month but as soon as every thing here is cut and dry which I think must be in a few days or a week I shall let you know."[20] In the interim, William was serving as a lieutenant in the 92nd Regiment in Canterbury and visited his Dochfour relative, Peter Baillie, who was a West Indian merchant, a partner in Bristol Old Bank, and member of Parliament for Bristol. "The old gentleman" undertook to exert his utmost effort to secure William a promotion.

Then, in May 1811, William set sail on the *Dorsetshire* with fourteen ships of the fleet. By September, he had landed in Bombay. John Gibson reported on the arrival and William's plans, commiserated with Isabella on Archy's maladies, and risked opening the obviously still festering sore of William's "unfortunate attachment."

We sincerely hope that his native air will reinstate Archy to his health ... William has arrived at Bombay & a letter from John Baillie this day tells us that he has most strongly recommended to him to come round to Calcutta to study the eastern languages & I have no doubt but he will arrive there soon. Most sincerely do we wish that he had been appointed [to Bengal] ... And we might have met or perhaps fortune might have stationed us at same place. I sh'd think that with so many votes in your families you might contrive to have his appointment changed but of this he himself should discuss with you. How I long to see him but know not when that may be. I do not think the Resident [John] will ever forget Inv. & the worthy folks there. He really has so princely a situation that few men would wish to leave it ... I think I may be pretty sure that if you were acquainted with Mrs. Inglis, your opinion of her would be more favourable. I cannot allow myself to believe that it is your own opinion, but that someone has been endeavouring to prejudice you, & the young ladies are really amiable.[21]

In a letter to his mother, William made clear that he had secured the introduction to Sir James Mackintosh that Macleod had ardently recommended. His "plans for future aggrandizement," including a relocation to Baghdad, bore the influence of Sir James. The reference to David Inglis, presumably a brother of his former intended, may, consciously or unconsciously, have been calculated to goad Isabella.

We are arrived here safe on the 6th of last month after a most favourable passage ... I was a good deal disappointed as you may suppose to find on my arrival here that Governor Duncan to whom I carried a letter of recommendation from Mr. C. Grant had died about three weeks previous to that time. It also added to my disappointment to find that David Inglis had gone round to Madras to find a passage from there to Europe, there being no opportunity, then, of getting to England from this quarter. I am not you know very apt to give way to disappointments, and on this occasion they were so much alleviated, by the attention and kindness I met with, from other quarters, to make me entirely forget them. I had been but two or three days on this island, when Sir James Mackintosh asked me to take up my residence with him, and ever since I have met with the utmost attention & friendly support from him. From the present acting governor Mr. Brown, and from General Abercromby I have also received some attention. The civility I have received from the former I attribute to Mr. Grant's letter to his predecessor the late Mr. Duncan, with the contents of which letter he has I believe become acquainted. The letter was referenced by a Mr. Chas. Forbes one of Mr. Duncan's executors, who remarked to me on having read it that "he feared the death of Mr. Duncan might be a great loss to me." This will not I hope be the case and I merely mention the circumstances to show you that Charles Grant concluded his favours to me in a handsome way.

Before going any further I must introduce you to Mr. James Calder son of the minister of Ferintosh with whom you are likely to drink tea pretty frequently in the course of our epistolary intercourse as he has undertaken to manage my matters in this part of the world, no very difficult task as you may imagine at present. Calder has maintained the utmost respectability of character in this quarter. Sir James Mackintosh thinks very favourably indeed of him. Having now introduced you to all my acquaintances in this quarter, of whom you are likely to hear in future, I must now proceed to give you some account of my professional views.

In a few days after my arrival here I was (as is usual) appointed a junior assistant to the Chief Secretary, Mr. Warden[,] with the customary salary of 250 rupees per month. The nominal value of a Bombay rupee is half a crown, its real value little better than two shillings, so that my income here is about £300 per annum. The value of money however is so very low here that it would be

impossible for any young man to live on this sum were it not that they
are usually accommodated for some time after their arrival here at the
houses of their friends. One or two plans for future aggrandizement
have suggested themselves since my arrival here on each of which Sir J.
Mackintosh has given me his advice. The first that occurred was to go
round to Calcutta to attend the College there, at which if I made any
figure I might hope to be appointed to the diplomatic line of the service, that is, assistant at one of the Residencys there which is no doubt
the highest line in India. While this plan was in agitation I wrote to my
cousin at Lucknow begging his advice, to which letter there has not
yet been time for an answer. His interest would no doubt have been
of the utmost use in this case. The plan however has been altogether
abandoned for another, by the particular advice of Sir James, which
seems somewhat more certain. It is to go up to Baghdad to study the
Arabic and Persian languages with a view to the ultimate succession
to the Residency there, and in order to give you some idea of my
prospect of success in these views I shall endeavour to make you
acquainted with the present state of things in that quarter. Mr. Rich,
son-in-law to Sir James Mackintosh[,] is now Resident at Bagdad; his
assistants are Dr. Colquhoun and Hyne both ass't surgeons on this
establishment; now Sir James is of opinion that, if Rich and I hit it,
of which he thinks there is every probability, an application from him
(Mr. R) to government beging to have me appointed his 3rd assistant
at Baghdad would be listened to, their point being once accomplished
there would be very little doubt of my succeeding to the Residence,
since, on any thing like equal terms a civil servant must be preferred to
a medical man. Indeed the Assistants at Baghdad hold their present
positions merely by sufferance as their doing so is expressly contrary
to the regulations of the Court of Directors. In order to carry this plan
into effect I have taken a passage on the Hon. Co's. ship The Tarnate,
for the Persian Gulph, which is to sail in a few days.

These are the plans which Sir James has kindly chalked out for
me and had he remained here there would not have been a doubt of
their realization. The same ship however which conveys this account
to you, bears him to his native shores. In him I lose a friend on
whom my hopes of success in this quarter would have firmly rested,
a loss wh. he has done every thing in his power to lessen by asking
me to write to him and assuring me of his exertions at home towards
the furtherance of my views ... The Tarnate sails on the 7th of next
month ... Mackintosh quite well.[22]

Ann Gibson supposed William to be in fine fettle.

> I wrote to William on his arrival at Bombay, but the lazy fellow, has
> not answer'd my letter yet. But I have heard he is quite well, & is
> appoint'd assistant to Mr. Birt [Rich] at Baghdad, who is the English
> Resident there. He is son in law to Sir James Mackintosh, who is
> lately gone home from Bombay with a very large fortune & has
> promis'd to use his interest at home in William's favour. Sir James
> cou'd very easily get Willy put on the Bengal Establishment (I mean
> exchang'd) – as it is done very frequently both by the Madras &
> Bombay servants & I assure you it wou'd make us very happy to
> have him so near us ... John & George Baillie are quite well thank
> God. They have made a very narrow escape with their lives from the
> carelessness of the servants not having their copper pans tinn'd prop-
> erly. John B. was only ill a few hours but poor George was confined
> to his bed & reduced to a compleate sckeleton but he is now poor
> fellow got quite well again. I hear frequently from them both.[23]

In little more than a year, however, John and George's illnesses paled by
comparison. By September, Isabella was aware that William had returned
to Bombay but had no idea why. And, despite William's observation that
managing his affairs in India would be "no very difficult task," a distraught James Calder was finding the responsibility singularly unenviable. In October 1813 Calder penned a note, presumably to his agent in
London, that William had suffered extreme mental disorder which neces-
sitated sending him home as soon as possible. "Your friend William
Baillie is now in the most deplorable of all situations suffering under a
disordered mind and he must go home by the first opportunity ... He has
been with me mostly ever since the appearance of the disorder & is since
become greatly deranged indeed. It has been a source of much distress to
me. I have yet written to no one in Europe on the subject, so keep this to
yourself for the present."[24] Yet, in his flustered state, Calder did not mail
the notification at the time; there is an addendum dated 22 December
informing the recipient that the letter would be delivered by one McLeod
of the Mills "to whose kind care I have committed our poor friend Wm
Baillie of whose deplorable fate [you] will probably be apprised before
this reach." Calder wrote that William

> leaves B[ombay] in a state of total mental derangement but may, I
> trust, regain health of mind to a considerable degree at least, during

the voyage. I am at a loss to whom to write or to whom to consign him in London, except yourself & I am sure you will gladly take charge of him & provide for him in his helpless pitiable condition. He talks of Mr. Alves as his chief friend in London.

I am writing particularly about his case to Sir James Mackintosh who is interested about him. There is an European servant named Morgan Richard, now attached to his person, who will attend him as long as you wish.[25]

Archibald Alves learned of his cousin William's arrival in London and reported to Isabella with what proved to be an overly optimistic assessment:

For three months William had had repeated attacks of fever attended sometimes with delirium which had reduced him so much that it was judged necessary to send him immediately to Europe as the only chance of saving his life ... The voyage I am happy to say has had the best effects and he now appears to have no other complaint than weakness, and a considerable dejection of spirits the natural consequence of debility. I have no doubt however that his native air will soon restore him to health. I wished him to consult Dr. Baillie, but he does not himself consider it necessary & seemed to have a repugnance to it. I did not therefore argue it. He is very desirous to go north ... I sympathize most sincerely with you my dear Madam in what you must feel on this distressing occasion. Let us however be thankful that his life has been spared – as to the rest, I trust the consequences will not be so injurious to his interest as might at first be supposed.[26]

Learning from Calder that William was considerably indebted and that Calder intended to correspond with her nephew John Baillie concerning William's affairs, Isabella importuned the resident at Lucknow "to investigate these matters & send us home a fair statement of Wm's debts that provision may be made to relieve those concerned." She observed that William's state was such that he was unable "to enter on any kind act for himself" and she was, accordingly, dependent on his friends. Isabella had obviously given a great deal of thought to the issue and had taken what was for her a bitter decision: "Our present views are to sell off at least a part of his paternal property. Should this be the case, it would gratify me exceedingly that you were the purchaser tho' God knows it would be the last wish of my heart to see it sold but my poor Wm's misfortune has made me calous [*sic*] to every other concern & were it the will of providence to restore him, I will thankfully, if he have not a six pence. I must tax your patience with burdening you with my distress but situate as I am to whom can I apply."[27] Isabella subsequently requested that John either send her a "fair statement" of William's debts or settle them and she would reimburse John's London agent. While the debts incurred were significant, resolution of them was relatively straightforward. Calder assumed the debts, the chief source of which seemed to have been "the attachment he [William] formed with an Asiatic."[28] "The Persian of whom he raves died soon after he sailed. He wrote me a deplorable letter on the subject from St. Helena. He may be told of his death to quiet him. That connexion unluckily proved the chief source of his expense, which I could not control till the last, & but for that his debt would have been far less, for I was at every pain to economize his other expenditure which he unwillingly allowed."[29] By 16 January 1816, although Isaac Ketchen complained that the resident at Lucknow "was a man of formalities" and had "acted lukewarmly" in the matter, John had discharged those debts, and Calder, on John's instructions, had sold William's Arabic books in Calcutta. There is some irony here in that John, this "man of formalities," had been a spendthrift in his youth and, in that regard, had accumulated debts to another man named Calder.

William's medical condition, on the other hand, was far from straightforward. Calder reported: "William was decidedly deranged before he reached Baghdad ... and was rescued by Sir W. Wiseman who by the bye on his arrival in England could give the most full and satisfactory acc't of the very beginning & progress of the malady for they went up together. I doubt not he will be detailing many equally strange visionary stories of me for he used to tax my cousin and me with the wildest and most improper actions & behaviour that could be imagined, & saw numberless things & scenes pass before his disordered eyes all day that never had existence ... but the lamentable reveries of this kind must long since be disregarded by his friends."[30] William was under Calder's care for some time before embarking for London, where he arrived in May 1814. One N. Smith informed Isabella that Sir Henry Halford and a Dr Munro had seen William two and three times respectively and that they both believed William was deranged and required restraint. More ominously, Calder had earlier noted:

They have given me a certificate of his derangement, in case he may again have recourse to law officers, which he has once done ... and he threatens it again, however I hope to hear from his friends before then; I do every thing in my power to keep on terms with him, and to prevent his acting foolishly; but I can neither do the one or the other, without giving offence, my utmost assiduity to please and to amuse him have been exerted in vain. And altho' he is never mischievous, yet he is far from being correct or coherent, and always perplexed me how to manage him. He now talks of a separation and living by himself. Wherein I have given him offence, God only knows, but he has taken an idea into his head that I am employed by you and the rest of his friends, and says that if he was once out of the way, it would better me no doubt. I hope 'ere this reaches you that your minds will have been made up as to the propriety of putting him under the care of one or the other of the medical men ... of late there have been several instances of his loss of memory, especially in playing a tune; he wanders into another and perhaps three or four, and then concludes with a few notes of the original. Mr. B has a cold & running at the nose, which he says, and indeed told the physicians was his glands suppurating, and that it was occasioned by undue means, such as various sorts of poison. He told them also that he lost five inches of his original stature, and this is now his constant theme ... However desirable that would have been, to be in possession of the manner in which the derangement originated, yet it would at present avail but little, so long as he is in possession of his present ideas, no remedy could change them but time and the probability is that when he is given to understand that he is under restraint, the mind may recover itself, and be restored to its wanted energy.

Should you not have come to a decision respecting what is to be done, I beg you may do so as soon as possible and transmit it to me without loss of time. Mr. B may elude all our vigilance and go by sea, and then the whole process is to go over again.[31]

The only positive news was that Calder had managed to obtain from the Bombay Civil Fund an allowance for William of £300 per annum for three years and then something at the end of that time.

Isabella began campaigning for some form of allowance for William from the East India Company. The Court recorded a letter from Isabella Baillie "on behalf of Mr. William Baillie, the writer on the Bombay Establishment representing that her son was obliged to return to England

on account of very severe ill-health which has terminated in mental
derangement and soliciting the Court to make him such an allowance as
will support him in his recent melancholy state."[32] Isabella's letter read:

I beg humbly to address your Honourable Court in behalf of my son
Mr. William Baillie Writer on the Hon'ble Company's Bombay
Establishment, who having discovered a predilection for the Hon'ble
Company's service was highly and very expensively educated accordingly, and he proceeded to India as Writer in the year 1811. This predilection was owing to his father the late Colonel John Baillie having
so long served in India, and more particularly his uncle Colonel
William Baillie whose life was sacrificed to the service of the Hon'ble
Comp'y, and whose services and sufferings must be well known to
many of the Honourable Directors. The premature death of both
these gentlemen has proved to the family a loss irreparable, and has
left the paternal estate exceedingly embarrassed. It becomes now my
painful duty to state, that although my son left this country for India
with a bodily & mental constitution equal to that of any of his relatives who have had the honour of holding such distinguished situations both civil and military in the Hon'ble Comp'ys service, he
returned to this country in 1814 in a deplorable state of mental
health, amounting I fear to absolute mental derangement. The
particulars of which will be more fully submitted to your Hon'ble
Court by Dr. Rees of London under whose charge he now remains.

For some time after my son's arrival in India I had the most flattering accounts of his indefatigable application to his duties which was
confirmed by his being appointed to a situation at Baghdad eventually most promising, and from every information I have yet been able
to obtain, it was in the zealous discharge of his duties at this station
during an unusually hot season, that he was attacked for the first
time with his present malady. By a letter I had from him dated
10th Jan'y, 1813 he appears to have recovered so far after his return
to the Presidency as to have received the highly respectable appointment of "Acting Collector General of Bombay," but he was finally
obliged to be embarked by his friends in the deplorable state in
which he now unfortunately continues.

I have requested of Thos. Gilzean Esquire of Inverness, who has
had the entire management of the family property for many years,
to make out a statement of its actual situation, and which I take the
liberty of annexing and submitting to your Hon'ble Court and by

which it will appear, that my unfortunate son, having in the discharge of his duties in India, been rendered incapable of further service either for the Hon'ble Company or for himself, has now no
resource, but in the consideration which his own services and sufferings, as well as the services and sufferings of his uncle the late
Colonel Baillie and other relatives may obtain from the liberality
and justice of your Hon'ble Court. I therefore beg humbly to sollicit
that the Hon'ble Court may be pleased to grant an allowance to
their unfortunate servant Mr. William Baillie of £300 per an. or
such provision as to the Hon'ble Court would appear adequate for
his maintenance.[33]

Isabella achieved a modicum of success since the Court ruled that
William could stay in Britain until the last ships of the next season and
commenced a quarterly "gratuity" of £30 from 24 May 1815. Meanwhile,
a cure for, or even a conclusive diagnosis of, William's malady remained
elusive. A Dr Rees determined that the cause of William's condition was
"brain fever" brought on by exposure to the sun in Baghdad. He described
the illness as an "idiopathic disease" which alters the brain structure
and observed that William considered himself a disciple of Mohammed.
William was put under restraint at Windsor where his mental state fluctu-
ated. His caregiver commented that at times William's only weakness was
"a fancy for the Mussulman costume and principles"[34] while on other
occasions he was extremely agitated and difficult to control. The mystery
of William's derangement and departure from India only deepened with
an allusion by his sister, Katharine Rose, to her mother of inappropriate
conduct on his part and a suggestion that she and Isabella get together to
discuss the rumour. "There is a report in the Country that William was
ordered to leave the Country in consequence of something he had done
– what I have not heard nor have I been able to trace the report of it to
any source."[35]

William took particular exception to his sister Anne's visits. Anne was
a headstrong and tenacious spinster who possessed an unerring ability
to irritate anyone with whom she came in contact. Her cousin, Archibald
Alves, had earlier encouraged Isabella's plan for her daughter. "I heard
of your intention of sending Anne to England which I approve very
much of – it will serve to polish her manners and (may I use the expression) rub off a little of the Highland rust – which you will allow prevent
her shining in society."[36] William appeared in such a confused state after
encounters with Anne that the medical practitioners sought to prevent

her "interfering" with her brother. When queried by his aunt, John guardedly responded: "On the propriety & probable result of Cousin Anne's proceeding with you to poor William I dare not hazard an opinion. That I wish most cordially for their success, she cannot doubt I am persuaded."[37] But that success was unattainable, and at one point William was so "disordered" by a visit from his sister that his servant, Andrew Fraser, threatened to leave his employ. In her turn, Anne "complained grievously of the Frasers, who she said had treated her with rudeness, and insolence, but particularly of her being prohibited from seeing her brother."[38] Indeed, the situation became so contentious that her cousins, John and Alexander, together with Archibald Alves, held a conference with Anne in which they agreed she could be "permitted to pay him a short visit occasionally under proper restrictions and Col. J. Baillie desired that she should distinctly understand what these were – that she should only be allowed to see her brother at such times as the persons under whose charge he was should think proper and only in their presence, or at least of one of them."[39] As time went by, a general consensus formed that Anne's interference was to her brother's detriment. Margaret expressed the family view of Anne's interventions: "I trust Cousin Anne will not attempt to interrupt poor William's quiet. We all feel really anxious about her conduct."[40]

Eventually, William, with the assistance of Andrew and Sarah Fraser, was able to retire to Dunain; by then, his mother had moved to Budgate, a Campbell residence. At Dunain, William became more settled and tranquil. His cousin John acted as *curator bonis* for William, Lord Cawdor agreed that his factor would manage William's affairs,[41] and the Frasers, Andrew and Sarah, assumed responsibility for his care.

Anne continued to annoy all and sundry. If anything, she became more adamant that she had every right to see her brother and repeatedly issued instructions to the mason to construct additions which would enable her to live in comfort at Dunain. William's guardian, Sarah Fraser, outlined the lengths to which Anne would go to intrude upon his peace of mind. "Mr. Baillie is very much in his usual way, quite well in his bodily health and for the last month he has been quiet and tranquil in mind. Nothing has happened in any shape to annoy or trouble us here since I last wrote, but we are all guarded & careful in going out. Andrew [her husband] observed a woman in the neighbourhood constantly on the watch to meet them, but as he knows her, he of course takes an opposite direction to where he sees her. She is a cottar on Dochgarnoch's estate in the neighbourhood of Miss Baillie's residence."[42] Anne insisted on living in the vicinity of William and took great exception when her cousin John, once again deputized by Isabella to read the riot act, advised Anne to move to Budgate with her mother. "She expressed herself much displeased with Colonel Baillie" because of that recommendation "but she accounts for his taking this view of the subject by having seen you [Isabella] first, for she said she knew your words from his lips & she acknowledged that she got quite out of humour with him."[43] John and Archibald Alves were not alone in supporting Isabella against her strong-willed daughter. Margaret chimed in with brutal frankness:

> Perhaps, strangers totally unacquainted with Anne's conduct for several years past might deem it hard to prevent her seeing her Brother, but we who know what unhappy effects their meetings have on poor William must admit the necessity of preventing them. I think Anne has entirely lost sight of prudence when she could permit Fraser to find out secretly her desire to take possession of Dunain, without William[,] since that evinces any thing but a disinterested wish for his recovery. You say nothing of his present state from which I fear it remains the same. May the Almighty restore him to human state. It appears a hopeless case, & certainly being under charge of his Sister would only render it worse. I sincerely wish you may prevail on her to return to Budgate.[44]

When Lady Arbuthnot learned of her cousin's plans to lease Ness House to enable Anne to walk to visit her brother at Dunain, she immediately advised Isabella to instruct her daughter to stay six months in Edinburgh.[45] Even the overbearing Isabella had limited influence on her daughter. At one point, Anne's refusal to speak to her mother led to Isabella's writing a missive in anything but placatory terms.

> When a young woman tells a parent that she can't bear to be spoke to there is nothing for it but to digest – you say you meant not to be contradicted or to use a harsher term to be repulsed – be it so you say you are willing to talk to me before a third person – I am most willing to give my sentiments candidly ... & will be happy to be corrected when I am wrong. We are all subject to errour & I think it's presumption in anyone (& very unlike the humility of a Christian) to set up their own oppinion as infallible – you may have been hitherto nursed in the lap of indulgence & know very little of the ways of the world.

Now in regard to my dear William I not only allowed your lead but in general you dictated tho' I must say that when I did take my own way I found I was right.[46]

With her mother's death in 1832, Anne felt no restraining hand and resumed her campaign to obtain the guardianship of her brother. The family factor clearly outlined to Anne the futility of her quest.

I received your letter of the 23'd instant and immediately transmitted a copy of it to Coll. Baillie without whose permission no application involving his name, could be made to the Court of Sessions.

I now have a copy of his answer which is to the effect which I anticipated, and which cannot surprise you, if you recollect what occurr'd at his house in Inverness a few years ago. It does not befit me to revive a discussion which at the time was unsatisfactory in its result to all parties; but before you compel Coll. Baillie to withhold his services I must not only state that all your true friends are of his opinion respecting the guardianship of your brother's person, but that in law the nearest male relation, however distant, is & must be, preferred to a female however near. The correctness of this any law-yer will confirm, and such being the law I do hope you will no lon-ger persist in an object which besides being imprudent cannot be legally obtained.

For added emphasis, Mackenzie enclosed John's response: "I feel so thor-oughly convinced of the great danger to herself and inexpedience as regards her unfortunate brother, of Miss Baillie's having any concern in the management of his person during his insanity that I consider it to be my positive duty to decline taking any personal interest in the affairs of the family if Miss Baillie persist and be supported by the Court of Sessions in her resolution to obtain the personal guardianship of her brother."[47] Anne did display some remorse as to the dissension with Isabella over the care of William but she persisted in her quest to obtain guardianship of him. "I have likewise to beg you will not touch upon subjects that are past, and are painful to me to look back to, as I am at present in a delicate state of health and I have no one now whose assistance or support I have claim on, my Mother and I never had a difference of opinion, but on the subject in question and I believe that now from the interference of others."[48]

"Mad" William's cousin Annie, who had become estranged from her family by marrying Munro, must have managed at least a partial reconciliation since she and Munro succeeded the Frasers in charge of William at Dunain. Archibald Alves wrote Isabella:

> Col. Baillie called on me a few days ago and read a letter he had received from you, in which you mention that his sister Mrs. Munro had offered (if it was thought she could be useful) to go to Dunain, & take charge of William, and asked my opinion. I said at once, that if Mrs. Munro would take the charge, I considered her by far the fittest person I knew – not only from the ties of blood and the affectionate interest she had always shewn for any part of her uncle's family, but from her own good sense and the zeal, temper and assiduity with which I was convinced she would discharge the trust if she undertook it. Therefore as far as my opinion is of any value, I think this would be a most desirable arrangement. Besides I think she might be more able to check any improper interference on the part of Anne than most other persons.[49]

At Dunain, when he wasn't bothered by Anne, William lived a quiet life during which he devised a new alphabet without consonants. He never recovered his mental health and died in 1869.

13

Estrangement

Why should we do anything for posterity, what has posterity
ever done for us?

Sir Boyle Roche

After his return to England in 1785, John's key concern relative to India
was to secure a commission for his sixteen-year-old nephew, Alexander
Baillie, the oldest son of John's deceased sister, Ann, and her husband,
George Baillie of Leys. Alexander had sailed to Madras as a cadet on the
Bellmont in 1782. Nelly described him as a good student and we know
that he studied in Edinburgh. Yet he was a taciturn and easily offended
soul. The only letter of his that we have on record is dated 21 October
1776 when he notified his uncles in India of his mother's death. Alexander
was appointed an ensign on 23 April 1784, well before John's departure,
but his commission remained elusive. While still in India, John applied
to Colonel William Fullarton on Alexander's behalf. Later, while returning to England by way of the Cape of Good Hope, he wrote to encourage
his nephew:

I had the pleasure of your letter at the Cape and hope you will meet
with many greater civilities on your unfortunate Uncle's acc't than
those mention'd. I also hope you will meet with some few in that
country who wish me well but those things are only mere mentions
of introduction and not to be depended upon by you. It is on yourself you must ultimately rely ... I have been very fortunate in my
passage hitherto – good accommodation, good livery, fine weather
and civility from my Danish friends. The only disagreeable circumstance is the ship's sailing badly but we must not expect every thing
our own way.

I am anxious about your getting the commission from F[ullarton]: but I fear he has been so much harried as a courtier to be a man of his word. This to yourself for your own sake as well as mine. I have by this ship wrote Spalding and Colonel Stewart about it and have still some hopes. I will at any rate, I think, be able to procure such recommendations in your favour to whoever is establish'd King's Commander in Chief that you will get a commission with leave of absence.

You must not expect to hear from me again untill my arrival on the Banks of the Ness. Remember me kindly ... to all my old acquaintances in the 19th and 20th Batt'ns: ... Write me freely and frequently for depend on it no one shall peruse your letters but myself.[1]

Acting on his promise, John sent a letter to Colonel James Stuart by way of his friend Alexander Fraser, apologetically bemoaning his need to rely on family connections. "I have as you will see touch'd on great relations a thing which I never did before in my life and which nothing but the welfare of a near relation would induce me to."[2] Although he mentions Jane Stuart, John, in fact, was the great-grandson of Sir Hugh Campbell, Thane of Cawdor, and Lady Henrietta Stewart, the third daughter of James, Earl of Moray.

Did the present application in the smallest degree interfere with any friend of yours, it wou'd be the highest of presumption in me to make it but as you may possibly be so situated as to have no partic- ular tie of friendship that wou'd sway you in giving your interest for a commission. In that case I wou'd take the liberty of recom- mending to your good offices my Nephew Ensign Alex'r: Baillie in the Company's service. I apply'd to Colonel Fullerton before I left India and he was so obliging as give a favourable answer so that if it has been in his power I have no doubt but the young man is already provided for. If not, I hope his being my Nephew and your distant relation may have some little sway, Lady Jane Stuart, a Daughter of Lord Murray's was my great Grand Mother and you are, I believe, of that family.[3]

In a roughly simultaneous letter to a Dr Spalding in Madras, John elab- orated on his nephew and his parents, affirming the Dunain family's view of their curmudgeonly brother-in-law, George:

Let me know when you write me how my Nephew goes on. He does
not want talents but he has a degree of obstinacy from a bent of a
Father which I fear will be a prejudice to him. But as no Brother was
ever fonder of a Sister than I was of his Mother, I am anxious about
his doing well. Shou'd sickness at any time make his going home
absolutely necessary, be so good as procure him the cash or give it
out of my funds. But get a draught on his Father and also an attested
copy of his letter of credit. That is[,] secure the payment of the
draught as much as you can for Papa is not to be depended on.
After what you heard Fullerton say, I think you might help through
Mr. Hipsley who is on very friendly terms with Colonel Stewart and
Fullerton to forward the commission for him I wish so much for.[4]

As late as 1789, when he again wrote to Spalding, an increasingly frustrated John was still endeavouring his utmost to obtain a commission for
what appeared, on the surface at least, to be a singularly ungrateful
nephew. He was skeptical that all Alexander's letters had been lost at sea
in view of the Company's common practice of placing duplicates of correspondence on various ships so as to increase the likelihood of the letters
reaching India House.

My Nephew is greatly obliged to you for interesting yourself in his
behalf. But God knows it is a cruel and hard case for me to think
there shou'd be occasion for any one twixt him and me. He was put
at the head of the list of volunteers of '84 in consideration of my
Brother's services and misfortunes and when I left India, he had his
choice of any corps on the establishment. During my stay in that
country after his arrival, I paid him every attention I cou'd have done
had he been my own son, in return for which I received an affectionate and kind letter at the Cape of Good Hope but no letter ever
since. What case there has been or what inducement he can have for
treating me and all his relations with such sovereign contempt is
unconceivable. His poor Sisters he has not only made miserable but
has injured their prospect of an eligible settlement in life. Did any of
his relations at any period hear from him, I cou'd give credit to his
having wrote but I am too well acquainted with the care taken of letters at the India House to believe that all shou'd be lost. No doubt
some are but not many. Upon the whole, my dear Sir[,] may I beg
and entreat that you will endeavour to induce my Nephew to write
his Father and his Sisters and also me if agreeable to himself. His

Father is now grown unwieldy and unlikely to live long and often says that the only, the last, and great comfort he cou'd receive on this earth wou'd be a letter from his Son and as a substantial proof of this, he is willing to answer his bills even to a considerable amount cou'd it be made appear that the money was properly laid out in the purchase of a company in the King's service if such a thing can be done. In that Alex'r has money and some friends ready and willing to interest themselves for him if they but know his situation, his wishes and what cou'd be done. When I left India he was strongly in the idea that I wou'd return and perhaps if I had not married and become the Father of a family, that might have happened. But as matters now stand it is as fifty to one my ever seeing the plains of Hindostan ...

I cannot help expressing my anxiety to hear what you are likely to do with Tipu. I hope in God you extirpate him and his law.[5]

John enclosed a note for Spalding to deliver to the unappreciative nephew. In it he implored Alexander to contact his father and at the same time cautioned him as to the expensive habits of his younger brother, John.

About two years ago your Father was induced by your Sister Margaret (who is very attentive to your interest) to make a trust disposition in my favour of all his subjects and in consequence granted him a bond giving him an annuity equal to the rents of them and obliging myself to give up the property to you or whoever became his heir. The reason of this transaction was your Father's fear that he might be pushed to sell some of his subjects. Indeed, he had immediately preceding the transaction sold his share of the King's Milns which he afterwards repented of. But notwithstanding this, there is still much in his power. But I hope in God you'll not provoke him. And in addition to the above cause your Father is now so much fail'd that he is unfit for business. Your Sisters are all well. William is in the planting line in Jamaica under the patronage of Mr. Cuthbert, Castlehill[,] and John is the apprentice to a Writer to the Signet. But as he is rather expensively inclin'd in case you correspond with him you will require to be cautious in what you write respecting money matters. I have now got a Son and two Daughters and have built a house at Dunain which has cost me about twelve hundred pounds sterling.[6]

In another letter John asked a friend in India to persuade Alexander to write his father, who owned property worth £200–300 that Alexander might well forfeit "by his own improper conduct."[7]

 beginning-ornament

On his father's death in 1789, Alexander inherited Leys despite his "improper conduct." The next year, on 21 August 1790, he received his long-sought commission as a lieutenant in the Madras Presidency; there is no way of knowing whether his uncle John had played a hand in this. In any case, Alexander laboured for another nine years before his next promotion to captain, which occurred auspiciously on 3 May 1799 while he was serving with the 11th Regiment Native Infantry under General George Harris at the siege of Seringapatam. The following day, an avenging David Baird stormed the fortress, overwhelming and slaying Tipu Sultan who, together with his father Hyder Ali, had been responsible for the deaths of Alexander's uncle, William, and his cousin once-removed, Francis. Further promotions soon came Alexander's way, to major in 1801 and to lieutenant-colonel of the 3rd Native Cavalry soon afterwards.

Yet India again proved a cruel place for Baillies. Not only did Alexander's health begin to decline after the Vellore mutiny in 1806, but he also lost two children. George and Mary, presumably, as we shall see, born to a native woman, were baptized and buried by an English missionary, C.W. Piazold, at Vepery, outside Madras, almost immediately after they were born, in March 1807 and July 1808 respectively. Alexander's brothers George and John were also in India at this time and were registered as sponsors at the christening.

A letter written by Ann Gibson in 1808 constitutes the only reference we have found to Alexander's role in the suppression of the 1806 mutiny and in part, at least, explains the illness that plagued him in India. The letter also mentions Alexander's brother John and Lord Minto, India's governor general at the time.

Mr. & Mrs. Edmonstone came to call for us a few hours after our arrival, gave me a very affectionate letter from John Baillie w[h]erein he says nothing wou'd give him greater pleasure than having an opportunity of showing me how faithfully he has cherish'd the genuine attachments we felt for each other in former days. She had also two very handsome Persian shawls for me sent by him, and a very

handsome palankeen. He has been very dangerously ill poor fellow
since we came to the country but is now thank God! Perfectly well.
I have heard twice from him since his recovery. God grant that he
may long live and be a comfort to his family. His Brother Col:
[Alexander] Baillie was extremely ill, dangerously so, brought on by
some vexatious conduct of his inferior officers at Vellore. You will
recollect the unhappy mutiny there. Doctor Ord told me it had such
an effect on his mind (tho' no blame was attach'd to him) that he
was absolutely derang'd for some considerable time and that he was
much affraid of not recovering but thank God, by the time we got to
Madras he was in a state of convalescence, had perfectly recover'd
his reason and had nothing of the disease left but extreme weakness.
His recovery was with the assistance of Providence and greatly
owing to the great attention of the woman who lives with him.[8]

Ann Gibson must, on another occasion, have relayed much more
distressing accounts of Alexander's health, for an obviously troubled
Margaret wrote to Isabella in 1809:

We have at last received a letter from my Eldest Brother dated at
Madras the 19th of Oct'r. & informing us that various circumstances
made him delay coming home for another year, had we got the letters
immediately on the fleet's arrival, his not coming home would be a
dreadful disappointment, but we're now so happy to hear of his
being alive & well in any part of the world, that it entirely reconciled
us to not seeing him so soon, indeed had I never heard Mrs. Gibson's
malicious stories, his remaining a little longer in India provided his
health held out tolerably would be no distress to me, though being
obliged to keep always near Madras he cannot reap all the advantages that otherwise he might. I wonder you have not heard from the
Gibsons & think they might even condescend to write me. However
if their letters bring no more pleasing intelligence than the last, long
may they keep silent.[9]

The mutiny of 1806, which likely gave rise to Alexander's illness, was
the first meaningful rebellion against colonial rule. The situation at
Vellore was potentially volatile owing to the presence there of Tipu
Sultan's twelve sons and eight daughters. They had been banished to
Vellore following the defeat and death of their father in 1799. A sub-
stantial number of their adherents had gradually infiltrated Vellore

and many of Tipu's former troops who had enlisted in the Madras army were assigned to the same city. At the time, four companies of the 69th Regiment, six companies of the 1st Battalion, 1st Regiment, and the entire 2nd Battalion of the 23rd Regiment, comprising 1,500 sepoys and 370 Europeans, were stationed at Vellore.

In the midst of this tinderbox, Sir John Cradock, the headstrong commander-in-chief at Madras, decided to improve the appearance of the army by issuing a revised Code of Military Regulations. The modified code required the sepoys to remove all caste marks and facial hair and to replace their assorted turbans with standard-issue helmets sporting a leather cockade – a stipulation that would have been anathema to both Muslims and Hindus. In decreeing the new standards, Cradock flouted the traditional British convention of leaving social and religious customs to be resolved by the natives themselves. His interference was particularly injudicious since the existing patterned turban had been sanctioned by the government in March 1797 after the Military Board had "given it every consideration which a subject of that delicate and important nature required."[10]

The disaffected Mysoreans fanned the flames by mocking the sepoys for submitting to the new regulations, which, they asserted, would inevitably lead to their conversion to Christianity. The troops were particularly susceptible to this intimidation given the sheer number of Mysorean sepoys at Vellore. On 17 June one sepoy, Mustafa Beg, notified the British officers of a planned rebellion. Lieutenant-Colonel Nathaniel Forbes, with perverse logic, queried the native officers, the very people implicated in the plot. Needless to say, they denied that anything nefarious was afoot and questioned Beg's sanity. In hindsight, the plot had been brewing for some time. The instigators had even sought the support of the French with a view to placing Tipu's eldest son, Fatteh Hyder, on the throne of Mysore. The uprising was scheduled for 14 July but Beg's betrayal accelerated it by four days. The insurgents struck shortly after midnight on 10 July, killing 114 officers and men and wounding countless more. They raised the flag of the Mysore Sultanate and declared Fatteh Hyder ruler of that kingdom.

Fortunately for the British, some of the officers escaped and notified Colonel Robert Rollo Gillespie at Arcot, fourteen miles distant. Gillespie acted immediately, setting out with the 19th Light Dragoons and the Madras Cavalry. While he was not stationed in Vellore, Alexander was lieutenant-colonel of the 3rd Native Cavalry at this time and, we surmise, took part in the relief of the city. He would have been involved in heavy fighting and a witness to dreadful carnage but that experience is unlikely to have triggered the mental troubles from which he later suffered. Rather, some of Alexander's hitherto trusted sepoy officers must have participated in the uprising. In any event, the British overcame the marauding rebels, who, having exhausted most of their ammunition, had abandoned themselves to plunder and pleasure. Three hundred and fifty Indians (the accounts vary) were put to death, with a few salutary examples blown from cannon and the remainder executed by musketry and hanging. Gillespie spared Tipu's family but dispatched them to Calcutta.

Alexander served as lieutenant-colonel of the 3rd, 5th, and 18th Native Infantry before retiring on 16 January 1810 on full pay. He moved to London where he became a proprietor of EIC stock. In 1815 he sold Leys to his younger brother, John, for the substantial sum of £12,052 plus an annuity to their father's widow (George had remarried after his first wife's death). To put the price in perspective, John and his heirs subsequently built Leys Castle and added the lands of Torbreck and Balrobert, purchased from the Frasers. Torbreck alone cost the estate £23,000. Subsequent owners disposed of the Fraser and other tracts of land over the years, and, over a century later, Leys sold for only £12,600.

∝

Besides the two children that Alexander lost in 1807 and 1808, he had another, a son, Alexander Charles (commonly referred to as Charles), who was born in India in 1800. Alexander was on furlough in England during 1802 and again in 1804–05,[11] and it was presumably during one of these furloughs that he brought Charles, who was educated at the Inverness Academy, to live with his formidable sister Margaret.

But that was not the end of Alexander's family. Back in England, he married Elizabeth Bournorvelle (*sic*) on 14 October 1822, well after the birth of their sons John, George, and William. Sister Margaret evidently viewed her new sister-in-law as less than a paragon and reacted sceptically to the encomia bestowed on her nephew and nieces. "After a residence of six weeks in Edin'gh to make matters even more secure Alick was married to the mother of his children … Under all existing circumstances the marriage was in some measure understandable & I trust the woman will in future conduct herself so as not to disgrace a man who has done so much for her. Kate [Catharine, her sister] & I have not only visited our new relation but the families have dined together both here & in Wimpole Street. The children are certainly promising enough but by no means the prodigies I was taught to expect."[12] Some taint obviously lingered since years later Cousin Anne was querying her mother as to the appropriateness of accompanying Elizabeth to her premarital haunts.

I wonder how much you should urge my going to Brighton with Mrs. Baillie, a place she was in the habit of going to for many years as Coll Baillie's mistress. She has had until now only a small house sufficient to accommodate herself and the children. Coll Baillie is still in London and will remain for a month or six weeks longer ... I have no objections to being seen with Mrs. Baillie any where in Scotland where she is known only as a married woman, and in many places I am likewise known, but certainly I must lose all sense of delicacy when I am seen with her at public places in England, untill she is more in society than she is at present ... What would my Aunt say if she was to look up to think those were the associates chosen for her Brother's daughter. Tho' I say this I rather like Mrs. Baillie. I think her a good hearted woman, and she has conducted herself with propriety ever since she became Coll Baillie's wife. She has a fine family and I wish they may do well, and Coll A Baillie has treated me with a degree of delicacy in regard to Mrs. Baillie that I esteem him for.[13]

They lived at Connaught Square and later moved to 33 Eastbourne Terrace, Paddington. In 1834 Alexander purchased Ness House, the building that now functions as the Columba Hotel in Inverness. Ness House was the former town residence of John and his sisters and the date suggests Alexander purchased it from his brother's estate. Alexander referred in a will of 1842 to "my mansion house affixed garden small park and other pertinences on the west side of the river Ness lying within the territory of the Burgh of Inverness."[14] Alexander and Elizabeth were "seriously talking" of moving to Inverness for three years.[15] That move, if it materialized, was evidently of limited duration, because we know from the same will that Ness House was occupied in 1842 by John Mackenzie, a banker in Inverness. Alexander presumably suffered a financial setback between the 1842 date of his original will and an 1850 codicil in which he declared "that my circumstances have greatly altered since the date of the within trust disposition and settlement"[16] and then ordered the sale of his "mansion house." Alexander died on 10 October 1854, at the age of eighty-eight, leaving the life rent in his properties and the use of the mansion house to Elizabeth "during all the days of her life so long as she shall continue my widow."[17] On the other hand, if she were to enter into another marriage, the proceeds of his estate would be divided among the surviving children "procreated" by the two of them. Elizabeth outlived him by ten years, dying at the age of seventy.

Their son George was born on 24 June 1818, educated at the EIC college, Addiscombe, and joined the Company as an ensign in 1837. After stints in Benares, Sangor, and Allyghur, George, in 1841–43, marched into Kabul as a lieutenant with the 64th Regiment Native Infantry in Sir George Pollock's Army of Retribution. The complacent Governor General George Eden, Lord Auckland, who knew little about India when he arrived there and even less when he departed in disgrace, had determined to restore the Sadozai Shah Shuja, to his throne. Despite the pro-British sentiments of the current incumbent, Dost Mohammed, and the implausibility of a perceived Russian threat, Auckland was intent on establishing a trustworthy ally on India's western front. Accordingly, he undertook in 1839 "the most unjust, ill-advised and unnecessary [war] that ever the British name or reputation was risked on."[18] Fortunately for George, he did not serve in that invasion of Afghanistan. Auckland's expedition did, indeed, restore Shah Shuja to the throne, but, in a pattern that has continued repeatedly to this day, the invaders alienated the proud and independent Afghans. They rebelled and drove the British from Kabul, destroying the occupying army as it limped back to India. As for George, his luck ran out when he died at Bhur-ke Chokey, near Delhi, while serving with his regiment on 29 July 1845. His demise was, in all likelihood, not combat-related since it preceded the outbreak of the First Anglo-Sikh War in 1845–46.

The second son, John, was baptized on 28 October 1820 at St Marylebone Church, London. He is mentioned in the 1823 will of Alexander's brother John, wherein he provides for a legacy to Alexander or his heirs by Elizabeth and gives preference to his godchildren John and Catharine. John appears to have died in 1827. In any case, he is not mentioned either in his uncle John's 1833 will or in Alexander's will of 1842.

The third son, William, was born on 28 October 1821, also educated at Addiscombe, and joined the East India Company in 1839, serving at Agra, Barrackpore, and Sebundy as a lieutenant with the 47th Regiment Bengal Native Infantry. He left India in 1841 and died, shortly thereafter, at 2 Southwick Place, Hyde Park, London, on 15 January 1842. Given his short service abroad, William, like his brother George, presumably died of afflictions incurred on the subcontinent.

Alexander and Elizabeth also had five daughters, of whom we have no trace: Catharine, born 1823; Helen, 1829; Elizabeth, 1831; Flora, 1834;

and Mary, 1837. By the time of Mary's birth, they were living at 9 Devonshire Place, Wimpole Street. When Alexander departed this world, the only living male heir, of whom I am aware, was Charles, but father and son had patently become estranged.

From all appearances, Alexander and Charles were on good terms at the time of the latter's nomination in 1817 as a cadet on the Bengal establishment. Charles Grant, member of Parliament for Inverness-shire and former chairman of the EIC, proposed Charles on the recommendation of Alexander's brother Colonel John Baillie. At the time, Charles was serving as a half-pay ensign in His Majesty's 81st Foot. His father endorsed the nomination and indeed, as an indication of the value of these appointments, both Alexander and John were required to provide undertakings that no money or other valuable consideration had, or would be, paid to secure the cadetship on the Bengal establishment. Perhaps Alexander was disappointed by his son's formal retirement from the Company's service at the age of twenty-six or at his lack of progress beyond the rank of lieutenant. Even worse, it appears that Charles had effectively retired in 1821 after only four years' duty for we have letters written in Scotland from him to his great aunt Isabella in that year enquiring as to whether any money from his uncle George had arrived for him. We know for certain that he was furloughed in London in 1824.

In any event, we are merely speculating as to the cause of the rupture between father and son. We have more secure grounds to believe the breach was exacerbated, if not caused, by Charles's marriage in 1829 to Mary Grant, for it is only after that event do we have any indication of family conflict. "I hear this is poor Charles Baillie's marriage day ... He has obstinately determined to listen to no advice on the subject, and for the last fortnight has kept entirely out of Mr. Fraser's sight ...They have gone through all the forms prescribed by the church of being publicly called etc. three successive Sundays, so that no clergy man could refuse to marry them now, unless forbidden by some of the young man's friends. His father has written to him some time ago but he paid no attention to his wishes. I am quite sure from his fickle disposition he will in a very short time bitterly repent the step he is about to take."[19]

Shortly thereafter, Charles lamented to Isabella that his only contact with his father was through his aunt, Annie Munro. "I am rather uneasy at not hearing from Mrs. Munro as I suppose it will now be through her that I may expect any communication from my father. I have some money due from him which I am in great need for, & which ought to arrive by this time."[20] The estrangement was again manifest in Charles's complaints that his father was treating him harshly in forcing him to walk thirty miles to receive the half-yearly interest on a legacy from his Aunt Margaret. Unfortunately for him, his father held the principal and authorized the interest payments. Charles resorted to pleading to Isabella that she act as an intermediary for him and lobby Munro and his father.

> This note which you can shew Mr. Munro. He can see by it he is authorized to pay me £7–10 sh. $^1/_2$ yearly, interest on £300 in my father's hands. I hope after seeing it he will raise no objection to immediately paying it, though from the lack of business between us I am not very sanguine in this subject. If it be however … The last time I got this same $^1/_2$ yearly int. he made me give him a blank receipt for £15, 7–10 of which had been given by my aunt & for which she never desired any receipt & I must say that I think rather odd to be giving blank receipts for such terms when the … £300 is with my father this 3 years without any acknowledgement. Although I believe my father's integrity can not be questioned I will not yield to him or Mr. M in hon'ble motives.
>
> I have nothing more to add but that I am entirely without cash, so if you can possibly prevail on Mr. Munro to send the money by you, you will extremely oblige.[21]

It is not known whether father and son achieved even a limited reconciliation. Alexander's will casts no light in this regard and in fact, if anything, deepens the mystery. The will, on first reading, appears to include Alexander Charles among his heirs, since it stipulates that Alexander's son of the same name is to share in the proceeds of his estate. The colonel even specifies that his mansion house is to accrue to his son, George, and failing George, to his son, Alexander. Further reading, however, gives rise to another possibility: that father and son had become estranged to such an extent that the colonel had excised the unworthy son from his life and given a hitherto undocumented child of his and Elizabeth the name Alexander. A number of reasons lead to that conclusion. In the will, the colonel reserves funds to "outfit" Alexander for his trip to India should the latter decide to join the EIC or the army. It is unlikely that Alexander Charles would require outfitting for India at forty-two years of age, particularly when he had already been outfitted previously and had since retired from the service. The colonel then includes Alexander in his listing of the children who had been "procreated" by Elizabeth and him and then refers to Elizabeth as the mother of all the heirs. Finally, the colonel refers to this particular heir as Alexander when the relatives invariably referred to Alexander Charles as Charles. I believe it is impossible to draw a firm conclusion but the circumstantial evidence points convincingly to a second Alexander.

Charles may have had to overcome unstated obstacles. He may well have been of mixed-race heritage and suffered that disadvantage. Were it not for the ban by that time on the appointment of Anglo-Indians to the Company's military, the balance of probability would point in that direction. That presumption is based on several facts: by 1800, there were still few single European women in India and the preponderance of British marriages and liaisons was with natives of the subcontinent; there is no mention in the India correspondence of Alexander having a wife, nor did a wife accompany him to Britain on his retirement; the records of the burials of Alexander's two children in Vepery in 1807 and 1808 refer to them as illegitimate; and Ann Gibson attributed Alexander's recovery from an illness to "the woman who lives with him." A European woman would presumably have attracted more notice. On the other hand, as we have seen, by 1800 no mixed-race progeny were admitted to the EIC's service, let alone to the officer category. Accordingly, whether Charles was Anglo-Indian remains an open question. In any event, his Anglo-Indian cousins, George and Neil Benjamin, built successful careers and lives despite that perceived handicap. We are then left with the impression that Charles was just a feckless character.

Although she left him a legacy, Charles's feisty Aunt Margaret continually fretted about his future. He and his household fell farther and farther down the socio-economic ladder in Inverness-shire until his death on 12 December 1858. His first son, Alexander, was born at Cawdor, Nairn, in 1831. He was listed as a draper's apprentice in 1851 and died in London on 10 June 1870. His second son, Charles, was born on 20 December 1835. He worked for a British railway and then immigrated to Saint John, New Brunswick, where he married Martha J. Hamilton in 1876 and died in 1917. It was only following the departure of Charles, the only surviving son, to Canada that this particular branch of the family gradually regained some financial security.

John of Leys and the Acquisition of Bundelcund

India is a geographic term. It is no more a united nation than the equator.

Winston Churchill

In 1791 the second of the next generation of Baillies arrived in Calcutta to join the East India Company. Despite the family's traditional connection with Madras, the new arrival was financially driven to opt for employment in more lucrative Bengal. He was William's and John's nephew and the younger brother of Alexander who, for nine years, had been stationed on the Madras establishment. John, born at Ness House, Inverness, in 1773, was the second surviving son of William's sister, Anne, and George Baillie of Leys. It is not known how much formal education he received, but it must have been more than adequate since he proved to be an exceptionally talented linguist and able diplomat. Though he initially apprenticed to a Mr Johnstone, a writer to the Signet, John had become disillusioned with the law and therefore sought new opportunities in India.

The elder John, the 13th Laird of Dunain, had earlier cautioned his nephew Alexander against John's free-spending ways, a subject about which he had first-hand knowledge. At the time of George Baillie's second marriage, he settled £1,000 on the four youngest children from his first marriage, with £250 as John's share. Uncle John wrote:

When John was bound apprentice to Mr. Johnstone his father granted a bond to me as trustee for John to that amount empowering me to lay out the money in such a manner as I thought proper for John's behalf. On receiving this bond John and I doubly as his trustee granted his father a discharge for the above sum as his patrimonie and all he had to expect from his father ... Of this sum prior to his running away I advanced one hundred and eighty five pounds and since that period thirty pounds. His father when last at Edin'g paid fifty pounds I believe indeed most if not all to J. Cawder on John's acc't ... so that first and last I can venture to say he has in all cost his father ... upwards of four hundred and I believe I shou'd not be far wrong were I to call it five hundred pounds sterling.[1]

Moreover, the correspondence suggests that Cawder maintained a further unpaid claim against John.

Alexander may well have taken to heart the advice to treat any monetary requests from John with circumspection since, in a letter to his uncle in which he referred to his youthful follies, John mentioned that his request for a short-term loan from his brother had elicited no reply. Necessity had then forced him to turn to his uncle, who, despite his skepticism, advanced him £85.[2]

In this same letter, besides ingratiatingly explaining and endeavouring to justify his further draw on his uncle, John displayed his considerable erudition by providing an incisive account of Lord Cornwallis's initiatives in the Third Anglo-Mysore War of 1789–92 and describing, prematurely as it turned out, the bankruptcy of what had been the Company's primary competitor in the East Indies. The Dutch or United East Indies Company was struck down by the venality of its employees, an irresponsibly generous dividend policy, and, most significantly, the loss of ships, trade, and territories to the British in the Fourth Anglo-Dutch War of 1780–84. In fact, while the Dutch leviathan was clearly in severe financial straits at this time, it did not formally declare bankruptcy until a few years later, in 1798, leaving outstanding obligations in the staggering amount of 219 million Dutch guilders. The company was nationalized shortly thereafter, burdening a relatively stagnant Dutch economy with a heavy millstone of debt.

On my passage from Madras, I wrote a few lines by the "Queen Indiaman" to Margaret which I suppose you will have seen before this arrive ... Indeed, so little has transpired worth notice since the date of it that I should hardly have troubled you at this time, except as a duty and just tribute to the tender and parental attention which you have always paid with pleasure to the most trifling interests of our family. You will see by that letter, and I am convinced that you will be happy to see, notwithstanding the many disadvantages which my own imprudence and your just diffidence of my future conduct subjected me to, on my first arrival in this country, I have not been near so unfortunate as might be expected. I have met with several friends and acquaintances, whose kindness has enabled me to live ever since my arrival most agreeably and comfortably, and without a farthing of expense, which you know my purse was very ill calculated to afford. I did not carry onshore with me at Madras £2 of the small sum your bounty allowed in England, and from want of every kind of necessaries on my arrival I was not able to bring away a single gold mohur of what you kindly authorized your friend, Mr. Tulloch[,] to allow me. You may easily conceive then how uncomfortable I should have been situated upon my arrival except that my good fortune afforded me an accidental meeting with some old friends. The gentleman I now live with, and most pleasantly do I live, is son of Provost Robertson of Dingwall, and after several misfortunes in India is now settled here for the present pretty comfortably, though I hope his situation will soon be much better and more independent. I have all the time hitherto shared with him all his comforts, both in his own house and with his friends in Calcutta, who are pretty numerous and respectable; and were it in his power, should not want the use of what he knows me very well to be quite destitute of. None of my pay has yet become due, as the army are two months in arrears, and were it even due I should not wish to draw it as I expect very soon, indeed almost every day, to be entitled to draw ensign's allowances, as there are more than vacancies already for all of us, I expect to have some arrears of pay to receive, which will be very acceptable. The allowance of an ensign in garrison, which is only a half batta station, are 140 rs. per month, and when our promotion appears in general orders, which we expect daily, if I have the luck to be allowed to join a corps in the field, or even up the country, my allowances will be fully double. These you know to be very far superior to those at Madras, and therefore wisely chose this establishment, of which I am now very glad, although the cadets of Madras were certainly sooner promoted. With regard to my brother [Alexander], who is in camp, I can say no more than what you can see in my former letter. I wrote him twice; my first I suppose from its size is miscarried.

The purport of both my letters was, I think, as nearly as possible the subject of our conversation in London. I explained to him briefly the state of my father's family, and mentioned his extreme anxiety, as well as yours, to hear from him, and pressed him earnestly to write. I concluded with mentioning my own situation, and that, if it was fully in his power, I should wish to be his debtor a short time for the small sum sufficient to furnish the articles immediately requisite for my military appearance, and which my own imprudence at home had prevented my friends from allowing me.

My not hearing from my brother hitherto, and my being joined to an European corps in Fort-William, have forced me, as you will see, to take a step which I much regret.

You will also see the reasons which urged me. I could not appear without the articles which I purchased, and had no credit. I do not even know that my having drawn for the sum will enable me to put off the payment till I receive pay sufficient to discharge it.

This was my sole motive, which you may perhaps condemn, but I am sure my situation justified. Were you to see a list of the articles and the expense attending the purchase, you would, I daresay, think as I do. You will be surprised when I tell you that my only regimental coat, and which I could not appear without, will necessarily cost near 80 rupees, and everything else in proportion. You know very well the expense of European articles in India, and need not mention it. They are here even more enormous than at Madras, and you may be sure the sum I have mentioned, and been obliged to draw, will not go far. I will not, however, say that I expect to be accepted, tho' I am sure, if my affairs in Edinr. have not turned out too pressing, you and my father will not wish to return it. I have not a doubt, if I live, of soon being able to pay all that I owe; and I shall be very happy that every farthing I have cost you and my father may be restored in one obligation to my sisters, which, if sent out, I will most gratefully sign, and with my first ability discharge. They are the chief, if not the only, sufferers from my extravagance, and the greatest cause why I now more than ever regret it, tho' I trust it may yet be the means of turning out to their as to my own advantage ...

Lord Cornwallis, at the head of the greatest army that ever was seen in India, then lay encamped about seven miles from Bangalore. He had lately sent out a large detachment, commanded by Colonel Stewart, to reduce Severndairg, a strong fort, about or near ten miles from the place of his encampment, and he himself remained with the

army to cover and protect the detachment in their operations, which
have hitherto been successful. Two other smaller detachments upon
the same service are encamped at the equal distances of seven miles
from the army; the one commanded by Lieut.-Colonel Cockerell, and
the other by Captain Walsh. When they succeeded agt. Severndairg,
which there seems no doubt of before this time, it was the intention
to proceed agt. Seringapatam, the destruction of which it is expected
will soon, tho' not till after very hard struggles and severe losses, put
a final conclusion to the war. With regard to the motions of the
Western Army, under Genl Abercromby, I am not so well acquainted,
and they are not very interesting at present ...

We have of late been a little surprised, tho' not much alarmed, to
hear of a smart action off Mangalore, on the coast of Malabar,
between a French frigate, with two transports in convoy, and His
Majesty's frigate, the "Phoenix," commanded by Sir Richd. Strahan.
The transports are supposed to have been loaded with supplys to
Tipu's army, and upon our Captain's requiring them to bring to, for
the purpose of examination, he received a broadside from the French
frigate, which did him very little damage, but only called forth his
just resentment, which he immediately exercised to the almost final
destruction of the Frenchman, whom he instantly boarded and took.

What effect this may have upon the politics of the two nations at
home, there is no surmise of. A packet has lately arrived over land to
Madras, which brings much interesting news about the French
nation in particular, and of the total bankruptcy of the Dutch E.
India Coy., as also of the destruction of their dock-yards and store-
houses at the instigation of the Empress of Russia, and that a similar
attempt had been vainly made in England. But I am only, I suppose,
reciting what you are already acquainted with. I do not even know
that I have said anything which will afford you amusement, or be
considered as news. If it is so, I have at least endeavoured, as I shall
always with pleasure do, to inform you of what I think will prove
amusing or interesting, and I have no doubt of your forgiveness if
I have failed ...

The length of this scrawl has, I am afraid, already displeased, if not
disgusted, you at me; therefore conclude it after paying you the compliments of the New Year. You are, I hope, fully persuaded of my
most sincere and grateful good wishes (all I can offer) for the health
and prosperity of you and your family. May I beg leave to be remembered to Mrs. Baillie and the dear little girl, if she at all remembers

her cousin Johnny, whom she used to oblige with the appellation of "Puppy," a term which, though I trust a little reformed, he has not yet lost all manner of title to. That the Supreme Being may many new years preserve and bless you, my dearest parent and benefactor, and every branch of your family, in which, as a mark of your goodness, I believe many of my own are included, is, believe me, the most ardent and sincere wish of your ever grateful and affectionate nephew.[3]

John adapted seamlessly to life in India, quickly becoming an intimate of Neil Benjamin Edmonstone and his social circle. Edmonstone, at the time, was deputy Persian translator to the governor general and later rose to the post of chief secretary to the government. "The handsome, brunette Baillie rarely followed convention; although he was, like Edmonstone, the younger son of an ancient but impoverished Scottish family."[4] John presumably took an Indian bibi shortly after his arrival in the country since his first child, Catharine, was baptized at Cawnpore in 1793. A second, George, was born in 1795.

Somehow – the precise means are unclear – John achieved an impressive fluency in native languages. This fluency shortly came to the attention of the governor general, Sir John Shore, who in 1798 selected John to translate from Arabic into English a compendium of the "laws and doctrines" of Shia Islam by Sir William Jones, a philologist and scholar of ancient India.[5] For this service, the Company paid John 10,000 rupees.[6] As Shore explained:

Some time prior to the death of the late Sir William Jones, a compilation was begun under his inspection of the law and doctrines of the sect of Muhamedans called Sheeas, but which was not completed until after his death; a translation of this useful work I conceive to be very desirable in a public point of view. During my residence at Lucknow, I had an opportunity of conversing with Lieutenant J. Baillie an officer in the Company's service whom from the great proficiency he has made in the study of the Arabic language I believe to be extremely well qualified for the task, and I therefore propose to the Board that Lieutenant Baillie be accordingly nominated for that purpose, and that such a recompense be made to him as the extent of the undertaking, and the manner of its execution may appear to the Board to merit.[7]

Soon afterwards, Richard Colley Wellesley was appointed governor general, a post he held until 1805. Wellesley, like Pitt, aspired to acquire a vast empire in India to compensate for the loss of America, and he also believed wholeheartedly in the value of education. In 1800 Wellesley established the College of Fort William to prepare East India Company servants to govern more effectively in India. To teach Arabic studies in the new college – Arabic being deemed second only to Persian on the basis that it was a classical language of Islam and was employed in many key Mughal texts – Wellesley chose John Baillie. The princely remuneration of 2,600 rupees per month contrasted markedly with the 140 rupees per month that John had been earning at the time of the letter to his uncle and attested to the importance that Wellesley attached to the position. Indeed, the amount of the stipend caused other professors at the college to complain. Nonetheless, John was obviously amply qualified, for, in addition to the *Compilation of the Laws and Doctrines of the Shiah Sect of Islam*, he later published a *Digest of Sheeah Law* (1797), *Sixty Tables Elucidatory of the First Part of a Course of Lectures on the Grammar of the Arabic Language* (1801), and *An Entire and Correct Edition of the Five Books upon Arabic Grammar* (1802). His son, Neil Benjamin Edmonstone Baillie, posthumously published John's *Digest of Muhamedan Law*.

John's linguistic proficiency was such that Francis Gladwin, professor of Persian and, incidentally, editor of the Calcutta *Gazette*, objected to his appointment to assist with instruction in that language. Neil Edmonstone, who also taught at the College of Fort William, had been forced by other obligations to relinquish his duties there and delegate much of the burden to Gladwin. Gladwin had withered under the load and sought assistance. However, the solution proved even more painful than the problem it was meant to solve when Gladwin determined that the proposed assistant was more qualified than he. Edmonstone gave vent to his frustration and, in doing so, emphasized just how exceptional were John's language skills. In an 1801 letter to the noted Orientalist William Kirkpatrick, he wrote:

> I am sorry to inform you that the Persian Dep't. of the College, during the last term, has been almost entirely at a stand. As my official avocations would not admit of my attendance at the College, the whole burthen of instruction was thrown upon Gladwin, whose state of mind was ill adapted to bear so heavy a weight, nor perhaps could the individual exertions & abilities of any man suffice for the instruction of 70 young men, the number to which the Persian class amounted. Gladwin was therefore extremely anxious for assistance. But it became extremely difficult to find any person whose services could be shared, sufficiently qualified. I therefore proposed the

expedient of uniting the Persian & Arabic Professorships. Mr.
Baillie's knowledge of Persian is very great & his proficiency in the
Arabic language gives him an advantage that no other European possesses. I was delighted with the notion of providing by this arrangement in the most effectual manner, not only for the success of the
institution, but (as I conceived) for the relief of Gladwin, who I concluded would be highly gratified ... But judge of my surprise when I
found that Gladwin absolutely refused to act with him, not upon the
plea of Mr. B's want of capacity, nor from any mistrust of his temper
& disposition, but declaredly because of Mr. Baillie's superior qualifi-
cations. Gladwin interpreted the arrangement into degradation & a
virtual dismission of himself, & under that impression, he withdrew
altogether, in a state of mind that exceeds all description.[8]

Edmonstone and Baillie employed every device in their arsenal to convince Gladwin that he was not being shunted aside. Nevertheless, not
until John offered to serve as Gladwin's assistant and "to act entirely with
Gladwin's advice & concurrence"[9] did the latter relent and agree to
resume teaching. The accommodation was short-lived: Gladwin soon
thereafter clashed with the provost, David Brown, and resigned. The
responsibility for both departments then devolved to John and an assistant, Matthew Lumsden, occasionally supported by Edmonstone.

As effective as the college proved in moulding raw recruits into capable
administrators, its cost ultimately rendered the College of Fort William
impractical. To 31 October 1801, the college devoured £79,000, an
amount well beyond the Company's ability or its appetite to provide on
a continuing basis. The death knell came with the opening of the East
India College at Hertford Castle in England in February 1806, the establishment of which undercut any rationale for a costly college in India.

ൠ

Following the defeat of Tipu Sultan in 1799, the effective subordination
to the Company of his Wodeyar successors in Mysore, and the annexation of the Carnatic in 1801, there remained two formidable native powers, Nizam Ali of Hyderabad and the Marathas. The British effectually
removed Hyderabad as a threat through a treaty with the nizam that
allowed them to station troops in the territory, ostensibly for Nizam Ali's
protection but definitely at his expense. In addition, the treaty provided
for the eviction of any French forces from the nizam's country. Thus, a
potential menace was transformed into a British vassal.

That left the Marathas as the lone challenge to British supremacy in India. Fortunately for the Company, the various Maratha chiefs, although theoretically under the rule of the peshwa, clashed among themselves and were seldom able to present a united front. By 1771, they had consolidated their control of central India, including the territories of Rajputana, Malwa, and Berar, but they subsequently split into five independent nations. While Gwalior, Indore, Berar, and Gujarat continued to acknowledge the titular suzerainty of the peshwas of Poona, the Maratha confederacy inevitably disintegrated in times of crisis and therein lay its adversaries' greatest advantage. The son of Ragonaut Rao, Baji Rao II, who reigned as the peshwa, and Daulat Rao Scindia, the maharajah of Gwalior, had alienated Jaswant Rao Holkar when they opposed his succession as ruler of Indore. In revenge, Holkar attacked Baji Rao II and Scindia, defeating them at Hadaspur on 25 October 1802.

The peshwa fled to Bassein, near Bombay, and petitioned the British to assist him in regaining his throne. Wellesley was in a position to dictate terms and he, as was his wont, took full advantage. The Treaty of Bassein, the primary purpose of which was to prevent the formation of a hostile union of the Maratha chiefs under the peshwa, ceded 2,600,000 rupees worth of land and provided for 6,000 British troops in the peshwa's territory. In addition, the treaty prohibited contact with other foreign powers, forbade the employment of Europeans without Company consent, and relinquished all the peshwa's claims to Surat. The British then succeeded in restoring Baji Rao II to his throne with little apparent opposition. That passivity was, however, deceptive. When the terms of the 1802 treaty became known, several of the peshwa's chiefs felt vulnerable and united with Scindia and the rajah of Berar to resist its provisions, particularly the ceding of Bundelcund, a province in central India lying between the Cane and Betwa rivers in what now constitutes part of Madya Pradesh and Uttar Pradesh. Their hostility prompted the British to issue a formal declaration that they intended to uphold the treaty. When the British representative at Scindia's court sought assurances of peaceful intent, Daulat Rao Scindia replied that the chiefs had not yet determined on a course of action but that, if they opted for war, he would inform Lieutenant-Colonel John Collins, the British envoy at his court. Wellesley took Daulat Rao's response as an affront and in July 1803 sent an ultimatum directing Scindia to withdraw his armies beyond the Nerbuddah and Ragoji II Bhonsla, the rajah of Berar, to return to his capital. The Maratha chiefs sent Wellesley soothing responses but did not withdraw their troops.

Wellesley treated his adversaries' failure to withdraw as a provocation and declared war in August.

Wellesley was cognizant of the overwhelming numerical superiority of the Maratha forces, which approximated 210,000 cavalry and 96,000 infantry under the capable command of European officers. He sought to dissuade as many of the chiefs as possible from participating in the hostilities. The most formidable Maratha commander, Jaswant Rao Holkar, was still nursing grievances against his fellow Marathas and opted to remain neutral. At the same time, the British were able to persuade Anand Rao Gaikwad of Baroda to resist the blandishments of Scindia and Bhonsla. As a result, the enemy could draw upon only half the Maratha forces but even so they remained formidable opponents. Wellesley, leaving no stone unturned, determined to pry the Mughal emperor from Scindia's control. Although the Mughal Empire existed in name only, the emperor still exerted symbolic power which Wellesley was anxious to harness. Rather than attacking sovereign powers to uphold a dubious treaty, he justified his aggression by claiming that he was defending the emperor, Shah Alam, from his refractory vassals. He then dispatched General Gerard Lake, a formidable and experienced soldier who had distinguished himself in Germany, America, and the revolutionary wars in France before commanding the British forces in the Irish Rebellion of 1798, to take Delhi and secure the person of Alam. Lake moved with alacrity and was able to confirm by September that Shah Alam had accepted British protection.

With the outbreak of the Second Maratha War in 1803, John, although still a professor at the College of Fort William, enlisted in the army and served at the September siege of Agra as an officer in the 1st Battalion, 4th Regiment of Native Infantry. However, Edmonstone, in his role as secretary in the Bengal government, was intent on employing John's linguistic and diplomatic skills in Bundelcund. Though it was not one of the larger states, comprising, as it did, only 4,896 square miles and a population of 900,000, Bundelcund was critical to maintaining British authority since it divided the Maratha powers and prevented them from utilizing the territory as a base for military offensives. Accordingly, Edmonstone sent a glowing recommendation to the commander-in-chief, General Lake, under Wellesley's signature. "Lt. Baillie's intimate acquaintance with the language and with the habits and disposition of the natives of India, and the judgment of abilities which that officer possesses, qualify him in a peculiar degree to aid your Excellency in the conduct of any political negotiations."[10]

The situation in Bundelcund was particularly complex. One of the provisions of the Treaty of Bassein was the cession of a portion of Bundelcund by the peshwa to the British. However, the peshwa did not, in fact, control this province in which Bundela prince skirmished with Bundela prince. In return for the peshwa's support in evicting the Afghan warlord Mahommed Khan Bungust and establishing him as the first rajah of Bundelcund, the renowned Bundela warrior, Chhatrasal, had adopted the first peshwa, Baji Rao I, and granted him one-third of Bundelcund. The Marathas continually encroached on Bundelcund. Finally, Ali Bahadur, a Maratha adventurer and an illegitimate grandson of Baji Rao I, with the assistance of Anupgiri Gosain of Moth, defeated the noted Rajput warlord Arjun Singh in 1790. Ali Bahadur and Anupgiri gradually became the dominant powers in Bundelcund as they consolidated ever increasing portions of the territory under the nominal suzerainty of the peshwa. When Ali Bahadur died at the siege of Kalinjar in 1802, Anupgiri became the primary force in Bundelcund. Ali's brother, Ghani Bahadur, proclaimed himself regent and placed his two-year-old nephew, Zulfikar Ali Bahadur, on the throne with Anupgiri's acquiescence. However, Ali Bahadur's elder son, sixteen-year-old Shamser Bahadur, disputed the succession. With military support from Holkar, Shamser seized his uncle at the Fort of Ajegarh and soon poisoned him. Overplaying his hand, Shamser then demanded a payment of 9,000 rupees from Anupgiri as a show of submission. Anupgiri refused and sought an alliance with the British.

Anupgiri had found it necessary to fend for himself his entire life. He had been born into a Brahmin family but his father's death left the family in poverty. As a result, Anupgiri's mother sold her two children as chelas to the guru Rajendragiri Gosain of Moth. Under his direction, Anupgiri and his brother, Umragiri, had become ascetic-warriors and served as mercenaries for various native princes. As he had in the past, Anupgiri had, undoubtedly, been contemplating a shift in allegiance for some time. He had recognized that the peshwa, by acceding to the Treaty of Bassein, had imperilled his authority over the Maratha warlords. It was therefore logical to turn to the British, who, in all likelihood, would soon prevail on the subcontinent. Anupgiri warned the Company that the Maratha chieftains Daulat Rao Scindia, Holkar, and Bhonsla were planning to attack the British using Bundelcund as a staging ground.

Wellesley immediately understood the benefit of controlling Bundelcund in a de facto as well as the existing de jure sense. He instructed Richard Ahmuty, the collector at Allahabad, as his delegate, and Graeme Mercer, as the commander-in-chief's representative, to negotiate an alliance with Anupgiri, whom the British styled the maharajah of Bundelcund. Anupgiri sought a jaidad of twenty-two lakhs to maintain his troops as long as the Bundela and Maratha warlords proved difficult; the eventual grant of a jaghir in the Ganga-Jumna Doab above Cawnpore; and the release of his brother, Umragiri, who had been confined by the British following an ill-fated conspiracy in 1799. By 4 September 1803, the two parties had reached a formal agreement enabling the British forces to join Anupgiri's troops in Bundelcund. Anupgiri possessed an impressive army comprised of 4,000 horse, 8,000 infantry, and 15,000 infantry commanded by a European adventurer, Colonel Johan Frederick Meiselbach, but he seemed loathe to employ it in battle.

As Anupgiri's reluctance became more evident, Ahmuty pleaded illness and was replaced as political agent in Bundelcund by John Baillie. It later surfaced that Anupgiri had been been bilking the Company. In that connection, suspicion arose that Ahmuty had been colluding with Anupgiri in some loose manner and that his supposed illness was in fact a ruse to escape Colonel Peregrine Powell's increasingly penetrating inquiries. Indeed, Powell complained in late October that "a much higher degree of importance had been attached to the force and military abilities of the Rajah, than they are either of them, entitled to."[11] Suspicions were further aroused when John determined, through Meiselbach, that Anupgiri was extracting twenty-four lakhs of rupees from the jaidad, which he had steadfastly insisted on increasing by two lakhs since he claimed that the existing grant was worth no more than eighteen lakhs. Even worse, Anupgiri continued to collect revenues in the territories he had assigned by treaty to the Company.

John was continually frustrated by his inability to determine the rough magnitude of Anupgiri's forces for the reason that they were continually employed in gathering the revenues of Anupgiri's jaidad. However, he estimated that the actual cavalry never exceeded twenty-five hundred and that the infantry, including Meiselbach's troops, approximated fifteen hundred men, a number much below the figure claimed by Anupgiri and, indeed, below the number for which the British were compensating him. John informed Graeme Mercer:

His [Anupgiri's] conduct upon this occasion has added to the many proofs which I possess; and which have been submitted to His Excellency the Commander in Chief as the grounds of my entire conviction, that exclusively of the assistance of the department of supply which the presence of the Rajah has afforded, and of the services of Colonel Meiselbach at present in the southern districts of Bundelcund, our connexion with this chieftain will in no degree secure to us the beneficial effects which might have been justly expected from the favourable terms which were originally granted to him.

His failure on the present occasion[,] however, will furnish an additional instrument of the success of my negotiation hereafter for the relinquishment of his Jaidad, and I shall not fail to apply it in the manner but calculated to accomplish His Excellency's views.[12]

John was clearly biding his time until Anupgiri's duplicity and inaction were incontrovertibly evident. Mercer apparently agreed wholeheartedly with John's strategy, for he replied: "My friend Himmut [Anupgiri] has certainly taken care of himself, and the sooner he is looked after the better; whenever you think it advisable to notice his laxity in the service, and deficiency of troops publicly, a letter to the purport you formerly mentioned will be sent by the Commander in Chief; but His Excellency says, that it would not be right for him to write it without some public grounds."[13]

Before he had sufficient evidence to indict Anupgiri, John received intelligence that the adventurer had fallen ill and was failing fast. He rushed to the dying man's bedside, where, he asserted, Anupgiri sought John's protection of his infant son. Anupgiri died the following day, 3 June 1804, whereupon his brother, Umragiri, attempted to take charge. John, unable to count on Umragiri's allegiance to the EIC and anticipating little support for Umragiri's ambitions, brought his vaunted diplomatic skills to bear and, by a baldly aggressive interpretation of Anupgiri's dying wish, expeditiously placed the rajah's heir, Nerinder Geer, firmly on the throne before Umragiri was able to take the initiative.

Whether or not John's actions were in keeping with Anupgiri's dying wishes, those actions were clearly in the EIC's interests. As John wrote to Mercer in June 1804:

As the solemn declaration of the Rajah to me on the day before his death left no doubt of his intention of bequeathing all his property and rights to his only son, an infant now in camp and the avowed inclination of the several sirdars pointed to this boy as the only heir of his father's property, and successor in command of the troops, whose rights they were disposed to acknowledge, I considered it to be indispensable to the important object of preventing tumult and disorder in the camp, to evince my own acknowledgement of those rights by a formal act and declaration vesting the command of the Rosala [cavalry] on Rajah Nerinder Geer till the pleasure of Government should be known.

I proceeded accordingly to the camp of the late Rajah this morning and having summon'd Rajah Umragiri and all the principal sirdars to his tent, I placed the boy upon his father's musnud and directed all the chiefs to make the customary presents and acknowledgements of his authority which were offered unanimously and with the greatest readiness and satisfaction by all, in my presence, excepting Rajah Umragiri who departed from the tent with some appearance of displeasure.

The general character of Rajah Umragiri and the limited influence which he possesses over the troops of his deceased brother, give me no ground to apprehend any ill effect from his dissatisfaction at the measure which I was induced to adopt and I have every reason to hope that my endeavours to prevent any new commotion or disturbance in the country upon this critical and arduous occasion, will prove to be completely successful and that no material difficulty will occur in the accomplishment of any objects which His Excellency the Commander in Chief or the Supreme Government may have in view respecting the Rajah's Jaidad.[14]

John's immediate response was effective as, despite the tradition that power passed from the guru to the chela, Umragiri in this case, there was no groundswell of support for Umragiri. In fact, within three days of Anupgiri's death, John was able to inform Mercer that "whatever may have been the principles or motives by which the conduct of the late Rajah was guided, and the objects to which the services of his troops were directed during his lifetime, I have not observed the smallest trace of disaffection or disorder in his camp since his death, and on the contrary, the conduct of all his relations, principal sirdars, and troops have been such as to inspire me with the fullest confidence in their attachment to the British Government, and in their ready submission and obedience to its will and commands."[15]

John handled this transition at a particularly delicate time since Colonel W.D. Fawcett had, with exceedingly poor judgment, detached Captain John Smith with an inadequate force to reduce a small village of no strategic importance. Smith's troops had been slaughtered with the loss of all their guns and baggage. Fawcett attributed the attack to Ameer Khan acting under the influence of Jaswant Rao Holkar but it transpired that the roaming marauders were neither large in number, not exceeding five thousand men, nor connected to the Pathan warrior Ameer Khan or Holkar. General Lake explained:

> By Colonel Powell's illness, and the death of Colonel [Thomas] Polhill[,] the command of the detachment in Bundelcund devolved to Colonel Fawcett, events not to have been foreseen; and had it devolved to any other man in the army, this dreadful event could not have happened I do really think. With four battalions of Sepoys and 450 Europeans, to have suffered these guns to have been carried away does seem most extraordinary. The folly of attacking a fort for no one reason whatever is beyond all belief, and then only sending two companies of Sepoys to protect the guns and batteries is not to be believed. I have ordered Colonel Fawcett to resign his command to Lieutenant Colonel Wittit, a most excellent officer, till Colonel Martindale can arrive for that purpose.[16]

The Company no longer seemed invincible and Wellesley determined that the setback demanded a strong response. "In the present temper of the durbars of Scindia and Ragojee, I should not be surprised if the misconduct of Lieut. Colonel Fawcett were to renew the war in every part of India, unless measures immediately be adopted, which shall convince all India that this disgrace is to be ascribed exclusively to the misbehaviour of a few incapable officers, and unless an immediate and severe blow be struck against the party of freebooters which has obtained this temporary triumph over the British arms."[17] He instructed Lake to appoint a senior officer in whom he had confidence to effect "the complete expulsion" of the invaders and to settle the province. The governor general undertook to vest the officer, under Lake's orders, with the entire civil and military government as commissioner for the affairs of Bundelcund. Subject to Lake's agreement, Wellesley intended to appoint Captain Baillie – he had been appointed to that rank on 30 September 1803 – secretary to the commissioner. Lake's approbation was a mere formality since John had served under him at Agra and had gained his confidence. In the interim, Baillie was to act in a civil capacity under the direction of the commanding officer in the province.

Meanwhile, John, as political agent for Bundelcund, had negotiated a supplemental treaty through which the peshwa, following his defeat at the Battle of Poona in October 1802, ceded the remainder of the province to the British as a condition of further protection. Despite the cession, the peshwa exercised little practical control of Bundelcund and Ali Bahadur's son, Shamser, retained claims to the territory. General Lake, recognizing that the British must deal with Shamser in one form or another, ordered Colonel Powell and Anupgiri to attack Shamser. Suffering a notable defeat, Shamser was obliged to retreat to Cabsah where he was overwhelmed and fled across the Betwa. Simultaneously, Lake instructed John to enter into negotiations with Shamser. John, in October 1803, scored another diplomatic success by inducing Shamser to accept monetary compensation instead of battling for his rights in the province. The EIC provided a pension of four lakhs per annum and undertook to convince the peshwa to permit Shamser to retain his houses and villages in the vicinity of Poona. John was then able to establish British influence in Bundelcund by conciliation rather than by warfare. General Lake was delighted with that outcome, eliminating as it did a potential combatant at a time when the Company was threatened by most of the Maratha chiefs.

John soon learned that he had earned "the Governor-General's highest approbation of the judgment, temper, and ability which you have manifested during the whole course of the negotiations."[18] In fact, Wellesley heaped praise on John in a dispatch to the Court of Directors:

At this period of time Captain John Baillie who conducted ... all political and civil duties in Bundelcund, resided at Banda, a place situated to the southward of the River Betwa, and nearly in the centre of that part on the Province of Bundelcund, in which the British authority had been established. The force with Captain Baillie consisted only of a small force of cavalry belonging to Shamser Bahadur, about 200 cavalry belonging to Rajah Anupgiri[,] and 1,000 Sepoys under the command of a European officer in the service of the latter chieftain. Notwithstanding the consternation which had spread throughout the Province of Bundelcund on the incursion of the predatory horse, whose numbers have been greatly exaggerated, Captain Baillie deemed it to be his duty to maintain his situation at all hazards, and the Governor-General in Counsel is satisfied that the preservation of tranquility in the districts in our possession south of the Betwa is to be ascribed entirely to the confidence inspired, and to the subordination maintained throughout those districts, by the firmness, manly prudence, and fortitude manifested by Captain Baillie on that occasion.[19]

John next set about negotiating treaties with the Bundela Rajputs in an attempt to detach them from their Maratha allies. By now his leverage had improved considerably in view of the devastating defeat suffered by Scindia and Bhonsla at the hands of Wellesley's younger brother, Sir Arthur Wellesley, at Assaye on 23 September 1803, a victory the future Duke of Wellington considered his greatest. Arthur Wellesley followed that triumph by almost totally destroying Bhonsla's army at Argaon. At the same time, General Lake inflicted a crushing defeat on Scindia's other army at Delhi and Laswari, with the result that both Scindia and Bhonsla sued for peace in December. However, a new threat appeared on the horizon as Holkar, in league with the rajah of Bharatpur, belatedly joined the fray and overwhelmed Colonel William Monson's force. Lake, however, subsequently trounced Holkar at Furruckabad on 17 November 1804.

As the year 1803 drew to a close, Wellesley established a commission to manage the affairs of the acquired territories under the superintendence of the Board of Revenue in Calcutta. It consisted of Thomas Brooke as president, Captain Baillie as agent to the governor general, and Lieutenant-Colonel Gabriel Martindale commanding the troops. Thereafter, the Company moved forthwith to conquer portions of Rath, Jalaldur, and Kharka from the Bundela rajah, Tej Singh, the forts and districts held by adherents of Shamser, and the districts of Panwari and Supa. The modest districts of Koni and Parsaita and a few villages of Raipur completed the list of British acquisitions in Bundelcund to the end of 1805. In each case, John agreed to confirm the chiefs of Bundelcund in possession of ancient territorial rights held under Ali Bahadur on condition of their allegiance and fidelity to the British power, their renouncing any future territorial aggrandizement, and their abandoning any of Ali Bahadur's former territories reacquired subsequent to Ali's death. In addition, John, by granting them some territory, negotiated mutually beneficial arrangements with several of the plundering bands whose predations were directed solely to obtaining subsistence. In that manner John sought to pacify the country and establish a buffer between Holkar and EIC territory.

He had other priorities too. The severity of the system of tax collection in Bundelcund had depleted the land and impoverished the people. That situation was particularly sensitive in Anupgiri's former jaidad, of which the Company regained control in August 1806. The troops who depended upon the revenues were so much in arrears that John concluded it would be folly to replace the acting managers immediately. Accordingly, he only gradually implemented a more just form of taxation. For that reason, the assessment for 1805–06 fell by a third from those of the two previous fiscal years. As we shall see, the poverty and oppression John encountered in Bundelcund markedly informed his later attitude to reform in Oude.

Despite Wellesley's victories, the Court of Directors in London grew weary of the costs and ordered an end to the conflict. Indeed, the common view was that, in conquering the Marathas, Wellesley had almost bankrupted the East India Company. So Wellesley was recalled and Cornwallis was reappointed governor general and commander-in-chief. However, Cornwallis died before he could arrange a final peace treaty and was replaced by a long-standing member of the Bengal civil service, Sir George Barlow, as acting governor general. Barlow did not continue Wellesley's expansionist policies but moved quickly to return the bulk of the Maratha lands. Even so, he was not confirmed as governor general by the Whig government, though he did obtain in compensation the governorship of Madras in 1806. The results were not good: "Unfortunate as his administration had been in Bengal, it was equally so in Madras."[20] His lack of tact quickly alienated most of his constituencies. He abolished a revenue system that had served Madras well, quarrelled with the grain contractors, and offended the army by cancelling a particular monthly allowance to officers. Barlow suspended four officers of rank and removed eight others from their command. A mutiny by the army erupted and was resolved only by the personal intervention of Lord Minto, the governor general, in 1807.

In the midst of these political machinations, John gradually and doggedly asserted British control of the province and secured submission of the various forts throughout the territory. In doing so, he diligently contracted treaties with native chiefs bearing an exotic array of titles – peshwas, gaikwars, nizams, nawabs, maharajahs, rajahs, soubahs, ranas, nanas, thakurs, and keladars. On 6 February 1804 he signed a Treaty of Peace and Alliance with the peshwa of the Marathas and Shiv Rao Bhoo, the soubah of Jhansi, whereby the soubah undertook not to molest any allies of the British or the peshwa, not to protect any enemies of either, and not to employ any European without British consent. In return, the Company would protect the soubah, at his expense of course, against any aggressors, with specific reference to Scindia.[21] The alliance with Shiv Rao Bhoo represented a critical milestone as Jhansi was the major town in Bundelcund.

In May 1804 Ameer Khan, a vassal of Holkar, invaded Bundelcund. Colonel Powell fretted that his reduced force would not be able to withstand Ameer Khan's forces. On the other hand, John surmised that Ameer

Khan, the very thought of whom had earlier overwhelmed Colonel Fawcett, wished to withdraw from Holkar's service. Consequently, he might well be induced to renounce the predatory warfare by which he had supported his troops in return for a small pension from the British government or, alternatively, a jaidad in the neighbourhood for the maintenance of 1,000 or 1,500 horse in service to the British. John then suggested that he "temporize" with Ameer Khan until Powell had reduced Gwalior and would be in a position to deal with Ameer Khan "with complete effect and prevent if possible his ... joining Ambajee [Scindia] or Holkar, both of whom have summoned him to their aid."[22] General Lake applauded the initiative: "Should Captain Baillie be successful in detaching Ameer Khan from Jaswant Rao Holkar's service, it will be a severe blow on that chieftain who has always looked upon him as his best officer and places the greatest confidence in him."[23] John succeeded in suborning Ameer Khan, thereby adding to an impressive list of accomplishments.

In September 1804 John concluded an "Obligation of Allegiance and Fidelity" with Maharajah Beekur Mageet Bejy which, in addition to the standard terms, included a provision compelling the maharajah to assist the Company in subduing any of his relatives who resisted the British. John confirmed the maharajah in the possession of ancestral properties yielding 4 lakhs and 488 rupees so long as he remained a faithful ally.

Notwithstanding all that John and his colleagues had achieved in Bundelcund, much remained to be done. Of the lands yielding 3,616,000 rupees ceded by the peshwa under the terms of the Treaty of Basscin, the British had only succeeded in acquiring territory yielding twelve lakhs, the jaidad of the late Anupgiri remained to be resumed, and the claims of the numerous Bundela chiefs were still outstanding. The governor general concluded that his objectives in Bundelcund could be achieved only by Captain Baillie and sent John once more to the province in December 1805.

Following Shamser's submission to British power, two to three thousand of his Naga warriors transferred their allegiance to the Bundela chief, Raja Ram, one of the main protagonists against the British in Bundelcund. These Nagas had made overtures to John and in late August 1804 he decided to employ almost two thousand of them. Commanded by Meiselbach, they served the British resolutely against their former paymaster and other Bundela chiefs for seventeen months. Yet, despite their yeoman service, the Nagas posed a threat to the stability of Bundelcund. By February 1806, John had resolved the Naga menace by giving them 110,000 rupees of back pay on the condition they depart Bundelcund and not "appear as an armed body in this province, on any future occasion."[24] He then set about recovering the jaidads of the late Anupgiri. Despite the resistance of the family and military chiefs in possession of numerous forts, John was able to effect the peaceable transfer of territory yielding eighteen lakhs of rupees per annum while only sacrificing a jaghir yielding one lakh.

In October 1805 Sir George Barlow instructed Captain Baillie to join him in Allahabad where the governor general assigned him to renegotiate some jaidads and allowances. John continued to build alliances and neutralize former enemies. On 17 October he signed an "Engagement" with Thakur Doorjun Singh whereby the latter undertook to provide no asylum to "marauders or refugees from the British" and to provide restitution or deliver the robber if any British merchant or traveller was plundered in his villages. In return, John granted Doorjun Singh a sunnud confirming him in the possession of the pergunnah of Mehur. On 23 October 1806 he signed a treaty with Govand Rao, nana of Calpee, recognizing that since his submission the nana had been an exemplary supporter of the British. As a result, he recovered the ilakas of Mohummedabad and Oorey in the first year and the pergunnah of Mohaba in the second. The nana ceded the Fort of Calpee and several villages on the right bank of the Jumna to the Company. In return, the Company delivered to Govand Rao territory equivalent to Calpee and pledged not to deprive him of any of the diamond mines under his management. Shortly thereafter, John suggested that a gift of two of the decrepit cannon obtained by Colonel Meiselbach at Boora Guch would satisfy Govand Rao's persistent pleas for military assistance, enabling him to subdue a few of his newly acquired forts without British assistance. John then concluded similarly advantageous treaties with Rao Rajah Pareechut of Duttecah and the rajah of Sumptur.

The only Muslim prince in Bundelcund, the nawab of Baonee, Nusseer-ood-Dowla, then sought assurance that the British recognized his right to the fifty-two villages in the vicinity of Calpee bestowed on him by the peshwa. The nawab had incurred the enmity of the Marathas by allying with the British. In response, his brother, Moulla Jah, sought Peshwa Baji Rao's support to overthrow Nusseer-ood-Dowla. John had undertaken to bring British influence to bear on the peshwa, had confirmed the nawab's possession of the fifty-two villages, and had assured the nawab that he would not be held accountable for any evil actions by his brothers, subject to the nawab's continuing to pay his brothers and their dependants their usual monthly allowances. The nawab was pleased with the arrangements but wrote that he would be even more comfortable with the same assurance from the governor general himself. Accordingly, on 24 December 1806, Barlow conveyed his satisfaction that the nawab's claim to the villages was valid.

That same month, John completed an "Engagement" with Luchmun Singh of Ajegarh resolving the constant threat to the Company of marauding bands through the ghats. Luchmun Singh undertook never to shelter enemies of the British and to guard the ghats so that plundering bands might neither enter nor depart the Company's territories. In addition, he undertook not to interfere with Juggut Raj and the peshwa's diamond mines. Luchmun Singh further agreed to deliver the fortress of Ajegarh to the British in two years and, in the interim, pay four thousand rupees per annum. Finally, he assumed responsibility for all damages caused by marauders who descended the ghats to loot British territory. Subsequently, he reported his inability to bring "the affected Zemindars in Kouch to a sense of their duty"[25] and proposed that Lieutenant-Colonel Thomas Hawkins, the commanding officer in Bundelcund, subjugate the Zemindars. Upon receipt of Barlow's approval, John instructed Hawkins to take the offensive. The latter sprang into action and quickly reduced several forts in Kouch. By March 1807, John was able to report the destruction of thirteen forts that were of no use to the British and a settlement of the land revenue in Kouch.

All in all, John's record was remarkable, and no one was more appreciative than Governor Barlow, who, sitting in Council in May 1807, sent the following dispatch – one of his last official communications before being replaced by Lord Minto – to the Court of Directors:

Your Hon. Court will observe, that on this occasion the Gov.-Gen. deemed it his duty to record the high sense which he entertained of the distinguished merits and exertions of Capt. Baillie, in the execution of the arduous duties committed to his charge, during his two missions to Bundelcund ...

With a degree of public spirit highly honourable to his character as an officer, Capt. Baillie, soon after the commencement of the war with the confederated Mahratta chieftains, although engaged in his duties as professor of Arabic and Persian in the college of Fort William, offered his services as a volunteer in the field, and proceeded to join the army then in the siege of Agra. At that time the precarious situation of affairs in the province of Bundelcund, requiring the superintendence of an officer qualified by talents and abilities to conduct the various important and difficult political negotiations, on which depended the establishment of British authority in that province, His Excellency the Com.-in-Chief, with the approbation of government, selected Capt. Baillie for the conduct of that arduous duty.

The original object of the British government, as connected with the general operations of the war, was to establish its authority, in the name of the Peshwa, over that portion of the province of Bundelcund, the command of which was necessary for the protection of our own territories against the hostile attempts of the enemy, who at an early period of time projected the invasion of our western provinces, by the aid of the chieftains possessing military power in Bundelcund.

The prosecution of this object the Nawab Shamser Bahadur ... had proceeded to occupy the province of Bundelcund in a state of enmity to the British power. The cause of Shamser Bahadur was supported by the Rana of Calpee, and other chieftains of the province, whilst, with a view to counteract this combination, the descendants of the ancient chiefs of Bundelcund were encouraged to employ their exertions in recovering the possessions wrested from them by the arms of Ali Bahadur, the father and predecessor of Shamser Bahadur.

The latter chieftain had been defeated, but not subdued, and it was deemed expedient, with a view to the accomplishment of our political objects in Bundelcund, to establish the influence of the British government by conciliation rather than by hostility. The transfer of a large proportion of the Peshwa's nominal possessions in Bundelcund, which occurred shortly after Capt. Baillie's mission, gave us a more direct interest in the province, and rendered necessary the occupation of most of the territories which the Bundela chiefs had been encouraged to seize.

To combine with the establishment of our authority over the lands ceded by the Peshwa, the conciliation of the chiefs who were to be deprived of them, at a time when the British government was engaged in a contest with the Mahratta power, and when the province of Bundelcund was menaced with foreign invasion and disturbed by internal commotion, became a duty of the most arduous and difficult nature, requiring the exertion of eminent talents, firmness, temper, and address. It was connected also with the duty of superintending and directing the operations both of the troops of the British government and of the auxiliaries, under the command of the Rajah Anupgiri, for the support of which, lands of the produce of twenty lakhs of rupees had been assigned. It embraced the reduction

of the power and influence of Anupgiri and the Native chiefs of
Bundelcund, without weakening their attachment or hazarding their
revolt, and the establishment of the British civil power and the collection of revenue in the province, under all the disadvantages of
impending invasion, and the desultory operations of numerous bands
of predatory troops.

Within the short space of three months, these objects were accomplished by the zeal and ability of Cap't. Baillie; and we have reason
to believe, that in the months of May and June 1804, when the regular force retreated on the invasion of the province by the troops of
Ameer Khan, and when the utmost disorder was apprehended in
consequence of the decease of Anupgiri, the British authority in
Bundelcund was alone preserved by the fortitude, ability, and influence of Cap't. Baillie. Even at that crisis of distress and danger,
Cap't. Baillie was enabled to frame an arrangement with regard to
the lands granted in Jaidad for the support of the late Anupgiri's's
troops which laid the foundation of their ultimate transfer to the
possession of the British Government ...

The services of Capt. Baillie were subsequently continued in his
capacity as a member of the commission appointed in July 1804, for
the administration of the affairs of Bundelcund: and the introduction
of the regular civil and judicial system into that portion of the province which had been subjected to the British authority principally by
the means of Capt. Baillie's ability and exertions admitted of his
return to the presidency in the month of July 1805.

Notwithstanding, however, the various arrangements concluded by
Capt. Baillie with the Nawab Shamser Bahadur, and other chieftains
of rank and power in Bundelcund, by which their interests were connected with those of the British government, much remained to be
accomplished for the complete establishment of our rights and interests in that province. Of the territory ceded by the Peshwa, under
the additional articles of the treaty of Bassein, to the extent of
3,616,000 rupees annual produce, lands of the value of 12 lakhs of
rupees per annum only, had been acquired. The Jaidad of the late
Anupgiri Bahadur yet remained to be resumed. The situation of the
numerous chiefs in Bundelcund relatively to the British government,
their claims and pretensions, together with various other important
questions connected with the establishment of the British authority
in the province, continued unadjusted.

The objects to be accomplished are accurately detailed in Capt. Baillie's able reports of the affairs of Bundelcund ... Those objects were, in our decided judgment, alone susceptible of attainment by the aid of Capt. Baillie's personal exertions, knowledge, influence, and abilities; and this conviction occasioned Capt. Baillie's second mission to Bundelcund in Dec. 1805 ...

The first success of his exertions was manifested in the peaceable dismission of the turbulent and ferocious body of Nangahs, the continuance of which in the service of government opposed a material obstacle to every salutary arrangement. The next and most important object accomplished by Capt. Baillie, was the complete resumption of the Jaidad lands of the late Anupgiri Bahadur, without the slightest commotion, although opposed by the powerful influence of his family, and a numerous body of military chieftains, in command of large bodies of troops, and in possession of numerous forts; thus effecting the peaceable transfer to the British dominions of a territory yielding an annual revenue of eighteen lakhs of rupees (£225,000) with the sacrifice only of a Jaghir of little more than one lakh of rupees per annum. The services of Capt. Baillie were further enhanced on this occasion, by the successful manner in which he resisted the extensive claims of the manager of the Jaidad, for arrears of pay to the troops, and balance of revenue ...

With a similar spirit of energy and zeal, aided by the exertion of his political talents and address, Capt. Baillie succeeded in accomplishing those arrangements with the principal chiefs in Bundelcund, which were prescribed by our instructions, and which have produced a degree of tranquility and security hitherto unknown within the limits of that turbulent province; and has finally placed the authority and relations of the British government in Bundelcund in a condition to admit of our conducting our affairs of the province under the ordinary system of administration established in other parts of the Hon. Company's dominions.[26]

John had indeed proved a skilful promoter of British interests. He knew how the game of imperial rule in the subcontinent was played, and he played it well, resorting to persuasion, manipulation, intimidation, or force – depending on the circumstances – to further the cause of Britain and the East India Company. He made enemies along the way, but also gained powerful friends. India had become his home, though he did not wish it to be the home of his mixed-race children, as we will now see.

15

Margaret and the Anglo-Indian Elmores

Better a diamond with a flaw than a pebble without one.

Chinese proverb

In the conclusion to his dispatch of May 1807, Barlow wrote that "we cannot doubt your honourable court's concurrence in our opinion, that Captain Baillie has established a peculiar claim to distinguished reward."[1] On the death of Colonel John Collins, the resident in the state of Oude, that reward materialized.

Instructed to transfer his duties as agent to the governor general in Bundelcund to John Richardson, John, as usual, left a detailed and thorough account of the situation in the province for his successor. While Bundelcund may have seemed modest in comparison to the grand court of Oude, the governor general's agent had charge of an extensive staff of forty or so – including writers, secretaries, court attendants, intelligence agents, and sepoy officers – at a monthly cost of more than one thousand rupees. John emphasized that "all of them" were "absolutely necessary for the conduct of your political duties."[2] With regard to territorial matters, there was much to report. He had investigated the claims of Daulat Rao Scindia against the chieftains of Kouch, the soubah of Jhansi, and the rajah of Duttee, and conveyed his findings to the resident at Scindia's court. The parties were now all assembled for the purpose of mediation by the resident. Meanwhile, not all the chieftains who submitted to British pressure obtained the EIC's protection. While the rajah of Sumptur had renounced his usurpations in Kouch and "received a public demonstration of the forgiveness of his offences,"[3] the British had intimated that they were not inclined to guarantee his possessions. All in all, John took a sanguine view of the political outlook: "It may be inferred that the political duties of your office, with ... reference to the northwest frontier of Bundelcund ... [are now] totally exhausted; and that the renewal of them at any future period must depend on circumstances or events which are not now in our contemplation."[4] As noted previously, John had sought to satisfy Govand Rao's pleas for military assistance by providing him with two of Meiselbach's cannon, but he had been prevented from implementing that measure when the guns were inadvertently shipped to Cawnpore. He did, however, implore Richardson to mollify Govand Rao by delivering "two pieces of heavy ordinance with their tumbrils, ammunition and stores"[5] at his earliest convenience.

Given the continual incursions into Bundelcund, the land claims were even more complex than the general chicanery and artifice that prevailed in India. The agent, of necessity, devoted a great deal of his time to resolving these claims. The rajah of Churkaree, Bujy Bahadur, and the rajah of Bujaour had each asserted his rights to the Tuppa of Isanee Gurh, located in Kistolah. The British had decided in favour of Bujaour, who held possession, even though the Tuppa was included in Rajah Bujy Bahadur's sunnud. John had deferred announcing the decision since he hoped to effect a mutually beneficial arrangement by appropriating a small portion of the unoccupied territory to the rajah of Chukaree in exchange for the Tuppa of Isanee Gurh. Similarly, John had considered relieving the government of responsibility for the pension (3,000 rupees a month) of Bakst Singh of Banda by assigning the rajah "a more considerable portion of the territory beyond the Ghats which was formerly possessed by his ancestors, and is now occupied by a person named Gopal Singh having no hereditary right to it."[6]

. Further complicating an already incestuous controversy was a common hereditary claim by Bujy Bahadur and Bakht Singh to three pergunnahs, a claim John had intended to settle in combination with Bakht Singh's pension. At the same time, John had not yet resolved the keladar of Kalinger's claim to the villages of Goorha, Nagawan, and Chutenee. These villages were not occupied under John's authority until March 1806 and Nagawan and Chutenee were of little value. John had determined to return them but retain Goorha since it was the site of the British cantonment. Before relaying the decision to the keladar, he learned of Richardson's appointment and so referred the matter to his successor.

John's most practical advice may have been that the collection of tribute from Luchmun Singh for the fortress of Ajegarh and from Dewan Poorun, the son and heir of Bujy Bahadur, would be more effectively handled by the agent rather than the Revenue Department because "the influence of the British regulations cannot be supposed to extend to the Keladar of Ajegarh (or Dewan Poorun), and would be executed in vain to recover his balances of revenue."[7] Finally, John reviewed the considerable and indispensable reduction in expense to the government by the disbandment of the irregular troops who had proved of such utility to the British during the Maratha war. Of those irregular troops, only Colonel Meiselbach's provincial battalion, consisting of the artillery and fifty horsemen, remained to be discharged. John had recently encouraged the commanding officer to proceed immediately to disband these remaining forces.

Although Barlow had abolished the office of compiler of Muslim law in 1805 as part of his effort to restore the war-ravaged finances of the EIC, John was authorized to draw his civil allowance both for this post and for his position as professor of Arabic and Persian. He was also to charge his expenses to the public accounts from the date he was relieved until his arrival at Fort William

John's new post, the residency of Oude, was quite a prize. Lucknow by the eighteenth century had displaced the splendid Mughal capital of Delhi as the unsurpassed precolonial city in northern India. It had become, without question, the grandest, most civilized and prosperous city, renowned as it was for its arts, cuisine and sophistication. When Delhi could no longer support the poets, musicians, scholars, and professional men who had subsisted on the bounty of the Mughal court, these people flocked en masse to Lucknow, transforming that city into the most urbane, literate, and brilliant society in India. It differed from Delhi in that it was populated by Shias rather than the doctrinaire Sunnis of Delhi. Also, unlike Delhi, Lucknow, under the influence of the British, absorbed a sprinkling of European culture. It boasted a population of 300,000 at a time when the greatest Scottish cities, Edinburgh and Glasgow, were modest in comparison, at 70,000 and 60,000 respectively.

By the time he made the journey to Lucknow by way of Cawnpore, John was the head of a large household. Besides his daughter Catharine and son George, born in 1793 and 1795 respectively, Neil Benjamin Edmonstone, the namesake of John's close friend, was born in 1799 and baptized at Calcutta. Charlotte Ann arrived in 1802. We do not know whether all four had a common mother, but John did follow the precedent of sending his Anglo-Indian sons, if not his daughters, to Britain. By this time, the prejudice against native Indians and their mixed-race progeny had become much more entrenched than in William's era. For example, during the period 1780–85, one-third of Bengal wills in the India Office provided a bequest for an Indian wife, companion, or natural children, and many more Britons in India presumably kept bibis without wishing to leave a formal legal record. However, by 1850, such provisions were negligible. The British broadly regarded Anglo-Indians as inferior in ability. Employment and opportunities with the EIC had become highly restrictive, and, socially, life was increasingly difficult. Indeed, Edmonstone's mixed-race daughter, Eliza, who remained in Calcutta, was barred from any EIC functions and held virtually no social standing despite her father's pre-eminent position in the Company, her marriage to the English deputy secretary of the Bank of Bengal, John Barker Plumb, and her substantial wealth as a result of a large dowry. This deprivation was taking place at a time when the Anglo-Indian population was expanding rapidly. Edmonstone, for example, believed that by the 1820s the Eurasian exceeded the European population of Calcutta.[8] Accordingly, for British parents, Europe was not only a means of enhancing the education of their mixed-race children; it was also a route to respectability for these children, if they could camouflage their Indian ancestry.

A contemporary observer, Munro Innes, gives us some idea of just how widespread was the phenomenon of sending Anglo-Indian progeny to Britain for schooling, while also making clear his own views on mixed unions. He wrote:

In this country, the women are kept perfectly idle and ignorant; those of the higher casts [sic] being either entertained as wives and concubines in the zenanas, or as dancing girls; excepting such as have lost caste, who, with the Portuguese wenches, a few Moorish and pariah women, generally fall to the lot of European soldiers as temporary wives. These are also the kind of ladies which European officers and civilians take such delight in supporting as kept mistresses; some gentlemen, of a singular (and I think a natural) taste, preferring them to white women. For my part, I consider them as at best a filthy and inanimate set of creatures having a strong smell; either of cocoa-nut oil, with which they constantly besmear their hair, or of the juice of betel nut which they are forever chewing, as a sailor does tobacco, and squirting over their clothes and apartments in the dirtiest manner. They also frequently rub themselves with ill-flavoured flowers and herbs, enough to disgust any man with a sound nose. Many allowances are, however, to be made for the ungovernable passions of those gentlemen which absolutely must have vent in this stimulating climate; but, I hope such parents will pardon my patriotism should I exclaim against transporting their offspring so frequently to

Great Britain. Measures might easily be fallen upon, both in the East
and West Indies, to give those mulattoes a decent education in the
country where they are born; and it surely would be more commend-
able by those means to render such children serviceable to their
native colonies, which are much better suited to their tempers and
constitutions, and consequently more conducive to their real happiness, than an education in Great Britain, where the birth which
nature has given them constantly exposes them, however unjustly[,]
to ridicule and reproach. If you were only to examine all the semi-
naries in Britain, for the education of youth, it would be found that
nearly one out of ten in the numbers they contain is of that description. I am, therefore, persuaded that the fathers of those children,
who are in any wise attached to their country, must as well as myself,
be convinced of the great danger which in course of time may arise
to the mother kingdom from this practice and surely government
never took the importance of this matter seriously into consideration,
otherwise a commerce, that may so sensibly degenerate the race and
give a sallow tinge to the complexion of Britons, would most certainly be prohibited. It was by this means that the Spaniards and
Portuguese got so much of a dusky hew in their accountancies, having kept up an unrestricted intercourse with their colonies till they
were seduced to their present despicable state; but, the French, sensible of its bad effects, issued an edict that none of those sable or
tawny-coloured foreigners should ever be permitted to remain above
eight days in France, and they must immediately return by the first
ship to their own country.[9]

Whereas Munro made the case that Anglo-Indians should remain in
the country of their birth, Edmonstone, who sired at least four half-caste
children with a native woman before marrying Charlotte Anne Friell in
Calcutta in 1803, believed that Anglo-Indians would fare worse in India
than almost anywhere else.

The great ... number of that class of the community of India denomi-
nated half-caste ... [are] generally speaking rejected and despised by
the European part of the society and held in very inferior estimation
by the natives. They belong in fact exclusively neither to the one nor
to the other. They are debarred from the rights and privileges of
British subjects, being deemed in law natives of the country, while
they are shut out from most of the advantages of their imputed

nativity by their religion, habits, manners and education. Precluded from holding any offices under Government but those of the most subordinate description; without capital, and consequently without the means of engaging in the commerce of the country, or establishing themselves as landholders, allied paternally with the European community, and maternally to the native population but disavowed by both[,] they form an insulated, degraded and consequently discontented body.[10]

Yet prejudice also lay closer to home. When a friend sought a place in Britain for his Anglo-Indian sons where their "birth and complexion would be no impediment to admission," the governor general, Lord Moira, who would prove John's arch adversary, found a school in Edinburgh. However, he reported back that there remained "one great objection to such plans of education ... I mean the Scotch language which boys cannot help acquiring ... [let us hope] it can be rubbed off by their removal to England before it is too completely fixed."[11] Thus, as late as 1805 Moira believed a Scottish accent could prove almost as damaging, if not equally so, for one's prospects as Indian blood or a swarthy complexion.

Both John and Edmonstone were anxious to have their male children, at least, raised in Britain. At seven years old, George was sent to live with his spinster aunt Margaret Baillie at Ness House in Inverness, and Edmonstone's two older sons, John and Alexander, also entered Margaret's household the same year, 1802. They were later joined by Ben, George's younger brother, and by Alexander Baillie's son, Charles. Margaret evidently was a formidable figure to take on such responsibility. Her cousin John Gibson remarked: "Margaret Baillie, my Cousin Peggy I mean, must be kept quite busy what with the boys, looking after Leys & then chasing votes etc. She is a noble lass."[12]

While Margaret dealt with the boys even-handedly, the fathers clearly did not. John Baillie treated his Anglo-Indian children as the equals of fully British offspring; his sons were raised by family, bore the Baillie name, and were university-educated. In contrast, Edmonstone, more representative of the era, had his sons raised well away from family, named them Elmore rather than Edmonstone, resisted sending them to college for fear such an education would raise their expectations beyond their rank, and never saw them once he returned to Britain. In fact, Marmaduke Edmonstone Browne, a descendant of Edmonstone, believes that the children of Neil Benjamin Edmonstone and Charlotte Anne Friell had no inkling that the Elmores existed.[13] When he interviewed that generation's only remaining survivor, she told him that she had never suspected the existence of another family but that she did remember Colonel Baillie visiting her father and a large emerald ring the colonel had given Edmonstone.[14] Indeed, the only hint of any tension between Edmonstone and Margaret arose from her decision to send the older Elmore to college.[15] As Margaret wrote in July 1812:

> I shall be extremely vexed & mortified at your removing the Boys from here till their future pursuits in life renders it necessary[,] particularly as I will believe such a determination proceeds from your displeasure at my having sent the Eldest to college without your approbation, which I certainly would never have ventured in had there been time to consult you on the subject, but I mentioned to my Brother the reasons that induced me to take such a step & hoped they might prove sufficient to excuse it. I never considered the charge of the Boys troublesome. On the contrary the hope of being in any measure useful to them afforded me infinite pleasure & I shall ever be most warmly interested in their welfare and happiness. John has lately expressed a wish to go into the mercantile line & should he remain with me I propose (if agreeable to you) that after spending one other year at his education he shall be under the direction of a respectable gentleman in trade here to ascertain whether his liking to business may be permanent.
>
> Alick though at first rather slow in learning now gets it much better and is a Boy of uncommon fine disposition. I shall indeed be both surprized and disappointed if he does not turn out remarkably well.[16]

The question as to whether the Elmores would remain with Margaret appears to have been resolved, for she subsequently wrote Edmonstone: "Your agreeable favour ... afforded me sincere pleasure, as it removed the painful idea of your being dissatisfied with the mode of education adopted for the Boys, particularly sending John to college. I now conceive the only objection arose from the fear that it might give the Boy ideas inconsistent with your views for him, to avoid which I constantly endeavour to impress his mind with a conviction that such education is given solely for the purpose of better enabling him to work his way through the world."[17] She could not, however, let pass that her brother's son George would be sent to university in London in a year or two to obtain his medical degree.

As the Elmore boys attained ages at which careers were chosen, Margaret engaged in a lengthy correspondence with both Edmonstone and his brother, Sir Charles. She outlined the two boys' circumstances in a letter to Sir Charles in September 1813:

John is nearly seventeen & Alick entered his fifteenth year. They have been educated at the Academy here, & had every advantage generally bestowed on the children of Scottish gentlemen in this country. The Eldest was 3 winters at King's College Aberdeen, where I presumed to send him along with my Brother's son, without any previous direction, but have since had the happiness to receive Mr. Edmonstone's approbation. Alick not having any great turn for classical learning did not go to college, but left the grammar school within these few months ... though of equal ability with his Brother, having been early rather backward in learning, he would certainly require some time longer at school. They are now 11 years under my care, & I can with truth say never were Boys of such docile & tractable dispositions. They are also very affectionate & most grateful for any good offered to them. John is decidedly inclined to the mercantile line, indeed their joint wish is to get out as merchants to Bengal, failing of which (with your approbation) John would have no objection to go into a counting house in London. He writes a good hand & has a sufficient knowledge of figures, having now left the Academy[;] he writes a few hours every day in the custom house here & attends a French class. As you are acquainted with their history I think it right to observe that the shade in their complexion is little conspicuous, since John might pass for a very dark native of Britain, & Alick would never be supposed otherwise by people unacquainted with his birth.[18]

Given Edmonstone's view of the shoddy treatment Anglo-Indians faced in their own country, it is not surprising that he put a stop to any thought of the Elmores' pursuing their careers in India. Nevertheless, the refusal came as a bitter disappointment to the boys, particularly when their contemporary, George Baillie, was preparing to embark for Bengal. Margaret recognized the firmness of Edmonstone's refusal to countenance any thought of India. "Mr. Edmonstone's letter & the perusal of it," she informed Sir Charles, "has now fully convinced me that he does not wish the Boys should go to India, therefore attempting to send either of them would be very wrong since he is certainly the best judge of the difficulties attending their comfortable establishment there."[19] Another letter in the same vein followed soon after:

> I should have earlier done myself the honour of answering your favour of the 1st, but judged it reasonable to allow John a little time to consider & reconcile his mind to the disappointment he appears to feel at losing his long cherished hope of getting out to India. Being[,] however, most desirous to conform to your wishes on views for him, he will not object to entering a counting house in Glasgow, but seems dreadfully averse to the manufacturers which he says he can by no means bring his mind to. The fact is that though without a legal claim to any rank in society he is sufficiently proud & has a great desire to be considered a gentleman. Therefore, he balks at any employment which he imagines might retard his being received as such; feeling the misfortune of his birth he eagerly grasps at what affords the quickest prospect of getting over it, & with this idea formerly thought of the army, but as the choice did not appear to proceed from any very decided partiality for the profession, I rather dissuaded him, for though a genteel line certainly a subaltern's pay scarce affords the means of subsistence. John however bids me say that with your approbation he would greatly prefer the army to the manufacturers' business, & indeed I now suspect to any other except his longed-for India ... a letter of my Brother's gave rise to the wish for he once mentioned the situation of a free mariner, that is getting out to Bengal with liberty to remain, & trade in the country[,] as eligible for his Eldest Boy (who however had taken a fancy to the medical line) but Elmore immediately declared he should like such an appointment extremely, & being led to believe it was not difficult to be obtained, I did not direct him from it. He entreated my Brother would propose the plan to Mr. Edmonstone, to which letter there could not yet be an answer. You enquired how the idea of John going to London along with my Nephew was raised, in answer to which I beg leave to observe that I only hinted to Mr. Edmonstone as those two boys' education had all along been carried on together, it might appear proper to him to send John from here at the same time with the other in order to place him by your direction & assistance in such a situation as should be thought most expedient for his further advantage but I would never have presumed to send him without positive orders to such purpose. Indeed, my Nephew is still here but preparing for his departure. Elmore requests me to mention that

should you decide in favour of the military profession for him, he would prefer a Scots regiment.[20]

John Elmore was not easily dissuaded from pursuing his dream of a military career, as Margaret explained in a further letter to Sir Charles:

Though John Elmore sees the propriety of relinquishing all idea of going out to Bengal, I much fear he cannot so cheerfully give up his wish to enter the army, since he has for some weeks past flattered himself with having your approbation to do so. I imagine Mr. Edmonstone's mention of the mercantile line for John proceeds partly from my having written him that the Boy inclined it, which at the time he really appeared to do, but ever since the army was again proposed to him his heart seems set on it. I say again proposed because [in] the second letter I had the honour of addressing to you (in answer to your question, whether any of the Boys had a partiality for the army) I mentioned that John early expressed a great liking, but that I endeavoured to divert him from it, as I thought a subaltern's pay not sufficient to support the rank of a gentleman, and in reply you had the goodness to say, that if he chose the profession, you should think yourself authorized to make him some additional allowance from which he inferred your support. And indeed I entertained the same idea & of course rather led him to view the bright side of a soldier's life, so that I cannot now with propriety use the same arguments I might formerly have done against it, though I tell him ... that in the mercantile line, he would probably acquire a handsome independence, which as a soldier he has very little chance of doing. Yet he perseveres in saying the army is decidedly his choice, & that he trusts the same goodness that led you to promise a little addition to his allowances while a subaltern will induce his worthy & hitherto so kind & indulgent father to assist him in getting beyond the rank which is all he could look for. I trust those hopes of John's may be realized, as though Mr. Edmonstone has the prospect of a large family, I should think a gentleman of his fortune & interest could never find it difficult to do all poor Elmore expects.

After thus expressing his wishes, John bids me say that if such is still your pleasure he will try the mercantile line, though I greatly dread with reluctance because he remarked that even if he tired of the army or did not succeed, then he could go into trade but after failing in business, it would be too late to enter the army with any chance of doing well. I repeat the above observation to let you men fully understand the young man's inclinations. After knowing which, it must rest with you Sir Charles to fix his future destiny. Only permit me to add that the sooner he knows your determination the better as a state of uncertainty prevents his paying proper attention to any thing.[21]

Margaret let Edmonstone know that Sir Charles had quickly responded, confirming that he would secure a commission for John.

Sir Charles[,] though he appeared to regret that Elmore had not continued study to the commercial line[,] had the goodness to promise him a commission, of course he now only waits till it can be conveniently procured ... I trust you will upon the whole think it best that the young man has been indulged & have no doubt of his still turning out well & giving satisfaction to his friends since he has ever been & continues entirely free from any vicious habits or inclinations ... As his Brother has written[,] Alick defers the happiness of addressing you to another opportunity but entreats me to tell you with his affectionate duty that he never had any desire for a red coat, & will some little time hence be most happy to enter into trade either at Glasgow or wherever else his friends may judge most proper. I can only add that I am & must ever continue very warmly interested in the success & happiness of both Boys, whose good temper & docile dispositions rendered them an easy & pleasant charge.[22]

Sir Charles made one last effort to induce John Elmore to enter the much more lucrative commercial line but relented in the face of John's insistence that the army was his desire. When Sir Charles offered him the choice between two regiments, and was met with indifference, Margaret suggested that the choice be governed by social practicalities. "Elmore is extremely grateful for your kind condescension in allowing him a choice but as the destination of both regiments is said to be the same & he has no acquaintance with either it cannot make any difference in which the commission is purchased. Perhaps going among entire strangers may rather be an advantage as I think those ignorant of his history will scarcely discover it from his appearance, which upon the whole is certainly prepossessing & the complexion not darker than I have seen in general natives of this country."[23]

John joined his regiment at Charlesfort and then embarked for Ireland. Margaret was later able to report to Edmonstone that she had received "most favourable reports of his conduct & character from all quarters. Indeed, I am assured there is no officer in his regiment of the same rank more respected than John."[24] Yet John's posting in Ireland as a full-pay officer was of relatively short duration, as John Baillie, upon his return to Britain, reported to Edmonstone: "My sister is with me in town and left your son John a halfpay Lieut. in Inverness Shire living with my relations whom he seems to prefer to his own naturally enough, poor fellow, as having been brought up with them since his childhood."[25] Subsequently, John wrote a letter to Edmonstone in which he revealed that he shared the gentleman-landowner's traditional wholehearted disdain of trade, even though he himself had earned rather than inherited his fortune:

The two lads who were brought up by my Sister unquestionably do credit to her care for them & are every way entitled to your name & the countenance of your family, tho' unfortunately for them deprived of the one & enjoying but a little of the other. John has lived with me nearly five months & is still with one branch of my family. I shall endeavour if I can see your brother to persuade him of the necessity of replacing John on the full pay of the army & if possible in an Indian reg't. His appearance is just as respectable as that of any young officer in His Majesty's Service. Poor Alick has been brought upon a line that I should not have approved. He is truly an amiable youth & would do credit to a more honourable profession than that of a manufacturer in Glasgow.

Edmonstone had asked John for a "settlement of accounts" with respect to his two sons' care and education over thirteen years, and John, while stressing that "I have no wish to mortify you by an idea that you owe me any thing on any score (I certainly owe you a great deal on many scores)," reported that the sum owing, less his own debts to Edmonstone, was £600.[26] And, since that is the last mention of the Elmores, we shall continue to wonder whether John regained full pay and distinguished himself in the army, and whether Alick persevered as a manufacturer in Glasgow or attained a "more honourable profession."

16

The Resident at Lucknow

Not Rome, nor Athens, not Constantinople; not any city I have
ever seen appears to me so striking and so beautiful as this.
William Russell on Lucknow[1]

On 20 July 1807 John reported that he had arrived in Lucknow and
assumed charge of the Residency and the balance of the treasury. Lucknow
was the seat of power of the nawabs of Oude, a Persian Shia merchant
family that had been ennobled by the Mughal emperor Bahadur Shah I.
In 1720 the emperor appointed Saadat Ali Khan governor of Agra and
in 1722 governor of Oude. Saadat greatly expanded the boundaries of
Oude and by 1740 Saadat Ali Khan I carried the titles of nawab and
vizier. As the power of the Mughals, who arrived in India from Central
Asia as "ruddy men in boots" and departed four centuries later as "pale
persons in petticoats,"[2] waned, the fortunes of the nawabs of Oude
waxed. As a result, the nawabs deferred less and less to the nominal overlord in Delhi.

As his assurance grew, the third nawab vizier, Shuja-ood-Dowla,
ordered the British to confine themselves to trade or be prepared to
defend themselves. As recounted earlier, the British had no intention of so
confining themselves and Hector Munro resoundingly defeated Shuja
and his allies, Mir Qasim, the nawab of Bengal, and Shah Alam II, the
Mughal emperor, at the Battle of Buxar in 1764. The victorious British
then prevailed upon the emperor to dismiss Shuja-ood-Dowla as governor of Oude. Only after the deposed nawab yielded to the East India
Company did the British relent and restore the bulk of his territory to
him through the Treaty of Allahabad. In a subsequent treaty of 1773 the
British sold back the remainder of the nawab's lands in return for fifty
lakhs, raised the nawab's expense of provisioning the British troops in
Oude, and established a resident at Shuja's capital, Faizabad. In effect,

the British created the buffer state of Oude to protect Bengal against the Afghans in Rohilkand and the Marathas in Delhi.

In 1774 the third nawab, the pleasure-loving Asaf-ood-Dowla, transferred the capital to Lucknow and began construction of the Residency, which was completed in 1800. The Residency eventually became a vast complex but a contemporary account suggests a smaller scale at the outset.

> By Lucknow standards the British Residency was a modest building. It had three storeys; and with its colonnaded west front, classical portico, semicircular fanlights, striped canvas awnings and Italianate roof balustrade gave the impression rather of a spacious summer villa than an embassy or palace. Only the somewhat incongruous decagonal tower, with its ribbed dome and finial, hinted at greater pretensions. Yet the overall impression was not unworthy of the symbol of British ascendancy. The building was situated on a low mound on the south bank of the River Gomti, to the west of the Farhatbakhsh palace – one of the most elevated and desirable sites in the city. Extensive gardens surrounded it on every side, full of mango, cypress, roses, oleander and scarlet hibiscus; and its yellow-washed walls were restful to the eyes even in the fiercest sunlight.[3]

The Residency later became renowned as the centre of British resistance in the Great Mutiny of 1857, and the site on which it stood was preserved as a museum to British grit and tenacity.

Following the death of Asaf-ood-Dowla in 1797, the British recognized Wazir Ali as his successor. Yet, within a year, Governor General Wellesley had forced his abdication, ostensibly because Asaf-ood-Dowlah's paternity of Wazir Ali was in question but in fact because Wazir's uncle, Saadat Ali Khan II, was seen to be more compliant to British demands. Tuhseen Ali, a crony of Asaf-ood-Dowlah, in league with the wife and the mother of the late nawab, spread a rumour that Wazir Ali had been purchased from his mother for five hundred rupees. An opponent of the nawab relayed the report to the governor general who, finding the rumour convenient, replaced Wazir Ali on the musnud allowing him no opportunity to rebut the charge. At the time of his elevation, Saadat Ali II agreed to raise the annual tribute to the Company to seventy-six lakhs of rupees, cede the Fort of Allahabad, and accept ten thousand British troops quartered and paid for by the nawab. The following year, Wellesley attempted to impose a new treaty on Saadat but the nawab was not entirely supine and threatened to abdicate rather than pay additional revenues and disband his army. However, the Company's pressure proved relentless and by 1801 Saadat Ali Khan II had ceded half of the kingdom and disbanded his troops in favour of British forces.

CR

In the same month that John assumed his duties as resident at Lucknow, Gilbert Elliot, Lord Minto, replaced Barlow as governor general. George IV insisted that India warranted an administrator of high rank, and Elliot fit the bill, having been created Lord Minto in 1797 and served as viceroy of the Anglo-Corsican Kingdom from 1793 to 1796. More significantly, he had gained valuable insight into Indian affairs as president of the Board of Control. Fortunately for John, the new governor general, a fellow Scot, proved to be supportive throughout his tenure. Minto had initially subscribed to the policy of non-aggression now espoused by India House, but, shortly after his arrival, Napoleon annexed Holland, which gave him control of Malacca and the Spice Islands. Minto expeditiously organized an invasion force which conquered the Spice Islands and the island of Java. He then deprived Napoleon of further possessions in the east by capturing the French islands of Mauritius and Bourbon.

During this time, John, as the resident at Oude, exerted great influence. "The Residents enjoyed among the European community immense power and authority, some of which was presumed by the community and not in fact possessed by the Resident, but which nevertheless did not detract seriously from his status. It is no exaggeration to say that from about 1800 onwards there were two courts in Lucknow, that of the nawab and that of the Resident."[4] Still, much of John's workload dealt with the mundane and his correspondence is peppered with references to pensions, the restoration of grounds and gardens in Goruckpoor to the nawab vizier, and the need for the nawab's government to undertake extensive reform. He later described his responsibilities:

> It was my duty to take cognizance of all the political transactions
> of the government to which I was accredited, and to guard against
> the adoption of any measure tending to infringe its political relations
> with our government ... to report every event or occurrence of
> moment, and in all practical cases to apply for and await the instruc-
> tions of government regarding these occurrences, to receive and com-
> ply with the requisitions of the allied sovereign for aid or advice
> on emergency, to direct and superintend the employment of British

troops in his dominions when their services were required for the purpose either of external defence or of maintaining internal tranquility, by suppressing disaffection or rebellion, and to attend to a variety of matters of detail which is unnecessary and impossible here to enumerate.[5]

Those tasks that he found "unnecessary and impossible to enumerate" undoubtedly entailed unravelling the endless intrigues at the court of Oude. First, he became involved in exposing a conspiracy by Mohammed Ali Khan to replace his brother as nawab vizier. Mohammed Ali Khan and his moonshee, Mahommed Saudik, fabricated a document addressed to Barlow that had purportedly been drafted by the late resident, Colonel Collins. The conspirators then arranged to have the report and other suspect letters, which criticized the nawab's conduct, delivered to the governor general. The plot was discovered, with the result that the resident and the nawab were able to apprehend the moonshee and to arrange Mohammed Ali Khan's "retirement" to Patna. Naturally, Mohammed Ali Khan vehemently disavowed having ever entertained any thought of subdividing the Kingdom of Oude or assuming the musnud until receiving overtures to that end in the name of Colonel Collins. Similarly, Mahommed Saudik solemnly denied ever having visited the house of Mohammed Ali Khan. Nevertheless, the circumstantial evidence was compelling and the enforced "retirement" took place.

Next, the deceased nawab's widow, Begum Shurrs Oodipa, complained continually of the current nawab's misconduct toward her. She solicited permission to live in the Company's dominions and sought to ingratiate herself by naming the EIC heir to her lands and possessions. Then, John became embroiled in investigating the nawab vizier's charge that his Delhi agent, Dola Ram, was embezzling funds but the accusation proved unfounded. No sooner had John dealt with these machinations than Inteaz Ali usurped the lands of John's moonshee, Ali Nuckee Khan, who had served John faithfully at the College of Fort William and Bundelcund and had distinguished himself in negotiating General James Stewart's release from the Sikhs.

ʒʒ

In the midst of all these intrigues, John fell ill. Ann Gibson had mentioned John's having been gravely ill as a result of a servant employing tainted pots. The illness presumably was serious, since the nawab vizier awarded Robert Wilson, a surgeon, 5,000 rupees for attending John during his sickness in January and February 1808 and John named his next-born son John Wilson Baillie. At roughly this time, too, John must have fallen in love with a grand noblewoman – known as the Begum of Oude. Mitchell asserts: "While the colonel was Resident at Lucknow he became a great favourite with the King of Oude, who presented him with one of the ladies of his court distinguished for her beauty, to whom it was said the colonel was married, and she brought with her a brilliant assortment of valuable jewels."[6] John appears to have addressed her as Lulu.[7] It is likely that John married the Begum, though no documentary proof of the marriage has been uncovered. John and Lulu had three children: Anne, born in 1809; John Wilson, born in 1811; and Henrietta, born in 1811. All three were baptized in Lucknow. There is some confusion as to the identity of John Wilson's mother since the British Army List indicates that his mother was Mary Martin or Baillie but the circumstantial evidence remains tilted toward the Begum of Oude.[8] Marla Chancey, in her book on Neil Benjamin Edmonstone, asserts that John married a native Indian and brought her back to Britain "dripping with jewels."[9] Since the Victorian purists religiously expunged any compromising references to great men having entertained Indian wives or mistresses, we have scant record of John's wife. There is no record that the Begum ever came to Britain nor any mention of the Begum on John's memorial plaque in the Grey Friars' Church in Inverness. But his descendants do have what, given the era, must be a photograph of a painting of Lulu, and the Baillies of Dochfour have a painting of *The Three Children of Colonel John Baillie of Leys and His Wife the Begum of Oude*. The Dochfour Baillies also have a portrait that appears to be of Wazir Ali Khan, the deposed nawab of Oude. Michael Baillie, Lord Burton, told me some years ago that a visitor had presented the family with the painting explaining that the subject was related to the Dochfour Baillies. From that, I surmise that Wazir Ali was the father of the Begum of Oude, who presumably remained in Lucknow after her father's banishment to Benares. A daughter would clearly have fared better remaining at the court of the nawab since Wazir Ali, after arriving in Benares, rebelled against the British who condemned him to spend the remaining seventeen years of his life in an iron cage in Vellore.

Mary Martin, on the other hand, most definitely was intimately connected to John. Not only is there the citation in the British Army List but John's will left Mary Martin, the "widow of John Chalcroft," a life annuity of £200, the use of his house in Connaught Terrace, and a legacy of

£100. Mary Martin was also to receive the furniture in the cottage at Finchley, Middlesex, and the use of the cottage for the remaining years of the lease.

During his years in Lucknow, the lives of John's relatives in Scotland were filled with marriages, births, career quests, and deaths. He corresponded regularly with Isabella, the widow of his uncle John Baillie of Dunain, and remained aware of that family's activities. His cousin Alick, the youngest of the three boys, died in 1805, the same year his cousin Katharine married Sir Hugh Rose of Kilravock. Katharine gave birth to Isabella Rose, named in honour of her grandmother, in 1806. The Roses tactfully flattered the grandparents, with Isabella soon followed by Hugh Rose in 1808 and then John Baillie Rose in 1809. Isabella's oldest son, William, as we have seen, attended the University of Aberdeen and the University of Edinburgh and then was engaged as an apprentice to Kenneth Mackenzie, a writer to the Signet, with a view to practising law. The younger children, Archy and Anne, were then still at school. John and Helen Alves's daughters had married earlier, Helen to George Inglis of Kingsmills, a business partner of George Baillie (Ardmore) and Archibald and William Alves, in 1796, and Ann to William Arbuthnot, lord provost of Edinburgh and later a baronet, in 1822. Their son, William, was a successful merchant in Demerara and distinguished himself in the defence of St Vincent against the French, an action in which he was wounded.

John's half-brother, George, who was born on 4 February 1787 to George Baillie of Leys and his second wife, Margaret Cumming, in Nairn, trained as a surgeon and was anxious to test his mettle in India. Fortunately for him and for many other local lads, Charles Grant simultaneously served as the member of Parliament for Inverness-shire and as chairman of the East India Company. Grant was successful in the petition he submitted in 1807 to the East India Company on behalf of George: "The humble Petition of George Baillie Sheweth That your Petitioner has applied himself with great Diligence to the Study and Practice of Surgery and is desirous of Proceeding to the East Indies as an Assistant Surgeon. He therefore humbly solicits your Honors Permission for that purpose being ready to give such Security as your Honors may require. Recommended for Bengal 1807 Charles Grant." By 25 January 1808, George had been examined as to his physical abilities and found qualified to serve in the station of assistant surgeon at any of the Company's presidencies in the East Indies. He joined his siblings in India later that year.

On the debit side, John's brother William, who was the only one of the immediate family to seek his fortune in the West Indies, died of unknown

causes in Jamaica on 5 May 1810. Other than a short note providing his
address a few years earlier, there is little record of his activities. Nevertheless, it seems a safe assumption, given the absence of any correspondence
among the potential beneficiaries, that the fortune to which he aspired
remained beyond his grasp.

John's younger sister, Annie, scandalized the family when she announced her decision to marry one Munro. The family banded together to
oppose the marriage but Annie was adamant. Munro's shortcomings were
never specified. Since throughout the correspondence Munro never merits
a Christian name, it is almost impossible to determine whether he was a
relative of Hector Munro, to whose actions, or lack thereof, the Baillies
attributed William of Dunain's deplorable fate. Yet, almost assuredly, the
family would not detest Annie's fiancé on account of a relative's perceived
shortcomings. Feelings ran so uniformly and so passionately against
Munro that he must have been regarded as no gentleman. William reported
to his mother, Isabella: "I have seen Coll: [Alexander] Baillie who looks
as well I think as when last in Britain. He has no idea that Miss Annie's
marriage with Munro can be prevented but hopes they will be prevailed
upon to stay in London. He expressed strong disapprobation of the thing
when first mentioned to him by his sister, but told her at the same time
that if she was determined upon it, her time of life put it out of his power
to give any opposition to it and that she must judge for herself. Margaret
& Kate Baillie are living with me at an hotel. They don't like to go to the
Commodore's for fear of meeting Munro."[10] Or as William said subsequently: "I forget whether I mentioned in my former letters that the Miss
Baillies & I live in the same lodgings, owing to Miss Annie's keeping
violent possession of the Commodore's."[11] Nevertheless, Annie persevered and the marriage took place. Sister Margaret, in her inimitable way,
must have expressed her opinion trenchantly. "You have heard that Annie
is married & that neither her Brothers or any of us were present. Both
Alick & Kate have[,] however[,] seen her since but none of them Munro.
I understand she talks of leaving this the week after next, and I will
remain as short as possible after, only to see how Kate gets on with the
Commodore ... My Brother [Alexander] declares that he has no wish any
of our friends should visit Anne; in all events she & I can have no intercourse, as she ordered me never to enter any house of which she was
mistress for my impertinence in daring to come here to interfere with her
happiness."[12] Even cousin Ann Gibson chimed in from Bengal: "Give
our love to Margaret & to poor unfortunate Annie Baillie ... I hope her
husband is sensible of the very great sacrifice she has made for him."[13]

Back in Lucknow, John was vexed by the nawab's arbitrary and excessive taxation, which both impoverished his subjects and depleted the land. Exacerbating his irritation were the nawab's constant demands to employ British troops not only to enforce payment of this oppressive taxation but also to destroy the forts the zemindars had built to protect themselves from the nawab's exactions. John believed that the iniquity was attributable more to the existing system, wherein the will of the sovereign "stimulated by a spirit of insatiable rapacity, constitutes the law,"[14] than to the malevolence of the nawab's officers. In the resident's view: "His Excellency's leading passion of avarice, and all its concomitant evils, have, as is natural, increased with his age, and the reluctance and impatience with which he ever listened to remonstrance against the inordinate gratification of this passion, or against any other unjust measure of his government, have lately risen to a degree of peevishness and irritation, which renders the efficient conduct of the duties of my station at this court, combined with the observances and offices of personal respect and conciliation, a great deal more difficult than before."[15]

During his posting in Bundelcund, John had witnessed the burdensome and oppressive taxation which had ground down the farmers. He was also conscious that the reforms implemented by the British in the territory ceded by the nawab of Oude had markedly improved the livelihood of the inhabitants and the productivity of the land. John firmly believed that an efficient system of reform was in the long-term interests of both the royal house of Oude and the people of the country. As a consequence, implementing such a system became almost an obsession with him. John first proposed a program of reform to the nawab in July 1808. He suggested that a representative of the nawab and of the resident jointly investigate the conditions of the various districts with a view to determining what the lands were capable of yielding "at a fair and moderate valuation."[16] He proposed that Oude then be divided into four or five zillahs, which would, in turn, be subdivided into districts producing one to three lakhs of rupees each. These districts would be entrusted to officers of undoubted character who would be compensated by a fixed salary and be allowed to reap a reward from the enhanced productivity of the districts. The zemindars would benefit from the assurance of fixed taxes for a three-year term, would have a right of appeal to the government against repressive taxation, and would have no need for fortresses which would be forbidden in the affected districts. The resident had modelled his proposed system on that in the Ceded Territories (land surrendered to the EIC by the nawab), a system that depended upon trustworthy ameers.

Accordingly, John suggested that the nawab select suitable candidates
and refer them to the resident for vetting. He also recommended including the phrase "with the advice and concurrence of the British Government"[17] in any proclamation on the rationale that such an insertion
would give comfort to the zemindars and farmers that the new arrangements would, indeed, be honoured.

As John surmised, the nawab had little interest in such reform. Saadat
Ali recognized that he would forfeit his rights to exact arbitrary assess-
ments and to confiscate the estates of defaulting farmers and collectors.
At first, he dismissed John's suggestions on the basis that he lacked trustworthy public officers, but the resident persisted. In fact, reform became
a fixation of John's, a fixation that was continually thwarted by the
nawab. But John was more resolute and tenacious than his adversary. In
addition, Saadat Ali was dependent on the resident to supply the troops
necessary to suppress resistance by the zemindars and to destroy the forts
in which they sought refuge from the nawab's exhorbitant demands. A
writer for the *Oriental Herald* contended that the resident and his supporters encouraged the zemindars to withhold their taxes so as to force
the nawab to submit to the proposed reforms. However, if there was such
a strategy, it clearly was undercut by the resident's employment, albeit
grudgingly, of the troops used to subdue the zemindars.[18] John's bargaining position improved when Lord Minto, in turn, urged adoption of
reforms upon the nawab. The governor general wrote:

That its interests were too deeply concerned in the reform of the
present vicious system of administration in his Excellency's dominions to permit the Governor-General in Council tacitly to acquiesce
in its continuance: that to the evils and abuses of that system, to the
oppression and injustice which naturally flowed from it, were principally to be ascribed those disorders which the British troops were
so frequently employed to suppress; that this Government had ever
viewed with painful regret the employment of its troops in services
of this nature, the general tendency of which had naturally been to
uphold and encourage those acts of violence, injustice, and extortion,
which a system erroneous in its principle and oppressive in its operation could not fail to engender.[19]

The communiqué concluded that the British government should "interpose
the weight of its influence" on the side of reform. It recognized that the

nawab would incessantly place obstacles in its path but that even "defective execution of the plan would be attended with some advantage."

The nawab remonstrated with John that the governor general would never have objected to the time-honoured taxation system had the resident not pressed the point. John responded that this reproach was proof of his conscientious discharge of his duty to both states since he had faithfully reported the proceedings at the nawab's court. He then remarked that the nawab had demonstrated a resolution to evade, if not resist, the salutary counsel of the governor general expressed in the language of friendship. He emphasized that the nawab's absolute rejection of Lord Minto's counsel was tantamount to a direct infraction of Saadat Ali's engagements. That rejection provided the British every right to impose their advice in all matters connected with the ordinary affairs of His Excellency's dominions.

With the governor general's steadfast stand on the issue of reform, the resident, after tedious and drawn-out negotiations, prevailed – or at least appeared to prevail. The nawab acquiesced and agreed to divide his dominions into zillahs and districts. In addition, he consented to appoint ameers but remained adamant that the resident should have neither a voice in the selection of the ameers nor a veto of the revenue arrangements. Such a voice or veto the nawab viewed as undermining his authority. John justified his involvement in the selection of the ameers on the basis that the nawab could not expect the support of British troops to quell resistance if the resident was not in a position to assess the justice of such a request. Nevertheless, John yielded on the question of vetting the ameers. The Council in Bengal confirmed the terms of the agreement. Minto commended the resident's "zeal, judgment, and ability which he had certainly displayed in concluding these discussions"[20] but was disappointed that Saadat Ali had yielded more to the energy and firmness of the resident than to the intrinsic merits of the reforms themselves.

Saadat Ali soon recanted, posing various objections and suggesting a trial of the new arrangements in one district only. Then, in July 1810, he requested British troops to suppress resistance in Sultanpore and Dalmow. John countered that the Company would agree to destroy forts only in situations where the possessors had opposed the just authority of the state. Lieutenant-Colonel Samuel Palmer was able to justify the destruction of twenty-two forts in three districts. John took the opportunity to insist once again on the proclamation of reform. Saadat Ali appeared to capitulate and sent his agent Mohummud Ashruf to the affected districts, ostensibly

to ensure the provisioning of the troops and determine a fair tax assessment. Ashruf totally subverted the purpose of his mission, acting as if his
sole purpose was to extract even higher taxes. Palmer was particularly
incensed since Ashruf had imposed exceedingly burdensome terms on
many of the zemindars, relying on Palmer's detachment to intimidate them
into submission. He observed that the proclamation had been received
favourably but the actions of Mohummud Ashruf had revived the zemindars' distrust. Accordingly, he was skeptical that subsequent proclamations would be given any credence. Needless to say, collection of revenues
would be attended with great difficulty, if not outright evasion.

John quickly prevailed upon the nawab to order Ashruf to abstain
from imposing excessive settlements but all recognized that the order was
mere form. The resident then informed the nawab: "Nothing but oppression to the ryots, disputes between Mohummud Ashruf and the zemindars, and finally disorder in the country, could be expected from his
[Ashruf's] deputation."[21] As a result, the objective he and Saadat Ali had
laboured so long and arduously to achieve could not be accomplished in
the current year. John finally threw caution to the winds and informed
Saadat Ali that, if he renewed existing leases without effecting the reforms,
"the future assistance or support of a single soldier of the British army to
the present baneful system of assessment and collection, or to any of its
instruments in the person of His Excellency's ameers, was totally out of
the question."[22] However, the government in Bengal indicated that it had
never contemplated carrying the negotiations to the extremes the resident was urging. Since the nawab's means of rendering the system abortive "were unlimited and beyond control," they were letting the initiative
lapse.[23] But John had other ideas.

The resident's unrelenting pressure for reform led to a plaintive outcry
by Saadat Ali. In January 1813 the nawab, temporarily rising from his
torpor, declared to Lord Minto that the indignities heaped upon him by
the resident had rendered his situation intolerable. "The wish of the
Resident is now to settle all matters in his own way, and merely apprise
me of the settlements; but your well-wisher will never consent to this;
and matters have come to such a pitch, that my statements are falsified
in every case, and the assertions of others are believed, which is extremely
distressing and disagreeable to me."[24] Yet Minto stood firm. "However
desirous Your Excellency may be to evade the performance of your
engagements, the British Government will not cease to require you to
fulfil them ... and no lapse of time and no change of circumstances will

induce the British Government to relinquish a measure which it considers
to be so essential to the welfare and happiness of Your Excellency's subjects ... and to the reputation and interest of both governments."[25] Saadat
Ali yielded, consenting to the reforms at the end of September 1813. A
month later, a public rapprochement occurred, the nawab embracing
John Baillie with "an affectionate hug" and banishing Huckeem Mehdi
Ali, the reputed source of the nawab's disaffection, from court "as a natural and necessary consequence of this reconciliation."[26]

CR

John's situation seemed increasingly attractive. His promotion to major
had been proclaimed on 2 January 1811, his lengthy and relentless campaign to improve the governance of Oude appeared to be bearing fruit, and
his half-brother, George, had been appointed assistant to the resident at
Lucknow on 5 March 1813. Lord Minto had proposed the appointment:

> I will confess that a very powerful motive with me in proposing this
> appointment is an earnest desire to promote the personal and official
> comfort of Maj. Baillie, and to meet his wishes on a point in which
> I know them to be warmly engaged. This arises solely from the high
> sense which I entertain of his great public merits, and if it partakes
> of the nature of a personal feeling, it is one which has its origin in
> public motives alone. Maj. Baillie is entirely unknown to me, except
> through the medium of his official correspondence and proceedings,
> and the high character which he bears for honour, integrity, learning,
> and talent. The sentiments of public respect, esteem, and applause,
> which a candid and impartial observation of his conduct has impressed
> on my mind, are known to the Board, and the proceedings bear testi-
> mony to the sense entertained by the present and former governments,
> of the ability, zeal, perseverance, and fortitude, displayed by Maj.
> Baillie, on various occasions of uncommon difficulty and delicacy, and
> by which he has resisted and overcome obstacles not to be surmounted
> by one possessing those qualities in an inferior degree. It is therefore
> with a high degree of satisfaction, in which I am persuaded I shall be
> joined by my colleagues, that I find myself able to propose an arrange-
> ment, which will combine with the indulgence of my cordial disposi-
> tion to gratify Maj. Baillie, an effectual provision for the necessities
> of the public service in the instance under consideration.[27]

In addition, John had just erected an elegant Banqueting Hall on the Residency grounds. The Baillie Gate, which provided refuge to the British during the Great Mutiny of 1857 and stands proudly to this day, was constructed in 1814 and John's elevation to the lieutenant-colonelcy of the Second Battalion, 4th Native Infantry, would materialize on 14 July of the same year. Finally, his eldest son, George, was scheduled to return to India as a surgeon in 1815, the Court of Directors having approved George's petition that he be permitted to return to Bengal "of which Kingdom he is a native, the Company being at no expense."[28]

For John, the resident at Lucknow, life indeed seemed good but disaster lurked.

Dismissal

There but for the grace of God, goes God.
Winston Churchill on Labour M P Stafford Cripps

He did not know it at the time, but the replacement of Lord Minto as governor general by Francis Rawdon-Hastings, Lord Moira,[1] in 1812 marked a turning point in John's career. Moira was a soldier by experience and education. He had served with distinction as Lord Rawdon in the American Revolutionary War, and then in the Low Countries, and owed his appointment to his friendship with the prince regent. Otherwise, he "had been a man of no great distinction in England."[2] In light of his military background, Moira was appointed both commander-in-chief and governor general. He possessed the mindset of a soldier, bluff and unsubtle; indeed, he was the model for the cad Rawdon Crawley in Thackeray's *Vanity Fair.*

Moira sincerely feared that the native princes would form an alliance to evict the British and was driven by a compulsion to establish British paramountcy in India. For that reason, he focused single-mindedly on military conquest at a time when Edmonstone and others in Bengal's government sought a period of tranquility. Edmonstone had supported Wellesley's conquests because he believed that the Company had no choice. However, he viewed Moira's wars as discretionary given that Britain had conclusively attained control of the subcontinent. The Marathas, the Pindari chief, Ameer Khan, and the founder of the Sikh Empire, Ranjit Singh, remained potential enemies of the British, but Edmonstone, like many others, calculated that no one of those groups could successfully oppose the British on its own and that, in the absence of provocation, their loathing of each other would preclude their uniting for that purpose.

Indeed, not only did Edmonstone view Moira's wars as gratuitous, but he also believed they were liable to create new perils. Whereas Wellesley had endeavoured to convert the native princes into allies, Moira gave the impression that he sought to transform them into vassals. At the same time, despite their extensive experience in the country, Moira paid little heed to his councillors and, in view of the royal favour he enjoyed, felt little need to justify his actions to the Court of Directors. Furthermore, Moira made no attempt to conceal his blatant preference for the military, whom he regarded as straightforward men of action, nor his disdain for the more effete diplomats, who engaged in what he regarded as unsavoury Eastern intrigue and other ungentlemanly pursuits. Understandably, then, Moira was far from popular with his colleagues, who resented both "the mode of his appointment and nature of his policies."[3] Sir David Ochterlony, the forthright hero of the Anglo-Nepalese War of 1814–16, former resident at Delhi, and unapologetic possessor of a harem of thirteen concubines, was not alone when he observed: "I do not like this new Viceroy, all noise and emptiness, like a drum ... I believe the old one was worth a dozen such."[4]

John's superb diplomatic, linguistic, and interpersonal skills had enabled him to earn the backing and respect of the preceding governors general. Shore as we have seen, had been sufficiently impressed with John that he commissioned him to translate a treatise on Muslim law and customs; Wellesley had presented him with a diamond ring in recognition of his services in Bundelcund; Barlow had praised him in a lengthy dispatch to the Court of Directors; and Lord Minto had appointed his younger half-brother, George, to his post at Lucknow in recognition of what Minto believed was John's exemplary service to the Company. This unqualified support was destined to end with the arrival of a governor general who differed so radically in his outlook from his immediate predecessors.

◌঵

Moira saw an opportunity in the tension that had been building for some time between Nepal and the Company. In 1804 the king of Nepal sent his military commander, the Gurkha leader Amar Singh Thapa, to annex the territories of the rajah of Palpa. Amar Thapa did not, however, stop at the Hills. He occupied Butwal in the district of Gorakhpore, even though the rajah of Palpa held that territory as a tenant of the nawab of Oude, to whose rights in Gorakhpore the Company had succeeded. Gorakhpore was a particularly desirable property owing to its fertility. Accordingly, the governor general demanded that the Gurkhas evacuate Butwal immediately. The Gurkhas refused to depart but did offer to pay rent to the

Company. The Company declined the offer but did not press its claim. Over the years, Amar Thapa appropriated more villages in the region, taking British quiescence as tacit recognition of Gurkha rights. Then in 1810 he announced his intention to occupy certain villages on the plains of Sirhind, on the grounds that these villages belonged to Sirmur and Hindur which were his by right of conquest. Initially, he desisted when Colonel Ochterlony, in his capacity as agent for the Sirhind Sikhs, declared he would contest any attempt to take the villages. But Amar Thapa was not easily dissuaded; in 1813 his forces seized six villages, two of which were under Ochterlony's protection. The king, not wanting to provoke a conflict with Ochterlony, ordered Amar Thapa to abandon those villages.

In a separate incident in 1811, Bir Krishna Singh, the rajah of Bettiah, a zemindar of the Company, on his own initiative, sent an armed body of men to seize a number of villages occupied by the Gurkhas. The Gurkhas claimed these villages as part of the conquered hill state of Makwanpur. The rajah, on the other hand, contended that they constituted a portion of the lands for which he had contracted to pay rent to the East India Company. During the encounter, the rajah's men killed a Nepalese soubah. The Gurkha rajah appealed to the Company, which concluded that the parties bore equal blame and, accordingly, the British would not condemn their zemindar. However, since the Butwal issue remained unresolved, the Company proposed an Anglo-Nepalese commission to settle the entire border question. The Gurkhas agreed but, still smouldering over the Makwanpur judgment, seized additional villages in Saran, for a total of twenty-two.

The Gurkha commissioner, Krishna Pandit, was well disposed toward the British and suggested that the Gurkha rajah concede British suzerainty in the lowlands in return for a lease to him of a tract along the foothills. Calcutta interpreted the offer as implicit admission of the British claims and Minto almost immediately dispatched an ultimatum demanding that the rajah surrender the lands or the Company would take them by force. The Company's chief commissioner, Major Paris Bradshaw, who was the head assistant at the Lucknow Residency, demanded that the Gurkhas withdraw from the twenty-two villages pending an investigation of the claims. The Gurkhas demurred but eventually consented. Once the Company was well ensconced in the hamlets, Bradshaw announced that there would be no investigation since evidence had already conclusively established the Company's right to the territory. In any event, Bradshaw believed that, in view of the Gurkhas' intransigence over Butwal, the Nepalese were liable to reject the findings. The Gurkhas naturally felt they had been deceived, as indeed they had. Calcutta ought to have allowed the investigation to proceed, particularly since the British were not yet aware the Nepalese had refused to evacuate Butwal and Saraj.

By now, Lord Moira was in charge. Upon the rajah's refusal to abandon the two territories, Moira sent a fresh ultimatum. The Gurkhas responded that they had no intention of forfeiting these lands to which an independent investigation had established their rights. The Gurkha commissioner terminated the negotiations and, upon the expiry of Moira's ultimatum, the magistrate of Gwalior ordered seventeen companies of native infantry to take possession of Butwal and Suraj. They met no resistance but, owing to malaria, the soldiers withdrew and the Gurkhas counter-attacked, inflicting several casualties on the Company's troops. The darogah had been wounded in the attack and surrendered, only to be tied to a tree and dispatched by arrows. Moira categorically stated that the two countries would be at war unless the Gurkha rajah disavowed responsibility for the murder of the darogah and punished the culprits. Amar Thapa's attempts to negotiate were dismissed and on 1 November 1814 Moira declared war.

John did not actively participate in the military campaign as he had at Agra in the Second Anglo-Maratha War, but his influence with the nawab, Ghazni-ood-din-Haider, was critical in supplying provisions and elephants as well as ensuring that Oude did not support the Gurkhas in any way. On 20 October, just prior to the declaration of war, John Adam, a councillor in Calcutta and later Moira's successor in the role of acting governor general, sent the resident a copy of Moira's proclamation. Adam sought to prevent subjects of the Company and its allies from engaging in the service of the government of Nepal and implored the resident to convince the nawab to forbid recruiting among his people. John was able to obtain a reasonable degree of intelligence and the loan of significant numbers of bearers, boats, horses, and elephants and even the offer of one or more battalions of Nujeebs for the war. The British graciously declined the offer of the Nujeebs but were very appreciative of the nawab's other assistance.

By December, the British commanders were seeking more help, and General John Sullivan Wood pleaded with the resident: "It will be impossible for me to move from Goruckpore, in a state of adequate equipment, unless you are enabled to send me 12 or 1500 bearers."⁵ At the same time, Wood sought a further fifty to sixty elephants. Baillie responded that he had sent three hundred bearers that day but it was difficult to procure more since in excess of one thousand had already been supplied. He had prevailed on the nawab to provide fifty elephants for Wood and a similar number for General Bennett Marley. At Adam's request, he undertook to ascertain the identities of the members of the former ruling families whose lands in the Hills had been usurped by the Gurkhas, with a view to restoring those whom the British deemed deserving.

John's primary contribution to the Nepalese War, however, lay in his ability to extract loans from the nawab. The Company's straitened finances meant that Moira's war had to be funded from external sources. Bengal was suffering a continual drain on its funds from a confluence of circumstances. Java, a recent acquisition, required subsidies, the China tea trade devoured resources, and, finally, creditors, owing to a sterling devaluation, were demanding cash in India rather than bills on England. Moira gave little thought to the long-run welfare of the people of Oude and grasped an opportunity to ingratiate himself with the nawab by rescinding John's hard-won reforms. For a time, Moira had ostensibly backed the resident's position on reform but his actions contradicted his professed support. In due course he directed that the plan of reform be suspended. In return, he anticipated that an appreciative nawab would lend the Company money from his ample resources, particularly since Oude would be a beneficiary of a successful British campaign. As we shall see, however, Moira, although unwilling to acknowledge the fact, depended on Baillie to wrest the loan from the nawab. In any event, that particular plan aborted when Nawab Saadat Ali suddenly died on 11 July 1814.

John handled the situation with the same aplomb and presence of mind he had evidenced at the death of Anupgiri in Bundelcund. Saadat Ali's brother-in-law, Rumzaun Ali Khan, had sought the resident's presence at the palace as soon as he heard that the nawab might be dying. Baillie, accompanied by the surgeon, proceeded there immediately and ordered the commanding officer in the cantonment, Colonel Philip D'Auvergne, to attend with his troops as soon as possible. Armed with secret instructions obtained from the nawab during an earlier illness in 1803, the resident requested the presence of the eldest son, Ghazni-ood-din-Haider, in the palace. Those instructions proved convenient, since the second son, Shums-ood-Dowla, who was less partial to the British interest, had clearly been his father's favourite. Sensing "untoward proceedings"[6] by Shums-ood-Dowla in concert with the resident's bugbear, Huckeem Mehdi Ali Khan, John sent for Shums and his younger brother, Nuseer-ood-Dowla, and "warned them both in their elder brother's presence of the ruinous consequences that must follow their opposition unavailing and vain, to the just views of our Government in the succession of their elder brother and natural head to the Musnud. Shums-ood-Dowla's language on the occasion was improper and indecorous in the extreme, but he ultimately declared his resolution to comply with my suggestion in all things, and Nuseer-ood-Dowla's language and deportment were in all respects proper and becoming."[7] Shortly after midnight, Colonel D'Auvergne arrived with his troops and was able to secure the treasury and the nawab's personal property. Shums evidenced a reluctance to surrender the keys to the treasury but the resident persisted. Once all these measures were in place, Ghazni-ood-din-Dowla ascended to the musnud.

The relationship between the newly enthroned nawab and the resident could not have begun more propitiously. John reported that Ghazni indicated his intention to be guided in all matters by the resident and to comply entirely with Moira's wishes. As his first act, the nawab confirmed the plan of reform. The transition proceeded so smoothly that by 13 July John had authorized the departure of the greater part of D'Auvergne's troops from the palace. He recounted that all the minor matters that had proved so vexatious with the late nawab had been resolved to the resident's entire satisfaction. Indeed, John reported to Moira with an air of self-satisfaction: "I may safely affirm to your Lordship that no event of such importance has ever occurred in Hindostan producing so little commotion & affording such universal satisfaction as the recent change in government."[8] Continuing in the same vein and, in all likelihood, exaggerating shamelessly, he wrote: "His Highness seems desirous indeed of making your Lordship's representative at his court the organ as well as the advisor of all the public measures of his administration, and the medium of conveying his wishes, and commands of his brothers, relations and dependants, as well as to the servants of his government; addressing me frequently by the appellation of uncle, and protector, and entreating my assistance as indispensable to the successful conduct of his affairs."[9] The relationship had become such that the resident and the nawab rode to the merchant and financier Claude Martin's massive edifice Constantia to check on the arrangements for a visit by Moira and, as a singular mark of royal affection, returned on the same elephant. Shums, however, continued to conspire and accordingly, was bundled off to Benares with an ample pension. Nuseer, on the other hand, proved steadfast in his support of the nawab and retained his official duties. Even Moira acknowledged that "Major Baillie's conduct was characterized by the greatest promptitude, vigilance & prudence and received my entire approbation."[10]

Meanwhile, Moira remained intent on extracting a loan from the nawab of Oude. To this end, consciously or not, he continued to undermine the resident by attempting to render Ghazni more dependent on, and favourably inclined toward, himself. The governor general reversed the ban on the insidious Huckeem Mehdi Ali Khan's attendance at court. He also encouraged the nawab in the latter's aspirations to remove the fetters of reform. His rationale is clearly evidenced in the following self-laudatory and misleading justification of his conduct.

Soon after my arrival in India, some British officers came to see me from the Nawab Vizier, Saadat Ali, sovereign of Oude, bringing me a representation of the degrading thralldom in which, through gradual and probably unintended encroachments on his freedom, he was held, inconsistently with the spirit of the treaties between the two states. The system from which he prayed to be relieved appeared to me to be no less repugnant to policy than to equity. On my professing a disposition to correct so objectionable a course, those officers who had been long in the Nawab's service assured me that any persuasion of my having such an inclination would cause Saadat Ali to throw himself upon me with such unbounded confidence, and to offer from his immense horde, the advance of any sum I could want for the enterprise against Nepal. The gratitude with which such a supply would be felt was professed. While I was on my passage up the river, Saadat Ali unexpectedly died. I found, however, that what had been provisionally agitated with him was perfectly understood by his successor; so that the latter came forward with a spontaneous offer of a crore of rupees, which I declined, as a peishcush [peshcush] or tribute on his accession to the sovereignty of Oude, but accepted as a loan for the Honourable Company.[11]

When the Company required additional funds to sustain the war effort, Moira asserted: "Luckily, I was upon such frank terms with the Nawab Vizier, as I could explain fairly my circumstances. He agreed to furnish another crore; so that the Honourable Company was accommodated with about two millions and a half sterling, on my simple receipt."[12] A crore equalled ten million rupees, which was the equivalent, at the time, to one million pounds sterling. Moira deceitfully attributed this success to his respectful and cordial relationship with the reigning nawab while castigating his own predecessors. "I obtained from Ghazni-ood-din-Haider, in an hour of exigency, an assistance for the Company which never could have been procured during the miserable backings of former management."[13]

There is no question that the nawab of Oude lent the Company the equivalent of £2,500,000. The controversy lies in the propriety and spontaneity of the loans and who convinced the nawab to grant them. Henry St George Tucker, then chief secretary in Bengal's revenue and judicial department, emphasized the Company's financial straits and suggested to Moira that Ghazni's accession to the musnud in Oude opened the prospect of a loan from that quarter. Tucker had checked with Edmonstone, who responded that in view of the immediacy of the nawab's elevation, any approach would be considered by the natives, and perhaps by the nawab himself, as extracted from a reluctant leader in return for recognizing Ghazni as nawab-vizier. Moira was not deterred by any such scruples and instructed the resident to seek a loan of a crore of rupees. At first, John baulked at what he regarded as extortion. Indeed, he later asserted convincingly that the loan had required considerable coercion on his part and that it was ludicrous to claim that the nawab had agreed to the loan out of an appreciation of the intentions of his predecessor:

> Any understanding between the late Vizier and the present sovereign of Oude on pecuniary, or other subjects connected with the British Government, is not only unfounded in fact, but absolutely inconsistent with the total estrangement that had subsisted between them for years; the second son [Shums-ood-Dowla] being the declared favourite and constant minister of Saadat Ali, and the elder excluded from the court till the hour of his father's demise. Lastly, that the present Sovereign of Oude, so far from making a spontaneous offer of a crore of rupees, or any sum of money to Lord Moira, was induced by my earnest entreaty, at the expressed desire of his Lordship, to offer with reluctance his first loan of a crore of rupees, in terms that were anything but gracious, as the words of his letter demonstrate. So true and so striking a picture of that first pecuniary transaction is given at the time of its occurrence, in my letter of 19th October, 1814, to a member of the Government in Calcutta, now my colleague in this Fort (Mr. Edmonstone) that I have been induced to keep an extract from that letter among the documents appended to the statement.

John then quoted from the aforementioned letter:

> Shall I tell you anything of my trip to Cawnpore, to meet the Governor-General? I had better not, I believe, for I have nothing very pleasant to communicate. I was desired to propose to the Nawab, that His Excellency should propose to Lord Moira to make a voluntary loan to the Company of a crore of rupees:

His Excellency did so accordingly, and his proposal was graciously received. To reconcile a proposal like this with my original disinterestedness, was an effort of diplomatic effrontery, you must admit; but mark the sequel and admire, His Excellency has proposed, in return, that Lord Moira should propose to His Excellency to put a stop to the system of reform, i.e., Huckeem Mehdi Ali Khan has drawn up a long string of extraordinary propositions (the above being one of them, of course), which he induced the poor Nawab to give in without understanding them himself; or informing me of their nature, and afterwards to support it, I am told with an offer of the crore of rupees as a gift instead of a loan, at a second conference with the Governor-General, indirectly and irregularly obtained from which the Resident was excluded, and of which the poor Nawab forgot the speech that was prepared for him, and made all the parties ashamed of themselves.[14]

In any event, John reluctantly sought the loan of a crore of rupees at the well-below-market rate of 6 per cent. Ghazni, acutely aware that a previous governor general had removed the rightful heir in favour of the more compliant Saadat Ali and that his brother Shums-ood-Dowla was angling to replace him on the musnud, had little choice and quickly acceded to the resident's request. As indicated in the documents quoted above, the nawab, feeling vulnerable and seeking Moira's support, even offered the crore as a gift rather than a loan. Moira reported to the Court of Directors that the offer had been spontaneous and sanctimoniously added that his probity would not allow him to accept the loan as a gift:

His Excellency the Vizier ... tendered to me as a proof of his friendship and of the cordial interest which he feels in the prosperity of the affairs of the Honourable Company an accommodation of one crore of rupees in the way of a loan. I deemed it to be my duty in consideration of the actual state of the public finances and the probable demands arising out of the prosecution of hostilities with the Nepalese and the eventual necessity of supporting by military preparations our political views with relation to Saugor and Bhopal to accept this offer with acknowledgement of the cordial and friendly spirit in which it was made.
     At a subsequent conference His Excellency solicited my acceptance of the sum as a free gift to the Hon'ble Company but for reasons which will be obvious to your Hon'ble Court I declared with

suitable expressions of my sense of this additional proof of His
Excellency's friendship, my inability to receive the accommodation
except as a loan.[15]

There was an element of hypocrisy in Moira's sanctimony given the low
interest rate on the "loan" as well as the fact that the interest was conveniently directed to paying for provisions for the nawab's dependants, an
obligation the British had guaranteed. With the loan in place, the situation could have been expected to return to normal. However, Moira soon
was informed that the Council in Calcutta had deemed it expedient to
employ 54 lakhs to discharge an 8 per cent loan and that the remainder
of the nawab's loan was required to meet current expenses. With unparal-
leled chutzpah, Moira instructed the resident to seek another crore from
the nawab. Moira apprised the Court:

At a subsequent period the heavy pressure of the war with Nepal ...
induced me to turn my thoughts to the expediency and practicability
of obtaining a further pecuniary aid from His Excellency the Nawab
Vizier, whose interest in the success of our measures is closely
interwoven with the British Government, whose attachment to the
Hon'ble Company is undoubted, and whose personal regard for
myself, I was disposed to think, would render him desirous of con-
tributing to the alleviation of our financial embarrassments, were he
once apprised of them. A private communication was accordingly
made under my orders to the Resident at His Excellency's court,
directing him to ascertain, as far as he might be able, the practicability of obtaining a further loan to the extent of one crore of
rupees, and to take advantage of any circumstance which might
appear to him as affording a prospect of success to open the matter
to His Excellency.[16]

Although Moira later implied to the Court that he had arranged the loan
directly with the nawab, there is no doubt that John personally negotiated the transaction with Ghazni. Indeed, the Council's following plea is
on the record. "According to a statement just received by His Lordship
from Edmonstone nearly three crores in addition to our surplus revenue
will be required to meet the war extraordinaries up to 30th April 1816 ...
Unless, therefore, you can enable me to rejoice His Lordship by informing him that you have succeeded in getting another crore from the Vizier,
fifty lakhs from the Begum and fifty lakhs from your monied men, we
shall be in a very desperate state."[17]

John reluctantly sought the additional crore from the nawab, who was persuaded by his advisers that the Company was not actually in want of money but that its true intent was to strip him of his treasure. Consequently, Ghazni begrudgingly offered only half a crore or fifty lakhs. Moira remarked: "The amount of this offer was not exactly commensurate to our probable wants; nor did the manner in which it was made, appear to me to be so frank as to render it advisable that I should accept the aid on the part of the Hon'ble Company." Accordingly, he declined the offer and instructed John to overcome the nawab's suspicions by explaining the extent of the Company's financial needs to prosecute the war and to protect the nawab's dominions, all the while expressing his confidence that he has "not committed or allowed a trespass on the kindness of the Vizier."[18] John, with the assistance of Agha Meer, chief minister of Oude, obtained the second crore. Commenting on these proceedings, one writer dismisses Moira's suggestion, in the wake of John's dismissal, that his resident was in fact an obstacle in the government's dealings with the nawab:

This delicate negotiation had caused Moira to suspend his ideas of removing Baillie, for he alone had the influence and the savoir-faire necessary to bring it to a successful conclusion ... It was certainly not true, as Moira implied, that Baillie was dismissed as part of a tacit bargain with the Nawab. Not the prospect of Baillie's absence, but the fact of his presence was the essential condition of these loans, and Moira only pretended otherwise because he was anxious to vindicate before the London authorities the removal of Baillie and the adoption of a non-interference policy. He implied that he had got the money by adopting a non-interference policy. In fact, he had risked wrecking that policy [by retaining Baillie] in order to get that money.[19]

As if this were not enough, Moira commissioned John to undertake yet another delicate task calculated to strain the resident's relationship with the nawab. The Bow Begum, wife of the late Nawab Shuja-ood-Dowla and the mother of Asaf-ood-Dowla, had become estranged from Saadat Ali Khan and Ghazni-ood-din-Haider and had indicated her intention to leave her jaghir, houses, property, and goods of every description, amounting to roughly seventy lakhs, to the Company. The resident was instructed to negotiate the terms with the Bow Begum and seek the agreement of the nawab. John obtained the Bow Begum's agreement to naming the Company as her beneficiary in return for the Company's guaranteeing the payment of pensions approximating one lakh, 99,608 rupees, and eight annas to her dependants, along with an undertaking that the Company would use its influence to obtain from the nawab a grant to her in perpetuity of villages in the Pergunnah of Puchumrath with an income of ten thousand rupees per annum. John succeeded on all fronts with the exception of an immediate assignment of sufficient of the Bow Begum's funds to ensure payment of the pensions and maintain her mausoleum. He dutifully informed the nawab, with as tactful an interpretation as he could place on the appropriation of a further portion of the Kingdom of Oude. John did, however, waive the Company's right to the estate in return for certain concessions. The nawab responded with suspect sincerity:

> Of a truth this Government had never, and can never have such a firm friend and ally. So sincere and disinterested in its friendship as the Honourable Company's Government, who regardless of its own advantage has rejected personal property to so very considerable an amount bequeathed by Her Highness, the Bow Begum, and determined to transfer the whole of that property to me, after providing for the payments of the legacies and annuities to the Begum's near relations and dependants which Her Highness so properly bequeathed to them, and which the British Government has justly guaranteed. Words are inadequate to express the sense which I entertain of this conduct; and of course I most cheerfully acquiesce in the arrangements, which His Lordship has proposed to me, regarding the assignment of lands in Puchumrath for the expenses of the Begum's mausoleum, and the other purposes of her will. Accordingly I hereby engage that when it shall please Almighty God to remove my venerable grand mother from this transitory scene, villages in the District of Puchumrath yielding a revenue of ten thousand rupees per annum shall be set apart and granted in perpetuity for the charges of Her Highness's mausoleum, and further that all the stipends and provisions, which Her Highness's relations enjoy and have hitherto received from this Government shall be continued to them and their heirs in perpetuity without any deduction whatever. Considering you as my sincere friend and well wisher, I request you to report these engagements for His Lordship in Council's satisfaction without any delay.[20]

On the Bow Begum's demise, the Company renounced its interest in the estate and transferred it to the nawab. But it did insist on a loan of 58 1/2 lakhs of rupees at 6 per cent to provide for the Begum's numerous bequests.

CR

Coincident with all these machinations was an intrigue of truly Asiatic proportions, one in which it is virtually impossible to keep track of the charges and counter-charges and the relation of the participants. Shortly after Moira's arrival, two army officers who had been in the employ of Saadat Ali for some time – undoubtedly Captain Malcolm McLeod and James Henry Clarke – approached him to ascertain his views on the reform project. According to Agha Meer, these officers "had a promise from His Excellency of the sum of a lakh of rupees as the reward for their labours" in undertaking this mission.[21] Based on their conversation with the new governor general, the officers gave the nawab some glimmer of hope. Then Moira himself wrote Saadat Ali permitting him to rescind the reform agreement and formulate a modified reform plan "in concert with the Resident." However, any progress on that front was set back by Saadat Ali's death. As we have seen, his successor, Ghazni-ood-din-Haider, purportedly accepted the reforms without reservation but any enthusiasm for them was, at best, transitory. He soon conspired to undermine the entire arrangement. To this end, he circumvented protocol by sending to Moira, via the glamorous Lady Hood rather than the resident, a letter in which he sought the suspension of reform. Upon receipt of a reply, the nawab told McLeod that Moira had "abandoned the enforcing [of] a most obnoxious measure."[22] Moira conceded that the conciliatory tone of the letter may have encouraged the nawab in the view that the new regime was not intent on reform "involving humiliation to himself." He did claim, however, that he would insist on "a reform in some other shape."

Shortly thereafter the exchanges descended to an unseemly pettiness. An anonymous letter denouncing the resident and his associates reached Moira. The letter accused John of plundering from the nawab's treasury, through his moonshee, Ulla Nuckee, lakhs of rupees and goods including a book outlining charges against the resident. The letter alleged that the resident had slighted the deceased nawab by neither attending his bier nor performing the dues of mourning. It cast aspersions on Agha Meer's character, claiming that his two-year-old son, Agha Ali, to whom the nawab had awarded one of the six zillahs, was the son of a prostitute and that it was by no means certain that Agha Meer was his father. It went on to accuse Agha Meer of embezzling Ghazni-ood-din-Haider's treasury and paying a portion to Ulla Nuckee to win favour with the resident. Another zillah had been awarded to Ulla Nuckee or his nephew, Kootub-ood-Deen. The nawab had been reduced to eating bang night and day and would not oppose the resident for fear of being replaced on the musnud by his younger brother, Shums-ood-Dowla. Finally, the author blamed

John and Ulla Nuckee for causing Captain McLeod "to be turned out in disgrace and ignominy."[23]

When the Calcutta Council, prompted by Moira, brought the charges to John's attention, he responded that the author was likely Inteaz Ali, a rival of Ulla Nuckee, assisted by an agent of Akbar Ali Khan and a vakil of Huckeem Mehdi Ali Khan. "These three persons are the only natives of India whom I could suppose to be inimical to myself, and the causes of their enmity are in the record. I were as bad as they are in my own opinion, if I were not the avowed enemy of such nefarious practices as some of their's."[24] With regard to the letter's specific allegations, he stated:

A production very nearly the same, except so far as my name is concerned, was stuck up against a wall in Lucknow several months ago, and His Excellency the Nawab offered a large reward to the author if he would come forward and avow it. The imputations against me are certainly quite novel, though as a continuation of the proceedings of October last they are not so much as to be wondered at ... The nominal collector of zillah Lucknow is certainly what the anonymous author states him to be or nearly so. He is a boy of three or four years of age ... The true circumstances of this case are as follow[s]. On the division of the country in zillahs, the Nawab very naturally gave the patronage of one zillah each to the Minister and Dewan, knowing of course that they could not be holden in their own names nor the duties discharged by themselves. The Minister himself being the naib of a boy, very naturally gave the name of his only son for the office, and recommended for the duties of the station, as his son's Naib, Sheikh Emam Bukhsh, an efficient revenue officer, who was put in nomination, as you know, for the high office of Minister by His Excellency, at the suggestion of the Sheikh's friend, Mr. Clarke ... Lord Moira is doubtless aware, that his Lordship's explicit instructions preclude any interference on my part in the appointment of the Nawab's officers; and, in fact, I know nothing of these matters but by ... reports ... and occasional communications from the Nawab which he makes to me now-a-days very rarely.[25]

John provided a similar defence of the award to Ali Nuckee. C.M. Ricketts, a future chief secretary, rejoined that "it is to be regretted, I think, that you did not report the circumstance of the appointment of the Minister's child to the important office of zemindar of the district of Lucknow, as your doing so would have given his Lordship an opportunity, had he judged it proper, of communicating his sentiments on the subject to the Nawab."[26] At the same time, Ricketts lamely attempted to distinguish between situations wherein the resident should and should not proffer advice to the nawab.

As that brouhaha began to subside, Ghazni, encouraged by Huckeem Mehdi Ali Khan, McLeod, and Clarke, sent a list of complaints about the resident to Moira. Moira then claimed that the nawab had sent him a request via Clarke for a private session excluding the resident. Moira held such a meeting, which was also attended by Ricketts, Adam, and George Swinton. Yet the nawab was anything but forthcoming. Grasping for an explanation, Clarke attributed the nawab's reticence to Swinton's known attachment to Baillie.

By this point, Moira's pettiness had descended to sending Captain Walter Raleigh Gilbert to Lucknow as his emissary to keep tabs on John. The nawab invited Gilbert to breakfast, where he purportedly unfolded a litany of grievances against the resident. Subsequently, Moira alleged that Ghazni confirmed to Ricketts everything he had said to Gilbert, closing with "cannot you get Major Baillie removed?"[27] Indeed, Ricketts prepared a report on his conversation with the nawab in which Ghazni confirmed his dissatisfaction with Baillie's conduct toward him.[28] McLeod claimed that, upon taking his leave early in the month of October 1813, the nawab entreated him thusly: "Captain McLeod, although I never opened my mind to you, you must be aware, from report, how degraded my situation is, and always has been, from the interference of Major Baillie in every branch and department of my Government. I believe you to be my well-wisher, and entreat of you to represent to Lord Moira that I am, under present circumstances, the most wretched being on the face of the earth, and that I wish death would put an end to my miseries."[29]

At a conference on the evening of 31 October, the nawab presented a document outlining his grievances against Colonel Baillie. One of these grievances was that the resident had allegedly "constructed a large and lofty Gate which overtopped all my buildings"[30] and extended beyond the original bounds of the Residency. Another involved Ghazni's desire to have a nobut, or large drum, beaten at the gate of his new palace. Since the palace was close to the resident's house, the nawab had been reluctant to beat the drum lest the noise should annoy Baillie. Even Moira was taken aback by this bizarre complaint, responding that surely there must be a misunderstanding and that Ghazni should refer the matter to the resident.

It is not clear what happened to cause the nawab to withdraw his complaints against the resident but retract them he did. The nawab "accused

Captain McLeod and James Henry Clarke of having instigated him to profess dissatisfaction with the Resident contrary to the real sentiments of his
own heart; the Nawab stated that he did not want the Governor-General
to remove from him the person whom he really regarded as 'his uncle and
his best friend.'"[31] Indeed, whatever resentment he may have been har-
bouring, Ghazni sent John a contrite apology on 7 March 1815. The
"Mr. De L'Etang" mentioned in this letter was the Chevalier Ambroise-
Pierre Antoine de l'Etang, whom Louis XIV had posted to India – without
the possibility of return to France – after word had reached him that the
chevalier was romantically involved with the queen, Marie Antoinette.
In 1814 L'Etang – who, incidentally, was the great-great-grandfather of
Virginia Woolf – was retained by the nawab to manage his horses.

> Mr. Clarke and Captain McLeod have been for some time past in
> the habit of saying to me, that a paper of faults to be imputed to you
> should be prepared and given to the Governor-General: but I never
> would consent to this suggestion. At length, yesterday, after the
> departure of Mr. Ricketts, they brought me a paper, and stated to
> me deceitfully that the Governor-General was displeased with you,
> and desirous of receiving from me a communication which might
> attach blame to you; consequently, that the giving in of such a paper
> would be pleasing and satisfactory to his Lordship.
>
> I being quite unaware of the deceitful and insidious views of those
> gentlemen, gave the paper in question to Lord Moira. Yet God is my
> witness, that my heart has never felt, and does not now entertain the
> least dissatisfaction with you, and that the friendship and unity sub-
> sisting between us have not suffered the smallest diminution or change.
>
> Be not, therefore, grieved or displeased with my conduct; because
> I have not been the origin of this matter myself, but on the contrary,
> it has proceeded alone from the deceit and incantations of those gen-
> tlemen. Mr. Clarke has another paper of the same description with
> those, and I know not whether he has given this also to Lord Moira
> or not.
>
> As these gentlemen have entered into such designs as those
> described, I have dismissed them both from my service, and with
> them Dr. Law and Mr. De L'Etang, who were also their associates
> in this affair; because the continuance in my service of such persons
> as interrupt the friendship between you and me is improper on
> every account.[32]

Whatever the reality, there seemed to be a goodly number of people who believed they would be well rewarded by furnishing the governor general with information that reflected badly on the resident.

The following day, Agha Meer conveyed a message from Ghazni to Adam and Swinton again disavowing his earlier complaints and reiterating that the supposed grievances were the work of Clarke. Moira attributed the change in attitude to the "delicacy and deference" he himself had evidenced toward Baillie relative to the beating of the nobut. He was supported in this by the dissembling McLeod, who claimed that Huckeem Mehdi Ali Khan and two others were present when Agha Meer cited the governor general's name to intimidate Ghazni into changing course. Agha Meer allegedly stated: "The Nawab had ruined himself; that the Governor-General was outraged at his complaints against Colonel Baillie, and even talked of removing His Excellency from the musnud; and that there was no remedy, but to declare that he had been misled by the artifices of others to profess what was most opposite to the wishes and dictates of his heart."[33]

Retraction or not, Moira was convinced and, in all likelihood, rightly so that the nawab harboured animosity toward the resident. Accordingly, the governor general continued to hound Baillie with niggling provocations and interventions. He inundated John with instructions as to his behaviour vis-à-vis the nawab, took issue with his suggested appointments to the nawab's court, and continued to pursue the propriety of the nawab's granting zillahs to Agha Meer's son and the resident's moonshee. While professing that the British should not interfere in land awards, Moira stooped to instructing the resident to seek the nawab's revocation of the zillah assigned to Ulee Nuckee and to have an Indian tribunal decide between the claims of Ulee Nuckee and his rival Inteaz Ali.

⌘

The tension between the governor general and his Lucknow resident was now reaching a breaking point. Seething with frustration and encouraged by Adam, John sent a dispatch to the Council in Calcutta in 1815 unleashing a torrent of accusations against Moira, his family, and his entourage. Although the insinuations may well have been valid, he was not dealing from a position of strength. Confronting a governor general, who was also a peer of the realm and an intimate of the prince regent, was a contest the resident was destined to lose. Among John's charges were: that

Moira "with the basest hypocrisy undermined privately that reform which he publicly commended to be carried into effect";[34] that Moira bypassed the resident, utilizing the duplicitous McLeod as his intermediary with the nawab; that, circumventing protocol, Moira had utilized Lady Hood to convey letters from the nawab to His Lordship without the resident's knowledge or involvement; that Moira had sent the nawab a private letter authorizing the suspension of the plan of reform; that Huckeem Mehdi's agent Tipoo Deen had joined Moira's suite and plotted against the resident; that associates of Moira were accepting extensive presents from the nawab in contravention of Company policy; that Moira had evidenced his "doubts of the veracity of his representatives at the Court of Lucknow ... by his deputation of Captain Gilbert";[35] that Moira invited the nawab to confer without the presence of the resident; that "he could only consider Captain McLeod and Mr. Clarke as authorized spies upon him";[36] that Indian emissaries of the governor general had undermined Agha Meer; that Moira vetoed the nawab's appointment of Mirza Jafeer as a minister owing to Mirza Jafeer's attachment to the resident; and that Huckeem Mehdi Ali Khan, McLeod, and Clarke had convinced Ghazni-ood-din-Haider that Moira was desirous of finding grounds for the removal of John from his post.

John had overreached, and Moira pounced. He informed John that, effective immediately, he was dismissed from the Residency of Oude. His successor was Richard Strachey, who had been serving as the resident at Gwalior.

You will hereafter receive a communication on the subject of your dispatch. For the present, I am instructed to state, that the tone and spirit which pervade that document, render it impracticable for the Governor-General to maintain with you that confidential intercourse, which the good of the public service requires should subsist between the head of the Government and his representative at the Court of a foreign prince. The Governor-General in Council has therefore thought proper to remove you from the office of Resident at Lucknow, and to desire that you withdraw from that Court as soon after you shall be relieved from the duties of the office as may be consistent with your personal accommodation.

... His Lordship in Council has been pleased to appoint Mr. Richard Strachey to be Resident at Lucknow, and you will deliver over charge of the office to Mr. Strachey on his arrival.[37]

Moira had clear and supportable grounds for firing Baillie for insubordination and might well have left it at that. However, he extended his vendetta by mean-spiritedly removing John's half-brother, George, from his post as second assistant at the Residency in Lucknow and, conscious that his own conduct was not beyond reproach, sought to vindicate himself to the Court of Directors by disparaging John's contribution and conduct.

There is no question that tension existed between the nawab and the resident. The issue is, first, whether that friction arose primarily because of the attempts to implement reform or because of John's attitude toward and treatment of the nawab; secondly, whether the benefits of reform warranted a strained relationship between the nawab and the resident; and thirdly, whether firm support from the governor general would have kept the discord well within manageable bounds.

With regard to the first point, Moira attributed the animosity to John's "captious disposition and a domineering tone of themselves highly calculated to excite irritation in a Prince whose situation would naturally render him acutely jealous of his independence"[38] and asserted that this impression had been confirmed by an unidentified "high authority," in all likelihood the ubiquitous McLeod. Moira cited as an example of John's overbearing manner his imposition of his protégé, Agha Meer, on the nawab as his chief minister. That accusation is called into question, if not completely overturned, by the nawab's reinstatement of Agha Meer as chief minister following the resident's removal. On the other hand, John contended that, for the first three years of his residency, the greatest collegiality had subsisted between him and Saadat Ali Khan, who had declared that "Baillie was the only Englishman he had known (with one exception) who could address a native of rank and reason with him on subjects wherein they differed without forgetting proper courtesy of expression."[39] It is also difficult to reconcile a "captious disposition and a domineering tone" with John's inability to introduce reform in the five years since undertaking the negotiations to implement the plan. Even Moira acknowledged that the reconciliation between John and the nawab shortly before Moira's arrival was "interrupted" when Saadat Ali Khan sought to retract some concessions which the Company had long sought relative to the plan of reform. John's record of concluding treaties with a host of native chiefs in Bundelcund at a time when he was unable to resort to military coercion similarly suggests that the conflict lay not in his personality but in opposing attitudes to reform.

Moira placed little value on the plan of reform, "the fitness of which with regard to his Dominion I had begun seriously to doubt and which I have been satisfied was injudicious,"[40] and, as we have seen, focused almost exclusively on conducting and financing the war with Nepal. The governor general also pronounced: "Still it is more likely that a system devised upon the model of that pursued in our Provinces should have failed in the territories of the Nawab, from the want of a class of public functionaries of approved integrity, free from sordid views to be accomplished at the expense of the country and unwarped by families or dependants whom they could be interested in aggrandizing."[41] That charge is easily rebutted. Reforms similar to those implemented in Oude had demonstrably brought material benefits in the Ceded Territories, and since the inhabitants of those territories and Oude were similar, it is not unreasonable to assume that these benefits could have been replicated in the latter. Indeed, John's plan of reform was almost identical to the arrangement finally introduced in 1856 when the British appropriated the entire province of Oude. Moreover, Agha Meer, who had prospered under the nawab and was therefore likely to be objective in his outlook, confided to a later resident, T.H. Maddock, that "the removal of the controlling influence of the Resident over the affairs of this government in the time of Lord Moira was the greatest misfortune that it could ever have sustained."[42] The implementation of the plan of reform was then clearly worth risking some dissension between the British as represented by the resident and the nawab of Oude.

Finally, would the firm support of the governor general have rendered the tension manageable? The nawab, whether Saadat Ali Khan or Ghazni-ood-din-Haider, plainly resisted the reforms and did whatever he could to oppose their implementation. However, the nawabs recognized where power resided and once Minto had unequivocally stated the necessity of reform, Saadat Ali reluctantly bowed to the inevitable. It was only when Moira succeeded Minto as governor general that Saadat Ali perceived an opportunity to overturn the policy. He found Moira, entranced by the vision of crores of rupees, receptive. Moira subsequently wrote indignantly in his defence: "The object of Major Baillie is visibly to fix upon me the charge of having endeavoured to defeat by my countenance of underhand intrigues those measures which I had publicly commissioned him to carry through."[43] Here the evidence, circumstantial and otherwise, strongly suggests that Moira did indeed undercut the resident's attempts to conclude a satisfactory plan of reform. John had achieved every point he required to effect reform within a month of Ghazni's accession but shortly thereafter the nawab felt empowered to retract his agreement. He would have had the temerity to undertake such a measure only if he had some encouragement from the governor general, since he was clearly cognizant that John was in no mood to compromise. In fact, the nawab, as we have seen, told McLeod that Moira had "abandoned the enforcing [of] a most obnoxious measure"[44] and his communication to Moira on the subject implied that the reforms had been suspended by the late nawab "in consequence of a letter" from the governor general.[45]

So the facts were on John's side, even if he emerged as the loser in the battle. Of course, being right was probably of little comfort as he contemplated what the future held. He had forged a remarkably successful career in India, only to see his reputation called into question by the crown's representative. Restoring that reputation – and achieving a measure of revenge in the process – was now his main priority.

18

Retribution

One must forgive one's enemies but not before they are hanged.

Heinrich Heine

As soon as possible but not before commissioning the cenotaph for his uncle William at Seringapatam, John left India for Britain. His nemesis back in India, meanwhile, remained focused on the Nepalese War, which, after a few setbacks, Moira successfully concluded. While reluctant to offend the Chinese by annexing Nepal, Moira did add some of the Hill territories to the British possessions and largely paid for the war by redeeming his debts to the nawab for land, particularly the fort of Khyragur which the nawab valued for its tiger-hunting possibilities.

John arrived in London on 30 June 1816. Circumstantial evidence suggests that his wife, the Begum of Oude, remained in Lucknow but that their three children, Anne, Henrietta, and John Wilson, as well as some of their half-siblings either travelled with him or joined him in England soon afterwards. A Court of Directors minute of 18 February 1818 resolved that "Ms. Charlotte Baillie be permitted to return to Bengal her Native Country, and to take with her a black servant, named Herigan, the Company being at no expense thereby."[1] Further, John's daughter Anne travelled to India in 1829, presumably to visit her mother. A codicil to John's will refers to Anne being "just embarked for India" and a letter of 1829 noted: "I know you will be glad to hear that we have at last had very agreeable letters from Anne written when she was just setting off for Lucknow."[2]

After twenty-five years in India, John found the climate of England a challenge but, all in all, he seemed in a reasonable frame of mind, writing to Edmonstone in India:

I landed at Brighton on the 30th of June, got to Town on the 2nd of July & have now been here twenty days. The climate is shockingly disagreeable but healthy I presume nevertheless. I have had only a little cold for a day or two & am now in astonishing health ...

I can say nothing of myself or my prospects in this country yet a while. I propose visiting Scotland next month & returning to winter in London where I shall in all probability live. The expense of living in any style is certainly very great but the necessaries & even the comforts of life on a small scale with the means of educating my children seem all within the compass of my fortune.

I have met with a number of old friends & a very great number of acquaintances. They all look happy enough & promise me happiness in England by & by. My next letter will inform you whether or not their promises are likely to be fulfilled ... I spent the morning the other day with Sir George Barlow who seemed very happy to see me. Lord Wellesley I have not been able to catch a sight of, & Lord Teignmouth was from home when I called. Some of the Directors have been civil. I dined with them all by invitation of the Chairman one day but have seen little of any of them since. I know nothing of their sentiments on the subject of Lord Moira's conduct to myself ...

PS I have taken a furnished house for a year at the amount 420 guineas.[3]

Given the plans of John's eldest son, George, to embark for India, Margaret was concerned that the young man might have departed the country before his father's arrival in London. She wrote Edmonstone: "I hope you will excuse my troubling you with a few lines to introduce my nephew George Baillie who goes out as surgeon of the Castlereagh Country ship. As my brother's last letters give us reason to hope for his speedily leaving India I have some fears his son may not encounter him then which would be a great loss & disappointment to the young man. Should this happen I presume to entreat your advice as to what course it will be most prudent for George to take since I know there is no friend on Earth in whose judgment John would rely so much."[4]

John quickly settled himself in a large terraced Georgian house at 90 Gloucester Place, Portman Square in the Marylebone area of London. The address later became the residence of Wilkie Collins, the author of the first modern English detective novel, *The Moonstone*. John subsequently undertook a major expansion of the buildings and grounds of the Leys estate he had acquired from his elder brother. His initiatives included a large walled garden erected in 1817. Eventually, he undertook what

Margaret suggests was a massive extension at Ness House (the present-day Columba Hotel) in the centre of Inverness. "I surely expect to be at Invss in May. My Brother still talks of following in June. I trust he will be satisfied with the improvements there & at Leys because they will cost money. Indeed I almost regret his laying out so much for the time he is likely to enjoy himself there."[5]

John cut a grand figure in the north. The Highland chronicler Joseph Mitchell recounted his arrival.

About 1828–29 the quiet town of Inverness was startled by the arrival of the colonel, who was reported to have acquired a great for-tune. This impression was increased in the minds of the inhabitants by an equipage of a very ornate and striking character. His carriage as it conveyed him to church created wonder; it was the handsomest ever seen in the North. The Baillie arms were emblazoned in the panels, the mountings of the harness and the peripheries of the wheels were silver gilt, gay footmen were behind, and a portly coach-man sat on a spacious hammer-cloth, the first ever seen in the capital of the Highlands.

The colonel, who was a handsome man, was in his manner bland and gracious to all. The magistrates and some of the principal people of the town waited on him; they exchanged hospitalities. He remained for some time in the North; he visited his paternal estate and obtained plans, and ordered a castle to be built on the precise site of the old house of Leys. He enlarged and improved Ness House, the residence of his sisters, which he made his temporary abode.[6]

In London, John maintained his Indian ties by joining the Asiatic Society of Great Britain, which sought to bring men of science and research together, and later by co-founding the Oriental Club "for the purpose of forming a point of union to persons connected with the East, without reference to Literature or Research."[7] The Duke of Wellington was the first president and "many persons of rank have already joined the Club." John's grandson Alexander F. Baillie authored a history of the Oriental Club and John's Canadian 5th grandnephew, Jonathan Baillie, revived a family tradition when he became a member in 2011.

CR

John returned from India as the wealthiest and most influential member of the Baillie family. While his aunts Isabella and Helen were the matriarchs of the extended family, John became the de facto head. Of his siblings, Margaret, who had raised his Anglo-Indian children, lived with him, ran his various households, and was the primary source of family gossip for her relatives in the north. Her nephews George and Charles, who were lodging together in London at the residence of someone identified only as the "Commadore," were constant sources of concern. Margaret wrote to Isabella in 1818: "Poor George is still idle & of course in disgrace. He & Charles stay at Betz Road which has put the Commadore nearly beside himself & keeps Kate in hot water."[8] And again, shortly afterwards:

> London is I believe extremely full & gay but I know nearly as little of what's going on as I should do at Invss except being occasionally distracted with noise ... more or less when my brother is engaged abroad. He has been at different times confined for days by trifling complaints but nothing seriously or interfered materially with his enjoyment of society, though his political affairs sometimes did ... Charles was appointed a cadet in the Bengal Establishment some time ago & is to sail the end of this week poor fellow. He has been very foolish & idle since coming to this wicked place where alas he had no one to take a proper interest in him. I still trust he may begin to think when among entire strangers & obliged to make the best of his own small means. George is not finally settled. At present there is a reasonable prospect of his soon being provided for but he has hitherto been so extremely unfortunate that I always fear something will happen to prevent it ... Charles has been with us this last week & says he would like to bid you adieu. In spite of his wildness he seems much affected at leaving his friends. I can hardly expect to see him again.[9]

Some years later, in 1825, Margaret shared this salacious tidbit: "Anne Rice who went out engaged to be married in Calcutta is I believe returning a spinster but her sister who accompanied her is now Mrs. Whiteford."[10] Margaret lost none of her feistiness and mordant wit and remained a going concern until her death in 1831.

John's sister Annie, as we have seen, was eventually hired with her husband to look after "Mad" Cousin William at Dunain. His other sister, Katharine, apparently managed the household of the "Commadore." John's brother Alexander lived in reasonable proximity at 27 Connaught Square. The two families visited each other frequently. George, the half-brother of John and Alexander, resumed his work as a surgeon in India after his dismissal by Moira as second assistant in the Lucknow Residency in 1815. He married Flora Loudon MacLeod in 1817 and together they had six children. Flora and at least some of her children visited Britain in 1828, as Margaret reported: "We had my sister-in-law Brother George's wife with two children, attendants etc. for a fortnight as guests in a London house all rather inconvenient though she certainly was as little troublesome as any we could possibly have. She left us on Saturday last for Leith ... but promises to meet us at Innvs after leaving her little boy with the grand folks."[11] Following a dispute with the Bengal government over his salary, George returned to Britain in 1833 with a reasonable fortune.

The only offspring of John's late Uncle William was Ann Gibson, with whom John corresponded regularly in India. At the time of her death from cholera in 1825, John represented the cousins in the dispute with the state and reached an eventual settlement distributing the not inconsiderable residual estate equally among the extant cousins. Of John of Dunain and Isabella's children, Archibald, whose illness had led to his brother William's obtaining a writership with the East India Company, died, as noted, one year after his cousin John's return to Britain, in 1817. Their sister Katharine, who had married Hugh Rose of Kilravock, died the following year. John was instrumental in securing positions with the East India Company for Katharine's sons, Hugh and John, writing in 1828: "I trust the poor Kilravock young men will have a pleasant passage to India. God grant them health & success particularly to Hugh on whom the preservation of the family depends. Their detention at Portsmouth was as you may believe attended with expense and inconvenience but they say a hard beginning often brings after luck, so let us hope the best."[12] The "Kilravock men" obviously reached India in good health, if not good spirits, since three years later Hugh provided some reflections on the country to his grandmother. "Isabella [his sister] says that I had been writing melancholy letters latterly and why I am sure I cannot say ... I have certainly no cause to grumble at this country when I have enjoyed so much better health than I ever possessed at home ... [the weather] is now perfect and in less than a month we ought to have the rains. This certainly has seemed to me by far the most oppressive year of the three and although I have not been unwell I am looking forward to the rains with more than ordinary impatience."[13]

In Britain, as already recounted, John and his brother Alexander expended a good deal of effort in the attempt, ultimately unsuccessful, to recover William's health, while also fending off the efforts of his sister

Anne to become his guardian. In 1770 John's aunt Helen became the second wife of Doctor John Alves of Shiplands, who brought four children to the marriage. Helen had worshipped her older brother, William, and named her first-born child after him. When that boy died in infancy, she flouted superstition and repeated the name with her second son, born on 29 June 1774. Their daughter, Helen, married George Inglis of Kingsmills, who had four children from an earlier liaison with a "free mulatto woman," Susanne Ker. Helen, like her cousin Bessie Rose, embarked for India. The Alves's younger daughter Anne married Sir William Arbuthnot, lord provost of Edinburgh and lord lieutenant of the city of Edinburgh. Their half-brother, Archibald became an intimate of John and took a house near him in London.

∾

Once back in Britain, John had one all-consuming ambition and that was to rehabilitate his reputation and to inflict retribution on his despised adversary, Lord Moira. Given the difference in their status and influence, John was undertaking an almost Herculean task. Only if Lord Moira overstepped egregiously could John expect any degree of success. Nevertheless, he immediately began his campaign of exoneration. He contacted India House to enquire whether there were any statements or opinions from the governor general which might require explanation or comment. He also requested a copy of Moira's dispatch concerning his removal and sought a suspension of the Court of Directors' decision relative to his dismissal "until he shall have been heard in reply."[14] But these efforts were to little avail; on 16 June 1817 James Cobb, the noted librettist and secretary of the EIC, communicated to John the directors' decision not to contest Moira's verdict. It was now abundantly clear to John that, since the government had determined to support Moira, the Company was unwilling to challenge the dismissal.

Unquestionably, 1817 was a year of great distress for John and his family. Not only had his brother George been deprived by Moira of his post at Lucknow and his son George was without employment or friends in India, but there were several deaths in his extended family, including his aunt Helen Alves, the last of the four Dunain siblings. As the year began, John's frustration came to the fore in a letter to Edmonstone:

I have been now more than six months in England & Scotland & have not heard from you once. This I confess is surprising. I have heard from my brother & son that the one is removed from Lucknow & the other without hope of employment. This too you may believe is distressing, and has a tendency by no means unnatural to impress me with a mortifying conviction that I am forgotten by my friends in Bengal. Of my situation and prospects in England I can yet say nothing satisfactory. The Gov't & consequently the Directors seem resolved to support my Lord Moira & of course I have nothing to look for but continued injustice & opposition should I appeal agst his Lrdshp's decision.

I have twice left a card at your brother's but have not had the pleasure of seeing him. I called on your sister at Cheltenham & kissed your three little girls. The boys that is Archy & Neil are at present I believe with your brother & of course I have not got a sight of them but I have learned that they are healthy & promising ...

With the exception of several colds & one sore throat I have enjoyed uniformly good health since I came back. My fortune with all my incumbrances is scarcely sufficient for my comfort. Yet many men are comfortable with less. Perhaps I shall learn to be content here. If not & Lord Moira come home I shall probably return to Bengal. While India is subject to his Gov't. I can never wish to be there. God bless you. Pray try to do something for my son & brother. I should certainly have exerted myself under similar circumstances for yours & therefore I have a right to appeal to a friendship which as sincere should be active.[15]

Discouraged, John resolved to gain membership in the two bodies to which Moira could be held accountable, namely Parliament and the EIC's Court of Directors. In the first of these arenas, politics, very few voters determined the success or failure of any prospective candidate. For example, in the late eighteenth century, only three thousand Scots chose all the Scottish members at Westminster, and John and his brother Alexander constituted two of the fifty-four voting freeholders of Inverness-shire in 1812. John became so embroiled in politics that Margaret observed: "John has done nothing yet in London but run after Hedon voters & dine at clubs and batchelor parties."[16] In 1817 the *Asiatic Journal* reported that John was "actively canvassing the Borough of Hedon in Yorkshire against the approaching election and with no doubt of success."[17] He did offer himself to the voters of Hedon, Yorkshire, in 1818 as someone "unconnected with any person or party,"[18] but while he was successful in Crail, he lost in the other burghs and withdrew. John returned to the fray in May 1819 when the leading candidate, Lord Advocate Alexander Maconochie, accepted a judgeship. However, John was soundly defeated in the ensuing election by Maconochie's successor as lord advocate, Sir William Rae. A tenacious John, in the 8 March 1820 election, finally prevailed, topping the poll. Together with the corn factor Robert Farrand, he became a member of Parliament for Hedon.

Politics, then as now, was not always a gentlemanly pursuit. In 1822 John described a recent experience in his constituency to his Aunt Isabella:

> I was worried out of my life almost, during the days of the last
> month by the knavery of some honest Yorkshiremen who were
> swearing against me at a terrible rate. But the rogues contradicted
> themselves at last, and so I got clear off, with the loss of a good deal
> of money which I could not well afford it is true but which I was
> far better pleased in expending towards the defence of my seat than
> I should have been in paying, (as they wished) into the pockets of
> the rogues who annoyed me ...
> But enough of myself & my vexations.[19]

While it took somewhat longer for John to accomplish the second and more ambitious objective, that of a directorship in the East India Company, he applied himself to the task with the same energy and dedication he employed in his parliamentary pursuits. As he informed Edmonstone, he had begun cultivating former governors general and EIC directors soon after his return to Britain. By 1819, his desire for a Company directorship was well known among his friends. It was an issue of significance in the north since EIC directors were widely perceived as being in a position to assist young men in advancing their careers. As one observer told Isabella in 1819: "Col. John Baillie & Miss Margaret have arriv'd at London long before this time. I see a new Director is appointed the other day after a powerful struggle. I heartily wish the Col. wou'd get in to the Directory. He wou'd be of service to many young lads who know not what to do with themselves."[20] In a lament to his aunt in 1822, John exclaimed: "Would to God that I were an East India Director were it only to give you what you want. At present I might ask to be Governor-General with just as much chance of success as for an office of any kind in the India House ...You may assure Mrs. Williams with great truth that both my brother & myself would most gladly do any thing in our power that you desired of us for yourself or any of your friends, but that the present object of her desire is totally out of my power & that she must wait till I am a Director if I should ever be so fortunate as to become one when she may confidently calculate on my friendship if she continues to possess yours."[21] Later that year, John bemoaned the longevity of the Company's directors and apologized for "my necessary detention in England as I thought it, altho' the result has shown that I was wrong. The Directors of the E I Co'y seem all determined to survive the candidates for their places, and my labours & privations as a candidate may properly last all my life. But if it be so, there is no doubt that many more desiring persons have suffered full as great a disappointment & that on this principle I should do wrong to complain."[22]

On 11 October 1820 Edmonstone was elected a director and John was placed on the April ballot for the next vacancy on the board. Achieving a directorship was no trifling matter. It required doggedness and endurance. In July 1821 John lobbied a former governor general, Sir George Barlow, explaining that he was waiving his claim on the first vacancy in favour of the banker Sir Charles Mills but was hopeful that Barlow would back him at the next opportunity.

> I have long thought of taking the liberty to announce to you my having offered myself as a candidate for the East India Direction, with the view of soliciting your recommendation of me to such of the Proprietors as might be known to you, but I have hitherto refrained from troubling you with a direct application on the subject, because I understood that your good offices were bespoken by some others of my fellow candidates for the Direction who had better claims to your support. I now take the liberty of informing you that … [I have] determined to waive my pretensions on the first vacancy in favour of Mr. Mills, for whose success I have heard that you are interested. I have obtained an assurance of support on the second occasion of a vacancy from a considerable number of the Proprietors, and look forward with some degree of hope to the accomplishment of the object of my ambition within a reasonable frame of time.
>
> May I flatter myself that you will take an interest in promoting the success of my canvas, when Mr. Mills shall have terminated successfully, and thus confer another important obligation on one who owes much of the success in life to the favour of your good opinion.[23]

Then in 1822 the proprietors received a notice signed by several of their prominent colleagues.

To the Proprietors of East India Stock
The friends of Lieut. Col. Baillie M.P. Candidate for the East
India Direction, and all such Proprietors of East India Stock as are
disposed to support his pretensions to a Seat in the Direction of
their Affairs, are most earnestly requested to meet at the City
of London Tavern, on Tuesday the 13th of August, at Two o'clock
in the Afternoon, for the purpose of taking into consideration
the most effectual means of promoting Col. Baillie's Election to
the Office of a Director of the East India Company.[24]

The session concluded that the Court of Directors had been deprived of
military knowledge and experience by the death of several distinguished
military officers with long experience in India and that Colonel Baillie
was an outstanding candidate who should be elected to the Court. Yet, at
the same time, they reached a consensus to defer John's candidacy until
his friends were in a position to assure him their votes.

That the services rendered to the Company by Lieutenant-Colonel
John Baillie, M.P. late Resident at the Court of Lucknow – Services,
the Magnitude and Importance of which have been so forcibly
and honourably testified by the Documents circulated among the
Proprietors – place that Officer in the highest Rank of those meritorious Servants of the Company who have contributed by their
Talents and Exertions to the pre-eminence of the British Power in
India, and demonstrate a combination of Military and political
knowledge, of judgment, energy, and local experience, which must
be deemed to qualify Colonel Baillie in an eminent degree for the
situation of a Member of the Court of Director ...
That this Meeting do, therefore, pledge themselves, to employ
their utmost endeavours to place Colonel Baillie in that distinguished Situation, at as early a Period as may be practicable; but
that, adverting to a confluence of circumstances, which has afforded
to another respectable Candidate the advantage of a pre-occupation
of the Votes of many of Colonel Baillie's most powerful Friends, it
is the opinion of this Meeting that Colonel Baillie should abstain
from proceeding to Ballot at the approaching Election of a Director
in the room of the late Mr. Inglis, and await the next Vacancy that
may occur; when it is hoped that the zealous exertions of his friends,
in support of his acknowledged pretensions, will accomplish the
object of his Ambition.[25]

With that the momentum accelerated. Margaret observed: "John is so constantly running after India proprietors that he neglects every thing else."[26] William Astell, a four-time chairman of the EIC, sponsored John's formal application as a candidate for a directorship while Barlow assured John of his backing and encouraged him to approach some of Barlow's friends. To this John replied: "I thank you sincerely & cordially for your kind letter of the 4th inst. I shall write to Mr. Morris again if you think it necessary. I did write to him if I mistake not early in October, but not having received an answer I fear that my letter has been mislaid. Mr. Dick I have waited on repeatedly. He is under obligations to one of the Directors whose influence I hope to obtain by & bye, & in that event your kind recommendation will not [only] secure Mr. Dick's 4 votes but also two or three others that I know to be uniformly influenced by Mr D. I have received a very polite letter from your brother Sir Robert assuring me of his vote if in Town & of any assistance in his power."[27]

Despite the promised assistance and encouragement, John despaired of ever realizing his dreams. As late as 1 May 1823, he foresaw as "little prospect as ever of any vacancy in the India directors."[28] But on 28 May his labours came to fruition. He gained election to the Court of Directors, replacing the London merchant and East Indiaman's ship captain, Joseph Cotton. There were allegations that John had been offered the seat on the Court of Directors as a quid pro quo for dropping his vendetta against Moira.

> On what other principle than this can it be at all explained that Colonel Baillie, the dismissed servant, whose removal from his office in India, was approved, not only by the government of the day in that country, but by the Directors here is now accepted as an honourable master in England? – that he who was deemed unworthy to serve in a land of despotism abroad, is thought quite worthy to rule in the company of despots at home? There are certain stories of threatened recrimination on each side, which led to this happy compromise; and of the dismissed servant being made an honourable master to prevent him from disclosing what he otherwise might have done, had he been not so satisfactorily silenced.[29]

The author of the above diatribe held a decidedly jaundiced view of the Court of Directors, as evidenced by his vivid description of the election process: "This board of despots and monopolists, and many are also acquainted with the mode of abject servility in which these future tyrants lined their devious way, through every dirty lane and alley in the city, to solicit, cap in hand, the 'honour of the vote and interest' of men whom, while they openly flattered, they inwardly despised! – not infrequently the whole of the members who are within the polluted precincts, club together the forces to keep the more pure from coming among them; and on the other hand they sometimes unite."[30] That tirade underlines the continuing envy directed toward the directors of the most powerful company in the British Empire. Yet the charge concerning John does not ring true. In truth, John sought the directorship as a venue for assailing Moira.

In this regard, Moira was his own worst enemy, as he continued to alienate his colleagues in India and paid little heed to instructions from India House. The first chinks in his armour appeared in 1819 when the Court of Directors debated a proposal to award a pension to the governor general. Charles Grant opposed the measure, ostensibly, at least, on the rationale that the traditional practice was to confer any such award upon completion of a governor general's term. Others seemed intent on finding reasons to deny the pension outright. The doctor and radical MP Joseph Hume, for example, asserted that the legality of the proposed pension was doubtful and that "it was, to use a strong term, rewarding a man for plunder."[31] More and more, the Court of Directors and Moira were at loggerheads.

Then, in 1821, the nizam of Hyderabad offered Moira £200,000 to build a new courthouse in Calcutta. The directors were aware that the nizam had recently borrowed heavily from William Palmer and Company to cover his debts. The interest rates on the loans were exorbitant and the Court objected to forcing the nizam to rely even more heavily on a lender who was unsavourily enmeshed with Moira. Accordingly, the Court declined the offer and censured some of Moira's entourage for their involvement with Palmer. Moira took offence and tendered his resignation, although he remained in India until 1823. As further details emerged, the Court became increasingly concerned about the relationship between Moira's government in India and Palmer. It transpired that a ward of Lord Moira's had married Sir William Rumbold, who subsequently became a partner in Palmer and Company. Moira granted an exclusive banking licence to that house and claimed that it was for the benefit of the nizam. Yet, in a minute revealing perhaps more naivety than calculation, Moira noted: "A person, in whom I take a very lively concern, from his having married a ward of mine, brought up nearly as if she had been my daughter, is a partner in that house. The degree to which his interest is engaged in the proposed transaction might, without my being conscious of the bias, warp my judgment."[32] He further reflected in a letter to Rumbold:

> The account you have given of the house of Palmer and Co. at Hyderabad is very favourable and certainly the details justify your inclination for going to that city to inspect the books. I enclose you a letter to the Resident couched in terms which will ensure to you his attentions and most earnest good offices. The partners speculate that your being one of the firm will interest me in the welfare of the house, to a degree which may be materially beneficial to them: it is a fair and honest calculation ... The amount of the advantage which the countenance of Government may bestow must be uncertain, as I apprehend it would flow principally from the opinion the natives would entertain of the respect likely to be paid by their own Government to an establishment known to stand well in the favour of the supreme authority here ... Perhaps a more distinct benefit may attend the firm, from the consequent discouragement to competition with you, by any other British partnership to which a similarly professed sanction would not be granted ... It is on the ground of the service to the Nizam, at the request of our Resident, that I have consented to let the good wishes of Government for the prosperity of this firm be signified. No new establishment could have such a plea.[33]

Notwithstanding Moira's protestations, the resident had never spoken in support of Palmer and Company. He had merely responded to Calcutta that the establishment of a commercial firm at Hyderabad based on English principles and conduct should prove a source of general convenience and benefit. Indeed, it turned out that Hans Sotheby, the assistant resident at the nizam's court, was a partner in Palmer and Company at the time when Rumbold swore a perjured oath that the partners in the firm were William Palmer, Sir William Rumbold, Hastings Palmer, George Lamb, and the Gujarati banker Bunketty Dos, and that "no other persons of any description have, directly or indirectly, any partnership with us, or any interest in any concerns, beyond such, as the public has in every other house of agency. We further declare, that no public functionary, at the head of any public office or department, ever had any avowed or direct partnership, directly or indirectly with us, or any interest in our concerns, which could influence him in countenancing our dealings with the Nizam's Government, or give him any means of deriving any personal advantage from them."[34] Sotheby never denied being a partner. In fact, he swore that Moira was aware of his interest in the partnership at the time His Lordship received Rumbold's oath but ignored it when furnishing information to the directors.

Normally, the affairs of a banking firm in India would not arouse a great deal of interest or controversy in Britain. However, William Palmer and Company had extended sizable loans to a critical British ally, the nizam, at rates that could be defended only on the basis that the banking house was undertaking the risk of lending to an Indian state. Moira's approval of the loans suggested that the influence of the British government would be utilized to ensure payment. If that were the case, the interest rates levied were clearly usurious. The Court of Directors took exception to being drawn into the affair. In 1821 an affronted Court charged Moira with approving loans by Palmer and Company to the nizam in contravention of an act predating Moira's arrival, accused him of withholding relevant and damaging information, and suggested that the loans were highly favourable to the lenders at the expense of the Company's ally, the nizam.

> In truth, you have, in substance, if not in form, lent the Company's credit in the late pecuniary transactions at Hyderabad, not, indeed, for the benefit of the Nizam's Government, but for the sole benefit of Messrs. Palmer and Co. You have not guaranteed the house the fulfillment of the engagements entered into with it by the Nizam's Government; but the house has received the support of the British Government, and it expects that the influence of that Government will be employed to secure satisfaction of its just demands upon the Government of the Nizam. Without this countenance and support, Messrs. Palmer and Co. declared that they never would have established an extensive mercantile concern (much less entered into large pecuniary dealings with the Government) in a country where there are no regular courts of judicature. With this countenance and support, they not only themselves feel secure, but they are placed in circumstances which enable them to secure a combination of the native monied interest.[35]

While Moira had claimed the interest rate was 10 per cent, the actual rates were in the 16–24 per cent range. The Court cited specific acts that both restricted interest rates to 12 per cent and forbade companies like William Palmer from making loans to native princes. In either case, the contracts would be void and the European-born partners subject to prosecution.

While a majority of the directors opposed Moira, the aristocrat and confidant of the prince regent did not lack supporters in an age in which, to paraphrase Jane Austen, many had a value for rank and consequence that blinded them a little to the faults of those who possessed them. As a result, India House heatedly debated the issue for a number of years. Upon assuming his directorship, John entered the fray, objecting, first, to Moira's assertion that Oude had been maintained in a state of thralldom in contravention of treaties, and, secondly, to Moira's claim that the nawab of Oude's loans were voluntary. When in 1832 the directors proposed sending a draft to India attempting to determine what limitations should be applied on loans to the nizam, John and Henry St George Tucker, the individual who had originally proposed a loan from the nawab of Oude, dissented on the ground that they wished the matter settled rather than prolonged. "The high interest common under the native Governments is, in great part, the consideration for insecurity... the principal part of that high interest, under such Governments, is in the nature of an insurance upon a risk. But if the influence of the British Government is to be employed in such a manner as to ensure payment and thereby to take away the risk, it will deserve to be considered how much, if anything, of that which may be regarded as the consideration for risk in the nominal rate of interest, it will be equitable to allow."[36] The two, after examining the correspondence, minutes, and representations of a number of parties including the late resident at Hyderabad, presented an addendum:

We cannot satisfy ourselves that the House of William Palmer and Co. have any just claim of debt on the Nawab Moneer-ool-Moolk, or that there are any grounds whatever for exerting the authority and influence of our Government to enable that firm to enforce any such claims. On the contrary, we are deeply impressed with the conviction that such an exertion of authority on our part would be an act of gross injustice, tending to violate our engagements with a Native Power, to produce a most proper interference in its domestic administration, to expose the rights and property of its subjects to be dealt with in the arbitrary manner, and finally to lower the character of the British Government, and to render our very name odious in the estimation of the people of India.[37]

Similarly, in response to a proposed motion largely vindicating Moira, the chairman of the East India Company declared: "Though upon consideration of all the transactions of Messrs. William Palmer and Co. with the Nizam's government at Hyderabad, I acquit the noble Marquess [Moira] of all corrupt and improper motives, I cannot, on the other hand, go so far as to say that his personal character is not at all affected by them ... I feel myself bound to state that in my opinion the noble Marquess has compromised his character by the proceedings at Hyderabad."[38]

In 1823 Moira's resignation was accepted. While the deference due a peer of the realm guaranteed him some supporters in the Court of Directors and at Westminster, virtually no one in India mourned Moira's departure. Although he did not benefit personally, the stench of corruption sullied his regime and left Moira, if not a broken, at least a blemished, man. "No Governor-General has ever returned from India more completely out of favour with all parties, than this unfortunate nobleman ... when he left the country, we believe there were scarcely a hundred individuals among the millions he left behind him who could conscientiously declare that they regretted his absence, or who could not hope for a much better ruler than himself ... he was believed to be hated as a tyrant by some, despised as a hypocrite by others, and pitied as one of the weakest of men by the greatest number of those who felt themselves bound to join in the clamourable applause, which they knew, while they swelled the shout, was entirely undeserved."[39] The Court of Directors displayed its "tacit disapprobation" of Moira by refusing to countenance the pension usually granted to retiring governors general. Indeed, although the prince regent had sought his appointment in India, at least in part as a means of repairing his shattered fortunes, Moira left the country with many unpaid bills, could not satisfy his creditors in England upon his return, and was obliged to take refuge in Brussels and Italy. The *Oriental Herald* skewered him on his leaving England: "We do not regard this as more than thoughtlessness in him, though in any but a man of noble blood it would be punished with imprisonment, and ranked as no small crime."[40]

With Moira no longer a factor in India, the way was open for John's return, as he himself had earlier intimated to Edmonstone. Yet, at fifty-one years of age in 1823, he was no longer young. Moreover, he was comfortably and influentially ensconced in Britain and many of his friends from India had returned to their native land. For his part, Moira, despite his demonstrated deficiencies, was appointed governor of Malta in 1824, only to die at sea two years later. With that, an effectively exonerated John was deprived of his main adversary. The fallout of Moira's intrigue continued, however, with the collapse of the once venerable William Palmer and Company in 1829.

19

Dissolution

Glory is fleeting but obscurity is forever.
Napoleon

With his detested adversary, Lord Moira, vanquished, John was undoubtedly able to take great pleasure in life. Politics were especially rewarding,
as on 6 November 1826 he was re-elected in the constituency of Hedon.
But then disaster struck. In 1829 he suffered a devastating personal blow
with the death of his beloved son John Wilson. Margaret had been excited
by Johnny's prospects, although she does leave us wondering as to who
was scheming what. "My brother is really distressed between parting
with his favourite & the schemes of another, though in several respects he
has been fortunate particularly in getting Johnny a writership in China
which prevents his being obliged to remain longer at college. Indeed he
will probably sail in late April."[1] Then came the dreadful news that John's
heir and "favourite" had drowned on the passage to China on 27 June
1829.

John was grief-stricken but gradually recovered sufficiently to take
advantage of a political opportunity that arose. A few years earlier, in
1824, he had begun to explore the possibility of a candidacy in his home
district of the Inverness Burghs, the seat held by Charles Grant, 1st Baron
Glenelg and son of the same Charles Grant who served as chairman of
the EIC. However, John withdrew his name from consideration for the
Inverness Burghs seat in 1826, deferring to Grant's brother Robert, who
was elected. As fate would have it, Charles Grant soon alienated Provost
James Robertson by thwarting the latter's bid for the lucrative post of
collector of customs which the provost, in keeping with tradition, sought
for a near relative. Provost Robertson then made it abundantly clear that
Robert Grant would not be returned in 1830. As a result, John was
unopposed in the Inverness Burghs in that year's election.

Unopposed or not, he campaigned vigorously. He declared his support for Wellington and Peel but remained careful to stress his independence: "While they follow the same course ... they shall generally have my cordial support; but I am not one of those who can be led by even the strongest partiality for a minister to lend my support to any measure which either my conscience or my judgment disapproves."[2] He also conveyed some sense of the complexity of the campaign when he sought to engage his Aunt Isabella and his cousin-in-law, Hugh Rose of Kilravock, in a little political intrigue.

> Here are a letter for you & a printed circular addressed to poor William by my friend & rival Lord McDonald. I wish you could come in some day and get Kilravock to come in with you to talk on some matters of importance to me. I would readily go out for the purpose but really have no time. Lord Cawdor's Barony of Arduries possesses a vote in the County of Inverness. With Mr. McPherson & Mr. Stubb's assistance this vote might surely be made useful, and Kilravock having it would be as good for me as my own. Regarding the Dunain vote also I am by no means sure that it is lost but writing on the subject is useless. If we could have a meeting with some legal advisor here before I leave the Country I should indeed be very glad.
>
> Pray show this note with my best regards to Col Rose who will perhaps have the goodness to come in some day this week & dine with me to talk on this subject.[3]

As a parliamentarian from 1820 on, John was a moderate Whig who supported the Tory ministries led by Lord Liverpool and the Duke of Wellington. He was firmly aligned with the conservative side on one issue, electoral reform. As a substantial landowner, he opposed such reform since it was against his interests and those of his backers. More than that, though, he saw the campaign for electoral reform as another manifestation of the French revolutionary principles which were rapidly infecting society. In 1830 the French ousted their last Bourbon king and Britain was roiled by landlords' attempts to offset a series of poor harvests through raising rents, displacing labour by machinery, and increasing import duties on grain. An address by John in support of a petition against the Reform Bill revealed the depth of his hostility to radicalism, as he saw it, of whatever stripe.

> This petition comes from a most respectable and influential, as well as intelligent class of the community, who are alarmed at the progress

of revolutionary doctrines and pray the House not to countenance any
such opinions by sanctioning any of the speculative notions of reform
now so much broached ... These petitioners do not come forth as the
uncompromising enemies of all reform, for they only declare themselves opposed to the extravagant doctrines advocated out of doors
on this subject. They are strongly attached to the form of Government
in this country, which has hitherto both in seasons of peace and war
secured to them the enjoyment of rational liberty and they come to the
House and beg that no measure may be sanctioned which can lessen
that security. They deprecate revolutionary projects and extravagant
changes as dangerous to the very existence of the country.

Such is the feeling of these petitioners, and I do most cordially concur in most of the sentiments expressed in the petition. I do hope, too,
from the declaration of a Noble Lord in another place, that he would
never countenance any measure of reform which could lessen the security of property or the just influence of it, and that the measure which
is to be submitted to the House will have that for its basis.[4]

John was less than enlightened on another subject as well. Despite his
personal experience with mixed-race children, John, in Parliament, was
surprisingly unsympathetic to the attempts of Anglo-Indians to achieve
basic civil and legal privileges. When John W. Ricketts, an Anglo-Indian
petitioning Parliament for better treatment of his people, sought support
from Robert Campbell, the deputy chairman of the EIC, Edmonstone,
and Baillie, he reached the conclusion that the first two "showed an apti-
tude to take a pretty fair view of the matter tho' the latter (Col. B) by no
means went to any thing like the same extent. As to Col. B[,] however
unpalatable it may be for me to do so, still a sacred regard to truth requires
me to say of him that the tendency of his observations savoured too much
of the rust of antiquity, and looked a very studied attempt to throw cold
water upon a fire of a laudable zeal, flowing from a good cause."[5]

Yet his opposition to electoral reform and lack of sympathy for Anglo-
Indians did not define the whole man. John was a consistent proponent
of Catholic relief and voted with the government when Wellington and
his home secretary, Robert Peel, passed the Catholic Emancipation Act
in 1829, opening Parliament to Catholics. He supported Jewish emancipation, repeal of the Test Acts (disabilities aimed at Catholics and non-
conformists), and abolition of the death penalty for forgery. And, on the
subject of British rule in India, his position was nuanced. In Parliament
he declared that "the natural effect of alliances such as ours with the

several states of India, i.e., of offensive and defensive engagements between paramount or powerful, and weak or subordinate states, so closely connected with each other, must be the gradual depression and ultimate subversion of the power of the one and the substitution of the other in its stead." But he then added: "As to the effect of this result on the general condition of the people, I should say that it must be greatly to their advantage, in as much as it never, I believe, has been doubted that the condition of the Company's subjects in India is preferable in every respect to that of those of the best governed of all the states of the Peninsula."[6] Even when offering these reflections, John could not resist a veiled criticism of his erstwhile adversary, Moira: "At the same time I am ready to admit that there have been cases of demand from some of our allies, and of interference in their internal concerns, which I should feel it difficult to justify, although the grounds of such demand and interference were considered to be satisfactory at the time by far higher authorities and more competent judges than myself."[7]

In the early 1820s John took a particular interest in the grievances of Calcutta bankers and voted for investigating them since he sensed rightly that, on this issue, Moira was vulnerable. He also secured appointment to the committee assessing the claims for compensation of the proprietor of the *Calcutta Journal*, James Silk Buckingham. The claims arose from the Bengal government's taking exception to some of Buckingham's published articles and compelling him to depart the country. As a result, Buckingham lost his periodical, which he valued at £40,000. In addition, on 9 February 1830 and again on 4 February 1831, John was placed on the Select Committee on East India Company Affairs, which was charged with investigating "the state of trade between Great Britain, the East Indies and China."[8]

In 1830 John's opposition to electoral reform didn't serve his interests well. When the Duke of Wellington misjudged and alienated the moderates by declaring that he would always oppose electoral change of any kind, even the most minor, the Tory government fell and was succeeded by that of Lord Grey, who was committed to the reform cause. The Tory-dominated House of Lords defeated Grey's initial Reform Bill, but after an election and King William IV's threat, albeit grudging, to create sufficient peers to ensure passage, the Reform Bill of 1832 became law. It was a limited achievement in that the electorate only rose from 6 per cent to 9 per cent of the male population, but it did abolish rotten boroughs and place suffrage on a uniform basis. Much of its importance was in setting the stage for further expanding the franchise.

Although he voted against the Reform Bill, John was a proponent of the Scottish variety of reform since it "proposes to take away but a little and to confer a great deal."[9] As a result, he lost the ensuing election to an anti-reformer. He had offered himself as "a friend of moderate reform," but after a discouraging canvass he withdrew. The setback, however, was temporary, for John was re-elected as a Conservative in 1832 in the revised constituency representing the Inverness Burghs. There were four candidates in the field and

at the nomination there was a regular row; all kinds of missiles such as kail stocks, potatoes, rotten eggs were thrown at Baillie and Bruce, the Tory candidates who were disliked by the majority of the crowd. The Colonel was allowed to address the electors first, but the noise of hissing and cheering were so great, that what he said could scarcely be understood, and for a long time he could not obtain a hearing; in one part of his address he said, "Boys of Inverness, what have I done that you will not let me be heard; did I not know your fathers, and did I ever see one of you in London, in need of assistance, but my hands were in my pockets for you?" This latter was quite true, for he was very kind to the Invernessians who were in distress in London.[10]

John celebrated with a great victory feast. "The colonel entertained his townsmen to a sumptuous banquet. The luxuries of the feast were enhanced by two great turtles brought down from London, a rarity never seen before in Inverness. The champagne circulated liberally – some of the new electors declared they never tasted such exquisite ginger beer."[11]

ભ

Upon Edmonstone's return to Britain in 1818, he and John spent a good deal of time together, much of it at India House. They embarked on a number of projects, one of which involved the teaching of Asiatic languages at the Company's college, Haileybury. Owing to their experience with the College of Fort William and Indian languages, Edmonstone and John were delegated by the Court to determine whether to revive the teaching of Eastern languages at Haileybury. There originally had been two learned natives of India as teachers of Persian and Hindi on staff but they had died or departed. As a result, the EIC had witnessed a decline in the "oriental acquirement" of the students. However, on the subject of employing native Indians as teachers, the Company had reservations, specifically:

the difference in religion, dress, customs & manners which has a tendency to lessen that respect on the part of the pupil towards his teachers which is indispensable to the former's improvement. 2dly – The total ignorance of the English language ... 3dly – The too frequently observed irregularity, or rather immorality of conduct of Mussulmans residing in this country, which may be productive of the greatest inconvenience, if not of most injurious effects as to the discipline of the College – and 4thly – the inconvenience and embarrassment to which the Court of Directors are subjected, by the experienced discontent & constantly recurring demands, of individuals of this class, arising from their habitual improvidence, and more especially by the pretensions of the family, which, in the event of death will generally be left in a destitute condition, dependants upon the bounty of the Company.[12]

The Company preferred Persian instructors, but Baillie and Edmonstone disagreed. Because the Persian dialect employed by many instructors did not resemble the colloquial Persian utilized in India, and because of the prevalence of Hindi throughout India, Baillie and Edmonstone felt that a native Indian would be preferable. Yet they changed their mind when it became apparent that the only available teacher was a Persian, Mirza Ibrahim. Fortunately, that gentleman possessed a number of advantages. He displayed a tolerable familiarity with the English language, dressed in the European manner, and, unlike the previous Muslims on staff, would be amenable to living with the other instructors. The Court evidently endorsed the recommendation, for in 1826 Baillie and Edmonstone offered Ibrahim the position of deputy or assistant to the professor of Arabic at £200 in his probationary year, an offer he readily accepted.

With the death of his Aunt Isabella in 1832, John and his cousin Archibald Alves were appointed executors of her estate. They instructed that the family pictures and papers be transferred to Dunain and that Isabella's property, for reasons of financial necessity, be sold. Almost immediately, John was fending off requests from Cousin Anne and for the first time contemplating his own mortality. "I have no objection whatever to your having the trinkets at the valuation & indeed if they were at my disposal you should have them for nothing with all my heart as the only remaining individual of your father's and mother's family capable of using them ... On the subject of Miss Whale's letter, it is entirely impossible for me to do any thing. With four nephews of my own to provide for, I have not the smallest prospect of serving any more customers for many many years to come even if Providence should spare my life far beyond the usual time."[13]

John was something of a celebrity in the north. He boasted the grandest carriage ever seen in north Britain. He was a member of Parliament, director of the East Company, and a substantial landowner in the environs of Inverness. In his honour, John W. Mitchell devised a *strathspey* or Scottish dance, "Lt-Col Baillie of Leys," based on a tune by the Scottish composer John Thomas Surenne. He had his portrait painted by Sir Henry Raeburn, one of the foremost artists of the era. Then in 1832 John commissioned Samuel Beazley, a British architect responsible for designing many of the leading theatres in Great Britain, to design a Mansion House at Leys, a house that would encompass the existing sixteenth-century tower. Lamentably, he did not live to witness its completion. John died at his home, 9 Devonshire Place, of influenza on 20 March 1833. He was buried in St Marylebone Parish Church where, as a result of extensive bombing in the Second World War, only a garden exists today. More tangibly, John is commemorated by a plaque in the High Church of St. Stephen in Inverness where, although they are interred in the Burying Ground of the Grey Friars, he also erected a plaque in memory of his parents, George and Anne, his eldest sister, Margaret and his daughter, Henrietta.

Not surprisingly, given his character as a "man of formalities," John left specific and detailed instructions regarding the disposition of his assets after his death. After returning from India, he had drawn up two wills, the first in 1823 and the second in 1833. His first will, dated 26 November 1823, designated John Wilson as his primary heir, but with the death in 1829 of "my dear boy" on his passage to China, his daughter Anne became the principal beneficiary of an estate valued at about £180,000.

A few years later, economic circumstances led to a change of plans. At the time of the first will, London was in the process of displacing Amsterdam as the world's financial centre and Britain was riding a strong economic expansion fuelled by the Bank of England's liberal monetary policy. The global bond market burst upon the scene, with London boasting twenty-three foreign bonds in 1826 whereas only one had existed in 1820. Exports and investments in Latin America boomed. Speculation rose to such feverish levels that even the fictitious Republic of Poyais managed to issue bonds. Fearing a bubble, the Bank of England began to contract the money supply and set off the financial panic of 1825. The stock market collapsed and close to seventy British banks failed. The crisis spread, leading to sovereign defaults in Latin America and a severe recession in Britain. John's losses in the panic – he observed that the "amount of my personal property has been diminished" – as well as the death of three of his beneficiaries and/or trustees led to the second, revised will of 1833. In that document he revoked a £5,000 legacy to Anne since she was first in succession to the estate and reduced the legacies to his children, George, Benjamin, Charlotte Anne, and Margaret Catharine, to £2,000 each. However, the provisions relating to the mysterious Mary Martin – a life annuity, furniture, and use of John's Middlesex cottage – remained intact. John also clarified the entail of the estate by stipulating that all the plate, jewellery, and books, along with his gold-mounted Persian sabers, were to be designated heirlooms, deposited at Leys, and forever made part of the entailed property. Until the estate was settled, Anne or her heir in possession of Leys would be paid £1,000 per annum from the estate but only if the heir spent at least six months of each year in the Mansion House of Leys.[14] In both wills, John had expressed the desire that his heirs expand the family landholdings, and, after his death, the trustees lost no time in acting on his wishes. By 1834, they had purchased Balrobert, Castle Hill, and the former Baillie estate of Torbreck, which included Knocknagael, from the Frasers, paying the substantial sum of £23,000 for Torbreck.

Anne married a distant cousin, John Frederick Baillie, the second son of Peter Baillie of Dochfour, in London in 1835. They had two children, John Baillie-Baillie, who was born in 1835 and served in the Coldstream Guards, and Alexander, born in 1837. Anne died relatively young at thirty-eight years old and her elder son took possession of the estate on attaining his twenty-first birthday. "Unfortunately neither of the sons took to any useful occupation. The revenues of their patrimony did not suffice for their expenditure. They broke the entail of the heirloom jewels, said to be worth £12,000, and they were sold."[15] Despite John's meticulous provisions to entail the estate in perpetuity, his grandsons lost no time in squandering his considerable fortune. They reputedly sold everything with the exception of John's books, which were bequeathed to Edinburgh University, and removed themselves to England. The sons died in 1890 and 1917 respectively but by 1882 the entailed estate of Leys was no longer in Baillie hands. Joseph Mitchell lamented: "The estate is now disentailed; the brothers, who are still alive, never visit the North, and Leys Castle lands were lately in the market. When I recollect the great affection the worthy colonel had for the North, the anxiety he displayed to have the Leys branch of the Baillies distinguished and honoured in the locality where they had resided for so many generations, I cannot help regretting that the legitimate ambition of this kindhearted and distinguished man should have been so early blighted."[16]

Alexander Brown Lawson of Clynelish purchased Leys in 1882. He was single with no heirs and, according to Hugh Saggers, the present manager of the estate, he stipulated in his will that "my sister gets nothing." On Lawson's death in 1889, Leys was bought by Charles George Olgilvie of Delvine, who held high office in Egypt and died during the First World War. The Countess of Southesk then leased the estate until it was purchased by Sir Francis Walker, a local architect and property developer, in 1925. His heirs subsequently sold the residual 3,173-acre estate in 2011 to a local industrialist, Doug McGilvray.

As the oldest of the oldest male descendant of George Baillie of Leys, I was the natural inheritor on two occasions but each time my claim was compromised. On the initial occasion, I would have been first in line to inherit Leys had my great-great-great-grandfather Alexander not sold the property to his younger brother and had my great-great-grandfather, Alexander Charles, not been estranged from his father. The second opportunity would have materialized, at least according to family lore, if my great uncle, Charles, who had no male heirs, had accepted the offer in the 1920s to inherit Leys on the condition that he reside there for at least six months of every year. The third opportunity arose when Michael Williamson died in 2010 and his heirs placed Leys on the market. Our family wrestled seriously with the proposition but in the end reason trumped emotion.

We owe an accounting of Colonel John's other children. Of the daughters, we know nothing more of Henrietta, who died in Inverness in 1822, and we have scant details of Charlotte Anne and Margaret Catherine. They only lived in Britain a relatively short time. Charlotte Anne returned to Bengal in 1818 and the following year married Thomas Richard MacQueen in Lucknow. MacQueen, who was born in County Armagh, joined the EIC in 1808 and served in the Third Anglo-Maratha War and the First Anglo-Burmese War. At his death, he was a major in the 45th Native Infantry. In 1820 Charlotte Anne gave birth to John's first grandchild, John Baillie MacQueen. Unfortunately, the child died within the month, but like her Great Aunt Helen Alves, Charlotte Anne gave little credence to superstition and named her fifth child John Baillie MacQueen. Charlotte left India with her daughter of the same name and died in Lanark in 1892. Margaret Catherine also returned to Bengal, two or three years after her sister, and married Henry Francis Caley in 1823. Caley, of English origin, arrived in India in 1807 and served in the Anglo-Nepalese War and the Third Anglo-Maratha War. Caley retired as a major-general and died in Rawalpindi in 1866. Margaret outlived him by a goodly margin, dying in 1890.

Of the sons, Neil Benjamin Edmonstone was a jurist of some standing in Calcutta and, like his father, published a book on Muslim law. Ben died in 1883. The oldest son, George, trained as a surgeon, went to India, and, perhaps finding his career thwarted by Lord Moira, returned to England by 1818, when Margaret referred to his still being "idle" in London. He married Harriet Garford and practised as a surgeon to the Metropolitan Police until his death in 1852. George and Harriet lived at Poplar. They had four sons, about whom George's cousin, Anne, conscious of George's heritage, observed to her mother: "Mr G. Baillie calls here pretty often ... His wife seemed like a good humoured pleasant like woman, and they seem a fine set of children, and not particularly dark."[17] The four boys and their cousins extended the family's engagement with India and the east into the fourth generation. Three of them found employment with the East India Company. John, born in 1826, joined the Company as a cadet in 1843 and served with the 1st Bengal Europeans. He saw action in the Sutlej campaign of 1845–46 (the first Sikh War), the Crimean War, and the Indian Mutiny of 1857. He was a garrison instructor at Agra and Allahabad from 1873 to 1875, attaining the rank of major-general, and died a bachelor in 1889. George became a professor of engineering at Rhookee and died in 1871. Neil Benjamin became a surgeon.

Meanwhile, Kate Innes, the granddaughter of Katharine Baillie Rose, daughter of John of Dunain and Isabella, was in Scutari in 1855 "to assist Miss Nightingale attending the wounded" during the Crimean War.[18] Shortly thereafter, Kate's brother Frank "made a marvellous escape from being butchered by the black fiends tho' three poor young fellows, brother officers of his, were barbarously murdered"[19] during the Indian Mutiny. George and Flora's son Hastings D'Oyly died in St Helena while serving with the 1st Bengal Artillery. Finally, William Alves's grandson John was active in Guiana but died at sea on his way to Demerara in 1882.

Despite the risks they undertook in venturing to India and its environs and the reasonable recompense that ensued, the Baillies of Dunain and those of Leys did not have many generations to savour their winnings. Neither household is represented in the Highlands today. The males of the Leys' branch are found anywhere but Scotland, and with the death of the last male heir of the Dunain family, poor "Mad William," in 1869, the senior line of a family that "had run an honoured course in the neighbourhood of the burgh of Inverness" for more than four hundred years came to an end. "Mad William" may also have been the last Highland Baillie to carry the benighted name William. William, the 12th Laird of Dunain, had dubbed William an unlucky name when his sister Nelly determined to call her second son by the same name as her first, and in this he proved prescient. He himself died at the age of forty-three in abysmal conditions in Seringapatam. His cousin, William of Torbreck, fell during General Abercromby's assault on Ticonderoga in 1758. Of the four nephews and one grand-nephew named in honour of the twelfth laird, William of the Leys family died at the age of thirty-nine seeking an unrequited fortune in Jamaica; William, the 14th Laird of Dunain, contracted "brain fever" in Baghdad in his twenties and remained mentally ill until his death; his nephew, Alexander's son William, died at age twenty, presumably of wounds incurred in India; Nelly's son William Alves died in infancy and only her second son, William, survived to have children of his own.

This outcome could have differed radically. What if Hyder Ali's rocketry had not, by a chance shot, destroyed Colonel William Baillie's tumbrils at Pollilur, if Hector Munro's army had marched the few miles to William's assistance, or if William had survived his imprisonment? Would he have returned to his native land with the power, titles, and influence of his fellow prisoner David Baird? Isabella had hoped and assumed that Colonel John of Leys would acquire Dunain. What if he had lived somewhat longer and purchased the principal Baillie estate?

In any event, as his uncle William of Dunain had been unfortunate in his adversaries and his commanding general, John was unfortunate in his choice of heirs. The prevailing primogeniture of the day would have designated the oldest male, George, as the presumed heir. However, the fact that John gave precedence to his children by the Begum of Oude suggests that he had indeed married her and regarded them as his primary heirs owing to their legitimacy. We have no way of divining whether John Wilson would have proven a better steward of the estate than Anne and her dissolute offspring, but the success of George and his children suggests that he would have been a much better choice. For that matter, Neil Benjamin or either of Charlotte Anne or Margaret Catherine in combination with their husbands would have been a marked improvement over Anne and her offspring.

For the Baillie clan, *Sic Transit Gloria* has proved a more appropriate motto than the family's own, *Quid Clarius Astris* (What Is Brighter Than the Stars).

Epilogue

As I noted at the outset of this book, I have travelled the world in search of my Baillie ancestors. These trips have left me deeply moved, providing a wealth of memories that I treasure still.

My family and I travelled to Scotland in 2002, 2005, and 2013. On the 2005 trip, we set out from our Inverness base on visits to the residences, places of worship, and burial grounds of generations of Baillies, touring Cawdor Castle, home of my seventh great-grandfather, Sir Hugh Campbell, and the reputed residence of Shakespeare's Macbeth; Dunain House, residence of my fourth great-grandmother, Anne Baillie, an imposing structure of forty-plus rooms; Leys Castle and surrounding grounds; and, finally, a distinctly more modest dwelling at 20 Wells Street in Inverness, from where my great-grandfather, Charles, set out on a journey of his own, eventually settling in Saint John, New Brunswick. Our stop at 20 Wells gave rise to the obvious questions: What could have transpired to reduce my family from the relative grandeur of the estates we had just visited to the respectable cheerlessness of 20 Wells? And did that transformation in their lives influence, in any way, their decision to immigrate to Canada? We pondered these questions as we stood and gazed upon Culloden Moor, where Cumberland's defeat of Charles Edward Stuart and his Highland allies put paid to any thought of a Stuart restoration. A mournful and misty atmosphere still pervades Culloden, yet the clans' defeat on that moor set in motion the series of events that would open to William Baillie and his cohort a vast array of possibilities unknown to previous generations of Scots.

On the 2013 trip, my family and I, including this time six grandchildren, basked in glorious weather during a week in which we rented Leys Castle from the McGilvray family. We found John Baillie's coat of arms liberally distributed throughout the castle, along with his paintings and furniture. We ate at his dining-room table, sitting on his chairs. We visited John's town residence, Ness House, which is preserved as the Columba Hotel. On an outing in search of the Loch Ness monster, our eight-year-old grandson Alexander sighted a fin and a tooth while our nine-year-old granddaughter Caroline spotted a flipper, but, lacking adequate documentation, we hesitated to report the discoveries. The grandchildren made some spears and painted shields which they brandished during charges on the bloody field of Culloden.

Then there was India. In 2008, in my pursuit of William Baillie, my wife and I, along with friends Peter and Bonnie Sacerdote, visited Chennai, known as Madras in William's time. We wandered about Fort St George, which has been conscientiously preserved and indeed is the most complete example of British military architecture in southern India. St Mary's Church, built in 1678–80 by Governor Streynsham Master, remains today much as it would have been when William and his fellow Company servants worshipped there in the late eighteenth century. It is the oldest Protestant church east of Suez and the oldest British building in India. Elihu Yale and Robert Clive took their marriage vows there. Later, we drove to Pondicherry, where William had been the commanding officer after the defeat of Bellecombe in 1778. The French presence remains pervasive but there was no trace of William. The trail became warmer when we reached Bangalore. Our local guide, Arun Pai, was a little flustered and confided to my wife that he was not sure how to handle the tour since any foreigners he had escorted to date had claimed victorious ancestors and my forebear had fared otherwise. Recently, Arun had taken a descendant of Lord Cornwallis on a roughly similar tour. Marilyn responded that she could understand how Seringapatam would appeal to Cornwallis's progeny but that I was well aware of William Baillie's fate. Accordingly, there was no need for Arun to gild the lily. Of Tipu's magnificent palace in Bangalore, only the Audience Hall remained in place. The area of Fort Bangalore, where Cornwallis breached the walls in 1791, was preserved, as was the dungeon, which had a plaque reading: "In this dungeon were confined Captain (afterwards Sir) David Baird and many others prior to their release in March 1785." Had William not died in prison, that exact dungeon would undoubtedly have served as a way station for him as well.

Upon arriving at Seringapatam, we could appreciate the impressive defensive position, protected as it was by the Kaveri River. Arun carefully orchestrated our visit, which began with a walk along the walls to the obelisk commemorating those who fell defeating Tipu in 1799, a campaign in which Lieutenant Alexander Baillie served. Had Alexander received his captaincy a couple of months earlier, I would have been able to determine his exact position in the battle, since a large memorial tablet outlined the location of the troops by officer down to the rank of captain. Arun then led us to Colonel Bailey's Dungeon where William, together with his senior officers, was imprisoned from 1780 until his death in 1782. At the entrance, on a slab of granite, we read the inscription: "In this dungeon were confined for many years the British officers taken prisoner by Tipu Sultan." The dungeon had an almost antiseptic appearance but the shackles were still in evidence and we had read enough of the historical accounts to realize how fetid and rat-infested the place had been for the unfortunates incarcerated there. Lying incongruously in the midst of the dungeon was a large cannon which, we understand, fell through the roof during the siege of 1799. Arun then took us to Tipu's summer palace, the Daria Daulat, built in 1784. The palace features a large mural celebrating victory at the Battle of Pollilur. It is a propaganda piece by an unknown Indian artist and has been restored liberally over the years. The mural confirms the old adage that history is written by the victors. The Mysoreans and their French allies appear as masculine exemplars with swarthy complexions and facial hair while their British opponents resemble women or, at least, creatures not fully male. The British lack facial hair and possess doe-like eyes, raised eyebrows, and pink lips. In addition, although many of the East India Company's soldiers would have fought in tartans and motley colours, the British in the mural are uniformly clad in red, the colour in India associated with eunuchs and women. Baillie, wounded and carried on a palanquin, and Fletcher are shown biting their pointing fingers, a sign non-Brahmins use to signify submission and defeat. The French commander, de Lally, looks through his eyeglass at the exploding tumbrils while a confident Tipu Sultan smells a rose. Interestingly, we could discover no depiction of the architect of the victory, Hyder Ali.

The signs forbade any photographs of the mural but Arun thought the site manager might allow an exception if I explained my connection to the central figure in the mural. I gave the gentleman, who proved a bureaucrat in the finest Indian tradition, a succinct – in retrospect, perhaps, too succinct – explanation of my relation to William Baillie. However, the manager preferred talking to listening and, after explaining at length that he could make no exceptions, added: "Who did you say was your relative?"

As the setting sun presented the site to its optimum advantage, Arun brought us to his pièce de résistance, the cenotaph to William erected by his nephew John, the resident at Lucknow. A minute of the Revenue

Department of Fort St George recorded: "We have great pleasure in sanctioning the grant of a small spot of ground as to the site of a cenotaph in memory of the late Colonel Baillie." It is a graceful and appealing work of Indian rather than European design, consisting of an octagonal and domed room with a pillared porch and funeral urns on each corner of the roof. A plaque bears the inscription:

To the memory
of
Colonel William Baillie
who
with a detachment of British troops under his command after a noble
and most gallant resistance to a superior force of the enemy on the
plains of Perumbaukum was ultimately compelled to surrender
to the united armies of Hyder Ali and Tipu Sultan on the 10th day
of September 1780
and
died in the Fortress of Seringapatam on the
13th day of November 1782
This monument is erected and inscribed
by his nephew
John Baillie Lieut.-Colonel on the Establishment
of Bengal and Resident at the Court of Lucknow
AD 1816

The cenotaph is even more impressive today since it has recently been restored by the British Monuments Commission but even at that time it had a powerful impact on me. While I was contemplating William's fate in a foreign land, a local man and his son approached us for money, presenting themselves as the grounds-keeping team that maintained the monument. In a vulnerable moment I gave them much more than the purported groundskeeper expected. The son extended his hand for more, causing his father to smack him and exclaim that they had done well enough. Afterwards, I asked Muneer, the guide coordinating our trip, if he thought they actually looked after the cenotaph; he responded, "Well, your heart was in the right place."

Two years later, in 2010, my wife and I returned to Lucknow, eager to visit John's "princely situation" and hoping to document the existence of the Begum of Oude. Lucknow itself is a city of faded grandeur with little prospect of recapturing its former glory. While in its day the Kaiserbagh, a palace of 400 square yards, rivalled any palace complex in Europe and the city abounded in impressive buildings, the British victors, after suppressing the Great Indian Mutiny of 1857, systematically destroyed the architectural glories of Lucknow in vindictive retribution for what they considered the city's central role in the insurrection. The British resistance at the Residency, where three thousand soldiers and civilians withstood the besiegers for ten months, assumed mythic proportions in imperial folklore. By the time the refugees boxed up in the Residency were relieved by Sir Colin Campbell, only a thousand survived. The heroic resistance inspired Tennyson's popular poem "Banner of England." At independence in 1947 the last Union Jack to be lowered in India was, tellingly, the flag over Lucknow's Residency.

Arguably, the destruction of Lucknow's architectural treasures need not have led to a precipitous decline in the city's cultural activities but any chance of retaining or rejuvenating its cultural dominance was forestalled in 1947 when the bloodshed surrounding partition drove the Muslim elite to decamp for the newly created Islamic country of Pakistan. As a result, we encountered a major city with imposing ruins and some grand remnants of its past but little in the way of tourist facilities. The Taj, and a modest Taj at that, seemed to be the only quality hotel, and, in contrast to our experiences elsewhere in India, the only good restaurant we were able to find was in the Taj itself.

Nevertheless, the Residency is imposing. The British had retained its grounds with their scarred and partially destroyed buildings as a museum to British valour. Astonishingly, after 1947, the Indians had rigorously maintained this symbol of foreign conquest. They modified the message somewhat by presenting the Great Mutiny as the first Indian war of independence, but essentially the Residency grounds remain a testament to British fortitude. Walking across them summons up an eeriness reminiscent of Culloden. Nor does it require much imagination to evoke the desperate position of the besieged taking refuge behind the Baillie Gate, a structure erected in 1814–15 by the nawab in John's honour.

While we thoroughly enjoyed our exposure to Lucknow, we failed to cast any light on the Begum of Oude. The records of the Residency had been destroyed in the Great Mutiny and we had no success in the local archives. We left India none the wiser about this mysterious part of John Bailllie's life, though deeply affected by what we saw as we toured the city that had been his home for nine years.

Finally, in 2012, my wife and I visited Ireland and while there we toured Kilkenny's St Canice's Cathedral, which contains a plaque to William's younger brother, John, the 13th Laird of Dunain, whose death at Bantry Bay while leading his Inverness Loyal Fencibles on an expedition to thwart a threatened Napoleonic invasion of Ireland effectively ended the Dunain family line.

In the course of all these trips, to say nothing of the hours spent in archives in Scotland and England poring over family correspondence and related documents, I came to have a much fuller appreciation of my ancestors' lives and their place in history. Gaps in the record still remain, but that is only natural – the past, as the novelist L.P. Hartley said, is a foreign country, one that can be understood in parts but never in its entirety, a place where, to a certain extent, facts and mystery must always exist side by side. If all I have accomplished here is to sketch the broad outlines of the story of several generations of Baillies, I can rest content, secure in the knowledge that the people featured in these pages – William, Alexander, the two Johns, and the other lesser characters, not least the formidable Margaret – have, after two centuries, emerged from the shadows, if only partially. I'm sure they would be pleased to have their stories told, however imperfect the results may be.

Colonial and Current Place Names

COLONIAL	CURRENT
Bangalore	Bengaluru
Bassein	Vasai
Benares	Varanasi
Bombay	Mumbai
Calcutta	Kolkata
Cawnpore	Kanpur
Chandarnagore	Chandannagar
Chingleput	Chengalpattu
Chintopilly	Chintapally
Cuddapah	Kadapa
Ellore	Eluru
Furruckabad	Farruckhabad
Kaveripatna	Kaveripattinam
Madras	Chennai
Madura	Madurai
Mangalore	Mangaluru
Masulipatam	Machilipatnam
Mysore	Mysuru
Pondicherry	Puducherry
Poona	Pune
Porto Novo	Parangipettai
Seringapatam	Srirangapatna
Singarpettah	Singarapettai
Tanjore	Thanjavur

COLONIAL	CURRENT
Tarrapore	Tarapur
Tranquebar	Tharangambadi
Trichinopoly	Tiruchirappalli
Trinomalee	Tiruvannamalai
Wandiwash	Vandavasi

Cast of Supporting Characters

ABDULLAH QUTB SHAH, seventh sultan of Golconda (?–1672), reigned from 1626 until his death. While he was a renowned patron of the arts, overall his rule was a failure. Abdullah captured Vellore, the last capital of the Vijayanagara Empire, but was compelled to surrender to the Mughals on punitive terms in 1636.

ABERCROMBIE, GENERAL JAMES (1706–1781), was a British army officer and parliamentarian. As commander-in-chief in North America, he directed the disastrous frontal assault at Fort Carillon (Ticonderoga) where his troops were virtually annihilated in 1758 by Montcalm's much smaller force. Abercrombie was recalled and replaced by Geoffrey Amherst.

ABERCROMBY, LIEUTENANT-GENERAL SIR JOHN (1772–1817), was a Scottish army officer and politician. He saw action in Flanders, the West Indies, the Batavian Republic, and Egypt before being appointed commander-in-chief of the Bombay army in 1809. Abercromby captured Mauritius in 1810 and was named commander-in-chief and temporary governor at Madras in 1812.

ADAM, JOHN (1779–1825), was a Scottish EIC civil servant. He served as private as well as political secretary to the governor general and was appointed to the Bengal Council in 1817. Adam became acting governor general on Moira's departure in 1823. In that capacity, he suppressed freedom of the press and withdrew support of the banking house Palmer and Company. He died off Madagascar while returning to Britain in broken health.

ADAMS, BRIGADIER-GENERAL THOMAS (c. 1730–1764), was a British army officer who, after service in the Netherlands and India, was given, in 1762,

command of British forces in Bengal. When Mir Qasim, the nawab, rebelled in
1763, Adams defeated him at Gheriah and Andwanala, thereby preserving the
EIC's still precarious position in Bengal.

ADDINGTON, HENRY, 1ST VISCOUNT SIDMOUTH (1757–1844), was a
British statesman and prime minister from 1801 to 1804. He entered Parliament
in 1784 and was appointed speaker in 1789. Addington served as home secretary
from 1812 to 1822 and chancellor of the exchequer from 1801 to 1804. As
prime minister, he secured peace with Napoleon through the Treaty of Amiens in
1802. Addington opposed most progressive legislation.

ALI BAHADUR, nawab of Banda (1758–1802), inherited Banda and Kalpi from
his grandfather, Baji Rao I, the peshwa. He ruled Banda from 1790 to 1802 and
established himself in Bundelcund by defeating Arjun Singh in 1790.

ALI MOHAMMAD (c. 1706–1748) was a Rohilla chief who founded the state of
Rohilkhand and reigned from 1719 to 1748. The Mughal emperor invaded
Rohilkhand and imprisoned Ali Mohammad whom he later pardoned and
appointed governor of Sirhind. Ali Mohammad took advantage of the Persian
sack of Delhi in 1739 to extend the territory and assert the independence
of Rohilkhand.

ALVES, ARCHIBALD (c. 1765–1839), was the son of Dr John Alves of Shiplands
and stepson of Helen Baillie Alves. He was a London merchant who by 1790
owned Carrapan Plantation in St Vincent in partnership with his brother William,
George Baillie, and George Inglis. By 1803 Alves and Company owned land on
Canje Creek which they named Rose Hall.

ALVES, THOMAS, was the youngest son of John Alves and his first wife, Jean
Campbell. He managed his brothers' plantations in Berbice and later became a
planter himself.

ALVES, WILLIAM (1774–1835), the son of Dr John Alves and his second wife,
Helen Baillie, was a West Indian planter in partnership with his stepbrother
Archibald Alves and George Baillie (Ardmore) and George Inglis. He acquired
land in Berbice and in 1817 purchased Rose Hall Plantation on the Corentyne
coast in partnership with John Cameron.

AMAR SINGH THAPA (1751–1816), the "Living Lion of Nepal," was a formidable warrior who commanded the Nepalese forces during the Anglo-Nepalese

War of 1814–16. He had previously annexed several western principalities and unified the country. Thapa fought bravely but lost roughly one-third of Nepal under the terms of the Treaty of Sugauli. Discouraged, Thapa, retired as an ascetic to Gosainkunda.

AMEER KHAN (1768–1834) was a Pathan warrior in the employ of the Maratha rulers Scindia and Holkar. For his services, Ameer Khan received extensive land grants and the title of nawab in 1798 from Holkar. In 1806 Ameer Khan established himself as ruler of the princely state of Tonk. Once the EIC subdued Scindia, Ameer Khan came to terms with the British and remained a faithful ally.

ANAND RAO GAIKWAD, maharajah of Baroda (?–1819), reigned from 1800 to 1819 but was a weak ruler. When a rebellion occurred, the EIC intervened to secure Anand Rao's throne. By the 1803 Treaty of Cambey, Anand Rao recognized British suzerainty.

ANWARADEAN KHAN, nawab of Arcot (1672–1749), held the governorships of Surat and later Rajahmundry under the Emperor Aurangzeb in recognition of his distinguished service in the Mughal army. Anwaradean became the highest-ranking official under the nizam of Hyderabad, Asaf Jah I, who appointed him nawab of the Carnatic in 1744. Anwaradean, allied with the British against the French, died fighting at Ambur and was succeeded by his son, Mohammed Ali Khan.

ARBUTHNOT, SIR WILLIAM (1766–1829), was a Scottish politician and administrator. He served as lord provost of Edinburgh from 1815 to 1817 and 1821 to 1823 and as lord lieutenant of the city of Edinburgh in 1821–22. Arbuthnot succeeded his father as secretary to the board of trustees for the manufactures and fisheries of Scotland. He married Anne Alves in 1800.

ARJUN SINGH (?–1792) was a Rajput warlord who served as commanding general of the troops and guardian to Bhakta Singh, king of Banda. He routed Anupgiri and the nawab of Oude in 1762. Arjun Singh emerged as the dominant force in Bundelcund following his 1784 victory at Gathyaura but, in turn, was defeated and killed by Anupgiri and Ali Bahadur in 1792.

ASAF JAH I (1671–1748) was a Mughal and Turkic nobleman who founded the state of Hyderabad, which he ruled from 1724 to 1748. He served as governor of Oude and then in 1712 was appointed soubah of the Deccan with the title Nizam-ul-Mulk (administrator of the realm). The emperor Muhammad Shah appointed Asaf Jah his prime minister, but, frustrated by the corruption at court, Asaf Jah returned to govern Hyderabad.

ASAF JAH III, sixth nizam of Hyderabad (Moneer-ool-Moolk) (1768–1829), was the second son of Asaf Jah II. He ruled from 1803 to 1829, during which time a British cantonment was established in the state. Asaf Jah III's reign was plagued with financial difficulties.

ASTELL, SIR WILLIAM (1774–1847), was an English merchant, banker, and politician. He was born William Thornton and assumed the Astell name upon succeeding to the estate of his great uncle, Richard Astell. Astell was a partner in Godfrey Thornton and Sons and a director of the Russia Company in 1802, the East India Dock Company from 1805 to 1835, and chair of the Great Northern Railway. He entered Parliament as a Conservative in 1807. Astell was a director of the EIC for forty-six years, serving as chair and deputy chair for several terms.

AURANGZEB (1618–1707) was the third son of the Mughal Emperor Shah Jahan and served his father as viceroy of the Deccan from 1636 to 1644 and 1654 to 1658. When Shah Jahan became ill, the four sons sought to assume the throne. Aurangzeb emerged triumphant and imprisoned his father in Agra Fort. He greatly expanded the empire but increasingly alienated the population by discriminating against non-Muslims.

BAHADUR SHAH I (1643–1712) was the Mughal emperor from 1707 to 1712. He served as governor of the Northwest Territories under his father, Aurangzeb. After a war of succession following Aurangzeb's death, Bahadur Shah emerged victorious and proclaimed himself emperor. He was much more liberal than his father and was able to maintain the strife-ridden empire until his death.

BAHADUR SHAH ZAFAR II (1775–1862) was the son of the Mughal Emperor Akbar II. He was the seventeenth and last Mughal emperor. During the Indian Mutiny of 1857, the rebels adopted Bahadur Shah as their nominal leader. Once the mutiny was suppressed, the British exiled him to Rangoon.

BAILLIE, ALEXANDER, 4TH LAIRD OF DOCHFOUR (c. 1735–1798), was the eldest son of Hugh Baillie. He joined the merchant and trading firm of Smith and Lambert in St Kitts in 1752. With his brothers, Alexander established the firm Smith and Baillies, trading throughout Africa, the Caribbean, and America. He married James Smith's daughter and had one child, Lieutenant-Colonel William, who died on his passage to join his regiment in the West Indies.

BAILLIE, CAPTAIN CHARLES (c. 1727–1758), is shown as the son of William of Ardmore in the records of the 78th Highlanders but he has likely been confused with General Charles. In any event, he transferred from the 21st Foot to the 78th and was appointed grenadier captain in 1757. Charles died at the siege of Louisbourg in 1758.

BAILLIE, EVAN, 5TH LAIRD OF DOCHFOUR (1741–1835), was the third son of Hugh Baillie. Following a stint in the army, Evan joined his brothers in a mercantile enterprise in the West Indies but returned to settle in Bristol where he established the highly successful firm of Evan Baillie Son and Company. He served as sheriff of Bristol in 1786–87 and in Parliament from 1802 to 1812. Evan married Mary, the daughter of Peter Gurley of St Vincent, and succeeded his eldest brother at Dochfour.

BAILLIE, GEORGE (c. 1755–1809), was a younger son of William of Ardmore. He arrived in St Kitts in 1770 and by 1773 was employed by the mercantile firm Garraway and Evan Baillie. George eventually became a large-scale merchant in St Kitts, St Vincent, and Grenada as George Baillie and Company. He took over James's business upon the latter's death but entered into disputes with his Baillie cousins. George's firm collapsed 1805.

BAILLIE, HUGH 3RD LAIRD OF DOCHFOUR (?–1798), was the eldest son of Alexander, 2nd Laird of Dochfour. He married Emilia Fraser, daughter of Alexander, 11th Laird of Reelig, in 1730. Hugh was the father of Alexander, James, Evan, and Katharine, who married Provost Chisholm.

BAILLIE, JAMES (1737–1793), was a West Indies planter and merchant and a British politician. He was the second son of Hugh Baillie of Dochfour. James joined his eldest brother, Alexander, in St Kitts from 1755 to 1771 and became a partner in Smith and Baillies. He purchased the Mount St Bernard plantation and, with Alexander, Hermitage Plantation in 1765. He married Colina Campbell of Glenure, the co-heiress of Colin Roy Campbell, whose assassination inspired Stevenson's novel *Kidnapped*. James was the first of the family to enter Parliament, in 1792–93. His heirs were compensated £73,700 for their 1,821 slaves in Grenada, Guyana, and St Lucia.

BAILLIE, JOHN FREDERICK (c. 1800–1865), was the second son of Peter of Dochfour and grandson of Evan, 5th Laird of Dochfour. He married Anne Baillie, the heir of Colonel John of Leys. John Frederick was the father of John Baillie of Leys and Alexander.

BAILLIE, MATTHEW (1761–1823), was the brother of the poet Joanna Baillie. He taught anatomy, for which he was renowned. Baillie then entered private practice, becoming physician extraordinary to George III. He was elected in 1790 to the Royal College of Physicians and to the Royal Society.

BAILLIE, PETER, 6TH LAIRD OF DOCHFOUR (1771–1811), was the eldest son of Evan, 5th Laird, and the father of John Frederick, who married Anne, the daughter of Colonel John Baillie of Leys. He was a Scottish West Indies merchant and politician who represented the Inverness Burghs in Parliament from 1807 to 1811. After serving in the army, he joined Evan Baillie, Sons and Company and became a partner in Bristol Old Bank in 1806.

BAILLIE, ROBERT CARNIBE (?–1779), was a great-grandson of Alexander Baillie, 9th Laird Dunain, and the son of Colonel Kenneth of Sunbury, Georgia. He was a lieutenant in the Third South Carolina Regiment and died at the siege of Savannah in 1779.

BAILLIE, WILLIAM OF ARDMORE AND ROSEHALL (1705–1779), was the second son of Alexander, 2nd Laird of Dochfour, and brother of Hugh and Evan of Abriachan. He was the father of General Charles, General Sir Evan, George (the West Indian merchant), and Captain Simon.

BAIRD, LIEUTENANT-GENERAL SIR DAVID (1757–1829), was a Scottish soldier who was captured at Pollilur in 1780 and was released at the conclusion of the Second Anglo-Mysore War in 1784. Baird served in the Third and Fourth Anglo-Mysore Wars, leading the charge which took Seringapatam in 1799. He commanded the Indian army which, with Abercromby, ejected the French from Egypt. Baird captured Capetown and distinguished himself in the Napoleonic Wars. He was named governor of Kinsale in 1819 and commander-in-chief of Ireland in 1820.

BAJI RAO I (1700–1740) was the son of the first Bhat peshwa, Baji Vishwanath. Baji Rao I ruled as peshwa from 1720 to 1740 and was a renowned warrior who created a formidable Maratha Empire by wresting what became Gwalior, Indore, Baroda, and Dhar from the Mughals.

BAJI RAO II (1775–1851) was the son of Peshwa Ragonaut Rao and reigned from 1796 to 1818. Following Baji Rao's defeat by Holkar, the British agreed to restore him as peshwa in return for the cession of vast territories to the EIC in the

Treaty of Bassein in 1802. The Maratha chiefs opposed the treaty and launched the Second Anglo-Maratha War of 1803–05. Baji Rao was deposed by the British following his defeat in the Third Anglo-Maratha War of 1817–18.

BAKHT SINGH (?–1837) was the rajah of Ajegarh in 1792–93 and 1807 to 1837 and rajah of Banda from 1792 to 1798. He succeeded his uncle, Guman Singh, on the thrones in 1792 but was deposed a year later by Ali Bahadur. With British assistance, Bakht Singh recovered the fort of Ajegarh and regained much of his former territory in 1807.

BALAJI BAJI RAO (1720–1761) was the son of Baji Rao I. He reigned as peshwa from 1740 to 1761, during which period he acquired Malwa in 1738 (confirmed by the emperor in 1741) and other territories. Maratha power reached its peak under Balaji but he suffered a devastating defeat which checked Maratha advances for some years at the Third Battle of Panipat in 1761 against an Afghan-Rohilla-Oude coalition.

BANNERMAN, ETHEL MARY ELIZABETH, COUNTESS OF SOUTHESK (1868–1947), was the daughter of Sir Alexander Bannerman of Elsick and Lady Arabella Diana Sackville-West. She married Charles Noel Carnegie, 10th Earl of Southesk, in 1891.

BARBOUR, JOHN (c. 1320–1395), was a Scottish poet and the first identifiable individual to write in the Scots language. He served in the household of his primary patron, Robert II, as an auditor of the exchequer in 1372 and as a clerk of the audit in 1373. *The Brus* is Barbour's best known surviving work. He was later appointed archdeacon of the Kirk of St Machar in Aberdeen.

BARLOW, SIR GEORGE HILARO (1762–1847), was an EIC administrator who joined the Company in 1778. He rose to chief secretary in 1796 and a member of the Supreme Council in 1801. On Cornwallis's death, Barlow served as acting governor general from 1805 to 1807 but was not confirmed by the Whig government. In compensation he was appointed governor of Madras. However, Barlow's rigidity gave rise to an officers' mutiny which led to his recall.

BARLOW, ADMIRAL SIR ROBERT (1757–1843), was the younger brother of George Barlow, governor general of India. He was a distinguished officer in the Royal Navy and saw action in the American Revolutionary War, the French Revolutionary Wars, and the Napoleonic Wars. Barlow was appointed deputy comptroller of the navy in 1806 and commissioner of the Chatham dockyard in 1808. He was elected a fellow of the Royal Society in 1819.

BEAZLEY, SAMUEL (1786–1851), was an English architect, novelist, and playwright. He fought in the Peninsular War of 1808–14 during which he assisted in the escape of Louis XVI's daughter, the Duchesse d'Angoulême, to Spain. Beazley became the leading theatre architect of his era. The Royal Lyceum and Drury Lane are examples of his work.

BEGUM SHURS OODIPA (BHOW BEGUM) (1731–1815) was the wife of Nawab Shuja-ood-Dowla and the mother of Nawab Asaf-ood-Dowla. Her immense wealth, derived from her family's service to the Mughals, enabled Shuja to redeem a substantial part of Oude from the EIC following his defeat at Buxar in 1764. She resisted her son's continual monetary demands and entrusted her remaining fortune, valued at seven million rupees, to the EIC.

BELLECOMBE, GENERAL GUILLAUME LÉONARD DE (1728–1792), was a French army officer and colonial administrator who served as governor general of Réunion from 1767 to 1774, of Pondicherry from 1776 to 1778, and of Sainte-Domingue from 1781 to 1785. He was active in the Seven Years' War in New France and Newfoundland. Bellecombe, as commander general in India, was compelled to surrender Pondicherry in 1778.

BENFIELD, PAUL (1742–1810), began as a writer with the EIC and became a financier in Madras. He amassed a considerable fortune through questionable loans to the nawab of Arcot. Benfield was recalled to Britain but reinstated after an investigation. He later entered Parliament and established a mercantile firm, Boyd, Benfield and Company, with William Boyd. Boyd's speculations cost Benfield his fortune and he died in poverty in Paris.

BLIND HARRY (c. 1440–1492), also known as Harry the Minstrel, was a Scottish poet who preserved the memory of William Wallace through his poem *The Actes and Deidis of the Illustre and Vallyeant Campioun Schir William Wallace*. He performed at the court of James IV.

BOURDONNAIS, BERTRAND-FRANÇOIS, COMTE DE (1699–1753), was a French military officer and colonial administrator. He was appointed governor of Île de France (Mauritius) and Île de Bourbon (Reunion) in 1735. As commander of the fleet, Bourdonnais relieved Mahé and Pondicherry and enabled the capture of Madras in 1746. He quarrelled with Dupleix, the governor general, over the terms offered the British and returned to France where he was imprisoned for corruption but eventually exonerated.

BRADSHAW, LIEUTENANT-COLONEL PARIS (1764–1821), was an Irish EIC army officer and administrator. He served as acting resident at the court of Scindia in 1797–98 and resident at Lucknow and Patna in 1816. In 1815 Bradshaw signed the Treaty of Sugauli, which imposed a resident on Nepal and transferred one-third of its territory to Britain.

BRAITHWAITE, MAJOR-GENERAL SIR JOHN (1739–1802), was an EIC army officer who captured Mahé in 1779 but was defeated near Annagudi and imprisoned by Tipu Sultan in 1782. He was released when peace was declared in 1784. Braithwaite served as commander-in-chief of Madras in 1792–96 and 1800–01. He captured Pondicherry in 1793.

BRUCE, ROBERT, KING OF SCOTLAND AND EARL OF CARRICK (1274–1329), opposed Edward I's choice of John Balliol as king but subsequently supported William Wallace's uprising. After Wallace's defeat, Bruce and his primary rival for the throne, John Comyn, were appointed guardians of Scotland in 1306. Bruce fled after murdering Comyn but returned and prevailed over Edward II's much larger army at Bannockburn in 1314 to re-establish an independent Scottish monarchy.

BURGOYNE, GENERAL JOHN (1722–1792), was a British politician and dramatist. In the American Revolutionary War, Burgoyne relieved Quebec but was decisively defeated by Horatio Gates at Saratoga in 1777. Saratoga was a turning point in the war in that it gave the French the confidence to intervene on the side of the Americans. Burgoyne was consequently stripped of his command but reinstated as commander-in-chief of Ireland and privy councillor in 1782.

BURGOYNE, MAJOR-GENERAL SIR JOHN OF SUTTON, 7TH BARONET (1739–1785), was a career army officer and the cousin of Lieutenant-General John Burgoyne. He served for many years in Ireland and in 1782 led the 19th Light Dragoons, the first European cavalry in India. Burgoyne became a major-general on the Madras establishment in 1783.

BURKE, EDMUND (1729–1797), was an Irish statesman, orator, author, political theorist, and philosopher. Entering Parliament in 1765 as a committed Whig,

Burke supported the cause of the American rebels, Catholic emancipation, and the impeachment of Warren Hastings, but opposed the French Revolution. He is regarded as the philosophical founder of conservatism.

BYNG, ADMIRAL GEORGE, 1ST VISCOUNT TORRINGTON (1663–1733), was a career naval officer and parliamentarian who played a critical role in securing the navy's support of William III during the Glorious Revolution of 1688. He stymied the French fleet attempting to invade Scotland in 1708 and routed the Spanish fleet at the battle of Cape Passaro, forcing the Spanish to accede to the terms of the Quadruple Alliance. Byng served as admiral of the fleet from 1718 to 1734 and first lord of the admiralty from 1727 to 1733.

CAMERON, CHARLES, 21ST LAIRD OF LOCHIEL (c. 1725–1776), was a younger son of the nineteenth clan chieftain. The crown had sequestered the Cameron estates following the Forty-Five and Lochiel's escape to France. He obtained a pardon and returned to Scotland where he enlisted Camerons in the service of the crown. Lochiel's estates were returned to his son, Donald, in 1784.

CAMPBELL, SIR ARCHIBALD OF CLUNAS AND BUDGATE (1668–1744), was the second son of Sir Hugh Campbell of Cawdor. He was a staunch Hanoverian who managed the estates for commissioners and was appointed sheriff-principal of Nairnshire for life. He married Anna Macpherson of Cluny in 1688 and their daughter Anne married Alexander Baillie, 11th Laird of Dunain.

CAMPBELL, MAJOR-GENERAL SIR ARCHIBALD (1739–1791), was a Scottish military officer, colonial administrator, and politician. In 1768 Campbell was appointed chief engineer of the EIC in Bengal. He made a fortune in shipbuilding and silk trading in India. After his exchange for the patriot Ethan Allen in the American Revolution, Campbell won battles at Savannah and Augusta. He was appointed governor of Jamaica in 1783 and later commander-in-chief and governor of Madras where he provided exemplary administration.

CAMPBELL, FIELD MARSHALL SIR COLIN, 1ST BARON CLYDE (1792–1863), was a Scottish army officer who served in the Peninsular War, the War of 1812, the First Opium War of 1842, and the Second Anglo-Sikh War of 1848–49. He led the Highland Brigade which distinguished itself at the battles of Alma and Balaclava. Campbell was appointed commander-in-chief of India at the outbreak of the Indian Mutiny of 1857 and twice achieved the relief of Lucknow.

CAMPBELL, SIR HUGH, 5TH LAIRD OF CAWDOR (1642–1716), was the son of Colin Campbell of Ardesier. In 1662 he married Lady Henrietta Stuart, sister of the 3rd Earl of Moray. Campbell undertook extensive building on Islay and at Cawdor. He represented Nairnshire in Parliament.

CAMPBELL, JOHN, 1ST BARON CAWDOR OF CASTLEMARTIN (1753–1821), was a British politician and noted collector of antiquities. He entered Parliament in 1777. Campbell was appointed governor of Milford Haven in 1780 and raised to the peerage in 1796. He became a fellow of the Royal Society in 1795.

CAMPBELL, SIR ROBERT (1771–1858), was a merchant at Madras from 1796 and a director of the EIC from 1817 to 1852. He chaired the EIC in 1831.

CARLETON, GUY, 1ST BARON DORCHESTER (1724–1808), was an Irish army officer and colonial administrator. After distinguished service as Wolfe's quartermaster-general at Quebec, Carleton was appointed captain-general and governor-in-chief of Quebec in 1768. He was instrumental to the passage of the Quebec Act of 1774, which gave French Canadians the will to resist the American invasion of 1775–76. Carleton was appointed commander-in-chief of British forces in North America in 1782–83 and was governor general of British North America from 1785 to 1796.

CAVENDISH-BENTINCK, LIEUTENANT-GENERAL LORD WILLIAM HENRY (1774–1839), was the second son of Prime Minister William Cavendish-Bentinck. He was a British army officer and statesman. After serving in the Peninsular War, Bentinck was appointed British representative to the court of Palermo where he was instrumental in the creation of the Kingdom of the Two Sicilies. He served as governor general of Madras from 1803 to 1807 and of India from 1828 to 1835.

CHAMPION, BRIGADIER-GENERAL ALEXANDER (?–1793), was a career military officer of the EIC. He fought in the campaigns of 1760–61 and served under Munro at Buxar in 1764. In 1773 Champion was appointed commander-in-chief Bengal and a year later routed the Rohillas at Miranpur Katra, thereby ending that war.

CHANDA SAHIB (?–1752) was the son-in-law and only male descendant of Dost Ali Khan, the nawab of the Carnatic. Nevertheless, on Dost's assassination in 1740, the feudatory suzerain, the nizam of Hyderabad, appointed Anawardean Khan to the nawabship. On the nizam's death, the French under Dupleix sought to instal Chanda as nawab. The French party prevailed and Chanda held the nawabship from 1749 to 1752. However, he was eventually captured by Clive at Arcot and put to death by Anawardean's son, Mohammed Ali.

CHHATRASAL, MAHARAJAH OF PANNA (1649–1731), was a renowned Bundela Rajput warrior who wrested a substantial portion of Bundelcund from the Mughal Emperor Aurangzeb. He captured Mahoba in 1680 and eventually established his own kingdom with its capital at Panna. With the aid of the peshwa Baji Rao I, Chhatrasal evicted the Afghans from Bundelcund. Chhatrasal, in turn, bequeathed much of Bundelcund to the peshwa, who had married Chhatrasal's daughter, Mastani.

CHISHOLM, PROVOST WILLIAM (1717–1807), was the second son of Roderick, twenty-first chief of the Chisholms. He was an eminent medical practitioner and served as provost of Inverness from 1773 to 1776 and 1779 to 1782. Chisholm married Colonel William Baillie's third cousin, Katharine of Dochfour, in 1775.

CLIVE, MAJOR-GENERAL ROBERT, 1ST BARON CLIVE (1725–1774), was a British military officer, administrator, and parliamentarian who turned the tide of the Anglo-French conflict in southern India by capturing Arcot in 1751. During his second posting, he established the military and political supremacy of the Company in Bengal by his victory over the nawab of Bengal at Plassey in 1757 and by securing the dewani of Bengal, Bihar, and Orissa from the Mughal emperor in 1765. He served as governor of Bengal from 1757 to 1760 and again in 1765–66. Clive declined the offer to command His Majesty's forces in America, and after a failed effort to censure him in Parliament, he committed suicide.

COBBETT, WILLIAM (1763–1835), was an English pamphleteer, journalist, politician, and farmer. He published the *Political Register*, which consistently opposed authority. Cobbett attacked rotten boroughs, corruption, and the Corn Laws. He was imprisoned for treasonous libel from 1810 to 1812 but finally entered Parliament in 1832.

COCKERELL, LIEUTENANT-COLONEL JOHN (1752–1798), was an EIC army officer who served as military secretary to Warren Hastings from 1767 to 1774. In 1770 he was quartermaster-general of the Bengal forces sent to relieve Bombay. Cockerell commanded the Bengal troops in the 1791 capture of Bangalore and siege of Seringapatam.

COLLINS, COLONEL JOHN ULRICH (?–1807), was an EIC career army officer and civil administrator. He served as resident at the court of Daulat Rao Scindia from 1795 until the outbreak of the Second Anglo-Maratha War 1803. Collins became the resident at the court of Oude in 1804. He was known as "King Collins" for his apparent cold, imperious, and overbearing manner.

COPE, GENERAL SIR JOHN (1690–1760), was a British military officer and parliamentarian. He distinguished himself in the Wars of the Spanish and Austrian Succession. Cope was appointed commander-in-chief Scotland in 1745 and was decisively defeated at Prestonpans. A court-martial exonerated Cope but his military career was at an end.

CORNISH, VICE-ADMIRAL SIR SAMUEL (1715–1770), was a British naval officer and parliamentarian. He joined the navy in 1728 and served at Cartagena in 1741 and in the Mediterranean in 1742. Cornish commanded the East Indies Station during the Seven Years' War and captured Manilla in 1762.

COSBY, LIEUTENANT-GENERAL SIR HENRY AUGUSTUS MONTAGU (1743–1822), joined the EIC's European regiment at Madras in 1760 and took part in the siege of Pondicherry. In 1771 he captured Vellore, of which he was appointed governor. Cosby resigned his commission in 1778 to command the nawab of Arcot's cavalry and was active in the Second Battle of Pollilur in 1781.

COTTON, JOSEPH (1745–1825), was an English mariner and merchant who left the Royal Navy to join the EIC where he accumulated a considerable fortune as captain of an East Indiaman, the *Royal Charlotte*. He retired to Britain where he served as a director of the EIC for a number of terms between 1795 and 1823. Cotton chaired the East India Docks Company in 1803 and was elected to the Royal Society in 1810.

CRADOCK, GENERAL JOHN FRANCIS, 1ST BARON HOWDEN (1759–1839), was an Irish army officer and politician. He served as quartermaster-general in Ireland during the Irish Rebellion of 1798. In 1803 Cradock was appointed commander-in-chief at Madras where he bore responsibility for the mutiny at Vellore in 1806. He was superseded by Wellington in 1809 in Portugal and given the governorship of Gibraltar. Cradock later served as governor of the Cape Colony from 1811 to 1814.

DALRYMPLE, LIEUTENANT-COLONEL JAMES (1757–1800), was an EIC army officer who was imprisoned with his cousin, David Baird, by Hyder Ali after the 1780 Battle of Pollilur. Dalrymple commanded the Company's forces in Hyderabad and took part in the conquest of Seringapatam in 1799. He married Mooti Begum, the daughter of the nawab of Masulipatnam.

DAULAT RAO SCINDIA (1779–1827) was the nephew and heir of Mahadji Scindia, maharajah of Gwalior. As ruler of Gwalior from 1779 to 1827, he greatly expanded his territories and exercised de facto rule of the Mughal Empire. Following his defeat by Gerard Lake at Aligarh and Delhi, Daulat Rao, under the terms of the 1803 Treaty of Surji-Arjungaon, ceded vast territories and accepted a British resident at his court.

DOST MOHAMMAD KHAN (1793–1863) was the founder of the Barakzai dynasty and emir of Afghanistan from 1826 to 1839 and 1845 to 1863. Dost Mohammad rebelled against the Afghan ruler Mahmud Shah and gained control of the country. His overtures to the British were spurned by Auckland, who had Dost deposed in 1839. Dost regained the throne in 1845 and became allied with the British through the offices of Sir Henry Lawrence.

DRUMMOND, HENRY (1730–1795), was the fourth surviving son of William, 4th Viscount Strathallan, a Jacobite who died at Culloden. Henry acted as agent to army regiments in the Seven Years' War and financial agent for New Jersey. In 1770 he was appointed joint paymaster of British forces in North America and later the West Indies. Drummond returned to the family bank in 1772 and entered Parliament in 1774.

DUFF, LIEUTENANT-COLONEL ALEXANDER, 2ND OF MUIRTOWN (1737–1778), was a Scottish army officer. He was the son of William, 1st Laird of Muirtown, and Mary Baillie, daughter of Baillie of Torbreck. In 1769 Alexander, in turn, married Christina, daughter of Hugh Baillie of Dochfour.

DUNCAN, JONATHAN (1756–1811), was a career civil servant with the EIC. In 1778 he was appointed resident at Benares, where he worked to suppress infanticide and established Sanskrit College in 1791. Duncan was appointed governor of Bombay in 1795, a position he held until his death.

DUNDAS, HENRY, 1ST VISCOUNT MELVILLE (1742–1811), was a Scottish advocate and Tory politician. He became solicitor general for Scotland in 1766 and lord advocate in 1775. Dundas entered Parliament in 1774 and served in several key cabinet posts. He was the de facto minister for Scotland and set policy for India. Although acquitted, Dundas was the last peer to be impeached in Britain.

EDEN, GEORGE, EARL OF AUCKLAND (1784–1849), was an English Whig politician and colonial administrator. He served as first lord of the admiralty three times, president of the Board of Trade from 1830 to 1834, and governor general of India from 1836 to 1842. Auckland declared war on Afghanistan in 1838 but was not prepared to commit the necessary resources to ensure success. As a result, he presided over a disastrous defeat.

EDMONSTONE, SIR CHARLES, 12TH LAIRD OF DUNTREATH (1764–1821), was a Scottish jurist and a Tory politician. He served as one of six clerks in chancery before entering Parliament in 1806.

EDMONSTONE, NEIL BENJAMIN (1765–1841), was a Scottish colonial administrator. He acted as private secretary to Governor General Richard Wellesley in 1798. Edmonstone was instrumental in effecting the system of subsidiary alliances. He became chief secretary in 1809 and vice-president of the supreme government in 1812. Following his return to Britain, Edmonstone was elected to the EIC directorate in 1820 and a fellow of the Royal Society in 1826.

ELLIOT-MURRAY-KYNYNMOUND, GILBERT, 1ST LORD MINTO (1751–1814), was a Scottish statesman who entered Parliament in 1776 as an independent Whig and joined the Privy Council in 1793. He served as viceroy of the Anglo-Corsican Kingdom from 1794 to 1799, envoy-extraordinary to Austria from 1799 to 1801, and president of the Board of Control in 1806. Minto was governor general of India from 1807 to 1813, and in that time he oversaw the acquisition of the French islands of Bourbon and Île de France and the Dutch possessions of the Moluccas and Java.

ELPHINSTONE, ARTHUR, 6TH LORD BALMERINO (1688–1746), was a Scottish army officer who fought for the Jacobite cause in 1715. After the Jacobite defeat at the battle of Sheriffmuir, he escaped to France. His father obtained a pardon but Elphinstone declared once more for the Stuarts, serving in the Forty-Five as colonel of the second troop of Horse Guards. He was captured at Culloden and beheaded on Tower Hill.

ERSKINE, ALEXANDER, 5TH EARL OF KELLIE (c. 1700–1756), was the only son of the fourth earl. He succeeded his father in 1710. Kellie fought on behalf of

Charles Edward Stuart and was imprisoned in Edinburgh for three years. Upon his release, Erskine regained his estates and title.

ERSKINE, JOHN, 6TH EARL OF MAR (1675–1732), known as "Bobbing John" owing to his shifting allegiances, was a commissioner for the union and secretary of state for Scotland during Queen Anne's reign. George I dismissed Erskine, who subsequently led the uprising of 1715. He was defeated by a much smaller army commanded by the Duke of Argyll at Sheriffmuir. Erskine fled to the continent with James, the Stuart pretender, but later intrigued against him.

ÉTANG, CHEVALIER PIERRE-AMBROISE ANTOINE DE L' (1757–1840), was an officer in the garde du corps of Louis XVI and superintendent of the Royal Stud Farm. Learning of De l'Étang's rumoured affair with Marie Antoinette, Louis had him posted to India with instructions that he not be allowed to return. He was eventually retained by the nawab of Oude to manage his stables. Following his dismissal, De l'Étang managed stud farms for the EIC.

FLETCHER, SIR ROBERT OF BALLINASLOE (1738–1776), was a Scottish military officer and politician whose father had fought for the Stuarts at Culloden. He joined the EIC in 1757 and was dismissed three times and reinstated. In 1775 Fletcher, as commander-in-chief at Madras, kidnapped and imprisoned the governor, Lord Pigot. Fletcher's large fortune was allegedly derived from the nawab of Arcot, the prime beneficiary of Pigot's discomfiture. He was censured and died at Mauritius of tuberculosis on his way to Britain.

FLETCHER OF SALTOUN, ANDREW (1655–1716), was a Scottish politician and commentator. As a result of his political activities, he was charged with high treason and temporarily lost his estates for participating in Monmouth's rebellion against Charles II. Following an amnesty, Fletcher returned to Scotland where he was a staunch supporter of the Darien scheme and where he became the leading opponent of union with England.

FLOYD, LIEUTENANT-GENERAL SIR JOHN WILLIAM (1748–1818), was a British army officer who took command of all forces on the coast of India in 1790. He led the cavalry against Tipu Sultan in the Third Anglo-Mysore War. Floyd later served as governor of Gravesend and Tilbury from 1812 to 1818.

FORBES, DUNCAN, LORD, 5TH LAIRD OF CULLODEN (1685–1747), was a Scottish politician and judge. He served as lord advocate from 1725 to 1737 and president of the Court of Session from 1737 to 174848. Forbes opposed the

Jacobites in the Rising of 1715 and was critical to maintaining the support of key clans for the Hanoverians in the Forty-Five.

FORBES, LIEUTENANT-GENERAL NATHANIEL OF AUCHERNACH (1766–1851), was a Scottish army officer. He served in India with the king's forces from 1782 to 1785 and with those of the EIC from 1787 to 1808 and from 1812 to 1822. Forbes inherited Auchernach in 1794 and purchased the estate of Dunnottar in 1836.

FRASER, COLONEL JAMES OF BELLADRUM (c. 1732–1808), was a Scottish soldier and plantation owner. He served in Germany during the Seven Years' War and in North America during the American Revolutionary War. Fraser owned plantations in Berbice and Demerara, one of which, Dochfour, was presumably named for his wife, Hannah Baillie.

FRASER, JAMES JR OF BELLADRUM (?–1834), was a Scottish planter and merchant who acquired a considerable fortune through the family estates in Berbice and Demerara. He soon owned plantations on the west coast of Berbice in his own right and established partnerships with, among others, Archibald Alves and George Inglis. Fraser sold his plantation Dochfour in 1803.

FRASER, LIEUTENANT-GENERAL SIMON (1726–1782), nineteenth chief of Clan Fraser, was the eldest son of Simon, 11th Lord Lovat, who was executed for treason and whose titles and estates were forfeited after Culloden. He was imprisoned but eventually pardoned and raised the 78th Fraser Highlanders to fight in the Seven Years' War, during which he served as acting governor of Quebec. In 1775 Fraser raised the 71st to fight in America. For his service, the crown restored his estates in 1774 but not the titles. Fraser represented Inverness in Parliament from 1761 to 1782.

FULLARTON, COLONEL WILLIAM (1754–1808), was a British army officer and politician. He entered Parliament in 1779 but raised His Majesty's 98th Regiment in 1780 and fought in the Second Anglo-Mysore War. He assisted in the suppression of the Kollars at Madura and in 1783 captured Dharapuram, Pálghát, and Coimbatore. Fullarton re-entered Parliament in 1784 and served as first commissioner for Trinidad.

FUTTY SINGH (SHRIMANT RAJASHRI FATEHSINRAO GAEKWAD), maharajah of Baroda and ruler of Gujarat (c. 1751–1789), was the third son of Maharajah Shrimant Rajashri Damajirao Gaekwad. He ruled as regent for his brother from 1771 to 1778 and in his own right from 1778 to 1789. Futty Singh concluded a treaty of alliance with the EIC in 1780.

GHAZI-OOD-DIN HAIDER (REFAUT-OOD-DOWLA) (1769–1827) was the third son of Saadat Ali Khan II, nawab of Oude. Ghazi reigned as the last nawab from 1814 to 1818 and as the first king from 1818 to 1827. At Warren Hastings's instigation, he declared Oude independent of the Mughals in 1818. Ghazi was a prolific builder responsible for many of Lucknow's major edifices.

GILLESPIE, MAJOR-GENERAL SIR ROLLO (1766–1814), was an Irish army officer who served in the West Indies before being assigned to India where he suppressed the Vellore Mutiny of 1806. In 1811 he led the British forces occupation of Java and was appointed commander-in-chief. Gillespie was killed at the battle of Nalapani in the Anglo-Nepalese War of 1814–16.

GODDARD, GENERAL THOMAS WYNDHAM (C. 1740–1783), was a distinguished EIC army officer. He arrived in India with the 84th Regiment and transferred to the EIC in 1763. During the First Anglo-Maratha War of 1775–82, Goddard commanded the Company's forces in Oude in 1776 and later the troops reinforcing Bombay after Wadgaon. Failing to secure a treaty with the Marathas, Goddard routed Holkar and Scindia's armies in 1780 and captured Bassein the same year.

GORDON, ALEXANDER, IST EARL OF HUNTLY (C. 1409–1470), was the son of Sir Alexander Seton. In 1437 he was appointed ambassador to England to negotiate a peace between the two countries. Gordon supported James II in the Douglas Rebellion and soundly defeated the Earl of Crawford (the Lindsays) at the battle of Brechin in 1452. He later forced the Earl of Douglas's rebel brothers, the earls of Moray and Ormond, to take refuge in the Western Isles. Gordon was created Earl of Huntly by James II in 1455.

GORDON, COSMO, 3RD DUKE OF GORDON (1720–1752), supported the government in the Forty-Five. Gordon sat as a Scottish peer in the House of Lords from 1747 to 1752. In 1741 he married Lady Catherine Gordon, who later raised the 78th Highlanders in which William Baillie began his military career.

GORDON, COSMO OF CLUNY (1736–1800), was the eldest son of John of Cluny, a successful Edinburgh merchant and factor to the 3rd Duke of Gordon. Cosmo entered Parliament in 1774 and served as baron of the Scottish Court of Exchequer in 1777 and trustee for fisheries and manufactures in Scotland in 1778.

GORDON, LORD GEORGE (1751–1793), was the third son of Cosmo George Gordon, the third duke. He served with little distinction in the Royal Navy from 1763 to 1772 and entered Parliament in 1774. Gordon opposed virtually all factions at Westminster and led the "Gordon Riots" against Catholic emancipation, an action for which he was imprisoned. He died of typhoid fever in Newgate Prison.

GORDON, WILLIAM, 2ND EARL OF ABERDEEN (1679–1746), was a Scottish peer, Tory politician, and Jacobite. He was the second son and heir of George, the first earl, and the father of Catherine, Duchess of Gordon, who raised the 89th Highlanders. Gordon served in Parliament from 1708 to 1709 and was elevated to the peerage in 1721. He died in Edinburgh intending to declare for Charles Edward Stuart.

GRAHAM, JOHN OF CLAVERHOUSE, 1ST VISCOUNT DUNDEE (1648–1689), was a Scottish politician and military officer. He led the forces of the established church in Scotland in suppressing the Covenanters and served on the Scottish Privy Council. Graham remained loyal to the Stuarts and rallied both Catholic and Protestant clans to oppose William III. He defeated William III decisively at Killiecrankie in 1689 but died in the battle.

GRANT, SIR ALEXANDER, 5TH LAIRD OF DALVEY (1705–1772), chief of Clan Donnachie, came from a family impoverished in the Jacobite cause. He sought his fortune in Jamaica where he established a trading enterprise which he expanded upon his return to Britain in 1739. Dalvey held properties in Scotland and represented the Inverness Burghs in Parliament from 1761 to 1768. At his death, he owned 7,000 acres and 457 slaves in Jamaica.

GRANT, CHARLES (1746–1832), was the son of Alexander, a rebel who died at Culloden. After serving with the EIC in India, he returned to Britain and represented Inverness-shire in Parliament from 1802 to 1818. Grant was elected a director of the EIC in 1804 and chairman in 1805. He was active in the Clapham Sect and campaigned vigorously for religious missions in India.

GRANT, CHARLES, 1ST BARON GLENELG (1778–1866), the India-born eldest son of Charles Grant, chair of the EIC, was a Scottish politician and colonial administrator. He entered Parliament as a Tory in 1811 but turned Whig over the Reform Bills. Grant held a number of cabinet posts, culminating in his service as secretary of state for war and the colonies from 1835 to 1839. He came under severe criticism for his handling of the 1837–38 rebellions in Canada.

GRANT, LIEUTENANT-COLONEL HUGH OF MOY (?–1822), went to India with His Majesty's troops and in 1765 transferred to the EIC where he commanded the 3rd Sepoy Brigade on the Bengal establishment. Grant returned to Scotland in 1774 and bought the estate of Moy the following year.

GRANT, SIR ROBERT (1779–1838), the India-born second son of Charles Grant, chair of the EIC, was a Scottish politician and lawyer. He entered Parliament in 1818 and served as judge advocate general from 1832 to 1843. Grant was governor of Bombay from 1835 to 1838. Like his father, Grant was deeply involved in social issues and was primarily responsible for passage of the bill emancipating Britain's Jews.

GRENVILLE, WILLIAM WYNDHAM, 1ST BARONET (1759–1834), was the youngest son of Prime Minister George Grenville and a British Whig statesman. He entered Parliament and held a number of cabinet posts, including home secretary in 1789 and foreign secretary in 1791. Grenville became prime minister in 1806 in the "Ministry of All Talents." His ministry failed to obtain peace or establish Catholic emancipation but it did manage to abolish slavery in 1807.

GREY, CHARLES, 2ND LORD GREY (1764–1845), was an English Whig politician who served as prime minister from 1830 to 1834. He entered Parliament in 1786 and held a number of cabinet posts. His administration passed the Reform Bill of 1832 and the Slavery Abolition Act of 1833.

HALFORD, SIR HENRY OF WISTOW HALL (1766–1844), was a British physician. He was born Henry Vaughan but in 1809 changed his name in expectation of an inheritance from his mother's cousin, Sir Charles Halford. Sir Henry was president of the Royal College of Physicians from 1820 to 1844 and was appointed physician extraordinary in 1793 and physician in ordinary in 1812 to George III. Halford served George IV, William IV, and Victoria in the same capacity.

HANOVER, PRINCE WILLIAM AUGUSTUS, DUKE OF CUMBERLAND (1721–1765), was the third son of George II. He gained fame by his victory over the Jacobites at Culloden in 1746 and ignominy by the atrocities he authorized following the battle. His subsequent military career was undistinguished. Cumberland suffered public disgrace after concluding the Convention of Klosterzeven, which provided for the disbanding of his army and the deliverance of his father's Electorate of Hanover to the French.

HARRIS, LIEUTENANT-GENERAL GEORGE, 1ST BARON OF SERINGAPATAM AND MYSORE (1746–1829), was a British army officer who served in the

American Revolutionary War, St Lucia, and Ireland before taking part in the siege of Seringapatam in the Third Anglo-Mysore War. Harris, as commander-in-chief of the Madras army, led the forces which took Seringapatam and ended Tipu Sultan's life in 1799.

HASTINGS, WARREN (1732–1818), was a British statesman who served as the first and most influential governor general of India from 1774 to 1785. He was appointed deputy governor of Madras in 1765 and governor of Bengal in 1771. Hastings completely altered the administration of India by removing the machinery of government from the nawab's court and instituting major judicial and tax reforms. Hastings was impeached for "high crimes and misdemeanours" at the instigation of Sir Philip Francis and only acquitted in 1795.

HAWKE, ADMIRAL EDWARD, 1ST BARONET (1705–1781), was a British naval officer who distinguished himself in the War of the Austrian Succession by capturing six French warships off the coast of Brittany in 1747. In the Seven Years' War, his victory at Quiberon Bay prevented the French from reinforcing their troops in Canada and put an end to French plans to invade Britain. Hawke served as first lord of the admiralty from 1766 to 1771.

HAWKINS, COLONEL THOMAS (1774–1818), was an EIC career army officer who was charged with transporting Tipu Sultan's sons to Calcutta following the suppression of the 1806 Vellore Mutiny. He commanded the British forces in Bundelcund at the time of its acquisition by the Company. Hawkins captured the fort of Chumar in 1807. He married, as his second wife, Elizabeth Friell, the sister of Neil Benjamin Edmonstone's wife, in 1803.

HAWLEY, LIEUTENANT-GENERAL HENRY (1679–1759), was a British army officer and reputed natural son of George II. He replaced Cope as commander-in-chief of Scotland in 1745 and was soundly defeated by the rebels at Falkirk. Hawley led the cavalry at Culloden and his subsequent brutality to the defeated rebels earned him the nickname "Hangman Hawley."

HEPBURN, JAMES, OF KEITH (1691–?), was a Jacobite who was taken prisoner with his father at the battle of Preston in 1715. Hepburn obtained a pardon but declared once more for the Stuarts in the Forty-Five. He escaped to Europe where he spent the next four years.

HOCHE, GENERAL LOUIS LAZARE (1768–1797), was a French military officer who commanded the army of Moselle and of the Rhine in 1793. He performed admirably but was imprisoned on suspicion of treason until the downfall of Robespierre. Reinstated in command, Hoche inflicted a decisive defeat on the royalists in Brittany. He led the abortive invasion of Ireland in 1796 but was more successful against the Austrians in 1797. Hoche was briefly minister of war.

HOOD, MARY ELIZABETH FREDERICA MACKENZIE (1783–1862), was the eldest daughter and heiress of Francis Mackenzie, Lord Seaforth, chief of the Mackenzies. She married Vice-Admiral Sir Samuel Hood, commander-in-chief of the East Indies Station, who died in 1814; and subsequently James Alexander Stewart of Glasserton.

HOWE, ADMIRAL RICHARD, 1ST EARL (1726–1799), was the second son of Emanuel Scrope Howe, 2nd Viscount, and the half-sister of George I. He was a British naval officer and politician who served with distinction in the American Revolutionary War but resigned in 1778. Howe was treasurer of the navy from 1765 to 1770, commander-in-chief of the Mediterranean Fleet, and commander of the North American Station. He was first lord of the admiralty from 1783 to 1788 and, as commander of the Channel Fleet, won the victory of the Glorious First of June 1794.

HOWE, GENERAL WILLIAM, 5TH VISCOUNT (1729–1814), was the third son of Emanuel, 3rd Viscount. He joined the army in 1746 and played a key role in the capture of Quebec in 1749. Howe led the British forces at Bunker Hill and assumed command of British troops in America in 1775. He captured New York and Philadelphia but resigned his commission in 1778. Howe entered Parliament in 1758 and was appointed a privy councillor in 1782.

HUGHES, ADMIRAL SIR EDWARD (1720–1794), was a British naval officer who saw action at Louisbourg and Quebec in the Seven Years' War. He commanded the East Indies Station from 1773 to 1777 and was commander-in-chief of the East Indies Station from 1780 to 1784. In the latter post, he held his ground against the gifted French admiral, Suffrein.

HURRY, PUNT (?–c. 1794) was the son of Purseram Bhow, the commander of the peshwa's armies. Punt allied himself with Nana Furnese and was confidential secretary to Peshwa Mahadeo Rao. Hurry was a formidable Maratha warrior who defeated the usurper Ragonaut Rao in 1774 and had a principal command in the defeat of the British at Wadgaon in 1779. In 1790 Hurry allied with Cornwallis against Tipu Sultan in the Third Anglo-Mysore War.

INGLIS, GEORGE OF KINGSMILLS (1764–1847), was a Scottish merchant and planter. He began as a clerk for George Baillie and by 1790 was a partner in a slave-trading venture in St Vincent with Baillie and the Alves brothers. Inglis was subsequently a partner in Fraser, Inglis and Company in Demerara where he owned the plantations of Phoenix Park and Bellefield. He returned to Inverness and married a stepsister of his former partners, Helen Alves (1782–1876), bringing with him four "free mulatto children" from a liaison in the West Indies.

JAHANGIR, 4TH MUGHAL EMPEROR (1569–1627), was the eldest surviving son of the 3rd Mughal Emperor, Akbar and ruled from 1605 to 1627. He rebelled against his father in 1599 but was confirmed as his successor by Akbar on his deathbed. Jahangir continued his father's tolerant policies and his rule was characterized by political stability, a healthy economy, impressive cultural achievements and an expansion of the empire's borders.

JASWANT RAO HOLKAR, maharajah of Indore (1776–1811), was the son of Maharajah Tukoji Rao Holkar. Jaswant Rao effectively ruled Indore as regent and later as maharajah from 1799 to 1811. He defeated the Peshwa Baji Rao II at Poona in 1802 and did not take part in the Second Anglo-Maratha War. Although the other Maratha states had submitted to the EIC, Jaswant Rao fought the British on fairly equal terms. Finally, in 1805, the two parties agreed to a treaty whereby all Jaswant Rao's territories were returned to him.

JENKINSON, ROBERT, 2ND LORD LIVERPOOL (1770–1828), was a British politician who, as prime minister from 1812 to 1827, achieved victory in the Napoleonic Wars and laid the foundations for economic prosperity. He entered Parliament in 1790 and served as secretary of state for foreign affairs from 1801 to 1804, home secretary from 1807 to 1809 and secretary of state for war and the colonies from 1809 to 1812.

JONES, SIR WILLIAM (1746–1794), was an Anglo-Welsh philologist, jurist, and scholar. He was appointed judge of Calcutta's Supreme Court in 1783 and co-founded the Asiatic Society of Bengal. Jones authored several books on Indian languages and law.

KEPPEL, ADMIRAL AUGUSTUS, 1ST VISCOUNT (1725–1786), was a British naval officer and parliamentarian. He joined the navy at the age of ten. Keppel commanded the Mediterranean Fleet in 1749 and the North American Station in the Seven Years' War. He played a critical role in the capture of Havana and commanded the Channel Fleet during the American Revolutionary War. He was appointed first lord of the admiralty in 1782.

KIRKPATRICK, MAJOR-GENERAL WILLIAM (1756–1812), was an Irish soldier and administrator who joined the EIC in 1771. In 1793 he was appointed aide-de-camp to Governor General Shore and was named resident at Hyderabad in 1795. He served as Persian interpreter to General Harris in the Fourth Anglo-Mysore War and was a member of the commission which negotiated the final settlement.

LALLY, THOMAS ARTHUR, COMTE DE (1702–1766), was the son of an Irish Jacobite, Sir Gerald Lally. He served as Prince Charles's aide-de-camp at Falkirk during the Forty-Five and escaped to France where he distinguished himself under Marshall Saxe. He was appointed governor general of French India in 1756. After some initial successes, de Lally was defeated by Coote at Wandiwash in 1760 and at Pondicherry in 1761. He was convicted of treason and beheaded in France in 1766.

LANG, LIEUTENANT-GENERAL ROSS, was a career EIC army officer who served in the siege of Madura in 1763 and the First Anglo-Mysore War of 1767–69. He commanded the army at Vellore. At the time of General Stuart's 1777 arrest, Governor Macartney appointed Lang commander-in-chief of the Madras army. Lang again commanded the Madras army from 1783 to 1785.

LAWRENCE, MAJOR-GENERAL STRINGER (1697–1775), saw action at Culloden and was subsequently appointed commander-in-chief of the EIC forces from 1747 to 1754 and from 1761 to 1766. He is credited with moulding irregular native troops into an effective fighting force. Lawrence generally prevailed against the French and strongly supported Robert Clive, whom he commanded.

LINDSAY, ALEXANDER, 4TH EARL OF CRAWFORD (1423–1453), known as "the Tiger Earl," was one of Scotland's most powerful nobles. In 1445 he was victorious at the Battle of Arbroath. Lindsay was appointed Scottish ambassador to England in 1451 but rebelled against James II after the latter's murder of William, 8th Earl of Douglas. He was defeated by Alexander Gordon at the Battle of Brechin in 1452 and submitted to the king.

LINDSAY, ADMIRAL SIR JOHN (1737–1788), was a Scottish naval officer and politician. He played a pivotal role in taking Havana. Lindsay was appointed commander-in-chief of the East Indies Station in 1769 with instructions to investigate the transactions between the EIC and the native princes. His handling of the assignment led to his recall in 1772. Lindsay served as admiralty commissioner in 1783 and commander-in-chief of the Mediterranean Station in 1784.

LINDSAY, MAJOR-GENERAL JOHN (1762–1826), the ninth child of the 5th Earl of Balcarres, was a Scottish soldier who was captured and imprisoned by Hyder Ali in 1780. He was released in 1784 and, under Cornwallis, led the attack on Bangalore in the Third Anglo-Mysore War of 1791–92. Lindsay later served in France. He married Charlotte, the daughter of Lord North, a former prime minister.

LOCKHART, GEORGE, 3RD LAIRD OF LEE AND CARNWARTH (1700–1764), came from a staunch Jacobite family. He served as personal aide-de-camp to Charles Edward in the Forty-Five and after Culloden joined the prince in exile in Paris. As Lockhart was attainted as a rebel, the estate would accrue to the crown upon his father's death. Accordingly, he staged his death and funeral in Paris, with the result that the estate passed to his younger brother, James.

LUMSDEN, MATTHEW (1777–1835), was a Scottish Orientalist who went to India as assistant professor of Persian and Arabic at the College of Fort William. In 1808 he became a full professor and in 1812 secretary to the Calcutta madrassa, where he superintended translations of English works into Persian. Lumsden was responsible for the EIC's press from 1814 to 1817.

MACARTNEY, LORD GEORGE, 1ST EARL MACARTNEY (1737–1806), was an Anglo-Irish statesman, colonial administrator, and diplomat. In 1764 he negotiated an alliance with Catherine II of Russia and in 1768 entered Parliament, where he served as chief secretary for Ireland from 1769 to 1772. Macartney was governor of Grenada from 1776 to 1779 and of Madras from 1781 to 1786. He refused appointment as governor general of India and led an unsuccessful embassy to China in 1792.

MACGILLIVRAY, CAPTAIN WILLIAM, 9TH LAIRD OF DUNMAGLASS (c. 1737–1783), succeeded his rebel brother, Alexander, as chief of Clan MacGillivray. He managed in 1750 to recover the family estates which had been forfeited in the Forty-Five. Dunmaglass undertook a rice-planting venture in Georgia in 1775 but, as a loyalist, returned to Scotland no better off. With the assistance of his brother John, Dunmaglass restored and expanded the clan fortunes.

MACKENZIE, SIR ALEXANDER, 5TH LAIRD OF COUL (?–1792), was the elder son of Sir Colin, the fourth laird. The baronetcy was created in Nova Scotia for the illegitimate grandson of Colin Cam Mackenzie, 11th Laird of Kintail, but forfeited as a result of the third baron's participation in the Rising of 1715. It was reclaimed by the third baron's brother. Jane, a daughter of the first baronet, married Alexander, 9th Laird of Dunain.

MACKENZIE, MAJOR-GENERAL SIR ALEXANDER, 6TH LAIRD OF COUL (?–1796), the elder son of Sir Alexander, 5th Laird of Coul, was a Scottish EIC military officer who held the post of provisional commander-in-chief of Bengal from 1790 to 1792.

MACKENZIE, MAJOR-GENERAL JOHN, LORD MACLEOD (1727–1789), the eldest son of the 3rd Earl of Cromartie, was a Scottish soldier of fortune and politician. He fought for the Jacobites and was taken prisoner at Falkirk in 1746 but pardoned on condition that he forfeit his claims to the earldom. Macleod rose to lieutenant-general and count in the service of Sweden before returning in 1771 to Britain where he raised Macleod's Highlanders, whom he led in the Second Anglo-Mysore War. He entered Parliament in 1780 and recovered the family estates in 1784.

MACKINTOSH, ANGUS (c. 1703–1820), succeeded his brother as twenty-second chief of Clan Mackintosh and twenty-third of Clan Chattan. He served as a captain in the Black Watch and fought for the Hanoverians in the Forty-Five. Mackintosh was captured at Prestonpans and paroled to his wife, Anne Farquarson-Mackintosh, who raised two battalions under the command of Alexander MacGillivray of Dumnaglass in support of the rebels.

MACKINTOSH, SIR JAMES (1765–1832), was a Scottish jurist, Whig politician, and historian. He gained renown for rebutting Edmund Burke in his *Vindiciae Gallicae: A Defence of the French Revolution and Its Admirers*. Mackintosh served as chief judge of Bombay from 1804 to 1811 and as an MP from 1813 to 1832. He was rector of Glasgow University from 1823 to 1825, became a privy councillor in 1827, and was a commissioner of the Board of Control from 1830 to 1832.

MACLEOD, LIEUTENANT-COLONEL DONALD OF ACHAGOYLE (?–1813), was an EIC army officer and an extensive landowner in Argyle, St Kilda, and Skye.

MACLEOD, MAJOR-GENERAL NORMAN, twenty-third chief (1754–1801), succeeded his grandfather as clan chieftain in 1772 and was able to restore the clan's finances. He raised a company of Fraser's Highlanders to fight in America but was captured entering Boston Harbour in 1776. In 1779 Macleod raised a battalion to fight in India. He saw action in the Second Anglo-Mysore War and in 1785 was appointed second-in-command of the army in India.

MACONOCHIE, ALEXANDER, LORD MEADOWBANK OF GARVOCK AND PITLIVER (1777–1861), was a Scottish advocate, judge, landowner, and politician. He was inducted into the Royal Society of Edinburgh in 1817 and served as solicitor-general for Scotland from 1813 to 1816 and lord advocate from 1816 to 1819. Maconochie entered Parliament in 1817.

MACPHERSON, LIEUTENANT-COLONEL DUNCAN OF CLUNY, thirteenth chief (1748–1817), was the son of Ewen, twelfth chief of the Macphersons. He served with distinction in the American Revolution with the 71st Fraser Highlanders and in 1784 recovered the estates which had been forfeited during the Forty-Five.

MADDOCK, SIR THOMAS HERBERT (1792–1870), was an English EIC civil servant and Conservative politician. He joined the Company in 1811, rising to resident at Lucknow from 1830 to 1831, secretary to the government of India from 1838 to 1843, and deputy governor of Bengal and president of the Council of India from 1845 to 1849. Maddock returned to Britain and entered Parliament in 1852.

MAHADAJI SCINDIA (1730–1794) was the illegitimate son of Ranoji Scindia, the first maharajah of Gwalior. He ruled the Maratha state of Gwalior from 1768 to 1794 and was instrumental in re-establishing Maratha power in northern India after the Third Battle of Panipat in 1761. Mahadaji restored the Mughal emperor, Shah Alam II, in Delhi under his tutelage in 1771 and humiliated the British at Wadgaon in 1779 during the First Anglo-Maratha War.

MALARTIC, LIEUTENANT-GENERAL ANNE JOSEPH HIPPOLYTE DE MAURÈS, COMTE DE (1730–1800), was a French army officer and colonial administrator. He saw action in the War of the Austrian Succession and in Canada during the Seven Years' War. Malartic commanded a regiment in the West Indies and was appointed commandant general of the French forces beyond the Cape of Good Hope and governor general of Île de France in 1792.

MARLEY, GENERAL BENNET (1754–1842), was a career EIC army officer. He was defeated by the Nepalese in 1815 during the Anglo-Nepalese War. Marley was appointed commandant at Allahabad in 1817 and served in that position for over twenty years.

MARTIN, MAJOR-GENERAL CLAUDE (1735–1800), was a French army officer, banker, merchant, and builder. He enlisted in the EIC army following the 1761 French defeat at Pondicherry and accepted a position as superintendent of the arsenal for the nawab of Oude in 1766. Martin was responsible for many of Lucknow's primary architectural achievements and is particularly remembered for his residence, Constantia. He amassed a considerable fortune through his bank and other business interests.

MARTINDELL, MAJOR-GENERAL SIR GABRIEL (1756–1831), was a career EIC army officer who distinguished himself in the 1774 Battle of St George against the Rohillas. He commanded the Company's forces in Bundelcund from 1803 to 1805 and acted as John Baillie's military counterpart. Martindell captured the fort of Aligarh in 1809 and Kallinger in 1812. He played a key role in the Anglo-Nepalese War of 1814–16 and the Pindari War of 1817–18.

MASTER, SIR STREYNSHAM (1640–1724), was an English career servant of the EIC. He served as acting president at Surat and successfully defended it against the Marathas in 1670. Master was agent at Masulipatnam and then Bengal before being appointed agent at Madras in 1678. He served there until 1681 and is credited with introducing the first administrative reforms. Back in England, he bought Codnor Castle in 1692.

MATHEWS, BRIGADIER-GENERAL RICHARD (?–1783), was an EIC officer who commanded the Bombay establishment. During the Second Anglo-Mysore War, Mathews captured Mangalore in 1783 but was suspended for procrastination in pursuing operations against Tipu Sultan. He later took Bednore but his lines were overextended. Mathews was defeated and captured by Tipu, who allegedly poisoned him.

MIDDLETON, NATHANIEL (1750–1807), was an EIC civil servant who was the Company's first resident in Oude where he served three terms, 1773–74, 1776–79, and 1781–82. His tenure at Oude was interrupted by the internecine conflict between Warren Hastings and his Bengal Council. Middleton amassed a fortune from a saltpetre monopoly in Oude and utilized that wealth to establish a banking house in London.

MILLS, SIR CHARLES OF HILLINGDON (1792–1872), was an English banker. He was a partner in the family banking firm, Glyn, Mills and Company. Mills was elected a director of the EIC in 1822 and was appointed to the Supreme Council of India in 1828.

MIR JAFAR, NAWAB OF BENGAL (1691–1765), was an Arab who assisted his cousin Ali Vardi Khan seize the government of Bengal in 1740. As a reward, he was appointed paymaster-general, commander-in-chief, and, in 1745, deputy governor of Orissa. On his succession, the new nawab, Siraj-ood-Dowla, dismissed Mir Jafar, who then conspired with Robert Clive. Following his victory at Plassey, Clive installed Mir Jafar as nawab in 1757. He remained nawab until 1760. With Dutch assistance, Mir Jafar rebelled but was defeated and replaced as nawab by his son-in-law, Mir Qasim. The British then reinstalled Mir Jafar, who ruled as nawab from 1763 to 1765. In Bengali, Mir Jafar became a synonym for traitor.

MIR QASIM (?–1777) was the nawab of Bengal from 1760 to 1763. He was the son-in-law of Mir Jafar, whose throne, with the assistance of the British, he usurped. Provoked by the demands of the EIC, he attacked Patna, killing the British resident and several Europeans in the process. Mir Qasim allied with the nawab of Oude and the Mughal emperor but in 1764 was routed at Buxar by Hector Munro. He was expelled from Oude by the nawab and died in poverty.

MONEER-OOL-MOOLK. *See* Asaf Jah III

MONSON, LIEUTENANT-COLONEL WILLIAM (1760–1807), was an English army officer and parliamentarian. He participated in the 1792 siege of Seringapatam and led the 1803 assault on Aligarh during the Second Anglo-Maratha War. Monson is remembered for his defeat by Jaswant Rao Holkar at the Battle of Mukandwara Pass and the utter destruction of his army during "Monson's Retreat" to Agra.

MONTAGU-SCOTT, CHARLES, 4TH DUKE OF BUCCLEUCH AND 6TH DUKE OF QUEENSBERRY (1772–1819), was a British landowner, cricketer, and Tory politician who was known as the Earl of Dalkeith. He represented various constituencies in Parliament from 1793 to 1807 and served as lord lieutenant of Selkirkshire, Dumfrieshire, and Midlothian.

MONTGOMERIE, ALEXANDER, 10TH EARL OF EGLINTON (1723–1769), was a leading Scottish proponent of agricultural improvement and a politician. He served as governor of Dumbarton Castle from 1759 to 1761, lord of the bedchamber from 1760 to 1767, and a representative peer from 1761 to 1769. He is remembered for his planned village of Eaglesham and for his violent death at the hands of Mungo Campbell whom Montgomerie accused of poaching.

MOODAJI BHONSLA I, rajah of Berar and king of Nagpur (?–1788), reigned from 1772 to 1788. He was the younger brother of the king, Janoji, and upon the latter's death in 1772 Moodaji killed his other brother on the battlefield of Panchgaon and succeeded to the regency on behalf of his infant son, Raghoji II, whom Janoji had adopted as his heir. Moodaji allied with the EIC and acquired Mandla and the upper Narmada valley in 1785.

MORRIS, GENERAL STAATS LONG (1728–1800), was an American who served as a British major-general during the American Revolutionary War although he was closely related to key American patriots. He was the grandson of Lewis Morris, New Jersey's first governor; the brother of Lewis Morris, a signer of the Declaration of Independence; and a half-brother of Gouverneur Morris, whom the historian Joseph Ellis claims had a greater influence than anyone else on the wording of the United States constitution. Morris commanded the 89th Highlanders, raised by his wife, Catherine. He was appointed governor of Quebec in 1797.

MUHAMMAD YUSUF KHAN (1725–1764) was an Islamic convert who attained the position of soubah of Nellore. Yusuf became a mercenary fighting on behalf of the French but, at Clive's instigation, defected to the EIC. He captured Madura in 1756 and, provoked by his overlord, Mohammed Ali, proclaimed himself governor of Madura and Tirunelveli, a claim recognized by the nizam and emperor. The British and various allies laid siege to Madura, with the result that Yusuf was taken prisoner and hanged as a rebel by Mohammed Ali.

MUNRO, GENERAL SIR HECTOR, 8TH LAIRD OF NOVAR (1726–1805), was a Scottish army officer and politician. Serving as commander-in-chief of India, he won a remarkable victory at Buxar in 1764. Munro returned to India in 1778 as commander of the Madras army, and although he captured Pondicherry that year, he was held responsible for a series of defeats at the hands of Hyder Ali in the Second Anglo-Mysore War. He represented the Inverness Burghs in Parliament from 1768 to 1802. Munro left no heirs since his two sons died in India, one after an encounter with a tiger and another with a shark.

MUNRO, LIEUTENANT-COLONEL INNES (?–1827) was a Scottish soldier and author. He joined Macleod's Highlanders (73rd Foot) as a lieutenant in 1777 and fought in the Second Anglo-Mysore War. Munro documented the campaigns in his book *A Narrative of the Military Operations in the Carnatic in 1780–84.*

MURRAY, GENERAL LORD GEORGE (1694–1760), was a Scottish army officer. He served under Mar in the uprising of 1715 but was later restored to favour. Nevertheless, Murray declared for Charles Edward in the Forty-Five. He was responsible for the victories at Prestonpans and Falkirk, counselled against invading England, and lost the friendship of Charles Edward when Murray insisted on withdrawing to Scotland. Murray escaped to the continent after the debacle at Culloden.

NANA FURNESE (1742–1800) was the capable first minister and effective strategist during much of the peshwa era. Opposed to Ragonaut Rao, Nana headed a twelve-person regency during the minority of Peshwa Mahadeo Rao II and was the primary adviser to Peshwa Baji Rao II in the early years of his reign. Nana was an ally of the French whom he viewed as a counter to British power.

NARAYAN RAO, fifth peshwa (1775–1773), was the third son of Peshwa Balaji Baji Rao. He served as dewan from 1770 to 1772 for his brother the fourth peshwa, Mahadeo Rao I. On the latter's death, Narayan Rao succeeded as peshwa but was murdered in 1773 by the order of his uncle, Ragonaut Rao.

NORTH, FREDERICK, LORD, 2ND EARL OF GUILFORD (1732–1792), was prime minister of Great Britain from 1770 to 1782. He entered Parliament in 1754. North served as secretary of state for home affairs in 1783 and chancellor of the exchequer from 1767 to 1782. A favourite of George III, he is remembered primarily for losing the American colonies.

OCHTERLONY, MAJOR-GENERAL SIR DAVID OF PITFORTHY (1758–1825), was an American military officer and colonial administrator in the employ of the EIC. After his role in the Second Anglo-Maratha War, Ochterlony was appointed resident at Delhi 1803. He led the British forces in the Anglo-Nepalese War of 1814–16 and engineered the victory over the Pindaris in 1817–18. Ochterlony in 1818 became resident at Rajputana, which was later combined with Delhi. Reputedly, he embraced Persian Mughal culture to the extent of having a harem of thirteen concubines.

OGLETHORPE, GENERAL JAMES EDWARD (1696–1785), was a social reformer, politician, and military officer who served with distinction as aide-de-camp to Prince Eugene of Savoy in the Austro-Turkish War of 1716–18. Oglethorpe obtained a grant for a colony in Georgia, which he founded in 1733. He led the colonists in repulsing the last attempted Spanish invasion of America at the Battle of Bloody Marsh. Returning to Britain, Oglethorpe took part in suppressing the Forty-Five.

O'SULLIVAN, GENERAL JOHN WILLIAM (1700–), was born in County Derry to a family, the lords of Dunkerron, whose lands had been confiscated by Oliver

Cromwell. He fought for the French in Corsica and accompanied Charles Edward Stuart to Scotland in 1745. O'Sullivan captured Edinburgh and was appointed quartermaster-general of Charles's forces. He escaped with Charles to France after the defeat at Culloden.

PALLISER, ADMIRAL SIR HUGH (1723–1796), was a British naval officer and politician who saw action in the War of the Austrian Succession, the Seven Years' War, and the American Revolutionary War. He served as governor and commander-in-chief of Newfoundland from 1764 to 1768 and was appointed comptroller of the navy in 1770. Palliser entered Parliament in 1774.

PALMER, LIEUTENANT-COLONEL SAMUEL (1762–1814), was the eldest son of Lieutenant-General William Palmer of the EIC. He was also an EIC career officer and commanded at Purtaubgurh during John Baillie's residency at Lucknow.

PALMER, BRIGADIER-GENERAL WILLIAM (1780–1867), was born in Lucknow, the son of General William Palmer and Fais Baksh, a descendant of the Emperor Shah Jahan. He was an officer in the army of the nizam of Hyderabad for twenty-four years and participated in the siege of Seringapatam in 1799. In 1814 Palmer founded a banking house, William Palmer and Company, in Hyderabad. It grew into the most successful commercial enterprise outside British India but became overextended in dealings with the nizam and failed.

PATERSON, SIR WILLIAM (1658–1719), prospered as a merchant in the Bahamas before returning to England where he conceived the idea of and co-founded the Bank of England. He amassed a sizable fortune through the Hampstead Water Company and the Merchant Taylor's Company. Paterson moved to Edinburgh where he played a key role in founding the Bank of Scotland and where he was the leading proponent of and force behind the ill-fated Darien expedition. He was also an active advocate of the Act of Union.

PEEL, SIR ROBERT (1788–1850), was an English Conservative statesman who served twice as prime minister, from 1834 to 1835 and from 1841 to 1846. He entered Parliament in 1809 and was appointed chief secretary for Ireland in 1813, founding the Royal Irish Constabulary in 1814. Peel became home secretary in 1822 and established the metropolitan police force in 1829. His repeal of the Corn Laws brought down his government.

PETTY, WILLIAM, 1ST MARQUESS OF LANSDOWNE (1737–1805), was an Irish-born British Whig statesman and army officer who was known as Earl of

Shelburne. He served as aide-de-camp to George III in the Seven Years' War and entered Parliament in 1760. Shelburne occupied several cabinet posts and, as prime minister in 1782–83, ended the war in America. He was criticized for agreeing to excessively generous terms, as a result of which his ministry fell from power.

PITT, WILLIAM, 1ST EARL OF CHATHAM (1708–1788), was the grandson of the governor of Madras, Thomas Pitt, who established the family fortune. He entered Parliament as a Tory in 1735 and was appointed paymaster general in 1746. Pitt alienated George II and was dismissed in 1755. Pitt became the de facto prime minister in 1756 and was credited with the strategy that enabled Britain to prevail in the Seven Years' War. He was an ardent imperialist and served formally as prime minister from 1766 to 1768.

POLHILL, COLONEL THOMAS (1747–1805), was an English career EIC military officer. He commanded the 1st Regiment of Bengal native infantry and Prince of Wales Island. Polhill died on duty in Bundelcund.

POLLOCK, FIELD MARSHALL SIR GEORGE (1786–1872), was an English army officer who took part in the Second Anglo-Maratha War, the Anglo-Nepalese War, and the First Anglo-Burmese War. Following the rout of the British by the Afghans 1841, Pollock was placed in command of the Army of Retribution and rescued the British hostages in Jalalabad and Kabul in 1842. He was appointed resident at Lucknow in 1843 and member of the Council of India in 1844 Pollock was elected a director of the EIC in 1854.

POWELL, LIEUTENANT-GENERAL PEREGRINE (1755–1835), was a career EIC army officer on the Bengal establishment. He marched his forces to the relief of Fort St George in 1781 and fought in the Battle of Cuddalore in 1783. Powell defeated Shamser Bahadur in Bundelcund in 1803 and jointly negotiated Shamser's submission with John Baillie.

PURSERAM BHOW was a Maratha warrior who allied with Governor General Cornwallis in the Third Anglo-Mysore War against Tipu Sultan. With British assistance, he captured Hooly Honore in 1791 and Shimoga 1792, both of which Hyder Ali had earlier taken from the Marathas.

RAE, SIR WILLIAM OF ST CATHERINE'S (1769–1842), was a Scottish Whig politician and lawyer. He entered Parliament in 1819 and served as lord advocate from 1819 to 1830 and from 1834 to 1835. Rae was appointed a privy councillor in 1830.

RAEBURN, SIR HENRY (1756–1823), was a Scottish portrait painter, the most prominent of his day. He was elected to the Royal Scottish Academy in 1815. Raeburn was knighted and appointed George IV's limner for Scotland in 1822.

RAGOJI II BHONSLA, rajah of Nagpur and Berar (?–1816), was the adopted heir of Janoji Bhonsla. Ragoji II reigned from 1788 to 1816 and added to Nagpur's territories. However, in 1803 he united with Daulat Rao Scindia to oppose the EIC in the Second Anglo-Maratha War. The British prevailed at Assaye and Argaon and forced Ragoji to cede one-third of his territory, including Berar.

RANJIT SINGH, maharajah of the Punjab (1780–1839), was a warrior who founded the Sikh Empire, which existed from 1799 to 1849. He captured Lahore in 1799 and Amritsar in 1802. Ranjit Singh gradually gained control of the entire Punjab and by 1819 had effectively annexed Kashmir. He reigned from 1801 to 1839 and came to terms with the British through the Treaty of Amritsar in 1819.

RICH, CLAUDIUS JAMES (1787–1821), was a British colonial administrator, author, and antiquarian scholar. After serving as assistant to the consul general in Alexandria, Rich travelled to Bombay where he married Mary, the daughter of the chief judge, Sir James Mackintosh. He was appointed British resident in Baghdad in 1808. Rich died of cholera at Shiraz.

ROBINSON, JOHN OF ISLEWORTH (1727–1802), was an attorney and steward who entered Parliament in 1764. He served as secretary of the treasury under Lord North and acted as North's political agent and liaison with the directorate of the EIC.

ROSE, SIR HUGH, 20TH LAIRD OF KILRAVOCK (1780–1827), was the son of Captain Hugh Rose of Brea and Broadley and Elizabeth Rose, heir of Sir Hugh of Kilravock. He held the positions of vice-lieutenant of County Nairn, colonel of the Nairnshire militia, and member of Parliament for Nairn from 1790 to 1820. Rose married Katharine Baillie, daughter of John, 13th Laird of Dunain, in 1805.

ROSE, HUGH, 21ST LAIRD OF KILRAVOCK (1808–1847), was the eldest son of Hugh, 20th Laird of Kilravock, and Katharine Baillie. He joined the EIC civil service in 1827 and served as deputy collector at Cawnpore around 1840. Rose died in India seven years later.

ROSE, JOHN BAILLIE, 22ND LAIRD OF KILRAVOCK (c. 1809–54), was the second son of Hugh, 20th Laird of Kilravock, and Katharine Baillie. He joined the EIC in 1827, served in Ireland, fought in China in 1842, and was stationed at Gibraltar in 1852. Rose, a major in the 55th Regiment, died at the Battle of Alma in the Crimean War.

ROSS, GEORGE OF PITKERRIE AND CROMARTY (1700–1786), served for many years as the confidential clerk to Lord President Duncan Forbes. Ross then established an army agency in London and amassed a considerable fortune. He purchased several properties in the north and first entered Parliament in 1780. Cromarty, which he created, remains today the finest example of an eighteenth-century European town.

RUMBOLD, SIR THOMAS (1736–1791), was a colonial administrator and parliamentarian. He served as Clive's aide-de-camp at Plassey in 1757, chief at Patna in 1763, and a member of the Bengal Council from 1766 to 1769. Rumbold returned with a large fortune to Britain where he entered Parliament and became a director of the EIC. He was appointed governor of Madras in 1777 but resigned in 1780, ostensibly for health reasons, and was subsequently dismissed for his role in Hyder Ali's invasion.

RUMBOLD, SIR WILLIAM, 3RD BARONET (1787–1833), was the grandson of Sir Thomas Rumbold, a governor of Madras. He was a partner in the banking firm William Palmer and Company and married Lord Moira's ward, Harriet-Elizabeth Parkyns, sister of Lord Rancliffe and the Princess de Polignac.

SALABAT JUNG (1718–1763), the third son of Asaf Jah I, nizam of Hyderabad, reigned as the fourth nizam from 1751 to 1762. He was appointed naib soubah (deputy viceroy) to his elder brother, Ghazi-ood-Din, the prime minister of the Mughal Empire. Supported by the French, Salabat succeeded his nephew, Muzaffar Jung, as nizam. However, he was deposed and slain in 1762 by his brother, Nizam Ali.

SHAH ALAM II (1728–1806) succeeded his father, Alamgir II, as the eighteenth Mughal emperor, reigning from 1759 to 1806. Following his defeat at the 1764 Battle of Buxar, Shah Alam by the Treaty of Allahabad granted the diwani of Bengal to the EIC. He was blinded by the Rohilla warlord Ghulām Qādir in 1788 and subsequently taken under the protection of Mahadaji Scindia and then the British in 1803 when they captured Delhi.

SHAH SHUJA DURRANI (1786–1842) ruled Afghanistan from 1803 to 1809 and from 1839 to 1842. He assumed the throne by overthrowing his brother and was, in turn, overthrown by his half-brother. Thirty years later, Shah Shuja regained the throne through British assistance but was assassinated by his god-son, Shuja-ood-Dowla.

SHEPERD, SIR SAMUEL (1760–1840), was an English barrister and politician. After his appointment as solicitor general in 1813, he entered Parliament in 1814 and served as attorney general from 1817 to 1819. Sheperd was lord chief baron of the Scottish Court of Exchequer from 1819 to 1830 and a member of the Privy Council.

SHIVAJI BHONSLA, CHHATRAPATI (1630–1680), was a formidable Maratha warrior who is regarded as the founder of the Maratha Empire. He rebelled against Muslim oppression of Hindus and seized extensive territories from the sultanate of Bijapur and the Mughals. Aurangzeb's troops finally subdued Shivaji in 1665 but Shivaji escaped and recovered the bulk of his former conquests. He was crowned king of the Marathas 1674 following which he undertook further conquests in southern India.

SHIV RAO BHAU, soubah of Jhansi (?–1814), was the son of Hurry Punt and the brother of Raghunath Hari Newalkar, whom he succeeded as soubah in 1796. Although nominally under the peshwa, Shiv Rao received a guarantee of British protection in 1804. A formidable warrior and confident in his alliance with the EIC, Shiv Rao declared Jhansi's independence.

SHORE, SIR JOHN, 1ST BARON TEIGNMOUTH (1751–1834), joined the EIC in 1768 and was appointed to the Supreme Council in 1787. His tenure as governor general was non-expansionist. On his return to Britain, Shore was appointed to the Board of Control but spent the bulk of his time on religious and philanthropic causes. He was the first president of the British and Foreign Bible Society.

SHUJA-OOD-DOWLA (1732–1775) reigned as third nawab of Oude from 1754 to 1775. In return for providing refuge to the future emperor, Shah Alam II, the emperor named Shuja grand vizier of the Mughal Empire. Shuja played a key role in defeating the Marathas in the Third Battle of Panipat in 1761. He, together with Shah Alam and Mir Qasim, was decisively routed by Hector Munro at Buxar in 1764. In the Treaty of Allahabad, Shuja relinquished vast territories to the EIC.

SIRAJ-OOD-DOWLA (1733–1757) was the last independent ruler of Bengal. Shortly after succeeding his grandfather, Ali Varda Khan, in 1756, he attacked the

British, capturing Calcutta and Fort William. The notorious Black Hole of Calcutta incident occurred after these victories. Clive exploited the dissension brewing at Siraj's court by allying with Mir Jaffar, whom Siraj had dismissed as paymaster of the army. After his defeat at Plassey, Siraj was executed by Mir Jaffar.

STRACHAN, ADMIRAL SIR RICHARD (1760–1828), was a distinguished British naval officer who saw action in the American Revolutionary War, the French Revolution, and the Napoleonic Wars. In the last battle of the Trafalgar campaign, Strachan captured four French ships at the Battle of Cape Ortegal. He was the last chief of Clan Strachan.

STRATTON, GEORGE (1733–1800), was an EIC career officer and parliamentarian. He joined the Company in 1750 and served as acting governor of Madras in 1776–77. He led the faction that arrested Lord Pigot and was indicted with others for murder after Pigot's death. The proceedings were quashed but Stratton was recalled and fined £1,000.

STUART, JAMES, 3RD EARL OF MORAY (1581–1638), was the grandson of James Stuart, a natural son of James VI. He was a privy councillor in 1607–08 and inherited the title when his father was murdered by his future father-in-law, George Gordon, 1st Marquess of Huntly.

STUART, LIEUTENANT-GENERAL JAMES (c. 1735–1793), was a British army officer who was suspended as second-in-command of the EIC forces in Madras in 1775 for arresting and imprisoning the governor, Lord Pigot. He was vindicated in 1780 and returned to India in 1781 as commander-in-chief at Madras. Stuart served under Coote in the Second Anglo-Mysore War. He assumed command at the time of Coote's death but was suspended by the governor, Lord Macartney, with whom he sparred continually.

STUART, LIEUTENANT-GENERAL JAMES (1741–1815), was a Scottish army officer who was distantly related to Colonel William Baillie through descent from the Earl of Moray. He served in the Second, Third, and Fourth Anglo-Mysore Wars. Stuart secured Ceylon for Britain in 1796 and was military governor of the island from 1796 to 1797. He was commander-in-chief at Bombay from 1797 to 1800 and at Madras from 1801 to 1804, during which he took part in the Second Anglo-Maratha War.

SUFFREIN, ADMIRAL PIERRE ANDRÉ (1729–88), was an exemplary French naval officer. He saved the Cape from capture by George Johnstone in 1781 and then fought several fierce but indecisive engagements with Edward Hughes in India in 1782–83. In the Battle of Cuddalore, Suffrein forced Hughes to withdraw, leaving Cuddalore vulnerable to an onslaught by the French and Hyder Ali. However, news of peace in Europe staved off the attack.

SWINTON, GEORGE (1780–1854), was a Scottish career servant of the EIC. He joined the Company on the Bengal establishment in 1805, served as Persian secretary, and from 1829 to 1833 as chief secretary to the government of India. He founded the Hindu College in 1816, the Calcutta School Book Society in 1817, and the Calcutta School Society in 1818.

SYKES, FRANCIS, 1ST BARON BASILDON (1732–1804), was a colonial administrator and politician. He amassed a fortune in the employ of the EIC at the court of the nawab of Bengal. Sykes served as governor of Kasimbazar.

THULJAJI, rajah of Tanjore (1738–87), was the eldest son of Rajah Ptrap Singh. He attacked the poligars of Ramnad in 1771, compelling Mohammed Ali, with the assistance of the EIC, to come to their defence. Thuljaji was forced to sign a humiliating treaty ceding lands and treasure. When he sought aid from the Marathas, the nawab and the EIC deposed Thuljaji. The Court of Directors restored Thuljaji to his throne but reduced him to a vassal of the Company.

TIDDEMAN, COMMODORE RICHARD (c. 1702–62), was a Royal Navy officer who served at the successful sieges of Louisburg in 1745 and Pondicherry in 1760. He was appointed second-in-command of the East Indies Station in 1761. Tiddeman was commodore under Sir Samuel Cornish of the expedition which took Manilla in 1762 but drowned when his barge capsized the day after the victory.

TONE, THEOBALD WOLFE (1763–98), was an Irish politician and revolutionary who co-founded the Society of United Irishmen. As a result of his revolutionary activities, Tone immigrated to America. He then persuaded the French Directorate to send an expeditionary force under General Hoche to Ireland 1796 in support of a planned rebellion. That invasion aborted but Tone was later captured during a raid at Lough Swilly in 1798 and executed.

TUCKER, HENRY ST GEORGE (1771–1851), born in Bermuda, was an EIC civil servant and financier. He served as military secretary to Wellesley in 1799 and accountant general from 1801 to 1804 and in 1805–06. In 1804 he joined Cockerell, Traill, Palmer and Company as managing partner. Tucker was appointed acting chief secretary in 1814 and governor of Java but left for Britain where he chaired the EIC from 1834 to 1847.

TUKOJI RAO HOLKAR (1723–1797) was the adopted son of Malha Rao Holkar, first ruler of Holkar. He commanded the army during Malha Rao's and Ahilyabai Holkar's reigns and together with Mahadaji Scindia humiliated the British at Wadgaon in 1779. Tukoji succeeded to the throne upon Ahilyabai's death and reigned from 1795 to 1797.

WALLACE, SIR WILLIAM (c. 1272–1305), launched a rebellion against the rule of Edward I by assassinating William de Hesselrig, the high sheriff of Lanark. Although most of the Scottish nobles submitted to Edward I, Wallace refused and in 1297 inflicted the most decisive defeat of the English to date at Stirling Bridge. Wallace was elected guardian of Scotland. In 1298 Edward's forces overwhelmed those of Wallace at Falkirk. He escaped but was eventually betrayed and hanged, drawn, and quartered as a traitor although he had never sworn allegiance to Edward.

WARDEN, FRANCIS, was a career EIC civil servant with extensive outside commercial interests. He was a member of the Council and chief secretary to the Bombay government. Warden owned the Bombay *Gazette* and held important positions in the Bombay Insurance Society, the Bombay Life Insurance Company, and the Bombay *Courier*. He served as a director of the EIC at various times between 1836 and 1850.

WAZIR ALI KHAN, fourth nawab of Oude (1780–1817), was the adopted son of Nawab Asaf-ood-Dowla. He assumed the throne in 1797 but was deposed four months later by Wellesley in favour of his more compliant uncle, Saadat Ali. Wazir Ali was removed to Benares with a pension but rebelled, killing the British resident. He was delivered to the EIC on the condition that he be neither hanged nor fettered. He spent his remaining seventeen years in an iron cage in Vellore.

WELLESLEY, RICHARD COLLEY, 1ST MARQUESS WELLESLEY (1760–1842), the eldest son of Garnet, 1st Earl of Mornington, was an Anglo-Irish politician and colonial administrator. As governor general of India, Wellesley extended the EIC's territories through subsidiary alliances and aggression, and his imposition of the severe Treaty of Bassein on the peshwa led to the Anglo-Maratha wars. Wellesley later served as foreign secretary from 1809 to 1812 and as lord lieutenant of Ireland from 1821 to 1828.

WEMYSS, DAVID LORD ELCHO (1721–1787), the eldest son of the 4th Earl of Wemyss, was the colonel of Prince Charles's Lifeguards in the Forty-Five. After Culloden, Lord Elcho fled to France where he obtained an appointment as colonel of the Royal Scots in the service of Louis XV. As an attainted rebel, Elcho's estates remained dormant until his death when a younger brother assumed them.

WHITEHILL, JOHN (1735–?), joined the EIC in 1752 and was promoted to chief at Masulipatnam in 1775. He served as acting governor of Madras in 1777–78 and as governor in 1780. However, he was dismissed 1781 by Warren Hastings, who believed that Whitehill's "senseless provocations" were the cause of Hyder Ali's invasion of the Carnatic.

WISEMAN, SIR WILLIAM SALTONSTALL OF CANFIELD HALL (1784–1845), was a captain in the Royal Navy. He succeeded his grandfather as seventh baronet and married Catherine, the second daughter of Sir James Mackintosh, chief judge in Bombay.

WOLFE, GENERAL JAMES (1727–1759), served on the continent and then as aide-de-camp to General Hawley in Scotland. Wolfe distinguished himself in the Seven Years' War in America and died defeating the French on the Plains of Abraham in Quebec City.

WOODFORD, COLONEL JOHN (?–1800), was a Scottish army officer and was active in the volunteer militia movement. He was appointed colonel of the North Highland Fencibles (the Gordon Highlanders) in 1793 and played a prominent role in suppressing the Gordon Riots which were led by his uncle.

WYNCH, ALEXANDER (1721–1781), was a merchant and career civil servant with the EIC. He served as deputy governor of Fort St David where he was captured by the French in 1758. Wynch resigned from the Company but was reappointed as chief at Masulipatam in 1768 and as governor of Madras in 1773. He was dismissed in 1775 for permitting the transfer of Tanjore to Mohammed Ali.

YALE, ELIHU (1649–1721), was a Massachusetts-born merchant and EIC official. He succeeded Streynsham Master as governor of Madras, serving there in 1684–85 and from 1687 to 1692. Yale accumulated a considerable fortune, primarily in the diamond trade, and was eventually dismissed for self-dealing. Collegiate School of Connecticut was renamed Yale College in appreciation of Yale's gifts.

Glossary of Anglo-Indian and Scottish Terms

ameer: the person in charge of collecting taxes and the chief administrative
  officer of government in an area; in Arabic, khabar (sing.) and akhbar (pl.)
bahadur: a military title comparable to that of a knight
bang: leaves and flowerhead of cannabis, used as a narcotic
Begum: title of rank and respect for an Indian Muslim noblewoman
bhatta: extra allowance to sepoys during time of war
bibi: Indian wife or mistress
bound hedge: a broad belt of land planted with bamboo, prickly pear, etc.
  to protect forts and villages
caffre: insulting and offensive term for a black African
chela: student or disciple; also a slave or adopted son
chhatrapati: Indian royal title equivalent to emperor
chubdar: an attendant on a prince or other important individual
chunam: polished lime plaster
circar: district or part of a province
cottar: Scottish peasant living on a farm owned by his landlord
crore: ten million rupees, or one million pounds sterling
darogah: officer overseeing police stations, bridges, and individual departments
  within a royal household
dewan: finance or prime minister of an Indian state
diwani: the right conferred to collect revenues and administer a territory for
  the Mughal emperors
doolie: a covered litter
dubash: interpreter
Dunain: Gaelic meaning hill of the bird
durbar: public audience given by native ruler to receive petitioners
  and ambassadors

farrier: blacksmith

feu: heritable, a feu interest gives the holder an equivalent of a freehold estate title subject to payment of feu duties and compliance with title conditions

firman: written royal order, decree, or grant

Gentoo: Indian of the Hindu religion

ghat: platform and steps leading down to a river, or a pass, generally through mountains

ghazi: holy warrior or jihadist

gillie: a male attendant or personal servant to a Highland chief

godown: warehouse or other storage space

gosain: generic term for ascetic

guinea: a coin approximating ¼ ounce of gold minted in Great Britain 1663–1814, originally worth 1 £ sterling (20 shillings); from 1717 to 1816 its value was fixed at 21 shillings

Gurkha: a Hindu Rajput people who gained dominion over Nepal in the eighteenth century

havildar: sergeant of sepoys

heritable subjects: lands and other properties that are to be inherited by the heir at-law

Hindustan or Hindostan: region of north India comprised of the modern states of Haryana, Delhi, Uttar Pradesh, and some parts of Madya Pradesh and Bihar where Hindustani is spoken

hiracarrah: trusted messenger employed to carry letters and obtain intelligence, commonly used as guides

ilaka: locality or vicinity

infestment: a provision in Scottish feudal law whereby freehold property or land was given in exchange for the recipient's pledge of service

jaghir: assignment of land entitling the holder to collect revenue

jaghirdar: holder of a jaghir

jaidad: assignment of revenue specifically for the maintenance of troops

jemindar: the junior native officer in a company of sepoys

keladar: commander or governor of a fort, a military title

kelat: robes of honour presented with the bestowing of titles

khan: title comparable to a lord

kutcheree (cutcheree): a public administrative or judicial office in India

lakh: one hundred thousand

madjum: sweets containing cannabis

maharajah: a primarily Hindu title for a great or high king

maharana/maharao/maharawal: variations of maharajah

mansabdar: Mughal nobleman and officeholder whose rank was determined by the number of cavalry he was expected to supply in battle

mirza: prince or gentleman

mohur: a gold coin that was minted by several governments including British India and several princely states; its value was generally equivalent to fifteen rupees

moonshee: native secretary or assistant

musnud: throne of cushions used by native princes

myar: town major

Nagas: a tribal people of northeastern India and Myanmar with a warrior tradition

naik: chief, leader, sepoy corporal

nangah: inhabitant of the mountains in northwest Kashmir

nawab: Mughal title denoting viceroy or deputy governor

nizam: Mughal title bestowed on the rulers of Hyderabad

nujeebs: semi-disciplined Indian infantry soldiers employed by native princes

omrah: pilgrimage, consisting of rituals performed by an individual at various shrines upon entering Mecca, often associated with the Haj; or nobleman

pagoda: gold or silver coins depicting a temple; widely used in southern India

peon: irregular infantry responsible for their own arms; generally employed in defence of forts and the collection of revenues

pergunnah: subdivision of territory containing several villages

peshcush: tribute paid by a subordinate to a superior

peshwa: originally the prime minister of the Mahratta confederacy and later titular ruler of the Marathas

pindari: marauder, usually associated with Maratha wars; they received no compensation but plundered for their own account

poligar: originally a subordinate feudal chief in southern India; latterly an inhabitant of mountains and woods, generally armed with pikes and matchlocks

rajah: Hindu prince or ruler

rajput: extended clans of Hindu warrior-rulers in northern India

rana: a Rajput title for monarch

rani: Hindu queen or princess, wife of a rajah

Rohilla: a Muslim Urdu-speaking Pashtun people who lived in Rohilkand in what is now the northern Indian state of Uttar Pradesh

rupee: silver coin

ryot: person who holds land as a cultivator of the soil

sasine: a provision in Scottish feudal law referring to the delivery of land and any property associated with it; in time, it was used to refer to the document recording the transfer rather than the transfer itself

sepoy: native Indian soldier in the service of the East India Company

sirdar: military chief or leader on the Indian subcontinent

soubah or soubadar: governor of an extensive territory

sultan: equivalent of king; title assumed by Tipu Sultan

sunnud: a charter or warrant; also, a deed of gift

superiorities: in Scotland the higher interest that remains after the sale of the feu; entitles the feudal superior to collect feu duties and ensure compliance with title conditions attached to the feu

tack: lease

tawing: turning hides into leather by soaking them in chemicals

thakoor: chief or master, used as a term of respect among the Kshatriya caste

Topasse: native Indian Christians, often with Portuguese blood

tumbrels: carts used for agricultural work or for carrying ammunition

umrah: nobleman

vakil: ambassador or representative

vizier: high official, particularly a minister of state in a Muslim country

wadset: in the Scottish Highlands an ancient tenure or lease of land similar to a redeemable mortgage

wāli: administrative title utilized during the caliphate and Ottoman Empire to designate governors of administrative divisions; the title employed by the ruler of the princely state of Swat

writer to the Signet: the Society of Writers to Her Majesty's Signet is a private association of Scottish solicitors dating from 1594; originally, members had privileges in executing documents requiring the monarch's seal

zemindar: owner of an agricultural estate

zenana: part of the house in which women are secluded

zillahs: districts into which provinces were divided for administrative purposes

Notes

CHAPTER ONE

1 Fraser-Mackintosh, *Letters of Two Centuries*, Lord Oliphant of Gask to his sister, Kennochan, March 1746, 225.

2 Fraser-Mackintosh, "Minor Highland Families," *Gaelic Society of Inverness*, no. 11, "The Baillies of Dunain," 117.

3 Charles Fraser-Mackintosh Mss., as quoted in Campbell, "Lieutenant-Colonel William Baillie," 1.

4 Mitchell, *Reminiscences of My Life in the Highlands*, vol. 1, 56.

5 Shaw, *Historical Memories of the House and Clan of Mackintosh and of the Clan Chattan*, 481.

6 Prebble, *Culloden*, 130.

7 Anderson, *The Scottish Nation*, vol. 3, 362.

8 Herman, *How the Scots Invented the Modern World*, 194.

9 Devine, *The Scottish Nation*, 177.

10 Herman, *How the Scots Invented the Modern World*, 21.

11 Miller, *Inverness*, 220.

12 Devine, *The Scottish Nation*, quoting Donald Withrington, 91.

13 Houston, *Scottish Literacy and the Scottish Identity*, 187.

14 Herman, *How the Scots Invented the Modern World*, 40.

15 Pincus, *1688*, 438.

16 Herman, *How the Scots Invented the Modern World*, 56.

17 Ibid., 57, 58.

18 This anxiety is reflected in Shakespeare's *Henry V*, act 1, scene 2: "'If that you will France win, / Then with Scotland first begin: / For once the eagle England being in prey / To her unguarded nest the weasel Scot / Comes

sneaking, and so sucks her princely eggs; / Playing the mouse in absence of the cat, / To spoil and havoc more than she can eat.'"

19   Herman, *How the Scots Invented the Modern World*, 96.

20   Home, *The History of the Rebellion in Scotland in 1745*, 21–2.

21   Buchan, *Crowded with Genius*, 43.

22   Ibid., 37.

23   Ibid., 48.

24   Ibid., 40.

25   Anderson, *Culloden Moor and the Story of the Battle*, chapter 6, "Butchery of the Wounded," n.p., quoting Robert Forbes.

26   Warrand, ed., "More Culloden Papers," vol. 5, 124, John Hossack to Duncan Forbes, Inverness, 9 Aug. 1746.

27   Miller, *Inverness*, 150.

28   Herman, *How the Scots Invented the Modern World*, 172.

29   Ibid.

30   Buchan, *Crowded with Genius*, 177.

31   Ibid., 117.

32   Ibid., 204, quoting Robert Louis Stevenson, "Edinburgh: Picturesque Notes," 99.

33   Herman, *How the Scots Invented the Modern World*, 26.

34   Ibid., 185.

35   Ibid.

36   Ibid., 87.

37   Devine, *The Scottish Nation 1700–2000*, 237.

CHAPTER TWO

1   Fraser-Mackintosh, "Minor Highland Families," *Gaelic Society of Inverness*, no. 11, "The Baillies of Dunain," 140.

2   Fraser-Mackintosh, "Antiquarian Notes" (1897), 53–4.

3   HAC, D456/A/10/9, James Bremmer to [?], Edinburgh, 11 Aug. 1792. Our understanding, as transmitted orally through the generations, differs somewhat from the account in Olivebank's papers. In our version there were three sons, of whom the eldest fled to Inverness, the second flew to Ireland where the family shortened the name to Bailie, and the youngest, who was not involved in the surgical procedure, remained at and inherited Lamington. The two versions may not, however, be in conflict as one of the sons may well have taken refuge in one of the family estates well removed from the scene of the incident.

4 HAC, D456/A/2/78, Alexander Baillie to William Fraser of Balnain, Dunain, n.d.

5 NAS, GD128/4/1/1, George Baillie to Alexander Baillie, Edinburgh, 20 Oct. 1757.

6 NAS, GD128/4/1/2, Alexander Baillie to Duke of Gordon, Dunain, 1 Feb. 1750.

7 HAC, D456/A/1/26, John Baillie to Alexander Baillie Edinburgh, 21 June 1744.

8 Miller, *Inverness*, quoting Dafoe, 122.

9 Ibid., quoting Edmund Burt, 122.

10 Newton, *The Life and Times of Inverness*, 4.

11 HAC, D456/A/ 2/78, Alexander Baillie to William Fraser of Balnain, n.d.

12 Waugh, *James Wolfe*, 101.

13 In conversation with the author, the eminent historian Niall Ferguson noted that when researching the two world wars of the twentieth century, he became interested in the fighting characteristics of various nations and concluded, not surprisingly in view of his Scottish ancestry, that the Scots ranked among the bravest and most fearless. He calculated that the Scots suffered (relative to the UK average) disproportionate casualties on a per capita basis in the First World War and, for the Second World War, cited examples of Scottish troops at Dunkirk refusing to lay down their arms after their English commander had determined that surrender was the most prudent option.

14 Harvey, *Clive*, 340; Tuck, *The East India Company*, 194.

15 Tilby, *British India 1600–1828*, 136.

16 Bowen, *The Business of Empire*, 16, quoting Philip Lawson and Jim Phillips, *Albion*, 225–41.

17 Ibid., 15, quoting from William Cobbett in "The Creevey Paper: A Selection from the Correspondence and Diaries of the Late Thomas Creevey, MP," vol. 1, 134.

18 Harvey, *Clive*, 346.

19 Keay, *The Honourable Company*, 366.

20 Quoted in Ferguson, *The War of the World*, 9.

21 Phillips, *1775*, 382.

22 McLynn, *1759*, 93.

23 HAC, D456/A/1/28, Alexander Baillie, Dochfour, to Alexander Baillie, Dunain, Nevis, 18 March 1752.

24 Fraser-Mackintosh, *Letters of Two Centuries*, Alexander Baillie, Dochfour, to Alexander Baillie, Dunain, St Christopher's, 26 May 1753, 240.

25 NAS, GD 128/4/1, Item F, Alexander Baillie, Dunain, to Alexander Baillie, Dochfour, Dunain, 8 May 1758.

26 NAS, GD 128/4/1 Item C, William Baillie to Alexander Baillie, Edinburgh, 30 Dec. 1758.

27 Ibid., Item D, Edinburgh, 6 Dec. 1758.

28 Ibid., n.d.

29 Ibid., Item B, William Baillie to Alexander Baillie, Edinburgh, 26 April 1759.

30 Ibid.

CHAPTER THREE

1 Campbell, "Lieutenant-Colonel William Baillie," 5.

2 NAS, GD 128/4/3/2, William Baillie to Alexander Baillie, Aberdeen, 6 Feb. 1760.

3 NAS, GD 128/4/3/6, ibid., Hastings, 22 March 1760.

4 NAS, GD 128/4/3/7, ibid., on board the *Admiral Watson*, 19 April 1760.

5 NAS, GD 128/1/1/22, William Baillie to Alexander Baillie, Pondicherry, 18 Oct. 1760.

6 Madison, *The World Economy*.

7 Dalrymple, "The Great and Beautiful Lost Kingdoms," 11.

8 Wylly, *A Life of Lieutenant-General Sir Eyre Coote KB*, 93.

9 NAS, GD 128/1/1/24, Fort St George, 6 Feb. 1761.

10 Hodges, *Travels in India during the Years 1780, 1781, 1782 and 1783*, 2.

11 Dodwell, *The Nabobs of Madras*, 110–11.

12 Ibid., 109.

13 Munro, *A Narrative of the Military Operation on Coromandel Coast ...*, Letter III, March 1780, 25.

14 Ibid., Letter IX, May 1780, 93.

15 NAS, GD 128/1/3/6, a diary incorrectly attributed to William Baillie, 3.

16 Hamilton, *Scotland, the Caribbean and the Atlantic World 1750–1820*, 96.

17 NAS, GD 128/1/3/6, a diary incorrectly attributed to William Baillie, 3–5.

18 Munro, *A Narrative of the Military Operation on Coromandel Coast ...*, Letter III, March 1780, 26.

19 Orme, *A History of the Military Transactions of the British Nation in Indostan from the Year MDCCXLV*, 5–6.

20 NAS, GD 128/1/3/6, a diary incorrectly attributed to William Baillie, 6.

21 Dodwell, *The Nabobs of Madras*, 108.

22 Godsman was a fellow lieutenant in the 89th. He returned to Britain with the regiment in 1763, leased Dunain from William, and served as

factor to the Duke of Gordon. William and Alexander Godsman's friendship evidently stood the test of time, since, on Godsman's return to Britain, he served as one of the three trustees of William's affairs in Scotland.

23 NAS, GD 128/1/1/25, William Baillie to Alexander Baillie, on the *Seaford*, 2 Dec. 1761.

24 HAC, D456/A/2/3, John Fraser to Alexander Baillie, 12 Feb. 1760.

25 HAC, D456/A/2/8, ibid., 5 Dec. 1761.

26 Campbell, "Lieutenant-Colonel William Baillie," 22.

27 Reports from Committees of the House of Commons, vol. 7, East Indies: Carnatic War, etc., First Report, Extracts of Letters from the Court of Directors, 19 March 1771 and 30 Dec. 1771, 190.

28 Wylly, *A Life of Lieutenant-General Sir Eyre Coote KB*, 122.

29 NAS, GD 128/4/3/8, William Baillie to Alexander Baillie, Fort St George, 10 June 1763.

CHAPTER FOUR

1 Grierson, ed., *The Letters of Sir Walter Scott*, vol. 6, Scott to Lord Montagu, 1 July 1821, 489.

2 Keay, *The Honourable Company*, 141.

3 Ibid., 281.

4 Bowen, *The Business of Empire*, quoting *The Yale Edition of Horace Walpole's Correspondence*, vol. 22, 498.

5 Ibid., quoting British Library, Egerton Ms., 218.

6 Keay, *The Honourable Company*, 113.

7 Ibid., 379.

8 Ibid.

9 Ibid., 364.

10 Ibid.

11 Wilson, *History of the Madras Army*, vol. 1, 213.

12 Parsons, *Seringapatam*, 124

13 Tritton, *When the Tiger Fought the Thistle*, 74–5, quoting a lieutenant in William Baillie's regiment.

14 NAS, GD 128/4/2, Item B, Henry Drummond to Alexander Godsman, 3 Jan. 1765.

15 Ibid., Item C, Alexander Godsman to [?], 29 June 1765.

16 Malleson, *The Decisive Battles of India*, 183.

17 NAS, GD 128/1/3/6, a diary incorrectly attributed to William Baillie, 26.

18 Llewelyn-Jones, *A Fatal Friendship*, 2.

19 Reports from Committees of the House of Commons, vol. 7, East Indies: Carnatic War, etc., Second Report, 272.

20 Ibid., 319.

21 NAS, GD 128/4/2 Item A, Evan Baillie to Alexander Baillie, n.d. [1760].

22 Campbell, "Lieutenant-Colonel William Baillie," 22.

23 Higginbotham, Men Whom India Has Known, 209.

24 Massie, Continental India, vol. 1, 393.

25 Reports from Committees of the House of Commons, vol. 7, East Indies: Carnatic War, etc., Second Report, Hyder Ali to Fort St George, 8 July 1769, 172.

26 Ibid., Hyder Ali to Fort St George, 7 March 1770, 175.

27 Ibid., Richard Church and J. Sibbald to Fort St George, 20 April 1770, 175.

28 Asiatic Journal and Monthly Register, 4 (July–September 1817): 571.

29 The East India Military Calendar 1823, vol. 1, 4.

30 Malleson, The Decisive Battles of India, 233.

31 Wilson, History of the Madras Army, vol. 1, 241.

32 Murland, Baillie-Ki-Paltan, quoting Joseph Smith, 30.

33 Wilson, History of the Madras Army, vol. 1, 245.

34 Murland, Baillie-Ki-Paltan, 29–30.

35 Campbell, "Lieutenant-Colonel William Baillie," 31.

36 Murland, Baillie-Ki-Paltan, quoting Thomas Fitzgerald, 32.

37 Mill and Wilson, The History of British India, vol. 3, book 4, 475.

38 Murland, Baillie-Ki-Paltan, quoting John William Fortescue, 36.

39 Rose, Newton, and Benians, eds., The Cambridge History of the British Empire, vol. 2, 277.

CHAPTER FIVE

1 NAS, GD 128, Robert Munro to Alexander Baillie, 19 Dec. 1767.

2 NAS, GD 128/4/2, Item D, William Fraser to Alexander Baillie, 9 Nov. 1767.

3 NAS, GD 128/4/2/1, William Fraser to Alexander Baillie, 16 Dec. 1765.

4 Fraser-Mackintosh, "Minor Highland Families," Transactions of the Gaelic Society of Inverness, vol. 22 (1897–98), no. 11, "The Baillies of Dunain," 148.

5 NAS, GD 128/4/2, Item E, Archibald Campbell to Alexander Baillie, 8 Jan. 1768.

6 NAS, GD 128/4/3/14, Robert Munro to Alexander Baillie, 16 April 1768.

7 NAS, GD 128/4/3/26, John Baillie to Alexander Baillie, 16 Nov. 1768.

8 HAC, D456/A/2/28, John Baillie to Alexander Baillie, Fort St George, 24 Dec. 1768.

9 NAS, GD128/4/2/2, Robert Sandilands to Alexander Baillie, London, 25 Oct. 1766.

10 Ibid., Robert Sandilands to Alexander Baillie, 18 Nov. 1768.

11 Ibid., Alexander Baillie to James Grant, Dunain, 14 June 1772.

12 NAS, GD128/4/3/14, Robert Munro to Alexander Baillie, London, 16 April 1768.

13 HAC, D456/A/2/26, Donald Campbell to Alexander Baillie, Airds, 4 Jan. 1768.

14 NAS, GD128/4/3/17, William Baillie to Alexander Baillie, Vellore, 8 Oct. 1769.

15 HAC, D456/A/2/39, Donald Campbell to Alexander Baillie, Airds, 20 Aug. 1770.

16 HAC, D456/A/16/3, Alexander Baillie to William Baillie, Dunain, 20 Oct. 1770.

17 HAC, D456/A/2/47, Margaret Campbell to Anne Baillie, Airds, 27 July 1772.

18 NAS, GD128/4/3/20, William Baillie to Alexander Baillie, Madras, 19 July 1771.

19 NAS, GD128/4/3/17, William Baillie to Alexander Baillie, Vellore, 8 Oct. 1770.

20 HAC, D456/A/2/34, William Baillie to Alexander Baillie, 20 Jan. 1770.

21 HAC, D456/A/3/4, Marie Baillie to William Baillie, Ardmore, 20 Jan. 1777.

22 NAS, GD128/1/3/5, William Baillie to Marie Baillie, 31 Jan. 1778.

23 HAC, D456/A/2/37, William Baillie to Alexander Baillie, Vellore, 4 April 1770.

24 HAC, D456/A/16/2, John Alves to William Baillie, Dunain, 23 March 1770.

25 HAC, D456/A16/4, John Alves to William Baillie, 20 Oct. 1770.

26 HAC, D456/A/16/3, Alexander Baillie to William Baillie, Inverness, 20 Oct. 1770.

27 HAC, D456/A/16/4, John Alves to William Baillie, Inverness, 20 Oct. 1770.

28 NAS, GD128/4/3/22, John Baillie to Alexander Baillie, Vellore, 24 Jan. 1771.

29 NAS, GD128/4/3/20, William Baillie to Alexander Baillie, Madras, 19 July 1771.

30 Fraser-Mackintosh, "Letters of Two Centuries," William Baillie to an unnamed relative, 4 March 1771, 295.

31 NAS, GD128/7/13, Arthur Cuthbert to Alexander Baillie, Fort St George, 6 Feb. 1771.

32 NAS, GD 128/7/12, receipt by Anne Baillie, Dunain, 29 June 1771.

33 HAC, D 456/16/6, John Alves to William Baillie, Dunain, 30 Nov. 1771;
    HAC, D 456/A/2/43, "State of Debts" following Dunain's death, compiled
    by John Alves, 11 Nov. 1771.

34 HAC, D 456/A/9/1, George Baillie to William Baillie, Dunain, 26 Dec. 1771.

35 HAC, D 456/A/16/7, John Alves to William Baillie, Inverness, 11 Jan. 1772.

36 HAC, D 456/A/16/5, Alexander Baillie of Dochfour to William Baillie, dated
    5 May 1771 but must be 1772.

CHAPTER SIX

1   Ballhatchet, *Race, Sex and Class under the Raj*, 96. The EIC minted
    the star pagoda in Madras. Its value fluctuated but in 1819 it was worth
    eight shillings.

2   Dodwell, *The Nabobs of Madras*, 202.

3   Ferguson, *The War of the World*, 20.

4   Chancey, *In the Company's Secret Service*, 25.

5   NAS, GD 128/1/3/6, a diary incorrectly attributed to William Baillie, 6.

6   Dodwell, *The Nabobs of Madras*, 14.

7   NAS, GD 128/4/3/47, John Baillie to Sir Thomas Rumbold, governor of
    Madras, Madras, 27 Dec. 1779.

8   Brendon, *The Decline and Fall of the British Empire, 1781–1997*, 72.

9   BL, IOR/Home Misc./398, 2.

10 Dalrymple, *White Mughals*, 40.

11 Ibid., 41.

12 NAS, GD 128/1/3, William Baillie to David Mitchell, 29 May 1775.

13 HAC, D 456/A/3/1, H. Woodhouse to William Baillie, Cuddalore, 28 Dec.
    1775.

14 HAC, D 456/A/3/3, David Mitchell to William Baillie, 16 March 1777.

15 NAS, GD 128/1/3, William Baillie to David Mitchell, 13 Sept. 1777.

16 HAC, D 456/A/4/6, William Baillie's account with David Mitchell, London,
    7 May 1778.

17 NAS, GD 128/1/3, William Baillie to David Mitchell, 29 Oct. 1778.

18 NAS, GD 128/4/3/50, Anne Baillie to William Baillie, 24 Jan. 1779.

19 NAS, GD 128/1/3/5, Anne Baillie to William Baillie, 23 Jan. 1778.

20 NAS, GD 128/1/3, William Baillie to David Mitchell, 10 Oct. 1779.

21 NAS, GD 128/1/3/5, William Baillie to Anne Baillie, 11 Oct. 1779.

22 Archibald was, I believe, the son of Colin Campbell, brother of William's
    mother and a younger son of Sir Archibald Campbell of Clunes.

23 HAC, D 456/A/16/8, Archibald Campbell to Wiilliam Baillie, 11 Jan. 1772.

24 HAC, D456/A/16/7, John Alves to William Baillie, 11 Jan. 1772.

25 HAC, D456/A/2/46, John Baillie to Ann Baillie, 18 Feb. 1772.

26 Harper, *Emigrant Homecomings*, 242.

27 HAC, D456/A/16/9, Helen Alves to William Baillie, 16 Nov. 1772.

28 HAC, D456/A16/11, Archibald Campbell to William Baillie, 28 Jan. 1773.

29 NAS, GD128/4/3/59, William Baillie to Anne Baillie, Trichinopoly, 22 July 1772.

30 HAC, D456/A/16/13, Archibald Campbell to William Baillie, 16 Nov. 1773.

31 HAC, D456/A/16/14, John Alves to William Baillie, 15 Dec. 1773.

32 HAC, D456/A/2/69, Francis Baillie to Anne Campbell, Fort St George, 27 Sept. 1774.

33 HAC, D456/A/16/10, John Alves to William Baillie, 28 Jan. 1773.

34 HAC, D456/A/16/15, William Baillie to John Alves, near Vellore, 2 Feb. 1774.

35 HAC, D456/A/2/71, Mohammed Ali to Joseph Smith, 7 Dec. 1773.

36 HAC, D456/A/2/71, Joseph Smith to Major Harper, Gardins, 2 Jan. 1774.

37 Ibid., officers to Major Harper, Vellore, 6 Jan. 1774.

38 HAC, D456/A/2/71, Mohammed Ali to Joseph Smith, 7 Dec. 1773.

39 Ibid., Joseph Smith to majors Baillie and Harper, Madras, 14 Feb. 1774.

40 Ibid., officers to Joseph Smith, 24 Feb. 1774.

41 HAC, D456/A/2/61, Mohammed Ali to General Smith, Chipauck, 8 March 1774.

42 HAC, D456/A/2/71, officers to General Smith, n.d.

CHAPTER SEVEN

1 Strachey, *Hastings and the Rohilla War*, 128.

2 Ibid., 132.

3 BL, OIOC, IOR354.541, selections 1772–85, vol. 1.

4 HAC, D456/A/2/68, William Baillie to Governor Wynch, Ellore, 14 Aug. 1774.

5 HAC, D456/A/16/16, John Alves to William Baillie, Inverness, 17 Oct. 1774.

6 HAC, D456/A/16/18, John Alves to William Baillie, 16 April 1775.

7 Ibid., Helen Alves to William Baillie, Inverness, 16 April 1775.

8 NAS, GD128/1/3/5, William Baillie to Alexander Godsman, Madras, 1 July 1775.

9 Ibid., William Baillie to John Alves, 11 Jan. 1776.

10 Ibid., William Baillie to John Alves and Alexander Godsman, 11 Jan. 1776.

11 Ibid., William Baillie to Anne Baillie, n.d.

12 Ibid.,William Baillie to Robert Fletcher, 7 January [no year].

13 Ibid., William Baillie to Arthur Cuthbert, Vellore, 20 Jan. 1777.

14 HAC, D456/A4/2, James Stuart to William Baillie, Fort St George, 14 Jan. 1777.

15 NAS, GD128/1/3/5, William Baillie to Alexander Godsman, Vellore, 22 Jan. 1777.

16 HAC, D456/A/4/4, William Baillie to John Whitehill, Poonamallee, 8 Sept. 1777.

17 Copies of Papers relative to the Restoration of the King of Tanjore, the Arrest of the Right Hon. George Lord Pigot etc., 10, s.56.

18 NAS, GD128/1/3/5, William Baillie to John Alves, September 1776.

19 Ibid., William Baillie to David Mitchell, 20 Sept. 1776.

20 Ibid., William Baillie to Alexander Godsman, Vellore, 22 Jan. 1777.

21 Ibid., William Baillie to John Alves, 1777.

22 Ibid., William Baillie to Arthur Cuthbert, Vellore, 20 Jan. 1777.

23 NAS, GD128/1/3, William Baillie to John Alves, Madras, 14 Sept. 1777.

24 NAS, GD128/1/3/5, William Baillie to David Mitchell, Madras, 13 Sept. 1777.

25 NAS, GD128/1/3, William Baillie to Alexander Godsman, Madras, 14 Sept. 1777.

26 HAC, D456/A/16/24, John Alves to William Baillie, Inverness, 8 June 1777.

27 NAS, GD128/1/3, William Baillie to David Mitchell, Madras, 23 Jan. 1778.

28 Rose et al., eds., *The Cambridge History of the British Empire*, 2: 283.

29 NAS, GD128/1/3, William Baillie to Alexander Godsman, 1 July 1775.

30 Fraser-Mackintosh, *Letters of Two Centuries*, Alexander Godsman to William Baillie, Dochfour, 23 Sept. 1775, 284–8.

31 NAS, GD128/1/3, William Baillie to Alexander Godsman, 11 Jan. 1776.

32 HAC, D456/A/16/19, Helen Alves to William Baillie, Inverness, 16 Jan. 1776.

33 HAC, D456/A/16/20, John Alves to William Baillie, Inverness, 16 Jan. 1776.

34 NAS, GD128/4/3/57, Archibald Campbell to William Baillie, Budgate, 22 June 1776.

35 HAC, D456/A/16/22, John Alves to William Baillie, Inverness, 30 June 1776.

36 HAC, D456/A/9/2, Alexander Baillie to William and John Baillie, Inverness, 21 Oct. 1776.

37 NAS, GD128/1/3, William Baillie to John Alves, September 1776.

38 HAC, D456/A/16/23, John Alves to William Baillie, Inverness, 3 Dec. 1776.

39 HAC, D456/A/3/5, Alexander Godsman to William Baillie, Dunain, 15 Oct. 1777.

40 NAS, GD128/1/3, William Baillie to John Alves, 1777.

41 HAC, D456/A/4/3, warrant from George Stratton to William Baillie, Madras, 9 Aug. 1777.

42 BL, OIOC, Transactions, Fort St George, 1 April 1778, 546–7.

43 NAS, GD128/1/3, William Baillie to Alexander Godsman, Poonamallee, 14 Sept. 1777.

44 NAS, GD128/1/3/5, William Baillie to David Mitchell, March 1778.

45 Ibid., William Baillie to John Alves, 11 March 1778.

46 HAC, D456/A/3/5, Alexander Godsman to William Baillie, Dunain, 15 Oct. 1777.

47 HAC, D456/A/16/25, Helen Alves to William Baillie, Inverness, 19 Feb. 1778.

48 BL, OIOC, Minute of the Council, Fort St George, 27 April 1778.

49 NAS, GD128/1/3, William Baillie to John Alves, Madras, 14 Sept. 1777.

50 Ibid., William Baillie to Alexander Godsman, Poonamalee, 14 Sept. 1777.

CHAPTER EIGHT

1 Auber, *Rise and Progress of the British Power in India*, vol. 1, 565–6.

2 NAS, GD128/1/2/14, [?] to William Baillie, Berrumpore, 21 May 1780.

3 NAS, GD128/1/3, William Baillie to David Mitchell, Pondicherry, 29 Oct. 1778.

4 Wylly, *A Life of Lieutenant-General Sir Eyre Coote KB*, 149.

5 NAS, GD128/1/3, William Baillie to David Mitchell, Pondicherry, 29 Oct. 1778.

6 Campbell, "Lieutenant-Colonel William Baillie," 64.

7 NAS, GD128/1/3, William Baillie to Alexander Godsman, 30 Oct. 1778.

8 NAS, 7/5, James Campbell to General Bellecombe, 24 Oct. 1778.

9 NAS, GD128/1/1/3, Articles of Capitulation, 17 Oct. 1778.

10 HAC, D456/A/16/26, William Baillie to John Alves, Pondicherry, n.d.

11 HAC, D456/A/4/23, Inventory of the Effects of Government House Pondicherry belonging to Col. William Baillie, 4 Nov. 1779.

12 HAC, D456/A/4/14, Comper to William Baillie, Pondicherry, 18 Feb. 1779.

13 NAS, GD128/1/3/5, William Baillie to Helen Alves, Pondicherry, 10 Oct. 1779.

14 NAS, GD128/4/3/51, Eyre Coote to William Baillie, Fort St George, 4 Jan. 1779.

15 HAC, D456/A/4/15, General Bellecombe to William Baillie, Pondicherry, 24 March 1779.

16 Ibid., near Madras, 2 April 1779.

17 NAS, GD128/1/3, William Baillie to John Alves, 10 Oct. 1779.

18 Ibid., William Baillie to David Mitchell, 10 Oct. 1779.

19 "Reports from Committees of the House of Commons, vols. 7 & 8, East Indies: Carnatic War etc. [hereafter Reports from Committees], First Report, Minute of Charles Smith, 10 Nov. 1779, citing Robert Clive, October 1766, 240.

20 Reports from Committees, First Report, Hyder Ali to Thomas Rumbold, 17 Dec. 1779, 22.

21 Ibid., Madras Council to Hastings, 7 Feb. 1779, 214.

22 Campbell, "Lieutenant-Colonel William Baillie," 63. A pioneer is a soldier responsible for engineering and construction. Traditionally pioneer corps undertook the construction of field fortifications, military camps, roads, and bridges.

23 Reports from Committees, First Report, Madras to Warren Hastings, 7 Feb. 1779, 214.

24 Ibid., Fort St George to Court of Directors, 3 April 1780, 245.

25 Tilby, *British India 1600–1828*, 126.

26 Reports from Committees, First Report, Hyder Ali to Bazalet Jung, n.d., 24.

27 Ibid., Second Report, Meer Raza Aly Cawn to Colonel Harper, 30 July 1779, 508.

28 NAS, GD 128/1/1/20, Madras Council to Colonel Harper, Fort St George, 23 Aug. 1779.

29 Reports from Committees, First Report, Colonel Harper to Thomas Rumbold, 13 Nov. 1779, 235.

30 Ibid.

31 BL, OIOC, H/249, William Baillie to Thomas Rumbold, near Inacunda, 5 Dec. 1779, 450.

32 Ibid., 24 Dec. 1779, 452.

33 Ibid., Minute of the Select Committee, Madras, 30 Dec. 1779, 456.

34 Fraser-Mackintosh, *Letters of Two Centuries*, William Baillie to Nabob Ameer ul Omrah Bahadur, 7 Dec. 1779, 296.

35 Reports from Committees, First Report, Select Committee Madras to Bengal, Madras, 30 Oct. 1779, 25.

36 Thomson, *Memoirs of the Late Wars in Asia*, vol. 1, 89.

37 Malleson, *The Decisive Battles of India*, 233.

38 Reports from Committees, First Report, Nawab of Arcot to Madras Council, 25 Nov. 1779, 26.

39 NAS, GD 128/1/2, Item 4, Hector Munro to John Baillie, 27 March 1779.

40 HAC, D456/A/4/26, William Baillie's account with A. Brodie, Fort St George, 15 Nov. 1779.

41 HAC, D456/A/4/13, James Baillie to William Baillie, London, 4 Jan. 1779.

42 HAC, D456/A/9/8, William Baillie, Spanishtown, n.d.

43 Bulloch, *Genealogical and Historic Records of the Baillies of Inverness* ..., 9.

CHAPTER NINE

1 Munro, *A Narrative of the Military Operation on Coromandel Coast* ..., Letter IX, 97.

2 NAS, GD128/1/3/2, 3, 4, "Hyder Ali, Tipu Sultan, Battle of Pollilur," manuscript account, sent by an EIC officer to his brother, of his service in the Battle of Pollilur, 1.

3 Reports from the Committees, First Report, 24–26 July 1781, 4.

4 Munro, *A Narrative of the Military Operation on Coromandel Coast* ..., Letter X, 100–1.

5 Tilby, *British India 1600–1828*, 126.

6 Wylly, *A Life of Lieutenant-General Sir Eyre Coote KB*, 185–6.

7 Wilks, *History of Mysore*, 2.

8 Reports from the Committees, First Report, minute of 29 July 1781, 5.

9 Ibid.

10 Ibid., Lord Macleod to Madras Council, 1 Aug. 1780, 5.

11 Wilson, *History of the Madras Army*, vol. 2, 5.

12 Wilks, *History of Mysore*, 13.

13 Campbell, "Lieutenant Colonel William Baillie," 71.

14 BL, OIOC, H/150, Hector Munro to Lord Macleod, Fort St George, 13 Oct. 1780, 551.

15 Fraser-Mackintosh, "An Account of the Overthrow of Lieut.-Colonel Baillie's Detachment by Hyder Ali's Army on the 10th Sept. 1780," attributed to General Macleod, *Celtic Magazine*, 13, no. 2 (November 1876): 2, secretary of Mohammed Ali to William Baillie, Chepauk, 4 Sept. 1780.

16 John Baillie provided these figures in a letter to his father from Fort St George on 14 June 1784 (BL, OIOC, H/223, J, 155). Others gave different figures. Wilson stated that Tipu attacked with 40,000 horse and foot and 12 guns (*History of the Madras Army*, vol. 2, 6); Baird and Thomson referred to 30,000 cavalry, 8,000 infantry, and 12 guns (Hook, *The Life of General the Right Honourable Sir David Baird, Bart.*, vol. 1, 18); and an unknown soldier who became a prisoner of Hyder Ali cited "10,000 Foot, 15,000 horses and Guns" (NAS, GD128/1/3/2, 3, 4, "Hyder Ali, Tipu Sultan, Battle of Pollilur," 4).

17 NAS, GD128/1/3/1, 21.

18 BL, OIOC, H/223, John Baillie to his father, Fort St George, 14 June 1784, 158.

19 Wylly, *A Life of Lieutenant-General Sir Eyre Coote* KB, 236.

20 NAS, GD 128/1/2, Item 17, "An Account of the Overthrow of Lt. Col. Baillie's Detachment by Hyder Allie's Army," 28 Aug. 1781.

21 Ibid., Item 12, "An Account of the Overthrow of Col William Baillie's Army by Hyder Ali 10th Sep 1780," 1.

22 Ibid.

23 Fraser-Mackintosh, "An Account of the Overthrow of Lieut.-Colonel Baillie's Detachment," 3.

24 Parsons, *Seringapatam*, 124.

25 NAS, GD 128/1/2, Item 12, "An Account of the Overthrow of Col William Baillie's Army by Hyder Ali 10th Sep 1780."

26 Munro, *A Narrative of the Military Operation on Coromandel Coast …*, Letter XII, 150, 158–9.

27 BL, OIOC, H/233, Captain Richard Chase to Captain Merit, 26 Oct. 1785, 123.

28 Ibid., H/223, Francis Gowdie to Dr Gowdie, 31 Oct. 1783, 2.

29 NAS, GD 128/1/2, "An Account of the Overthrow of Col William Baillie's Army by Hyder Ali 10th Sep 1780."

30 Browne, *A History of the Highlands, and of the Highland Clans*, vol. 8, 4.

31 Fraser-Mackintosh, "An Account of the Overthrow of Lieut.-Colonel Baillie's Detachment," 4–6.

32 Thomson, *Memoirs of the Late War in Asia*, vol. 1, 161–2.

33 Hook, *The Life of General, the Right Honourable Sir David Baird, Bart.*, vol. 1, 24–5.

34 NAS, GD 128/1/2, Item 7, "An Account of the Action Fought the 10th September," 1.

35 BL, OIOC, H/223, John Baillie to his father, Fort St George, 14 June 1784, 161.

36 Ibid., H/211, Narrative of Hyder Ali's Battle from M. Wood, 246–7.

37 Wilks, *History of Mysore*, citing Francis Robson's *The Life of Hyder Ali*, 25–6.

38 BL, OIOC, H/150, 553, Hector Munro to secretary of war, Fort St George, 14 Oct. 1780.

39 Parsons, *Seringatpatam*, 106.

40 NAS, GD 128/1/3/2, 3, 7, 4, "Hyder Ali, Tipu Sultan, Battle of Pollilur," 7.

41 Thomson, *Memoirs of the Late War in Asia*, vol. 1, 167.

42 Reports from the Committees, First Report, Anthony Sadleir to Warren Hastings, Fort St George, 23 Sept. 1780, 75–6.

43 Ibid., H/150, Macleod to [?], 548.

44 Higginbotham, *Men Whom India Has Known*, 205.

45 Thomson, *Memoirs of the Late War in Asia*, vol. 2, 167–8.

46 NAS, GD 128/1/3/1, "On the 10th Sept'r."

47 Hook, *The Life of General, the Right Honourable Sir David Baird, Bart.*, vol. 1, 32.

48 NAS, GD 128/1/2, Item 11, Francis Baillie to John Alves, Fort St George, 28 Nov. 1780.

49 Fraser-Mackintosh, "An Account of the Overthrow of Lieut.-Colonel Baillie's Detachment," 4.

50 BL, OIOC, Mss Eur Orme 197, 150–1.

51 Munro, *A Narrative of the Military Operation on Coromandel Coast ...*, Letter XII, 155–6.

52 Ibid., 160.

53 Parsons, *Seringapatam*, quoting the Rev. Edmund Bull, 107.

54 NAS, GD 128/1/2, Item 7, "An Account of the Action Fought the 10th September," 3.

55 Buddle, *The Tiger and the Thistle*, 16.

56 Thomson, *Memoirs of the Late War in Asia*, vol. 1, 163.

CHAPTER TEN

1 Rafter, *Our Indian Army*, 157.

2 NAS, GD 128/1/2, Item 7, "An Account of the Action Fought the 10th September," 2.

3 Higginbotham, *Men Whom India Has Known*, John Lindsay's account of his imprisonment, 257.

4 Munro, *A Narrative of the Military Operation on Coromandel Coast ...*, Letter XII, 164–5.

5 BL, OIOC, H/223, John Baillie to his father, Fort St George, 14 June 1784, 165.

6 Higginbotham, *Men Whom India Has Known*, John Lindsay's account of his imprisonment, 258.

7 Ibid., 261–2.

8 Dalrymple, *The White Mughals*, 21.

9 BL, OIOC, H/223, John Baillie to his father, Fort St George, 14 June 1784, 179.

10 NAS, GD 128/1/3/1, p. 26.

11 Thomson, *Memoirs of the Late War in Asia*, vol. 2, 53–5.

12 BL, OIOC, IOR 354.541, "Selections 1772–85," vol. 2, 891.

13   HAC, D456/A/16/27, John Alves to William Baillie, Inverness, 8 Feb. 1781.

14   HAC, D456/A/16/28, John Alves to John Baillie, Inverness, 31 May 1781.

15   NAS, GD128/1/2/2, David Mitchell to William Baillie, London, 11 July 1782.

16   HAC, D456/A/16/29, Helen Alves to John Baillie, Inverness, 18 Jan. 1783.

17   NAS, GD128/4/3/35, John Alves to John Baillie, Inverness, 18 Jan. 1783.

18   Wylly, *A Life of Lieutenant-General Sir Eyre Coote K.B.*, 200.

19   Reports from the Committees, Third Report, Supreme Government to the Court of Directors, Calcutta, 29 Nov. 1780, 604.

20   Miford, *The Correspondence of Horace Walpole, Earl of Orford and the Rev. William Mason*, 166.

21   Colley, *Captives*, 271.

22   Brendon, *The Decline and Fall of the British Empire*, 61.

23   Thomson, *Memoirs of the Late War in Asia*, vol. 1, 188.

24   NAS, GD128/4/3/35, John Alves to John Baillie, Inverness, 18 Jan. 1783.

25   HAC, D456/A/5/8, "An Account of the Effects of the late Lieut. Baillie."

26   Thomson, *Memoirs of the Late War in Asia*, vol. 1, 200.

27   Wilks, *History of Mysore*, vol. 1, 122.

28   Wylly, *A life of Lieutenant-General Sir Eyre Coote* KB, 333.

29   HAC, D456/A/4/37, David Mitchell to William Baillie, London, 11 Sept. 1783.

30   NAS, GD128/1/4, Item 3, John Baillie to Spalding, n.d. [1785].

31   NAS, GD128/1/2, Item 1, Alexander Fraser to John Baillie, Seringapatam, 10 Jan. 1783.

32   Thomson, *Memoirs of the Late War in Asia*, vol. 1, 82.

33   NAS, GD128/1/4, Item 1, John Baillie to John Alves, n.d.

34   Wylly, *A Life of Lieutenant-General Sir Eyre Coote* KB, 374, quoting Lady Louisa Stuart.

35   NAS, GD128/1/4, Item 2, John Baillie to Brodie, Madras, 2 Feb. [presumably 1784].

36   Wylly, *A Life of Lieutenant-General Sir Eyre Coote* KB, 374.

37   Ibid. 374–5.

38   Munro, *A Narrative of the Military Operation on Coromandel Coast …*, Letter XVII, May 1784, 370.

39   NAS, GD128/1/4, Item 3, John Baillie to [?], Inverness.

40   Compton, *A Particular Account of the European Military Adventurers of Hindustan*, 49.

41   Dirom, *A Narrative of the Campaign in India Which Terminated the War with Tippoo Sultan in 1792*, 11.

42   Ibid., 188.

43   Buddle, *The Tiger and the Thistle*, 33.

44 Wilks, *History of Mysore*, vol. 2, 689.

45 Ibid., vol. 2, 743.

46 Chancey, *In the Company's Secret Service*, 122.

47 Ibid., 123.

CHAPTER ELEVEN

1 NAS, GD 128/1/4, Item 1, John Baillie to Stewart, n.d.

2 Ibid., Item 2, John Baillie to Alexander Godsman, n.d.

3 Ibid., Item 1, John Baillie to Stewart, n.d.

4 Will of William Baillie, Pondicherry, 28 July 1779.

5 NAS, GD 128/1/4, Item 3, John Baillie to Captain Cumming, n.d.

6 Ibid., Item 2, John Baillie to Archibald Campbell, n.d.

7 Ibid., Item 1, John Baillie to David Mitchell, Madras, 7 June 1783.

8 NAS, GD 128/1/13, Captain Grant to John Baillie, 30 June 1784, and GD 128/1/1/17, David Baird to John Baillie, Arcot, 3 July 1784.

9 NAS, GD 128/1/4, Item 2, John Baillie to David Mitchell, Madras, 5 Sept. 1783.

10 NAS, GD 128/1/4, Item 1, John Baillie to David Mitchell, Madras, 7 June 1783.

11 Ibid., John Baillie to Helen Alves, n.d.

12 Ibid., John Baillie to David Mitchell, Madras, 7 June 1783.

13 BL, OIOC, IOR, B/107, 20 Aug. 1788.

14 Ibid., 4 June 1788.

15 Fraser-Mackintosh, "Minor Highland Families," 149.

16 NAS, GD 128/4/3/29, Margaret Baillie to Isabella Campbell, Inverness, 3 June 1786.

17 NAS, GD 128/1/4, Item 3, John Baillie to Doctor Spalding, Inverness, n.d. [1785].

18 Ibid., Item 1, John Baillie to John Alves, n.d.

19 Fraser-Mackintosh, *Antiquarian Notes, Historical, Genealogical and Social*, 37.

20 HAC, D456/A/10/3, William Ford to Alexander Godsman, Inverness, 4 Dec. 1790.

21 HAC, D456/A/13/3, Isabella Baillie to the freeholders of Inverness, 1809.

22 HAC, D456/A/10/21, William Ford to John Baillie, 1 March 1794.

23 HAC, D456/B/16/10, Duke of Gordon to John Baillie, Elsmont House, September 1795.

24 HAC, D456/A/10/16, Archibald Campbell to John Baillie, Budgate, 19 March 1793.

25 HAC, D456/A/10/27, Keith Macalister to Alexander Macalister, Inverness, 14 June 1794.

26 HAC, D456/A/10/17, John Woodford to John Baillie of Dunain, Aberdeen, 14 April 1793.

27 HAC, D456/A/10/29, William Gordon to John Baillie of Dunain, Camp, 5 July 1794.

28 Ibid.

29 HAC, D456/A/10/33, Duke of Gordon to John Baillie, Gordon Castle, 7 Nov. 1794.

30 HAC, D456/B/21/2, Duke of Gordon to John Baillie, Edinburgh, 27 Feb. 1795.

31 HAC, D456/A/13/3, Isabella Baillie to the freeholders of Inverness, 1809.

32 Ibid.

33 Ibid.

34 HAC, D456/A/31/1, William Baillie to Isabella Baillie, Edinburgh, 18 April 1806.

35 HAC, D456/A/55/2, Donald Macleod to Isabella Baillie, Glasgow, 19 April 1806.

36 HAC, D456/A/40/1, John Gibson to Isabella Baillie, Musselburgh, 6 May 1804.

37 HAC, D456/A/31/3, William Baillie to Isabella Baillie, Edinburgh, 24 June 1806.

38 HAC, D456/A/40/3, Ann Gibson to Isabella Baillie, Calcutta, 10 Feb. 1808.

39 HAC, D456/A/40/5, John Gibson to Isabella Baillie, Arrah, 14 Nov. 1811.

40 HAC, D456/A/40/7, Ann Gibson to Isabella Baillie, Arrah, 22 July 1812.

41 HAC, D456/A/40/13, Margaret Baillie to Isabella Baillie, London, n.d.

42 HAC, D456/A/40/12, John Baillie to Isabella Baillie, London, n.d.

43 HAC, D456/A/30/23, Margaret Baillie to Isabella Baillie, London, 18 Feb. 1825.

44 HAC, D456/A/40/9, Opinion of Sir S. Sheperd, 31 Jan. 1826.

45 HAC, D456/A/23/53, Statement prepared by Anne Baillie, n.d.

46 HAC, D456/A/40/10, John Baillie to Anne Baillie, London, 27 Jan. 1827.

CHAPTER TWELVE

1 HAC, D456/A/55/7, Donald Macleod to Isabella Baillie, Edinburgh, 19 May 1808.

2 HAC, D456/A/13/1, Charles Grant to Isabella Baillie, London, 22 June 1808.

3 HAC, D456/A/17/5, Archibald Alves to Isabella Baillie, London, 20 Jan. 1810.

4　HAC, D456/A/30/1, Margaret Baillie to Isabella Baillie, Inverness, 19 May 1809.

5　HAC, D456/A/31/7, William Baillie to Archibald Baillie, Kilravock Castle, 29 July 1809.

6　HAC, D456/A/26/5, Archibald Baillie to Isabella Baillie, London, 28 Aug. 1809.

7　Ibid., Donald Macleod to Isabella Baillie, London, 28 Aug. 1809.

8　HAC, D456/A/31/8, William Baillie to Archibald Baillie, Budgate, 6 March 1810.

9　HAC, D456/A/17/5, Archibald Alves to Isabella Baillie, London, 20 Jan. 1810.

10　HAC, D456/A/31/12, William Baillie to Isabella Baillie, London, 2 March 1811.

11　HAC, D456/A/55/5, Donald Macleod to Isabella Baillie, Edinburgh, 30 June 1807.

12　HAC, D456/A/7/2, State of the debts, receipts, and expenditures of Dunain, 3 Sept. 1807.

13　HAC, D456/A/55/7, Donald Macleod to Isabella Baillie, Edinburgh, 19 May 1808.

14　HAC, D456/A/40/6, Ann Gibson to Isabella Baillie, Arrah, 26 Feb. 1812.

15　HAC, D456/A/31/47, William Baillie to Charles Grant, n.d. [1810].

16　HAC, D456/A/31/10, William Baillie to Isabella Baillie, London, 16 Jan. 1811.

17　HAC, D456/A/30/5, Margaret Baillie to Isabella Baillie, London, 12 Jan. 1811.

18　HAC, D456/A/55/14, Donald Macleod to Isabella Baillie, Edinburgh, 26 Jan. 1811.

19　HAC, D456/A/31/11 William Baillie to Isabella Baillie, London, 4 Feb. 1811.

20　HAC, D456/A/31/12, William Baillie to Isabella Baillie, London, 2 March 1811.

21　HAC, D456/A/40/5, John Gibson to Isabella Baillie, Arrah, 14 Nov. 1811.

22　HAC, D456/A/31/17, William Baillie to Isabella Baillie, Bombay, 22 Oct. 1811.

23　HAC, D456/A/40/7, Ann Gibson to Isabella Baillie, Arrah, 22 July 1812.

24　HAC, D456/A/31/22, James Calder to [?], Bombay, 28 Oct. and 22 Dec. 1813.

25　Ibid.

26　HAC, D456/A/17/6, Archibald Alves to Isabella Baillie, London, 8 June 1814.

27 HAC, D456/A/27/11, Isabella Baillie to John Baillie, Dunain, 1814.

28 HAC, D456/A/8/5, N. Smith to Isabella Baillie, London, 11 Sept. 1814.

29 HAC, D456/A/48/5, James Calder to Isaac Ketchen, Bombay, 23 June 1815.

30 Ibid., 20 Nov. 1815.

31 HAC, D456/A/48/5, James Calder to Isaac Ketchen, Bombay, 23 June 1815.

32 BL, OIOC, B/161, Court of Directors, 16 June 1815, 233.

33 HAC, D456/A/7/4, Isabella Baillie to Court of Directors, Inverness, n.d.

34 HAC, D456/A/8/17, Macarthur to Isabella Baillie, 9 Oct. 1815.

35 HAC, D456/A/28/21, Katharine Rose to Isabella Baillie, n.d.

36 HAC, D456/A/17/1, Archibald Alves to Isabella Baillie, 17 May 1809.

37 HAC, D456/A/40/12, John Baillie to Isabella Baillie, London, n.d.

38 HAC, D456/A/17/24, Archibald Alves to Isabella Baillie, London, 23 Dec. 1829.

39 Ibid.

40 HAC, D456/A30/30, Margaret Baillie to Isabella Baillie, London, 9 July 1828.

41 HAC, D456/A/13/11, Lord Cawdor to Isabella Baillie, Castle Howard, 14 Jan. 1816.

42 HAC, D456/A/39/15, Sarah Fraser to Isabella Baillie, Dunain, 14 July 1829.

43 Ibid.

44 HAC, D456/A/30/47, Margaret Baillie to Isabella Baillie, London, n.d.

45 HAC, D456/A/19/18, Anne Arbuthnot to Isabella Baillie, 14 Feb. 1826.

46 HAC, D456/A/27/29, Isabella Baillie to Anne Baillie, Edinburgh, 30 Jan. 1821.

47 HAC, D456/A/ 53/6, Thomas Mackenzie to Anne Baillie, Edinburgh, 5 March 1832, and John Baillie to Thomas Mackenzie, London, 1 March 1832.

48 HAC, D456/A/15/61, Anne Baillie to Thomas Mackenzie, n.d.

49 HAC, D456/A/17/24, Archibald Alves to Isabella Baillie, London, 23 Dec. 1829.

CHAPTER THIRTEEN

1 NAS, GD128/1/4, Item 3, John Baillie to Alexander Baillie, n.d. [1785].

2 Ibid., John Baillie to Alexander Fraser, n.d. [1785].

3 Ibid., John Baillie to Colonel Stuart, n.d. [1785].

4 Ibid., John Baillie to Spalding, n.d. [1785]

5 Ibid., John Baillie to Spalding, Inverness, n.d. [1789].

6 Ibid., John Baillie to Alexander Baillie, Inverness, n.d. [1789].

7 BL, OIOC, L/MIL/9/130, John Baillie to Dr Spalding, n.d. [1785].

8 HAC, D456/A/40/3, Ann Gibson to Isabella Baillie, Calcutta, 10 Feb. 1808.

9 Ibid., D456/A/30/2, Margaret Baillie to Isabella Baillie, Inverness, 10 June 1809.

10 Wilson, *History of the Madras Army*, vol. 3, 169.

11 BL, OIOC, IOR E/4/895, Governor-in-Council, Fort St George, Court Minute, 5 June 1805.

12 HAC, D456/A/30/19, Margaret Baillie to Isabella Baillie, London, 9 Nov. 1822.

13 HAC, D456/A/23/20, Anne Baillie to Isabella Baillie, Rectory, St Luke's, 1 July 1830.

14 PRO, Cat. Ref. 11/2200, pgs. 78–80, Will of Lt.-Col. Alexander Baillie, dated 16 Feb. 1842, written in Edinburgh, and sealed in London with a codicil dated 17 Dec. 1850.

15 HAC, D456/A/23/14, Anne Baillie to Isabella Baillie, St Luke's Rectory, 5 April 1830; and D456/A/23/11, Anne Baillie to Isabella Baillie, St Luke's Rectory, 25 Jan. 1830.

16 PRO, Will of Lt.-Col. Alexander Baillie.

17 Ibid.

18 Higginbotham, *Men Whom India Has Known*, 8.

19 HAC, D456/A/39/16, Sarah Fraser to Isabella Baillie, Dunain, 26 Nov. 1829.

20 HAC, D456/A/20/5, Alexander Charles Baillie to Isabella Baillie, 2 May 1831.

21 HAC, D456/A/20/7, Alexander Charles Baillie to Isabella Baillie, 9 Nov. 1831.

CHAPTER FOURTEEN

1 NAS, GD128/4/3/45, John Baillie to James Fraser, Dunain, n.d.

2 HAC, D456/A10/48, invoice from Alexander Mackintosh to John Baillie n.d.

3 Fraser-Mackintosh, *Letters of Two Centuries*, 321–5.

4 Chancey, *In the Company's Secret Service*, 27.

5 BL, OIOC, F/4/35/913.

6 Ibid., F/4/35/2445.

7 Ibid., F/4/35/913, "Extract of Bengal Public Consultations 26th Jan'y 1798," minute by Governor General Shore.

8 Chancey *In the Company's Secret Service*, 150–1 quoting BL, OIOC, Mss. EUR F/228-9, N.B. Edmonstone to William Kirkpatrick, Calcutta, 1 May 1801.

9   Chancey, *In the Company's Secret Service*, 151.

10 Ibid., 170, quoting BL, OIOC, "Secret Consultations on the Mahrattas," f.503, Richard Wellesley to Gerard Lake, 24 Sept. 1803.

11 Pinch, *Warrior Ascetics and Indian Empires*, 133.

12 Ibid., John Baillie to Graeme Mercer, 14 Dec. 1803, 137.

13 Ibid., Graeme Mercer to John Baillie, 30 March 1804, 138.

14 Ibid., 138–9; BL, OIOC, "Bengal Secret and Political Consultations," John Baillie to Graeme Mercer, 4 June 1804.

15 Ibid., p. 140, no. 234, John Baillie to Graeme Mercer, 6 June 1804.

16 Martin, ed., *The Despatches, Minutes and Correspondence of the Marquess Wellesley*, vol. 4, Gerard Lake to Wellesley, Camp Hindoun, 28 May 1804, 74–5.

17 Ibid., Wellesley to Gerard Lake, Fort William, 8 June 1804, 83.

18 Chancey, *In the Company's Secret Service*, N.B. Edmonstone to John Baillie, Calcutta, 2 Feb. 1804, 171.

19 Martin, ed., *The Despatches, Minutes and Correspondence of the Marquess Wellesley*, vol. 4, Wellesley to the Court of Directors, Fort William, 15 June 1804, 128.

20 Higginbotham, *Men Whom India Has Known*, 15.

21 BL, OIOC, H/636, 169–75.

22 BL, OIOC, H/491, no. 246, 181–2, John Baillie to Graeme Mercer.

23 Ibid., 181, General Lake to [?], camp near Soorut, 11 Feb. 1804.

24 Pinch, *Warrior Ascetics and Indian Empires*, 137.

25 BL, OIOC, Z/P, John Baillie to [?], 18 Dec. 1806.

26 *The East India Military Calendar*, Sir George Barlow to Court of Directors, 1 May 1807, 64–70.

CHAPTER FIFTEEN

1   "The East India Military Calendar," Sir George Barlow to Court of Directors, 1 May 1807, 64–70.

2   BL, OIOC, F/4/216/4747, John Baillie to Richardson, 1807, no. 2.

3   Ibid., no. 7.

4   Ibid., no. 8, 109.

5   Ibid., no. 10, 110.

6   Ibid., no. 16, 113–14.

7   Ibid., no. 20, 119.

8   Chancey, *In the Company's Secret Service*, 28.

9   Munro, *A Narrative of the Military Operation*, Letter V, 49–51.

10 Chancey, *In the Company's Secret Service*, 28.

11 Dalrymple, *White Mughals*, 40.

12 HAC, D456/A/40/5, John Gibson to Isabella Baillie, Arrah, 14 Nov. 1811.
13 Cambridge University Library, Elmore Papers, Mss. 7616/3/1, concerning a passage in "The Early life of N.B.E. in India" by Marmaduke Edmonstone Browne.
14 Ibid.
15 Ibid., Margaret Baillie to N.B. Edmonstone, Inverness, 23 May 1811.
16 Ibid., 17 July 1812.
17 Ibid., Margaret Baillie to N.B. Edmonstone, Inverness, 28 Aug. 1813.
18 Ibid., Margaret Baillie to Sir Charles Edmonstone, 17 Sept. 1813.
19 Ibid., Margaret Baillie to Sir Charles Edmonstone, Inverness, 7 Sept. 1813.
20 Ibid., 11 Oct. 1813.
21 Ibid., Margaret Baillie to Charles Edmonstone, Inverness, 18 Dec. 1813.
22 Ibid., Margaret Baillie to N.B. Edmonstone, Inverness, 4 Feb. 1814.
23 Ibid., Margaret Baillie to Charles Edmonstone, Inverness, 29 May 1815.
24 Ibid., Margaret Baillie to N.B. Edmonstone, London, 22 July 1816.
25 John Baillie to N.B. Edmonstone, London, 22 July 1816.
26 Ibid., London, 25 Jan. 1817.

CHAPTER SIXTEEN

1 Llewelyn-Jones, ed., *Lucknow*, 89.
2 Lane-Poole, *Aurangzeb and the Decay of the Mughal Empire*, 19.
3 Pemble, *The Raj, the Indian Mutiny and the Kingdom of Oudh*, 33.
4 Llewelyn-Jones, *A Fatal Friendship*, 99.
5 *Appendix to the Report from the Select Committee of the House of Commons on the Affairs of the East-India Company 16th August 1832 and Minutes of Evidence*, no. 6, point 5, p. 25–6.
6 Mitchell, *Reminiscences of My Life in the Highlands*, vol. 1, 60.
7 Cambridge University Library, Elmore Papers, Mss. 7616/3/1, "The Baillies of Leys," 56.
8 Since writing this manuscript, I have become aware of an affidavit (BL, OIOC, IOR/J/1/43) dated 18 July 1827 wherein Colonel John stated, "I John Baillie do make oath and swear that Mary Martin or Baillie, the mother of my son John Wilson Baillie was the offspring of European parents to the best of my knowledge and belief and was so believed and declared to be by her adoptive parents in India." On that evidence, it would seem reasonable to conclude that Mary Martin was, indeed, the mother of John Wilson. However, the painting of *The Three Children of Colonel John Baillie of Leys and His Wife the Begum of Oude*, which, judging by the ages of the children, must have been commissioned by John shortly after his return to Britain in 1816, raises the question of why, if a

woman of European extraction was the parent of one or all of the three children, John would present his offspring as Anglo-Indian in a society in which mixed race was a decided disadvantage. Furthermore, if he was actually married to Mary Martin, D.R. Fisher in *The History of Parliament* would have had little cause to describe John's children as "bastards." On the other hand, by the time of the 1827 affidavit there was a clear incentive to present John Wilson as fully "European" given the prohibition on Anglo-Indian sons entering the employ of the EIC. Could John have persuaded Mary Martin, who, as we have seen, remained close to John and may well have been his mistress in Britain, to allow her name to be used to secure John Wilson's EIC appointment?

Whether or not the Begum of Oude was the mother of John Wilson, I am convinced she gave birth to the two girls and was the woman John regarded as his de facto and perhaps de jure wife. His designated heirs were not his eldest sons but the children attributed to the Begum of Oude, John Wilson and, following his death, Anne. Indeed, Anne travelled to Lucknow as a young adult and I am able to envisage little reason for such a trip in that era other than to visit her mother.

If the Begum of Oude was the mother of Anne, John Wilson, and Henrietta and the probable wife of Colonel John, who was Mary Martin and what was her relationship to John? In view of the affidavit, we can be reasonably certain that she was an orphan of European parentage, adopted by a couple of the same ilk, and that she lived in Lucknow at the time of John Wilson's birth in 1811. Otherwise, Colonel John's 1827 affidavit would have no credibility. In that regard, a distant cousin, Alan Tritton, has found in the Bengal baptism register a Mary Martin baptized 12 November 1781 by her parents, Robert Martin and Mary of no surname. If that is our Mary Martin, she would have been thirty years of age when John Wilson was born. Whatever her relationship with John, I do not believe they ever married as, in his will, John referred to her as the "widow of John Chalcroft," whereas had they ever been married, it would have been much more natural to refer to Mary Martin as his wife or former wife and a distinct advantage to John Wilson to have his "European" ancestry acknowledged. There was undoubtedly an intimate connection with Mary Martin as attested by the citation in the British Army List, the petition on behalf of John Wilson, and the meaningful legacy from John.

9   Chancey, *In the Company's Secret Service*, 27.

10   HAC, D456/A/31/9, William Baillie to Isabella Baillie, London, 24 Dec. 1810.

11   HAC, D456/A/31/10, William Baillie to Isabella Baillie, London, 16 Jan. 1811.

12   HAC, D456/A/30/5, Margaret Baillie to Isabella Baillie, London, 12 Jan. 1811.

13 HAC, D456/A/40/6, Ann Gibson to Isabella Baillie, Arrah, 26 Feb. 1812.

14 *Appendix to the Report from the Select Committee of the House of Commons on the Affairs of the East-India Company*, no. 26, point 3, p. 415.

15 Ibid., point 33, p. 421.

16 Ibid., point 21, 1st, p. 418.

17 Ibid., point 140, p. 450.

18 *Oriental Herald & Journal of General Literature*, 7, no. 22 (October–December 1825): 321.

19 *Appendix to the Report from the Select Committee of the House of Commons on the Affairs of the East-India Company*, no. 26, point 48, p. 424.

20 Ibid., point 116, p. 445.

21 Ibid., point 27, p. 420.

22 Ibid., point 150, p. 452.

23 Ibid., point 153, p. 453.

24 *Oriental Herald & Journal of General Literature*, 7, no. 22 (October–December 1825): 327.

25 Pemble, *The Raj, the Indian Mutiny and the Kingdom of Oude*, 62.

26 *Oriental Herald & Journal of General Literature*, 7, no. 22 (October–December 1825): 410.

27 *The East India Military Calendar*, Extract of a Minute of the Right Hon. the Earl of Minto, 5 March 1813, 70–1.

28 BL, OIOC, B/161, Court of Directors, 9 June 1815, 200.

CHAPTER SEVENTEEN

1 Later in life, the new governor general became the Marquess of Hastings but he was titled Lord Moira during his years in India.

2 Tilby, *British India 1600–1828*, 187.

3 Pemble, *Britain's Gurkha War and the Invasion of Nepal*, 48.

4 Ibid., 249.

5 *Papers regarding the Administration of the Marquess of Hastings in India*, 23 Nov. 1814, 395.

6 BL, OIOC, "Extract [of] Political Letter from the Governor-General dated 15th August 1815," para. 6, 45.

7 Ibid., "Extract [of] Bengal Political Consultations the 26th July 1814," John Baillie to Lord Moira, 12 July 1814, para. 7, 45–6.

8 Ibid., "Extract [of] Political Letter from the Governor-General dated 15th August 1815," John Baillie to Lord Moira, Lucknow, 23 July 1814, para. 2, 130.

9 Ibid., John Baillie to Lord Moira, Lucknow, 15 July 1814, para. 4, 66.

10 Ibid., para. 2, 3.
11 *Oriental Herald and Journal of General Literature*, 7, no. 22 (October–December 1825): 311.
12 Ibid., 423.
13 Ibid.
14 Ibid., 423–4.
15 BL, OIOC, "Extract [of] Political Letter from the Governor-General dated 15th August 1815," para. 9, 3.
16 Ibid., para. 11, 5.
17 Pemble, *The Raj, the Indian Mutiny, and the Kingdom of Oude*, 79.
18 BL, OIOC, "Extract [of] Political Letter from the Governor-General dated 15th August 1815," para. 11, 10.
19 Pemble, *The Raj, the Indian Mutiny and the Kingdom of Oude*, 78.
20 BL, OIOC, H/638, Refaut-ood-Dowla to John Baillie, Lucknow, 4 Aug. 1814, 609–11.
21 *Oriental Herald and Journal of General Literature*, 7, no. 22 (October–December 1825): 416.
22 BL, OIOC, "Removal of Lt. Col: Baillie from the Office of Resident at Lucknow," Lord Moira to Court of Directors, 30 March 1816, point 44.
23 Ibid., point 158.
24 *Papers respecting a Reform in the Administration of the Government of his Excellency the Nawaub Vizier ...*, John Baillie to C.M. Ricketts, Lucknow, 8 June 1815, 1007.
25 Ibid., 1006.
26 Ibid., C.M. Ricketts to John Baillie, Futtygurh, 29 June 1815, 1007.
27 *Oriental Herald and Journal of General Literature*, 7, no. 22 (October–December 1825): 406.
28 Ibid., 405; *Papers respecting a Reform in the Administration of the Government of His Excellency the Nawaub Vizier ...*, Report signed C.M. Ricketts, Lucknow, 2 Nov. 1814, 876.
29 Ibid., Captain McLeod's Statement, 900.
30 Llewelyn-Jones, ed., *Lucknow*, 196, quoting BL, IOR [OIOC], Bengal Political Consultations, 7 March 1815, no. 16.
31 *Oriental Herald and Journal of General Literature*, 7, no. 22 (October–December 1825): 407.
32 *Papers respecting a Reform in the Administration of the Government of His Excellency the Nawaub Vizier ...*, Refaut-ood-Dowla to John Baillie, Lucknow, 7 March 1815, 900.
33 *Oriental Herald and Journal of General Literature*, 7, no. 22 (October–December 1825): 406.

34 Ibid., 411.
35 BL, OIOC, "Removal of Lt. Col: Baillie from the Office of Resident at Lucknow," Lord Moira to Court of Directors, Fort William, 30 March 1816, point 61.
36 Ibid., Moira's note of 30 Nov. 1814, point 74.
37 *Papers respecting a Reform in the Administration of the Government of His Excellency the Nawaub Vizier …*, John Adam to John Baillie, Fort William, 13 Oct. 1815, 964.
38 BL, OIOC, "Removal of Lt. Col: Baillie from the Office of Resident at Lucknow," Lord Moira to Court of Directors, Fort William, 20 Jan. 1816.
39 *Oriental Herald and Journal of General Literature*, 7, no. 22 (October–December 1825): 410.
40 BL, OIOC, "Removal of Lt. Col: Baillie from the Office of Resident at Lucknow," Lord Moira to Court of Directors, Fort William, 30 March 1816, point 46.
41 Ibid., point 109.
42 Pemble, *The Raj, the Indian Mutiny, and the Kingdom of Oude*, Agha Meer to Braddock, 30 Sept. 1831, 67.
43 BL, OIOC, "Removal of Lt. Col: Baillie from the Office of Resident at Lucknow," Moira to Court of Directors, point 3, Fort William, 20 Jan. 1816.
44 Ibid., point 44.
45 Ibid.

CHAPTER EIGHTEEN

1 BL, OIOC, B/166, 1090.
2 HAC, D456/A/30/33, Margaret Baillie to Isabella Baillie, Ballmare, 29 Dec. 1829.
3 Cambridge University Library, Elmore Letters, Mss. 7616, John Baillie to N.B. Edmonstone, London, 22 July 1816.
4 Ibid., Margaret Baillie to N.B. Edmonstone, Inverness, 29 May 1815.
5 HAC, D456/A/30/47, Margaret Baillie to Isabella Baillie, London, n.d.
6 Mitchell, *Reminiscences of My Life in the Highlands*, vol. 1, 58.
7 *Oriental Herald and Colonial Review*, 2, no. 5 (May–August 1824): 143.
8 HAC, D456/A/30/14, Margaret Baillie to Isabella Baillie London, 28 Jan. 1818.
9 HAC, D456/A/30/16, Margaret Baillie to Isabella Baillie, London, 20 April 1818.

10 HAC, D456/A/30/23, Margaret Baillie to Isabella Baillie, London, 18 Feb. 1825.

11 HAC, D456/A/30/30, Margaret Baillie to Isabella Baillie, London, 9 July [1828].

12 HAC, D456/A/30/31, Margaret Baillie to Isabella Baillie, London, 31 Dec. 1828.

13 HAC, D456/A/62/1, Hugh Rose to Isabella Baillie, Shahjahanpore, 24 May 1831.

14 BL, OIOC, B/164, John Baillie to Court of Directors, London, 3 March 1817.

15 Cambridge University Library, Elmore Letters, Mss. 7616, John Baillie to N.B. Edmonstone, London, 15 Jan. 1817.

16 HAC, D456/A/30/14, Margaret Baillie to Isabella Baillie, London, 28 Jan. 1818.

17 *Asiatic Journal and Monthly Register*, 4 (July–September 1817): 633.

18 Casey, John Baillie Bibliography, in Fisher, *The History of Parliament*, quoting the Hull *Advertiser*, 20 Sept. 1817, 23 May 1818; House of Commons *Debates*, 1790–1820, 2: 446.

19 HAC, D456/A/29/49, John Baillie to Isabella Baillie, London, 5 March [1822].

20 HAC, D456/A/42/8, Alexander Grant to Isabella Baillie, Cawdor, 8 Jan. 1819.

21 HAC, D456/A/29/49, John Baillie to Isabella Baillie, London, 5 March [1822].

22 HAC, D456/A/29/56, John Baillie to Isabella, London, 25 December [1822].

23 BL, OIOC, Mss. EUR, f.176, John Baillie to George Barlow, London, 21 July 1821, 23.

24 BL, OIOC, Mss. EUR, f.176, Resolutions dated 13 Aug. 1822, 13.

25 Ibid., 14.

26 HAC, D456/A/30/19, Margaret Baillie to Isabella Baillie, London, 9 Nov. 1822.

27 BL, OIOC, Mss. EUR, f.176, John Baillie to George Barlow, 7 Nov. 1822, 19.

28 HAC, D456/A/30/20, Margaret Baillie to Isabella Baillie, London, 1 May 1823.

29 *Oriental Herald and Journal of General Literature*, 7, no. 22 (October–December 1825): 563.

30 Ibid.

31 *Asiatic Journal and Monthly Register*, 8 (July–December 1819): 53.

32 *Oriental Herald and Journal of General Literature*, 4, no. 13 (January–March 1825), Moira's minute of 15 July 1820, 407.

33 Ibid., Lord Moira to Sir William Rumbold, 4 Jan. 1825, 436.

34 Ibid., Oath of Sir William Rumbold, 457.

35 Ibid., Court of Directors to Lord Moira, 28 Nov. 1821, 407.

36 Kaye, *The Life and Correspondence of Henry St. George Tucker* ..., 396.

37 Ibid., 409.

38 *Oriental Herald and Journal of General Literature*, 4, no. 13 (January–March 1825): 399.

39 Ibid., 2, no. 5 (May–August 1824): 35.

40 Ibid., 49.

CHAPTER NINETEEN

1 HAC, D456/A/30/31, Margaret Baillie to Isabella Baillie, London, 31 Dec. 1828.

2 Casey, John Baillie Bibliography, in Fisher, *The History of Parliament*, quoting from NAS, GD23/6/573/10; Inverness *Courier*, 25 Aug. 1830.

3 HAC, D456/A/29/68, John Baillie to Isabella Baillie, Inverness, n.d.

4 Barrow, *The Mirror of Parliament*, vol. 1, 1831, 503.

5 M.M. Stuart, "The Baillies of Leys," *Scottish Genealogist*, vol. 28 (1981), journal 2, 54.

6 *Appendix to the Report from the Select Committee of the House of Commons on the Affairs of the East-India Company 16th August 1832 and Minutes of Evidence*, 26–7.

7 Ibid., 26.

8 Barrow, *The Mirror of Parliament*, vol. 1, 1831, 40.

9 Casey, John Baillie Bibliography, in Fisher, *The History of Parliament*, quoting from NAS, GD23/6/614/8/11, Inverness *Courier*, 27 April and 11 May 1831.

10 Munro, *Recollections of Inverness by an Invernessian*, 41.

11 Mitchell, *Reminiscences of My Life in the Highlands*, vol. 1, 59.

12 BL, OIOC, J/2/5, "Report by Neil B.J. Edmonstone and John Baillie," India House, 31 July 1826, 279.

13 HAC, D456/A/29/69, John Baillie to Anne Baillie, London, 25 Dec. [1832]. In 1834 D.H. Mackenzie, the corrupt factor of the Baillies of Leys, fled Scotland with between £400 and £500 of Isabella's estate. HA, D456/A/45/17.

14 BL, OIOC, L/AG/34/29, 477–504,Will of John Baillie of Leys, County of Inverness and of Devonshire Place in the Parish of Saint Marylebone in the County of Middlesex, 11 May 1833.

15 Mitchell, *Reminiscences of My Life in the Highlands*, vol. 1, 60.

16 Ibid., 60–1.

17 HAC, D456/A/22/49, Anne Baillie to Isabella Baillie, Rectory, St Luke's, 31 December [no year].

18 HAC, D456/A/47/49, Isabella Innes to Anne Baillie, Edinburgh, 21 Dec. 1855.

19 HAC, D456/A/54/75, N. McLean to Anne Baillie, Inverness, 25 Sept. 1857.

Bibliography

PRIMARY SOURCES

Archival Resources

British Library (BL). India Office Records, Oriental and India Office Collection (OIOC). London.
Cambridge University Library. Elmore Papers. Cambrigde.
Highland Archive Centre (HAC). Inverness.
National Archives of Scotland (NAS). Edinburgh.

Printed Documents, Journals, Contemporary Accounts

Aitchison, C.U. *A Collection of Treaties, Engagements, and Sunnuds, relating to India and Neighbouring Countries.* Vol. 3. Calcutta: P.M. Cranenburgh, Bengal Printing Company 1863.
Appendix to the Report from the Select Committee of the House of Commons on the Affairs of the East-India Company 16th August 1832 and Minutes of Evidence, nos. 6 and 26. London: J.L. Cox and Son 1833.
Asiatic Journal, January 1821. London: Cox and Baylis.
Asiatic Journal and Monthly Register for British India and Its Dependencies, vol. 4 (July–September 1817); vol. 6 (June–December 1818); vol. 8 (July–December 1819); vol. 10 (July–December 1820); vol. 16 (July–December 1823). London: Black et al.
Auber, Peter. *Rise and Progress of British Power in India.* London: W.H. Allen and Company 1837.
Barrow, John Henry. *The Mirror of Parliament.* Vol. 1. London: William Clowes 1831.

Broom, Arthur. *History of the Rise and Progress of the Bengal Army*. London: W. Thacker and Company 1850.

Browne, James. *A History of the Highlands, and of the Highland Clans; with an Extensive Selection from the Hitherto Unedited Stuart Papers*. Vol. 3. Glasgow: A. Fullarton and Company 1838.

Burke, Sir Bernard. *A History of the Landed Gentry of Great Britain and Ireland*. Vol. 1. London: Harrison 1871.

Calcutta Magazine and Monthly Register. Vol. 4 (1830). Calcutta: Samuel Smith and Company.

Celtic Magazine. Vol. 13. No. 2 (November 1876). Inverness: A. & W. Mackenzie.

Compton, Herbert. *A Particular Account of the European Military Adventurers of Hindustan*. London: T. Fisher Unwin 1892.

Copies of Papers relative to the Restoration of the King of Tanjore, the Arrest of the Right Hon. George Lord Pigot, and the Removal of His Lordship from the Government of Fort St. George, by Sundry Members of the Council. Vol. 1 (1777).

Dirom, Major. *A Narrative of the Campaign in India Which Terminated the War with Tippoo Sultan in 1792*. London, 1793.

Dodwell, Edward, and James Samuel Miles. *Alphabetical List of the Officers of the Indian Army*. London: Longman et al. 1838.

Duff, James Grant. *A History of the Mahrattas*. Vols. 2 and 3. London: Longman et al. 1826.

The East India Military Calendar; containing the Services of General and Field Officers of the Indian Army. Vol. 1 (1823); vol. 2 (1824); vol. 3 (1826). London: Kingsbury, Parbury, and Allen 1823 (OIR 335.321).

Extract of Bengal Public Consultations. British Library.

Fisher, D.R. *The History of Parliament: The House of Commons 1820–1832*. Cambridge: Cambridge University Press 2009. Includes John Baillie Bibliography by Martin Casey.

Fraser-Mackintosh, Charles. *Antiquarian Notes regarding Families and Places in the Highlands*. Inverness: Advertiser Office 1865.

– *Antiquarian Notes, Historical, Genealogical and Social on Inverness-shire*. 2nd Series. Inverness: A. and W. Mackenzie 1897.

– *Letters of Two Centuries*. Inverness: A. and W. Mackenzie 1890.

– *Minor Highland Families No. XI: The Baillies of Dunain*. Inverness, 1898.

– *Minor Sects of Clan Chattan*. Glasgow, 1896.

Grant, John, and William Leslie. *A Survey of the Province of Moray: Historical, Geographical, and Political*. Aberdeen: Isaac Forsyth 1798.

Grierson, H.J.C., ed. *The Letters of Sir Walter Scott 1819–1821*. Vol. 6. London: Constable 1934.

Higginbotham, J.J. *Men Whom India Has Known.* 2nd ed. Madras: Higginbotham and Company 1874.

Hodges, William. *Travels in India during the Years 1780, 1781, 1782 and 1783.* Sold by J. Edwards, London, 1794.

Home, John. *The History of the Rebellion in Scotland in 1745.* Edinburgh: Peter Brown 1822.

Hook, Theodore Edward. *The Life of General the Right Honourable Sir David Baird, Bart.* Vols. 1 and 2. London, 1832.

Houston, R.A. *Scottish Literacy and the Scottish Identity: Illiteracy and Society in Scotland and Northern England, 1600–1800.* Cambridge: Cambridge University Press, 2002.

"Hyder Ali; Tipu Sultan; Battle of Pollilur." Manuscript account, c. 1780, by an officer of the East India Company describing his service in the Battle of Pollilur.

Johnstone, G. *Account of the Late Discontent of the Madras Establishment.* London, 1809.

Kaye, John William. *The Life and Correspondence of Henry St. George Tucker, Late Accountant-General of Bengal and Chairman of the East India Company.* London: Richard Bentley 1844.

Lindsay, Robert. *Lives of the Lindsays.* Vol. 2. London: John Murray 1849.

Malcolm, Sir John. *The Government of India.* London: John Murray 1823.

Malleson, George Bruce. *The Decisive Battles of India.* London: W.H. Allen 1888.

Marsh, Charles. *A Review of Some Important Personages in the Late Administration of Sir George Barlow, Bart. at Madras.* London, 1813.

Martin, Montgomery. *The Despatches, Minutes and Correspondence, of the Marquess Wellesley, K.G. during his Administration in India.* Vol. 4. London: William H. Allen and Co. 1837.

Massie, J.M. *Continental India.* Vol. 1. London: Thomas Ward and Company 1840.

Mill, James, and Horace Hayman Wilson. *The History of British India.* Vol. 3. London: James Madden et al. 1858.

Mitchell, Joseph. *Reminiscences of My Life in the Highlands.* Vols. 1 and 2. Printed by the author, 1883.

Munro, Innes. *A Narrative of the Military Operation on Coromandel Coast against the Combined Forces of the French, Dutch and Hyder Ally Cawn from the Year 1780 to the Peace in 1784: in a Series of Letters.* London: T. Bensley 1769.

Neill, James G.S. *Historical Record of the Honourable East India Company, First Madras European Regiment.* London: Smith, Elder and Company 1843.

Oriental Herald and Colonial Review. Vol. 2 (May-August 1824). London: J.M. Richardson.

Oriental Herald and Journal of General Literature, January-March 1825, October–December 1825.

Orme, Robert. *A History of the Military Transactions of the British Nation in Indostan from the Year MDCCXLV.* London: John Nourse 1763.

Papers regarding the Administration of the Marquis of Hastings in India. 3 March 1824. London: J.L. Cox

Papers respecting a Reform in the Administration of the Government of His Excellency the Nawaub Vizier, and the Employment of British Troops in His Dominions, from the 1st January 1808 to the 31st December 1815, also Relating to the Negotiation of the Several Loans Contracted with the Vizier between the Months of October 1814 and May 1815. London: J.L. Cox 1824.

Parliamentary History and Review; containing Reports of the Two Houses of Parliament during the session of 1826. London: Longman et al. 1826.

Prinsep, Henry Thoby. *History of the Political and Military Transactions in India during the Administration of the Marquess of Hastings 1813–1833.* London: Kingsbury, Parbury and Allen 1820.

Rafter, Captain. *Our Indian Army: The Military History of the British Empire in the East.* London: E. Bryce 1855.

Reports from Committees of the House of Commons, Volumes VII and VIII East Indies: Carnatic War etc. – 1781 and 1782. London, 1806.

Shaw, Alexander Mackintosh. *Historical Memories of the House and Clan of Mackintosh and of the Clan Chattan.* London: R. Clay, Sons, and Taylor 1880.

Smith, George. *Twelve Indian Statesmen.* London: John Murray 1897.

Stewart, Major-General David. *Sketches of the Character, Manners, and the Present State of the Highlanders of Scotland.* Vol. 2, 3rd ed. Edinburgh: Archibald Constable and Company; London: Longman et al. 1825.

Strachey, John. *Hastings and the Rohilla War.* Oxford: Clarendon Press 1892.

Thomson, William. *Memoirs of the Late War in Asia: with a Narrative of the Imprisonment and Sufferings of our Officers and Soldiers.* London: Printed for the author and sold by J. Murray, 1788.

Wilks, Colonel Mark. *Colonel Wilks's Sketches of the South of Ind*ia. Vols. 1 and 2. Madras, 1869.

Wilson, W.J. *History of the Madras Army.* Vols. 1, 2, and 3. Madras: E. Keys 1883.

SECONDARY SOURCES

Anderson, Fred. *The War That Made America*. New York: Viking 2005.

Anderson, Peter. *Culloden Moor and the Story of the Battle*. Inverness: Eneas Mackay et al. 1920.

Anderson, William. *The Scottish Nation: or the Surnames, Families, Literature, Honours and Biographical History of the People of Scotland*. Vol. 3. London: A. Fullarton and Company 1863.

Ballhatchat, Kenneth. *Race, Sex and Class under the Raj*. London: Weidenfeld and Nicolson 1980.

Barlow, Glyn. *The Story of Madras*. London: Oxford University Press 1921.

Bate, Jonathan. *Soul of the Age*. New York: Random House 2009.

Bowen, H.V. *The Business of Empire: The East India Company and Imperial Britain 1756–1833*. Cambridge: Cambridge University Press 2006.

Brendon, Piers. *The Decline and Fall of the British Empire, 1781–1997*. New York: Alfred A. Knopf 2008.

Brendon, Vyvyen. *Children of the Raj*. London: Weidenfeld and Nicholson 2005.

Buchan, James. *Crowded with Genius: The Scottish Enlightenment: Edinburgh's Moment of the Mind*. New York: Harper Collins 2003.

Buddle, Anne. *The Tiger and the Thistle*. Edinburgh: National Galleries of Scotland 1999.

Bulloch, J.G.B. *Genealogical and Historical Records of the Baillies of Inverness Scotland and Some of Their Descendants in the United States of America*. Washington, 1923.

Campbell, Keeta. *Lieutenant-Colonel William Baillie 1739–1782 East India Company Army*. Unpublished manuscript.

Cashin, Edward J. *Lachlan MacGillivray: Indian Trader: The Shaping of the Southern Colonial Frontier*. Athens: University of Georgia Press 1992.

Chancey, Marla. *In the Company's Secret Service: Neil Benjamin Edmonstone and the First Indian Imperialists 1780–1820*. Gainesville, FL: Florida State University Press 2003.

Colley, Linda. *Captives: Britain, Empire, and the World, 1600–1850*. London: Pantheon Books 2002.

Dalrymple, William. "The Great and Beautiful Lost Kingdoms." *New York Review of Books*, 21 May 2015.

– *The Last Mughal*. New York: Alfred A. Knopf 2007.

– *White Mughals: Love and Betrayal in Eighteenth-Century India*. New York: Viking 2003.

Devine, T.M. *The Scottish Nation, 1700–2000*. London: Penguin 2006.

Dodwell, Henry. *The Nabobs of Madras*. New Delhi: Asian Educational Services 1926.

Farrington, Anthony. *Trading Places: The East India Company and Asia 1600–1834*. London: British Library 2002.

Ferguson, Niall. *The War of the World*. London: Allen Lane Penguin Books 2006.

Gilmour, David. *The Ruling Caste*. London: John Murray 2005.

Hamilton, Douglas J. *Scotland, the Caribbean and the Atlantic World 1750–1820*. Manchester, UK: Manchester University Press 2005.

Harper, Marjory. *Emigrant Homecomings: The Return Movement of Emigrants 1600–2000*. Manchester, UK: Manchester University Press 2004.

Harvey, Robert, *Clive. The Life and Death of a British Emperor*. New York: Thomas Dunne Books 2000.

Herman, Arthur. *Ghandi and Churchill*. London: Hutchinson 2008.

– *How the Scots Invented the Modern World: The True Story of How Western Europe's Poorest Nation Created Our World and Everything in It*. New York: Crown 2001.

Hibbert, Christopher. *The Great Mutiny, India 1857*. Middlesex, UK: Penguin Books 1980.

Hodson, Vernon Charles Paget. *List of the Officers of the Bengal Army 1758–1834*. Vol. 1. London: Constable 1927.

Jasanoff, Maya. *The Edge of Empire: Loves, Lives, and Conquest in the East 1750–1850*. New York: Albert A. Knopf 2005.

Keay, John. *The Honourable Company: A History of the English East India Company*. London: Harper Collins 1991.

Lane-Poole, Stanley. *Aurangzeb and the Decay of the Mughal Empire*. Oxford: Clarendon Press 1896.

Llewelyn-Jones, Rosie. *Engaging Scoundrels: True Tales of Old Lucknow*. New Delhi: Oxford University Press 2000.

– *A Fatal Friendship: The Nawabs, the British and the City of Lucknow*. New Delhi: Oxford University Press 1985.

Llewelyn-Jones, Rosie, ed. *Lucknow: City of Illusions*. London: Prestel Publishing 2008.

Love, Henry Davison. *Vestiges of Old Madras, 1640–1800*. Vol. 3. London: John Murray 1913.

Luce, Edward. *In Spite of the Gods*. London: Little Brown 2007.

Madison, Angus. *The World Economy: A Millennial Perspective*. Paris: OECD 2001.

Mason, Philip. *The Men Who Ruled India*. London: Jonathan Cape 1985.

McLynn, Frank. *1759: The Year Britain Became Master of the World*. London: Vintage Books 2008.

Miller, James. *Inverness*. Edinburgh: Birlinn 2004.

Mitford, Rev. J. *The Correspondence of Horace Walpole, Earl of Orford and the Rev. William Mason*. Vol. 2. London: Richard Bentley 1851.

Moorhouse, Geoffrey. *India Britannica*. London: Harvill Press 1983.

Moorhouse, Roger. "Darien: The Scottish 'Empire.'" *BBC History Magazine*, July 2001.

Munro, Robert. *Recollections of Inverness by an Invernessian*. Inverness: Printed for the Author 1863.

Murland, H.F. *Baillie-Ki-Paltan: Being a History of the 2nd Battalion, Madras Pioneers 1759–1930*. Uckfield, UK: Naval and Military Press 2006.

Newton, Norman. *The Life and Times of Inverness*. Edinburgh: John Donald Publishers 1996.

O'Toole, Fintan. *White Savage: William Johnson and the Invention of America*. New York: Farrar, Strauss and Giroux 2005.

Parsons, Constance E. *Seringapatam*. Oxford: Oxford University Press 1931.

Pemble, John. *Britain's Gurkha War and the Invasion of Nepal 1814–16*. London: Frontline Books 2008.

– *The Raj, the Indian Mutiny, and the Kingdom of Oudh, 1801–1859*. Cranbury, UK: Associated University Press 1977.

Philipart, John. *The East India Military Calendar*. London: Kingsbury, Parbury, and Allen 1823.

Philips, Cyril Henry. *The East India Company: 1784–1834*. Manchester: Manchester University Press 1940.

Phillips, Kevin. *1775: A Good Year for Revolution*. New York: Viking Penguin 2012.

Pinch, William R. *Warrior Ascetics and Indian Empires*. Cambridge: Cambridge University Press 2006.

Pincus, Steve. *1688: The First Modern Revolution*. New Haven, CT, and London: Yale University Press 2009.

Prebble, John. *Culloden*. London: Atheneum 1961.

– *The Lion in the North: A Personal View of Scotland's History*. London: Secker and Warburg 1971.

Richards, Frederick B. *The Black Watch at Ticonderoga and Major Duncan Campbell of Inverawe*. Ticonderoga, NY: Fort Ticonderoga Museum 1926.

Roach, Stephen. *The Next Asia*. Hoboken, NJ: John Wiley and Sons 2009.

Rose, John Holland, Arthur Percival Newton, and Ernest Alfred Benians. *The Cambridge History of the British Empire*. Vol. 2. Cambridge: Cambridge University Press 1933.

Rothschild, Emma. *The Inner Life of Empires: An Eighteenth Century History*. Princeton, NJ: Princeton University Press 2011.

Scottish Genealogist. Vol. 28, Journal 2. Edinburgh: Scottish Genealogy Society 1981.

Swamy, L.N. *History of Srirangapatna*. New Delhi: Harman Publishing 1996.

Tharoor, Shashi. *India from Midnight to the Millenium*. New York: Arcade Publishing 1997.

Tilby, Wyatt. *British India 1600–1828*. Boston and New York: Houghton Mifflin Company 1914.

Tritton, Alan. *When the Tiger Fought the Thistle*. London: Radcliffe Press 2013.

Von Tunzelman, Alex. *Indian Summer*. London: Simon and Schuster 2007.

Warrand, Duncan. *More Culloden Papers*, vol. 5, February 1746–December 1747. Inverness: Robert Carruthers and Sons 1930.

Waugh, W.T. *James Wolfe: Man and Soldier*. Montreal and Kingston, ON: McGill University Press 1928.

Weller, Jac. *Wellington in India*. London: Greenhill Books 1972.

Wilks, Mark. *History of Mysore*. New Delhi: Asian Educational Services 1989.

Wylly, H.C. *A Life of Lieutenant-General Sir Eyre Coote KB*. Oxford: Clarendon Press 1922.

Zakaria, Fared. *The Post-American World*. New York: W.W. Norton and Company 2008.

Index